05   1/4/21   2.00

Family & Relationship

Mother-Daughter Wisdom

Mother~Daughter Wisdom

Creating a Legacy of Physical and Emotional Health

Christiane Northrup, M.D.

BANTAM BOOKS

MOTHER-DAUGHTER WISDOM
A Bantam Book / February 2005

Published by
Bantam Dell
A Division of Random House, Inc.
New York, New York

Many of the stories that appear in this book are composites; individual names and identifying characteristics have been changed. Nevertheless, they reflect authentic situations in the lives of the thousands of women I've seen in my practice over the years. Other stories were generously contributed by readers of my newsletter specifically for publication in this book. If you think you recognize yourself in these pages, the similarities are strictly coincidental unless you submitted your story with the clear understanding that it might be published.

Book design by Glen Edelstein

Bantam Books is a registered trademark of Random House, Inc.,
and the colophon is a trademark of Random House, Inc.

Library of Congress Cataloging-in-Publication Data

Northrup, Christiane.
Mother-daughter wisdom : creating a legacy of physical and emotional
health / Christiane Northrup.
p. cm.
Includes bibliographical references and index.
ISBN 0-553-10573-6
1. Women—Health and hygiene. 2. Women—Mental health.
3. Mothers and daughters. I. Title.

RA778.N795 2005
613'.0424—dc22
2004065614

Printed in the United States of America
Published simultaneously in Canada

www.bantamdell.com

10 9 8 7 6 5 4 3 2 1
BVG

This book is dedicated with love and compassion
to all the mothers who came before me:
 my mother, Edna Margaret,
 my grandmother Ruth,
 my great-grandmother Margaret, who died when my
  grandmother was only three,
 and my great-aunt Edna, who raised my grandmother starting at
  the age of eleven. (My mother's name bears witness to these two
  motherless daughters who are part of my legacy.)

And to my two daughters, Annie and Katie—
 and all the mothers who will come after me.

Contents

ROOM TWO:
Seven to Fourteen Years

ROOM THREE:
Fourteen to Twenty-one Years

EPILOGUE

List of Figures

Acknowledgments

Like all creations, this book would never have been born without the support of many people. Much gratitude and appreciation go to the following key individuals:

Irwyn Applebaum, whose patience, vision, and unconditional support for this prolonged gestation gave me the confidence I needed to hang in there and do the job right.

Ned Leavitt, my agent and friend, who has believed in this "baby" from the beginning.

Leslie Meredith, my first editor and the person who convinced me to do this book so many years ago.

Toni Burbank and Beth Rashbaum, my editors, who kept their shoulders to the wheel and never let up until this manuscript was fit to see the light of day. You two are brilliant.

Barb Burg and Theresa Zoro—what a pleasure to have your promotional gifts and talents for getting the word out.

Karen Kinne for her can-do attitude and transcription skills.

Katy Koontz for cheerful and efficient research and fact-checking.

Paulina Carr for being willing to do whatever needs to be done with skill and humor.

Janet Lambert for establishing and maintaining such precise, skillful, and user-friendly financial order in my life.

Charles Grover, who has been an enthusiastic and humorous supporter of my work for all these years (and also an awesome dancer).

Sue Abel, for the care and dedication that has kept my home organized and beautiful no matter how crazy things have been. Your presence in my life is a blessing.

Paul and Chris Bourgeois, the father-son dream team who have helped me keep hearth, home, and office all in good working condition during this writing process.

Mike Brewer, handyman extraordinaire. For your role in keeping things up and running.

Abby Shattuck for supporting my environment with your botanical magic.

Fern Tsao, my (and my daughters') acupuncturist, healer, and all-around amazing health-care practitioner. You have helped me and my girls maintain good health through many years and several books. We are so fortunate to have you.

Joseph Saucier for helping me see myself in a new light.

The staffs of the Royal River Grillhouse and Harraseeket Inn for providing such delicious and healthful sustenance during this process.

Louise Hay, Reid Tracy, Donna Abate, Margarete Nielson, and all the staff at Hay House who have been instrumental in getting this message out to the world through my newsletter and public television. To Niki Vettel and Dennis Allen for their crucial roles in producing my PBS show. And to Judie Harvey for her talented editing of my e-letter and newsletter.

Dr. Mona Lisa Schulz—what would I have done without your scientific brain, intuitive and aunting skills, and your willingness to escape to as many movies as needed to keep my brain vacuumed during this process? With deep respect and enormous gratitude for our working partnership and friendship.

Diane Grover, my first office nurse and now the CEO of everything. Kahlil Gibran wrote that "work is love made visible." Your work with me for over twenty years bears witness to that truth. Words cannot express my appreciation for all you do and all that you are.

And finally, to my family, who have helped hone my soul qualities from the beginning: my late father, Wilbur, my mother, Edna, my sister Penny, my late sister Cindy, my brothers, John and Bill, and, of course, my two soulmate daughters, Ann and Kate.

Prologue

PROLOGUE

1

Mothers and Daughters

The Bond That Wounds, the Bond That Heals

The mother-daughter relationship is at the headwaters of every woman's health. Our bodies and our beliefs about them were formed in the soil of our mothers' emotions, beliefs, and behaviors. Even before birth, our mother provides us with our first experience of nurturing. She is our first and most powerful female role model. It is from her that we learn what it is to be a woman and care for our bodies. Our cells divided and grew to the beat of her heart. Our skin, hair, heart, lungs, and bones were nourished by her blood, blood that was awash with the neurochemicals formed in response to her thoughts, beliefs, and emotions. If she was fearful, anxious, or deeply unhappy about her pregnancy, our bodies knew it. If she felt safe, happy, and fulfilled, we felt that too.

Our bodies and those of our daughters were created by a seamless web of nature and nurture, of biology informed by consciousness, that we can trace back to the beginning of time. Thus, every daughter contains her mother and all the women who came before her. The unrealized dreams of our maternal ancestors are part of our heritage. To become optimally healthy and happy, each of us must get clear about the ways in which our mother's history both influenced and continues to inform our state of health, our beliefs, and how we live our lives. Every woman who heals herself helps heal all the women who came before her and all those who will come after her.

A mother's often unconscious influence on her daughter's health is so profound that years ago I had to accept that my medical skills were only a drop in the bucket compared to the unexamined and on-going influence of her mother. If a woman's relationship with her mother was supportive and healthy, and if her mother had given her positive messages about her female body and how to care for it, my job as a physician was easy. Her body, mind, and spirit were already programmed for optimal health and healing. If, on the other hand, her mother's influence was problematic, or if there was a history of neglect, abuse, alcoholism, or mental illness, then I knew that my best efforts would probably fall short. Real long-term health solutions would become possible only when my patient realized the impact of her background and then took steps to change this influence. Though health-care modalities such as dietary improvement, exercise, drugs, surgery, breast exams, and Pap smears all have their place, not one of them can get to the part of a woman's consciousness that is creating her state of health in the first place.

Before birth, consciousness literally directs the creation of our bodies. It is also constantly being shaped by our life's experiences, most especially those of childhood. No other childhood experience is as compelling as a young girl's relationship with her mother. Each of us takes in at the cellular level how our mother feels about being female, what she believes about her body, how she takes care of her health, and what she believes is possible in life. Her beliefs and behaviors set the tone for how well we learn to care for ourselves as adults. We then pass this information either consciously or unconsciously on to the next generation.

Though I acknowledge that the culture at large plays a significant role in our views of ourselves as women, ultimately the beliefs and behavior of our individual mothers exert a far stronger influence. In most cases, she is the first to teach us the dictates of the larger culture. And if her beliefs are at odds with the dominant culture, our mother's influence almost always wins.

MATERNAL ATTENTION:
AN ESSENTIAL LIFELONG NUTRIENT

When a TV camera focuses on audience members in the studio or at sporting events, what does the person on camera shout out? More often than not, it's "Hi, Mom!"

Each of us has a primal need to be seen and noticed by our moth-

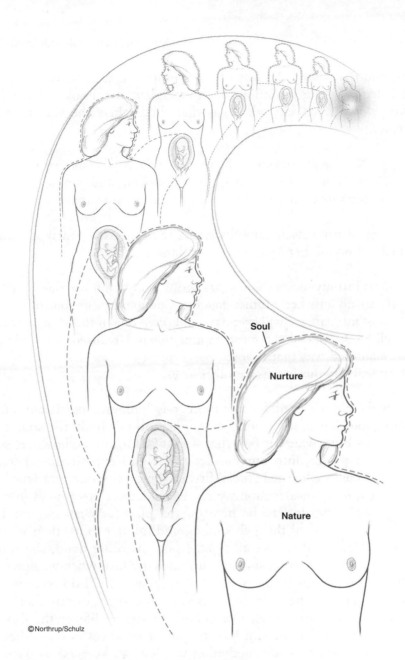

Soul

Nurture

Nature

©Northrup/Schulz

EVERY WOMAN IS A DAUGHTER

A woman's health is the soil out of which all humanity grows. Enhancing a woman's health fertilizes and replenishes this soil for everyone—men, women, children, plants, animals, and the planet itself. The mother-daughter bond in all its beauty, pain, and complexity forms the very foundation of a woman's state of health. This primal relationship leaves its mark on every cell of our being throughout our lives.

ers, and that's why the loss of one's mother can be so devastating. In a letter at the beginning of Hope Edelman's book, *Motherless Daughters,* a woman whose mother died when she was thirteen wrote:

> No one in your life will ever love you as your mother does. There is no love as pure, unconditional, and strong as a mother's love. And I will never be loved that way again.

One of my newsletter subscribers recently used nearly the same words, although her loss came much later in life:

> I lost my mother four years ago when I was forty-nine. And I sure do miss her. Mother-daughter relationships are one of the most intimate we will ever have and often one of the most complicated. One of the most painful things I realized when my mom died was that I would never again be loved as unconditionally (in this life) as a mother loves.

A daughter's need for her mother is biologic, and it continues throughout her life. Not only was our mother's body the source of life for us but it was her face that we looked to, to see how we were doing. By gazing into our mother's eyes and experiencing her response to us, we learned crucial first lessons about our own worth.

The quality of attention we receive as babies determines in part how worthy we feel to be here on the planet. When our mother shows her approval through smiling and talking to us, then we encode the idea that we are all right. If, on the other hand, she is not present for whatever reason, or withholds her love when we don't do what she wants us to do, we feel abandoned. We'll do whatever it takes to get that attention back. As young children, our mother's approval or disapproval felt like either the kiss of life or the kiss of death. No wonder she still has the power to affect our well-being. No wonder, even as educated adult women, we keep going back to the same well of maternal attention to see if we're okay and lovable and to check out how we're doing.

I firmly believe that the mother-daughter bond is designed by nature to become the most empowering, compassionate, intimate relationship we'll ever have. How is it, then, that when we go back to that well to be refilled, the result is so often disappointment and resentment on both sides?

Too many of my patients and friends have told me painful stories about going home for the holidays. Here's one of them:

> During my junior year in college, I went home on the Friday night before Mother's Day. I'd already told my mom that I'd be unable to stay and have a family dinner on Sunday because I had to get back, write a paper, and study for my final exams. When I walked into my house, my mother burst into tears. I said, "Mom, what's wrong?" She continued crying and said, "The ones you love the most hurt you the most. Don't get close to anyone."
>
> I said, "Mom, are you upset because I'm not staying down here for Mother's Day?"
>
> She replied, "I can't talk about it."
>
> Of course this made me feel as though I was being a terrible daughter (which is exactly what my mother wanted to convey). I said to her, "Mom, you haven't been happy with me since the day I moved out to go to college." She obviously wasn't willing to talk about what was really going on. She refused to address this and just kept cleaning the kitchen counter. She finally said, "I promised your father we were going to have a good day. So let's have a good day."

This sort of thing went on around Mother's Day and every other major holiday for years, but my friend couldn't stay away. "Not going is just not an option," she told me. No wonder she goes, despite the anxiety, headaches, and upset stomach that often ensue. She keeps going back to the well of maternal attention to try to slake her thirst for unconditional recognition and approval, because for generations her cells have been programmed to do this. Though she sometimes gets a few sips of her mother's approval, there is never enough to truly fill her up, and the price is very high. She is being called upon to bear the brunt of her mother's unhappiness and lack of fulfillment. At the very time when she most needs her mother's support to move ahead in her own life, her mother is calling her back. The message may take many forms, from tears to anger to stony silence, but the subtext is always the same: if you really loved me, you'd stay here and suffer with me.

My friend's relationship with her mother needn't be this difficult. To help heal it, she must first identify and name the common web of expectations, needs, and miscommunication in which she and her mother both feel trapped. And then she needs to look below the surface of her mother's behavior and her habitual response to it. When she does, she'll see that her (and her mother's) behavior stems seamlessly from our cultural inheritance as women. Appreciating this is the first step toward healing.

MATERNAL AMBIVALENCE:
OUR CULTURAL LEGACY

Both men and women in this society are encouraged to view having a baby and raising a child as the most significant achievement in a woman's life. And on many levels, it is. For a significant number of women, however, motherhood brings up far more conflict and ambivalence than we feel comfortable admitting lest we be labeled as "bad" mothers whose love for our children is suspect. To admit our ambivalence about motherhood and the ensuing loss of control and status that so often accompany it is to fly in the face of one of our most cherished cultural myths.

The epidemic of undiagnosed and untreated postpartum depression and the toll it takes on society speaks volumes. Who wouldn't be ambivalent about the one decision in a woman's life that totally changes her future? Though the biological act of becoming pregnant requires little thought or planning for most, raising a healthy, secure child is, hands down, the hardest job on earth. It requires a degree of maturity and altruism for which there's no way to adequately prepare. Today it also means the loss of independence and freedom that women have fought so long to attain.

Contrary to the myth, nurturing isn't an innate default setting in the human female. It is active and requires strength, stamina, will, intelligence, and determination: all of the qualities that we tend to associate with maleness. And yet, because femaleness has so long been seen as inferior to maleness, the work of nurturing and raising our young has also been denigrated.

Instead of being honest about the less than wonderful aspects of motherhood, however, we oversentimentalize it on the one hand, while undersupporting and downplaying the actual work involved on the other.

No human mother was ever designed to be the sole source of sustaining life energy for her child without also receiving outside support for herself and her own individual needs. Although we mothers nurture initially through the very substance of our own bodies, and later through our hearts, minds, and souls, the energy we expend in nurturing must always be replenished with self-care and self-development if we are to mother optimally. No one would expect a field to produce bumper crops year after year without replenishing the soil regularly, yet we expect mothers to do this. And most mothers don't feel they can ask for help.

When the fuel required for mothering and nurturing others is not replenished regularly, or when mothers don't get their need for self-development met separately from their children's or family's needs, breakdowns and failures in the nurturing system manifest as depression, anxiety, and even violence that affect both mothers and children. Illness then becomes the most socially acceptable way to get nurturance needs met.

DOCTOR, HEAL THYSELF

I first wrote the proposal for this book in 1996 when both my daughters were still living at home with their father and me. At the time, I thought I knew what it was going to be about. After all, I had raised two healthy daughters, had a solid relationship with my own mother, and as an obstetrician-gynecologist, had helped countless other mothers give birth to and raise healthy daughters themselves. With great enthusiasm, I began writing what I thought of as an "owner's manual for raising a healthy daughter."

But every time my writing got under way, it was interrupted by another project. It took more than five years of starting and stopping before I finally understood why this kept happening. I wasn't ready. In order to write the book that needed to be written, I first had to come to grips with my own beliefs about mothering. I had to be willing to allow my own denial and sentimentality to be burned away so that I could clearly see how these primal mother-daughter bonds had influenced every cell in my body and every aspect of my life for more than fifty years. In retrospect, I saw that every project or event that appeared to interrupt the writing of this book was a necessary step in its preparation.

One of those intervening projects was writing *The Wisdom of Menopause,* a book that describes how and why the menopausal transition is, in essence, a biologically supported opportunity for major personal growth and transformation. It boils down to this: Grow or die. And the choice to grow always involves clearing up any unfinished emotional business from the first half of our lives.

My own midlife transition included the end of my twenty-four-year marriage. During the soul-searching that was part of this painful life change, it came to me that I had married my mother. Not every part of my mother, of course. Just the parts from our past together that were still crying out for resolution and healing. My relationship with my husband had been an opportunity to reenact, and thus bring to consciousness, some outmoded beliefs about myself that had been formulated years earlier in response to my mother. As a result of this new awareness, I was able to bring more love, joy, and health into all areas of my life, but especially into my relationship with my mother and my daughters.

None of this was easy, however. There were many days during the dissolution of my marriage when I was certain that I was a total failure as a woman and as a mother. After all, on the surface, I had it all—a physician husband, two lovely children, a nice home, and a career that has always felt like the work I was born to do. Why push it? I wasn't sure I was worthy of more.

The truth is, a part of me had always felt that I had to prove myself in order to be loved. So, like many women, I overgave—both to my daughters and to my husband. I fell into the pattern easily enough, given that motherhood and sacrifice are still nearly synonymous in our culture. The needs of mothers are assumed to come last—after everyone else's. It was shocking to realize that even with all my outward success, I still lost myself at home. And now that I was divorced, I had to face the same issues with both my mother and my daughters.

Opening My Eyes

By this time, both daughters were in college. I'd look forward to their holiday and summer vacations and stock the house with their favorite foods. If I didn't have something they wanted, I'd feel awful about it. I'd fantasize about all the fun we'd have when they came home, only to be disappointed when they had already scheduled other activities with their friends that didn't include me. The problem was that I didn't know how to stop my automatic "mothering" behavior and the emotional needs that were fueling it. I didn't really know how to tell the difference between my healthy desire to nurture and care for my daughters, and my need to earn their love to affirm my worth.

My relationship with my mother was also changing. Ironically, she and I were now the only single adult women in my extended fam-

ily with no children living at home. When she was my age, my
mother had been forced by widowhood to individuate from her former role as wife and mother. She responded by becoming the mayor
of her town for five years. After that, she fulfilled a dream of hiking
the entire Appalachian Trail and also of climbing the hundred highest peaks in New England.

Now that I was in a similar situation, however, I remembered
more difficult parts of the story. How, after she was widowed, my
mother's social life changed dramatically, because she was no longer
invited to the events that she and my dad had attended for years.
How she had been unable to take out a loan in her own name, even
though she owned the farm where we grew up. (My own social and
financial situation was different, but no less challenging to my sense
of worth.) I also discovered that, as two single women, we were automatically paired as a "couple" at all family events. Did my newly
single status mean that I was now expected to be both my mother's
companion and caregiver?

Old memories kept coming up with new significance. I recalled
that my mother had always been happiest when she was on the
move. (Even today, at the age of seventy-eight, a perfect day for her
involves participating in several different sports, then mowing the
lawn and watering all the flowers on the property.) As a child I don't
remember her ever lingering at the table after a meal. She'd begin to
clear the table and get the dishes washed as soon as possible so she
could get on to the next thing. Often I was not yet finished eating.
Now I realized that from as far back as I could remember, she had
had a kind of "caged lion" feel about her when she couldn't be active. I believe that stopping would have caused her to feel something
she didn't want to feel. I also believe that, as a child, I sensed her uneasiness and unconsciously took on the responsibility of soothing
her. This was my own soul choice, not my mother's doing, but it created a pattern that was now painfully outdated.

One day during this period of intense inner work, my left eye
suddenly began to feel irritated. I took out my contact lens and
cleaned it. That didn't help. Every time I put it back, there was still
irritation. By the time I went to an eye specialist in Portland, the vision in my left eye was so clouded that I couldn't read the top line of
an eye chart. At the Massachusetts Eye and Ear Infirmary in Boston,
I was diagnosed with infectious crystalline keratopathy, a very rare
form of corneal ulcer that is usually seen only in patients who are im-
munocompromised in some way. The prognosis was blindness in
that eye. I was terrified.

Even while I was searching out the most sophisticated medical care I could find, I kept asking myself, "Why this? Why now?" A chance remark by a female resident at Mass Eye and Ear really caught my attention: she said that when women have eye problems such as mine, it's always in the left eye. I knew that the immunosuppression that had led to this infection was related to the suppressed memories I had recently dredged up. This is not surprising, given that our first emotional center, which affects our blood, immune system, and sense of safety and security in the world, is heavily influenced by our relationship with our mother. The left eye is associated with the right brain, the part that is in touch with emotions that the left side of our brain, our intellect, often tries to deny. The left side of the body, including the organs on that side, are also said to represent the mother in traditional Chinese medicine.

Finally things turned around when, in addition to the antibiotic drops I was prescribed, I began to use very high doses of vitamin C (vitamin SEE, as a friend of mine pointed out) and also worked with several different healers. In retrospect, I see that my eye infection came about because of an obsolete belief I was carrying. I believed that in order to maintain my standing as a good mother and a good daughter, it was my job to care for my family in ways that were no longer appropriate for me. In traditional Chinese medicine, eyes are in the liver meridian. And the liver is associated with anger. (Are we surprised?) Unbeknownst to me, I was angry about what I believed I was "supposed" to be and do as a mother and daughter.

My eye infection was really my body's wisdom, letting me know, through a brush with blindness, that there was a different way to see the situation. I had to see that my mother and my daughters were all strong, capable adults who didn't need me to sacrifice anything for them or rescue them in any way. It was time for me to envision my role as both a mother and a daughter in a new, healthier way for all concerned. And as usual, this insight came to me through my body—quite literally through my eyes, which were signaling me to illuminate a previously dark and unexamined area of my psyche.

It was following this that I finally recognized the real book that was trying to come through me: not a doctor's parenting manual for daughters, but an entirely new and empowering way of looking at the mother-daughter relationship. I wanted to find a way to help women of all ages—*whether or not they are raising a daughter*—heal themselves physically and emotionally at the deepest possible levels.

ENERGETIC BREAST AND HEART DISEASE PREVENTION

A loving, nurturing mother tends to become the very center of her family's health and happiness. She is like the family umbilical cord that everyone taps into for sustenance at all levels: physical, emotional, psychological, and spiritual. This nurturing role can be enormously fulfilling. It can also deteriorate into martyrdom if a mother gives her children and spouse the love and care she doesn't feel that she herself is worthy of receiving.

The energy of giving and nurturing others unconditionally strengthens all the organs of the fourth chakra, or energy center: the breasts, heart, lungs, upper spine, and shoulders. (See figure on page 45.) But the love that makes maternal nurturance so life-affirming must be replenished regularly, otherwise it leads to health problems in those same organs. When a woman puts her own personal and emotional needs on the back burner—or forgets entirely that she has them—the energy of her fourth chakra inevitably becomes diminished by resentment, anger, grief, longing, pining for contact, and pure fatigue. This is the energy pattern that invites breast, shoulder, heart, and lung problems. And diseases in those areas cause the majority of deaths and disabilities in women.

You can't legislate caring and compassion. But the minute a woman decides that she is worthy of love and care, things begin to change. A woman who has the courage to break the martyrdom cycle will be ensuring her own health and helping her daughter or other loved ones do the same. The only way to teach your daughter how to recognize and state her emotional needs is to do so yourself. And when your daughter witnesses this, she will be less likely to carry the mother burden on into her own life.

Risking the Truth

Taking on the health implications of the mother-daughter relationship was not easy. I often felt as though I were walking on eggshells simply by telling the truth about my experience. When one of my friends sent me a story about her own mother, she said that writing it had made her feel guilty—even though her mother, a very difficult and jealous woman, has been dead for over twenty years! Whenever there's this much discomfort around telling a simple truth, there's also enormous suppressed energy that is keeping a secret in place.

If I were going to write a book that could really help women, I needed to be willing to name "what is" and feel my feelings fully, especially the ones that weren't comfortable. I also had to get clear that telling the truth is not the same thing as blaming our mothers (or our daughters) for their shortcomings. Blaming is a dead-end street that doesn't help anyone. But until we risk telling the truth to ourselves about how we really feel, nothing in our lives can change or improve. When it comes to your mother or your daughters, you've got to risk changing any habitual beliefs and behaviors that aren't healthy for you. And you have to be willing to do this even if your mother or your daughter doesn't like it. Otherwise, neither of you will be able to enjoy optimal health or freedom.

Then you must do something that is a paradox. No matter what happened to you and no matter how wrong it feels, you must step into the world of grace and possibility where you're willing to accept responsibility for every aspect of your life. And that includes your relationship with your mother, your daughter, and yourself.

Part of taking responsibility is first naming your unfinished business with your mother, including any past hurts or resentments. Then you need to shine a spotlight on the ways in which your own behavior in the present is keeping those hurts and resentments alive—and even carrying them on to the next generation. You must check to find the ways in which you are complicit with the culture of self-sacrifice and illness behavior that too many mothers unwittingly pass on to their daughters.

Yes, there is a way to create healthy, sustainable relationships with our own mothers and daughters without getting sick, feeling sucked dry, or being resentful. Yes, we can relate to and support each other and still be free to live our lives as fully as possible, without the tyranny of guilt and obligation that so often plays itself out in this relationship. And yes, we can create a legacy of health for our daughters and their daughters to come. *Mother-Daughter Wisdom* will show you the way.

BREAKING THE CHAIN OF PAIN

One day, as I was near the end of writing this book, I received a special report called "Touch the Future: Optimum Learning Relationships for Children and Adults." A compendium of solid research on the importance of mother-child bonding for optimal brain and emotional development in children, it included documentation about how modern obstetrical practices, lack of maternal-infant bonding, lack of breast-feeding, institutional day care, and media violence have all conspired to create an epidemic of bullying, depressed, violent, or suicidal children.

Even though the research in the report wasn't new to me, and even though I agreed with much of it, it still triggered some very old and very deep abyss of maternal guilt within me. I was paralyzed and couldn't read further, overcome with the feeling that I hadn't done enough for my children. I felt guilty because I had had help with child care when I was working. I felt guilty for wanting to have a career and a family. I felt guilty because I hadn't carried my children next to my body for the entire first year of life. Descending into that abyss of maternal guilt, I was blinded to everything I had done right.

It took me over twenty-four hours to begin coming to my senses. When I finally recovered enough to think and feel clearly, I asked myself, "What is really going on here? Why am I feeling so bad about myself as a mother?"

And then I made the connection. I didn't like some of the choices one of my twenty-something daughters was making at the time. But instead of letting those choices be her responsibility, I assumed that her mistakes were my fault—a reflection of how she had been mothered. What if I had done it differently? What if I hadn't worked? What if I had been stricter? Did I give her too much in some areas? Too little in others? When did my responsibility end and hers begin? The article that had triggered my guilt had been about early childhood bonding. What about now? And regardless of what I had or had not done in the past, I realized that going back to dissect my errors of omission or commission as a mother was a dead end. Driving down that particular road over and over again brought nothing but more pain and guilt.

Blaming our mothers for their shortcomings (and subsequently our own) or feeling guilty for our own failures as mothers are sure-fire ways to stay in the victim mode as women, a state that removes us from our personal power and sets us up for illness and more failure. Though we must be honest with ourselves about our own childhoods, though we must acknowledge the ways we ourselves have fallen short, it doesn't serve us in any way to stay stuck in blame. Instead, we need to learn how to move on consciously with our eyes and hearts open.

Regardless of how we were mothered, we must eventually internalize and update the nurturing function originally provided for us by our mothers and learn the additional skills necessary to mother and care for ourselves optimally. We must become the ideal mother we wanted while letting our human mothers off the hook. And we must turn our loving compassion on ourselves and our own lives.

If you have a daughter, the work you do to make peace with your own mother and your nurturing history will be the best legacy for health and healing you can pass on to her. And if you don't have a daughter or don't plan to, know that by healing your relationship with how you were mothered and nurtured, you will become for women and men everywhere a role model of that rarity—a well woman who has made peace with her past and looks forward to creating her future.

WISDOM CHALLENGE: *What Do We Owe Our Daughters? What Do We Owe Our Mothers?*

When you have an "easy," empathetic child who sails through life taking responsibility for herself and knows when and when not to ask for help, then a mother's job is as easy and natural as breathing. Your daughter will go through normal "growing pains," of course, but she manages to be responsible for her own life most of the time. Things become far more challenging when a daughter doesn't easily negotiate the emotional and physical milestones that lead to maturity.

If a daughter becomes developmentally stuck at some stage of her life, whether it be at age five, sixteen, or twenty-five, what is a mother's responsibility? Where does it begin? Where does it end? And how and when do you wean yourself from your role in trying to help your daughter succeed? When are you off the hook if she fails? What is a mother supposed to do for a seven-year-old who has no friends? What about a sexually precocious eleven-year-old who wants to start dating? What do you do with a fifteen-year-old who smokes or drinks alcohol regularly? What if she's twenty-five and doesn't have a job? What if she's thirty and wants to move back in to save money on rent?

And what about your own mother? If she is unhappy or alone, what is a daughter's responsibility? If she is widowed, chronically ill, or can no longer live by herself, what does she expect of you? What do you expect of yourself? Do you enjoy each other's company or is your relationship based on guilt and obligation: "I did it for you. Now you should do it for me." Is your willingness to "give back" related to how much your mother did for you, or is it simply part of being a daughter?

There is no one right answer to the questions above, but you cannot answer them for yourself until you clarify your own beliefs and behaviors. This book will help you do that.

EMBRACING YOUR UNIQUE MOTHERING STYLE

Guilt and worry about whether or not we're being good enough mothers has only intensified as more and more choices for self-development have become available to women. Increasingly, mothers are expected to keep perfect homes and prepare home-cooked meals, while also working full-time outside the home. Our culture then holds up the ever-popular and unrealistic "celebrity mom" profile as an example of how working mothers are supposed to look and act.

But there is no one right way to be a mother. I've found it helpful to think of mothering styles—or *nurturing* styles, if you don't have children—as falling somewhere along a spectrum. Once you identify your mother's style and also your own, you'll be better able to appreciate and understand how you've influenced each other, and what choices are right for you.

At one end of the spectrum is the nontraditional mother or nurturer, the woman who is primarily turned inward toward meeting creative needs that come from deep within her. This type of mother has to take care of these needs if she is to remain emotionally balanced and physically healthy. My mother falls into this category. In women like my mother, activating the motherhood and nurturing circuits tends to take a toll physically unless they also have a lot of practical support. Though they love their children as much as anyone, they are not biologically wired for motherhood to fulfill them totally at the deepest levels. For my mother, skiing and other outdoor activities were as necessary as oxygen. When we were little, instead of missing a day of skiing, she'd bundle us all up and take us with her, putting one of us on skis between her legs and one in a back-pack. We all learned to ski by the age of two!

My mother has often told the story of how, when she was a twenty-year-old new mother with her first child, my older brother, she sat on the back stoop wanting to run over the back hill to get away from the crushing responsibility of caring for her new baby. My father, sensing this, immediately hired someone to help her. My mother was neither temperamentally nor immunologically suited for the demands of motherhood in the 1950s, an era when women's roles were far more circumscribed than they are now. Like most of the postwar brides of that time, she was expected to devote her life to taking care of her husband and her children. (She bore six children over a span of fifteen years, one of whom, my sister Bonnie, died within six months of birth.) This included the shopping for and preparation of three meals a day for over thirty years!

At the other end of the spectrum is the traditional mother, the classic "natural mother" or "earth mother." Having babies and caring for them is the happiest and most fulfilling activity of her life. Her touch seems to automatically make things grow. She often keeps a garden. She likes nothing better than creating a home, baking cookies, and being available for her children. This mother's focus is primarily on her children and she often doesn't feel the need for a career or other interests. A woman with this temperament tends to adore and notice babies from the time she is a little girl. These women feel at their best when pregnant, nursing, or having their children around the house and underfoot. The motherhood circuitry seems to enhance and fulfill them and they have no problem caring for a number of children simultaneously. The traditional mother may go through considerable difficulty at midlife if she perceives that she is no longer needed by her family. She often continues her caregiving role throughout her life by doing such things as volunteering to care for her grandchildren or hosting holiday gatherings at which she prepares most of the food.

Somewhere near the middle of the spectrum is the woman who combines both the traditional and nontraditional types of mothers. I fall into this "combination mother" category. Like my mother before me, I was never interested in babies until I had my own children. And my need to pursue a career in women's health was an all-consuming passion, just as my mother's love of sports was for her. When my first child was three months old, I, like my mother before me, had some problems with immunologic compromise. Part of this came from the stress of working full-time and also trying to provide breast milk as my daughter's exclusive diet. I always had full-time help but could have used even more given my on-call schedule.

Eventually my two worlds of nurturing and career collided with each other. When my children were age two and four, I stopped delivering babies in order to spend more time with them. This decision was very difficult, especially since I had gone into ob-gyn because of my love for delivering babies. Still, mothering my children and spending a significant amount of time with them was now my highest priority.

The Combination Challenge

Because of the way in which society has changed, many women who are traditional mothers by temperament are now being forced into being combination mothers. This presents enormous challenges. The biology of motherhood combined with our culture's relentless 24/7 addiction to productivity and work makes mothering young children enormously difficult when both parents work. We don't yet have good solutions in place for young families. Still, things were far better for me than they were for my mother. I don't know what I would have done had I been a wife and mother back in the 1950s when my mother had her children. And I'm also very grateful that my work has given me the foundation for a very fulfilling second half of life now that my children are adults.

No matter what our individual temperament may be, our choices, like my mother's, are shaped by the culture of our time and place. Many women of my mother's generation have told me that they feel sorry for women in my generation. They look at the mothers of today, running around trying to get it all done, and just shake their heads. Compared to us, they say, they had far more free time and far more support. They expected their husbands to provide for them and for their children. The rules were simpler. There were fewer choices. Still, it would be naive to believe that all mothers willingly settled into the blissful domesticity of the post-WWII years, the "Happy Days" portrayed on the television sitcoms of the 1950s and '60s. For many women, including my mother to some extent, having children and caring for their homes and husbands came at the expense of their own hopes and dreams for self-actualization.

Niravi Payne, a specialist in the psychological aspects of fertility, has pointed out that the baby boom generation was the first in human history to collectively delay childbearing beyond the age when their mothers had their first children. We were going to do it differently. Unlike our mothers, we were going to have it all: fulfilling careers, functional families, and partnership marriages with men who would understand and meet us halfway with everything from parenting to moving to a new city for a job promotion. But by saying "no" or at least "wait" to the strong biologic pull of fertility and motherhood in favor of career achievement in a male-dominated world, we were thrust unwittingly into completely new territory for which there were no road maps and no guidance available from either our mothers or society, let alone the men in our lives. Our generation had to make it up as we went along. And our daughters will pick up where we left off—and create even more balance.

Where We're Going

What I didn't know back then as a young mother was that my inner creative blueprint was knocking on the door, urging me to find the fulfillment I was seeking through creating a life in which the joys and fulfillment of motherhood and nurturing my children could be combined seamlessly with my work as a physician.

Thousands of other women were simultaneously asking the same questions and making the same kinds of changes in their work and personal lives. The generation of girls who are now coming of age, our daughters, are the result of this experiment.

Together, mothers and daughters are now ready to forge a legacy of true health and freedom for themselves and for each other. Deep in my heart, I know that this is the work for which I was born. And my mother, Edna, has been my mentor and greatest teacher from the beginning.

Collectively we are at a new frontier in which countless women, having tasted the heady fruits of individuation and personal power, are no longer willing to go back to the unconscious, unexamined caretaking roles that have been handed down to us for generations. Nor are we willing to accept the notion that getting older always means getting sick and needing care.

Most of us also want and need the satisfaction that comes from creating a home and a family. And despite our independence and economic clout, nearly every woman I've ever met also wants to be loved and cherished in an intimate partnership, though not if giving up control of her money, body, career, or time is the price she must pay.

Feminine energy is now rising up all over the planet to support us as we move into the new partnership archetype that is signified by the number 2 of this millennium. It is this energy that is supporting both men and women to create new family stories, new health and longevity stories, new work and fulfillment stories.

A SPIRITUAL PERSPECTIVE

From a higher perspective, the journey I'm describing in this book isn't really about our mothers or our daughters at all. It's about coming home to our deepest selves and being happy with our own company. This is a challenge all women face. Only by transforming ourselves can we hope to create the lives we're longing for in the outer world.

I believe that all mothers and daughters are old friends on a soul level who are here to help each other bring love, skill, and discipline to the parts of our personalities that we took at birth to develop more fully. Because each of us was born with different gifts and challenges, no two of us will ever have exactly the same idea of what is right or what is best. But we can work toward a lifelong relationship in which each supports the full evolution of the other regardless of her life stage or age.

I am not my daughters' Higher Power and I never have been. I gave them the best beginning I was able to, just as my mother did for me. What they do with this legacy is now up to them in partnership with their souls.

ENTER THE MOTHER BEAR

What is the most dangerous beast in a forest? A mother bear who is protecting her young. There is no more ferocious or dangerous creature. She knows what it takes to keep her young safe. And they are her first concern. Period. But she also knows what to teach them so that when the time is right, they can live independently without her.

Raising children in general and daughters in particular or healing our own relationships with our mothers and learning how to nurture ourselves requires that each of us bring back our instinctual knowledge—the parts of our biology that have been systematically routed out by our culture for thousands of years. This energy is symbolized by the Mother Bear in many traditional cultures.

The only way to raise a healthy, proud daughter or heal our own relationship with our mothers is to enter bear territory. The only way to become the mother you always wished you had is to enter bear territory. Listening to your instinctive maternal wisdom and allowing it to rise up through you and guide your mothering of yourself or someone else requires that you become ferocious and receptive simultaneously. If you are raising a daughter, you must be willing to open yourself to the place inside where you would willingly sacrifice your own life or that of someone or something else for your daughter. And paradoxically, it also means that you must know when to stop the sacrifice for her sake as well as your own. Likewise, if you are healing your relationship with your mother, you must learn when to take care of yourself and when to give to others.

We are each born with some Mother Bear energy in us. The processes leading up to the birth of a baby—gestation, labor, delivery, and the postpartum period—are designed to saturate us with the hormones and emotions we need to access this energy. But there are precious few truly ferocious Mother Bears guarding their young these days. Where has that Mother Bear energy in humans gone, and how can each of us get it back? For too long, our womanly instincts have been belittled, ignored, or degraded by the culture, leaving most women more than a little ambivalent about what we know deep within. We don't talk about this much because we don't want to appear too foolish, unsophisticated, or unscientific. And of course, we also want everyone to love us, including our daughters, our husbands, our friends, or our lovers.

Where is the Mother Bear? How is it that so powerful an instinct has gone underground or become so distorted? What is the full expression of this naturally? How can each of us remember it and apply it as needed to our *own* lives? Don't get me wrong. Unconscious biologic instinct and biologic instinct that is honed and refined by consciousness and choice are two different things. Remembering our instinctual wisdom doesn't mean negating our intellect or the contributions of science. It means using our intellect in partnership with our instinctive, or natural, wisdom.

Opening yourself to the power of your Mother Bear instinct will open you to depths of feeling that you never knew you possessed—and to the most heart-melting love you can imagine. At the end of my first book, *Women's Bodies, Women's Wisdom,* I wrote, "We carry in our own bodies not only our own pain but that of our mothers and grandmothers—however unconsciously." In writing this book, I have felt the truth of that statement more acutely than ever. I hope that you will feel it too, because when you do, you will soon find that that feeling place is the gateway through which you must walk if you are to create a truly joyous, creative, and full life for yourself and your daughters.

2

Life Is a Series of Wombs

The Inner Blueprint for Creation and Growth

In every mythology the world over, the hero's journey figures
prominently. These heroes, with rare exceptions, are males who
leave their homes and families to go out into the world to seek
some kind of treasure. They encounter and overcome obstacles, ene-
mies, and danger, and also endure loss. Eventually, they return home
to be reunited with family and loved ones, utterly changed and with
far more wisdom than when they started.

We are all heroes. And the hero's journey begins at the moment
of our birth. But the hero's journey for women is different. The ene-
mies, obstacles, and battles women encounter are seldom as straightforward as those faced by men. They often exist within our own
psyches and have been handed down to us by a culture that is only
now becoming comfortable with feminine ways of being in the
world.

A woman's heroic journey always begins in partnership with her
mother, the woman from whom she takes the imprint of what it
means to be a woman. Her journey picks up speed when she leaves
the comfort of the womb and goes through the process of birth.
From then on, she must travel through a series of developmental
stages that can be likened to a series of wombs.

OUR JOURNEY BEGINS AND ENDS AT HOME

Because women so often dream of houses—a very concrete symbol of our psyches and our bodies—I have depicted the female hero's journey as a journey through a house. Each room of this house contains challenges that we must face in order to find the treasure that also awaits us in that room. Our mother's womb is the foundation or "basement" of our house. We enter the first room by going through physical labor and birth, followed by a period of postpartum adjustment. The energies of conception, gestation, labor, and birth that brought us into physical life will then repeat themselves metaphorically as we move from one room to the next, meeting the challenges associated with that room and also reaping the rewards and finding the treasures.

To grow and evolve to the subsequent stage of development—the next room—we must go through labor and birth yet again. Appropriate timing for this process is as crucial to our health and happiness as is the timing of labor during a pregnancy. Failure to progress and move on when we have reached the end of a developmental stage, or trying to skip a stage and moving on too soon, are associated with health risks—even, in some cases, premature death.

As an obstetrician-gynecologist, mother, and author, I have come to see that every significant creation in our lives, whether it be a child, a work of art, a home, a relationship, or our life itself, requires an investment of life energy similar to that of a human pregnancy. And each of our creations, like each of our children, is also shaped and influenced by our own consciousness.

That's not all. Each creation also requires a support structure to sustain and nourish it, just as the human placenta nourishes the unborn child. And most intriguingly, each of our creations goes through essentially the same stages that women go through when we create and birth new life into the world. The biological and cosmic processes of conception, pregnancy, labor, birth, and the postpartum period are physical metaphors for how we create everything in our lives. These processes are the mechanism through which we carry out the dictates of our internal blueprint for creation. All mothers give their daughters this profound legacy.

Why Seven Years?

An impressive number of world traditions have acknowledged the seven-year cycle in human development. In the Jesuit tradition, for instance, a child is said to have reached the age of reason by age seven. Rudolf Steiner, the founder of the Waldorf school movement and Anthroposophical medicine, taught that children are biologically and intellectually ready to read only after their secondary teeth come in at about age seven. The famous modern psychologist Erik Erikson also divided the life cycle into developmental stages—though not of seven years—each of which is associated with specific challenges, conflicts, and achievements.

Based on tradition and my own experience, I have assigned seven years to the passage through each room in the house of life. This, however, is not meant to be a straitjacket of "shoulds" that you must follow to be healthy and successful. It is meant rather as a broad framework to give you an idea of the terrain you or your daughter will be covering in your unique journey through life.

Just as there's no way to predict exactly when one will go into labor and give birth, there's no way to predict the timing of one's journey through a given room. There is considerable normal variation in how long it will take to meet the challenges and find the treasure associated with the room in which they are cached. Some women move through a given room in two or three years. Others need ten years or even more for the same passage. Sometimes you may even need to go backward for a while, revisiting a room that you thought you'd left for good. An accident or illness will often force you to do just that.

The Goal of Our Life's Journey

I firmly believe that each of our lives is imbued with a unique purpose and meaning from the very beginning. Our thoughts, emotions, and behaviors are the way in which we tap into and further develop our life's purpose and innate creativity. Each time we encounter one of life's obstacles or tests, no matter what their timing, we have the opportunity to either blame our outward circumstances for our problems or go within ourselves and make contact with our souls and our creativity. If we do this consciously and repeatedly throughout our life cycles, we develop significant inner resources and skills that help us carry out our unique purpose. And as a result, we become a gift to ourselves and to the world. Our life, regardless of our circumstances, becomes a blessing that adds richness and goodness to our families and our world.

On this journey, mothers and daughters are in partnership from the very beginning. The circumstances of a mother's conception, pregnancy, labor, and birth with her daughter form the original imprint that her daughter encodes about what to expect as she moves from one room to the next on her life's journey. Yet it is the baby who initiates labor, and the mother whose body must relax into the process. These experiences form the very foundation for every subsequent developmental stage. They are the grist for the mill that our souls will grind and refine repeatedly throughout life.

One of my friends notes that whenever she's involved in a project, her "pregnancies" are overdue. She spends an inordinate amount of time in the gestational period, gathering information, collating it, and fact-checking. Then she tends to "deliver" her project precipitously. She was astounded when she found out that her mother's pregnancy with her was nearly a month overdue. Her mother finally went into labor and had a very quick birth after taking castor oil and driving over bumpy roads. The daughter's creative challenges were different, but she mirrored her mother in how she met them.

The treasures associated with our life's journey include health, love, a sense of gratitude, creativity, joy, freedom, abundance, and success. All of these qualities contribute greatly to our state of physical health. These treasures are found by meeting the challenges of each room.

If we have not successfully met the challenges associated with a given room and can't apply the skills developed in appropriate ways, then we're apt to get stuck in that room. As a result, our physical and emotional health may be at risk. Our relationships may also suffer if we try to keep our children and/or loved ones in that same room with us long after it's time for them to move on.

The Significance of the Stairs

Though each seven-year developmental stage has its own set of challenges, the times when we must ascend the "stairs" from one floor of the house to the next have special significance. Each stairway is a particularly potent birth canal, offering the opportunity for the same kind of astounding growth that was present at our birth. Because the dramatic developmental energies available at these times inevitably bring up the unfinished business of our lives, our stairwell experiences often test our faith in the process of life far more acutely

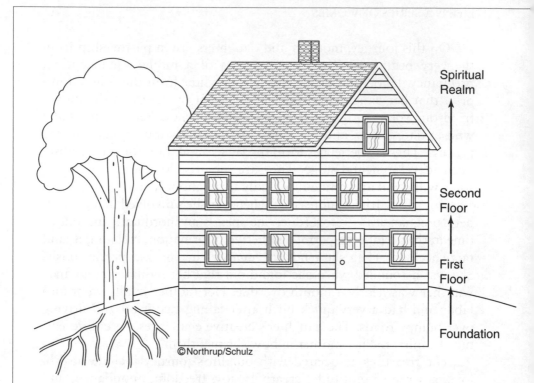

Spiritual
Realm

Second
Floor

First
Floor

Foundation

©Northrup/Schulz

LIFE AS A HOUSE:
THE INNER BLUEPRINT FOR OUR JOURNEY

Each developmental stage of life can be likened to the room of a house.
The foundation for the entire house is created by our gestation and birth
from our mother's womb, the first room of our physical lives. To enter the
first floor, we must go through labor and birth, followed by a postpartum
readjustment period as we make our debut into independent physical life.
In each successive room, a child, and later a woman, has the opportunity
to meet the challenges of that room by further refining and updating the
skills and goals appropriate to that room. Because none of us is ever
completely independent, we must also become adaptable and resourceful
enough to create a support and nurturance network to help sustain us in a
given room. This network performs the same function as the maternal
placenta, our original organ of support and nurturing.

than the minibirths required to move from room to room on the
same floor.

When we are born, we must move from the foundation level of
our mother's womb to the first floor of our house, a time when we

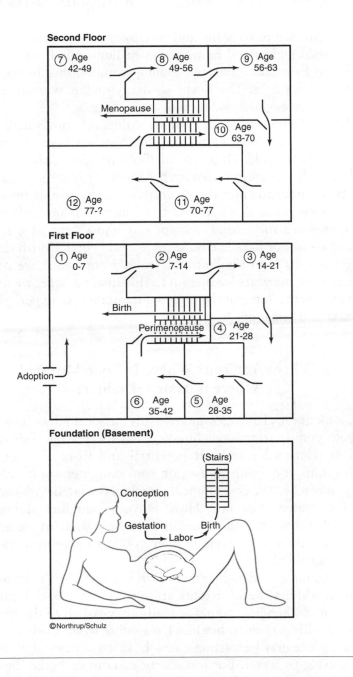

Second Floor

⑦ Age 42-49
⑧ Age 49-56
⑨ Age 56-63

Menopause

⑩ Age 63-70

⑫ Age 77-?
⑪ Age 70-77

First Floor

① Age 0-7
② Age 7-14
③ Age 14-21

Birth

Perimenopause ④ Age 21-28

Adoption

⑥ Age 35-42
⑤ Age 28-35

Foundation (Basement)

(Stairs)

Conception

Gestation
Birth
Labor

©Northrup/Schulz

are maximally vulnerable to the influence of our environment, especially that created by our mother's mind, body, and emotions.

At midlife, we must ascend the stairs to begin work on the second floor of our lives. Perimenopause, which coincides with the well-known midlife crisis, is a biologically and psychologically supported opportunity for total rebirth and rejuvenation of body, mind, and spirit, one that results from addressing and healing the unfinished business of the first half of our lives. That's why so many midlife women remember and then let go of childhood trauma at this time.

Our soul's journey through these vulnerable times is very much like that of a newborn kangaroo which, when born, is extremely small and vulnerable. Once out of the birth canal, she must climb blind, naked, and unprotected up her mother's body, guided only by instinct, in order to enter the protective and nurturing environment of her pouch. Some don't survive this journey. Years later, when we have completed the second floor of our house, and have moved to the rooftop of our lives, we must once again enter a birth canal that delivers us—back to the spiritual realm from which we originally came. During the years leading up to this final passage, we may once again experience some of the same vulnerability we experienced as a newborn, only this time in reverse.

Where Are You? Where Is Your Mother? Where Is Your Daughter?

A look at the challenges and treasures associated with each room will help you determine where you, your mother, or your daughter stand in relationship to your potential and to each other. Notice which rooms you, your mother, or your daughter are in. How well have you reached the developmental tasks associated with each room you've transited thus far? How is your daughter doing? Your mother? Has each of you moved into the next room at the appropriate age, or are you or your mother trying to stay in a room that you've outgrown?

For example, a daughter who is too anxious to risk life in the outside world may decide to stay at home or move back home in her twenties just when her mother is ready to move on to the next room in her own life. On the other hand, a midlife woman whose children have left home may be starting a new business, a new relationship, or be preparing to travel. But just as she's about to "take flight," her mother begins to experience a variety of physical complaints and to make demands on her daughter's time and energy. The real problem may be the mother's fear of moving on to the next room—which can worsen or even create the health problems of aging.

While there are times when an adult child legitimately needs temporary shelter, or when an older mother needs care and assistance, these arrangements do not generally work well if either party believes she can get the nurturance she's seeking only by going to her mother or her daughter. If either mother or daughter falls into this nurturance trap, it may prevent them from developing the feminine powers that are the treasures of every "room" in their lives.

ACCESSING THE POWER OF CONSCIOUSNESS

Consciousness, working through and with the laws of nature, creates and sustains our bodies from the beginning to the end of our lives. To have maximal access to our ability to maintain or achieve optimal health and happiness, we need to know how to acknowledge, embrace, and access the power contained in this consciousness. Then we must learn how to consciously and skillfully use that power at each stage of our life journey.

Owning and using power has traditionally been a troubling issue for women, so I'd like to be clear about what I mean when I talk about feminine power.

Science defines power as the energy needed to do work or change matter from one state to another: turning water to steam, or lifting a boulder. In other words, power is the energy necessary to make something happen.

Eastern cultures, particularly the teachings of Taoism, divide power into two types—yin and yang. Yang power is what most Westerners think of when we hear the word "power." It moves actively and deliberately toward a goal in the outer world. We use yang power to step on the gas and propel us toward our goals. Yang power is associated with masculinity. When it is unbalanced by its partner, yin power, it becomes a force that is used to control and dominate others. An excess of yang power within an individual leads to overstimulation of the sympathetic nervous system and the stress hormones it produces. This leads to overwork, burn out, and chronic disease.

Yin power, on the other hand, is the power of expectancy and faith. We use yin power to change our minds and our beliefs so we are better able to attract what we want. Yin power knows how and when to wait and hold back. It knows that sometimes the best action is to do nothing. The essence of yin power is knowing that you can't force a harvest of any kind without compromising its quality and quantity. Yin power is the power of the egg that sends out a signal for the sperm—and then sits and waits for the sperm to come to it. It is also the power that causes the seed to germinate in the darkness. Yin power is associated with femininity. An excess of yin power results in passivity and dependency in life and in relationships. Unless it is balanced by yang power, yin power can lead to lethargy, lack of motivation and initiation, and stasis.

Both yin and yang are integrated in what I am calling feminine power. In assessing my own life, I've found it useful to think of this power as divided into five different facets, all of which are seamlessly interrelated. Your mother provides the basic scaffolding for how you yourself will use the five facets of power in your own life. It is your job to remodel this scaffolding to suit your own unique soul's purpose by examining and updating your beliefs and behaviors in each area.

THE FIVE FACETS OF FEMININE POWER

One: Feminine Biology. The processes of your female body are not some "mistake" to be hidden or medicated. To raise a daughter who is healthy and comfortable in her own skin, a mother needs to appreciate and work consciously with the biologic processes in her own body, knowing that all of them—the menstrual cycle, pregnancy, labor, birth, breast-feeding, and menopause—are gifts that contain wisdom designed to help a girl or woman lead a happy and healthy life.

The functioning of every cell and every organ in our bodies is heavily influenced by our thoughts, beliefs, and behaviors. As in all areas of life, the law of attraction—that like attracts like—operates on a biologic level. Our thoughts literally become their physical equivalents. If a mother believes, for example, that menstruation is a painful nuisance, then she (and her daughter) will be quite likely to experience it that way. If, on the other hand, a mother honors her menstrual cycle as a time for monthly reflection, meditation, cleansing, and renewal, she and her daughter are likely to experience it as a comfortable and meaningful part of their lives.

Two: Relationships and Bonding. Throughout our lives, our health and immunity depend upon our ability to create and sustain healthy relationships. And our relationships with our mothers provides us with a potent imprint for what relationships look and feel like.

The placenta is the quintessential organ of relationship. It is co-created between a mother and her child to sustain a child's intrauterine life. No one quite understands how the maternal body is able to immunologically tolerate the fetus without rejecting it as foreign. Such tolerance for new life that literally feeds off one's body is the essence of the maternal relationship. But one need not be a mother to appreciate the fact that many new relationships begin with one person helping to sustain another. The reward that a mother gets for this is a warm feeling of satisfaction that enlivens and strengthens her heart and also changes her brain so that it's more adaptable.

But there's a limit to this tolerance. Once a baby has reached full-term growth, placental blood vessels begin to calcify and shut down, signifying that it's now time for the baby to be born into more independent life. Both mother and child go through labor to prepare them for their new roles. The same is true for all relationships. They must undergo constant change and growth—not all of which is comfortable—if they are to reach their full potential.

The placenta also models healthy boundaries in relationships. The maternal and fetal blood flow remain separate. The mother—the one who is donating her resources—either provides or withholds blood flow to her baby by the effect of her thoughts, emotions, and behaviors. If she's angry, stressed, or doesn't want to be pregnant, her body is likely to create an abundance of stress hormones, which narrow the blood vessels and restrict the blood supply to her child. If, on the other hand, she is relaxed, happy, and feels well cared for, the blood flow to her baby will be optimal.

Once we are born, the flow of our mother's breast milk is just as crucial to our health and well-being. Later, as children, we crave our mother's approval and attention in the same way that we craved her placental blood flow and breast milk.

As they are nurturing and sustaining us, our mothers also need an outer placenta of people, places, and things that support and replenish them.

Ultimately, each of us has to outgrow our mother's care and create in turn an outer placenta to provide us with sustainable nourishment at each stage of our lives.

Three: Self-care. Our bodies are the homes in which our souls are housed. If we don't care for our bodies well, how can we expect to live well?

We internalize our mother's care of our bodies as the standard for our own self-care. Starting in utero with the experience of our mother's blood flow to us, our early feeding experiences determine whether or not we believe that there will be "enough."

Breast-feeding is a good example of the self-care principle. When you are nursing a child, the quality and quantity of your milk is directly linked to how rested and well nourished you, the mother, are. You can't slake another's thirst if your own cup is empty. If you're exhausted from too much work, worry, grief, sadness, or anger, the quality and quantity of your milk supply suffers.

This same principle applies if you have too many "fight or flight" stress hormones surging through your body. Then you won't be able to engage the "rest and restore" chemicals elaborated by the parasympathetic nervous system. Over time, chronic illness and tissue breakdown is the result.

Bottom line: All self-care must balance yin and yang—waking and sleeping, eating and fasting, stretching and strengthening.

Four: Passion and Purpose. Each of us is born with an innate sense of purpose and the passion to manifest our heart's desires here on earth. And we were each born with an individual will to accomplish this task.

We are the only ones who can really know that purpose, so it's up to us to decide how we will manifest it. Responsibility to ourselves and to our soul's purpose is the basis for personal autonomy and freedom. This doesn't mean that we're free to do everything and anything, or to ride roughshod over others. Our passion and purpose must be aligned with our souls, and our will must be motivated by love and appreciation, not by unexamined compulsions, external circumstances, or the unconscious conditioning we have inherited from our parents or society. Like an actor who has infinite freedom to perform her role within the confines of a script, we too must manifest our passion and purpose within the confines of our soul's script.

We are born with an individual will, which then gets shaped by our experience. We discover the boundaries between our will and the will of others through painful experiences and by hearing the word "no." "No" doesn't mean we're supposed to give up; it means that we must allow ourselves to entertain other options. The old saying "Where there's a will, there's a way" is a statement of the truth.

Our emotions are designed to guide us in the direction of our greatest fulfillment. Feelings of love, awe, and appreciation mean that we're going in the right direction. Feelings of anger, fear, and pain mean that we've just crossed a boundary or taken a wrong turn. Time to readjust.

When our will is truly aligned with our soul and motivated by love, we eventually attract the circumstances that fulfill our passion and purpose. But the pursuit of our life's passion is rarely a straight line. It involves getting off track and then readjusting. And it is refined over a lifetime.

Five: Resourcefulness and Adaptability. In order to manifest our passion and purpose, we need skills that help us navigate in the world and the ability to respond to changing circumstances. We need to recognize when we must depend on others and when we must act independently with minimal support. We need a firm sense of self-esteem and self-worth. We also need financial literacy and the education required to fulfill our dreams. Financial literacy includes the knowledge that money is nothing more than a manifestation of what our society values. Wealth is infinite and money, like biology, follows well-defined laws. One of those is that we must trade value for value, and that our time itself has financial value.

In addition, we must know when to lead and when to follow; when to speak up and when to keep to ourselves; when to follow the rules and when the rules can be bent.

Above all, resourceful people understand the law of attraction and how to align themselves with it. Like a charming young child who knows how to win her mother's attention, a resourceful person knows how to attract helpers and mentors. She also maintains a sense of humor and perspective no matter what is going on around her.

Fortunately, no matter where we currently are in our lives, we each have guidance available with which to access all aspects of our feminine power. That guidance comes directly to us through our maternal legacies when we ask for it. And it's as individual as our fingerprints. Let me explain.

WELCOME THE GRANDMOTHERS

Years ago, when I was leading a workshop in women's health at the Omega Institute, I started one of our sessions with a matrilineal naming circle. Here's how it worked: I asked each woman present to say her name out loud and then add "daughter of," going as far back as she could recall. I started with, "I am Christiane, daughter of Edna, daughter of Ruth, daughter of Margaret." Then I took the hand of the next woman who named herself and her maternal foremothers. As each of us named the women of her maternal heritage, and then joined hands with the next woman, the room was filled with evocative antique names: Zoe, Mabel, Gertrude, Sophy. Some women's heritage went back for seven generations. When we had finished, I said, "Now let's invite all of these women to be with us today. Feel their presence. Accept what they have to teach us." Within moments, many women in the room had started to sob. This sobbing escalated as women shed tears and voiced the grief that had remained dormant and unacknowledged in their bodies for years, perhaps centuries.

Inviting our mothers, maternal grandmothers, and maternal great-grandmothers into the room that summer day taught me something very powerful and important, something every woman interested in her health needs to know: if you want to experience the health, joy, and freedom that are possible for you, you must journey to the headwaters of your consciousness as a woman. You must be willing to drink at the place in the earth from which your lifeblood sprang, your relationship with your mother and your maternal inheritance. When you do this, you will probably find yourself weeping. But each tear you shed will help you heal.

Don't worry about doing this alone. Each time you pick up this book or feel overwhelmed by emotion, invite in the grandmothers, all the women who came before you. Name them out loud if you can. Don't worry if you don't know their names. Just say, "I invite my personal grandmothers, from seven generations ago until the present, to be with me now." They will be there. Thank them for coming. It's that simple. Their blood is still coursing through your veins and through your heart. If you ask them to come, they will be there for you, ready to help you heal and become a woman who is healthy and joyful. The first step toward joy and health in your present life may require shedding the tears that your grandmothers were never able to shed. Feeling and releasing the grief of the unfulfilled lives of our foremothers lifts the weight of our maternal legacies from our shoulders. When we no longer have to carry this heaviness, we are free to remember and develop the many gifts and talents that we have also inherited from them.

If you are reading this book, you're feeling enough love in your life to help you dissolve any blocks about your health or your life that you may have unconsciously inherited from your maternal line. Congratulations! This is cause for great celebration! Welcome to the work that heals all of us: our mothers, our grandmothers, and all the women who came before us. Imagine them cheering you on and sending you blessings. Let's begin.

The Foundation of
Mother-Daughter Health

3

The Miracle of Conception

Igniting New Life

✿

From the moment I gazed into the eyes of my firstborn child, I was enchanted. Up until I actually went into labor I had remained totally immersed in my career, approaching my impending motherhood in a detached clinical way, mind-body split firmly in place. Like my mother, I had not been particularly interested in babies, but I always knew I wanted to be a mother someday. Once my residency training in ob-gyn was finished, I knew that it was now or never. I got pregnant and gave birth to Annie, my first daughter, when I was thirty-one. Despite having spent much of the previous five years delivering babies and marveling at how infinitely varied were the ways in which their mothers responded to them, I was completely unaware of my own internal blueprint for motherhood. Nor had I ever given any thought to how each woman's mothering blueprint is shaped by the way she herself had been mothered. Through the process of labor and birth, however, the innate creation and nurturing skills that had lain dormant within me were now awakened—quite suddenly and unexpectedly. Seeing the imprint of my own mother on my particular way of mothering would start to happen only many years later.

One of the things that amazed me at the time was that I instantly had the urge to have a whole lot of children. I was thrilled with the baby I had just produced, a fact that both surprised and delighted me, given my prior take-it-or-leave-it attitude toward babies. I was caught up in the wonder and abundance of biologic creativity at that moment in a way that I will never forget. Like my mother before me, I had never doubted my ability to care for a baby. It seemed like common sense. What I wasn't prepared for was the amount of heart-bursting unconditional love I felt for this little being. The very day she was born, Annie laughed—a tiny laugh, I'll admit, but coming out of her perfect rosebud lips, it sounded like the voices of the angels themselves. I had the distinct feeling that she had spent a good deal of her time with the angels. And she looked as though she hadn't quite left the spirit world behind. I knew that I would do everything in my power to protect her, provide for her, and let her know that she was loved. I thought she was the most precious child ever born.

But despite my immediate postpartum enthusiasm for making babies, it was two and a half years before I gave birth to my next child, my daughter Kate. And by the time I turned thirty-seven, with two small children in the house, I realized that although I felt a strong biologic urge to have a third, I didn't have enough life energy available to both mother another child in what I considered the optimal way—which involved breast-feeding for at least a year and a half and being available to my children as much as possible—and write the book that I knew was waiting to be born through me. I chose the book.

I adore my children and have found motherhood fulfilling beyond my wildest dreams, but being a mother is only one aspect of who I am. As a physician and a writer, I have strong needs for inward focus, solitude, and scholarly pursuits—lifestyle qualities not easily available to the mothers of large families. To be a truly happy and healthy woman, and therefore a happy mother, I have needed a focus other than my home and family, just as my own mother had.

Once I made the decision not to have more children, I had a tubal ligation to firmly and consciously close the door to my biologic fertility. I had seen far too many women in my practice get pregnant at midlife "by mistake." I didn't want any creations by default, even though I know that for some women deciding not to decide can be a blessing. Looking at my own life, it seemed clear to me that I wouldn't be able to get where I wanted to go in my career and my life unless I was willing to keep a firm grasp on the reins of both my creativity and my fertility. I needed to consciously direct them rather than leave them to chance. My first book, *Women's Bodies, Women's Wisdom,* was "born" seven years later.

PURPOSE AND PASSION

Whether or not she chooses to use it, every woman has within her the ability to give birth to creations of all kinds. For many women, having children is their life's major passion and purpose. For others, a child would be a significant detour from what they feel they were meant to do, perhaps even making it impossible. Then there are those, like me, who know that their life purpose includes having children but who feel other callings as well. We want children and, when we have them, we love them as ferociously as those who stay at home full-time with their kids. But to be completely happy, healthy, and fulfilled as individuals, we need to combine our mothering with other creative endeavors. Failure to do so can result in one or more of the following physical and/or emotional problems: infertility; chronic feelings of guilt, anger, or depression, with an increased risk for illnesses of all types as a consequence; overinvolvement in the lives of our children; rerouting of our unfulfilled ambitions through our children; or jealousy of our children, especially our daughters. This is why the great psychiatrist Carl Jung said that the greatest unconscious force in the lives of children is the unfulfilled dreams of their parents. I couldn't agree more.

Regardless of which path is right for you, the key is to bring full consciousness to the choice of how best to realize the potential of your feminine creative power. Fortunately, we are all born with innate instructions for accessing and using the creative energy available to us at each stage of our lives. We simply need to learn how to "read" those instructions.

One of the primary jobs of being a mother is to encourage our children to achieve happiness and fulfillment by reading and acting on their own innate instructions—a job that is much easier if we ourselves have done such work, and been honest with ourselves about the extent to which we have followed our hearts and lived up to our potential. But being honest about how you're using or wish to use your creative energy can be very difficult in a society in which women are still socialized to believe that there is a "right" way to use feminine power, and that that necessarily involves having children. Sometimes honesty will mean acknowledging that you have channeled your energy into an "unwanted" or "default" pregnancy or creation simply because you weren't willing to take responsibility for using this energy more purposefully. Which is not to say that such detours are necessarily mistakes. At all times, keep in mind that the soul part of you may have an agenda that you simply cannot control.

Condoms break. Women get pregnant even when they take the pill correctly. Often the children who come into their lives as a result bring them great joy. Conversely, women who desperately want children sometimes find themselves unable to conceive, and then discover fulfillment in ways they had never dared to imagine possible.

Defining and Refining Our Purpose and Passion

Just as we are born with hundreds of thousands more eggs than we will ever use, we also have far more creative ideas than we will ever be able to bring into being. Some of these eggs and ideas are destined to take root and grow if we're willing to fertilize and support them. Others end in miscarriage or stillbirth. This is not a sign of failure. Nor is it a design flaw. Instead, this process simply reflects the adaptability of Nature, a force that keeps creating and experimenting with form and function in a variety of changing environments. When one thing doesn't work, she tries another, and just keeps sending out more eggs, sperms, seed pods—and ideas!

Pruning—Ideas and Brain Cells

Interestingly, the same shaping and pruning that has to take place in our procreative and creative lives also occurs in our brain cells and the connections among them. We have more brain cells before we are born—approximately 200 billion neurons when we are twenty weeks old and still within the womb—than we will ever have again. But a lot of these neurons and their connections are flawed, so the brain kills them off, in a process called apoptosis—cell death. Thanks to pruning, by the time we are born we have "only" about 100 billion neurons. If, however, something goes wrong and there is insufficient pruning, the result will be neurological "static," due to faulty connections or too much information for us to be able to process. That's why there is such a large die-off of brain cells beginning while we are still in utero, and continuing, at a slower rate, throughout our lifetime. You can't progress developmentally unless you and your ideas, like your brain cells, undergo regular pruning.

The biological wisdom of nature teaches us to reduce the inessential in order to help us focus, shape, and define our purpose. As we mature, we learn to discard goals that are no longer relevant to our lives. We learn to concentrate on fewer creations, but with deeper involvement and greater mastery.

Conception Choices

Every time we say yes to a given choice, we're simultaneously saying no to something or someone else who will never see the light of day. The endless possibilities available to us, as to what, where, when, how, and with whom we might conceive, force us to make choices. We will have full access to our procreative and creative powers only when we are willing to make conscious choices about what we're willing to gestate to full maturity. This can be difficult. A woman who chooses to have a child instead of going to college must say no—at least for now, and probably for some time to come, if not forever—to everything that college could bring. A woman who chooses to remain childless to pursue her career or other interests is saying no to the gifts and joys of motherhood. Each choice we make has consequences.

❧ WISDOM CHALLENGE: *To Conceive or Not to Conceive*

It takes a great deal of faith to conceive, bear, and raise a child. It also takes a lot of resources, inner and outer, and, ideally, planning, for child rearing is surely one of life's most passionate and consuming endeavors. When deciding about whether to bear a child every mother must ask herself the following questions: Do I have what I need—physically, emotionally, practically, financially—to raise a child? Am I in good health? Are there any genetic legacies I need to be concerned about passing on? Can I provide a good home? a loving family? an education? Do I have adequate income? Will I have support from a partner? my family? friends? community? What resources do I currently have available to help me take on this responsibility? Which ones will I need to acquire later? Although it is not always possible, it is best to give these issues some thought and put some support structures in place before conceiving.

Perhaps the most fundamental of all questions a woman must ask herself is whether she wants a child. Some women feel "forced" into motherhood by cultural pressures when, on a deep soul level, they'd prefer to do something else with their creative energy. Just as it takes faith to decide to have a child, it requires courage to say no to having a baby, for the woman who does so knows that she is putting herself at odds with what the prevailing culture expects of women.

Releasing the Illusion of Perfection and Control

When you embark on conceiving either a child or an idea, there are no guarantees on how it will turn out. An attitude that is perfectionistic or overly controlling may result in paralysis that adversely influences both fertility and creativity. Or it can result in becoming so overwhelmed that you adopt a default attitude of "deciding not to decide," and abdicating responsibility for the consequences. Although we must learn how to work consciously and respectfully with our fertility, enhancing it when we have decided to conceive, controlling it when the time is not right (see Preconception Program, page 51), we must also accept that life has a way of throwing us curve balls on a regular basis, no matter how carefully we plan. Writer Annie Dillard put it this way: "That something is everywhere and always amiss is part of the very stuff of creation."[1]

Multiple Umbilical Cords

Once you've found or homed in on your life's purpose, if it involves more than marrying and having children, how do you fit it in with the needs of a mate or a family? All creative pursuits require energy to grow and develop. As any artist or writer will tell you, the process of creating a painting, a beautiful song, or a piece of literature is very much like conceiving, gestating, and giving birth to a child. The same is true for anything we make, whether or not we think of it as a "creative" endeavor. Each of our projects and creations has an umbilical cord attached to it that draws life energy from our bodies for nourishment, just as a child developing within us does. The energy it takes to plan, shop for, and prepare a meal, for example, comes out of the same place as a human pregnancy—the second chakra of the body, which comprises the pelvic organs, lower bowel, and lower back.

Tending to the needs of a child, a life partner, and/or a career, as much as you love any or all of them, can put a lot of stress on the

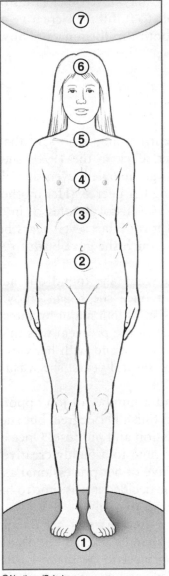

©Northrup/Schulz

CHAKRAS: THE EMOTIONAL CENTERS

The chakras are the energy centers in the physical body where one's beliefs and emotions are transformed into one's state of health. Their locations parallel the body's neuroendocrine and immune system pathways and form a link between our energy anatomy (our family legacy together with our current thoughts, feelings, and beliefs) and our physical anatomy (the health of our tissues and organs). The holographic energy system of the chakras carries information for the growth, development, and regeneration of every part of the body.

second chakra. When too many demands are made on it, your body won't be able to sustain and gestate anything fully. You literally deplete your own creative soil. Nothing can take root. Sometimes this happens in a very literal sense. Women who experience a conflict between their drive to go after what they want in the world versus their need to be loved and accepted may find themselves having fertility problems. If they are unable to replenish their energy through self-care and support from others, they may have other kinds of gynecologic problems, too—or be unable to fulfill their creative ambitions. The following story illustrates both the dilemma and how one woman found a way out of it.

ARIEL: Rediscovering Her Creativity

Ariel was a forty-three-year-old patient of mine who said that she had always wanted to be an architect. Back in the 1970s she had dropped out of architectural school to get married, even though she had only a year to go before completing her degree. (Her mother before her had left a very satisfying job as a history professor in order to get married and have children, but it took her seven years before she was finally able to conceive, after which she gave birth to Ariel, her only child.)

After divorcing her first husband when she found out he was having an affair, Ariel remarried; but once she began enjoying a highly satisfying career as a design assistant in a major architectural firm, this marriage, too, fell apart. Part of the problem was that her second husband wanted children right away and with her career finally taking off, after being stalled for several years, she wasn't yet ready.

After her second divorce, Ariel had a number of job opportunities as well as a chance to go back and finish her degree, but she still found herself unable to sustain her passion and purpose. Once again she fell in love and got married—this time to a highly creative and charismatic attorney who was supportive of her professional aspirations. Not long after their marriage, she decided it was time to have a baby, whom she conceived and gave birth to easily.

During her pregnancy and the first few years of her daughter's life, Ariel collapsed herself into her husband's and her child's identities as if they were an architectural project to be made perfect in every detail. She redecorated and redesigned every room of a large old Victorian home, dressed herself and her daughter impeccably, and accompanied her husband on his every business trip, for fear that without her presence he would have an affair, as her first husband had done.

While Ariel continued to say that she wanted to work in architecture, she felt conflicted. Every time she took on a couple of clients, she became distracted by what she perceived as the needs of her husband and child and failed to do the work necessary to move forward with her work. As a result, her frustrated clients would invariably leave. She felt angry and abandoned, unable to figure out why she was always losing clients or how to fit her professional life into her all-consuming family life.

Ariel was stuck in the same creativity limbo as her mother before her. And, like her mother before her, she was unable to conceive the second child she and her husband had planned to have.

But Ariel was on the way to wisdom. During a visit for peri-menopausal complaints of PMS and headaches, when I asked her what was going on in her life, Ariel began to see the pattern that had become her undoing: every time she had had a chance to launch a creative enterprise, she became fearful of losing control over her other life creations—her marriage, her house, and her child—and sabotaged herself so that she ended up spending 100 percent of her time taking care of her family.

Over time, Ariel began to let go of her need for perfection at home and to allow others to assist her. With respect to her child, she learned that part of mothering is learning to let go. Once she stopped being consumed by her home life, she was able to reopen the channel to her creative wisdom and return to doing the work she loved. A part-time job at an architectural firm allowed her to enjoy both family and professional life. Her home may have lost its perfect appearance, but her health and happiness improved enormously, and her daughter, age eight at the time, blossomed as well, making many new friends once her mother was no longer so enmeshed in her life.

What Were You Thinking?

Pregnancy is best approached as a freely chosen or accepted opportunity to participate in bringing forth a new life. But research indicates that nearly 60 percent of all pregnancies in the United States are unintended.[2] This is not just a teenage phenomenon. Although 82 percent of pregnancies in women aged fifteen to nineteen are unintended, accidents are also widespread in women over age thirty-five, accounting for 56 percent of their pregnancies. Accidental pregnancies aren't necessarily a problem. Many women make the adjustment from the initial shock and dismay to acceptance and delight. But this is not always the case, and the results can be tragic for both mother and child. The percentage of unplanned pregnancies that still occur, in an age when birth control and sex education are so widely available, speaks volumes about how far we have to go to truly bring full consciousness to sexuality and fertility.

A mother's intentions when she becomes pregnant can influence how she nurtures and what she feels toward her child. Of course many women conceive accidentally, without any intention. Others conceive consciously, with joy and love. But some women conceive as a way to keep a marriage alive or hold on to a man; and some conceive because of a perceived hole in their lives. One of my patients once confessed that she wanted a baby because she was lonely and wanted someone to love who would not leave her. Having a child is rarely a good way to compensate for some area in your life that is lacking. Not only is it unlikely to give you what you need but it puts far too heavy a burden on the child.

Creations that are lovingly conceived and carefully nurtured and guided have a far greater chance of reaching their full potential than those that lack the unconditional love that mothering in optimal circumstances can provide. This is true whether the creation is a child, a relationship, or a garden. No matter which "room" of our lives we're currently residing in, the way our bodies were conceived, birthed, fed, and cared for establishes the lifelong foundation for our health and well-being.

THE BLUEPRINT FOR CREATION

The processes of conception, gestation, labor, and birth contain the very blueprint for creation and, because of this, are imbued with wisdom that can teach us how to live our lives. For example, once we've conceived an idea, whether it has come to us spontaneously or as the result of many days and nights of hard work, we must attend to it, just as we would attend to a child growing within our body. We must have the physical strength and stamina to bring together the necessary resources to feed and nurture it, so that it can grow into what it needs to become. And we must have commitment.

As I was writing this book, I knew that a few things were necessary if my ideas were ever going to grow into a full-fledged book. First, I needed to devote enough time and energy to the writing process for the conception to take on a life of its own within me. This finally happened in July of 1998. Up until that time, I had been working sporadically on the project for several years, gathering research and writing when I had the time. Though a slow gestation process was going on within me during those years, the project hadn't really taken root in me yet. Then I realized that this creation would never really see the light of day if I didn't devote a solid block of time and energy solely to it. So like good mothers everywhere, I waited until my two daughters were away for three weeks before setting aside the requisite chunk of time. Then I said no to all other commitments, and sat every day with the material, until one magical moment when I felt this book quicken within me. It was as though the placenta that could nourish the project had finally insinuated itself deeply enough into my creative process to keep it going. The book had at long last taken on a life of its own, fueled by my commitment, focus, intent, and surrender to the process. I couldn't wait to get to it every day. I knew that like every child, this creation was not really me but was coming through me and was part of me. My job was to take care of myself and my creation by attending to both our needs. If we tune into our Mother Bear wisdom, we will find that the same environmental factors that support optimal pregnancy and birth can help support maximal creativity, happiness, and vibrant health in all our endeavors throughout our lives.

Conception Wisdom

The fertilization of an egg by a sperm is one of the greatest wonders of nature, an event in which magnificently small fragments of animal life are driven by cosmic forces toward their appointed end, the growth of a living being. As a spectacle it can be compared only with an eclipse of the sun or the eruption of a volcano. . . . It is, in fact, the most common and the nearest to us of nature's cataclysms, and yet it is very seldom observed because it occurs in a realm most people never see, the terrain of microscopic things.
—GEORGE W. CORNER

Many women have told me that they remember the moment when they conceived a child. One put it this way: "Somehow I knew the night I conceived. It felt as though something fundamentally changed in my body . . . that I was no longer just me. Someone else was with me. I knew I had conceived my first child."

Nature is extravagant when it comes to conceiving new creations of all kinds. She is also very fertile and very persistent. Think of all the seeds that dandelions produce and all the burrs that get stuck on your dog or your socks. Our female bodies—as well as our minds and spirits—are likewise alive with creative potential, starting even before we are born.

When we are five-month-old fetuses developing in our mothers' wombs, we have 6–7 million eggs. By the time we're born, the total number of eggs in our ovaries has already begun to decline, but we still have 1 to 2 million. At puberty, when we become biologically able to conceive a child, we have an average of 400,000 eggs ready and waiting to develop, and by age thirty-six, the number has declined to about 36,000[3]—still tens of thousands more than a woman will ever need, no matter how many children she wants to have!

Interestingly enough, the account I just gave, based on what has been until now the conventional biological doctrine of the twentieth century—that there neither is nor can be any addition to the millions of eggs originally formed in the fetal ovary—may not give sufficient credit to nature's infinite regenerative capacities. New research from Jonathan Tilley, Ph.D., and colleagues at Harvard Medical School has found that female mammals are able to create new eggs even into adulthood. This preliminary work has significant implications for how we view fertility, and it certainly forces us to rethink the "old egg theory."[4]

All women are creators by nature. Every part of us, including our biological fertility, participates in Nature's creativity directly. But creativity is not limited to our biology. Nature in her benevolence has blessed us with far more ideas, as well as eggs, than we can possibly bring into being. The creative force within us is very strong. If we learn how to channel it, we can make ourselves available for all kinds of conceptions, be they ideas or babies.

You Are a Miracle

Some creations are consciously and eagerly planned. Others happen by default. Nevertheless, from a soul perspective, a child who makes it to birth was meant to be here. Part of her purpose may be to acknowledge the pain associated with being called a mistake. In some circumstances, such "mistakes" are later acknowledged as major blessings in disguise. One of my friends found out she was pregnant when her oldest child was age sixteen. Once she and her husband recovered from their initial shock, they decided to continue the pregnancy. Both parents now say that this child has been one of the best things that ever happened to them.

Regardless of the circumstances of your conception, be assured that your existence is a miracle. The odds against any one of us being born are staggeringly high. Your mother's body had tens of thousands of eggs to choose from. Only one of them ripened the month you were conceived. That egg accepted just one of millions of sperm available to her from your father at that moment. Then, guided by biology, destiny, and your soul qualities, the embryo that was you had to make it through the multiple stages of development necessary to launch your unique life into being. For a variety of reasons—genetic, environmental, or a combination of both—most conceptions never reach maturation. Of the relatively few eggs that do get fertilized, 80 percent never make it to the embryonic stage. The statistical probability of a particular egg and a particular sperm coming together to create the unique human that you are is infinitesimally small. On a soul level, of course, statistics mean nothing. If a creation or individual is destined to be born, it will happen. I've seen this repeatedly. Babies get conceived under mysterious circumstances in which conception is considered biologically impossible or highly improbable. One of my patients conceived after ten years of infertility with a husband whose sperm count was theoretically zero.

The fact that you are alive and reading this is, therefore, an absolute miracle—the result of an agreement between your soul and your mother's soul.

PRECONCEPTION PROGRAM: CREATING A HEALTHY FOUNDATION FOR YOUR DAUGHTER

Given the fact that our bodies are self-renewing and in a perpetual state of change, it's always possible to enhance your chances of conceiving and bearing a healthy child. No matter how many bad lifestyle choices you may have made in the past, you can choose a different way of life that will get your baby off to a good start.

Good nutrition, for example, is vital to a healthy pregnancy and healthy baby. Research has indicated a link between the mother's diet in the first trimester and all of the following conditions: sterility, miscarriage, prematurity, and low birth weight, as well as many of the most common birth defects, for example spina bifida and other neural tube defects, heart defects, urogenital anomalies, cleft palate, club foot, missing digits, and so on.

The following do's and don'ts will help you start preparing for pregnancy as far in advance as possible, which is a great idea since it's often a month or two before a woman knows she's pregnant—and that first trimester can be crucial. In fact, results are best if a couple begins a preconception program at least six months before conception. After the do's and don'ts, I've included a dietary program, which is a good one to follow both before you've conceived and after you're pregnant.

PRECONCEPTION DO'S:

Get enough natural light. Natural light is a "nutrient" that affects fertility. Make sure you are exposed to natural light daily. If you can't get outside enough, then use full-spectrum lightbulbs that recreate all the frequencies of natural light. (See Resources.)

Sleep in the dark, without a night light. Nighttime darkness enhances normal levels of melatonin and helps fertility.

Consume eighteen hundred to two thousand calories per day. This is about the right amount for the average one-hundred-forty-pound woman.

Maintain a healthy weight. Many formerly infertile women conceive naturally once they achieve a normal weight, and in general it's a good idea to start your pregnancy at a healthy weight (BMI of 25 or below). Once pregnant, don't gain more weight than necessary. A weight gain of twenty-five to thirty pounds is healthy if a woman begins her pregnancy at a normal weight. Overweight women can afford to gain less than this and still give birth to healthy babies. For example, a woman with a BMI of 27 could eat well and gain only about ten pounds during her pregnancy, but still have a healthy baby. The quality of what a pregnant woman eats is more important than the quantity. Healthy cells develop from having enough of the right nutrients available.

Pregnant women who are quite thin (BMIs of 19 to 22) do best when they gain more than twenty-five to thirty pounds. One of the most encouraging things I've noticed in the media reports on the

Hollywood baby boom is that stars like Kate Hudson and Gwyneth Paltrow—women who are very thin—have reportedly gained forty or more pounds during their pregnancies.

PRECONCEPTION DON'TS:

Don't drink alcohol. Research has shown that alcohol can decrease sperm count, impair sperm motility, and cause malformation of sperm. Recent work on fetal alcohol syndrome (FAS) by Anne Streissguth, Ph.D., has shown a seven-point decrease in IQ in children whose mothers had consumed just one alcoholic drink daily during pregnancy. It is now recognized that there are children who do not bear the physical characteristics of FAS but who have subtle mental or behavioral difficulties from being exposed to alcohol in the womb and are now identified as suffering from fetal alcohol effects (FAE).

Don't smoke tobacco. Smoking is by far the most common contributor to prematurity and low birth weight. Women who smoke have a higher incidence of children with birth defects such as cleft lip and palate. Even when the mother does not smoke, if her partner smokes over ten cigarettes a day, they are two and a half times more likely to have a child with congenital malformations. One of my ob-gyn colleagues refuses to see pregnant women who smoke. She tells them, "When you continue to smoke while pregnant, it means that I care more about your baby than you do. That's not okay with me." I call this tough love. And I agree with her.

Avoid caffeine. Even one cup of coffee per day has been shown to double the rate of miscarriage.

Don't use marijuana or any other recreational, mood-altering drugs. These all contain chemicals that affect the developing brain and nervous system of the child, and among other kinds of damage may predispose a child to a higher-than-average chance for drug-seeking behavior later in life.

Don't use birth control pills for at least three months prior to conception. It is well documented that oral contraceptives lower levels of zinc, manganese, vitamin A, and a number of the B complex vitamins, especially pyridoxine (B_6). They may also lower magnesium and raise copper. So you want to be sure that your body has had a chance to replenish these vital nutrients before conceiving.

Avoid over-the-counter drugs. You should also minimize use of prescription drugs as much as possible, though obviously some medications, such as anticonvulsants for someone with epilepsy, are necessary. Check with your doctor before going off any prescription drugs.

Don't use any products containing industrial toxins. For a book listing these toxins see S. M. Barlow and F. Sullivan (1982), *Reproductive Hazards of Industrial Chemicals: An Evaluation of Animal and Human Data.*

PRECONCEPTION AND PRENATAL DIETARY PROGRAM

The following principles of good nutrition apply both to women who are intending to get pregnant and to those who are already pregnant. But the longer in advance of conception you begin to eat in a healthful manner, the better for both you and your baby.

Eat three meals a day incorporating a minimum of five servings of fruits and vegetables, preferably organically grown and free of pesticides. And be sure to eat breakfast. Eating in the morning sets up a series of metabolic events that will help stabilize your blood sugar throughout the entire day and help keep your appetite under control.

Eat organic, natural foods as often as you can, including organic meats, eggs, fish, vegetables, fruits, nuts, beans, seeds, soy, and low-fat dairy foods. Although it may not be possible to eat 100 percent healthy all the time, it's much easier when you're pregnant, or preparing to conceive, because your body will often crave the healthy foods that the baby needs.

Eat enough protein, including a source of protein with each meal. If you're vegetarian, you can get your proteins from dried beans, nuts, soy products, and low-fat dairy foods. (See next chapter for more information about adequate nutrition for vegetarians.) The average woman, who is about five feet three inches and 135 pounds, needs about sixty grams of protein per day once she is pregnant. You'll need more protein if you're taller or have a heavier frame, less if you're shorter or have a very small frame.

Grams of Protein in Foods	
Animal protein, such as pork, beef, or fish	7 g/oz (average, depending upon leanness of meat)
Eggs	Whole: 6 g/egg Albumin (egg white): 4 g/egg
Hard cheese	6–7 g/oz
Beans, white	17 g/cup
Skim milk	8 g/cup
Tofu	10 g/1/4-cup

Source: Protein Equivalency Chart A, Appendix to *Protein Power*, by Michael and Mary Dan Eades

Drink pure filtered water, one ounce per every two pounds of body weight. For example, if you weigh one hundred and forty pounds, drink seventy ounces of water per day.

Get enough omega-3 fats, which are crucial to a baby's brain, cardiovascular, and immune system development, and can also help prevent postpartum depression. Wild salmon is one of the best foods on the planet for replenishing or maintaining omega-3 fatty acids, especially one known as DHA (docosahexaenoic acid). A 3.5-ounce serving of wild Alaskan sockeye salmon contains a minimum of 1.2 grams DHA and EPA, another of the fatty acids. Sardines, omega-3–enriched eggs, dark green leafy vegetables, ground flaxseed, flax oil, ground hemp seed, and hemp seed oil are also good sources. You need at least 400 mg of DHA per day. Some experts suggest taking 800 to 1,200 mg per day, given that so many women are seriously deficient in this type of fat. An enormous and impressive body of scientific literature has shown that insufficient levels of DHA and other essential fatty acids may put the child and/or her mother at increased risk for a myriad of health problems, including mood disorders, autoimmune disorders such as lupus and multiple sclerosis, and brain disorders such as attention deficit and dyslexia.[5] You can get DHA in capsule form (see Resources) if you don't get it through foods.

Avoid partially hydrogenated fats, which occur mainly in packaged foods and will be identified as such on the label. They interfere with the metabolism of essential fatty acids and have a known deleterious effect on cellular membranes. In fact, the introduction of hydrogenated fats into the food supply has been associated with the increase in ADHD, depression, learning disabilities, mood disorders, etc.

Avoid excess consumption of "white" foods, such as pasta, white bread, and other foods prepared with refined flour and/or sugar, which rank high on the glycemic index and cause rapid rises in blood sugar.

Minimize consumption of sweets or eliminate them. When you do add sweeteners, it's best to use honey, maple syrup, or barley malt. These have a lower glycemic index than sugar and also more micronutrients. They are "whole" foods. Agave syrup is particularly good and has a low glycemic index.

Avoid chemical additives such as aspartame and MSG.

PRECONCEPTION AND/OR PRENATAL SUPPLEMENTATION PROGRAM

Both before and after conceiving, follow a daily regimen of supplemental vitamins and minerals. Make sure your supplements' potency are guaranteed and that they are manufactured according to GMP standards (Good Manufacturing Processes), a term that denotes high quality. (See Resources.) The following suggestions for a vitamin and mineral regimen indicate ranges that are deliberately very broad, because I know that it's difficult to find supplements with the exact amounts of everything you need. My own preference is generally to go with the upper range of the values, but the lower ranges will be very helpful even if not absolutely optimal.

Vitamins

Folic acid[†]	800–1,000 mcg
Beta carotene[††]	15,000–25,000 IU
Vitamin D	400–1,200 IU
Vitamin E[†††]	200–400 IU

Vitamin C	500–2,000 mg
Glutathione	2–10 mg
Vitamin K	60 mcg
Thiamine (B_1)	9–100 mg
Riboflavin (B_2)	9–50 mg
Pyridoxine (B_6)	10–100 mg
Niacin (B_3)	20–100 mg
Biotin	100–500 mcg
Vitamin B_{12}	30–250 mcg
Pantothenic acid (B_5)	30–400 mcg
Inositol	30–500 mg
Choline	45–100 mg

Minerals

Calcium	500–1,500 mg[††††]
Magnesium	400–1,000 mg
Boron	1–3 mg
Chromium	100–400 mcg
Copper	1–2 mg
Iron	30 mg
Manganese	1–15 mg
Zinc	12–50 mcg
Selenium	80–120 mcg
Potassium	200–500 mcg
Molybdenum	20–60 mcg
Vanadium	50–100 mcg
Iodine	150 mcg

Trace minerals—from a marine mineral complex or from eating
    sea vegetables such as hiziki, dulse, wakame, nori.

[†] This has been shown to reduce the incidence of cleft lip and palate as well as neural tube defects such as spina bifida.
[††] Vitamin A at levels greater than 10,000 IU per day may be associated with fetal malformations. Beta carotene, which is converted to Vitamin A in the body, is safe.
[†††] as mixed tocopherols (including some tocotrienols)
[††††] amount depends upon dietary sources

Research on the efficacy of a preconception program similar
to that contained in the Do's and Don'ts and the dietary supplementation recommendations outlined above has been
done at the University of Surrey. The study monitored the
progress of 367 couples, many of whom had previously had
difficulty conceiving, miscarriages, premature babies, etc.,
as they followed the "Foresight Preconception Care Programme." The women ranged in age from twenty-two to
forty-five years, the men from twenty-five to fifty-nine years.
By the end of the study 89 percent of the couples had had babies. The average gestational age was 38.5 weeks. Forty-two
percent of the babies were males whose average weight was
seven pounds four and a half ounces (3,299 g) and 58 percent were females whose average weight was seven pounds
two ounces (2,368 g). There were no miscarriages, perinatal
deaths, or malformations, nor did any of the babies have to
be admitted to Special Care. For more information, go to
www.google.com and type in "Foresight Preconception Care
Programme."[6]

Connect with Your Child's Soul

While you are preparing your body for conceiving, you can
also prepare your mind and your spirit. You can consciously "call
in a soul." Envision your little one and invite her in when you
make love. Or try a meditation. Many cultures have a tradition in
which a woman who wants to conceive goes off into nature and
sits in meditation. When her mind is clear and her heart is open,
she invites a special soul to join her. After you do the inviting, you
have to let go and give it over to God, trusting your own soul to do
the rest. In other words, don't let this become another exercise in
control and perfection. You can do the same thing before adopting
a child. A very good and practical reference book for how to do
this is *Parenting Begins before Conception: A Guide to Preparing
Body, Mind, and Spirit for You and Your Future Child,* by Carista
Luminare-Rosen, Ph.D. I also like *Conscious Conception: An Ele-*

mental Journey through the Labyrinth of Sexuality, by Jeannine Parvati Baker and Frederick Baker.

You may also want to keep a preconception journal and write down any thoughts or dreams that arise about your baby. Sometimes your baby will communicate with you, even before she has been conceived. Remember, everything is vibration. You can "lighten" your vibration by consciously lifting your mood—with beautiful music, inspirational literature, affirmations, or even massage. Feeling good around the time of your baby's conception will help get her off to the best possible start.

4

Pregnancy

Trusting the Process of Life

❀

Our female bodies are imbued with and sustained by the wisdom of self-care, starting with the egg itself. Anything we create needs to be fed, repaired, and nurtured into being. The female egg performs these tasks naturally, keeping the genetic code on track without any conscious input on our part. Eggs have powers the likes of which are not seen in any other cells in nature.

EGG WISDOM:
MICROSCOPIC GUIDANCE AND NURTURANCE

Although we've been led to believe that the egg merely sits there and waits to be "acted upon" by the sperm, newer research has shown that the egg is not a passive participant in reproduction. First of all, the egg actually sends out a signal that attracts sperm to it. And it selects the sperm that will enter it. Once fertilized, eggs become the original mothers. They see potential and facilitate it into becoming reality. In fact, the very word *egg* means "to incite to action." The egg literally "eggs on" new life, like a cheerleader helping her team to achieve its goal. This is achieved via mitochondrial DNA—cytoplasmic genes within the egg that reside in the tiny intracellular organs called mitochondria. Mitochondria are tiny holograms of nurturance and guidance that are critical for metabolizing the fats and sugars that provide fuel for embryogenesis (development of new life) once the egg is fertilized.[1] They are also capable of interacting with and influencing the way in which genes from the sperm get expressed. They can repair damaged genes from the fertilizing sperm, thus putting the creation back on track and helping to ensure the health of the developing fetus. Think of it this way: The male brings his genes to the table. The woman brings her genes, too; but she also brings food and shelter to give their resulting creation a place to grow and thrive. And as if this weren't enough, she brings the tools to fix things up if the house requires repair.[2,3] That's why a female biologist once quipped that instead of seeing fertilization as the triumphant penetration of the egg by the sperm, the process should more aptly be called "the egging of the sperm."[4]

Mitochondrial DNA is decidedly female, being inherited strictly through the maternal line. Every person, male and female alike, carries these little nurturers in every cell of their body throughout their life, courtesy of their own mother. And every daughter passes this maternal legacy on to all of her children. This is especially apparent in mothers and daughters. How often have you heard a woman exclaim, "I sound just like my mother!" Like women everywhere, I too find myself saying exactly the same things that my mother has said, using identical intonations and hand gestures for emphasis. My daughters in their turn find themselves channeling my words and gestures.

Yet I've rarely heard a woman say, "Oh, I sound just like my father!" Perhaps this is because our maternal legacies, and the mitochondrial DNA that wires them into place, keep our mothers' voices alive within us in a particularly powerful way.

In truth, male and female alike, we've had a woman "egging us on" with nurturance and guidance from the very beginning. This doesn't end in utero. Sometimes it doesn't end after childhood either. We mothers often feel compelled to do this for our loved ones throughout our lives. It's not surprising then, that a daughter's health is far more apt to be adversely affected by a disengaged, indifferent, sick, or abusive mother than by an equally challenged father.

Even though we take our father's surname in this patriarchal culture, to truly identify our biologic or tribal heritage, we must look to our maternal lineage. This is why forensic pathology units identify dead bodies through maternal DNA testing. And why, in the traditional Jewish faith and in many Native American tribes as well, children are considered to be part of the tribe only if their mother has tribal blood in her. In much of Native American culture, property is handed down through the maternal line.

Just as it's true that dead bodies can be identified by maternal DNA, it is also true that behind every successful, healthy, living woman, one can find outstanding maternal DNA. One of the purposes of this book is to teach you how to "read" this maternal DNA and your egg wisdom, so that you can keep yourself—and your daughter, if you have one (or more)—on track.

Nature Gets It Right

The ability to become pregnant and create a child is direct and incontrovertible evidence that women's bodies contain the blueprint for creation. And it is a testament to that blueprint that most pregnancies are normal and that the vast majority of children are born healthy.

An ob-gyn colleague of mine recently participated in the birth of a healthy baby girl to a forty-three-year-old woman who hadn't known she was pregnant until she began having labor pains. (Variations on this theme are more common than you might think.) Since this woman had been infertile for years, when she stopped having her periods, she simply figured that she was entering menopause. And since she was about forty pounds overweight, she didn't really notice any difference in the size of her abdomen during the pregnancy. That she also managed not to feel the baby kicking simply speaks to the totality of her mind-body split! In any event, she delivered a healthy baby girl amidst much weeping for joy and celebration, once she and her husband saw that their child was perfectly healthy. What had bothered her most, when she discovered that she was actually in labor, was not that she was about to have a baby but that something would be wrong with it because she hadn't known she was pregnant! If she had known, she would have eaten better and abstained from drinking wine and beer.

This story illustrates something that I experienced repeatedly in my obstetrical practice: when it comes to pregnancy and birth, Nature gets it right most of the time, in spite of our human imperfections. That's very reassuring to know, because the major organ systems of a human fetus are already formed by the time most women realize that they are pregnant and begin making the necessary changes to their behavior as a result. However, Nature's wisdom should not be used as an excuse for taking undue risks. We should work in concert with Nature, helping her to do her job.

Sometimes, despite our best efforts, Nature makes a mistake—or what appears to us, with our limited human vision, to be a mistake. For the approximately 2 percent of women whose babies have birth defects of some kind, the experience can be devastating as well as guilt provoking, often resulting in a mother obsessively reviewing her pregnancy looking for any sins of omission or commission she may have committed during those months. In the majority of cases, however, the cause of these abnormalities remains a mystery, even after exhaustive testing.

Messages from Within

To come to peace with Nature's apparent failures, we have to trust the process of life. But how do we learn to trust without simply lapsing into passivity or irresponsibility? By reclaiming the Mother Bear wisdom that is encoded in every cell of our female bodies. This means listening and acting on the messages from our inmost selves, while also accepting the reality that Nature has her own reasons, not all of which we can always understand. The following remarkable story comes from a woman who learned how to do that listening, and through it found both the ability to conceive and the confidence that she and her child had everything they needed to have a healthy pregnancy and birth.

JANE: Connecting with the Soul of Her Child

After a long period of ambivalence about whether she would be able to balance a demanding career in academia with the challenges of family life, Jane successfully conceived a child—which she did despite an infertility diagnosis. Her first step was learning to listen to what her body needed in the way of food and activity:

> My doctor told me I would never be able to conceive. Rejecting the surgical and drug "treatment" that was recommended, I began to care for my own body and life. After letting

go of the doctor's insistence that conception was impossible, I eliminated all dairy and meat products from my diet and started to walk in the sunshine for thirty minutes a day. Within one month, I discovered that I was pregnant.

At the end of an uneventful first nine weeks, I began to bleed. I bled at the end of each work week for a total of four weeks. The bleeding would start when I got home on Friday night from my thirteen-hour days as a college professor. I rested in bed each time, scared to death that I would miscarry but unaware of the deeper issue that was causing my problem.

After this had gone on for four weeks and I had already taken to my bed for the weekend, a good friend called. I suddenly blurted out to her: "I am such a failure. I knew that I couldn't do this." I surprised myself. I had never allowed such thoughts to come to my consciousness. I cried. Within one hour the bleeding became significant. After the interrupted and annoyed on-call doctor whom I consulted insisted that this was "quite usual" and that I was overreacting, I went back to bed. And into deep thought.

Within twelve hours, I was not only bleeding but had also begun to vomit—throwing up all of the fear that had filled my gut. I threw up even when there was nothing to throw up. And I bled. I remained in bed for a whole week. I had never missed a class or workday before—certainly not for "personal reasons." I sat. I thought. I cried. I felt at the deepest level that if I didn't figure out what was going on with me, my baby would die. Then, almost suddenly, an epiphany. I realized that I feared losing myself by giving birth. I was convinced of it.

But even as I felt the fullness of my fear, I felt my child—my daughter. It seemed to me that we were communicating, that we were having a silent conversation. I remember "hearing," "You *can* do this. I am not going to die. You can do this. We can do this." I was so overtaken with the experience that I told no one— not even my husband. I went to sleep, got up the next morning, told my husband that the baby and I were fine, and cleaned the house. The bleeding had completely stopped and I knew I was fine.

I completed a normal pregnancy and gave birth to Elena in May of 1997. Now some would say that her conception and birth can be understood using rather conventional medical explanations. I know that the experience is significantly more profound than these explanations allow.

Not only did I not lose myself in giving birth and mothering her, but I have begun to find my deeper self. And for that, I owe my daughter.

The Daughter's In Utero Contribution to Her Own Destiny

As Jane's story illustrates, the health of a baby is a two-way street from the beginning. Both a mother and her daughter make contributions, with the baby being a very dynamic force in the partnership. Anyone who doubts the child's participation has only to look at how a pregnant woman's food cravings are directly affected by her child. Many mothers will tell you that they craved different things with each pregnancy.

A baby interacts with her mother from the beginning via changes in the molecules of communication—hormones. These hormonally mediated changes affect the health of both mother and child. Here are a few examples:

~ The placenta is a source of steroid hormones that can contribute to a sense of well-being in the mother.

~ The fetus signals the mother's body that she is pregnant by producing the hormone HCG (human chorionic gonadotropin), which signals the corpus luteum (the short-lived progesterone-producing endocrine organ that forms in the ovary after every ovulation) to continue making progesterone, in order to sustain the pregnancy.

~ The baby's adrenal glands are responsible for providing DHEA, a precursor for estrogen, to the maternal portion of the placenta. The estrogen produced by the DHEA is necessary for growing placental tissue and the muscle layer of the uterus. If the baby's body is unable to produce the necessary amount of DHEA, her mother will not be able to supply enough estrogen to sustain the pregnancy.

~ The baby is also responsible for the initiation of labor, probably through a combination of factors involving the adrenal and pituitary glands. It is satisfying to think that some signal from the baby's brain and adrenal glands puts the fetus in charge of its own destiny by orchestrating its own time of birth.[5]

Clearly a daughter has been a partner with her mother in her own well-being from the moment of conception. And this partnership continues throughout life.

The Medium of Mother-Daughter Communication

Mothers and daughters "talk" to each other about their feelings right from the beginning, though not necessarily in words. They talk through soul communication, as Jane and her baby did. And, as mentioned above, they communicate via a whole series of complicated hormone and neurotransmitter messengers. Though mothers and daughters have different bloodstreams, they are so intimately connected that virtually all of the neurotransmitters and hormones that a mother's body makes affect her baby, and that means that every emotion and subsequent biochemical change associated with that emotion affects her child.

For example, a mother's sense of well-being or lack of it results in changes in stress hormones such as cortisol, epinephrine, and vasopressin that help regulate placental blood flow and thus affect the amount of nutrients and oxygen the child is receiving. (See vasopressin discussion, page 101.) When a woman's cortisol levels are high from maternal anxiety or fear, the result is a metabolic cascade that produces elevated levels of other hormones known as cytokines, which regulate the immune system. If cortisol and cytokine levels remain chronically elevated, a woman's immune system and that of her developing baby may become compromised.[6] Chronic maternal anxiety also increases the risk for prematurity, labor complications, breech presentation, stillbirth, and miscarriage.[7] These same problems may be exacerbated by a nutrient-poor diet. Conversely, if a woman is well nourished, feels supported in her pregnancy, and enjoys a wide range of emotional and physical intimacy with her partner as well as her friends and family, her levels of the hormone oxytocin, one of the so-called molecules of belonging, will be increased, which enhances her and her baby's immunity and helps her to bond with her child even before it is born. The neurotransmitters circulating through the mother's body create a physical imprint on the developing brain and body of the child, hardwiring her sense of safety and security. Her very biology tells her, "All is well. I will be cared for. I am at peace."

A large body of research has documented what many have always known: babies have the capacity to learn from and remember—in their bodies if not their conscious minds—many aspects of their prenatal life, and also the events of their birth. These events get translated via hormones and other messengers into an indelible biologic imprint that impacts us at some level for the rest of our lives.

The following story illustrates how a mother's emotions during pregnancy can have an enduring impact on her daughter.

SUZANNE: Healing Her Fears

When I was forty, I began descending into a darkness that had me thinking that my life was over, that I would die soon, that there was nothing left for me to do here, that I could not offer anything of worth or value. I wasn't suicidal but rather depleted of any sense that life for me would go on. I developed fears of dying, even though there was absolutely no reason to think that was happening. I would find myself planning my funeral, having fantasies of what it would be like, what my family would do afterward. I would come out of these fantasies with a sense that it was just a forgone conclusion that it would happen soon. This went on for two years. And a number of attempts to address it had only short-term effects.

Then one evening while I was talking with my mother, I mentioned these fears to her. Our relationship up to that time had not been one in which we shared much emotionally. In fact, I felt quite distant from her, and I don't know what made me tell her about my fears at that point. Without missing a beat, my mother said, "Of course you have a lot of fears about dying. When I was five months pregnant with you, I was told that I was in danger and that I could die giving birth to you. I lived in fear of my life from that point on, and I'm sure that my fears passed on to you." She also told me that throughout every pregnancy after mine (there were five more) she lived in fear for herself, and that the two she carried after the age of forty were especially difficult.

This revelation hit me like a thunderbolt. Something in my body shifted dramatically. I knew in that moment that these fears were not all mine, and I began the process of sorting out mine from hers, which led me into the deepest healing work of my life and to studying body-centered healing and therapy. Ten years later I am fully alive, vibrant and excited about life, and fully expecting to live through my nineties. I am very grateful to my mother for telling me about her fears. I have healed my relationship with her, and appreciate what happened to me at age forty so that I could take charge of my own life and well-being.

This story is a great example of how we can take a maternal legacy of anxiety and depression that may be passed down from gene to gene, blueprint to blueprint, and courageously take responsibility for transforming it in our own lives without blaming our mothers.

Regardless of your relationship with your mother, it is very illuminating to understand the power and mystery of your connection throughout your lives.

Violence and the Pregnant Woman

Many women in our culture experience trauma and violence from the men in their lives, either directly or indirectly. Unfortunately, pregnancy does not decrease this violence; it just changes the nature of the attacks, so that a woman's pregnant abdomen becomes the target.[8] In general, approximately 17 percent of pregnant women are physically abused during their pregnancies. Those who have had a history of abuse are more likely to experience such abuse while pregnant. What must it be like for the sensitivities of a baby developing in the womb to feel the effects in its own body of abuse that is directed at that womb? Since minute changes in hormones affect how cells grow and develop, the fact that the child is actually growing its nervous system, brain, and organs while swimming in a biochemical soup of fight-or-flight hormones is bound to have an effect.

It wasn't until I was in my forties that I learned that as a baby my mother slept in a crib beneath a bullet hole that was made during a shoot-out between the police and my grandfather, who was a bootlegger. My mother was an infant at the time and doesn't remember any of what happened, but her younger sister does remember being told about it and passed that information on to me. Since there are large chunks not just of her infancy but of her childhood that my mother doesn't remember, I suspect that there may have been more instability and violence during my grandmother's pregnancy than my mother or I will ever know about.

There's No Such Thing as a Perfect Beginning, a Perfect Mother, a Perfect Daughter, or a Perfect Life

Remember that there is no such thing as a perfect pregnancy and birth. Life has a way of happening. Things don't always turn out the way we want them to, regardless of how much effort we make to control all the variables. A mother may avoid alcohol, cigarettes, and drugs, eat well, exercise regularly, listen to Mozart daily, surround herself with white light, take supplements, and go to the "best" ob-gyn in the "best" hospital in the world. And still, her unborn child's foundation might be unavoidably affected by the death of her father, an illness in the family, the day-to-day chaos of life, or some other factor which we cannot identify. Regardless of the events and conditions that went into the making of your foundation, remember this: Even if you or your daughter's individual life journey may have gotten off to an adverse start, you were both born with the inner wisdom and soul qualities to overcome this. There are individuals whose foundations are so leaky and shaky as to be nonexistent—for instance the child of an abusive mother who did drugs, drank alcohol, smoked cigarettes, and neglected or abandoned her infant either physically or emotionally. Yet such people often have an amazing ability to tap into their soul qualities and the universal energies of creation. They overcome seemingly insurmountable challenges and go on to live happy, successful, productive lives. Others may begin life with the firmest foundations possible, yet go on to live unhappy, unproductive, unfulfilled lives.

THE BOTTOM LINE: Neither the circumstances of our births nor the actions of our mothers have the power to write the script for our lives or to prevent us from taking the unique journey we were meant to take in life. We do that for ourselves, in partnership with our souls.

Pregnancy and the Wise Placenta: The Biologic Organ of Human Connection

From the very beginning, mother and daughter are involved in a dynamic dance between nurturance and rejection, dependence and independence, that will go on for the rest of their lives. It starts with the formation of the placenta, which is an organ of both relationship and nurturance. The placenta is the very embodiment of the way in which both relationships and food sustain our physical and emotional health.

Once the fertilized egg has traveled down the fallopian tube and been implanted into the uterine wall, mother and child begin to co-create the dynamic organ that connects them, the placenta. The placenta is a living, responsive physical boundary that both separates and connects mother and child for the first nine months of life, mediating the dynamics of our very first relationship.

I have always been fascinated by the placenta, the wondrous life-support system that nourishes the child in utero, and have closely examined it following the birth of nearly every baby I've delivered. Many times I've encouraged the new parents to take a look with me. Although some are initially reluctant, they soon end up fascinated and grateful for the chance to understand the wonder of this remarkable organ. Once the newborn is safely in the external womb of her mother's arms, having been released into her earthly life with the cutting of the cord, we pay tribute to the organ that sustained her for the preceding nine months. Holding up the membranes, I show the parents how and where the placenta was attached to the uterine wall, and how the umbilical cord tethered the baby to the placenta for nourishment, allowing her to float in a miniature ocean within her mother's womb.

The creation of the placenta begins soon after fertilization, when the embryo begins to make the cells that insinuate themselves into the uterine wall. Nature has set it up so that the mother's body does not automatically reject this intrusion, even though the fetal cells that are attaching themselves to her body are not immunologically identical to her own, and would, if they were an organ transplant, undergo almost certain rejection and death. In almost a half century of intense research by the world's most outstanding biologists, no one has been able to fully explain how this is possible. It defies all the laws of immunology and transplantation. One theory is that the mother's body, through a group of specially formed lymphocytes, controls the degree to which the embryo invades her body.[9] But once the pregnancy is established, the fetus contributes to its own acceptance by making HLA antigens on the placental surface, which ensure its survival by blocking rejection by the mother.

The ability of the placenta to nourish and sustain a baby depends so directly upon the health of both the mother and her daughter that it can be thought of as the physical metaphor for their relationship. All mothers need to learn to set healthy boundaries on their nurturing of others, including their children. Placental wisdom can offer us guidance on how to do this. When we are pregnant, it is not possible to separate our needs from those of our baby. They are essentially the same—whatever keeps us healthy and happy will do the same for the growing baby. Nevertheless, there are some substances that the placenta does not allow to cross from mother to child or child to mother. That is why the placenta keeps most of the fetal cells from reaching the mother. But the boundary is porous, and some fetal cells do slip past it. (Fetal cells do not have any negative consequences for the mother, but if there are too many of them and she and her baby have different blood types, for example Rh negative mother, Rh positive baby, then the mother's body may produce antibodies that damage the blood cells of a baby in a subsequent pregnancy.) Recent research has shown that up to 70 percent of pregnant women have fetal cells circulating in their bloodstream by the final trimester of pregnancy. And some have been detected in the circulation of women up to twenty-seven years postpartum![10] In commenting on these findings, Sarah Berga, M.D., professor of obstetrics and gynecology at the University of Pittsburgh wrote:

> When contemplating the never-ending job of motherhood, I like to joke about the "Teflon umbilical cord" that cannot be severed. Little did I know that the fetus may truly always be there in both a literal as well as an emotional sense. This notion gives new meaning to the biological sacrifice inherent in reproduction.[11]

Dr. Berga is absolutely right. As I was writing this section of the book, my older daughter had just graduated from college and moved to New York City to begin her first job. I awoke every morning with a bloody nose, a symptom that is very rare for me but which my daughter has had frequently during stressful times since childhood. I knew that this symptom was symbolic of my worry for her—and our lifelong blood tie to each other.

Some other recent research, on stem cells, suggests that fetal cells might eventually be able to help a mother regenerate damaged organs in her own body. Another amazing example of the mutually healing power of blood ties![12]

ONE LIFE BECOMES TWO

Though it is often thrown away and ignored in our culture, the umbilical cord is a highly significant and symbolically charged piece of tissue. I remember seeing my first umbilical cord when I was about five years old. My mother and father took the time to show us the dried umbilical cord remnant that had recently dropped off the newest baby in the family. I was intrigued. Native cultures such as the Sioux Indians used to weave the dried umbilical cord of their sons into the mane of the boys' horses to give them protection when they first came of age and left the comfort of their mothers and original homes.

I was present when my niece was born, and saved her umbilical cord. I dried it into a thin sinewy spiral by wrapping it around a small cardboard cylinder and putting it in a very warm dry place. When she is older, I intend to give it to her at an appropriate coming-of-age ceremony. I didn't think to do this with my own daughters' cords, but when they saw the one that had been set aside for their cousin, they wanted to know what had happened to theirs. How I wish I had saved their cords too!

THE CHANGES OF PREGNANCY

Yes, having a child changes you forever. And the experience of being pregnant also brings about profound changes—in how you look and feel, how others respond to you, your appetite, your sexuality, even your dreams. Your reaction to all of these changes lives in your body—and in your daughter's body.

Appearance

It's true—your feet do get bigger. But that's of course the least of the changes you will experience. Many women fear that pregnancy will result in the permanent loss of their figures. One woman told me that her mother always resented having had children because she felt that the process had ruined her body for good. I've heard women say

that what they're most proud of about their pregnancy was the fact
that no one could tell that they were pregnant until the very end.
Think about this for a minute. How sad it is that we live in a culture
that encourages many of us to be proud of being able to hide the fact
that our bodies are growing new life! What kind of impact do you
think this has on our daughters?

Most of us have inherited to some degree our culture's deep split
concerning maternity and sexuality, sometimes called the virgin-
whore split. The physical changes of pregnancy seem only to exacerbate that split: pregnant women aren't supposed to feel sexy or look
sexy. Or at least they weren't until recently. But new ad campaigns
for maternity stores now proclaim "Motherhood is hot!" and show-
case beautiful pregnant women in beautiful, sexy maternity clothes.
So at least in some pockets of the culture we are making progress.

Many men love the way their wives look when they are pregnant.
My husband did, and it made me feel much better about myself. But
many others do not like the weight gain that is inevitable with pregnancy, and they nag their wives constantly about their eating.

A WORD ABOUT PREGNANCY WEIGHT GAIN

I deplore our society's overemphasis on thinness, which has
resulted in an epidemic of disordered eating, chronic dieting,
reliance on diet pills, and anorexia, so that the "soil" of
many women's bodies has been depleted of the essential nutrients they need to nourish a child optimally. That said,
pregnancy is *not* a time to throw caution to the wind and
"eat for two." In fact, the extra metabolic demands of pregnancy require only an additional three hundred calories per
day on average—the equivalent of one McDonald's hot apple
pie, or six ounces of baked wild Alaskan salmon—if you are
eating an appropriate diet to begin with.

The best approach to losing weight after delivery is to
have been moderate in weight gain during pregnancy. But if
you find after you have delivered that your weight gain is
much in excess of the six pounds that is about average, be patient with yourself about taking off the additional pounds.
The sooner you learn how to deal with food in a healthy, realistic way, the better able you will be to create a firm foundation for your daughter.

In years past the medical establishment reinforced such attitudes. Until the early 1980s, many doctors were trained to overly restrict pregnancy weight gain, urging that generation of mothers to diet during their pregnancies. They also prescribed diuretics, in a misguided attempt to minimize weight gain and decrease ankle swelling. What the women actually needed was more protein and better-quality food, not a drug that depletes blood volume at the very moment the baby needs it most! Fortunately, the medical establishment now has a better understanding of the amount of weight gain desirable for a pregnant woman. (See "Pregnancy Program" below.) Let's hope husbands will follow suit—not to mention the women themselves!

Sense of Well-being

Many women truly enjoy being pregnant and will tell you that they felt better during this time than at any other time in their lives. Some women, for instance, become multiply orgasmic during pregnancy even though they never were before, probably from a combination of increased blood flow to the pelvis combined with an elevated mood from the hormones of pregnancy. For this reason, pregnancy can be a peak time for some women sexually. The major hormonal change of pregnancy is an increase in progesterone, which has a distinctive calming effect on nerves, similar to the effect of Valium. No wonder many women radiate such an air of calm and well-being during pregnancy.

But there is a wide variation between women in terms of how comfortable they are during pregnancy. Some women have morning sickness the entire time, or low-grade abdominal discomfort and low back pain. Women who suffer from back pain often benefit from regular massage or osteopathic adjustments. And those with nausea often find relief by drinking ginger tea or taking ginger capsules, eating small, frequent meals, and avoiding food preparation when possible. (Being around the smell of food is often the problem, not the eating of it. Conversely, the strong aromas of ginger and peppermint essential oils can be very effective against nausea.) Also, all pregnant women need a lot more sleep, especially in the first trimester when the body is doing profound work that isn't yet visible. Many pregnant American women who work outside the home don't get enough rest, and this contributes to physical distress.

But even women who for whatever reason have difficult pregnancies may also have wonderful memories of the feelings of joy and anticipation they experienced during those months—memories it is inspiring to pass on to their daughters. Knowing how happy her mother's pregnancy made her gives the daughter a sense of safety and security about her place in the world. I remember that I was lying out in the sun on the back deck of our first home in Milton, Massachusetts, when I first felt my daughter Annie move in my sun-warmed belly. It felt like a little butterfly was inside me—a truly magical sensation. Annie always loved hearing me describe that happy memory.

Dreams and Fantasies

Because the hormones of pregnancy allow the curtain that usually separates body and soul to become more transparent, pregnant women are more emotionally porous and susceptible to intense dreaming than at other times in their lives. This is not a weakness. It is a gift of discernment which, if heeded, will give them intuitive insight into everything from choosing the right foods to choosing the right companions. The downside of this porousness is that they are also more apt to become depressed, moody, and anxious, if those emotions are in the environment around them. That's why it's so important when pregnant to surround yourself with as many supportive people and as much positive energy as possible.

While our culture overromanticizes that "special glow" associated with the process of growing new life in pregnancy, it also paradoxically reduces the highly intuitive, emotionally porous state associated with pregnancy to "mood swings," "paranoia," and "irrational" food cravings. Once we understand that our brains were designed to become more receptive during pregnancy, we will view our emotional volatility in a much different light, opening ourselves to the insights now available to us.

Fear, Worry, and Guilt

Our cultural inheritance concerning pregnancy, labor, and delivery virtually guarantees fears and worries during pregnancy. I've never met a single pregnant woman who didn't have at least some concerns about the health of her unborn baby. These fears often get expressed in dreams, and may take the form of dreams about leaving the baby in a cellar, or about forgetting you have a baby and allowing her to come to harm because of your forgetfulness.

Of course it's natural to have some concerns about what is to come. The question is, are they maladaptive or adaptive? It's adaptive to worry about your food quality while pregnant and then take steps to improve it. It's maladaptive to avoid meat and fish because you're worried that they contain pesticide residues and mercury, but then gain sixty excess pounds from eating too much whole grain pasta and bread, and organic ice cream. Ultimately it is your skillfulness at handling your fears, not the fears themselves, that will make the most difference to your own health and that of your daughter.

Most pregnant women feel guilty about something, given our heritage. Some women take on a particularly heavy burden of guilt, for example those who were given DES, a synthetic estrogen that was thought to prevent miscarriage but was later found to produce reproductive system abnormalities in the daughters born to these women. Having seen many DES daughters, I can assure you that the level of pain and guilt in their mothers, who were simply following their doctors' orders when they took it, is often so big that to address it and talk about it openly is well nigh impossible.

No matter what emotions we feel, however, it is the emotions that we cannot talk about or work through that do the most damage to the next generation. The more you're able to forgive yourself and allow your heart to process what has previously seemed unacceptable, the healthier you and your daughter will become. I guarantee it.

PRENATAL TESTS: RISKS AND BENEFITS

WISDOM CHALLENGE: *Prenatal Testing*

Almost all women worry about whether their children will be born healthy. Women with genetic legacies that may predispose their children to certain problems, and women over the age of thirty-five, may be particularly concerned and may want to avail themselves of the various options for prenatal testing, such as amniocentesis. As with all medical decisions, you have to learn to pick and choose among your options, using not just statistics and your intellect to guide you but your true Mother Bear wisdom as well.

Once you become a mother, you will be faced with making innumerable decisions about your child's health. The question of how to approach prenatal testing is just the beginning, but it is an ideal place to start tuning in to your gut feelings. As you do, keep in mind that even though much of prenatal care today focuses only on what can go wrong and what tests you should have to assure that nothing is wrong, pregnancy and birth are natural life processes that the vast majority of women and their babies can go through completely safely and healthfully. There is certainly something to be said for the innocence and trust in Nature that were present before the culture of medicine began to offer testing to virtually everyone, not just to women at high risk for conditions such as Down syndrome, Tay-Sachs, and spina bifida and other neural-tube defects.

I never even had an ultrasound when I was pregnant, even though they were routine at the time. Didn't feel I needed it. Of course, I was thirty-one and thirty-four when I had my children—just "under the wire" before age-related risks would start to increase significantly.

The Purpose of Prenatal Tests

It's a great paradox that prenatal testing, which is designed to reassure women, can sometimes cause more anxiety than it allays. This is the nature of testing, which always has limitation and dangers and is subject to the vagaries of human interpretation. Once you have educated yourself about the pros and cons of the various tests, you'll have to make up your own mind about which, if any, tests to have.

Prenatal tests are done for a number of different reasons. They include the following:

- Screening for treatable conditions in the mother that can affect her baby's health. This includes screening for gestational diabetes and high blood pressure.

- Screening for fetal characteristics, including size, sex, gestational age, and placement of fetus and/or placenta. Examples would be checking for a breech presentation or a placenta that is covering the vagina.

- Screening for congenital defects, e.g. spina bifida or cardiac defects.

- Screening for genetic defects, e.g. Down syndrome.

Screening for treatable conditions in a mother that may affect her baby is medicine at its best. Obviously all pregnant women should have their blood pressure monitored and also be screened for diabetes. The same goes for venereal diseases. And if there is a problem, every effort should then be made to help a woman become as healthy as possible during her pregnancy.

When it comes to fetal screening with ultrasounds, or to testing for genetic or congenital defects, however, the issue becomes far murkier.

The Fetal Screening Dilemma

Over the past twenty years, more and more tests have become available to help determine a baby's health status before she is born. These include routine ultrasounds, blood tests for alpha fetal protein that can help determine risk of spina bifida and other neural tube defects as well as Down syndrome, and genetic screening for over 250 different diseases.

Though these tests can be reassuring, especially when there is concern about a family history of a genetic disease, such as Huntington's chorea or Tay-Sachs, they are too often a double-edged sword. For example, many children with cystic fibrosis, which is one of the conditions that prenatal tests screen for, can live for years and years and have a fairly high quality of life. But no one knows for sure which child will do well and which won't.

What if you have no family history of a genetic disorder (the vast majority) and you just go in for routine testing? For example, let's say that you have the second trimester blood test that screens for neural tube defects and Down syndrome, and it reveals a slightly elevated alpha fetal protein in your blood. You get worried. More testing is required. Standard testing for maternal serum alpha fetal protein levels if done at the right gestational age will detect approximately 80 percent of open spina bifida and 90 percent of anencephaly.[13] But MSAFP levels can be elevated for a variety of other reasons that are not related to fetal neural tube or abdominal wall defects, so this test is, unfortunately, not 100 percent specific. In fact, the most common cause for an elevated MSAFP is a wrong estimation of the gestational age of the fetus, not a fetal abnormality!

However, even if you know that, getting an abnormal test result causes all kinds of stress hormones to flood through your system. Now you have "tentative pregnancy" which means that you're worried about your baby and aren't sure you can truly commit to it and allow yourself to truly invest in the pregnancy until further testing reveals that all is well. And the mind being what it is, you imagine the worst. To be certain that all is well, you have an amniocentesis. But this is not a benign procedure. It can cause needle injury to the baby, bleeding, infection, and even result in a 1 in 100 risk of losing the baby from ruptured membranes. All this because of a routine test!

Or let's say that you're having a routine ultrasound just because you want to know the sex of the baby. But the test reveals that your placenta is too low—a fairly common condition in the second trimester, which often resolves itself later. Though you know that this is so, you still worry about whether or not the placenta will move. If it doesn't, you could have a placenta previa which can cause severe bleeding. To make sure, you need yet another ultrasound. Though another ultrasound is not necessarily a big deal, the procedure has created doubt and worry about a "possible" adverse outcome that, most of the time, would go away on its own. Another thing that happens with routine ultrasounds is that they sometimes pick up echo patterns known as artifacts that may or may not be a fetal or placental abnormality. This really sends the mother into a tailspin. The "cure" is to get a follow-up ultrasound. Meanwhile the mother is frantic with worry (and her baby is awash in stress hormones) until her next appointment.

Another form of prenatal testing is chorionic villus sampling, which is done at ten weeks gestation to screen for genetic problems such as Down's. Again, the procedure is not benign. There's the chance of miscarriage and possible damage to the limbs of the fetus.

The problem with testing and technology is that they are not infallible. There are false positive and false negatives for every test that is done. This is the nature of science. And all of it is subject to human interpretation, which differs depending upon whom you ask!

What If There Is an Abnormality?

And what if the testing does reveal an abnormality? What then? Most women choose to terminate the pregnancy. Some do not. (A very moving account of deciding to give birth to a Down syndrome child is Martha Beck's *Expecting Adam*. It's stunning and brilliant.) You should try to think through in advance what you would choose to do if there is an abnormality—though admittedly this is something you can't fully imagine until you are facing it. Whatever you decide is right for you and your family is what you should do. But be aware that these decisions can have long-term emotional reverberations. One of my patients, who terminated a pregnancy because of spina bifida and then became infertile for a time, told me that the termination experience was very traumatic for her because she could feel the baby move. She said, "I kept thinking, 'What if the doctors are wrong? What if my baby is really normal'?" After doing some deep work to release her grief, she eventually conceived another child. But, years later, she still questioned whether or not she had done the right thing. Contrary to popular belief, her subsequent child did not "make up" for the child she lost. The bottom line is this: pregnancy loss, for whatever reason, is very difficult for women. It needs to be acknowledged and grieved. (See Resources.)

A CONSERVATIVE APPROACH TO PRENATAL TESTING

Prenatal testing has become routine in nearly all pregnancies even though there is no universal agreement on its efficacy. There have never been any long-term, double-blind, controlled, randomized studies on the use of routine ultrasound or alpha fetal protein screening. Instead, our culture tacitly agrees that more screening is better, without fully appreciating the limitations of that screening. Instead of making prenatal testing your default approach, think through the pros and cons before proceeding.

Determine your risk. Some chromosomal disorders are inherited, but most are caused by sporadic errors in the genetics of the egg or sperm. The chance of a child having these disorders increases with the age of the mother. For example, according to the ACOG, 1 in 1,667 live babies born to twenty-year-old women have Down syndrome. That number changes to 1 in 378 for thirty-five-year-olds and 1 in 106 for forty-year-olds. Remember, the risk from an amniocentesis is 1 in 100 (some sources say 1 in 200). A good overview of the subject of genetic screening can be found at http://www.kidshealth.org.

If you have any serious genetic conditions in your family, such as Huntington's disease, hemophilia, or sickle-cell anemia, you may want to consult with someone who specializes in medical genetics who can help you sort through all the testing options and assess your risk as objectively as possible.

Be clear about the limits of testing. There are no perfect tests. All have the potential for false positives and false negatives. Understand that prenatal genetic and fetal screening can cause a lot of stress. I remember what that was like, because I participated in the initial studies for alpha fetal protein serum testing during both of my pregnancies. I didn't really rest easy until the tests came back as "normal."

Invest your energies in the place where the biggest payoff is. If our culture spent the same amount of time, money, and effort on preconception and prenatal nutrition and well-being that we now spend on prenatal testing, the incidence of congenital anomalies would probably plummet! And so would the rate of other common pregnancy complications, such as prematurity and pregnancy-induced hypertension.

WAITING FOR BABY

Communicate with Your Unborn Child

Once pregnant, you can regularly communicate with your baby. Visualize your child in a pink bubble (or another color of choice—I suggest pink because it is associated with love) and send the message that she is safe and loved. This is an especially useful exercise during times of stress or when you are scared or anxious. You can also read to your baby and talk to her regularly. Hearing begins to develop in the first trimester! And remember, pregnancy is a two-way street. If you tune in carefully, you may sense that your daughter is also communicating with you.

Good Vibrations

Make listening to music, dancing, and singing a regular part of your pregnancy. It helps tune both of your bodies. Layne Redmond, an accomplished drummer and author of *When the Drummers Were Women,* points out that the original beat our bodies were exposed to was our mother's heartbeat. And that's why the beating of drums still stirs us right to the bone. Vibrational healer Deena Spear, who is also a violin maker, says that everything vibrates and has energy, whether it's a person or a potato chip. And if it vibrates, it can be tuned for improved clarity and health.

An exciting new body of scientific research is proving that musical harmony is part of our very essence. For example, the late Dr. Susumu Ohno, a geneticist, explored the music of genes by assigning musical notes to them according to their molecular weights. An enzyme called phosphoglycerate kinase, which breaks down glucose in the body, revealed itself to Ohno as a lullaby. A malignant gene sounded much like Chopin's Funeral March. Mary Ann Clark, a professor of molecular biology at Texas Wesleyan University, writes: "Every generation of cells in every living organism plays the genetic score of its species. However, while the history of music as we know it goes back some 1,000 years, the history of genetic music is at least 3.8 billion years in the making."[14]

Music has been shown to reduce anxiety, heart rate, and respiratory rate. It also decreases stress hormone levels, boosts natural opiates, relaxes laboring women, and has beneficial effects on the physiology and behavior of the newborn, including contributing positively to weight gain in both normal-weight and premature babies.[15] When you play music and sing to your child, you're causing pleasurable vibrations that literally tune up the cells of both your bodies.

Listen to music you love. It doesn't have to be Mozart, but I'd definitely make sure it's calming, inspirational, and uplifting. Pregnancy is no time for heavy metal or any hip-hop with misogynistic lyrics! Some women get a definite signal from their babies about what the child likes, for example when hearing music she loves, the baby will move around more vigorously. Remember that the best way to increase the kind of intelligence that really matters—heart intelligence—is to send feelings and thoughts of love and support to your baby. It's particularly nice to set those loving feelings to music. (See Resources.)

Don't Wish Away Your Pregnancy

When she was diagnosed with breast cancer, comedian and writer Erma Bombeck wrote down some of the things she wished she had done while she still had the time. One of those was savoring her pregnancies. She wrote, "Instead of wishing away nine months of pregnancy, I'd have cherished every moment and realized that the wonderment growing inside me was the only chance in life to assist God in a miracle."[16]

Use the Power of the Mind-Body Connection

Take advantage of your emotional porousness. Use birth affirmations regularly during your entire pregnancy to help you program your body and mind for optimal birth. In her book *Ina May's Guide to Childbirth,* midwife Ina May Gaskin points out the amazing power of the mind to influence the body during labor. She told one pregnant woman that during her labor her vagina, vulva, and cervix would become huge openings to allow her baby to pass through easily. When she gave birth, that is exactly what happened!

Put affirmations all around your environment—your refrigerator, bathroom mirror, Palm Pilot, journal, and phone—to remind you of your birthing power. Say them out loud or in your head regularly. Write them down repeatedly. Let the power of your emotions and thoughts do its magic with your body. Here are some examples:

- ⁓ My body is strong and capable. It knows exactly how to birth normally and joyfully.

- ⁓ My body is flexible. It is the perfect channel to allow my baby to emerge from my body.

- ⁓ My baby and I are *soul* friends. We are enjoying this adventure together.

For further ideas about using affirmations, I recommend *The Pocket Midwife* by my friend and nurse-midwife colleague Susan Fekety, C.N.M. This spiral-bound book is small and will stand up by itself, making it easy to do your affirmations while you cook, brush your hair, or go about your day. (To order, log onto www.pocketmid wife.com.)

Create an Outer Placenta

Pregnancy, labor, and birth are physically demanding events that require a large outpouring of life energy. Every woman who is going through the changes of pregnancy needs to replenish that energy, not just through proper nutrition but through the love and support of those around her—the nourishing environment I call the outer placenta. Just as the developing baby cocreates her own placenta in partnership with her mother, so too must the mother "implant" herself into her community to cocreate this outer placenta.

The urge to reimplant yourself into your own mother is particularly strong at this time. If you don't have a mother, or have an inadequate or abusive mother, you'll need to enlist one or more "surrogate mothers" to help out. They can be friends, family members, or colleagues—anyone loving, caring, and supportive.

The quality of the mother's outer placenta influences her health as well as her ability to create a healthy environment for her child. Obviously a supportive mate is a major plus in a woman's ability to care for herself optimally. A carefully chosen, committed health-care team can also make a big difference. In general, the more effective and diverse your community of support, the better.

SELF-CARE PROGRAM FOR PREGNANCY

Your body forms the very soil in which your child takes form. As any farmer will tell you, the quality of one's crops is directly related to the quality of the soil. Pregnancy, labor, birth, and the postpartum period are beautiful illustrations of two self-care principles: you reap what you sow, and you can't give to another what you don't have yourself, on either the body or the soul level.

DIET

Follow the diet outlined in the Preconception Program. I chose to put the entire prenatal and preconception program in Chapter 3 to emphasize that the further upstream you start taking care of your baby, the better! (See pages 51–57.)

WHAT IF YOU'RE A VEGETARIAN?

If you are a vegetarian, it's still possible to have a healthy pregnancy, but it's more of a challenge. I recommend that you read *Your Vegetarian Pregnancy* by my friend and colleague Dr. Holly Roberts, who is a board-certified ob-gyn physician and a vegetarian herself. There are many kinds of "vegetarians." Some include a little animal food in the form of eggs and milk (ovo-lacto vegetarians). And some are "vegans," avoiding all forms of animal foods. In general, even if you're a vegan, I suggest that during pregnancy you follow your cravings and consider eating some animal food in the

form of fish, eggs, or even an occasional serving of organic
red meat.

EXERCISE

Get moving. Women who are physically fit have easier, more comfortable pregnancies than those who are out of shape. I always told
my pregnant patients that the only two sports they absolutely
couldn't participate in were sky-diving and water-skiing (the former for obvious reasons, the latter because there is too much risk
of water being forced into the uterus during a fall). Regular exercise is important when pregnant. Aim for at least three days per
week. My mother skied when pregnant, with all of us, right up until she went into labor. (Of course, she was an experienced skier
and in excellent physical shape. I don't recommend taking up the
sport for the first time when you're pregnant!) I did Pilates, yoga,
and tai chi, and a lot of walking with both my pregnancies. But I
stopped running when pregnant with my first because it felt so uncomfortable, and I've never resumed it—just don't have the right
body type! Walking, swimming, dance, stationary cycling, and
yoga are all ideal exercises for pregnant women. However, some
yoga positions are not appropriate for pregnant women. Check
with a qualified yoga teacher. Better yet, join a class for pregnant
women.

Avoid competitive sports during this time unless you are a highly
trained competitive athlete already. And forget running a marathon,
engaging in any kind of endurance sports, or staying on your feet for
hours on end. Make sure your heart rate doesn't get above one hundred forty beats per minute. Don't do strenuous exercise for longer
than fifteen minutes at a time. Don't get overheated.

ACTIVITIES

Don't quit your job if you have one. Most studies have shown a
health benefit for working outside of the home. However, there is a
limit. For example, studies of pregnant female ob-gyn residents who
work more than eighty hours per week have shown an increased risk
of preterm labor, preeclampsia, and fetal growth restriction compared to the pregnancies of the partners of their male counterparts![17]
So don't overdo.

PREMATURITY: A NATIONAL HEALTH CRISIS

Preterm labor is the leading cause of hospitalization among pregnant women, and preterm delivery is the second leading cause of death among infants, second only to deaths from severe birth defects. The crisis is particularly acute among African-Americans. Complications from preterm births are the leading cause of death for African-American infants today.

This national epidemic of prematurity affects 12 percent of all births in the United States and 17 percent of births among African-Americans.

In her testimony on the challenges of prematurity before the U.S. Senate in 2004, Eve Lackritz, M.D., chief of the Maternal and Infant Health Branch, National Center for Chronic Disease Prevention and Health Promotion at the CDC, summarized the current problem:

> We have very few health threats of this magnitude, and this health threat goes well beyond the burden of infant mortality. Preterm delivery is the leading cause of developmental disability in children, including cerebral palsy and mental retardation, and is an important cause of blindness and chronic lung problems. Infants who are born premature are more than two times more likely to have a birth defect than infants who are born at term. Premature infant births extract a huge financial toll on our health-care resources. Hospital care of preterm infants costs over $13 billion each year. This is just for hospital care at their birth. Additional costs include hospitalization of mothers and continued care of children, including costs for repeat hospitalizations, medical visits, rehabilitation, and special services for children with special needs. But the toll of preterm delivery is not just financial. It tears at the fabric of our families and our communities, and takes an enormous emotional toll on mothers and fathers. Taken together, it is clear that preterm delivery is a public health priority.[18]

What Causes Prematurity?

As with cancer and cardiovascular disease, prematurity is caused by cellular inflammation. And many factors contribute to this excess inflammation. Though researchers in the past felt that that inflammation was the result of low-grade chronic infections such as vaginal infections or gum disease, a decade of research has failed to show that treating infections with antibiotics prevents preterm labor.

It is the inflammation itself, not the bacteria, that is the culprit. Inflammation is the result of a cascade of different metabolic reactions that result from both physical and psychological stress.

PREMATURITY PREVENTION PROGRAM

To decrease the risk of prematurity, you need to decrease cellular inflammation. Here's how:

Stop smoking. Tobacco use remains a major preventable cause of low birth weight.

Don't douche. Vaginal douching has been shown to be associated with low infant birth weight and bacterial vaginosis.

Follow the preconception and prenatal supplementation program on pages 56–57. Research has shown that vitamin supplementation *prior to* conception significantly decreases the risk of prematurity.

Eat enough omega-3 fats, especially DHA. Essential fatty acids (also called polyunsaturated long-chain fatty acids, or PUFA's) often halt inflammation by giving the body the right precursors to prevent it. Studies have shown that women who have given birth prematurely before and who eat 1,000 mg of DHA and 1.3 grams (1,300 mg) of EPA (another type of essential fat) per day in a subsequent pregnancy experience a far lower risk of preterm delivery. And their babies are also bigger.[19] (See Resources.)

Talk to your doctor about taking progesterone. Studies have shown that receiving a progesterone shot (17 hydroxyprogesterone 250 mg IM) every week from week sixteen through thirty-six of gestation dramatically decreases the risk of premature labor in women at high risk. Progesterone can also be given as a vaginal suppository. Progesterone is very well tolerated, and even though shots are uncomfortable, and suppositories can be irritating, they sure beat having a premature baby![20]

Get psychological support. Studies have shown that psychological support can decrease the rate of premature birth in those who are at increased risk. It has also been documented that meditation and guided imagery can be helpful interventions.[21]

5

Labor and Birth

Accessing Your Feminine Power

No other experience puts a woman in touch with the process of creation as literally and vividly as that of giving birth. And no birth experience can connect her to the source as directly as a natural birth. Going through natural childbirth can empower a woman for the rest of her life, leaving her with unshakable trust in her own Mother Bear wisdom. Women who have been in touch with that wisdom rarely develop the postpartum depression or other mood disorders that are so common in our culture. And because they don't fear birth, they don't fear death either.

Women labor as they live. The process of labor tends to lay bare a woman's inherent adaptability and inner resources for everyone, including herself, to see. If she's well supported by her labor team and her loved ones and able to tune into her Mother Bear wisdom by taking part in the process consciously, then she will emerge from it with greater resources and adaptability than she had going in. Perhaps the most important thing she will get out of it is the experience of surrendering to a natural process that is enhanced by full consciousness but cannot be controlled with the intellect—exactly the skills required to raise a child (or follow a life passion) successfully.

What Is "Natural Birth"?

Natural birth is labor that proceeds without unnecessary medical interventions—for example, cesarean section, epidural anesthesia, artifical induction of labor. Such interventions have their place, of course, when there are problems, but for the vast majority of women, they aren't needed.

Neurologically speaking, labor is a series of motor movements that your body knows how to engage in. They are as natural and automatic as the reflexes that cause your knee to kick out when a doctor taps it in the right place.

Anatomically speaking, no drug or medical procedure has ever been invented that can improve upon the original design of the female body when it comes to birthing. Let's start with the uterus, the baby's home during the nine months of pregnancy. Once labor begins, the uterus is a muscle that knows exactly how to do the work of pushing the baby down toward the cervix and, once the cervix has dilated to about ten centimeters, into and through the birth canal.

The cervix, which is the opening at the bottom of the uterus, consists of muscular tissue which remains tightly closed during pregnancy, keeping the baby safely within, until labor begins and it gradually opens.

The pelvis is almost always adequate in size to allow the passage of the baby, even a very large one, because the four bones that make up the pelvis are joined together by ligaments, which loosen up during late pregnancy and labor. This ensures that the pelvis can widen enough for birth to take place without damage to either mother or child. Yet many ob-gyns have been taught to routinely do pelvic measurements or ultrasound to determine whether or not a woman will need a cesarean section. My ninety-pound four feet eleven inch maternal grandmother delivered my mother and my aunt at home. Both weighed over nine pounds. Good thing no one ever told her that her pelvis wasn't adequate to birth those babies.

The American Way of Birth

The kind of birthing I'm describing is common elsewhere. In the Netherlands, for example, as in a number of other medically advanced countries in Europe, many women give birth at home. They don't expect that they'll need drugs to assist or to numb labor, and, as a result, they don't. How different from our experience here in the United States. In this country, birth is medicalized to such an extent that if labor doesn't proceed rapidly enough, the doctors may recommend cesarean section, which is major abdominal surgery. In many hospital settings the "timer begins ticking" the minute you get admitted. You have only so much time to get that baby delivered. You need to "produce" according to a standard known as the Friedman labor curves, a series of criteria for the rate of cervical dilation and pushing that have become part of the culture of obstetrics. Doctors here aren't trained to trust the normal process of labor. When I first started delivering babies, I thought it was an emergency situation if a woman came into the birthing room too close to delivery for me to be able to start an IV and hook her up to a fetal monitor! Now I know that the simple act of starting an IV changes birth, impeding the woman's ability to move around and giving her the subliminal idea that she can't labor without it, or without any of the many other interventions typical of our delivery rooms.

Medicalization of labor has major consequences. The rate of cesarean deliveries (27 percent of all deliveries), epidural anesthetics (70 percent or more in many hospitals), labor inductions (which have doubled between 1989 to 1998 from 9.2 percent to 19.2 percent), and premature cord clamping (in approximately 95 percent of labors) that goes on in U.S. hospitals[1] is directly related to our failure to appreciate the biological wisdom of the female body, and the resulting lack of faith in a woman's innate ability to birth normally. The amount of unnecessary stress and trauma associated with this attitude and the resulting interventions is incalculable, for both mother and child. However, even though many mothers and their daughters have been talked out of their innate birthing wisdom, it remains available to us if we will simply recognize that it is there, and allow it to guide us. One area in which there has been significant improvement is in the rate of episiotomy, which has decreased from nearly 70 percent in 1983 to 20 percent in 2000. Interestingly, black women and those with government versus private insurance have consistently lower episiotomy rates.[2]

Perfection in Action: A Woman's Body in Labor

I've often said that if you want to know where a woman's true power lies, look to those primal experiences we've been taught to fear—not coincidentally the very same experiences the culture has taught us to distance ourselves from as much as possible, often by medicalizing them so that we are barely conscious of them anymore. Labor and birth rank right up there as experiences that put women in touch with their feminine power, along with the menstrual cycle and menopause. But imagine what would happen if our culture believed that we required medical help to have our monthly periods. What if all women went to medical centers for menstrual "anesthetics," to help them avoid feeling the passage of menstrual blood, or for a procedure to extract menstrual blood quickly and painlessly, so they wouldn't have to go through this monthly "nuisance."[3] If, when reading this, you notice that the idea of menstrual extraction appeals to you, you will probably also be drawn to birth interventions. This is simply a sign that you've been talked out of some of your feminine power.

At no other time than in the act of giving birth does your body serve so directly as a channel for the life force—if you do not interfere with that life force. And at no other time can you see Nature's wisdom so palpably in action—if you are willing to allow Nature to do what Nature does best.

The process of birth is one of Nature's highest achievements. Nature in all her wisdom has designed it so that the experience teaches a woman about her inner resources and how to access them. If participated in consciously and fully, labor will also cement the relationship between mother and child, and, if the mother's mate is present, among all three of them.

The teaching is embodied in the rhythms of labor, which entrain the body and brain of the mother with strength, flexibility, and resilience. You experience contractions, which force you to find the resources to deal with the discomfort and to go deep within. And then you have a period of rest and relaxation, during which you can change positions, get more support, drink some water, and prepare yourself for the next contraction. You learn to go with a situation you cannot control, which may involve pressure and pain. And you learn to trust that the process will give you the time and strength you need to ready yourself for the next wave of contractions.

The bonding occurs thanks to the extraordinary biochemistry of labor, which primes the body and brain of both mother and child with high levels of two potent neurotransmitters, oxytocin (which causes uterine contractions as well as intense feelings of love) and beta-endorphins (the body's natural opiates, which cause euphoria and numbing of pain). Together these hormones create a biological imprint in the bonding circuits.

All of these processes occur naturally, and most women do not need any of the numerous interventions, mechanical and drug-mediated, that make childbirth in this country resemble a medical emergency rather than a normal physiological event. But pregnant women tend to go along with this overmedicalized approach unthinkingly, assuming that their doctors know best. If, however, you understood that birth interventions such as IVs, electronic fetal monitoring, episiotomy, epidural anesthesia, labor induction, vacuum extractor and forceps deliveries, and cesarean sections might have adverse consequences for yourself and/or your baby, would you still participate in them under circumstances when they're not medically necessary—which in most cases they aren't? Birth interventions that bypass the normal processes of labor and birth are the equivalent of clamping the umbilical cord before the baby has had a chance to adjust to breathing on her own—another medical procedure that is all too common in the rushed environment of today's delivery rooms, as will be discussed below.

No one speaks more clearly about the perfection of the design of the female body for giving birth naturally than Ina May Gaskin, a professional midwife who is the founder and guiding spirit of the Farm Midwifery Center and who has been delivering babies for over thirty years. From their birthing center in a rural community in Tennessee, Gaskin and the other midwives at the Farm have overseen the prenatal care and attended the births of more than 2,200 babies, most of them born in their parents' homes or at the Farm. They have a safety record for mother and child that would be the envy of any medical center anywhere, despite (or probably because of!) the fact that fewer than 2 percent of their births were cesareans, fewer than 1 percent were assisted by forceps or vacuum extractors, and none of their births were drug assisted, except in cases of medical emergencies.

"Remember," Ina May says, "your body is not a lemon. You are not a machine. The Creator is not a careless mechanic."

PRINCIPLES OF BIRTH WISDOM: WHAT EVERY WOMAN SHOULD KNOW

I invite you to have trust in the natural principles that govern labor and birth—physiological, psychological, biological, and biochemical. The following section describes these principles, which are important to know and understand, not only because they will help ensure an optimal start for our daughters but because they can be applied to creations of all kinds, including our own state of health.

Principle One: Labor proceeds on its own schedule.

Pregnancy forces us to have patience with the process of growth and development. As a culture, we want everything instantly. But Mother Bear wisdom doesn't work that way. You have to allow your pregnancy to reach fruition. And you have to wait for labor to begin.

Toward the end of their pregnancies, many women feel the need to "get it over with." "When is this baby coming?" "When will I go into labor?" These questions are, quite frankly, unanswerable. Each pregnancy has its own gestation period. The baby will give the signal that she's ready to come when she is ready. Going along with this program teaches us how to wait on the will of heaven—and that of our child.

A child is actually much easier to care for while it's inside your body. Yes, your back may ache toward the end of pregnancy and you may walk with a waddle. Yes, you have to slow down. And sleeping isn't always as comfortable as you might like. But this is part of the process. You learn to pace yourself and parcel out your life energy. You don't want your baby to be swimming in a sea of stress hormones. And you want the baby to have all the advantages of waiting until she is ready to be born.

❊ **WISDOM CHALLENGE:** *Elective Induction of Labor*

Some labors need to be induced for the safety of either the mother or the baby, or both. This would be the case if a mother has severe pregnancy-induced hypertension, for example, and is at risk of having seizures.

Increasingly, however, women are being told that it's fine to plan and control the timing of their deliveries. They want to know when to tell their mothers to come. They want to schedule their work and be able to tell their bosses when they will need time off. That is why labor inductions, and the risks associated with them, are now on the rise once again. The same thing was going on when I was a medical student. Then inductions declined for a while. Now they're back in full force.

Induction of labor is simply not the same thing as spontaneous labor. It involves rupturing the membranes prematurely, giving oxytocin via IV, and/or applying prostaglandins to the cervix directly. Most women are surprised by how painful these induced contractions are. Because artificially induced contractions are often stronger than normal ones, they're more apt to result in fetal distress and to cause the laboring woman to request pain-relief medication. Spontaneous labor, on the other hand, has its own rhythms and is far easier to tolerate. Induction of labor increases the risk of cesarean delivery, uterine rupture, fetal distress, jaundice, and premature birth. Though we'd all like to believe that a baby's readiness to be born can be assured with complete accuracy, given our high-tech ultrasounds, the truth is that this technology doesn't always give conclusive readings. And inducing a baby before she's mature is more common than many in my profession would like to admit.[4]

Pregnancy requires flexibility in your mind and in your environment. It cannot be approached in the same way as running a Fortune 500 company. But the lessons it teaches are applicable to many other areas of life. You cannot control the progression of pregnancy. You can only surrender to it. This flies in the face of one of the core values we all internalize in our culture: the illusion of control. When you let go of that, you find that your body (and your soul) has a wisdom that surpasses that of your conscious mind.

THE BOTTOM LINE: Allow me to be a loving but tough-minded mother (and doctor) for a minute and ask you something: If you can't allow yourself to be "inconvenienced" by the onset of spontaneous labor, how do you expect to deal with the inconvenience of a child's needs? Sorry. Couldn't help myself.

Principle Two: Childbirth is designed by nature to be a peak experience, characterized by joy, love, ecstasy.

Labor and birth are designed by nature as a numinous peak experience that a mother will never forget, thanks to the two key neurotransmitter hormones, oxytocin and beta-endorphin. During labor, the frontal and temporal lobes of a mother's brain are flooded with these hormones, which makes them more active and receptive than usual. This means that all her senses are heightened. Time seems to stand still. She may even feel a mystical sense of being at one with the universe.

Oxytocin is a hormone that is important for every known type of animal bonding. Levels of oxytocin increase during sex and nursing and other types of social bonding activity, and they are particularly high during labor. The neurotransmitter beta-endorphin, a naturally occurring morphinelike substance, is also produced in large amounts during unmedicated labors, saturating the bodies of both mother and baby. It is associated with euphoria, a sense of reward, and decreased perception of pain. (This same neurotransmitter is produced during exercise and meditation.)

The combination of oxytocin and beta-endorphin–flooding during labor creates an altered state of consciousness characterized by a sense of love and well-being—sometimes so intense that it is known as *ekstasis*.[5] Because of these hormones, labor can put a nonmedicated woman into a hyperreceptive state characterized by an enhanced memory of everything that happens to her, heightened intuition, and exquisite sensitivity to her environment. When a baby is born under such conditions, the participants experience a striking elevation in mood that is contagious, affecting everyone in the room. This is why I always recommend that even if a woman is having an elective C-section, she should plan on going into labor beforehand, unless there are medical contraindications to labor. That way she and her baby will be better primed to meet each other.

When I was a medical student, one of the patients whose birth I attended told me at the time of her postpartum visit that she was having recurring dreams about falling in love with and dancing with the obstetrician who had attended her labor, a wonderful man who was an important role model for me. Since then, I've heard many other women make similar remarks. I used to think that these women were simply grateful for the skills of their obstetricians, the only men other than their husbands who knew their bodies intimately (though clinically), and like damsels everywhere, had, at least in their dreams, expressed their gratitude by giving these men their love. But now I know that they had been affected by oxytocin, which acts as a biological Cupid's arrow, bonding the women to their babies—and incidentally to the caregivers who were in the room with them during their labors and had offered them such good support. Women who give birth by cesarean, particularly those who don't go into labor before the C-section, don't experience the oxytocin priming of labor, and may not bond as easily with their babies. I've even heard some cesarean-birth mothers ask: "How do I know if the baby is mine?" Technology has made it so easy to bypass the process of creation that they don't recognize the child their own body has produced. Can you imagine a chimpanzee in the wild having this concern?

Nature if left unimpeded enables you to meet your new baby in a hormonally induced wave of euphoric pleasure, so that you will fall in love with her instantly. This is Nature's way of seeing to it that the new baby will be well cared for, and that the bonds of love among mother, father, and child will be strengthened.

Although our culture does not acknowledge this, there is no doubt that neuroanatomically speaking, birth can elicit the same intensely pleasurable feelings as orgasm. One of my patients once told me that her pleasure was so great when she birthed her daughter that she said to her doctor, "If I had known before that it could be this good, I'd have been tempted to have ten children." The kind of ecstasy I'm describing here is very rare in hospital births, because this setting by its very nature precludes the kind of intimacy that allows a woman to feel safe enough to go deeply into herself.

Women who have had these ecstatic childbirth experiences say that they are at once physically pleasurable and intensely spiritual. Yes, the same transcendent energy, altered states of consciousness and feelings of bliss described by saints and holy people during profound religious experiences may be experienced by women in childbirth. Physiologically speaking we know this to be true because the same areas of the brain that are activated during childbirth (the temporal lobes) also figure very strongly in intuitive and mystical experiences of all kinds, including near-death experiences. This may explain why so many midwives and labor and delivery nurses find themselves doing hospice work with the dying at some point during their careers. There seem to be some people who are just naturally drawn to the energy at the gateways between life's passages.

WISDOM CHALLENGE: *Elective Cesarean Delivery*

There are certainly times when cesarean sections are necessary for the health and well-being of both mother and child. But the issue of elective cesarean delivery for no medical indication is highly controversial. Though fewer than 10 percent of women will require a cesarean if they are well supported during labor and attended by skilled caregivers, there are still many women who request this procedure because they are so frightened of childbirth that they will do anything to avoid it. To say that this bypasses Mother Bear wisdom is an understatement. Although I don't want to be unduly alarmist, I do want women to understand that C-sections are major surgery and they have some serious risks.

Following is a partial list of some of these risks, as compiled by the Coalition for Improving of Maternity Services:

~ Women run five to seven times the risk of death with cesarean section compared with vaginal birth.[6,7]

~ Complications during and after the surgery include surgical injury to the bladder, uterus, and blood vessels (two per one hundred), hemorrhage (one to six women per one hundred require a blood transfusion), paralyzed bowel (ten to twenty per one hundred mild cases, one in one hundred severe), and infection (up to fifty times more common).[8,9]

~ One in ten women report difficulties with normal activities two months after the birth,[10] and one in four report pain at the incision site as a major problem. One in fourteen still report incisional pain six months or more after delivery.[11]

~ Twice as many women require rehospitalization as women having normal vaginal birth.[12]

~ As is true of all abdominal surgery, there may be internal scar tissue, which can cause pelvic pain, pain during sexual intercourse, and bowel problems.

~ Reproductive consequences compared with vaginal birth include increased infertility[13] and premature birth.[14]

C-sections also pose hazards to the baby:

~ Especially with planned cesareans, some babies will inadvertently be delivered prematurely. Babies born even slightly before they are ready may experience breathing and breast-feeding problems.[15]

~ One to two babies per one hundred will be cut during the surgery.[16]

~ Studies comparing elective cesarean section or cesarean section for reasons unrelated to the baby with vaginal birth find that babies are 50 percent more likely to have low Apgar scores, five times more likely to require assistance with breathing, and five times more likely to be admitted to intermediate or intensive care.[17]

~ Babies born after elective cesarean section are more than four times as likely to develop persistent pulmonary hypertension compared with babies born vaginally.[18] Persistent pulmonary hypertension is life-threatening.

THE BENEFITS OF VAGINAL BIRTH FOR THE BABY

The skin is derived from the same embryonic layer as the brain and the central nervous system. For that reason, the skin functions as a sort of "external nervous system." Stimulation of the skin directly affects the function of all the internal organs via the autonomic nervous system. The process of going through labor involves an enormous amount of tactile stimulation for the baby, which tunes up her internal organs, getting them prepared for life outside the womb. Labor also wrings out her lungs, which are full of fluid in the womb. Babies who go through normal birth are far less likely to end up in the intensive care unit from a condition known as transient tachypnea of the newborn. This condition results, in part, from having too much fluid in the lungs at birth. And it is far more common in babies who have undergone little or no labor.

STRESS URINARY INCONTINENCE IN THE MOTHER

There has been a lot of publicity lately about the link between vaginal delivery and subsequent development of stress urinary incontinence, a condition that affects about 25 percent of women, particularly as they get older. Though it's true that vaginal childbirth is a risk factor for incontinence, the vast majority of women do not become incontinent from vaginal birth, so this should not be used as a justification for cesareans. If birth attendants minimized the common football coach–style encouragement to push, and instead focused on helping women use more effective muscle relaxation techniques, there would be less stress on the pelvic support structures during vaginal birth and the already low incidence of birth-related stress urinary incontinence would be further lowered.[19]

Principle Three: Birth is sexual.

As we've already seen, Nature has designed the labor and birth process to enhance a woman's ability to bond with her baby. But the process can also do the same thing for her and her mate. After all, birth is the natural extension of sex. Childbirth educator Sheila Kitzinger put it this way, "Birth itself is always a sexual act, with all the passion and intensity of a love affair which binds together mother, father, and baby." If this process is interrupted by emotional and physical separation, a woman's relationship with both her husband and baby may suffer.

It's very easy for mothers to understand why they should keep their babies with them following birth. But what most do not appreciate is that it is very important to have one's mate present as well.

Marilyn Moran, a pioneering lay researcher who championed "do-it-yourself" home births, reported on the experience of hundreds of couples who gave birth at home without anyone from the medical community in attendance. Although I know that few women would choose an unattended birth, what interests me about her research is how big an impact there is on a couple's subsequent love life when the father of the child is present and very intimately involved in the process. For the majority of women in our culture, sexual desire for their husbands wanes considerably after they give birth. The result is that the woman becomes a sexual gatekeeper, who frequently keeps the gate closed, and the father commonly feels shut out of the intimate bond between mother and child. I can certainly relate!

The couples studied by Moran had a very different postpartum experience. About 70 percent of these couples had sexual intercourse during the early stages of labor. Although this may seem a radical concept, in other cultures intercourse is used to induce labor in women whose contractions are intermittent. Stimulation of the breasts and nipples—which causes the release of oxytocin—can do the same, a fact well known to doctors in other areas of the world who are able to induce labor predictably by having their patients use a breast pump during the last days of pregnancy, and by doctors in this country who use nipple stimulation to induce contractions (in what is called the contraction stress test) so that they can see how well a baby will tolerate labor.

Like Ina May Gaskin and others, Moran found that giving birth in intimate settings with a partner who is physically supportive and affectionate can be an orgasmic experience for the mothers, and that it also greatly enhances the quality of their subsequent love life. In a study that compared couples who delivered at home in an intimate setting with those who delivered at the hospital using the conventional medical model, Moran found very significant differences in the quality of the couples' sex and love relationship at four and twelve months postpartum, with the do-it-yourself home-birthers showing far more compatibility in their marriages than their hospital-delivering counterparts.[20] The frequency of sexual intercourse was either unchanged or increased in 64 percent of the do-it-yourself home-birth couples at four months postpartum. And 21 percent of them were having sex much more than before the baby was born! In the conventional hospital-birth couples, on the other hand, 58 percent were having sex less frequently than before and 26 percent were having sex much less frequently, while only 11 percent were having sex at a frequency that was unchanged and only 5 percent were having it much more than before.

Given my own experience with waning postpartum libido as well as that of the hundreds of mothers I've cared for, the results of Moran's study really had an impact on me. I know that do-it-yourself home-birthers are not your average couple! And in my role as a physician I would not presume to recommend do-it-yourself home birth to anyone in this litigation-saturated culture. But in my role as a visionary in women's health, I find the experiences of the people in her study intriguing. Every instinct and intuitive cell in my body tells me to pay attention to Moran's work because it underscores the biologic and creative potential that is available at birth. I believe that the experience of birth was designed by nature to enhance a couple's pleasure bond. Birthing in a way that makes this more likely amounts to a solid-gold investment in the health and happiness of a family.

Principle Four: How we are born imprints both mother and baby.

The events of our birth remain with us for life, as a sort of blueprint for what to expect here on earth. If we are welcomed by a calm, joyful, trusting mother who is deeply supported in her inherent power and beauty, if we are gathered immediately into her loving arms, held to her breast and gently rocked, then kept close to her body for our first weeks of life, we will internalize a sense of safety, trust, and security that will inform all of our days, and create healthy brain chemistry that will serve us throughout our lives. As explained above, this is what happens when a mother gives birth under optimal conditions, because the saturation of oxytocin and beta-endorphin receptors in her brain and body makes her maximally available for bonding with her baby and her caregivers, and for experiencing a sense of euphoria.

But the converse is also true. If we are separated from our mothers for significant periods of time immediately after birth or cared for by a mother who is depressed or emotionally unavailable, this too may have a lifelong impact. This happens, in part, because of another brain chemical, vasopressin, which is produced during potentially stressful events like labor but which has the exact opposite effect of oxytocin on bonding.[21] In contrast to oxytocin, vasopressin is important for creating vigilance and preparing the body for fight or flight. It tells you that something is wrong, that there is danger, something you need to be concerned about. Though it is present to some extent in all labors, it doesn't have any adverse effect if it's balanced by oxytocin. The balance between oxytocin and vasopressin is a key marker for the quality of the social support we receive.

When a woman's labor doesn't go well—for example, she perceives her caregivers as insensitive, she feels alone, she doesn't get the care she needs, she feels overwhelmed by all the medical technology, or she has to undergo an emergency medical procedure—then her heightened sensitivity and increased levels of vasopressin may make it harder for her to bond with her baby.

❀ WISDOM CHALLENGE: *Electronic Fetal Monitoring*

Electronic fetal monitoring was introduced when I was a resident. And, almost overnight, it became the standard of care to hook up everyone to a fetal monitor, as a way to practice defensive medicine, even though today, more than thirty years later, it has yet to be demonstrated that routine monitoring improves outcomes!

What fetal monitoring has done is to put more focus on making sure the lines on the monitor strip are visible to the birth attendants than on making labor as comfortable and efficient as possible for the laboring woman! She may have to go through all kinds of awkward maneuvers so that the monitor strip can be easily read, and she has to stay relatively immobile lying on her back in bed when she'd be better off being free to move around. When a baby is working its way down the birth canal, the process is aided immensely if the mother can choose her laboring position. Upright positions—sitting, squatting, standing, kneeling—can sometimes significantly speed up labor and also increase the size of the pelvic outlet, because they are working with rather than against gravity.

Fetal monitoring has not only interfered with a woman's freedom of movement but has also created an atmosphere of fear surrounding the birth process. The laboring woman loses trust in her own body. She watches the monitor strip, believing that its little lines, not the natural forces of birth, are what are keeping her baby safe. Instead of watching the strip, she should look within—going inside, connecting with her baby, letting her know she is safe and will be taken care of. And she herself needs the same kind of reassurance from her caregivers, but they may be too preoccupied with the monitor strip to give it to her.

For their part, the birth attendants use the monitor as a talisman of normalcy, becoming overly quick to suggest or even insist on a C-section if the lines on that strip show anything potentially amiss, because they want to cover themselves legally in the event anything goes wrong. No wonder C-section rates have ballooned.

Having been in this situation far too many times as an ob-gyn myself, I can tell you that it doesn't help the process of labor one bit! The focus on a piece of technology is the result of our collective anxiety about the safety and security of birth. All of our fears get played out unconsciously in the typical hospital delivery room. Sometimes I wonder if those who are drawn to this arena (including me) are working out our own unresolved birth trauma.

Principle Five: Natural birth is safe.

Although we don't often hear about this, a series of studies in Europe has demonstrated that home birthing is as safe as hospital births in healthy mothers with no risk factors for birth complications.[22] Those who choose it are generally healthy, well-educated, and highly motivated women who are more apt to trust themselves and their bodies in the first place. They are also likely to have arranged to be well-supported by skilled caregivers.

The same conclusion about safety emerges from the births at the Farm. Ina May Gaskin has documented that for *every* mother who was given prenatal care by the Farm midwives, whether she had a home birth attended by them or a hospital birth attended by physicians near the Farm, the rate of complications affecting both mother and child was exceedingly low. This is true despite the fact that she includes in her statistics even the "high-risk" births (breeches, twins, premature labors, etc.) that other birth centers exclude. Of the 2,028 pregnant women cared for by Farm midwives between the years 1970 and 2000, 95.1 percent completed birth at home or at the Farm. Only 1.3 percent required emergency transport to a hospital. The C-section rate was a mere 1.4 percent.[23]

Principle Six: What we believe affects how we give birth.

Childbirth practices say more about a culture's values and beliefs than any of its other customs. In our own culture, as reflected in everything from sitcoms to Hollywood dramas, birth is typically depicted as a major life-threatening event that is intensely painful. There's also the belief (part of Judeo-Christian teaching) that labor pain represents God's punishment for "Eve's sin" in the Garden of Eden. "She will bring forth children in pain and suffering." Talk about a setup!

How often have you seen a laboring woman depicted as an out-of-control hysteric begging for drugs to put her out of her agony? The crisis-intervention, technology-fixation, emergency mind-set of our culture gets played out daily, in the obstetrical suites of hospitals as in the psyches of individual women.

The belief system surrounding birth was beautifully illustrated on a talk show I listened to a while ago, in which four 911 emergency operators were heralded as heroes because they talked four ill-prepared husbands through the deliveries of their wives' babies. These were healthy women whose labors had proceeded so well that they found that their babies were coming before they had time to get to the hospital. In listening to the taped playbacks of the 911 operators and the husbands, what stood out the most for me was the fact that both the operators and the husbands were concentrating solely on the mechanics of catching the baby, forgetting the needs of the mother completely. Although you could hear the mothers' voices in the background meekly asking for their husbands to hold their hands or connect with them, no one seemed to recognize the fact that at the moment of birth, a mother's emotional and physical well-being is profoundly connected with how safe, supported, and encouraged she feels. Because a woman is far more emotionally porous when pregnant and in labor, she is maximally receptive to her environment. This heightened sensitivity makes her particularly vulnerable to her caregiver's fears or to any other discord in her environment.

Given the ways in which birth wisdom is passed down in our culture and depicted in the media, it's little wonder that so many women are afraid of labor. Births are often presided over by highly trained and technologically proficient individuals who believe that their job is to control a process that is inherently dangerous and painful, to heroically snatch the mother and baby from the yawning jaws of death and disaster. This attitude was embedded in the title of an article that appeared in the professional journal, *Obstetrics and Gynecology*: "Induction of Labor in the Nineties: *Conquering* the Unfavorable Cervix" [my italics]. By approaching the cervix as an organ to be forced open and conquered, we are at risk for missing the inner wisdom that the woman's cervix is trying to impart: if a woman's cervix is not softening and ripening as it should, there's a deeper reason for it—and any approach that serves to subdue or "conquer" the message the cervix is trying to convey may, on some level, be perceived by the body as an assault. We keep overlooking the fact that it is possible (and desirable) to engage our souls and psyches to help with the natural work of labor, without forgoing the assistance of technology if it should be needed.

When nearly all births moved into hospitals in the 1940s and '50s in the name of safety and modern maternity care, there is no doubt that lives were saved that would otherwise have been lost. But when we as a culture embraced the medical model of birth as our standard and reduced this miraculous event to a potential medical emergency, we paid a huge price and lost something precious, something that we are just beginning to reclaim: the knowledge that birth is set up biologically to be a time of heightened awareness, euphoria, and receptivity for the mother, the father (or significant other), and the newborn, a passage that sets the stage for that family's relationship from that moment forward.

Like the talk show host who focused on the beaming 911 operators and the puffed-up heroic husbands, we have also lost sight of another central truth: the true heroes of the births being described on that show were the mothers and their miraculous bodies—bodies that knew instinctually exactly what to do, and could have done it well, or even better, without all the frantic phone calls. Though an unplanned home birth is not ideal for anyone, all of those mothers and their babies would have been fine without any of the dramatics.

Principle Seven: Who you choose to have with you in the delivery room can change your experience.

One of the ways in which delivery-room practices have definitely improved in recent years is the welcome now extended to fathers. The fathers or life partners of the woman in labor are not just allowed to be present but in many places expected. When I went through labor with my first child, I had my husband and my nurse with me the whole time. The experience was so intense that I couldn't imagine having done it alone.

This gave me a whole new appreciation for the deprivation of my mother's experience. Giving birth in the 1940s and '50s was very different from what it is today—and my mother did it six times!

MY MOTHER: Alone in the Delivery Room

I didn't get to see any of my children born, or to hold them right after birth. I know you were born at night and I never got to see you until the early-morning feeding. When I went to the hospital, I was put in a room alone and strapped down. A nurse came in every now and then to check on me, but basically, no one was there. Your father couldn't come in. Then, when it was time to deliver, they wheeled me down the hall and put me out.

I can't imagine anything more difficult than going through labor alone, frightened, and strapped down to a bed in a hospital room. But almost all of the mothers of the children of the baby boom generation (and there are five times the number of children in that generation than in those who came before or after the baby boomers) had a similar experience. And it took its toll. Many mothers adapted to this level of deprivation by becoming stoic noncomplainers who learned to "suck it up"—and to expect those around them to do the same.

We now know that many (though not all) women need and want the support of their loved ones while they are in labor. These may include not just the father of the child but friends, family, even other children.

John Kennell, a pediatrician, and Marshall Klaus, an obstetrician, coauthored a book, *Parent-Infant Bonding,* reporting on a number of well-controlled, scientific studies they have done on the birthing practices that best support mothers, babies, and fathers during birth.[24] Some of their work has focused on how good psychological support during childbirth has positive effects on the creation of healthy bonds among family members, and some of it has focused on how good psychological support can also have physical benefits for the woman in labor. For example, they documented that when a mother has the continuous labor support of a doula, a person (usually but not always a woman) certified as a labor caregiver who has been trained to "mother the mother" and to offer reassurance to the mother's partner as well, the cesarean section rate can be cut in half, the labor shortened because there is less stress and pain, the number of drugs used in labor decreased, and the number of babies sent to the intensive care unit with various problems significantly decreased. In a lecture at the American Holistic Medical Association Annual Meeting in the early 1990s, Dr. Kennell proposed that if every woman in labor were to be supported by a doula, it would save the country $3 billion annually in unnecessary medical costs associated with birth interventions.

The benefits go beyond the labor room too. Women who are cared for and mothered in labor are more apt to care for their children well, even if their own self-care has been lacking. For example, a study of low-income, uneducated women in Houston found that those who had the support of a doula's steady hand and reassuring voice during labor were more affectionate with their babies two months later, compared to those who received standard care.[25]

These kinds of results speak clearly for the benefits of well-trained psychological support and healing touch. It is clear to me that if the beneficial effects of a doula could be obtained by a drug, it would be unethical not to use it right now. Yet, as of this writing, the vast majority of labors are carried out without doula support.

Principle Eight: Who you choose to listen to about labor can change your experience.

Many, many women have been told birth horror stories by other women. These "veterans" ' stories work their way into the psyche and adversely affect the course of labor, especially when the story comes from your own mother. Such stories become self-fulfilling prophecies that play themselves out according to what a woman believes will happen.

The all-too-common ritual of recounting these pregnancy war stories takes on the flavor of a fraternity hazing, complete with an I-went-through-it-therefore-you-should-too tone. Baby showers tend to be a natural place for this kind of health- and confidence-undermining female talk. Not uncommonly a pregnant daughter will be told by her mother, "Now you'll see how I suffered giving birth to you." If I start to overhear these stories on an airplane, restaurant, or anywhere else, it's all I can do to keep myself from running over and doing an immediate "intervention."

Despite my objections, I know that there are good reasons why women feel the need to tell their labor stories. One is that the arena of pregnancy and birth has been the only place where women have historically wielded any power and authority compared to men. No wonder they feel the need to relive their experience and tell it in the same way a veteran tells his tale of battle. Another reason is that the heightened spiritual energy that's available at birth, even if misunderstood, exerts a pull on us that we need to express. When we journey during labor to that numinous territory at the gateway between being and nonbeing, we're compelled to tell the tale upon our return. But once we better understand the energy emanating from this life passage, we will be more apt to empower our daughters or sisters with birth stories that are positive, albeit still heroic.

Here's a really positive view of labor and delivery that the mother of one of my newsletter subscribers passed on to her:

> Mom made being pregnant sound like the most wonderful experience a woman can have. She would tell me about how her doctor would have her wait a little longer in the waiting room so other expectant mothers would see how happy and healthy a pregnant woman could be.
>
> When my turn came I went into it expecting good health and looking forward to delivering a healthy baby. And that's exactly what I got. I had about two weeks of mild morning sickness and minor water retention with my pregnancy. The rest of the time I was happy, healthy, and busy making baby clothes. I was staying with my mom when labor started and she took me to the hospital. About two hours later she heard a baby cry, and since I was the only person in delivery at that time (small hospital), she knew it was her grandchild. My son practically fell out. He was eight pounds four ounces, and we were home in two days. This was in 1962.
>
> I know that it takes more than a good attitude to create a comfortable pregnancy and that complications can happen in the healthiest of women, but I also believe that being indoctrinated

with horror stories, such as "I was in labor for eighty hours, and my body's ruined after giving birth to you," can do real harm and set a woman up for a more difficult time than needs to be. I will always give Mom full credit for setting up an atmosphere and giving the support needed for the wonderful experience of my becoming a mother.

I couldn't agree more.

Principle Nine: Fear hurts.

Perception and expectation often determine our experience of things. In the United States women are indoctrinated with a techno-medical model of birth based primarily on fear. They believe that the pain of labor will be intolerable. But fear has consequences, beginning with the fact that because they believe their pain will be intolerable, they experience it that way.

Fear stops the progression of labor and increases the rate of interventions—including cesarean birth and forceps delivery—that are associated with an increased risk for infection, bleeding, and bonding difficulties. According to a new survey of 1,600 women conducted by Harris Interactive for the Maternity Center Association (MCA), a nonprofit organization dedicated to improving maternity care, 61 percent of the women surveyed experienced between six and ten medical interventions during their labor and deliveries, ranging from being hooked up to an IV to being given Pitocin to speed up labor. Pitocin increases the amplitude of contractions and makes them more painful. It also increases the risk of fetal distress and neonatal jaundice. Nearly half (43 percent) of the women in the survey had between three and five major interventions, including induction, episiotomy, C-sections, and forceps delivery. Eight out of ten women had pain-relief medication during labor; that number increased to 91 percent for first-time moms. Donald Coustan, M.D., chief of ob-gyn at Women and Infants Hospital in Providence, Rhode Island, speaking of the survey results in *Parenting* magazine, said, "What we're seeing is that most women want to minimize their discomfort. We've actually been disappointed that our alternative birthing center, where women labor drug-free and without monitors, has been underutilized."[26]

In *Women's Bodies, Women's Wisdom,* I told a story about how when my older daughter was around three, she cut her finger on a sharp stick while outside playing and ran into the house crying. As I held her finger under some running water to reveal a very small cut, she said, "It didn't hurt until I got scared." Truer words were never spoken. Women are quite willing to go through painful procedures if they're convinced that the outcome is desirable and that the procedure is safe. Leg waxing, plastic surgery, and eyebrow plucking—not to mention going to medical school and staying up all night on hospital rotations—are all examples of our willingness to endure pain for a good cause. And what could be a better cause than a healthy child with whom we feel immediately bonded?

The main problem with childbirth is the legacy of fear that surrounds it. And fear changes the dynamics of labor, affecting nerve and muscle function. Fear is based on our beliefs and perceptions. These beliefs trigger behaviors such as muscle tensing, racing heartbeat, and increased rate of breathing, all of which make the perception of pain much worse than it need be! Fear overstimulates the sympathetic fight-or-flight nervous system and causes the uterus to clamp down and the cervix to close. I've seen countless women who were in active labor when they came to the hospital only to have the process stopped by the stress of going through admitting, having an IV started, and having a parade of strangers enter the room. The hospital atmosphere and the fear that permeates it is very contagious. And the heightened sensitivity of the laboring woman makes her very susceptible to "catching it." The result is often a dysfunctional and overly painful labor.

By being well supported, using her own ability to focus, and changing her perceptions, a pregnant woman can access her inner Mother Bear and dissolve her fear and its adverse consequences.

Principle Ten: Labor can be hard work. Labor can hurt. The rewards are worth it.

Birth is hard work. And it can also be painful. But as mentioned above, women voluntarily choose to go through all kinds of processes that aren't particularly comfortable. Women go through these processes to build self-esteem, to feel better about their bodies, and to achieve long-term life-changing goals that they believe will make everything they go through worthwhile. Yet going through natural childbirth holds far more power to transform a woman's sense of self-esteem than any of those other things.

Still, we're advised to avoid the pain of childbirth at all costs because we don't understand that this pain provides important feedback during the process of labor. And worse, the implication is that we must have pain relief because we're too weak to "take it."

Remember, the pain of a normal labor is not the pain of injury or danger, though that is the message we are given when it is medicated away. Once you know that nothing bad is going to happen to you from the pain (you're not going to burst open), you can deal with it—almost always without resorting to medication. Gas pain can also be excruciatingly painful. But because you know that it is only gas, you don't get scared. You relax, and eventually the gas passes. It's the same with labor pains. They exist as feedback to enable you to move around, change positions, and better adapt to the passage of the baby through the birth canal. The pain of labor also changes during each stage of the process. For example, after the cervix is fully dilated, the body will often go into a period of no contractions, during which a woman can rest and prepare herself for the final push!

We need to give different messages about labor pain—what it means, what purposes it serves, and how to get through it. Think about the following:

~ Labor gets you to slow down completely and find a safe place to birth your baby.

~ Labor sensations provide important feedback about how and when and into what position to move to better facilitate the process. (See "Wisdom Challenge: Epidural Anesthesia.")

~ Labor puts you in touch with yourself and your body more deeply than ever, bringing you completely into the moment. During labor you are living from one contraction to the next. Time stands still. Labor forces you to surrender to a power greater than your intellect. It's the ultimate experience of "letting go and letting God." Think of the contractions as ocean waves. If you stay on the surface of the pain and fight them with your intellect, you're more apt to crash against the rocks of the shore. In other words, you'll just create more suffering. The trick is to dive deep down under the surface to the calm center below—the same place that yogis reach during profound states of meditation.

~ Labor asks you to find resources within yourself that you didn't know you had. It increases your self-esteem. You emerge from the process knowing that you can handle whatever comes your way. It is perfect preparation for the rigors of parenting.

~ Labor is a biological rite of passage into motherhood. No other biological process is as dramatic—or needs to be. Motherhood is the true "change of life."

One of my patients once told me about her first birth experience this way: "During labor, I felt as though I were floating above myself, looking down with great wisdom and compassion. Labor forced me to open up to a place in myself that I didn't know existed. I came out of it with absolute confidence and unshakable belief in my body."

WISDOM CHALLENGE: *Epidural Anesthesia*

Currently about 70 percent of women get epidural anesthesia for birth because of their fear of pain and mistrust of their body's ability to birth normally. There's no question that an epidural can provide much-needed relief in labor. In fact, I've watched women dilate very quickly after being given an epidural because they were finally able to relax and let go. Unfortunately, more frequently I've seen just the opposite: women whose labors slowed to a crawl after they received their epidural, and who eventually ended up undergoing a C-section that could have been avoided.

Like all interventions, epidural anesthesia is a double-edged sword, not a universal panacea. When the anesthesia is given under the right circumstances, at the right time, by a highly skilled anesthesiologist, it can be ideal. This is especially true in Pitocin-augmented labors in which the contractions are unusually painful. And it's also true if a woman has been progressing slowly, is exhausted, and needs some relief.

But an epidural is not a benign procedure; it's a major intervention. Epidural anesthesia involves having a large-bore needle inserted into the space around the dura (the coating over the spinal cord) so that anesthestic can be injected into that space to numb the spinal nerves. Getting that needle into the right place takes a lot of practice. And the laboring woman has to curl into a little ball while in active labor to allow the procedure to take place; it isn't comfortable at all, and it doesn't always work. Sometimes the level of anesthesia is too high, sometimes it's too low. Some people are far better at giving epidurals than others, but most women aren't given a choice of anesthesiologists. You get the one on call. So it often happens that the woman's labor will be disrupted by repeated attempts to "get it right." As with all complex medical procedures, there are no guarantees.

Besides the disadvantages cited above, epidural anesthesia also blocks the body's wisdom and interferes with the two-way communication between a baby and her mother. This is because epidural anesthesia blocks the sensory nerves of the uterus, cervix, pelvic floor, and abdomen so that the mother doesn't feel the sensations of the baby moving through her body. As a result, she won't feel the feedback her body is giving her about how to change her laboring position in order to respond to her baby's progress through the birth canal. This is one of the functions of labor pain. To relieve it, you naturally move your body into the positions that most benefit the process of labor.

Dr. Mona Lisa Schulz says that from a neurological point of view, labor is a well-orchestrated dance between the mother's and the baby's neurologic systems. When you numb the organs and muscles of a mother's birth canal, you have, in effect, numbed the conductor of this orchestra. You block the mother's ability to move freely in response to her bodily sensation, you block the function of her pelvic floor muscles (which can cause the baby's head to engage in a less favorable position, making forceps or vacuum extraction more likely), you block the mother's ability to know when to push and when to stop, and you change the quality of uterine contractions. As a result, baby and mother are far less likely to "dance" well together!

Epidural anesthesia also changes the levels of beta-endorphins in the mother's bloodstream, thereby decreasing the potential ecstasy associated with birth. And it is associated with unexplained maternal fever in a significant number of women for reasons that aren't clear. Though the fever does not usually signify an infection, we can't be sure that none is present, so the baby has to be taken to the nursery and worked up for sepsis. This involves drawing blood, doing a spinal tap, starting an IV in the newborn, and putting her on antibiotics "just in case." All in all, not a great welcome to the world for the little one.

UMBILICAL CORD WISDOM

After the baby is born, the umbilical cord, which has been her life support system during all the months of gestation, will continue to pulsate for ten to thirty minutes if it is not cut. The cord provides the baby with a backup oxygenation system while her heart and lungs are adjusting to the move from the water environment in which she was nourished via her mother's bloodstream to an air environment in which her lungs must expand and begin the process of respiration. Until it stops pulsating, the umbilical cord is a living, viable organ that also helps ensure that the baby gets enough blood volume for optimal circulation to her brain, lungs, and other organs. Once the baby's blood volume is normal and the lungs have adjusted to breathing air directly, the cord will stop pulsating on its own.

While the cord is still pulsating, the newborn should rest in her mother's arms or on her abdomen while both of them go through the most profound bodily changes of their lives. The cord should not be cut until it has stopped pulsating completely, indicating that the backup support from the placenta is no longer needed and that the child's respiratory and circulatory systems are now ready to supply the brain, lungs, and other organs.

Because birth is so often approached as an emergency, however, this gradual and gentle transition time is usually cut short by clamping the cord immediately at the moment of birth. No wonder we as a culture get the feeling that we need to hurry up. We've been programmed since birth to be hurried—to cut to the chase, to get on with it. And our bodies also get programmed to believe that "there's not enough time" (or oxygen). In other words, starting with the way we are born, we're being taught to bypass our own internal rhythms and comfort zones.

It's not just the fact of feeling hurried that is at issue here, however. There is a substantial body of evidence that too quick clamping of the umbilical cord, particularly in premature or sick newborns, can result in hypovolemia, a condition in which there is not enough blood volume for optimal organ perfusion in the baby. This puts the baby at risk for respiratory distress syndrome as well as brain injury. It also leads to the necessity for transfusions in the neonatal intensive care unit, in order to supply the blood that the placenta and cord were designed to provide naturally.

Although doctors are taught that the cord needs to be clamped immediately to prevent the baby from getting too much blood, this does not happen if you simply keep the baby and mother at the same level, while the placenta provides its final contributions to the baby's well-being. Even with a sick or premature baby, when a neonatologist is part of the delivery team, it's entirely possible for neonatalogists to do their part in resuscitating the baby while she is still attached to the cord, thereby giving the child the best of both worlds. This is rarely done, however.[27]

A PROGRAM FOR OPTIMIZING BIRTH WISDOM

The birth of a baby is an unforgettable experience that brings a woman's entire maternal legacy to the surface. The time surrounding birth is imbued with the energy of new beginnings, growth, and change. It's as though all the old inherited patterns in a woman's life get scrambled so that they can be reassembled in newer, improved forms. Because birth can go a long way toward helping a woman heal her past, it's important to plan for it carefully.

Choose your birth companions. You'll want to think very carefully about who you want to have present with you during labor and after birth. Make sure you genuinely like everyone who is going to be present at the birth of your baby. This is no time for trying to make "peace at any price." For example, don't give in and allow your husband's cousin Sarah or your sister-in-law to be with you during your labor and birth if you don't really want them there, just because you know it would please the family.

Choose your caregivers. Most women are pretty clear about what type of caregiver they want for their labor. Some want a doctor, some want a midwife. I have taken care of many women who've had good experiences with home births attended by midwives, and have also taken care of women who feel safe only in a hospital setting. To labor well, you must be in a setting in which *you* feel safe and secure, regardless of what your mother or sister-in-law, your best friend, your doctor, or anyone else—including me—thinks!

If you choose to be attended by a midwife, keep in mind that there are big differences among them. Some work in hospitals and are very technology focused. Others support home birth. And some are in-between. You'll need to interview the ones in your area to see who is the right "fit" for you.

When it comes to doctors, there are family doctors who deliver babies and there are board-certified obstetrician-gynecologists who are trained to handle any obstetrical emergency that might arise. Ask your prospective birth attendants what their birth philosophy is: do they believe that most women can labor and birth normally?

Regardless of whom you've chosen for medical care, as I said earlier, I'd highly recommend hiring a doula, who can help mother you during labor and birth, and also ideally tend to you postpartum for a week or two at home. I certainly wish that this option had been available to me. A mate can't take the place of a doula. A mate's job is to love the laboring woman unconditionally, but not to be an expert in labor support! So do yourself and everyone else a favor. Free your loved ones from the technical details of labor support and let them put all their energy into just being there for you and with you! (See Resources for how to find a birth assistant.)

Choose your labor facility. The midwives, physicians, nurses, doulas, and other birthing professionals who make up the Coalition for Improving Maternity Service (CIMS) have established what they call "mother and child-center criteria" which they believe all labor facilities should aspire to meet. Although there are currently only two birth services that meet these standards so completely that they have officially qualified as "mother-friendly," when choosing your own labor facility you might want to consider some of the following criteria from their list:

- ⁓ unrestricted access for the mother to the birth companions of your choice, including family, friends, midwives, doulas, etc.

- ⁓ freedom to walk around and to labor in any position of your choice, unless medically counterindicated

- ⁓ induction rate of 10 percent or less

~ episiotomy rate of 20 percent or less (with a goal of 5 percent or less)

~ cesarean rate of 10 percent or less in community hospitals, 15 percent or less in hospitals treating high-risk pregnancies

~ a policy of not routinely employing practices not supported by scientific evidence, including: shaving, enemas, IVs, early rupture of membranes, electronic fetal monitoring

~ staffed by people educated in nondrug methods of pain relief

(For more complete information on the evidence-based guidelines compiled by the coalition, see Resources.)

Other options you may want to keep in mind when choosing your birth facility are the availability of hot tubs that women can labor in to reduce pain and enhance relaxation. Also ask about family-centered care, which allows you, your baby, and your mate to stay together in the same room where you gave birth.

Keep your baby with you. Every species of mammal that has been studied has been shown to have a "sensitive" period, a window of time just after birth during which the offspring becomes attached to its mother. If the baby, be it a lamb, a goat, or an elephant, is removed from its mother during this sensitive period, the mother will often reject it and not allow it to nurse.[28] The pioneering work done by Drs. John Kennell and Marshall Klaus has turned up evidence for a similar sensitive period in human beings. Before getting involved in bonding research, Dr. Kennell had been instrumental in setting up the first neonatal intensive care unit in the country. He noticed that babies who had been born prematurely and immediately taken from their mothers to the neonatal intensive care unit were much more likely to end up in the emergency room as victims of battering or neglect at a later age. Having spent thousands of hours and dollars successfully keeping these children alive, Dr. Kennell was deeply concerned about what had gone wrong. His subsequent research on bonding showed that when the events of birth interfere with the bonding time and activities that Nature in her wisdom has put into place, there may well be a tendency on the part of the mother to be more detached from or, in the worst case, even abusive to the child.

For all these reasons, anything that causes unnecessary separation of mother and baby after birth should be avoided. This has been demonstrated not just in the studies done by Drs. Kennell and Klaus (whose work on the kind of birthing practices that best support laboring women was cited earlier), but also by midwives such as Polly Perez, who runs a doula service. The concept of family-centered maternity care that has emerged from their work is reflected in hospitals and birth centers that allow mothers to labor and deliver in a home-like setting, often with doula support. After the baby is born, the mother and significant others of her choice remain with the child until it's time to be discharged from the hospital. Importantly, the mother's nurse and baby's nurse are one and the same, which discourages any artificial division of the mother-baby dyad during this crucial time period, when the two are getting to know each other. Support for breast-feeding with the maternity nurses is also built into the system as well.

Even if you are not able to find such a hospital or birth center, you can make sure ahead of time that the place you will be giving birth will support you in your wish to keep your baby with you after delivery. But do check this out in advance, because a significant degree of both maternal and newborn deprivation has been built in to the obstetrical care of mothers and babies over the last fifty years (as my mother's birthing experiences attest), and it is a legacy that is still present in many settings. When a mother and her baby are separated at birth for any reason, the stress of the situation partially blocks the effect of the molecules of belonging, which can make it more difficult to bond with a child. You don't want Cupid's arrow to go off course!

All that having been said, it's important to acknowledge that relatively few people have experienced the kind of ideal birth and bonding experience described above, yet most of us love our children deeply and are in turn loved by them. A child's sense of safety, security, and love is wired in by repeated experiences occurring during the course of an entire lifetime. Pregnancy, labor, and birth are just the beginning. Oxytocin will continue to pulse and create a bond throughout all the years of your relationship with your daughter. It pulses even when you're just thinking about a loved one. The oxytocin pulse that is part of our inner wisdom helps sustain the nurturing bond between individuals as long as they both live.

Be informed. A very good place to start is by reading *Ina May's Guide to Childbirth*. It is filled with uplifting and empowering birth stories that you can use to imprint yourself with the right words and affirmations about birth, and with good, solid, detailed information about prenatal care and labor. The guide is also chock-full of national resources that you can use to find the midwives, doulas, and birth centers that will provide you with the right atmosphere to birth normally.

Have faith. Professionals who support Mother Bear birth wisdom work in every hospital and clinic in the world. You'll find them through the law of attraction once you start looking for them. Remember, "That which you are seeking is also seeking you."

6

The Fourth Trimester

Creating the Outer Placenta

❋

BEING WITH YOUR BABY

Once you have given birth, you and your baby will enter the vulnerable postpartum period known as the fourth trimester, which lasts for three months. During this time, mother and child are still very much a physical unit, your bodies in synchrony with each other as the baby makes her gradual transition to a more independent life.[1] This transition began with the severing of the umbilical cord.

At no time is the Mother Bear instinct more unbridled than now. And if you allow yourself to tap in to it, you will find yourself able to access wellsprings of maternal wisdom you didn't know you had. You may discover that you feel more connected and at one with the process of life than ever before, and you may have vivid dreams that reinforce that sensation of oneness. Although your feelings can sometimes drop into depression, more often they will open you up to the intuitive, mystical side of life during this important time, when your baby is still brand-new to you and the world.

Years after her daughter was born, one mother could still vividly recall what those early days with her newborn were like:

> I would wake up with a start, because I would be holding
> the baby in my dream, and I would feel her body and the

warmth of it on me. I would wake up frightened that I would drop her, and I found that I always awakened just before she woke up to be fed. It was like we were totally wired together. This gave me so much confidence as a mother. The connection was so profound. How could I doubt myself?

I could always tell if she had gone to sleep versus just resting there, because our hearts beat in time to the same rhythm. I mean, I would feel this one big heartbeat going through her and through me. It was very physical, an unmistakable physiological feeling, and I always knew that at that point it was okay to lift her off my shoulder and put her back in her crib. It was so much bigger than me. And it puts you in life in a whole different way.

Birth Opens an Emotional Window

In these first months of your new life with your child, your hormones blast you open, and these biological modulators will amplify whatever emotions you are feeling—happiness or sadness, anxiety or peacefulness. The fourth trimester is a time when you are likely to experience a degree of emotional openness, rawness, and lability different from anything you have ever felt.

The same mother who wrote the beautiful description of the complete unity she felt with her baby had this to say about her feelings in the world beyond the mother-child cocoon:

> On the other hand, if someone looked at me cross-eyed during those early days, I'd cry. It was hard going out onto the street because the world felt so harsh. I felt so thin-skinned. Literally.

The External Fetus and the Outer Placenta

A newborn baby has just spent almost forty weeks living as part of her mother's body. During all that time, her mother's biological rhythms—heart rate, respiration, sleep-and-wake cycle, and all other biological rhythms—were entrained with and setting the tone for her own. After being born, as she makes the transition from intrauterine to extrauterine life and her body undergoes the enormous physical changes that are part of this transition, she continues to have a profound need for her mother. In fact, the mother's support of essential life-sustaining functions is still so critical to the health of her child that the early infant has been referred to as an "external fetus."

Similarly, the maternal body can be likened to an external placenta—sort of like a kangaroo pouch. Even after the cord is cut and the placenta has been expelled, the mother's body continues to serve a placental function. Designed by nature to support and nurture her newborn optimally, her body now sends nutrients to the baby through her milk, her touch, and her physical presence. And when she holds her baby or when she nurses her, she is still helping to regulate basic biological functions and rhythms—heart rate and blood pressure, sleep-wake-and-dream cycles, as well as skin temperature, breathing, brain chemistry, and mood—until these processes can be regulated by the child herself. No wonder the best and safest place for the baby is right next to her mother, the person to whom her body is most closely linked.

Although I didn't know this when my children were born, there are many good reasons why it is best not to take a new baby into the outer world for the first few weeks of life. She is still adjusting physiologically to being outside the womb. So why stress her system further by introducing her to too many external stimuli?

EARLY INVESTMENTS IN YOUR CHILD'S HEALTH YIELD BIG PAYOFFS LATER

The messages, both implicit and explicit, that a child receives from her mother about her body and bodily functions, her emotions, her food, her medical care, and her relationships, all form an indelible imprint on that child's mind and body. This imprint will affect her immune system and her overall health for the rest of her life. It will also set the stage for how she cares for herself on all levels.

Think of a child's health and well-being as a bank account that accrues compound interest over time. The earlier in a child's life that a mother invests in her child's health, the greater the return. Every one of us has the capacity to change and improve her health and circumstances at any age. But no one can ever go back and recapture the kind of physical, mental, and emotional resilience and sense of safety and security in the world that a child absorbs at the cellular level from a healthy mother in touch with her inner Mother Bear wisdom.

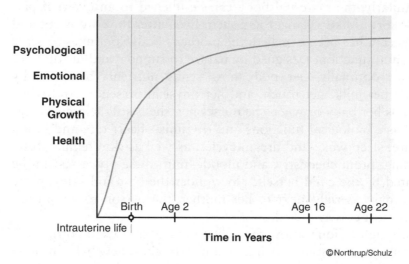

MATERNAL INVESTMENT AND
THE HEALTH OF THE CHILD

Psychological

Emotional

Physical
Growth

Health

Birth   Age 2   Age 16   Age 22

Intrauterine life

Time in Years

©Northrup/Schulz

Early "deposits" yield far bigger gains over time than deposits made
later in life.

❀ WISDOM CHALLENGE: *Baby versus Career*

Whenever you've created anything of significance, you need to acknowledge your creation, assess how it fits into your life, and allow
yourself time to rest and regroup. Although many women with newborns have to return to work after a six-week pregnancy leave or
even less, leaving a newborn baby too soon can feel as though it's
tearing your heart in two. Every pregnant woman should do everything she can to ensure that she can be home with her new baby for
at least the first three months of that child's life. There will be plenty
of time later to pursue career plans. A baby is only newborn for a
short time. Use this time to focus your passion and nurturance on
your new creation.

    If you don't *have* to go back to work for financial reasons after
that first six weeks or three months or whatever, deciding when or
whether to go back requires enormous self-knowledge as well as
courage, because it's so difficult to find the right balance between
your own needs and your baby's. Many women find themselves
racked with guilt over their decision, especially those women who
don't do well when they stay at home full-time with young children.

I'm one of those women, and you may be, too. If so, it's far better for both you and your child if you go back to work.

Still, even women who love their work and want to get back to it as quickly as possible are often happiest if they can shape their career path in a way that allows them to accommodate the needs of their children. That's the reason I decided to stop delivering babies when my daughters were two and four. Being on call at all hours of night and day was taking away too much of our time together, so I changed my work life and co-created the Women to Women health care center in 1985.

Of course there are also women who go back to work and are shocked to find how much they miss being at home with their baby. As a result, they may decide to stay home, even if it involves making financial sacrifices. Often these sacrifices can be considerable, because as a culture we may talk a lot about family values, but we do far too little to actually support families with adequate maternal and paternal leaves (or with high quality day care afterward). The United States is the only Western country where a mere six-week maternity leave is the norm. In Australia and Europe, women routinely take a year off with each child, receive some work compensation, and have their jobs waiting for them when they go back. Talk about cultural support for the fourth trimester—and well beyond! For women who live here, however, deciding whether or when to go back to work can be a very difficult choice, both emotionally and financially.

Whatever your situation, your Mother Bear wisdom will help you tune into what's right for both you and your baby. And the first rule of Mother Bear wisdom is that a mother needs to be happy and fulfilled to do her mothering optimally.

Breast-feeding as an Extension of the Placenta

When a baby is born, her immune system is still very undeveloped. Her immunity up until now came mainly from her exposure to her mother's amniotic fluid, which is full of antibodies. But once she has left the protection of her mother's womb, it's easy for infectious agents to enter her body. The mother can meet her baby's newfound need for protection against disease and infection through her breast milk, which can be thought of as a continuation of the nourishment she received through her connection to the placenta when she was inside her mother's body.

The colostrum, and following it, the mature milk, are loaded with immunoglobulins and antibodies that target the very organisms the child is most likely to encounter in her new environment, organisms to which her mother is already resistant. Breast milk has been shown, for example, to kill parasitic intestinal protozoa that can cause intestinal disease in children.[2] (See "Feeding Your Baby.")

The Wiring of Immunity and Disease Resistance

The mother plays a role in immunity and disease resistance that includes but is not limited to the breast milk she provides. From the moment of birth, the mother's role in regulating the baby's bodily functions, and in helping her to feel safe and secure in the world, has a direct effect on the child's immune system. The physical and emotional support she offers helps set down communication networks in the child's first emotional center, the locus of feelings of safety, security, and belonging, and the place where the immune system, the blood, and the bones get hooked up together. While humans vary widely in their innate resilience in the face of all kinds of stresses, including infection, the mother-child relationship is a crucial factor in the development of the child's resilience. And studies demonstrate that one's lifelong vulnerability to disease is influenced by early experience.

The reason infancy is such a critical period in the development of resilience is that this is the period when the nervous system, the endocrine system, and the immune system are all learning how to talk to each other. A mother's interactions with her child actually pattern the way in which this happens via the biological effects of human contact, as well as via the immune-enhancing properties of breast milk.

Immunologist Edwin Blalock, Ph.D., explains the workings of the immune system this way:

> The immune system may sense stimuli that are then recognized by the central nervous system. These stimuli are termed "neurocognitive," and include bacteria, tumors, viruses and antigens that would go unnoticed, if it were not for their recognition by the immune system.[3]

The immune system operates like an additional pair of eyes. The recognition of such stimuli is converted into information in the body via peptides, hormones, lymphokines, and monokines. And these, in turn, are the signals that tell the immune system cells what to do.

This information is simultaneously conveyed to the brain and the neuroendocrine system so that all these systems—nervous, endocrine, and immune—can work together, prompting appropriate physiological changes in the body.

Through her interaction with her child—through touch, feeding, talking, singing, eye-to-eye contact, and her physical presence—the mother is training the child's body to recognize what is safe and what is not safe in the world. She is not only training her eyes to see the world and her ears to hear the world, she is also entraining all of the white cells of her child's body to react to that world. If the mother-daughter bonding doesn't occur or is disrupted, the child's body may be literally blind to these stimuli, and as a result, far more vulnerable to disease.

MILLY: Impaired Immunity

Aware of the connection between a sense of safety and security in the world and a healthy immune system, I once asked one of my patients, a woman with a great deal of immune system dysfunction, what her early childhood had been like. Her mother, a first-generation daughter of immigrants who came through Ellis Island, had proudly told her the following story, which was part of her maternal inheritance:

> The day you came home from the hospital, you cried constantly. In fact, you cried for two days. I said to myself, "Oh yes, I know what this is all about. We're not going to start this way. I'm going to train this child from the very beginning that she can't pull this with me! We're going to establish a pattern right away that this child will only be fed and picked up at certain times—according to my schedule, not hers. I'm not going to spoil this child."
>
> You cried constantly for two days and then finally stopped. You finally figured out that your crying wouldn't work with me. And after that, you calmed down and would entertain yourself for hours in the playpen and would never cry. You were a perfect baby and we never had a problem with you.

Remarkably enough, Milly has turned this painful beginning into one of her strengths. She is an incredibly bright and well-educated physician who brings an amazing sense of vulnerability as well as humor to everything she does. Her presence has helped many others to heal their lives, the way she has healed hers. She knows that if she had had a different relationship with her mother, she would never have become who she is today. But she's paid a high price for her gifts, not just in her body but in her sense of herself. As she puts it, "I carry around this feeling that I am somehow flawed because of my lack of a healthy mother-daughter bond. But I also know that that same flaw, though painful, has contributed to my genius."

YOU CANNOT SPOIL AN INFANT

Unfortunately, many of us and many of our parents were raised at a time when holding and cuddling a baby "too much" and picking her up when she cried was seen as "permissive" and considered "spoiling" a baby. But it is really not possible to "spoil" a newborn baby, given the incontrovertible evidence we have that optimal growth and development are fueled by generous amounts of human contact.

In the United States, the almost universally held policy of expecting female employees to return to work when their newborns are only six weeks old reinforces the idea that babies don't really need this kind of physical contact, depriving mothers and children of each other's presence right at the time they most need to be together. Leaving an infant alone in a separate room and insisting she somehow has the ability to deal with this, after spending nearly forty weeks intimately connected to her mother's body, flies in the face of what mothers instinctively know—children do best when they're held and cuddled a lot.

Failure of the brain to develop has been known to occur after sensory deprivation of any kind, whether that be touch, sound, or the smiling faces of loved ones. On the other hand, holding, rocking, and singing to a newborn provides her with the kind of sensory stimulation that is needed for optimal postnatal maturation of areas in the brain stem important for wakefulness and sensitivity to changes in the environment.[4]

Despair and Loneliness:
A Postpartum Legacy of Our Culture

Most of us have some degree of despair encoded at the cellular level because the culture we live in is not supportive of the importance of mother and child staying in close and constant contact with each other during the first months of the child's life. I remember, for example, taking my first child to visit relatives, and being told to "leave the baby upstairs in the crib." This upstairs was very far away from where we were sitting, and I would never have done such a thing because I wouldn't have been able to hear her cries. I was horrified at the way this older couple, themselves parents of five grown children, expected me to treat my new baby.

The infant emotion associated with being left alone in a room without another body nearby is despair. This is probably one of the reasons why adopted children have a higher incidence of depression.[5] Though today's adoptions do not usually involve a period of separation before the new parents take her home, at some cellular level, the baby knows that her mother has been switched, and may later have feelings of "not belonging," of being inexplicably "different." This is why it's always best to be honest about the fact of adoption. (Note: On a soul level, I strongly believe that we always end up with the right parents, including those of us who are adopted.)

The separation of a mother from her baby during the fourth trimester is a setup for postpartum deprivation and despair in both mother and baby. In striking contrast to this is the joy that is so often evident in the people of cultures that keep their children close to their bodies in infancy, guided by their innate Mother Bear wisdom. In Bali, for example, children aren't allowed to touch the ground for several months following birth. They are always held by someone. Constant physical contact with her caretakers helps a child's right brain to develop optimally as the circuitry of emotions is being laid down.

Co-Sleeping: Nature's Way of Soothing Your Baby

In his book *The Happiest Baby on the Block* (see Resources), pediatrician Harvey Karp, M.D., points out that there are many cultures in the world that simply don't have colicky, fussy babies. Those are the cultures in which mothers and other family members carry their babies with them on their bodies, sleep with them, and swaddle them when they are infants. In contrast, 50 percent of babies in America cry or fuss for more than two hours per day! This can lead to depression in mothers and even child abuse in those who are stressed and who have little support.

American babies cry because we don't follow our Mother Bear instinct and carry them around with us and sleep with them. It seems inhumane to expect a little mammal to sleep in a room by herself after having spent her first nine months in her mom's uterus. I recommend co-sleeping with your child until she is about six months old. There are now wonderful co-sleeping units that attach to your bed so that your child will have her own little protected area next to you. I had a bassinet near our bed when Annie was a baby. That way I could easily pick her up and nurse her as needed.

I know that not all mothers or fathers will feel comfortable co-sleeping. If that's true of you, don't do it. Your child will pick up on your discomfort and as a result, will not be comforted.

HOW TO ELICIT A CHILD'S NATURAL CALMING REFLEX

It's very harmful to expect a baby to be able to soothe and settle herself during the first few months of life. Instead, think "womb" and try to re-create the same feelings she had there! Most infants can start learning how to put themselves to sleep by the age of six months or so. Some can do this earlier. Dr. Harvey Karp's two books offer very practical, humane approaches for training your baby to sleep well and self-soothe at every age from birth to four years. If I were still delivering babies, I would give *The Happiest Baby on the Block* and *The Happiest Toddler on the Block* as gifts to all of my new moms.

To help a child develop healthy sleep patterns, you first need to know how to elicit her calming reflex. Here's how:

Use white noise or a shhh-ing sound. Put on a CD of white noise or get a machine that produces it for the child's (or your) room. The inside of the womb is as loud as a vacuum cleaner. Putting a baby in a quiet room is unsettling to them. But taking her for a car ride—with the noise of the engine and the motion of the car—often puts her to sleep. Shushing your baby—as loud as she is crying, and right near her face—can also elicit the calming reflex because it re-creates the sound of the womb.

Rock your baby or put her in a swing. Motorized swings are a godsend for parents. (I used a wind-up Swing-a-Matic for Annie and it worked beautifully—but I had to keep rewinding!)

Wrap your child tightly in a receiving blanket. If it's hot, use a small sheet. This will re-create the same feeling of security she had in the womb and will immediately calm her down.

Hold her on her side or on her stomach. The side and stomach positions elicit the calming reflex because they imitate the baby's position in the womb where she is never on her back. Tucking the child's head down a little, touching her on her stomach, and then laying her on her side activate position sensors in her head that trigger the calming reflex. This is, of course, the classic "fetal" position that is comforting even for adults! Karp says that trying to calm a fussy baby on her back is like calming her and pinching her at the same time. The position often makes an infant feel insecure. This is because putting her on her back will often trigger her "Moro," or startle, reflex, causing her to cry and fling her arms out to the sides. Once you put her down for the night, however, she should always be on her back. If you swaddle her before putting her on her back, in the manner that Dr. Karp suggests, this position also can elicit the calming response. Ever since the "Back to Sleep" campaign was initiated in 1992, the annual SIDS rate has declined by more than 50 percent.[6]

Allow your baby to suck on a pacifier or put her to your breast. You can use the calming reflex any time your baby is fussy. For more detailed information on swaddling and on helping your baby or young child develop healthy sleep patterns, please see Harvey Karp's two books, *The Happiest Baby on the Block* and *The Happiest Toddler on the Block*. His advice is invaluable and it works.

Touch Is Good Medicine

When a child is in the womb, her delicate skin is caressed and stroked regularly by the mild daily contractions of her mother's uterus, and also by the vibration of her heartbeat and voice. The baby's transition to a healthy life outside of the womb is greatly aided by the intense tactile stimulation she gets through the process of labor, which stimulates and prepares all of the baby's internal organs, preparing them for birth. (See "Labor.") Then, once the child is born, her growth and development is further advanced by regular touching, cuddling, and massage.

The skin is the largest sensory organ and is derived from the neuroectoderm, the same embryonic layer that develops into the brain. So we could think of our skin as a kind of external brain. Touch needs to be thought of as a nutrient. Without adequate touch, both humans and other animals fail to thrive and may also die. This has been proven repeatedly throughout history, and in the lab with animals. The most recent widely publicized example of this phenomenon occurred in the 1990s, when thousands of Romanian orphans were "warehoused" in their cribs with almost no experience of being touched or held for up to two years. Many have been subsequently found to be severely, often irreversibly, impaired, with problems ranging from attachment disorders to mental retardation.

There are as many as 5 million touch receptors in our skin—three thousand per fingertip. These receptors all send messages via the spinal cord to our brain. It has been scientifically demonstrated that a simple touch can lower blood pressure and heart rate. Touch has been shown to stimulate the production of beta-endorphins in the brain, a biochemical associated with euphoria. Deep touch, such as that used in massage, can enhance immune function and lower stress hormones such as cortisol and adrenaline.

Touching increases the production of growth hormone, which is a master hormone that affects all the endocrine functions of the body. This explains why babies who are fed but not touched often suffer from a syndrome known as "failure to thrive," meaning that they don't grow and develop.

Touch is another of the factors that help the baby's immune system to develop. Psychobiological studies of early experience and its effects on immunity show that touch during the preweaning period increases antibody response, and if the mother is separated from her baby during this time, it can cause immune system depression.

The research of Tiffany M. Field, Ph.D., of the Touch Research Institute in Miami and others has demonstrated that touch is good medicine and positively affects a variety of conditions ranging from migraines to diabetes. When premature babies are given three fifteen-minute massages a day for ten days, they are more alert, active, and responsive compared to controls, they gain weight on an average of 47 percent faster, and they can be discharged from the hospital a full six days sooner than the babies who didn't receive this treatment, at a cost savings of $10,000 per baby. It is felt that the weight gain is partly a result of better absorption of food by the massaged babies, thanks to the ability of massage to stimulate the vagus nerve, which innervates the gastrointestinal system and is involved in the release of glucagon and insulin.[7]

There are volumes of scientific reasons why you should hold and caress your baby as much as possible. Tactile stimulation is believed to have a lifelong impact on the body's immune health.[8] If the mother is separated from the child prematurely, before weaning, that can lead to a lowering of immune response in adulthood. Studies of monkeys suggest that if the mother and the child are prematurely separated, the offspring's immune system may become suppressed for years afterward.[9] Not touching a child is like not feeding her, only instead of not feeding her stomach, you're not feeding her brain and nervous system.[10] If you don't touch your child enough, it's a form of weaning.

Rocking an infant, one of the most instinctive behaviors we humans experience, is also beneficial to a baby. Rocking repeats the blissful state of being in the womb and is very calming. It stimulates the vestibular system in the brain, which has many connections with the vagus nerve and with the parasympathetic nervous system, the part of the system that helps our bodies rest and repair.

Despite the well-documented benefits of touch throughout our lives, we in America are largely a "nontactile" society. We don't touch enough. And I believe this may be one of the factors in our national penchant for violence. It has been documented that cultures that show more physical affection toward their infants and children tend to have lower rates of adult violence.[11]

Touch is so important yet so lacking in our culture that I wish we doctors could prescribe it, for both its health benefits and its potential to prevent violence. Interestingly enough, this is one of the areas in which gender bias has resulted in a distinct advantage for girls. As Ashley Montagu explains, "Touch is considered an act of intimacy and privilege . . . as a token of power exercised nonreciprocally at the discretion of one's betters and reciprocally between equals. . . . Since in the power structure of Western societies females are regarded as inferior to males, and are treated as if they belong to an inferior class or caste, females from their earliest days receive a good deal more touching than males." Montagu's observation is borne out by studies that have shown, for instance, that both parents touch daughters more frequently than they do sons. Since repeated experience is one of the key factors that wires the brains of children, it is no wonder that the brains of little girls are more relational. Their external brain—their skin—gets repeatedly stimulated from birth onward.

Evidence suggests that the disease of "touch abuse" and violation of the bodies of children is actually increased when we pathologize touch and make people afraid to act on their natural impulses to hold and touch little children. The result is a touch-starved society in which any and all touch too often becomes sexualized because our "skin hunger" hasn't been routinely fed in appropriate ways. Boundary violation and sexual abuse of girls (and boys) will not be stopped by outlawing touching in our homes, schools, hospitals, and child care centers—those places where touch is needed more than ever.

FEEDING YOUR BABY

An entire generation of mothers, many of whom wanted to breast-feed, were talked out of it by the prevailing medical opinion of the late 1940s, '50s, and '60s. During this time, baby formula was felt to be scientifically superior to human breast milk. And a timed feeding schedule for babies was deemed preferable to the natural instinct that would tell a mother when her child needed to feed. Left-brained intellect, unbalanced by Mother Bear wisdom, triumphed for several decades, but is now being overturned, as science begins to acknowledge what mothers have known since the beginning of time. Although the "scientific" legacy still lives on in many women, we now know much more about both the physiological as well as the emotional benefits of breast-feeding, and of feeding when the baby is hungry, not when a predetermined schedule deems that it's "time."

How We Are Fed Sets the Stage for How
We Will Feed Ourselves

The whole process of learning about healthy attachment begins with how we attach to our mothers through oral feedings. On a very basic level, it is true that the way to our hearts is through our stomachs. How and what we are fed in infancy creates the basic wiring diagram we will follow when we attach ourselves to others in the future. The way our mothers feed us teaches both our brains and bodies what to expect from nourishment and intimacy, setting the stage for how well we will be able to meet both our nutritional and emotional needs for the rest of our lives.

When my daughters were babies, I felt strongly that they should have maximum access to my body—and my breasts—when I was home. I thought of my body as a kind of storehouse of maternal nourishment, both physical and emotional, that my daughters needed to be healthy.

Breast-feeding Is Self-care and Child-care Simultaneously

Breast-feeding was designed by nature to help a mother care for both herself and her baby optimally. Breast-feeding demonstrates the same principle as pregnancy: you can't give what you haven't got. To breast-feed successfully you need good nutrition, adequate social support, and adequate rest. Breast-feeding offers mothers and their babies the following benefits:

~ **Improves the mother's health**
Women who breast-feed have an easier time losing the weight that they gained during pregnancy. Breast-feeding also offers the mother protection against breast cancer, ovarian cancer, and post-menopausal osteoporosis. It is also far more convenient than carrying around bottles and formula. It is effortless nurturing.

~ **Promotes a sense of safety and security in the baby**
Putting the baby to your breast in an unrestricted, unscheduled way lets her know that all is well. She can relax and simply be nurtured. She gets the idea that there is enough to go around and she will always be provided for.

~ **Offers the baby protection from disease**
Thousands of studies continue to demonstrate the health advantages of breast-feeding, including decreased incidence of infant ear infections, allergies, diarrhea, and bacterial meningitis. Recent findings from Scotland's Dundee infant feeding study, for instance, show that babies who are breast-fed exclusively for at least the first fifteen weeks of life are nearly 50 percent less likely to develop respiratory illnesses during childhood than their bottle-fed counterparts. In addition, these

children tend to have lower blood pressure and are thinner than children who began solid foods before four months of age.[12] Research also strongly suggests that breast-feeding protects against childhood lymphoma, sudden infant death syndrome, and diabetes.

~ **Meets the child's primal need to suck in the most physiologic and healthy way possible**

Babies suck their thumbs in utero. Sucking is a primal need. In fact, the areas of the brain controlling the tongue and mouth are huge—with more nerve cells devoted to these body parts and functions than almost any other. Babies suck on everything—their thumbs, your fingers, the faces of their caregivers, etc.

~ **Promotes optimal facial and jaw development**

The development of a baby's facial muscles, palate, teeth, and gums is affected by how and what she sucks. Nursing at the breast is hard work, and therefore better exercise, for the baby's tongue, cheek, and jaw muscles than sucking from a bottle. As a result of the exercises of these muscles, the hard palate and upper jaw get well developed, which contributes to a facial structure in which there is more room in the sinuses and nasal passages, all of which are connected to the mouth and the back of the throat. So breast-feeding is the best possible way for a child to develop a healthy mouth, teeth, and jaws, as well as nasal passages.

~ **Promotes optimal breathing**

Newborn infants are considered obligate nasal breathers—in other words, nasal breathing is the norm for them. Although they can breathe through their mouths, this is distinctly abnormal and is a stress response. Breast-feeding simply reinforces a baby's normal tendency, because the milk goes down slowly enough that the baby can simultaneously breathe through her nose and swallow while she is nursing, a process that further contributes to the development of her nasal passages. Bottle feeding has the opposite effect. Because milk from the bottle goes down so much more quickly than milk from the breast, the baby is forced to gulp the milk down and then possibly gasp for breath from her mouth between sips. This has a profound impact on the development of a child's respiratory system, including the sinuses, nose, and mouth structures. Bottle feeding is a setup for mouth breathing and suboptimal development of the teeth, the jaw, and nasopharynx. The effect on both the mouth and nasal structures can predispose a child to allergies and sinus problems later in life.

~ Promotes optimal intelligence

Research has shown that breast-fed babies tend to be smarter. A recent study from New Zealand that followed children from eight to eighteen years showed that longer periods of breast-feeding were associated with consistent and statistically significant increases in IQ at ages eight and nine; in better reading comprehension, mathematical ability, and scholastic ability at ages ten to thirteen years; in higher teacher ratings of reading and math ability at eight and twelve years; and in higher levels of achievement on final exams. The reason for this may, in part, be related to the fatty acids present in breast milk (but not in formula). Nerve cells are made almost exclusively from the metabolic products of fatty acids, so their presence in breast milk may help promote optimal brain development and long-lasting neurophysiological health.[13]

~ Breast-feeding is neuroprotective

New research is also revealing another aspect of feminine wisdom. Breast-fed infants have naturally higher levels of bilirubin, a pigment in blood that turns skin yellow and has a number of potential effects on health as well. "Babies with higher bilirubin levels are more disease-resistant," reported Sylvain Dore, Ph.D., of Johns Hopkins University School of Medicine, speaking at the 33rd Annual Winter Conference on Brain Research at Breckenridge, Colorado. "Bilirubin also protects against retinopathy in premature babies." Dr. Dore's research indicates that bilirubin also has neuroprotective effects in the area of the hippocampus, and that high concentrations of bilirubin decrease free-radical mediated injury to body tissues, suggesting that bilirubin could act as an antioxidant.[14]

Whether Breast or Bottle Feeding, Serve Up Love Along with the Milk

The quality of the food that is offered is important: its temperature, purity, and nutrient content. But the way in which the food is offered may be just as important. Optimal nourishment will include all the emotional nutrients that can go into the feeding process. This means that even though breast milk is the ideal food for babies, it's also possible to offer a good healthy dose of life-giving sustenance through a bottle that is held and administered by a present, engaged, loving human being who is simultaneously cooing to, rocking, and looking at the child.

How You Feed Matters as Much as What You Feed

How you feed a baby conveys as much information to the baby's developing brain and body as what you feed her. A baby who is either bottle or breast-fed in an unrestricted manner according to a mother's finely tuned intuition has a very different experience from one who is breast-fed on a strict schedule by a mother who is anxious about the whole process.

I recall one of my patients, whom I'll call Amanda, who seemed to be allergic to everything, including life itself. After she had her first child, she obsessively and compulsively avoided everything one "should" avoid while breast-feeding. She always looked fatigued and depressed and pretty much devoid of joy, a condition worsened by the fact that everywhere she turned, she found new things she thought might be a problem. She seemed to be depriving herself of everything she loved because it was the "right thing to do for the baby," and because to do anything else, such as eating an ice cream cone or having a glass of wine, "wouldn't be safe for the baby."

A professional woman, Amanda had her child brought in to work by the nanny. When the baby arrived, Amanda would sit down and mechanically "apply" the child to her breast as though to a feeding machine. The child's dose of milk was administered as though it were a dose of medication—without any joy or animation, or talking to the child, or being emotionally engaged in the process. By approaching breast-feeding this way, she was feeding her child insecurity directly through her breast.

This is in stark contrast to another of my patients, Ada, who always lifted her baby to her breast while talking to her in her usual animated fashion. Ada's baby was clearly an integral part of Ada's life. Though Ada generally followed a healthy diet, she indulged in an occasional hot fudge sundae or order of French fries simply because sometimes this is good for the soul.

❀ WISDOM CHALLENGE: *Breast or Bottle?*

There is a good reason why Mother Nature put optimal nutrition and erotic pleasure in the same bodily vehicle: food and pleasure are both related to bonding and both necessary to our well-being. Feeling good about our breasts and *both* of their functions is an important self-care principle.

But because we've been acculturated to feel good about one function of our breasts (their attractiveness to men) at the expense of the other (the nourishment they provide to children), many women have an internal split that decreases their access to their feminine power.

The American Academy of Pediatrics recommends that mothers breast-feed for a year, and continue for as long after that as is mutually desired by the mother and baby. Currently, about 60 percent of new mothers breast-feed, but only about 50 percent continue through the first six months of a child's life.[15] The reason these numbers aren't higher has everything to do with the price tag our culture has put on women's sexuality. Deciding whether or not to breast-feed can force a woman to weigh her mate's desires against her baby's needs.

Women in patriarchal cultures such as our own have inherited the deeply ingrained belief that their worth is determined by how attractive they are to men. Since the female breast is such an obvious symbol of female sexuality and desirability in our culture, women's breasts are viewed by many as currency of considerable value for buying male attention and support. Given this widespread attitude, it is not surprising that the main reason why women don't breast-feed, even when they are aware of the advantages of the practice for their babies, is because they are afraid that breast-feeding will decrease their value in the eyes of their husbands or boyfriends.[16] And given the law of attraction, women who hold this belief are the ones who are most likely to be partnered with the kind of men who feel that female breasts are their territory, not the territory of a baby.

It's a sad indictment of our culture that a woman would ever feel she needed to choose between her baby and her mate. Perhaps this is why, despite the very obvious medical health implications for encouraging breast-feeding at every turn, relatively few ob-gyn and pediatric residency training programs require the doctors in these specialties to receive any formal training in the art and science of breast-feeding. And even then, doctors hesitate to stress the benefits of nursing lest we make mothers feel guilty for choosing bottles. No wonder most women who breast-feed today do so for only a few weeks or months at most, and suckle their babies no more than eight times in twenty-four hours.

Breast Implants

Breast implants, which make nursing nearly impossible and mammograms and other breast-disease-screening tests more difficult, have now become "the norm" in mass media images of women, for instance the Victoria's Secret catalogue, television shows, rock videos, and so on. As a result, we're losing our sense of what normal breasts actually look like. I find it ironic that the only time the average woman's breasts will ever approach the size and shape of the artificially enhanced breasts we've come to think of as standard is when she is nursing! Our Mother Bear wisdom has programmed men and women both to appreciate this abundant look, but now, instead of getting true nourishment, we get plastic! The number of women getting breast implants has increased dramatically over the last decade despite the fact that their safety is not well established. In 1992, 32,607 women got implants for cosmetic reasons. By 2002, that figure had climbed to 225,818.[17] Louise Brinton, Ph.D., of the National Cancer Institute found that women who've had breast implants are more likely to die from brain tumors, lung cancer and other respiratory diseases, and suicide compared to other plastic surgery patients. She also found a 21 percent overall increased risk of cancer for women with implants compared with women of the same age in the general population.

I believe that it's not so much the implants themselves that are causing health problems as it is the reasons a woman is having them. If she feels that she needs to enhance her breasts in order to attract male attention, it means she doesn't feel good about herself, which puts her at risk for various health problems. I have had several patients who've gotten implants after having their babies and nursing them. And they've done well. But many young women get them right after high school—the prime time for having the proper "bait" to hook a man. This will lead to a lot of children not being breast-fed and missing out on key developmental nutrients. And it is also likely to have an impact on the health of the women. Yet the cultural taboo against bringing this information to consciousness is very strong.

The rapidly increasing incidence of breast implants is a perfect ex-

ample of how thoroughly women's maternal wisdom has been undermined in our culture. Can you imagine any other species of mammal
in which the female would put her babies at increased risk for health
and survival problems for the sake of a cosmetic "improvement" she
believed would help preserve her relationship with her mate?

BONDING WITH YOUR BABY

How We Bond as Babies Sets the Stage for How We Bond as Adults

Though the bonding process begins in utero, most mothers never
forget the first few days with their new babies, a time when they may
be overcome with more love and tenderness than they have ever felt
in their whole lives.

The quality of the mother-daughter bond at birth and in the first
few months of life helps set the template for all subsequent intimate
relationships in life. It is a baby's first experience of being loved and
cherished. This experience influences the growth and development of
the actual areas in the brain and body that form the physical substrate for emotional attachment and physical health in future years.

Research has clearly demonstrated that the strength and diversity
of our relationships in adulthood are predictive of better immune
system functioning, hence more resistance to disease.[18,19] The postpartum period is when the groundwork for forming such relationships in later life is established.

The quality of the love and support the mother gives her daughter entrains her daughter's brain and body with an imprint of "how
relationships should be." This, in turn, will influence who she picks
to bond with in the future, including the kind of mate she attracts
and the kind of mother she herself will become.[20]

Emotional Circuitry Is the First Thing Laid Down in the Brain

The neural pathways that govern the emotions and their influence on bodily organs are some of the first to be set down. For example, warmth and touch from the mother's body have an effect on the
neurochemistry of a baby's brain, including the levels of dopamine
and epinephrine, neurochemicals important in regulating a baby's

experience of fear, anxiety, learning, attention, and memory. The mother also regulates a child's autonomic nervous system, which innervates all the organs of the immune system, including the thymus, lymph nodes, and spleen.[21] These immune organs are also connected seamlessly with the other organs of the body, including the heart, lungs, GI tract, and pelvic organs. Physical and emotional well-being are thus seamlessly linked.

During early postnatal life an area of the brain known as the right orbitofrontal cortex—the area of the brain associated with the capacity for bonding, as well as for emotional communication and intuition—begins to grow rapidly in the baby.[22] Its optimal growth and development are highly influenced by the quality and intensity of attention and care the child receives in her early years.

There is some evidence to suggest that this area of the mother's brain also undergoes heightened function in the aftermath of childbirth, just as it does premenstrually. And this is certainly borne out by women's descriptions of their intense sensitivity at this time, when their innermost feelings come to the surface and they can often instantly intuit the needs of their babies. It makes sense that both mother and child would experience heightened activity in the area of the brain related to emotional communication in the period when the two of them are laying down the biologic foundation for their lifelong connection with each other.

A mother's ability to intuitively know what is going on both emotionally and physically with her child is crucial to the child's health, and to the quality of her social development. When a mother reflects back to her daughter that she feels and understands the child's needs, both emotionally and physically, then her daughter will be able to internalize these functions for herself. Later in life, a child who has had this experience with her mother (or other caregivers) will in turn know how to bond and connect intuitively with others.[23]

The Birth of Emotional Regulation and Resilience

It is crucial to a child's lifelong adaptability and resourcefulness that she experience appropriate bonding early on. If her brain is not adequately stimulated by a consistent caregiver, she may not be able to trust her gut feelings and her inner knowing later in life. Although you can't do anything about the soul qualities or temperament your daughter will have, you can maximize her emotional resilience by making an effort to maximize your own. You do this by learning to trust the process of conception, by developing a sense of patience through the long course of pregnancy, by surrendering to the rhythms of labor, and by giving yourself ample opportunity to rest, rejuvenate, and truly take joy in your creation during the postpartum period.

If you skip any of these steps or fail to develop these resources within yourself, then your bonding and attachment to your child may be compromised. As a result, certain areas in the right or-bitofrontal area of her brain may fail to develop properly, and she may then have problems later in life with exactly those same skills: trust, patience, resilience, rest and rejuvenation, and so forth. She may also have difficulty with identifying what she is feeling or being able to intuit the emotional reactions of others. The physical mani-festation of this inability to access her own feelings is that she may be out of touch with her needs for food or rest, or fail to recognize when she's in pain.

The Mother-Daughter Bond Helps Wire Emotional Regulation

An infant is born helpless and vulnerable. She has many needs and few means of meeting them. How these needs are satisfied is cru-cial to her sense of well-being and ability to maintain a stable mood. A loving, attentive mother gives her daughter:

The sense that all is well.

The ability to regulate her own mood and self-soothe.

The development of a healthy inner representation of self—a sense that she belongs, she matters, and she has a self that is separate from her mother and others.

A mother's resourcefulness and ability to adapt help a child wire in the ability to maintain mood stability throughout life. Few things are more important to living a healthy and successful life than the ability to regulate one's emotions and stay on an even keel in the face of the inevitable ups and downs of life. Emotional regulation is the ability to experience a feeling, know that the feeling signals a need, then have the ability to get that need met.

When a mother looks lovingly at her baby, holds her against her heart and physically and emotionally bonds with her, she is actually providing her daughter the stimulus needed for optimal development and organization in the areas of the brain that will enable her to know how to express her emotions, both in public and in intimate relationships. These areas of the brain are important for developing the skills necessary to soothe and modulate her emotions, whether they be anger, sadness, loneliness, fear, joy, or love.

The Importance of a Good Parenting Bond

The quality of the bond between a mother and a father has definitely been shown to enhance the mother's ability to care for and bond with her child. In fact, marital woes are one of the most common factors associated with poor pregnancy outcome, higher rates of prematurity, labor and delivery difficulties, and health problems in the first three months of life.

Though fewer studies have been done with gay couples, I am certain that the same correlation holds true: the quality of the parental relationship will affect the baby's sense of security in the world, as well as the mother's ability to be present with the child. If the mother hyperbonds with her child to the exclusion of her husband, for example, this can set the scene for a very unhealthy family system that does not benefit her, her husband, or her baby. I've often seen this in women who don't let their husbands hold the baby. They let him know in any number of subtle and not-so-subtle ways that he doesn't know how to carry, feed, dress, or change the baby properly. This effectively shuts him out at the very time that his presence is most needed. Many women do this because, having few other such opportunities, they view child care as their own locus of power and control.

Temperament: What the Daughter Brings to the Situation

Bonding is a reciprocal process. The mother may be doing everything she can and her relationships with her husband and family may be fine. But if a child's brain or soul is underreceptive for the formation of a biologic or emotional bond, for whatever reason, or if the child is excessively needy, then there may be glitches with bonding. Oxytocin secretion must occur on both sides of the mother-daughter bond. Interestingly, autistic children have almost no ability to form normal social bonds with people. They tend to bond with things such as numbers, plastic car models, etc. These children have been found to have abnormally low levels of plasma oxytocin.[24]

When I was delivering babies, I became aware of how fascinating, individual, and fully human babies are right from birth. Babies are not born equal. They are all born different. And they are equipped from birth with the ability to influence their caregivers and affect their own quality of care by virtue of their innate temperaments. Quite simply, some people are more likable than others. I can remember countless times in the delivery room when I'd have a real sense of the personality of the child I had just delivered. Some were docile and calm, others seemed to be born cranky and in need of a lot of extra attention. And this had nothing to do with anything their mothers did or didn't do. Stephen Porges, Ph.D., and others have shown, for example, that even premature babies display a wide variation in temperament. Some are easy to feed and gain weight quickly, while others are fussy and don't take nourishment well. Some are innately twitchy and irritable while others are calm and collected. These temperament differences manifest in the two aspects of the autonomic nervous system. Some babies display more fight-or-flight–type activity, some more parasympathetic "rest and restore" activity.[25]

My delivery-room experiences as well as what I've read—and what I myself witnessed when I gave birth to two daughters who were different from the very beginning—have convinced me that though a child's body is formed and influenced by her mother, there is another aspect of her that is forever and always separate and independent of her mother. This aspect is her soul. And it is her soul qualities more than any other factor that determine her temperament. My second daughter was so easygoing and nondemanding from the moment of birth that she seemed to be saying to me, "It's okay, Mom. Just do what you need to do. I can soothe myself."

The soul of an individual lives beyond space and time and cannot be explained entirely by genes, environment, nature, or nurture. It's in the realm of the mysterious.

Once you have a child, you have to acknowledge your part in the creation but also understand that this is just the beginning of a lifetime of exploring who this new person is. A mother is the vehicle an individual soul rides into physical life. She also provides her with a place to grow. But she doesn't own that child, nor is the child a mere reflection of her.

A child is born with a fully formed soul. What happens to her after birth will influence how her innate soul qualities get expressed, just as it will influence how her genes get expressed, but it cannot change those qualities. She is who she is. And her temperament will profoundly affect her ability to attract the kind of care and attention we all need. There are babies who are able to charm everyone in the room. And there are babies who are much less fun to be around and pick up, so you don't feel that you're getting much out of the interaction. As a result, that kind of child will have a very different experience from one who is equipped from birth for delightful social interaction.

Of course, there are some mothers who are able to bond with just about any child; others bond effectively only with babies who are a good psychological "fit" for them. Both partners bring their own temperaments to the dance of love.[26] And that is why, when you asked your mother the inevitable question, "Do you love me as much as you do my brother and sister?" and she said, "I love all of you the same," she wasn't telling the entire truth. She, like all mothers, will find it easiest to love the children whose temperaments match her own. Some temperaments are just a better "fit" with each other. This continues throughout life with every individual we meet. We "click" with some and not with others. In my family, my sister Penny, a born athlete and competitor, was a better "fit" with my mother's temperament than I was. When we were little, I was calmer and more docile, while Penny was a risk-taker who at age three set fires in wastebaskets and ran into town naked one day.

The Original Sin of Being Born Female
Can Disrupt Bonding

Being born female may be enough to disrupt the bonding process. In a 1975 study of maternal satisfaction during the postpartum period, researcher Dana Breen found that 70 percent of the women who had given birth to sons described themselves as content whereas only 13 percent of those who had given birth to daughters felt as satisfied.[27]

Though I feel strongly that this is changing, it is still a very potent part of the maternal legacy of many women I know. One of my patients, who had her children in the late 1960s, told me that when her first daughter was born, she and the baby were showered with gifts and cards. When the second daughter was born the gifts decreased. And by the time the third daughter was born, she said she didn't receive more than a single gift. But then she had her son. And she said,

"Even though I really didn't care one way or the other, you'd have thought I'd given birth to the Christ Child himself, I got so many cards and gifts. To tell you the truth, it made me very angry."

It's fairly common to meet women whose parents regretted that they weren't boys, or who regret that they didn't give birth to the "right sex," but it's almost unheard of (except in transgendered populations) for a male to regret that he isn't a female or a daughter. If there are any men who feel this way, they certainly aren't admitting it publicly.

I'll never forget the time that a female physician, the wife of one of my ob-gyn professors, was having her fourth cesarean for the birth of her fourth child, who like the previous three was a girl. She was very clear that she didn't want any more children—or operations. At the last minute, her husband ran into the operating room and told her doctor: "Her tubes are mine. Don't touch them." (This was at a time when a woman couldn't get a tubal ligation without her husband's written permission!) With that, he stormed out. He was holding out for a son. I always wondered how this affected the health and happiness of their marriage—not to mention the feelings of both of them toward their daughters.

Although it is not politically correct to say this, there is no question that some men fear either they or their wives are inferior if they cannot have a son. That means that a daughter, especially if she is a second or third daughter, may be put into the role of being the hoped-for son or family heir who will carry on the family name. I have talked to countless patients over the years who told me they knew they were a disappointment to their fathers because they weren't boys. Their mothers felt the same way. I know of many cases in which the parents were hoping for a boy, and when the child was born a girl, the parents named her after the father anyway but feminized the name. For example, the father's name is John, so the daughter is called Johnna; the father's name is Paul, so the daughter is called Pauline. It's okay to masculinize a girl, but you certainly don't see many boys named after their mothers. That's taboo. In the same vein, the worst thing a boy can be called is girly. This is part of the reason that gay men, who tend to be more in touch with their feminine nature, have been so ostracized in our society. Given the fact that the male gender is still preferred over the female, and masculinity is preferred over femininity, it's a tribute to the strength and resilience of the inner Mother Bear that women and girls (and gay males) do as well as we do throughout our life cycles! Take a moment to appreciate yourself for it.

THAT GENDER THING

When I gave birth to my second daughter I could hear the words "I'm sorry, honey" come right up into my consciousness to be directed at my husband. I didn't say them out loud—I had heard them uttered far too often by my patients when they had given birth to girls. I was horrified that the thought even entered my head! All along, I had been sure that I was having a boy. I called her William throughout the entire pregnancy because she moved around so much more than her sister. Talk about sexist thinking! I wanted to wash my subconscious out with soap! I've apologized to her repeatedly for this.

Of course, this gender preference may get worked out in ways that are not necessarily damaging to the child—at least if parent and child have a good temperamental "fit." My mother, who has always loved activities traditionally associated with males such as hunting, fishing, and sports, has told me:

> I am sure that my father wanted to have a boy, because when Mother named me Edna, he immediately called me "Eddie," and, of course, that has stuck with me—a lot of people have called me that my whole life. And it is not distressful to me at all, but as I look back, I realize that that is probably what happened [he wanted a boy]. And he also taught me things that most fathers generally don't teach girls, but maybe that's the bent that I had anyway. I did like doing things that were different from a lot of girls.

Other Factors That Can Make
Postpartum Bonding More Difficult

Physiologic changes and poor health habits during pregnancy can affect an infant's temperament, making her more difficult to care for after she is born and a source of stress to the mother. The mother's stress may then lead to postpartum depression, which will be communicated to the daughter through the physiological and hormonal changes associated with depression, further compromising the quality of the mother-infant interaction. Or a woman may be depressed by marital problems or upset by economic or social needs that are not being met, and the resulting depression can affect the baby and her relationship with her baby. This is another time when good self-care on the part of the mother translates into good care of those around her.

TAKING CARE OF YOURSELF

Postpartum Replenishment

When your baby is born, the creative process has come full circle. Your body, and your child's, have just accomplished the profound work of gestation, labor, and delivery. Now you need time to rest, repair, and take stock of the changes in your life on every level. If you allow yourself to take this time, the postpartum period will teach you to do all of this, and give you the deepest possible experience of bonding with what you've just created.

However, the postpartum period, like pregnancy and labor, is apt to be rushed in our culture and in our individual psyches. We want to get up and go on to the next thing. It feels self-indulgent to rest.

Despite all the pressure to do otherwise, the postpartum period is not a good time to go back to work, much less move or start planning a new career. One profound life change is enough! Not knowing this, and being in my most "macho" phase, I did all three of these in the month after my first daughter was born. I left the hospital the same day I gave birth. The next day I started packing up the house my husband and I had been living in for four years so we could move to Maine two weeks later where he would be setting up his first private practice. It never occurred to me to rest. Compared to being on call in my residency, I felt as though I were slacking off.

On the night that my second daughter was born two years later, I personally cooked dinner for my mother. I told myself, "I feel fine. I'm not sick. Why not?" It was stupid. I didn't know any better. I didn't really allow myself to bask in the miracle of each daughter's birth. Though I adored both of them the minute they were born, apart from breast-feeding them and keeping them close to my body physically, I did not spend as much time with them as I should have—or as I would have liked. I had been on such a rigorous schedule for so long that I didn't understand how much I needed rest and replenishment. Now I wish I had spent more time with them during the postpartum period, simply "taking them in." Looking back, I shake my head in disbelief at how driven I was, and hope that my daughters will do better.

A new mother is likely to be unprepared for how much love she feels for this new baby. But sometimes her postpartum emotions will be so raw, and she'll feel so vulnerable and unprotected, that she'll have difficulty bonding with her child. This can make her feel guilty and very alone.

Whether you instantly fall head-over-heels in love with your child or have difficulty bonding at first, having a baby and caring for her changes your priorities from that moment on. You need to rest and nurture both of you well, so that you can learn how to shift gears into your new life. A mother can gain a great deal of self-esteem and self-confidence from her ability to feed and care for her child optimally. A new mother also needs to make arrangements ahead of time to get as much help and support from others as she thinks she will need—and then to be prepared to get more if it turns out she needs more.

I Want My Mother

When you give birth, a part of you longs for connection with your own mother. The bonding circuits that laid down the foundation of your relationship with your mother get reactivated because the same hormonal milieu has now been re-created. Just as when you were born, every cell in your body cries out for your mother—it's primal. This is true even if your relationship with her is poor, or she's no longer living—or you don't even know who she is! This biologic need for one's mother is so strong that it can sometimes heal the relationship between an estranged mother and her daughter. The following story is a good illustration.

ANGIE: Reconnecting with Mother

I was born in Manchester, England, the daughter of an unwed mother who obviously didn't want me. I didn't really know who my father was, and my mother wouldn't talk about it. I felt as though my presence in her life had ruined her hopes and dreams. Eventually I left home and worked around the world at various jobs—always searching for a better life. Even though I had cousins and other family members around, I never felt truly at home with my mother. I eventually ended up in the United States, where I worked as a nanny and met my husband. When we had our first child, my mother came over to stay with us. Being with her first grandchild seemed to cause something to break loose inside of her. She started to tell me all kinds of things that I hadn't known before: how I was taken care of by my grandmother so that my mother could go back to school, etc. But my grandmother died, and my mother was then stuck with me. She didn't know the first thing about caring for babies. And at the age of eighteen, she felt she was too young to be saddled with a baby. I picked up on her resentment and internalized it. But upon seeing her first grandchild, all the past was suddenly brought to consciousness and we were able to forgive each other for all the years of secrets and misunderstandings. She says that my baby is the best thing that ever happened to her. She is so happy that she had me. And she's the best grandmother in the world.

Sometimes the mother-daughter bond cannot be healed, even after the daughter herself gives birth. Or there may be reasons that a mother cannot be present for her daughter after the birth of her grandchild. Both of these sets of circumstances, by denying a woman the longing she feels for her mother at this time, can tip the scales toward postpartum depression. (See "Program for Preventing or Healing Postpartum Depression" on page 155.)

One of my patients has a mother who is an alcoholic. Her alcoholic mother had full-time nannies for her children, did not breastfeed, and never got up at night with any of them. When my patient had her first child and wanted her mother with her for support, she was devastated when her mother arrived at her house drunk, expecting her daughter to take care of her! My patient found that her mother needed far more care and support than she gave. It was a setup for the severe postpartum depression that ensued. When she had her subsequent children, she knew that she could not have her mother come visit again. And she did not have a recurrence of her depression.

The Postpartum Adjustment Period

If maintaining order, control, and independence is something that has always made you feel secure and contributed to your sense of mastery, then having a newborn can, at first, be exceedingly unnerving. When my first daughter was three days old, I bounded out of the house to go to the grocery store. As soon as I hit the porch, the reality of my new life hit me like a thunderbolt: "I have a baby. I have to take her with me. Oh God, what have I done!" Eventually, I, like new mothers everywhere, learned to relax my standards of order and control, and became much more flexible.

The postpartum period, like labor, forces you slow down and surrender to a process that is much bigger than you. This is the time to really take in and appreciate what you've just accomplished, allowing your body to relax and your stress hormone levels to return to normal. As you discover that this new baby is your first priority, everything else eventually takes its rightful place around her. But you may also have to overcome fears of all kinds, including doubts about whether you will be able to care for her properly.

When we modern women deny our need for this postpartum time with our new babies, we suffer as much as the babies do. The pull between our innermost needs and those of the outer world can be particularly acute postpartum because we don't feel that we have the right to take this special time. It feels too good—too fragile, too magical. I certainly felt that way. What right did I have to just stay in bed and nurse my baby? I was still very much a left-brained animus-possessed doctor in those days, even though I was into natural mothering in a big way, and I definitely had more opportunities to be with my children immediately postpartum than my mother did. When I first went back to work after my first child was born, she was three months old. Resuming work then seemed reasonable, and besides, I took her to work with me until she was six months old. Many of my patients, however, had to go back to work and leave their babies after only six short weeks—far too soon!

Creating an Outer Placenta for the Mother

Having tried the macho, or superwoman, approach to the postpartum period, I recommend doing the opposite—taking plenty of time for yourself, and getting plenty of help. Every mother needs an outer placenta of friends, family, and perhaps paid professionals, like doulas or baby nurses, to help her in those early months after giving birth. And you'll want to have as much of this set up in advance as possible.

Regardless of how well your mother took care of herself or you, know that the Mother Bear energy that created your body is still present for you. You can tap into it right now by starting a self-care regimen that will make you stronger, for both your baby and yourself.

One more thing. Remember that your daughter's soul picked you for her vehicle to get here. She knew what she was getting into. So just do the best you can and trust your (and your daughter's) Higher Power with the rest.

POSTPARTUM MOTHERING PROGRAM

Get as much rest as possible. Even if you're not tired, rest as much as you can and enjoy your baby. Don't do any household chores for at least a week (two to four weeks is even better).

Wear your baby. Keep your baby close to you as much as possible during the first three months of life so that she can get the tactile stimulation, as well as the eye-to-eye contact, which helps develop the frontal brain connections to the autonomic nervous system in the body. Hold her, cuddle her, talk to her, sleep with her next to you. Remember, touch is a "nutrient" that a child needs, especially during these early days.

If you cannot spend this much time, for whatever reason, find someone else who can be fully engaged and present with your baby. In the traditional extended family, this role is automatically filled by older children, grandparents, aunts, uncles, etc. In today's nuclear family, the role may have to be filled by hired caretakers.

Babies can also derive some "touch nourishment" by lying on lambskins, which give them comfort and tactile stimulation. Studies have shown that infants and premature babies gain more weight, lose less body heat, consume less oxygen, and are generally more peaceful when they are placed on a lambskin versus regular sheets. Lambskin protects the premature infant's delicate skin from abrasion that can result from regular bed linens. It also puts less pressure on the head. Infants placed on lambskins after feeding are more content and will often lie peacefully awake for an hour without requiring additional attention. The danger of suffocation is almost entirely removed since circulation through the wool is so thorough.

Breast-feed, if possible. Breast-feed your baby for as long as possible. One to two years is ideal. In addition to antibodies and other immune system benefits, breast milk provides a baby's sole source of DHA, the omega-3 fatty acid that is essential for normal brain development. As explained earlier, it is felt that the DHA in breast milk is one of the reasons why numerous studies controlled for socioeconomic status have continued to show that children who were breast-fed are more intelligent than their formula-fed peers. If you breast-feed, supplement your diet with DHA. (See Resources.)

Even if you only breast-feed for a week, and even if you supplement that minimal amount of breast-feeding with a bottle, you will be helping your baby's body.

It is important that a baby's oral needs get met—and get met fully. One of my breast-feeding patients once told me, "I think that it's important for my baby to get all the sucking she needs now . . . and then later in life, when she needs to suck something, she'll be discriminating."

There's a great deal of wisdom in that statement. I remember once going to the kitchen at the age of five and asking my mother if I could have some milk in a bottle. She said, "Sure," and gave it to me, and I distinctly recall lying down on the living room rug, contentedly sipping the milk. She didn't shame me or tell me that big girls don't use bottles. She must have realized that, given all the bottles and babies around me, it was natural for me to want to "regress" now and then. (I didn't take my milk in a bottle routinely and don't remember asking again.)

If you can't or don't choose to breast-feed, warm the formula. Use a bottle with a nipple designed to imitate the experience of sucking on a human breast as closely as possible—such as a NUK nipple. I used a NUK nipple when using a bottle, but today there are better options. Use formula that is supplemented with DHA. A good brand is Enfamil Lipil, which contains the highest levels of DHA and arachidonic acid (another essential fatty acid) found in baby formulas. Another good choice is goat's milk.

Get support from others. Mothers do much better with the support, help, and company of others, particularly a supportive mate. Of course, that depends on the mate. Almost every mother I know will tell you that her response to her child's cry for comfort in the night is heard and attended to differently by her than by her mate. Maddening as this is, it may be a matter of pure instinct. In the wild it has been observed that when a mother and father monkey are sitting together and the baby monkey cries, the father won't react. It's as if he doesn't even hear the baby. So the mother gets up to soothe the infant. But if the mother isn't around and the infant cries, the father will hear the cries and get up to attend to the infant![28] This "monkey business" isn't true of all men, of course. One of my friends has a husband who got up every night with their new baby, brought him in to be breast-fed, and then took him back to his crib when he was finished.

The postpartum time is also an ideal time for you to get help from your mother. My mother came for a week when each of my daughters was born. I wish I had had the sense to have her stay longer. I needed much more help than I got, but I didn't know that at the time. My mother would have willingly stayed, but in my typical macho fashion, I didn't want to bother her for longer. I felt that having her stay longer would be "selfish" of me.

I would also highly recommend that you hire a postpartum doula to help out at home for at least a week. As is the case during labor, this gives family members a chance to adjust to the new baby without the enormous fatigue that often accompanies having a new baby at home.

Give up the illusion of perfection. The kind of bonding that I advocate need not be a full-time professional career. The optimal development of the orbitofrontal area of the brain requires what has been called "an average expectable environment," or what is known in psychiatry as "good-enough" mothering. So you needn't be perfect; you just need to have a certain amount of regular, high-quality emotional connection with your child—which is really just a matter of doing what comes naturally.

Postpartum Mood Disorders

Depression in mothers has been described as far back as written history. And although it is more common than gestational diabetes, preeclampsia, or premature delivery, postpartum depression receives much less attention in contemporary medical literature, training, and clinical practice. Childbirth is one of the major physical, psychological, and social stressors in a woman's life, so it is not surprising that, of the approximately 4 million births that occur annually in this country, an estimated 40 percent are complicated by some type of postpartum mood disorder.[29] But these disorders are under-recognized and treated, often because patients are embarrassed about feeling unhappy during a time when society expects them to be elated.

We need to look at both the dark and light sides of childbirth: it opens our hearts and is often a peak experience; but sometimes, when conditions are not optimal, this life-changing event can be a major risk factor in the development of mental illness. One study of 35,000 women, which used data gathered at ninety-day intervals beginning at birth and continuing over a two-year period, showed a seven-fold increase in the risk of psychiatric hospitalization in the first three months following delivery.[30]

About 10 to 17 percent of new mothers suffer from postpartum depression that goes on to become a major depressive disorder. Symptoms include difficulty concentrating or making decisions, irritability, jumpiness, feelings of either sleepiness or agitation, fatigue, changes in appetite or sleep, recurrent thoughts of death or suicide, and feelings of worthlessness or guilt—especially focused on failure as a mother. There can also be excessive anxiety that focuses on the baby's health.[31]

Postpartum depression, whether mild or severe, is the result of a complex mixture of heredity, fluctuating hormone levels, and psychological, physical, and emotional stress that alter hormonal levels. It is also associated with low levels of DHA, the omega-3 fatty acid I refer to as the physical substrate for bonding. DHA is one of the substances in the mother's body that the baby literally sucks up when creating its own body. Given that so many mothers are depleted in this substance to begin with, it is not surprising that by the end of pregnancy, many do not have sufficient stores of their own to maintain optimal brain and emotional functioning.

When so many women suffer postpartum depression following what is supposed to be a normal physiologic process, it is time to evaluate the culture that surrounds that event. Our bodies were not designed in such a way that so many mothers would end up depressed and even psychotic following birth. Given the prevalence of postpartum depression, we need to devote much more energy and allocate many more resources to preventing it, and to early intervention as a means of healing it.

At the personal level, you should be aware that you may be at particular risk for postpartum depression if your mother had it, or if you and your mother do not have a good relationship. Following is a list of conditions associated with postpartum depression:

~ History of postpartum depression in previous pregnancy

~ Lack of emotional, physical, or psychological support

~ A difficult labor and birth

~ A personal or family history of depressive disorders, which increases risk of PPD to 30 percent

~ Unstable marital relationship

~ Lack of satisfaction with your educational achievement

~ Difficult relationship with your mother or father.[32]

I believe that every mother in our culture is at some risk for postpartum depression, simply because there is so little support for new mothers built into the fabric of our society. Each of us needs to do everything we can to prevent this condition from arising in the first place, through optimal support of mothers and babies from birth forward—physically, psychologically, and emotionally.

If you are at risk for postpartum depression and plan to get pregnant or are currently pregnant, don't risk passing the effects of this on to your child. The following suggestions describe how to take extra care to ensure that your postpartum experience is a good one.

PROGRAM FOR PREVENTING OR HEALING POSTPARTUM DEPRESSION

Step One: Shore up your own first chakra. Line up help *before* the delivery, so that it is in place when you go home. Don't risk making depression worse with isolation. In addition to hiring a doula or other help if possible, enlist your friends and family members to bring you meals, do housework, and cook. Ask them to check in on you regularly, even if you don't call them first.

Step Two: Get hormonal support. A good way to do this is to use natural progesterone beginning right after delivery, to help support your hormonal balance through the first few weeks or months postpartum. The pioneering work of Katharina Dalton, M.D., in England has shown that if natural progesterone is given to women at risk for postpartum depression within a day or two of giving birth, their depression is often prevented.[33] The usual dose is 100 to 200 mg per day. I recommend transdermal progesterone obtained from a formulary pharmacy. It can also be given as an intramuscular shot by a doctor or nurse about once per week. Natural progesterone is also available as a vaginal gel (Crinone) or oral micronized capsule (Prometrium). All of the above require a prescription. For some women, however, an over-the-counter 2 percent natural progesterone cream rubbed into the skin will provide adequate hormonal support. Usual dose is one-quarter to one-half teaspoon applied to the skin per day. (See Resources.)

Estrogen has also been used.[34] I prefer progesterone, however, because it does not interfere with milk supply.

There is no evidence that progesterone will harm the baby if you are breast-feeding. In fact, the evidence is in the other direction—natural progesterone (but *not* synthetic progestins such as Provera) given to pregnant women during the first trimester of pregnancy is associated with superior intelligence in the children. Natural progesterone has also been shown by Dalton to help prevent and treat preeclampsia (toxemia) in pregnancy.

Step Three: Get professional help and counseling if necessary. Depression can usually be successfully treated. In some cases antidepressant drugs may be necessary. But cognitive behavioral therapy—therapy that results in thought and behavioral change—has been shown to create the same changes in brain chemistry as antidepressant drugs in those who are willing to institute behavioral change in their lives. (See Resources.) Interestingly, social support, even in the form of internet chat rooms devoted to postpartum depression, has also been found to be very effective.

Room One

Three Months to Seven Years

7

The Emotional Brain

Empathy, Will, and Shame

❊

William Ross Wallace's poem "What Rules the World" contains the much-quoted line, "The hand that rocks the cradle is the hand that rules the world," which praises motherhood as the preeminent force for human well-being. Though one could debate how much power mothers have over the world in general, there's absolutely no question that the hand that rocks the cradle is the crucial influence on the development of the new being who has been placed in her care.

It is during the earliest years of a child's life that mind and body, emotions, and experience all become woven together in a seamless biological web that will influence her health and well-being as long as she lives. Optimal brain, nervous system, and bodily organ development are dependent on adequate amounts of the right kinds of emotional, mental, physical, and spiritual experiences. Although the brain and bodily organs continue to change and develop throughout life, experiences before the age of seven are especially critical because of the rapid rate of growth and change during this time.

In a famous neuroscience experiment, newborn kittens were raised with only vertical stripes to look at. After a critical stage of brain development had passed, they could no longer perceive anything horizontal in nature and actually ran into horizontally positioned objects. The brain area required to see what is horizontal was never stimulated

by experience in the outer world, and therefore, the pathways to imprint it into the visual cortex itself never developed.[1] Although far
more complex, the same type of visual development occurs in humans.
And, to some extent, our early experiences also teach us what to "see"
and not to see in the emotional and social world around us.

THE ORBITOFRONTAL AREA:
THE MIND-BODY-EMOTION CONNECTION

Everything that goes on around us and everything that happens
to us during these formative years creates a biochemical imprint in
the area of the brain called the orbitofrontal cortex. (*Orbit* stands
for "eye" and *frontal* for "frontal lobe"—see the diagram on page
163.) This brain center is critical for maintaining a stable mood and
having healthy relationships;[2] it gives us the capacity for empathy, intuition, emotional communication, and the ability to relate to self
and others. Its growth and development are highly influenced by the
quality and intensity of attention and care the child receives.

Orbitofrontal wiring for relationship and empathy starts when a
child looks into her mother's eyes and sees how her mother feels about
her and her behavior: loving, disappointed, or indifferent. The information this area processes—how your mother feels about you—is then
transferred to the rest of the body and all the bodily organs. The orbitofrontal area can be thought of as a relay station that transmits the
quality of one's moods and relationships directly to every cell, affecting
every aspect of a child's health, including bowel, heart, reproductive,
lung, and skin function.[3] If a child is to feel really good about herself
and have optimal health, her orbitofrontal area needs to be adequately
wired in by her relationship with her mother or early caregivers.

The Wiring between Emotional and Physical Health

Very specific connections develop to link the orbitofrontal cortex
to the areas in our bodies that regulate respiration, gastrointestinal
function, the cardiovascular system, and the hormonal system. If the
brain registers emotional distress—even if we are not conscious of it
or cannot express it—all of these physical systems then speak to us
through symptoms that are meant to tell us one of three things:

1. An emotional need isn't being met.

2. Something in our own lives needs to change to meet that need.

3. Something in a loved one's life is out of balance and needs to be attended to.[4]

In short, the optimal growth and development of the right orbitofrontal area of our brains and its connection with our bodies is key to the healthy functioning of every organ system, and also to our ability to connect emotionally and intuitively with others. This system can be thought of as the hardwiring of the body-mind connection.

Not surprisingly, the growth and development of the orbitofrontal area and its connections with our organs is regulated and affected by the quality and intensity of attention and care we receive. And this may affect our health, for better or for worse, for years to come.

DEMYSTIFYING THE BRAIN

Though I am not a brain scientist, my best friend, Dr. Mona Lisa Schulz, is. Dr. Schulz is a board-certified psychiatrist and also has a Ph.D. in behavioral neuroscience. As a medical intuitive, she helps people rewire their thought patterns to help them create physical and emotional health. As a neuropsychiatrist, she evaluates people with head injury, stroke, dementia, autism, and a wide range of behavioral problems. Her approach is to find out what's working well in an individual's brain and then help them capitalize on their strengths and work around their weaknesses. She has helped me, my daughters, and a number of family members learn to appreciate and work more effectively with our unique brain styles.

In short, Mona Lisa's enthusiastic knowledge of the brain and her scholarly desire to know more have been the perfect match to my years of clinical experience in women's health. You might say that she speaks fluent "brain" and I speak fluent "body." We like to think of ourselves as the Rodgers and Hammerstein (or at least the Laverne and Shirley) of women's health. Her forthcoming book, *The New Feminine Brain,* is designed to help women access their intuition and unique genius by understanding how to work optimally with their moods, anxiety, attention, and memory.

Dr. Schulz has shown me a very simple yet elegant way to understand how our brain experiences, interprets, and modulates emotions, thoughts, and behavior. The following is a basic schema of the functional areas of the brain and how they develop in childhood:

The Limbic System: The Emotional Brain This part of the brain is important for emotions and memory. It is where memories—both the ones we talk about and the nonverbal memories that are stored in our bodies—are processed. Much of this part of the brain is fully functional at birth. All of the following areas are included in the limbic system: the temporal lobe, the orbitofrontal area, the amygdala, and the hippocampus. Many writers erroneously refer to this area as the "reptilian brain"; this term turns Dr. Schulz into a fireball because it implies that the emotional brain is the most "primitive" part of the brain. Studies of neurodevelopment have shown that this simply is not true. In addition, calling emotions more "primitive" suggests that they are somehow "inferior." And nothing could be further from the truth!

The Frontal Lobe: The Executive Brain This part of the brain comes on board as we grow and develop. It is extremely "plastic," so that it can be shaped by experience during early childhood. Although the brain retains some of this plasticity throughout life—being self-renewing and able to rewire itself in response to changing circumstances—it does become more "committed" to certain thoughts and beliefs once the hormones of puberty cement its circuitry into place. This part of the brain modulates limbic-system emotions so that we can fit them into our relationships and work, thus allowing us to become functional and contributing members of society. The function of the frontal executive area—also known as the dorsolateral prefrontal cortex (DLPC)—is to direct what the rest of the body and brain should be feeling, doing, and saying. It enables us to act appropriately, inhibit our impulses, and reflect thoughtfully on our actions.

The Right and Left Hemispheres The functions of the right and left hemispheres are very complex and there is a wide range of difference among individuals. Still, Dr. Schulz boils it down to this: Generally speaking, in the left hemisphere, the executive brain's thoughts and judgments dominate the emotions of the limbic system.

In the right hemisphere, the emotional limbic system dominates the executive brain's judgment circuits. Right-hemisphere-dominant individuals exhibit more spontaneous, less inhibited behavior and emotions. The right hemisphere also has more connections to the bodily organs than does the left hemisphere. Most women tend to have more right-hemisphere contributions to their brain function than do most men.

Although both hemispheres process and interpret emotions, research suggests that they process different types of emotions. The left limbic area is said to process emotions of joy, contentment, and happiness and the right limbic area is associated with fear, anger, and sadness.[5]

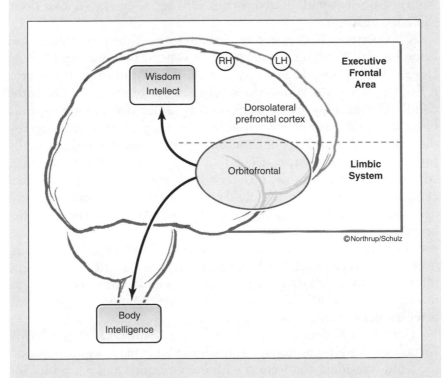

The Basic Emotions: Joy, Love, Anger, Sadness, and Fear

A child comes into the world biologically primed to move toward what feels good and away from what doesn't. These pure and powerful instincts are one component of the inner guidance system that a child innately knows and trusts. During the first year to eighteen months of life, a baby is wired to go after what she wants, but doesn't have the capacity to understand or deal with the consequences. Her behavior is appropriate for her age—she isn't capable of controlling her drives yet. She is the center of her own universe, and everything—and everyone—else exists only to fulfill her needs.

When a baby sees something she wants, she gets excited. Her heart beats faster and her face lights up. Her entire sympathetic nervous system sings with the thrill of connecting with what feels good, like eating chocolate, playing in the water, or going after a toy. (I'll never forget the unbridled joy of my daughter Kate's first encounter with chocolate. I'd bought a cake to celebrate her first birthday, and she nearly fell into it, shoving fistfuls into her mouth with great enthusiasm.) Conversely, when a child isn't fed or can't get what she wants, she howls with discomfort. And when someone slams a door, she cries with fear.

Chocolate and other bodily pleasures aren't the only things that bring her joy, however. Attachment to others, bonding, and feeling close also feel good. The quality of a child's relationships at this critical stage shapes the connections between her brain and body. If the child's relationships are characterized by a healthy and appropriate blend of all the basic emotions—joy, love, sadness, fear, and anger—then her mind-body imprint is more apt to be healthy and optimally functional. In contrast, if a child's mother is chronically unstable, constantly angry, irritable, upset, or frightened, then this emotional chaos gets imprinted in the child's body and mind simultaneously. The result is often lifelong health challenges. And if a child's mother or primary caregiver is indifferent, depressed, preoccupied, or expresses only overly controlled or "sanitized" emotions, then the connections between the child's brain and body are also more likely to be muted and difficult to access. Later in life, a child born to this type of mother may have difficulty knowing how she feels and what her body is telling her.

Until a child develops the frontal-lobe brain areas that control, curtail, or inhibit emotional expression, she experiences a pure, direct, and unbridled connection with her emotions and her body. She knows what feels good and what doesn't. Mothers help reinforce a child's emotional connectivity and ability to feel passion when the child first starts interacting with her environment. Research has shown that until ages twelve to eighteen months, 90 percent of most mothers' behavior consists of affectionate play and caregiving, while only 5 percent is involved with saying no and prohibiting her child from going after what she wants.[6] The mother herself creates the safe space in which the baby can connect physically and emotionally with the world around her.

First Steps to Independence

I remember a particular family hike when my first daughter, Annie, was about two. She refused to allow either her father or me to hold her hand, even though several months before she still had enjoyed walking between us and holding both our hands so that she could swing whenever possible. But now, despite the rough terrain and the fact that she slipped and fell a lot, she was adamant that we not help her. When we attempted to grab her hand, she pulled it away and told us that she was going to do this on her own. And to our amazement and amusement, this little tyke marched along for the entire one-and-a-half-mile hike completely unassisted—and with a sense of determination that was impressive.

From the age of about eighteen months onward, a child rapidly develops the muscular coordination and nervous system maturation necessary for her to individuate from her mother and caregivers. She learns to walk, talk, control her bowel and bladder functions, and begins to explore and manipulate her outer world. It is at this life stage that the seeds of healthy independence, initiative, and drive are sown that help support a girl to go after what she wants in life with confidence. Simultaneously, she is beginning to lay down the brain circuitry necessary to direct, curtail, and inhibit her drives appropriately in order to fit into relationships and society.

The Dance of Individuation: Running Away, Coming Back

Children learn their most significant and lasting lessons about autonomy and independence before the age of five. As a child begins to test her legs in the world, most of her initial walking is away from her mother. With her newfound skills, the child feels elated. At this stage, it is crucial that the mother share the child's sense of accomplishment and elation and mirror it back to her. This helps to establish a bedrock sense of self-confidence. If a mother fails to do this or doesn't actively nudge her child away to enjoy her freedom, the daughter, depending upon her temperament, may end up finding it difficult to assert her independence and ability to go after what she wants in the world.

Toward the end of the second year, however, she'll probably spend most of her time not running away but running back. A good friend of mine was very surprised when her daughter started clinging and crying whenever she left the house. She said, "I don't understand it. I've been leaving her with sitters for six months and she's never done this before." She relaxed when she realized that her daughter was just going through the normal "clingy" stage. The child has now gotten some perspective on what she has lost by leaving her mother. So now she returns. Once a daughter leaves her mother, she actually discovers her in a new way when she returns. This developmental stage marks the first time that a child actually experiences what it feels like to miss someone who is not there. She is now internalizing the concept of togetherness versus separateness, and the fact that she and her mother are two different beings. She is no longer the center of the universe.

During this stage a child realizes that her mother (and others) may have different wishes from hers. And because she now has the ability to go after what she wants, conflicts between mother and child inevitably arise. The basic patterns for healthy, mutually satisfying relationships are laid down now. A child must work through this stage of conflict and resolution if she is to get along in the world. She must learn that there are multiple needs, not all of which are hers. To get her needs met in a balanced way, she must begin to consider other people's points of view. ("How will Mommy feel if I do this?")

DEVELOPMENT OF WILL:
THE BEGINNINGS OF PASSION AND PURPOSE

At about the same time she learns to walk, a child begins to develop her will, which helps solidify her inner drive to go after what she wants in the world. Will is the power the mind and soul have over one's thoughts and behavior. It is synonymous with decisiveness, determination, resolution, and the ability to choose one's own actions and purposes. Will comes directly from a child's soul. It manifests as drives she must learn to channel into a unique expression that reflects her soul's passion and purpose. Every daughter needs a strong personal will and enough ego strength to accomplish this task. A disciplined will used responsibly becomes her steering wheel for personal autonomy and freedom.

At some time during the second year of life, a child discovers that her wants and needs are different from those of her parents. Her personal will is tested by the strength of her desire to go after these anyway! And her resourcefulness will determine how she manages to negotiate her way around her parents, siblings, and other caregivers. A child will develop and express her will somewhere along a continuum of two opposing extremes, neither of which is desirable or healthy: on the one hand, she may become paralyzed by shame, fear, or guilt. And on the other, she may try to impose her will on others by becoming oppositional, defiant, and rigid. The foundation for all of this begins now, with a child's first no.

Amazing Twos—The Blossoming of Ego Strength and Personal Determination

Though we call this time the terrible twos, there's nothing terrible about it. What's really going on is that the child is developing her will by pushing against the limits created by her parents or her surroundings. At this time, a mother must start to introduce more restrictions in her child's environment and curb some of the child's wishes. And her interaction with her child changes from one based primarily on unlimited approval to one that requires disapproval of some of her behavior. During this time, a child will attempt to have her way, despite knowing what her parent wants. As one of my patients told me, "My precious two-year-old who used to be so sunny and cheery now says no to everything. Even the things she really likes, like having ice cream. It feels as though she says no just to say no!"

The stage is now set for sustained conflicts of will, and the parent's role makes a dramatic shift from primarily being a caretaker to that of being a socialization agent. The ensuing struggle between a mother and her daughter, though at times exhausting, is crucial for the healthy balance between determination and adaptability, self-love and accommodation to others. When a mother forbids her daughter to indulge in some activity and the child is prevented from achieving a thing that she desires, her natural instincts get frustrated and she experiences anger. Learning to deal with this frustration is an important life skill.

The child is also now old enough to know and consider what others think of her. And because humans are herd creatures, her health and survival depend upon a sense of belonging, fitting her needs with those of others, and being loved. A child has to learn to weigh her personal desires for herself against what others think and feel about her. She's laying the foundation for the lifelong dance of "bob and weave" that all mothers are familiar with: the constant compromise between going after what she wants in the world while at the same time making sure she has the love and acceptance that she also needs. The lessons she learns now about how and what she can go after in life actually shape the brain circuitry for inhibiting her unbridled drives, learning how to delay gratification, and channeling her drives into constructive outlets.

A Temperamental Difference

Each of us is born with a distinct temperament when it comes to how we go after what we want. And although this temperament is somewhat shaped by how we were raised, our basic approach will remain unchanged for most of our lives. My sister and I were as different as we could be, though only eleven months apart in age.

When my sister Penny was about three or four, she frequently got out of bed and wandered around in the middle of the night. Sometimes, in the summer, when it was still light outside in the evening after bedtime, she'd even wander down the street. Once she showed up in the middle of a party my parents were giving, stark naked, at 11:00 P.M.

Our baby-sitter, Matilda, who was sixty-five at the time she started helping my mother, used to tie my sister to the porch or sometimes in bed with a large hemp rope. My parents even used a hospital restraint—a straitjacket, really—on several occasions. But my sister, being the three-year-old blond version of the great Houdini, always managed to get out of these contraptions and come into my room to sleep with me. I recall at the age of five being amused by this. I generally did what I was told and my parents didn't have to resort to physical restraints.

By current standards of parenting, tying your child up with a rope to restrict her movement is certainly not optimal—and perhaps even likely to create emotional wounds. Not so with my sister. I called her to ask what she thought of being tied up as a child now that she's a mother with three sons (all of whom as little boys tempted me to tie them up at least some of the time). Anyway, her response was telling, and a great testimony to the temperament she was born with—a temperament that, in my view, actually attracted the rope. She said, "I remember accepting it all as an incredible challenge. In fact, once when Till [our name for Matilda] was looping the rope over and over the bed and around me, I said to myself, 'This is going to be incredibly easy.'" She went on, "As far back as I can remember I've had this sense that I will bow to no one. And anything that happened to me I put in that context."

As an adolescent, this same persistence and physical activity level propelled my sister onto the U.S. Alpine Ski Team.

Balancing the Inner Yes (Will) and Inner No (Morality)

As a parent, none of us wants to raise an individual who has no internalized sense of empathy or social conscience—an antisocial personality or a "sociopath." No one wants to raise a child who wreaks havoc by running willy-nilly after everything she wants. On the other hand, it's important that a child not become so inhibited and obsessive about acting on her urges that she is immobilized. There needs to be a balance.

In order to modify your needs so they fit in with those of others, you first have to be able to key into what other people are thinking and feeling. If a child is developing normally, this ability builds on the already established empathy circuits in her brain, the areas associated with the ability to understand and process nonverbal language.

Once you have the ability to anticipate what another person thinks and feels in a given situation, it becomes possible to ask the following questions before acting: How is that person likely to respond? And how much do their feelings matter to you? Let's say, for example, that you want another cookie but your mother has told you that you can't have another one before dinnertime. You also know that you could climb up to the cookie jar and get one when she goes into the other room. Is getting the cookie worth your mother's disapproval if you climb up and sneak it when she isn't looking?

As with all things, there's a healthy balance here. Some children, by temperament (and soul qualities), value their mother's approval of them more than they value the satisfaction of eating another cookie. For this type of child, the joy of getting the cookie would be significantly sullied by the anticipated disapproval of the mother. For others (who are considered more willful), getting the cookie would far outweigh their need to have their mother's approval.

Dr. Mona Lisa Schulz describes such bonding circuit differences in terms of "Teflon" versus "Velcro." The child who cares more about the cookie than her mother's feelings has bonding circuits that are like Teflon. The one who cares more about her mother's feelings than the cookie has Velcro bonding circuits.

The way in which a child's empathy circuits develop—and also operate later in life—is, to some extent, controlled by the child's will. If it serves her to win her mother's approval in order to accomplish a goal she's interested in, she will be far more likely to pay attention to how her mother feels about her behavior. In other words, she will quickly learn how to "butter up" her mother. Watch a three-year-old stroke her mother's cheek, do something cute to make her laugh, or say "I love you, Mommy"—all so she can reach her goal of staying up a little later, having another cookie, or petting the bunny for five more minutes. She knows how to activate the empathy bonds that open her mother's heart.

But sometimes a child needs to learn that no means no, and that nothing she does or says is going to change that. At such times, trying to butter up a person to get her way would be manipulative and disrespectful. A child needs to develop the emotional and mental flexibility to know when to push for what she wants despite the feelings of others, and when to defer her needs for the needs of others. This is a process that gets refined over a lifetime.

Most children are also naturally empathetic when they sense that Mom (or someone they love) is upset. A friend wrote me, "My son sent us a heartbreaking e-mail after 9/11. He described himself and his wife sitting stunned and grieving in their New York City apartment while their daughter, sixteen-month-old Molly, was at her most affectionate, charming, and well-behaved all day, doing everything she knew to do to comfort them." I've also seen very little kids attempt to provide comfort at funerals or when a family member isn't feeling well.

KNOWING WHAT YOU THINK
AND HOW YOU FEEL

The connections between thoughts, feelings, and language are formed between the ages of two and five. It is during this time that a child learns to think about right and wrong and also to feel these concepts in her body. Healthy connections between thoughts, feelings, language, and the physical body are crucial for a child to be able to express her thoughts and feelings out loud—and also to know which thoughts and feelings support her fully and which don't.

The body is the first place in which we feel emotions. Fear is embodied as a sinking sensation in the solar plexus, a stomachache, sweaty palms, or a racing heart. Anger may be accompanied by clenched fists, overall muscle tension, and a red face with a scowl. The key to a lifetime of emotional and physical health is being able to name the emotion and, eventually, the event or thought that prompted that emotion in the first place. (Remember, an emotion is always preceded by some belief or perception. No two people will respond to the same thought or event with the exact same emotions. It's all relative.) The emotion needs to be validated and felt fully. It will then move through the body spontaneously once its message is heeded. (*E-motion* is simply energy that is in motion.) And very often, once the emotion is named and validated, a spontaneous solution to the problem or situation will arise.

Even very distressing emotions, from anger to anxiety to embarrassment, do not cause long-term problems unless they are invalidated, feared, or have no way to be expressed. This fact is the basis for an effective new therapy known as DBT (dialectic behavioral therapy), which teaches individuals skills for naming and dealing effectively with the full range of emotions which, if not addressed, often result in a wide variety of somatic symptoms. (See Chapter 18 for a fuller discussion.)

Most mothers instinctively know when their children are emotionally upset even if the child doesn't recognize it. You can help her by observing her behavior and pointing it out to her in a nonjudgmental way. For example, one of my patients noticed that her daughter Susie was looking very dejected after a play date with a friend. She said, "Susie, would you like to tell me what you're feeling? I see that your head is hanging down and you are walking slowly." (A simple open-ended question generally works better than asking "Is something wrong?") Then just listen. This alone will convey more to your daughter about her worth and the validity of her emotions than anything else you can do. You don't need to comment every time a child has a difficult feeling. Emotions come and go naturally. The main thing is simply to validate the ones that you intuitively know are giving your child a hard time.

Teaching Heart Wisdom

Once you have really listened, and it's clear your child doesn't have anything further to share, ask her to put her mind into her heart area and have her put her hand over her heart for emphasis. The heart is where emotions really get healed, not the intellect. Now ask her to think of something she loves, like her pet dog, cat, Mommy, or her grandmother. Encourage her to bask in that feeling for a moment. Now ask her to think about the troubling situation and check to see if her heart has a solution for her. You will be amazed at how often kids know exactly what needs to be done. In Susie's case, she was sad because her friend's older brother had been making fun of her new pink sneakers. When she and her mother did the heart wisdom exercise together, Susie decided that she really loved her sneakers and was going to continue to wear them no matter what her friend's older brother said. Her mother's validation of her emotions had made all the difference. Her mood immediately shifted and she went off to play with her toys.

Communicating Love and Respect

Even toddlers who can't talk understand when they're listened to and respected and when they are not. When a person is upset, whether a toddler or an adult, the strategy that conveys the most love and respect is to repeat back to her what she just said or expressed. In his book *The Happiest Toddler on the Block* (the best and most fun book I've ever read on how to raise an emotionally and physically healthy toddler), pediatrician Harvey Karp calls this strategy the Fast-Food Rule. When you drive up to a fast-food window, the server says, "Can I take your order?" say, "A burger and fries, please." The server then repeats your order back to you: "That'll be a burger and fries." He doesn't say, "Do you know how many calories are in that?" or "Don't you really want a salad?" No—he can't go to the next step until he has repeated your order exactly as you gave it. Just so, a child who is upset can't go to the next step of being soothed and redirected unless her needs are first validated.

It's easy to see how this works with an adult or older child. For example, my younger daughter became really upset when she forgot to recharge her new Palm Pilot and lost all the data she had spent hours entering. When she told me this, I didn't cut her off, give her a hug, and say, "There, there, honey. You can do it again. By the way, did you fill up the car with gas like I asked you to?" or worse, "Well, you should have read the instructions."

Instead, I commiserated with her, sharing a story about how I had lost a whole day's writing because I had forgotten to press Save. "You keep hoping that there's some way to fix it," I said, "but there isn't. It really sucks." Soon afterward, her mood lifted, and she was able to collect herself enough to redo the work.

Similarly, when a young child is upset, the first thing they need is to have their upset validated—not overlooked, soothed, or bypassed. And this has to be done sincerely, with your heart. Karp says that parents often make the mistake of saying "It's okay" over and over again in an attempt to calm the child. Then the toddler has to ramp up the message because she hasn't been heard.

Karp teaches parents to use "Toddler-ese," a language style that exactly mirrors the short phrases, repetition, intensity, and gestures of the toddler. I watched one of my friends do this with her two-year-old. We were having coffee together and her daughter began to get agitated and whiny because she was bored. My friend said to her—with great empathy, giving her child her full attention: "Bored, Casey, bored. So bored. Out, out. Get out. Home, Mommy, home. Go home." Casey immediately calmed down, knowing that her mother had gotten the message. When her mother pulled a new toy from her purse and told the now calmer Casey that they would go home very soon, Casey was willing to settle down and play.

Karp writes, "I sometimes think of the Fast-Food Rule as a rescue mission. Your toddler is stuck deep in the jungle of her Stone Age emotions. The only way you can rescue her is by finding her in her jungle. And the only way to find her is by mirroring her feelings."

Why Emotional Validation Is So Important

Over the years I've seen literally thousands of women both in my practice and in everyday life who are out of touch with what they think and what they feel. As a result, they have difficulty knowing what is right for them and what is wrong. Their natural ability to tune in to their inner guidance system, know who they are, what they like, and then express this to others was programmed out of them at an early age because their parents didn't know how to listen to them or because they were shamed for having valid needs.

In our grandmother's day, the dictum was "Children should be seen and not heard." So it's no wonder that so many of our parents were handed down the legacy that a child's thoughts and feelings weren't important. They then internalized the idea that the feelings themselves were bad or unworthy—and, in turn, found it difficult to acknowledge uncomfortable feelings in their own children.

In contrast, of course, there are also a vast number of adults who have never learned to restrain either their behavior or their expression of feelings. They suffer from insufficient shame and self-restraint. And their health and relationships also suffer as a result. Either extreme, too much shame or insufficient shame, is not healthy. Both extremes can make living authentically from your true self a lifelong challenge. The solution is for mothers to learn how to listen to their children, really listen, without expecting themselves to have all the answers or to be able to "fix it" for the child all the time.

SHAME: AN ESSENTIAL EMOTION

Once the orbitofrontal circuits for healthy emotional dependence and connection have been well established, a new brain area comes on board: the dorsolateral prefrontal cortex (DLPC), which wraps around the sides and top of the orbitofrontal area. The dorsolateral area is where we encode rules, regulations, rational reasoning, and social mores—in other words, our "shoulds," "shouldn'ts," and "oughts." This area of the brain helps a child restrain her behavior once she's aware—based on the empathy created in the orbitofrontal area—of how others are likely to feel about it.

The ability to feel embarrassment or to restrain oneself begins to appear sometime between twelve and eighteen months,[7] when the dorsolateral prefrontal cortex begins to develop.[8] When you're old enough to walk around, you're old enough to learn not to touch a hot stove, hit your brother, or run out into the street. In other words, your brain is developed enough to curb motor movements voluntarily to some extent. As this area continues to develop, it also leads to the ability to control bowel and bladder function. At about the same time, temper tantrums appear, peaking between the ages of two and three.

In contrast to the playful approval of the first year, researchers have observed that mothers of eleven- to seventeen-month-olds tell the child to stop doing something on an average of every nine minutes. These minute-to-minute interactions about not playing with the dog's water or not pulling the books off the shelf can wear mothers down, but they're actually helping the child develop control or inhibition.[9] Once a child is about eighteen months old and beyond, however, she begins to lay down the pathways in the DLPC that enable her to feel shame. This is the beginning of her cultural and moral education.

Another interesting thing happens about this time. A mother may notice that the baby's father is starting to get more engaged and involved with her. In general, older children with more reasoning power are more interesting to men than younger children. And the very time when fathers are more apt to interact more with their children is also when the dorsolateral prefrontal cortex comes onboard—the part of the brain that encodes rules and regulations. As a girl grows older, the personal attributes of her father will become an important part of her internal representation for how the rules and regulations of our culture work. If her father routinely runs red lights or belittles his wife, for example, then she is apt to encode this behavior as a cultural norm that is within the bounds of morality.

It's intriguing that the dorsolateral prefrontal cortex area works in direct opposition to the orbitofrontal brain, which develops first and governs emotions and intuition. The development and function of these two brain areas is so strikingly similar to the traditional functions we attribute to mothers versus fathers that I have been tempted to call the orbitofrontal bonding area the "mommy" brain and the dorsolateral prefrontal cortex the "daddy" brain! The orbitofrontal brain area tells you to act on your impulses and to stay in the feeling mode, while the dorsolateral prefrontal cortex inhibits these messages.

TEMPER TANTRUMS: EMOTIONAL INCONTINENCE AND "LOSING IT"

According to Dr. Mona Lisa Schulz, a temper tantrum is the physical manifestation of the child's struggle to learn how to contain and direct her emotions in a socially appropriate fashion. When she wants something, she has developed the motor skills to reach for it. However, the mental apparatus to restrain her wants in a socially appropriate way is not yet solidly on board. As a result, she shrieks, screams, or dissolves into tears when an external control is placed between her and what she desires. This frustration comes out in a temper tantrum, which

Dr. Schulz refers to as emotional incontinence. This term fits the neurodevelopment of this stage perfectly, given that temper tantrums tend to begin at about the same age as bladder control. Learning to control one's bladder and bowels is a process that takes place over several years, and so does the process of acquiring social restraint. It's not surprising that when adults cry or fly into a rage, we say they're "losing it." Old people who are demented also lose both bladder and emotional control as their frontal-lobe circuits deteriorate.

Both emotional incontinence and loss of bladder control are far more apt to happen when a child is overexcited or overtired. Although these full-scale emotional meltdowns tend to diminish by age four or so, she will still tend to lose it by crying, yelling, or withdrawing when she gets too tired or frustrated. How and when she experiences emotional incontinence will also depend upon her temperament. All humans occasionally need to lose it in a way that doesn't harm anyone else. After all, temper tantrums are like thunderstorms: full of noise and light, followed by a refreshing clearing of the air!

As a mother faced with a tantrum, you might be ready to lose it yourself (and that is part of the problem). You must maintain your own emotional continence. Do not spank or hit your child. Take a deep breath, remain calm, and, depending on the situation, first try what pediatrician Harvey Karp calls the Fast-Food Rule. (See page 172.) If that doesn't work, remove your child to a quiet area as quickly as possible. Do not reward her, bribe her, or try to comfort her. Withdraw all stimuli and allow her to be alone with herself. That means you sit in the front seat of the car with your back to her, or wait in another room of the house while she has her time out. She'll get over the tantrum in several minutes and may well fall asleep for a while.

The Healthy Use of Shame

We learn our first lessons about what to approach and what to avoid from our parents. As we get older, they also teach us more complicated lessons about how to act in public and in private. These instructions get laid down in both the orbitofrontal cortex, which says, "Yes, it's okay to feel that and go after that," and the dorsolateral prefrontal cortex, which says, "No, better not do that right now. Look before you leap. That's not appropriate." We need both parts of our brains to be fully functional. Neither part is right or wrong; each of these areas, and the bodily organs and functions they govern, need to be trained in ways that support our full health and self-expression.

If a girl is to become a woman of character, integrity, and honor— or a mother who is able to raise a daughter with those qualities—then she must, somewhere along the line, internalize a healthy sense of what behavior is honorable and what is improper. Our health throughout our lives is affected by the degree to which we live in accordance with an appropriate value system. In order to learn what is appropriate and what isn't, the child will have to experience some shame.

The *Random House Unabridged Dictionary* lists a number of definitions for *shame*. The one that captures the concept of healthy shame is "the painful feeling arising from the consciousness of something dishonorable, improper, ridiculous, etc., done by oneself or another." Or, "Shame is a painful feeling caused by the consciousness or exposure of unworthy or indecent conduct or circumstances."[10] (The emotion of guilt, by the way, is the result of feeling ashamed about something you believe you should have done or should not have done. Like shame, there is healthy guilt and unhealthy guilt.)

Every child needs to be taught appropriate social behavior so she can express her passion and purpose in a way that is respectful of both herself and others. We do this by providing structure, rules, and proper discipline. Shame works to restrain behaviors that are not appropriate in a social setting, thus allowing a child to fit in and get the health benefits of belonging. Most people, especially when they are children, will do anything to be accepted and loved by their family or group. When they are shamed, they know that their behavior is not acceptable and that they could risk losing approval and love if they continue that behavior. They restrain inappropriate behavior to win the approval and love almost all children so desperately need.

Researchers have found that in order to achieve optimal growth and development as humans, a child needs small doses of shame in the socialization process beginning in early childhood.[11] This accomplishes three tasks: making a child conscious of her behavior and its impact on others; teaching right from wrong (the basis of morality);

and instilling the ability to distinguish appropriate from inappropriate behavior.

However, the way in which she is told about her inappropriate behavior is key. A respectful parent who is in touch with her own feelings, her own emotional vocabulary, and who has worked through her own unjustified thoughts and feelings of shame will make a very clear distinction between the unacceptability of a child's behavior (justified shame) as opposed to the unacceptability of the child herself (unjustified shame). I watched a two-year-old girl crawling over people's feet in an airport terminal recently. Her mom gently picked her up, took her aside, and told her she had to stop because her behavior was upsetting others. The girl resumed quietly playing with a toy—self-esteem intact, but inappropriate behavior curbed.

The parent who ridicules the child, on the other hand, and leads her to believe that she is bad because her behavior is unacceptable may create a feeling of unjustified shame so painful that the child shuts down emotionally so as not to feel it. I once saw a child stumble at the beach. Her father yelled, "Pick up your feet, you clumsy idiot." This sort of treatment, if continued, can result in "clipped circuits" between a child's body and brain. This has lasting consequences for physical and emotional health and also for one's ability to live a meaningful life imbued with passion and purpose.

Shame is perhaps the most painful emotion that we humans experience. If you've ever left the ladies' room with your skirt tucked into your pantyhose, you know what I'm talking about! Most children—but not all—will do whatever it takes to avoid it. When a child is shamed in a way that damages self-esteem, the results may be paralyzing, both emotionally and physically, depending upon her soul qualities and temperament. Shaming a child in an unbalanced and unhealthy way can damage her sense of joy, independence, self-esteem, and bodily acceptance. The decisions that a child makes about her worthiness become programmed into her very cellular tissue. When a child is made to feel ashamed for normal bodily functions, feelings, or behaviors, then she may begin to believe that she is inherently flawed as a human being. And then, long after the original shaming is over, the beliefs and behaviors that result will continue to play themselves out into adult life, often in ways that are debilitating to a woman's sense of herself as a worthy, whole, capable human being. There can also be health consequences such as autoimmune diseases. (See Chapter 9.)

The unjustified use of shame as a socializing technique is only now being appreciated by our culture for its long-lasting, deleterious effects on our health. Research has shown that the excessive use of shame can also lead to depression, depending upon a child's temperament.[12]

Shame and Gender

Down the millennia, in almost every culture on earth, women have been shamed for exactly the same behaviors for which boys are rewarded; i.e., behaviors that are associated with being autonomous, independent, and adventuresome. When a little girl starts climbing a high tree or a piece of furniture, she is often told, "Get down off there or you'll hurt yourself," or "Don't you realize that people can see right up your skirt?" or "It's not ladylike to climb up there. Get down here right away." A little boy doing exactly the same thing would probably hear, "Look at him, he's really athletic, isn't he?" or "Look at how fearless, brave, and coordinated he is."

When a girl acts her emotions out physically, she is also much more likely to be shamed for her behavior than is a boy. When a boy does exactly the same thing, we look the other way or exclaim, "Boys will be boys!"—a stance that simply perpetuates behavior in boys, and later in men, that is too often destructive to society. As a result of this double standard, the majority of women have areas of their lives in which they feel overly controlled or overly fearful. And too many learn to use manipulation to get their emotional needs met.

ELAINE: Unjustified Shame Changes Heart Rhythm

Elaine was fifty-seven years old when she first saw me for a routine checkup. Her past medical history revealed some social anxiety, and also a history of heart palpitations and an irregular heartbeat. When I asked her about the heart problems, she told me the following story.

> In my late forties, I started to develop irregular heartbeats. Missed beats at first. Nothing serious, I was told. Then the palpitations started. They frightened me greatly. My heart felt as though it was out of control. The more fear I experienced, the worse the problem became. I eventually ended up in the emergency room, had several EKGs, carried a monitor for several days, walked the treadmill, and had an echocardiogram. I was

told that my heart was fine and that I'd just have to live with the problem. My doctor said, "Consider them a 'skip in your heart's CD.' " The image worked well for me. Things got better for a while.

Toward menopause, when I was in my fifties, I became very interested in tennis, a game I had enjoyed in high school but hadn't had time to play for years. Soon it became an important part of my new life. I wasn't having any problems and was now playing in a doubles league. But then the idea started creeping in that maybe those palpitations would come back. And sure enough, I began to experience them occasionally. If I stopped whatever I was doing and took a few deep breaths, they'd go away. I noticed that I got them especially when I was afraid of messing up during a doubles match. One day, during a game with a partner I didn't know very well, I began to experience strong palpitations. I felt embarrassed, not wanting to show my weakness in front of my partner. But what could I do? I made a quick decision: I would stop, lie down, and relax. I explained to her that it happened to me sometimes and that she should not be frightened. She sat by my side, holding my hand. At that point, I felt that I was letting go, that what would happen did not matter, and I experienced a deep feeling of warmth and love within my heart. The palpitations stopped, like magic. . . . And I suddenly heard my mother's voice saying, "You look like an idiot. Stop making a spectacle of yourself!" . . . I laughed. . . . I did not care anymore. . . . I was lying down there, vulnerable and pitiful, in front of my friend, and I did not care. . . .

Then the episode when my mother had uttered those words came back to me. I was four years old, standing in the front yard during my older sister's birthday party. I was so excited, I started to sing "Happy Birthday" and dance around—before it was "time." Everyone started to laugh. My sister said, "Don't be an idiot." My mother said, "You're making a spectacle of yourself in front of all these people." Then my sister and I got into a fight and my mother sent me to my room. I missed the rest of the party and felt ashamed to come out for the rest of the day. After that, I had trouble singing and speaking in public, though I'll admit that I was always somewhat nervous and shy as a child. I finally realized that my "performance anxiety" compounded by my fear of not being up to par with a task in front of both my mother and father was quite a setup. And to think that I had carried this in my body all those years. After my body finally offered up this information, my heart calmed down. I've never had another problem.

One of the notable parts of Elaine's story is the fact that the hormone changes of perimenopause uncovered her childhood shame patterns. And these patterns were uncovered in part through heart palpitations, a very common symptom that is the result of increased estrogen relative to progesterone. These same hormonal changes also affect the memory areas of the brain, uncovering information from the past that needs to be addressed and healed. The healing work a mother does at this stage can greatly improve a daughter's chances for breaking free from unhealthy patterns herself.

HARRIET: Shamed for Anger

Here is another example of how shame can get hardwired into a susceptible child's brain and body.

Harriet feels ashamed every time she gets angry, even when the anger is completely justified—for example, when a co-worker shows up late day after day, leaving Harriet to pick up the slack. She was never allowed to express her anger as a child—only her mother got to be angry! She learned that anger was a "bad" emotion. When she feels anger, she feels bad and thinks she is bad. Harriet's shame also spills over into how she feels about her own body. So when she feels bad for whatever reason, she also feels as though she's too fat, even though her weight is normal, or even low.

All women need to understand that anger is filled with energy and information that can mobilize us to make needed change. And that certainly beats the immobilizing emotions associated with helplessness, hopelessness, and depression. As one of my patients put it, "It took me a while, but I now embrace my anger, knowing that it is always a message from my inner guidance system telling me that something needs to change. And sometimes that change is simply my perception about how things should be!" The first step with anger is to allow yourself to feel it fully in a way that is harmless to yourself and others. Many times you'll need to remove yourself from the situation that is causing you anger, much like the child who is having a tantrum. With practice and intent, you'll be able to name both the prompting event and the underlying message for the anger and then make necessary changes in your life.

Obsessional Behaviors Are Shame Neutralizers

Obsessional behaviors such as excessive cleaning or obsessive thoughts of being too fat or too stupid often develop to cover up feelings of shame and anxiety. Obsessionality begins when the dorsolateral prefrontal brain area comes on board. It results when the two main areas of the frontal lobes are in opposition. It's like stepping on the brake and the gas at the same time. Obsessional thoughts or behaviors are strategies to repress our normal emotions and normal drives toward food, sexual pleasure, independence, or power and cover them over with repetitive behaviors or thoughts. People who are prone to compulsive or obsessional behavior or thoughts feel enhanced anxiety when they feel emotions that they are uncomfortable with. Sometimes, but not always, these are emotions they were shamed for in childhood.

FEELING YOUR SHAME: GETTING BEYOND IT

Step One: Acknowledge that shame is painful. The only way to get beyond it is to feel it and talk about it. Otherwise it can't be dissipated. Shame is perhaps the most painful emotion that we humans experience. That's because of the way shame is used to control our behavior. Instead of learning that our behavior is inappropriate in a given situation, we end up believing that something is inherently wrong with us. Most people will do anything rather than feel the pain of that. This is one of the reasons why addictive behavior is so common—it takes the edge off and makes us feel better temporarily.

Step Two: Address your addictions. The purpose of an addiction is to keep us out of touch with what we know and what we feel. And we wouldn't overuse addictive substances like alcohol and sugar, or addictive processes like work, exercise, or sex, unless we had painful feelings that we didn't want to feel. The problem is that when you continually use an addictive substance or process to cover up what you're really feeling, you can't identify your own needs in a healthy way. And if you can't do that, chances are pretty good that you won't be emotionally available for a relationship either. If you are in a close relationship with someone who uses drugs, cigarettes, alcohol, food, work, or sex addictively, you have to be very clear with yourself about why you are in a relationship with someone who isn't present for himself or herself. If you're the one with the addictions, you have to ask yourself whether or not you'd want to be in a relationship with someone like yourself.

Step Three: Release the myth of "terminal uniqueness." Many women stay locked in disabling cycles of shame and avoidance because they've been led to believe that they're the only ones with the problem. They are unique. No one could possibly understand how bad it is for them. Everyone else is "normal" except them. This is part of the "disease" of shame.

In fact, adverse childhood events that lead to adult shame and illness are remarkably common. Back in the early 1980s, I realized that every case of severe PMS I saw was in a woman who had come from an alcoholic home or was currently residing in one. Many others with chronic pelvic pain had been sexually abused. This sort of information was what prompted me to write *Women's Bodies, Women's Wisdom* in the first place. My original work was based on my observations in a small town in Maine. Since that time, I have found that women's experiences are the same the world over.

The huge 1998 ACE (Adverse Childhood Experiences) study conducted by the Kaiser Permanente Health Care Center in San Diego found that adverse childhood experiences are vastly more common than is recognized or acknowledged. Slightly more than half of the seventeen thousand middle-class, middle-aged study participants in the ACE study had grown up in dysfunctional alcoholic homes, homes with a depressed or mentally ill person, or homes in which they had experienced sexual, physical, or emotional abuse.[13]

You can't change the past, but you can definitely change the decisions you've made based on past experience. The past is not responsible for how you feel now. You can take steps to feel better. When you do this, you rewire your brain and body in ways that support health and well-being. It isn't the actual abuse or shaming that is so painful for the child. It is the meaning that the child ascribes to it that does the damage. For example, a child decides that she is inherently bad because she had been abused or beaten. Or she decides that she can't trust her instincts because the person she loves and depends upon is not trustworthy.

In the end, the only way to recover from these adverse events is to talk about them, get them "off your chest," and understand that we humans have the ability to heal from anything and everything—and that we are inherently worthy and lovable!

Insufficient Shame Also Uncouples the Mind-Body Connection

In contrast to the burden of unjustified shame, parents who are self-centered or disengaged may cause another kind of problem. If a child is allowed to go unchecked, if she does not learn that her behavior has consequences, she will not develop an adequate sense of healthy shame. Depending on the child's temperament, the result can be a child who is out of control in social settings, wreaks havoc in her environment, fails to learn how to have mutually satisfying relationships, or takes no responsibility for herself or her behavior.

I once had a patient who sat quietly in a chair and read while her three-year-old daughter trashed the surrounding exam room—pulling apart every tampon, overturning the trash can, taking all the freshly folded exam gowns from the drawer and flinging them all over the floor. By the time I entered the room, the place looked like a tornado had hit it. The child's mother never lifted a finger to restrain her child. Nor did she apologize to me or my staff for the mess her child had created. Instead, she made a comment about how much she encouraged her child to be expressive and free because "I never got to do that when I was a child." (Many baby boomer parents who grew up questioning authority of all kinds have let the pendulum swing very far in this direction.)

Children who don't internalize enough shame and morality do not learn to take responsibility for themselves or appropriately restrain their behavior. They may internalize an overinflated sense of self that is not tempered by humility. Paradoxically, these children are often very angry and demanding, even with all their so-called freedom. Such a daughter grows up as an entitled "princess," one who expects that others will clean up her messes, meet her needs, and keep her amused. She's a classic Queen Bee-in-training. She may become an unreliable adult who tends to be surrounded by others who pick up the slack for her.

SELF-LOVE VERSUS SELF-ABSORPTION: WHERE IS THE BOUNDARY?

All children are born both self-loving and self-absorbed. They also have an innate desire for the best that life has to offer. An example of this is the fact that nearly all young children who board a train or a plane are drawn to the first-class seats and want to sit there. They instinctively know that these seats feel better. These desires are a gift from the Divine and should be honored and cultivated as a critical part of a child's innate passion and purpose. When these desires are regularly shamed or dismissed—"Who do you think you are, the Queen of Sheba?"—a child's ability to appreciate and use her innate desires to create a healthy and prosperous life can be truncated as surely as a kitten's visual cortex can develop with the inability to see horizontal forms. The result could be a life of self-sacrifice for the perceived benefit of others, without ever making sure she herself is included in the "benefit" column. Self-sacrifice is a very real health risk that is especially common in girls and women. There is a balance, however.

The Birth of Unhealthy Narcissism

A child who is raised to believe that she is the center of the universe, that she is entitled to receive everything she wants and can do no wrong, may construct her sense of self very differently from someone who was raised with appropriate amounts of shame and self-restraint: she becomes a narcissist-in-training.

Narcissism gets its name from the Greek myth of Narcissus, who fell in love with his own reflection in the water and pined away when he could not embrace it. The sine qua non of unhealthy narcissism is an overinflated sense of self-love and self-worth coupled with the inability to recognize any flaws. It goes hand in hand with a lack of mutuality, or even curiosity about others. Other people exist only to mirror the narcissist back to herself.

Narcissists cannot accept criticism because they feel they must be "perfect," without any foundation for that belief. If they are criticized, they are crushed, because they feel either superior to others or terrible and worthless. And there's nothing in between.[14]

Excessive narcissism stems, in part, from the failure to accept one's humanity—both the flawed and limited parts as well as the good ones. Narcissists lack the ability to see when they are doing well and when they aren't measuring up. Not surprisingly, narcissistic personality traits are far more common in boys than girls, given our cultural history and preferences.

Do You Know a Narcissist?

Narcissists are particularly impervious to authentic shame. They control negative feedback from the outer world and think that they're "above it all." They are hypersensitive to criticism, but, ironically, very critical of others so as to maintain their "one-up" position, which is why they often appear arrogant and superior.[15] Their highest aspiration in life is to look better than others, thus keeping the attention on themselves and their needs.

As a result, narcissistic individuals feel intense anger if criticized when they do something that is insensitive or hurtful to another. But they can't admit their anger because that would make them look bad. If you tell them that they have hurt you, they will look angry— and then often deny it and insist they're hurt and ashamed instead. This shame isn't real, otherwise they'd show remorse by making an effort to change their hurtful behavior. But that almost never happens. Instead, they use pseudoshame or sometimes crocodile tears (a tactic generally, but not always, directed at the opposite gender) to make others feel sorry for them. This gets the heat off them and puts it back on the person who complained about the unskillful or hurtful behavior in the first place!

An empathetic person will be stopped dead in her tracks by this—because she's certain that the narcissist has the same depth of feeling and sense of responsibility that she does. This simply is not true. Although narcissistic people don't feel empathy in the same way as someone with normal bonding and shame circuits, they know how to use empathy to get their needs met at the expense of others. Their crocodile tears "act" is so skillful that others learn never to bring up the subject again.

What the person with normal empathy does is try to put themselves in the narcissist's position and imagine what and how they are feeling. The narcissistic person is actually a "blank screen" onto which a person with empathy projects how they themselves would feel. The empathetic person then makes excuses for the narcissist, assuming that their emotions run so deep and that they've been so deeply hurt that they simply can't go near that painful place within them. That must be why they don't want to talk about or change anything.

This is the story that those in a relationship with a narcissist always tell themselves. It becomes so uncomfortable and so unproductive to be around the emotional manipulation of a narcissist that most people never ask the narcissist to change his or her behavior again. They just go along. The following true story is an illustration of how this can play out.

NANCY: Lessons in Entitlement

Nancy was raised by her parents to be the golden girl, the special princess of the family. Her parents thought that the sun rose and set in her. She was always given the best of everything and was clearly favored over her younger sister, Sally. Nancy's Hispanic maternal grandparents had immigrated from Puerto Rico, and her mother, like many first-generation immigrants, had been raised to be ashamed of her background. Her people were known as greenhorns in the community where they lived. So when Nancy's mother married a white American man of Swedish ancestry, she felt as though she had "hit the jackpot." Things got even better when Nancy was born, because she had fair skin and blond hair. She looked "white." Her younger sister, Sally, on the other hand, looked just like the rest of her mother's family, olive-skinned with a prominent nose that matched her mother's.

Nancy was given everything—the latest shoes and dresses. Her younger sister got the bargain-basement stuff and hand-me-downs. While Sally worked hard in school and got straight A's, Nancy preferred to get by with doing as little work as possible. Though she was asked to do chores, she never did them, preferring to leave them to her sister, Sally, who had to do both her share and her sister's share as well.

During her childhood and adolescence, Nancy always expected her mother or father to bail her out of every tight spot in her life—and they obliged. After she learned to drive, for example, she frequently forgot to put gas in the car. She'd call her father in tears (crocodile tears) and he'd come and "rescue" her. Nancy moved out of the house when she got married. But she stayed close by her parents and still called on her father whenever she had a problem. Later when she had children, her mother frequently took care of them. When they were little, Nancy still put her own needs first. For example, she often slept late on weekends, neglecting to give her children breakfast. When her mother arrived to help out on Saturdays, she'd often find Nancy and her husband still in bed at 11:00 A.M. Meanwhile, the baby would have crawled out of her crib and up the stairs to try to get her parents to feed her.

Although she started out with low self-esteem, Nancy's sister, Sally, compensated by excelling at school. She became very self-reliant at an early age. While her sister felt entitled to everything, Sally was the opposite. She worked for everything that she got. By the time both sisters reached midlife, their paths had widely diverged. Sally had had a lot of therapy and had recovered from the excessive shame that had marked her childhood. She was now a full professor at an Ivy League college, adored her highly creative work, had published widely, and enjoyed her students, her home, and her prosperous life. Her sister, on the other hand, had gone through two divorces, looked far older than her age, and had two grown children who no longer wanted to visit home. Her truncated life still revolved around her parents.

Making sure a child internalizes an appropriate and healthy amount of shame—and also learns how to truly contribute to society and family—is the best way to prevent this disorder later in life.

The Tragedy of Narcissism

Narcissists do not have the ability to care for or "mother" others. This causes enormous suffering in those around them—the ones who pick up the "mothering slack." If a mother is narcissistic, her daughter may well end up mothering her—and may also marry a narcissistic husband whom she must also "mother." If a daughter is narcissistic, chances are good that she will end up overtaxing her mother's empathy and resources—monetary and otherwise—for a lifetime. Sometimes, both mother and daughter are narcissistic, and live in their own isolated little world of entitlement.

On some level, narcissists are truly tragic individuals who teach the rest of us that if we are to find the truth, we have to look beyond appearances. Though they may have a few decades of glory depending upon how good they look, most narcissistic individuals do not age well because their values are only skin-deep. In fact, they tend to fall off the growth curve relatively soon—high school or college. This is because the outer world of work and achievement never grants anyone exclusive status unless they earn it. Because of their inner emptiness and neediness, narcissists never feel the genuine warmth of true partnership with another, or the sense of accomplishment that comes from knowing that you did a job well, even if no one was looking! In the end, we always sow what we reap. And the sooner a child learns this, the happier and more content she'll be.

The Shame Donor/Shame Recipient Syndrome

Many families have narcissistic members who maintain their superior status by shaming others. Sometimes this shaming is very subtle and sometimes it's obvious. Either way, an empathetic child or adult will feel its effects. Because of their overinflated sense of self-esteem, narcissists don't feel shame themselves but know that others do. They are often extremely skillful at sensing another's emotional Achilles' heel, so their shaming hits a vulnerable target. They see the paralyzing effect that shaming has on others. They maintain their superior status by making others shame "recipients" who are kept in their place by being made to feel bad. This maintains their narcissistic position of being one-up. I think of these narcissistic individuals as shame "donors." They "donate" the shame that they ought to feel (but don't) to others who feel it acutely. These are the "shame recipients."

In my own extended family, one of the shame donors was an aunt who regularly put people down in a critical, smug way. When I was about five years old my older brother, who was seven, gave a rabbit's-foot key chain to our grandmother for her birthday. I recall the intense shame I felt when this aunt—who was a pediatrician, no less—ridiculed him for giving what she considered a foolish gift.

His self-esteem plummeted right in front of my eyes. His face fell and his shoulders dropped. Only moments before, he had happily anticipated the joy he would feel at giving his grandmother this treasure. Now he felt bad about his gift and, ultimately, bad about himself. My brother's shame had become contagious. And I "caught" it just by watching this scenario. Gift giving suddenly became an occasion for anxiety. It's difficult to give in a joyful, uninhibited way when you're worried that your gift, or yourself, will be judged as stupid.

How Shame Is Passed Down in Families

There are generations of people who come from overcontrolled, repressed families who use shame to control others. They maintain tight control of everything, from money to emotions such as joy and happiness. This behavior and brain style gets passed on from one generation to the next. Individuals from these families are often afraid of spontaneity and full emotional expression (unless assisted by alcohol) because these qualities are equated with being out of control.

These "shame donors" are most comfortable setting up rules to control the emotions, thoughts, and behavior of others. They tend to be rigid and overly moralistic and are often very staid, upstanding citizens. Their only connection with their emotions is an occasional foray into anger or crocodile tears to get attention directed back to them. They also tend to be over-intellectual and, quite literally, disconnected from their bodies and their orbitofrontal and intuitive areas. Chances are they have never developed a healthy dialogue between the two parts of their brains that is necessary for maximal adaptability. Consequently they have difficulty with the three skills necessary for fulfilling relationships: identifying their own needs, balancing these needs with those of someone else, and recognizing the needs of the relationship as a whole.

Individuals from such families admonish their children to "keep their voices down" and not "laugh so much." Unfortunately, excessive emotional control also shuts down a child's capacity to feel all emotions fully, which can be a setup for depression.[16] I witnessed the following scene from a "shame-donating" mother during one of my daughter's tennis matches when she was in junior high school. I'll never forget it.

SARAH: The Tennis Court Shaming

One of my daughter's teammates was finishing up a tennis game against a competitor from another school. Her mother drove up and walked briskly over to where her daughter was engaged in a match competition, clearly enjoying herself. Her mother rolled in looking angry and impatient and went right up to the fence and yelled, "Sarah, we have to go now. And I mean *now*." She wouldn't wait until her daughter had finished the game. And she was not about to be talked out of her need to have her daughter leave the court immediately. Instead, her shaming behavior stopped the game dead in its tracks.

Sarah, obviously shamed in front of her entire team and all her peers, hung her head and left the courts with her mother. Her mother's behavior said it all. "You shouldn't be doing this right now. We've got to go and you should have known better." Apparently the mother had arranged some kind of doctor's appointment for her daughter that they needed to go to. I do not know the details. What I do know is that this mother's shaming behavior was so intense that every one of us who was watching that day felt it intensely and will never forget how it made us feel.

When a woman from a "shame donor" family has a child of her own, that child will one day come running up to her very excited about finding a bug, a new toy, or even, heaven forbid, discovering that it feels good to touch certain parts of her body. The mother's job is to acknowledge the child's joy of discovery and then redirect her behavior as appropriate. But if the mother meets her child's excitement and discovery with disapproval or with her own discomfort or shame, then the child registers that there is something wrong or bad about what she is doing or feeling. And the vicious cycle of shame continues.

If this kind of shaming occurs regularly, the child may eventually feel as though she herself is bad or dirty, and will learn to distrust her natural instincts and feelings. This is a setup for addictions of all kinds. What's more, she is very likely to attract an abusive, narcissistic mate who treats her in the same way as her shaming mother did. She's also at increased risk for raising a daughter (or a son) who treats her poorly. Regardless of her inherent gifts and talents, she may have great difficulty discovering her unique passion and purpose for two reasons: 1) she's likely to suffer from health problems and addictions that serve to keep her out of touch with the pain of feeling bad about herself, and 2) her addictions and health problems will serve to further remove her from her feelings and inner guidance about what is right for her.

If you have a shame-donating, self-centered mother whose attention and love you're still trying to win, you are more apt to raise a child who is also self-centered and who you will also try to please. If this isn't recognized early on, you may find yourself sandwiched between the needs of both your mother and your daughter!

HOW TO SPOT OVERLY NARCISSISTIC INDIVIDUALS (SHAME DONORS)

~ Very little modesty; will often run around the house naked. Or they may have naked pictures of themselves openly displayed in the house.

~ Appear very independent but have difficulty being alone. Must always be surrounded by family or adoring "mirror holders." Noting the fact that these individuals are the opposite of martyrs, neuropsychiatrist Mona Lisa Schulz quips, "These individuals have homes with a very high mirror-to-crucifix ratio."

~ Have few or no real friends because they lack mutuality in relationships. Main relationships will be with family members or employees who "have" to be with them. They won't admit this—ever.

~ Will often participate in activities that make them look like heroes, such as athletics, climbing, swimming in cold bodies of water, or hiking mountains.

~ Will almost always be in a relationship with someone who doesn't look as good as they do. But the person who doesn't look as good will actually be very reliable and very skilled. She (or he) will be the "wizard behind the screen" who is always pumping up the self-esteem of the one who looks good.

~ Motivation for giving to others or to causes is always to look good.

~ Usually stingy with gifts, tips, and praise. Very comfortable letting others pay for them.

How to Spot Overly Empathetic Individuals (Shame Recipients)

~ Always give everyone the benefit of the doubt.

~ Want to be liked so desperately that they allow others to use their goodwill.

~ Are willing to accept responsibility for the unskillful behavior of others rather than face life without their "love."

~ Often grew up in a family in which a narcissistic individual had more power to control than did other family members.

~ Have difficulty keeping weight off.

~ Quickly reimburse others who have paid for them. Uncomfortable when others pay for them.

~ Have lots of close friends; are "universal donors" of friendship and empathy.

~ Tend to go into the "helping" professions such as psychology, nursing, social work.

~ Go overboard in the gift-giving department.

~ Carry more than their share of the responsibility for the outcome of situations.

MARIAN: The Relationship Dance between Shame Donors and Shame Recipients

The following story is an example of how shame donors and shame recipients tend to relate to one another in love relationships later in life. This imbalance often results in health problems suffered by the shame recipients.

It's Friday afternoon, and Marian and her boyfriend have a date. He is picking her up at work and they plan on a romantic dinner for two at their favorite restaurant. He has already made the reservations and is looking forward to turning over a new leaf, following their altercation the week before. He arrives at the office building at the appointed time of 6:00 P.M. with flowers in the back-seat. Marian is late again—this time by fifteen minutes. But she shows no signs of remorse. She swoops out of the building and says in a cold, defensive tone, "I'm sorry, but I had an important conversation I had to finish." Met with his girlfriend's dismissive tone, her boyfriend swallows his annoyance, though his body recoils with irritation. But he doesn't dare bring it up again because her tone communicates that he shouldn't. And he doesn't want the evening to be spoiled. So he tells himself, "Well, at least she apologized . . . sort of . . . this time."

Once Marian gets into the car, her face lights up perceptibly, and in an animated voice she turns to her boyfriend, and says, "Oh, by the way, how was your day, anyway?" He's about to open his mouth to respond when she cuts him off, and tells him, "Oh, I forgot to tell you, the people at the office are having a cocktail party right now and I think it's important that we be there. It might increase my chances of getting that promotion I want." Marian looks at her boyfriend, and says matter-of-factly, "I told them I'd come, and I assumed that you wouldn't mind coming along. . . ." Her voice trails off as she ends the discussion abruptly and starts to fidget in her purse, looking for her lipstick. Marian's nonverbal activity with her purse signals to her boyfriend that she is finished with the communication and not really interested in his response. Her boyfriend, after a long uncomfortable silence, clears his throat nervously, and says in a quavering voice, "I would have—uh, uh—appreciated it if you had asked my input before accepting that cocktail party invitation. It took me a long time to get our dinner reservation and I was really looking forward to a special evening after our last argument." He hesitates and says, "I'm kind of upset about it. Do you know what I mean?" Marian shoots him a cold, angry look, and after another long silence, says, "I just asked for your input and I've been really busy lately. A lot of stuff has been coming at me. All you're thinking about is your feelings. You're not thinking about my needs at all, just your own feelings."

Marian's body language and speech patterns lack empathy for her boyfriend. She is a shame donor. Her boyfriend's stammering speech and throat clearing are indications that he is the shame recipient in this situation. If they go on to marry, this pattern may be passed down to another generation.

HOW TO DEAL WITH A SELF-CENTERED MOTHER

Women who have mothers who were disengaged or self-centered may be left with a legacy of self-doubt that they try to repair for their entire lives. The following steps will help you recover from this legacy more quickly, and avoid passing it on to your own daughter.

Acknowledge that you can't make things right for your mother (or your daughter). No matter how hard you try, you do not have the power to make her happy or content. So the best thing to do is stop knocking yourself out trying. One of my patients told me:

> You can't do right by my mother. She rarely appears pleased or truly happy. When I was growing up, she was angry whether or not I tried to please her. It didn't seem to make any difference. Over time, I realized that my values didn't fit in with hers. And I finally realized that whether or not I went along with her "program," she didn't approve of my life and my choices. My life and my health started to improve greatly when I finally realized that the only choice I had was to be happy with who I was and stop trying to please her!

Practice radical acceptance. On some level, it doesn't matter who your mother was or is. She is the only mother you've got. One of my patients told me:

> My mother hated me. She never wanted me. She even told me that I was the reason she never had the career she wanted. Now that I'm an adult and I've done a lot of work on myself, I've come to the conclusion that in the end, it doesn't matter! The way I think of it is this: I just used my mother's uterus to get here. My childhood was pure hell. But now my life is pure joy. I no longer waste any time wishing my mother were different. But I severely limit my visits with her and don't allow her much space in my life. If I did, she'd engulf me. And I'd get sick.

Value yourself as much as you value your mother and her opinions. If you have a mother who is difficult and controlling, it is very possible that you're the kind of woman who knocks herself out to be pleasing to others. You doubt your inherent worth so you spend a lifetime trying to prove to others that you're worthy. This pattern stops only when you start affirming your own worth and believing it!

Stop the legacy. Women whose mothers were difficult or impossible to please often have daughters who are eerily like their maternal grandmothers. If this pattern is not stopped, a narcissistic daughter may take advantage of her mother for a lifetime.

My patient Helga had a very difficult mother who was smitten with Helga's father but never really there for her children. Helga has suffered from various autoimmune illnesses for most of her adult life. She has a nine-year-old daughter named Ingrid who has always been given everything that Helga didn't get as a child. Unfortunately, Ingrid treats her mother very poorly, is demanding, and has few friends. Ingrid is very much like Helga's own mother. And Helga now realizes that she has to do something about this or the situation will get worse. Helga wants to go back to graduate school but has been afraid of leaving Ingrid.

The solution is clear: Helga needs to enroll in graduate school, assign a regular schedule of chores at the house, and create more expectations for her daughter. She will also, of course, have to deal head-on with her fear of losing her daughter's love. Bottom line: You will never lose your daughter's love by providing her with guidelines and discipline. If you don't provide such things, she will lose respect for you. And ultimately, you will lose respect for yourself.

The game stops only when you learn how to feel good about yourself and start valuing your time and energy enough to stop throwing it into the abyss of the self-centered individual, whether that be your mother or your daughter.

Release your guilt. The overempathetic individual is easily manipulated by guilt. She lives in fear of being called selfish or uncaring. She worries that if she stops donating to her mother or daughter, they will talk badly about her. They will, but the truth always wins—you must know that you have the strength to handle whatever happens.

8

Mouth and Gut Wisdom

The Roots of Self-care

EXPERIENCING THE WORLD
THROUGH THE MOUTH

How a child is fed and soothed creates her core beliefs about whether or not there is enough of everything she needs and whether or not she will be provided for. This is one of the most important ways in which a child internalizes the feeling of safety and security that is so crucial for healthy immune-system function.

A child's first and most persistent way of soothing herself is by sucking. It is also the primary way in which she experiences the world, which is why a young child will always put things in her mouth. It is well documented that babies sometimes suck their thumbs while they are still inside their mother's womb! Food is not only necessary for physical survival but is also a powerful source of comfort. A child's need to suck and experience oral pleasure is primal and even in adults, it never truly goes away. As my father, who was a dentist, used to say, "The mouth is the center of the personality."

A child's oral needs are met, in part, by both the quality and quantity of the food that she is given. But *how* she is fed is even more important. When a child's mother gazes lovingly at her while feeding her, the child wires in healthy connections between the orbitofrontal brain area and her stomach, bowel, and heart. She learns to feel good about herself and her physical needs. Emotional nourishment and physical nourishment are one and the same at this age.

Prolonged separations between mother and child, or caregivers who are disengaged from the child, can result in faulty connections in these same areas. If you are a cat lover, you know that kittens that are prematurely separated from their mothers often develop an alternative and very destructive way to get their oral needs met: they suck on and chew wool, fabric, plastic, or other household items. They may even suck their own fur to the point of creating bald spots.[1] All mammals need to suck. (My sister-in-law recently nurtured back to health a miniature horse that was born prematurely and had to be separated from her mother. The adorable little thing chews gravel to get her oral needs met.) In the same way, a human infant who does not get her oral needs met during infancy will continue to revisit this area in an attempt to re-create a crucial developmental step. The human equivalent of a cat sucking wool includes smoking cigarettes, pipes, or cigars, biting fingernails, sucking one's thumb after early childhood, overeating, substance abuse, sexual addiction, and alcohol addiction—just to name the most common ones. Interestingly, in cats as well as humans, drugs that increase serotonin levels in the brain and thus enhance mood are sometimes used to successfully treat these sucking disorders. In cats, giving crunchy dried food also helps, just as, in humans, eating a whole-food diet with enough variety helps meet oral needs.

MONICA'S PHOTOS

A mother's behavior with her daughter—in feeding and every other area—encodes behavior patterns in the brain, organs, and muscles of her child's body. I vividly recall a series of photographs in one of my medical school textbooks that demonstrated this point. A baby named Monica was born with a congenital anomaly that required her to be tube-fed. A photo showed Monica's mother tube-feeding her. The next photo showed Monica, now a mother, with her own child. She is holding the child away from her body—as though the bottle were the tube that she herself was fed through. The text explained that Monica never held the child close to her body while feeding her, even though her husband and other caregivers held the baby in the normal way.

Providing Motherly Comfort

One of the reasons I breast-fed my daughters until they were two, despite the hours I spent at the hospital, was that breast-feeding was the one thing that only I could do for them. They couldn't get this kind of nourishment or mothering from anyone else. I gave them NUK-brand pacifiers, which are physiologically designed to ensure healthy jaw development. Both of them gave up the pacifier by the age of three or so, and neither one ever sucked her thumb, though it wouldn't have bothered me if they had. (They were breast-fed long enough and often enough to prevent any possible adverse jaw and mouth development from thumb sucking.) I also gave them soy milk, goat's milk, or watered-down juice in bottles as long as they wanted it. Though I don't recall exactly when we stopped tripping over bottles in my house, I do know that I had no agenda whatsoever about the age at which children "should" stop using a bottle. My philosophy was this: young children need to suck on things—that's how they were designed to take in nourishment and love at the same time. If they don't get their needs for love and sucking met in childhood, they're more apt to get those oral needs met in adulthood through smoking, sex, food, and alcohol. I'd rather help a child get her oral needs met through using a bottle or a pacifier or prolonged breast-feeding than increase her risk for unhealthy behavior later.

I'm always amazed at how afraid many of the World War II generation are of "spoiling" children, simply by allowing them the emotional comfort of sucking their thumbs or sleeping with a special blanket. One of my friends with young children recently e-mailed me about the pressure she was getting from her parents:

> My parents think it's horrible that I let my kids keep their baby blankets and feel I should have forced them to give them up by now. My feeling is that they'll give 'em up when they're ready, and since this is the worst habit they've got, they're still just perfect. Sometimes I tell my mom and dad that they already had their chance to screw up their own kids, it's my turn now. Not surprisingly, that goes over like a pregnant pole-vaulter— not too well. My children never have nightmares. I think my daughter has had three in her whole life, and I don't think my sons have ever had them.

I agree with my friend. Anything that gives a child comfort and doesn't harm either her or her parents is worthwhile. My daughters often slept with me on and off during their childhood, especially when their father was on call or out of town. (Though in fact he was a very sound sleeper and having the children in our room never bothered him.) When they were beyond the crib stage, we kept a futon under our bed and dragged it out whenever the girls wanted to come in—whether because there was a thunderstorm or they were just feeling insecure. They gradually outgrew this behavior. And then I missed it!

The most secure and fearless children are, by and large, the ones who were allowed to develop their inner core of strength gradually over time. They're not the ones who had their bottles or blankets snatched from them prematurely in a misguided attempt to "toughen them up."

Of course, in many cases, grandparents of the World War II generation are simply passing on their own childhood legacies. One of my newsletter subscribers, a seventy-five-year-old woman, wrote me the following amazing story about the kind of tactics once used to wean children. It powerfully illustrates the seamless connection between our emotions, our oral needs, and our bodily health.

> My mother had a little story about my weaning that she used to tell in quite an offhand joking manner. I've repeated the story to friends and received wide-eyed looks of amazement. So it has set me to thinking that perhaps what she did back then might have had something to do with my own actions when I became an adult.
>
> My mother said that she nursed me until I was about four years old and began embarrassing her in company by climbing up on her lap and proceeding to unbutton her dress. Try as she might to teach me to drink from a cup, I was absolutely adamant and insisted on breast-feeding only. Finally in desperation, she painted her bare breasts with stove blacking. (This was back in the days when folks used woodstoves.) When I was presented with the smelly, greasy, black bosom, I began crying. She claims that I screamed my way through three days without milk before giving up and allowing her to feed me from a cup.
>
> This story became a family anecdote. I'm sure that I didn't resent her for her action, which, of course, I didn't remember. I may have even thought that I was an especially feisty and spirited child. But by the time I was eighteen, I had developed large, hard, and painful breasts which were full of cysts and mastitis.

On my rather thin frame, I had to have brassieres altered to fit size 34D because back in the '40s and '50s, that size wasn't produced. I was too shy to mention my problem to a doctor. I simply didn't want anyone to touch them. When I married, I had to tell my husband about my discomfort and he, being the kindest of all husbands, was understanding.

My first child arrived three years later and the doctor informed me that my nipples were inverted and nursing could cause infections. I was, of course, delighted to have a legitimate excuse to avoid having the baby touch my sensitive breasts. We went on to have five children and nearly as many doctors since we moved around the country. They were all happy to relieve my anxiety about breast-feeding. Now, too late, I know better. My children missed out and so did I. I don't really blame my mother for giving me "breast phobia," but it's something to think about, isn't it. By the way, my mastitis disappeared after my first child and I happily went down to a 34B, but my nipples remain inverted.

In this case, the writer's childhood legacy was complicated by her doctors' misinformation. In fact, inverted nipples can be everted easily by wearing special nipple shields in one's bra during the last couple of months of pregnancy. Nursing itself also everts nipples.

FEEDING YOUR CHILD:
THE IDEAL VERSUS THE REALITY

It's too bad that a primal comfort like food has become one of our most obsessive anxieties. Of course, maybe that's why it causes so much anxiety! If we think we can't get what we need, we go into full survival mode. Throughout my career, I've been asked more questions about nutrition than about any other topic. Health-conscious mothers sometimes become frantic about this issue, particularly when their child hits the conservative won't-try-anything-new stage at about age two. You can fill up your shelves with books about what a child should be fed and when, but then you still have to face the gap between the ideal and what your child is actually willing to eat.

Feeding a child doesn't need to be complicated. Breast-feed for as long as possible (at least a year) and hold off on solid food for at least four months (preferably six months). This prevents the introduction of food allergens that the child's developing GI system is not yet ready to assimilate, and it has been shown to reduce the risk of later allergies and ear infections. Studies are increasingly showing that introducing foods such as cereal grains before the age of three months, can, in genetically susceptible individuals, increase the chances of developing type 1, or juvenile-onset, diabetes. This may also be true for cow's milk, which is known to cause allergies if introduced before the child is a year old.[2]

When you do introduce solids, use whole natural food that is organically grown whenever possible.

HOW TO HELP YOUR DAUGHTER DEVELOP A HEALTHY RELATIONSHIP WITH FOOD

~ Allow your child to meet her oral needs in her own way and her own time. Remember that you can't spoil a baby who is younger than a year.

~ Breast-feed exclusively with no solid foods until four to six months.

~ Cuddle your baby regularly without offering food. If you feed your baby every time she signals that she is distressed, you are programming her to eat in order to soothe emotional needs, whether or not she needs the food energy.

~ Allow your daughter to expend energy and calories by encouraging freedom of movement instead of restricting her in carriers, infant seats, or close-fitting clothes. (Swaddling for comfort is usually unnecessary after about three months.) For the older infant, encourage playing and crawling and minimize sitting.

~ Incorporate regular touch and hugs into daily life. Let your children sleep with you when they want to.

~ Acknowledge your own need for nurture and learn how to soothe yourself in healthy ways so your child can model her behavior after yours.

~ Assume that your daughter understands what you are saying, even if she can't talk yet. Know that a child is exquisitely sensitive to the emotions behind words.

A Whole Foods Legacy

My parents were years ahead of their time. We were brought up on the whole food advice of Adelle Davis, who wrote *Let's Eat Right to Keep Fit*. My mother made yogurt and whole wheat bread, and our orange juice was spiked with extra vitamin C. So it seemed natural for me to raise my own children on whole foods, including brown rice, lots of vegetables, tofu, miso soup, and some fish. When they were really little, I just bought a Happy Baby food grinder and ground up whatever food my husband and I were eating at the time. I never bought prepared baby food. There was no need.

We followed a macrobiotic, mostly vegetarian diet until the children were about four and six years old. We didn't drink milk or eat cheese, but my daughters did drink soy milk. I gave them daily multivitamins, which I believe all children should have. No matter how hard a mother tries, it's just not possible to get your child (or yourself) to eat optimally every day. Giving a comprehensive multivitamin and mineral supplement helps mothers relax, especially on those days when a toddler won't eat more than a few crackers! (See Resources.) My children were almost never sick.

In retrospect, I believe that we ate too much grain and bread back then, and when the girls were in their early teens, our diet changed to one that was higher in animal protein, but still rich in fruits and vegetables. It has been demonstrated that in some individuals, eating cereal grains actually increases insulin resistance over time and contributes to obesity. I certainly found myself putting on weight by my late thirties from my grain-based diet. (I will have much more to say about this issue in Chapter 13, where I discuss the crucial topic of insulin resistance.)

You want your child to have a whole foods diet, but you should avoid power struggles over food, if at all possible. Remember, the emphasis here is on self-care—the child has to learn to become self-regulating around food. I once watched a macrobiotic mother wrestle her child to the ground because he was trying to pick up a piece of wrapped candy from the sidewalk. A kid is going to go for the bright colors of candy and bubble gum and also the sugary flavor. They love this stuff. The key is to keep it really limited. Where you draw the line is up to you. (I'd certainly nix the fourteen-ounce blue Slurpee I recently saw a little kid drinking, a "treat" loaded with chemicals and sugar.) But they won't be harmed by the occasional french fry or chicken tender. If a kid is cut off from normal life, including the junk foods of their culture, their bodies do not learn how to process an occasional toxin. They get sick when they encounter them.

Even when we were macrobiotic, my children went to birthday parties and ate the food that was served. (And in the beginning, they *did* get fevers and runny noses afterward.) I admit, when my youngest first went to a birthday party at McDonald's and came home and announced that she'd had a hamburger, I got upset with her. She cried. I soon realized that I could not erect a wall to protect her from the "real world." I apologized and never did it again. I knew that if I continued to put myself in the position of "food police," I'd eventually have a daughter with an eating disorder!

And because we ate a healthy dinner together on weeknights and also packed healthy school lunches (which I knew they sometimes traded in for junk), I finally relaxed. I began to see fast food as a sort of condiment—one I never brought into the house. When we went out to eat on weekends, my children ate their share of chicken fingers. But I figured that they would eventually associate the healthy and delicious foods they ate at their own dinner table with home and comfort. And that is exactly what has happened. To this day, when my daughters go into a vegetarian restaurant, the brown rice, vegetables, and miso soup bring back childhood memories of home. Believe it or not, the human body is designed for healthy foods. Over time, that's what we begin to crave.

I, like many mothers before me, had to learn how to keep food in perspective. Yes, it's important. But it doesn't have the power to make or break a child's health all by itself. The way in which a food is digested is also affected by who cooked it, how it was served, and what kind of beliefs and emotions surround it. In the end, family emotional dynamics are far more important to a child's health than food quality. Too many mothers focus on food (something they can control) as a way to avoid emotions and circumstances over which they have no control. Bottom line: a child will be far healthier eating canned spaghetti and meatballs served in a loving and harmonious atmosphere than she ever will eating 100 percent organically grown vegetables and tofu in an alcoholic household!

EATING FOR COMFORT

Comfort foods are the ones we eat when we are lonely or feel empty. They tend to be the foods we remember from our childhoods such as macaroni and cheese and mashed potatoes. When a woman is told she shouldn't eat these foods for health reasons, she may become irrational. One of my friends recently told me that she couldn't eat beans because they contained "too many carbohydrates." But the day before that, she had had no qualms about eating a piece of cheesecake, a piece of French bread, and a plate of pasta all at the same sitting! When a mutual friend asked her why she doesn't eat more fruits and vegetables, she said, "My stomach can't handle it." Whenever you encounter this level of rationalization you can be sure that you are dealing with beliefs and feelings that stem from our preverbal days before the age of two when our bonding with our mothers was the most intense.

WHEN FOOD IS LOVE

The bond between a woman and her food supply is rooted in the bond between a healthy mother and her child. That's why, despite study after study on what constitutes a healthy diet, modern science and medicine have utterly failed to change people's attachment to what they put in their mouths. Take the maternal influence on smoking, for instance. It is well documented that children whose mothers smoke have an increased risk for smoking during adolescence.[3] Recent research has found that the breast milk of mothers who smoke also tastes and smells like cigarettes. The changes in the odor of the milk parallel the changing concentrations of nicotine in it. We already know that exposing a developing baby's brain to nicotine increases the risk for later addiction. Now we know that in addition to this, early experiences with the flavor of tobacco in breast milk and even amniotic fluid can influence the likelihood that exposed children will find these flavors appealing in later life. This doesn't mean that women who smoke occasionally should stop nursing. But knowing how this habit affects the flavor and smell of breast milk is an additional reason to avoid the habit in the first place.[4]

MARIA: A Lifelong Struggle with Obesity and Addiction

Maria's grandmother was mentally ill with schizophrenia. She married several different times, but her marriages never lasted. As a result of this instability and her own temperament, Maria's mother, Sophia, never developed a healthy relationship with either food or cooking. Maria told me that her mother was an awful cook, resorting mostly to boxed or canned foods as the staple meals in her house. A can of creamed corn was often used to feed a family of five, even though money was not an issue. The only meal that the family consistently ate together was pasta on some Sundays with homemade sauce, the one food Sophia had mastered. Sophia also spent a great deal of time driving to and from the mental institution where her own mother was often in residence. So there was no nurturing presence in the kitchen.

Because neither Sophia nor her daughter, Maria, had grown up with the pleasures and comforts of a good home-cooked meal prepared by a loving caregiver, each of them inherited a nurturance pothole around food and emotional nourishment. Maria never felt fully seen and nurtured by a loving presence during her oral stage of development, she found herself continually drawn to food, drink, and smoking as a substitute. By early adulthood, her weight had ballooned, and though she often lost twenty to thirty pounds by dieting, she invariably gained it back. She also smoked, and she sometimes worried that she was drinking too much.

As the regional manager of a cosmetics company, Maria was an efficient, skilled, and disciplined professional. She rarely ate during the day, but at night, when she went home, her emotional oral needs took over. She felt compelled to have a beer or two (to relax) and then ate a major meal that always contained hearty portions of bread or pasta. These carbohydrate-rich foods are noted for their ability to increase brain levels of serotonin and therefore alter one's mood, so they are comfort foods par excellence. And interestingly, these meals were always prepared by her partner, a person who functioned in a motherly way in the household by taking care of the shopping, cooking, and cleaning.

After a particularly grueling series of corporate reorganizations in her business, Maria developed heartburn and an ulcer. Her gastroenterologist told her that the only way for her to cure her problem permanently was to stop smoking, drinking, and also to eat regular meals. Though she was able to stop smoking over a period of a year or two, and limited her drinking to the weekends, she actually gained more weight. But her ulcer at least helped her eat a somewhat healthier diet.

Maria's health and weight didn't change permanently, however, until her mother, Sophia, was diagnosed with breast cancer. At this time, Maria became so fearful and distraught about losing her mother or getting sick herself that she entered therapy and also became a member of Overeaters Anonymous, where she learned how to follow a healthy diet.

The last time I saw Maria she was losing weight and looking healthier than ever. She told me:

> It finally dawned on me that my addiction to pasta, bread, and other carbohydrates was a substitute for my need for a nurturing mother who would feed me and adore me. I know intellectually that my own mother couldn't give me what she herself never got. So, in a way, I appreciate how my cravings go back over several generations. I've stopped beating myself up for having them.
>
> When I finally allowed my cravings to speak to me and tell me what I really needed, I discovered that when I came home each night, I felt anxious and empty. I used food and alcohol to fill this void within me. Finally, instead of medicating it, I allowed myself to begin feeling this emptiness. It wasn't easy at first, but gradually, little by little, it's going away. I also got myself on a healthy diet to balance my brain chemistry.
>
> There may always be a part of me that will feel empty from time to time. But now I also know that I don't need to feed that emptiness inside with oily pasta, I just need to get a back rub, a hug, or go for a walk. And I also need to turn my inner emptiness over to my own Higher Power. The feeling always goes away when I do this and also take care of myself. I now feel as though I can be my own mother, and I feed my heart regularly, as well as my stomach.

Maria's story illustrates the trap of filling nurturance potholes with comfort foods and other addictive substances. These quick "hits" make us feel better temporarily. But over time, as we become habituated to them without addressing our core issues, we require more and more of them to get the same result. What we're really looking for is a sense of self-worth, self-esteem, and self-nurturance that can only come from within.

Our Cultural Legacy: Unmet Oral Needs Are Epidemic

Though the details of Maria's history are unique to her, her problem is very common. Nurturance potholes from early childhood are the real reason why I'm asked so many questions about diet. And no matter what dietary topic I write or speak about, whether it be dairy food allergies or the fact that some people need more protein than others, and no matter how much science supports what I'm saying, the responses I receive often border on fanaticism. For example, a woman wrote, "I can't believe that dairy food could ever harm anyone. Where do you get your information? It seems to me that if milk could cause problems, I'd have heard about it by now from the Dairy Council!" Another told me how grossly misguided I was to suggest that some individuals did better with some meat in their diet. Still others are certain that soy foods are causing everything from cancer to premature puberty.

The vehemence of opinions about specific food dos and don'ts and the shaming way in which the information is delivered also point up another problem: too many women feel ashamed for having an appetite! By the time most girls are six or seven years old, they've already received adverse messages about what they should or should not be eating. I remember once visiting a woman who had adopted a baby girl. This woman's husband, like many men, constantly criticized his wife about her weight and her eating. He wanted to make sure she never gained a pound. So, like many women, she hid chocolate and ate secretly when he wasn't around. When their adopted daughter was about two, and displayed a healthy appetite, they both made fun of her for "eating like a redneck"!

Many mothers (or fathers) say to their daughters disapprovingly, "I see that you're eating again." Enough of this kind of shaming, and she'll wire in the feeling that her desire to eat makes her a bad person. How many women do you know who approach the dessert tray with the statement "I'm going to be a bad girl now and eat this pie"?

The Real Nourishment We're All Longing For

When a woman wants to know what to eat, she's really asking for the ideal diet plan that will take care of all her emotional and physical needs and guarantee that she'll be safe and healthy as a result—if she follows this diet to the letter. Such a plan doesn't exist and never will. The only "diet" that even comes close to meeting these requirements is breast milk that is provided by a loving, will-ing, and well-nourished mother. But even breast milk composition changes from day to day according to the needs of the baby and the condition of her mother!

What we're all really looking for is the mother that few, if any, of us ever had: a superhuman being with two ever-full breasts who is al-ways there for us, meeting our every need and gazing into our eyes with pure, unadulterated love, a being so powerful that she can pro-tect us from all the inevitable discomforts and challenges of life, and soothe all our feelings of self-doubt, self-criticism, and self-blame. There's no such being. And the sooner we learn how to nurture ourselves, the better we'll be at being realistic role models for our daughters.

THE WEIGHT-HEALTH CONNECTION: HOW AND WHEN OBESITY DEVELOPS

Many women alternate between worrying that their child is not eating enough to support life and worrying that she is going to get fat. This concern is understandable given that research has shown that the "set point" for body size and weight is heavily influenced by what happens in our early years. It's now alarmingly clear, for exam-ple, that once established, childhood obesity often becomes chronic and resistant to treatment.

On the other hand, children need enough of the right kinds of foods to support the growth and development of their organs, in-cluding the density of their bones and the health of their brains. The nutritional focus during the early years should be on preventing fu-ture problems by providing healthy food choices and modeling healthy behavior around food. Once this is done, weight will usually take care of itself over time.

The Challenge of Our Fast-Food Nation

In general, if a child is breast-fed for at least a year and is then presented with lots of whole food choices, her innate wisdom will choose the foods her body needs. But here's the problem: Our food supply has been altered in order to influence the appetite centers in our brains. Additives such as MSG, which is widely used as a flavor enhancer, trick the appetite center, overriding our innate satiety signals. Much of today's food is designed to make sure that "you can't eat just one." It is well documented, for example, that giving lab rats MSG makes them fat. Hundreds of studies have documented its contribution to obesity. (To view these studies, go to www. PubMed.com and type in the keywords "MSG obese." You will be amazed and dismayed by the number of studies that have been done.)

Given the choice between flavor-enhanced chips or crackers versus plain carrot sticks or broccoli, what do you think the vast majority of toddlers will pick—not to mention the vast majority of mothers? Therein lies the problem. We have been tricking our own brains and bodies with our food choices.

But knowledge is power. Each of us is responsible for using that knowledge to help our kids and ourselves maintain a healthy body composition. Here's what every mother needs to know.

I'm Fat and My Mother Is Fat: Is My Daughter Doomed?

The answer to this is an emphatic No! Many women worry about getting the same diseases as their mothers, including obesity. Although it's tempting to think that we inherit a tendency for obesity primarily through our genes, this simply is not true. Our genes are not autonomous entities that "have their way" with our bodies. Instead, it is the environment surrounding our genes (the epigenetic factors) that determines how they get expressed. That environment is determined in part by how we apply the feminine facet of power related to self-care and nourishment. It is also profoundly affected by the legacy around food that we inherited from our mother, our maternal grandmother, and all the women who came before her.

I define *legacy* as the huge amount of information about our own past, and our family's past, which affects our energy, health, and potential for change in each generation. This information is passed on *unconsciously* through repeated behavior and *consciously* in the form of advice. For example, if we were taught to "clean our plates" and to please Mama by always taking second helpings, then we're likely to have a tendency toward weight gain, especially if we also have a sedentary lifestyle and eat too many of the wrong kind of calories. (See Chapter 13.)

Instead of believing that it is our genes that make us fat, we need to face the truth. It is the legacy we've inherited from our mothers around food and physical activity that is affecting our weight in the present. Look at Oprah Winfrey. She has completely changed her genetic inheritance around obesity and diabetes by changing her behavior around food and exercise. I know this one well myself. If I ate whatever I wanted, whenever I wanted, and didn't exercise every day, I would be obese in a month. And so would one of my daughters. Period. End of story. Simple, but not easy!

Healthy Body Composition Begins in the Womb

There are three critical periods when a girl is most likely to develop weight problems that too often persist into adult life. These are the pre- and perinatal periods, the time around age two, and again during adolescence.

PERINATAL PERIOD

The intrauterine environment lays the foundation for a child's relationship with food and body weight. It affects the number of fat—and other—cells that develop in organs, the satiety centers within the brain, and the function of the endocrine system. All of these working together favor either restricted or exuberant growth.

Infants with low birth weight for gestational age (less than five pounds eight ounces or 2,500 grams for a full-term pregnancy) appear to remain smaller than those whose birth weights are normal. However, some large longitudinal studies have shown that growth restriction in utero may lay the foundation for type 2 diabetes and cardiovascular disease later in life. This is because some growth-restricted infants have a tendency to get fat once they have enough to eat. The theory is that they have developed a "thrifty" metabolism in the womb. In short, they're like little dieters, whose bodies learn to make the most of whatever calories come their way.

Maternal smoking is associated with growth restriction in fetuses. So is inadequate weight gain during pregnancy. Researchers have documented a very clear association between thinness in infancy and impaired glucose tolerance or diabetes in young adulthood. However, crossing over into higher categories of body-mass index (a measure of the relationship between weight and height) after the age of two is also associated with these disorders.[5]

On the other hand, infants with high birth weights (newborn weight exceeding eight pounds thirteen and one-half ounces or 4,000 grams) also appear to have an increased risk for subsequent overweight. Mothers who gain too much weight, or who have gestational or other types of diabetes, are apt to have babies who are big.

Breast-fed infants are rarely obese. If they are, it's because of the early addition of solid foods that provide excessive calories. Nursing naturally provides a child with the right kind of nourishment because the composition of breast milk continually adapts to meet the unique needs of a growing child. For example, the fat content of breast milk increases toward the end of a feeding. This is known as the hind milk. It's sweeter and richer than the earlier milk, which is more watery to quench the baby's thirst. Hind milk is nature's own "dessert."

TODDLER WEIGHT GAIN

A second indicator of later problems with obesity and cardiovascular disease is known technically as the adiposity rebound. During their first year, it is normal for babies to have a relatively high percentage of body fat. They often become dramatically leaner when they start to walk and move around more. The adiposity rebound refers to a return to a higher body fat percentage. If their weight gets beyond what is considered normal for their age and height, then they may be at increased risk for problems later.

Though much more research needs to be done in this area, one thing is clear: Childhood weight problems are far easier to prevent than to fix. The current approach is to have your child "grow down the percentiles." In other words, she should not be expected to lose weight; the goal is simply to slow down her rate of gain so that her height can catch up.

WATER: WHY CHILDREN NEED TO DRINK IT

It is estimated that fully 30 percent of the average American child's calories currently come from soda pop! Soda is a nonfood that shouldn't be part of any child's diet. Although I never gave my children soda, like many mothers at that time I overdid it on the apple juice—which is basically sugar water. Believe it or not, a child's main beverage should be plain water. Here's why.

In a Nutshell

Though no one can go back and change her birth weight or the circumstances of her pregnancy, seven basic guidelines are sure to make weight control easier for mothers and daughters.

~ Keep blood sugar and insulin levels stable by eating a diet rich in lean protein, fruits, and vegetables, and healthy fats such as those found in nuts, seeds, and cold-water fish.

~ Make sure to get regular moderate exercise. "Mommy and me" swim or gym programs are an ideal way to exercise together.

~ Avoid foods that stimulate the appetite center abnormally, such as MSG, refined sugar, and caffeine.

~ Change your daughter's legacy by making healthy eating a family affair.

~ Take a good multivitamin/mineral supplement rich in antioxidants.

~ Practice emotional hygiene so that addictive eating is less likely.

~ Make sure that you and your child enjoy a variety of pleasurable activities that don't include food. Regular massage is right up there on my list!

The research of Fereydoon Batmanghelidj, M.D., author of *Your Body's Many Cries for Water,* points out that many people are dehydrated in part because our natural thirst mechanism is turned off by drinking beverages such as soda, juice, and tea. Dr. Batmanghelidj reminds us that life started in water and that evolutionary paths included sophisticated mechanisms to maintain the body's water supply. Water plays a dynamic role in maintaining the body's chemistry. It carries oxygen, nutrients, and other substances throughout the body; it is also needed to remove waste from the cells. For the body to function optimally, its water supply needs to be "topped up" regularly. This makes sense—75 percent of the body is made up of water and only 25 percent is solid matter.

In medical school, we learned that a dry mouth is a reliable sign of dehydration. But it is not the only one. It is very common for a child (or adult) to feel hungry when in fact she is thirsty. The body also gets "thirst pains" the same way it gets hunger pains, so another sign of dehydration is actual aches and pains.

Though the body can survive some dehydration, it eventually pays a price. In adults, chronic dehydration can lead to conditions such as dyspepsia (heartburn), arthritic pain, back pain, headache (including migraine), colitis pain and associated constipation, anginal pain (from the heart), and leg pain (on walking). This is in addition to the common symptom of fatigue, particularly in the mid-afternoon.

In modern society, most of us believe that all fluids are equal. But most conventional juices, coffee, nonherbal tea, and soft drinks *deplete* the body's water supply because they contain dehydrating substances such as caffeine and sugar. These agents actually draw water from the body's reserves. Worse still, once an individual has cultivated a taste for these beverages, she will lose her natural thirst for water. That's one of the reasons people don't realize they're dehydrated. Health can improve rapidly once a child drinks enough water every day.

The optimal amount for a child to drink is one half her body weight in ounces. In other words, if a child weighs thirty pounds, she needs fifteen ounces of water a day. (Don't force this. Just have water available at all times.) Babies generally get all the fluid they need from breast milk or formula, though it's fine to give them water now and then. I currently keep my refrigerator stocked with bottles of filtered water so that it's easy to grab one as needed. I recommend that you do the same. Drink spring or filtered water—tap water is not pure enough in many places. You can still give your child other healthy beverages such as green tea, amasake, or freshly made juices as long as she drinks enough water. (See Resources.)

Do Your Kids Need Milk?

Despite what most people have been led to believe, it's completely possible for a daughter to develop healthy bones and teeth without drinking cow's milk. As I've said, my own two daughters never drank it. We didn't even have it in the house until they were teenagers, and even then, no one drank it by the glass. We used it on cereal or in tea occasionally. The girls drank soy milk and also a rice beverage known as amasake.

The fact is, the majority of the world's population doesn't drink milk after infancy. Cow's milk is designed, after all, for baby cows. Human milk is designed for baby humans. (Even breast-fed babies can suffer from cow's milk allergy if their mothers are drinking cow's milk.)

Milk is not the miracle food it's cracked up to be. In his book *The Wellness Revolution* Paul Zane Pilzer writes:

> A typical cow in nature can produce up to 10 pounds of milk per day whereas today's tortured modern dairy cows produce up to 100 pounds of milk per day. This is because cows today are given massive amounts of specialized hormones like bovine growth hormone to increase milk production—making udders so large they often drag on the ground. This results in frequent infections and the need of constant antibiotics—the USDA allows drinking milk to contain from 1 to 1.5 million white blood cells (that's pus to non-biologists) per milliliter.[6]

The bovine growth hormone (BGH), pus, and antibiotics remain in the milk after processing and result in all kinds of health problems for those who consume dairy products, especially children. Gas, constipation, allergies, and ear infections are common. It is not *always* clear if symptoms are from lactose intolerance, antibiotics in milk, or allergens in the milk itself. It has also been my experience that some kids are sensitive to conventionally produced milk but not to organic milk. But what concerns me even more is the effects of BGH. The age of puberty has lowered and breast size in teenagers has increased since the introduction of BGH and other hormones into our food supply. I'm convinced that these hormones have disrupted human growth and development and have contributed not only to increased breast size but also to the increase in breast and ovarian cancer.

And to make matters even more confusing, there's convincing evidence that drinking milk doesn't prevent osteoporosis. For example, a study published in *The American Journal of Public Health* compared milk and calcium consumption in 77,000 women over a twelve-year period to determine the incidence of hip and forearm fractures. Those with the highest intake of dairy food had more fractures than those who drank less milk! In fact, the authors concluded that the data do not support the hypothesis that consuming milk and other food sources of calcium protects women against hip and forearm fractures.[7] In another study, those who consumed more milk and cheese in their twenties were found to have an increased rate of hip fracture later in life.[8]

The Calcium Connection

Instead of cow's milk, I recommend that children receive a calcium/magnesium supplement. Magnesium is a mineral that is as important to bone health as calcium. It also helps calcium assimilation. In fact, there's evidence that children are more apt to be magnesium-deficient than calcium-deficient. Chewable tablets are available. The dose for a toddler is 400 mg per day of calcium and 100 mg of magnesium. The requirement gradually increases to 1,300 mg per day of calcium for an adolescent and about 400 mg of magnesium. (See Resources.)

Beans, blackstrap molasses, sardines, and dark green leafy vegetables are also rich in calcium, as are a whole host of other foods. The problem is, of course, that many children, especially toddlers, can go for weeks without going near a vegetable! So for peace of mind, I recommend using supplements. If your children won't chew them, then you can add ground-up or liquid calcium with magnesium to soups or even bake it into cookies or breads. They won't be able to taste it.

And if you feel strongly about giving your kids milk, just make sure it's organically produced and free of BGH.[9]

SUNLIGHT: AN ESSENTIAL NUTRIENT

Though today we're taught to be afraid of the sun, all of us, including children, need regular sunlight to be healthy. Our inner wisdom knows this, and that's why, despite all the propaganda about the dangers of sun exposure, millions of people still flock to the beach. The sun just feels too good to be all that bad! In addition to increasing serotonin levels in our blood and helping to balance melatonin, the sun's UV rays enable our bodies to manufacture vitamin D in the fat layer under the skin.

The current RDA for vitamin D is based on the amount a child needs to prevent rickets, a condition characterized by abnormal bone formation. But prevention of rickets isn't the only benefit of optimal vitamin D levels. There's a paradigm shift now going on in medicine as new research reveals a far greater role for vitamin D than was previously understood. Vitamin D is both a vitamin and a precursor hormone that has an essential role in the maintenance of bone, breast, brain, immune system, and gut health. Throughout our lives, adequate vitamin D helps build bone mass, maintain healthy cholesterol and blood pressure levels, and build joint health. Researchers have even shown that supplementation in infants less than a year old of 2,000 IU of vitamin D per day reduced the incidence of type 1 diabetes by 80 percent.[10] It also decreases the risk of multiple sclerosis and helps prevent some cancers, including breast, ovarian, prostate, and colorectal cancer. In fact, suboptimal levels of vitamin D may be one of the reasons why breast cancer incidence is higher in northern latitudes than nearer the equator. It is estimated that adequate exposure to vitamin D either through sunlight or supplementation would save more than 23,000 American lives per year due to reduction in cancer mortality![11]

It is now clear that the Food and Nutrition Board's previously defined upper limits (UL) for safe intake of vitamin D of 2,000 IU per day was set far too low. The physiologic requirement for adults may be as high as 5,000 IU per day and at least 1,000 IU for children.

Vitamin D toxicity is far less common than previously thought. Induction of vitamin D toxicity generally requires one to four months of 40,000 IU per day in infants. Adult toxicity requires at least 100,000 IU per day for several months!

Exposure to outdoor sunlight is a much more reliable predictor of vitamin D levels in your blood than your dietary intake. This is partly because oral vitamin D requirements have been found to vary tremendously among individuals. In addition, vitamin D researcher Dr. Michael Holick of Boston University School of Medicine points out that the vitamin D content of enriched dairy foods varies widely, especially in low-fat dairy foods. (Vitamin D is a fat-soluble vitamin, and fat-free or low-fat dairy doesn't contain enough fat to dissolve it.) And while it is possible—though extremely rare, as I've pointed out above—to take in toxic levels of vitamin D from supplements, it is impossible for sun exposure to result in too much vitamin D. Our bodily wisdom contains a built-in mechanism whereby we manufacture exactly what we need from the sun—no more and no less.

To bring vitamin D levels into the healthy range, all that is needed is for a child to play outside with face and hands exposed for twenty minutes without sunscreen three to five times per week for four to five months a year (between April and October in northern latitudes). Her body will make enough vitamin D from this exposure to last the entire year. The more body area that is exposed, the better. Full-body exposure to sunlight on clear days at equatorial latitudes can easily provide the equivalent of 4,000 to 20,000 IU in less than thirty minutes in those with lightly pigmented skin. Those with darker pigmentation need more. The key is moderation and avoidance of sunburn. Early morning or late afternoon sun is the safest. Avoid midday sun whenever possible.

We don't store up vitamin D very well as we age. Miriam E. Nelson, Ph.D., author of *Strong Women, Strong Bones,* notes, "If a 65-year-old woman and her 35-year-old daughter take a ten-minute walk on a sunny day, the mother's skin will manufacture only a third of the amount of vitamin D that her daughter's does."[12]

I realize that it may be a challenge to get your child (and yourself) outside regularly if you work or live in a city, but it's worth the effort. It also helps prevent her overreliance on television or the computer for entertainment.

If a child is going to be out longer than twenty minutes or so, sunscreen should be applied to prevent sunburn. UV exposure beyond pre-erythema levels (reddening of the skin) doesn't enhance vitamin D levels. However, if your daughter has very dark skin, she needs to be in the sun longer—even an hour or two to get the same amount.

While it is nearly impossible to get the high levels of vitamin D you need in your blood without adequate sun exposure, supplementation is still helpful. Children should take at least 400 IU of vitamin D (as cholecalciferol, vitamin D_3) daily until age four and then increase it to a minimum of 1,000 IU. A very good source is cod liver oil, which my parents used to give us regularly in winter. These days, there are brands that taste much better than the stuff we took. (See Resources.) For information on the correct dosage of vitamin D at different ages, proper serum levels, toxicity, and health issues, check the Web site of the Vitamin D Council, a nonprofit organization working to promote awareness of the adverse effects of vitamin D deficiency (www.Cholecalciferol-Council.com).

HOLDING ON, LETTING GO: THE BIOLOGY OF BOWEL AND BLADDER FUNCTION

The ability to use the toilet is a major step toward autonomy and independence. If toilet training is negotiated well, a daughter develops a sense of power and control around her own body and a deep trust in her ability to allow her body to do what it knows how to do naturally. She also begins to move more freely in the wider world outside her home. Indeed, many preschools and day care centers will not accept children who are not toilet trained.

Most children reach the neuromuscular development necessary for bowel and bladder control somewhere between the ages of two and four. However, there is a very large individual variation among children when it comes to the development of full voluntary control. There is also a large variation in how often a child has a bowel movement.

A Healthy Approach to Toilet Training

When I asked my mother how she approached toilet training, she told me:

> I didn't make any big deal out of it. When you kids got to a certain age, you didn't like the way diapers felt when they were soiled. So I put you in underpants. Then, before you'd go out to play, I'd ask you if you had to go to the bathroom. If you said no, I simply said okay. And let you go. Then if you came in a bit later with wet or soiled pants, I'd say, "Guess you had to go, didn't you?" You'd say, "Yep," take off your soiled clothes, put on clean ones, and go back out. It didn't take long for all of you to learn that it was more comfortable to go to the bathroom before going out to play than waiting until you were wet and cold. There was no shaming involved.

When I was growing up we hiked and camped a lot. So I learned from a very early age how to relax and perform normal bowel and bladder functions in the woods or by the side of the road. Except for the drawbacks of the female anatomy in this regard, I was as adept in the out-of-doors as my brothers. I also learned how to use leaves as toilet paper. (You have to be able to identify poison ivy, of course!) I've taught my daughters the same, so that they are comfortable with taking care of these normal bodily functions in a wide variety of settings.

Early toilet training—the gold standard of mothering for our grandmothers' generation—is no longer the norm. In fact, the age of potty training is edging upward. Studies suggest that while about 90 percent of kids were out of diapers by age two and a half in the 1960s, not even a quarter are trained that early now. The largest recent study, conducted in suburban Philadelphia, found that half of boys and 30 percent of girls weren't toilet trained by age three.[13] The makers of major diaper brands are now making their products in larger and larger sizes, including Pull-Ups, underwear-shaped diapers for kids, which are Kimberly-Clark's largest seller. The well-known pediatrician T. Berry Brazelton appeared in TV ads for the larger-size Pampers, telling parents, "Don't rush your toddler into toilet training or let anyone else tell you it's time. It's got to be his choice."

Brazelton believes that children are less likely to develop problems such as bed-wetting and chronic constipation if parents avoid potty power struggles. I agree. I also believe, however, that allowing a child to remain in diapers too long may indicate a parent's need to keep the child a baby, or a child's fear of growing up and becoming independent. Most children, especially girls, are ready to begin the process of toilet training at about age two.

Many women have grown up in families where there is some squeamishness about bowel function. One of the gifts of having a baby is that several years of diaper-changing followed by another year of so of potty talk help you get over it. All humans take in food and excrete waste products. All bowel movements smell bad (except in an exclusively breast-fed baby), and we all pass malodorous gas from time to time as well. These things are just facts of life and nothing to be ashamed of. All the supermodels, the international jet set, and even the pope go through the same process of daily elimination. Make peace with this. Relax and join the human race.

If you have a daughter, leave her BMs alone. And leave your child alone as she is moving her bowels. Don't hover. Teach her how to wipe herself properly (from the front to the back so that fecal bacteria don't get into her vagina or urethra), help her if she "messes up," and then leave her alone.

The Mind-Body Connection in Bowel Health

The physical ability to control one's own bowel and bladder is associated psychologically with the emotions related to holding on versus letting go. Holding on equals constriction, while letting go equals expansion. The only way to hold on to urine or feces is to contract the sphincter muscles. The only way to evacuate the bowel or the bladder is to relax and expand those same muscles. To become and remain healthy, a child needs to develop a balance between these two polarities, not just physically but emotionally as well. During the years when she moves from diapers to the toilet, the stage is set for how well she achieves this balance in later life. (See "Temper Tantrums: Emotional Incontinence and 'Losing It'" in Chapter 7.)

The mind-body connection is extremely powerful when it comes to bowel health. Most bowel problems in children begin as an imbalance in the neurotransmitter levels that affect bowel function. Since these neurotransmitters are exactly the same as the messenger chemicals within the brain, a "gut reaction" at any level, including the colon, is really a child's "lower" brain giving her messages. Emotional distress can affect a child's bowel function even when she is not consciously aware of her distress. Changes in diet, environment, activity level, and the dynamics of her relationships also affect neurotransmitter levels—and bowel function. Of course, this is true for adults, as well.

Sphincter Law

We receive both conscious and unconscious messages about whether or not it is safe to let go at a given time or place. In general, the more relaxed and safe we feel, the more relaxed and effective our elimination will be. Ina May Gaskin, the renowned midwife and author of *Ina May's Guide to Childbirth,* refers to this as sphincter law. (The cervix is also a sphincter.) *You can't force a child's (or an adult's) sphincter to relax when she doesn't feel safe and comfortable.* It's that simple.

It's very common for both children and adults who are traveling to be unable to move their bowels for a few days. Many women also find it difficult to have a bowel movement in a public restroom. The minute they walk into their own homes, they can go! Recently, a sixty-five-year-old woman told me that she went on a Windjammer Cruise in Maine and didn't move her bowels for an entire week because the toilet was located up on deck in a conspicuous location. She couldn't relax and let go, even when her traveling companion stood at the door to make sure that no one would enter. Obviously this woman had internalized some messages about bowel function at an early age that were still impeding her ability to be fully functional in the world. Sphincter law strikes again.

Sphincter law results from one of the body's most basic processes, the function of the autonomic nervous system. The autonomic nervous system comprises two branches. The sympathetic nervous system (SNS)—the "fight-or-flight" part—contracts muscles and blood vessels in response to a perceived challenge or threat. The parasympathetic nervous system (PNS)—the "rest-and-restore" part—relaxes muscles and blood vessels once the threat has passed or when we know we are safe. The SNS can be thought of as the gas and the PNS as the brake. All of the body's organs, including normal bowel function, depend upon balance and coordination between both of these systems and the neurochemicals they produce.

When a child doesn't feel safe or secure, the rhythmic contractions of her bowel wall may either speed up, resulting in diarrhea, or slow down, resulting in constipation.

Irritable bowel syndrome, a common condition that is exacerbated by emotional distress, results from an imbalance between the parasympathetic and sympathetic functions of the gut wall. It is characterized by constipation alternating with diarrhea. The common tummy aches that many children experience are related to the same kind of emotional distress that produces IBS in adults. The vagus nerve, the main nerve in the PNS, is connected to the amygdala of the brain and also to the temporal lobe. These are the very areas that are associated with strong emotions and intuitive information.

Though constipation is sometimes due to the lack of fluid and fiber in the diet, it is far more commonly associated with what is called neurogastroenterologic disturbance, a very long word for problems with the mind-bowel connection—usually stemming from childhood.

If there are power struggles or undue fears around toilet training, a child may also develop a personality style referred to as anal and withholding. She will grow up to have difficulty relaxing and letting go psychologically in ways that appear to have nothing to do with her sphincters. Such a person is overly concerned with perfection, cleanliness, and details, and finds it difficult to open up and allow her emotions to flow freely and organically. People with sphincter issues also try to prevent the free flow of expansive activity enjoyed by others. In short, they become "cultural sphincters."

Maternal Ambivalence and Toilet Training

When the child tries to individuate from total dependence on her mother, her mother may well experience some ambivalence about this, particularly if she has especially enjoyed her role as primary caregiver of an infant. She may also feel empty inside at the prospect of her children growing up and not needing her.

A mother may, unknowingly, become fixated about what her

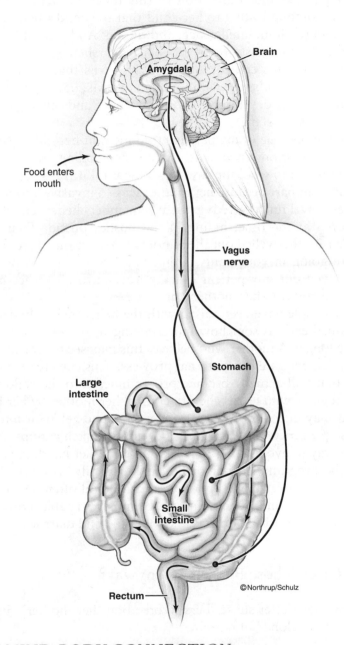

THE MIND-BODY CONNECTION
IN BOWEL FUNCTION

daughter produces on the toilet, want to check every movement, and generally pay too much attention to this function. When she does this, she is communicating to her child that the child's body doesn't have its own wisdom, intelligence, and timing. And since it is the nature of the child to trust herself and her body, she begins to struggle with her mother for control. She quickly learns that she can exert control over her mother by withholding her BMs, having them in the wrong location, or developing "stomachaches" and other symptoms related to her GI system.

For example, one of my patients told me that her older sister developed a condition known as encopresis—soiling of underwear from holding on to stool for days at a time until it leaks. This condition resulted in part because her mother was so invasive about monitoring her bowel function. My patient remembers her sister, who was about seven at the time, hiding in the bushes outside their house while their mother yelled out the window, "You're out there. I know it. You're going in your pants, aren't you!" Having seen how this drama played out, my patient quickly learned to move her bowels privately, away from her mother's prying eyes.

Many people have been raised with the belief that a child who is toilet trained early is somehow more intelligent or superior to those who take longer. A mother who believes this may see toilet training as a way to demonstrate her maternal prowess. This can create a power struggle that will actually become programmed into the child's biology. A daughter who learns she can control her mother by her bodily functions may unconsciously carry over the same behavior into later relationships; for example, she may develop stomach cramps or diarrhea as a way to avoid going to work. On the other hand, the daughter may be programmed out of her innate bodily wisdom entirely. Power struggles over bowel function in childhood often set the stage for such chronic and debilitating problems as irritable bowel syndrome, chronic constipation, gas and bloating, and diarrhea.

PATRICIA: Whose Body Is It Anyway?

One of my newsletter subscribers wrote about her mother's attempt to make her a "clone" of herself:

> Her needs and my needs were decreed to be identical. I was mostly forbidden to speak unless spoken to, and even then there was only one right answer which I had to figure out in advance

in order to survive. There was nothing I could say that anyone would want to hear, and no one would ever be available to help me. I was an only child.

A specific incident I remember from about age five of having to go to the bathroom during a long car trip. I bravely asked my parents repeatedly but they would not stop. Finally they got so fed up with me that we stopped by the side of the road and my mother watched while I peed on the ground. I distinctly remember her saying, "Oh, you really did have to go." And I remember thinking (but not saying), "She didn't believe me." My mother actually thought that if she didn't have to go then neither did I.

I had to eat all the food served to me, which was usually more than I wanted or needed, and I learned never to have to go to the bathroom at an inconvenient time. In other words, all my body's signals were invalidated or turned off: decades later I am still trying to reclaim and reset them.

DEBBIE: Smothering Mothering

Debbie's daughter was three when she developed constipation and recurrent bladder infections. Debbie, who was my patient, took her to a number of different doctors, all of whom were unable to determine the cause of the problem. Though the little girl was treated with everything from laxatives to antibiotics to homeopathic remedies, the symptoms always recurred.

Debbie was forty years old at the time. She'd given birth to her daughter after years of treatments for infertility. Debbie described her first year with her new baby as "the best time of my life." Debbie told me, "I loved having an infant. I never wanted my daughter to change or grow up." She'd been having a series of dreams, she said, the main theme of which was that someone was coming to take away her baby. She was terrified of losing what she had worked so hard to achieve—her child.

But you can't stop the process of life, especially when it comes to the rapid evolution of a child. In fact, the degree to which your identity is dependent upon being a caregiver or a mother is the degree to which you may have difficulty letting your children become autonomous and independent.

Not surprisingly, each time Debbie's daughter took a developmental step—first when she started to walk, and later when she began nursery school—Debbie found herself becoming somewhat panicked. She responded by continuing to treat her daughter as though she were an infant: making every food, clothing, and activity choice for her and hesitating to let her go on play dates with her new friends. She constantly monitored the perimeter, making sure her daughter didn't get too dirty and didn't engage in any potentially dangerous activities, such as swinging too high on the playground swings. And she followed her daughter into the bathroom and checked every time she used the potty.

Clearly, Debbie's daughter had some feelings about her "smothering mothering," but being a child, she didn't have the sophistication to articulate these feelings. So she developed symptoms— constipation and urinary tract infections—in the very area of her body where control is a primary issue.

Debbie is not unique. Many women unconsciously find themselves trying to keep their children dependent on them to some degree, the payoff being that if the child doesn't grow up and move on to their next stage of life, they won't have to either. I have come to believe that this is also why so many women, when they reach the turning point of age forty or so, decide to have another baby.

Because Debbie was open to looking at her own role in her daughter's medical condition, she entered therapy and realized that she couldn't continue to use her daughter as a way to get her own mothering and nurturing needs met, needs that she had put off for all the years that she was trying to have a baby. As time passed, she learned how to change her behavior around her daughter. Eventually, both the constipation and the urinary tract infections cleared up.

A PRACTICAL APPROACH TO VULVAR IRRITATION

It's fairly common for little girls to have occasional vulvar redness, irritation, and itching. This can be associated with an overgrowth of yeast in the area from an antibiotic, irritation from chemicals in bubble bath, toilet paper, or for unknown reasons.

The treatment I prescribe is the same one I used for my daughters with great success. Give your daughter a bath in warm water, and wash the vulvar area gently with mild, unscented soap like Ivory. (If it's too irritated to use even mild soap, just let her soak in water for a while.) Dry her off gently and apply Resinol ointment. (See Resources.) I grew up using this salve, and it remains one of the most effective remedies for minor skin irritations of all kinds. It's available in most pharmacies without a prescription. In my opinion, every household should have a jar of this in the first-aid kit. If symptoms persist, seek medical attention. Occasionally a child will insert a foreign object such as a button into her vagina, which causes irritation.

The Cultural Programming of Bowel Function

I grew up seeing TV ads showing cheery mothers handing out laxatives to their family members because they were suffering from the uncomfortable effects of what was called irregularity. As a child, I could never figure out what the ads were referring to. They always ended with a happy family group whose vacation had been saved because Dr. Mom handed out the laxatives! We didn't even question how ridiculous these ads were.

Bowel function is as normal and natural as breathing. Instead of monitoring their children for regularity, mothers would do better to stay away from their children's elimination patterns except in the most matter-of-fact way. The child will then internalize the fact that in the vast majority of cases, bowel and bladder function were designed to take care of themselves. After all, there is no universally agreed-upon standard about when, how much, and what texture healthy bowel movements should be.

Despite this too many girls are given messages about bowel and bladder function that can set the stage for a lifetime of fear and concern. I've had countless patients over the years tell me about their childhood "bowel programming." One woman was not allowed to go out and play in the morning until she had moved her bowels. Many others were given enemas regularly if they didn't produce the requisite spontaneous bowel movement in a given time period. Still another had a mother who would cancel family outings if her daughter hadn't produced a bowel movement before they were scheduled to leave. Talk about a heavy sphincter burden!

It always does a child's newly developing sense of automony and body trust a disservice to give them the idea that some kinds of bodily functions are better or more deserving than others. Judging a morning stool as more valuable than one produced in the evening, or a "floater" as better than a "sinker," is an example of this thinking. It makes bodily functions the enemy to be controlled.

CONSTIPATION AND COW'S MILK ALLERGY

Laxative use is a way of life in some families. But laxatives and enemas are rarely necessary. In fact, regular use of any type of laxative can create dependency and result in chronic bowel problems.

Constipation is a frequent problem among infants and children. In one U.S. study, 16 percent of parents of twenty-two-month-olds reported that their children had constipation. In the United Kingdom, 34 percent of four- to seven-year-old children have been reported to have constipation.

Most constipation is short-lived with no long-term consequences and doesn't require treatment. All that is necessary is making sure your child drinks more water and also gets enough fiber from regular servings of fruits and vegetables. Normal bowel function at all ages also depends upon eating a diet with balanced amounts of whole food sources of protein, fats, and carbohydrates so that your body makes the proper proportion of eicosanoids, the evanescent hormones that govern virtually all cellular functions.

Sometimes, however, constipation is caused by cow's milk allergy that results in anal inflammation and even fissures. Intolerance of cow's milk occurs in 0.3 to 7.5 percent of otherwise normal infants, 82 percent of whom have symptoms within four months of birth and 89 percent by one year of age. The symptoms include vomiting and diarrhea but can also include runny nose, asthma, and eczema. Intolerance of cow's milk isn't something that goes away. If it is present in infancy, it may well also be present in the same child at age six.[14]

If you or your daughter was constipated as a child, stop all cow's milk for at least two weeks and see what happens. If you don't notice an immediate improvement, reintroduce the cow's milk after two weeks or so. Usually symptoms such as diarrhea, constipation, or a runny nose will recur almost immediately. If they don't, you probably don't have a problem. If they do, take the child off cow's milk and milk products.

Fear of "Catching Something" in a Public Restroom

Too many little girls are still taught all manner of paralyzing half-truths about the dangers of public restrooms, even though these dangers are largely unfounded. Fear of catching something from a public toilet seat then becomes part of their biologic inheritance right at the time when they should be developing increasing confidence in the world around them and their ability to negotiate it safely.

Whenever I'm traveling, I overhear mothers unwittingly programming their daughters for potential bowel problems. When a little girl goes into a toilet stall, she'll often be told not to touch the seat with any part of her body, not to touch her own body, and not to touch the door handle. One of my favorite overheard warnings: "Don't ever sit on the seat because sometimes people stand on the seats and you don't want the dirt from their shoes to get on you!" One of my older daughter's college friends told her: "Make sure you always flush the toilet with your foot. Don't *ever* touch the handle on a toilet." During her freshman year in college, my younger daughter roomed with a group of four girls. They were the only ones who used the bathroom in their suite. Yet one of the girls lined the toilet seat with paper every time she used it.

When you are little, it's nearly impossible to hover over a toilet seat without touching it while at the same time relaxing enough to go. Inserting fear and anxiety about germs and disease into this process is a fertile setup for adversely programming sphincter function. Television ads of mothers taking antibacterial spray everywhere they go to sterilize toilet seats and doorknobs don't help. They simply feed a child's sense of vulnerability.

It's far better to teach your child that her body's immune system is well equipped to deal with the germs in the outside world. There are no studies that show that spraying public toilet seats with germ killers will enhance a child's health. In truth, cultural programming of fear is much more dangerous and debilitating over the long run than anything a woman is apt to encounter in a restroom. After all, the skin of the buttocks is stratified squamous epithelium complete with sebaceous glands—all of which provide a very effective barrier against invasion by germs. In more than twenty years of gynecological practice, I never saw a single case where a woman caught a disease from a toilet seat—not *one*! Avoiding contact with a surface in a public restroom doesn't offer protection against sexually transmitted diseases. Women "catch" things from sexual partners, not from toilet seats.

A Healthy Approach to Using Public Restrooms

Adverse childhood programming about bowel function and one's safety and security in the world can lead to a lifetime of discomfort and shame. You can stop this cycle by teaching your daughter how to trust her body and her immune system's ability to keep her safe. A good place to teach this is in public restrooms, places where women's beliefs about their bodies and their safety play out very clearly.

~ Make sure the toilet seat is dry. Sitting down on a wet toilet seat is a very unpleasant experience.

~ Allow the child to sit on the seat and get comfortable. (Line the seat with toilet paper if you must, but remember that what too many children really "catch" in restrooms is a permanent feeling of vulnerability.) Sitting on the toilet versus squatting over it helps to relax the requisite muscles. The seat is simply too high for a child to relax adequately if she's trying to squat over it.

~ Give the youngster plenty of time. Make sure she is finished before getting up. Ask her to check in with her body about this.

~ Teach her how to wipe herself properly from front to back to be sure that fecal material doesn't get into the vagina or urethral areas. Girls need to know that there are three openings in their bottoms, from front to back: one for urine, one for making babies and birthing them, and one for stool. Learning this anatomy at an early age will serve them for life.

~ Teach her to use the right amount of toilet paper for the job. Many mothers reinforce the "dirty" issue by using wads and wads of paper.

~ Have her wash her hands before leaving the bathroom. If the line is too long, there aren't any paper towels, or you're in a hurry, you may occasionally skip this step unless you work in a restaurant or in a health-care setting.

~ Teach your child how to relieve herself in the woods if necessary and wipe off with leaves.

From one end to the other, our gastrointestinal system allows us to "take in and digest" the world around us. We can also trust our guts to provide us with clues about what is safe to take in and what isn't. Learning to trust our gut wisdom will serve us well for a lifetime, and this learning begins in earnest in early childhood.

9

The Immune System

A Mirror on the Mind and Environment

❀

S tarting in utero, and continuing through adolescence, a child's immune system matures through constant interaction with her environment. An infant's first environment is, quite literally, her mother's body, which is host to millions of harmless, and often helpful, microbes, including those in breast milk. Breast-fed babies have sweet-smelling, yellow stools because the bacteria in breast milk don't produce noxious smells. The minute the child is fed formula or other food, the gut bacteria change and so do the smells produced. A baby's gut is sterile at birth. Beneficial bacteria in breast milk help colonize the baby's bowel with bacteria that promote healthy digestion and gut function. These gut flora help to prevent allergies and asthma as well.

A child's environment includes the beliefs, emotions, and ideas that she is exposed to, just as surely as it includes germs, air, food, medicines, and water. All of these factors contribute to the maturation and programming of her immune system as she grows into young adulthood. A mother's choices in each of these areas (including her beliefs and behavior about germs) strongly influence her child's immune competence and ability to protect herself.

Our first line of defense is on the surface of the body. Though it's not widely appreciated, the bulk of the immune system is located in the mucosal membranes that come into direct contact with the environment through eating food, breathing air, and touching people, plants, and animals. The mucosal immune system comprises the conjunctiva of the eyes, the lining of the mouth, gastrointestinal and reproductive systems, and the nasal passages, trachea, and bronchial tree of the lungs. The breast and breast milk are also considered part of the mucosal immune system, as is the skin. Each of these surface areas is colonized with its own beneficial bacteria that are necessary for immune system health and balance.

Several centuries of study have clearly demonstrated that every part of our immune system communicates with every other part. When your body encounters a foreign protein in the form of a germ, for example, the rest of the body is alerted and the immune cells on the surface mobilize to investigate and do what is necessary. If the immune system surveillance alarm goes off and the germ is recognized as "harmful," then it will mount an inflammatory response of some kind to kill the invader. The immune cells in the bloodstream are called into service only when mucosal immunity has failed.

For reasons that aren't yet clearly understood, the immune system may also overreact when it encounters certain environmental stimuli such as foods, pollens, animal hair, and so on. This is the basis for allergic reactions and also asthma, a condition in which the immune system becomes chronically overactivated, triggering inflammation and narrowing of the airways.

The immune system is imbued with all the characteristics of our other sense organs, like the eyes and ears. And just as in the famous discovery that kittens raised with only vertical stripes eventually lose the ability to see anything that isn't vertical, so too are our immune systems programmed for what to "see" and not "see" by our childhood experiences and environment.[1]

The function of an individual's immune system is inextricably associated with her mood and behavior. Changes in neuropeptide levels (the molecules that the brain makes when it thinks and feels) affect immune function. Things get even more interesting, however. Immune-system cells *themselves* make the same neuropeptides as the brain. In fact, J. Edwin Blalock, Ph.D., an immunologist at the University of Alabama at Birmingham School of Medicine, calls the immune system a "mirror on the mind."

Because immune function is intimately associated with mood, we cannot defend ourselves against disease or allergies simply by retreating into a hermetically sealed environment that is free of dust and germs. In fact, trying to rid the environment of microbes is, itself, a health risk. That's because optimal immune-system development depends upon exposure to a healthy mixture of bacteria both inside and outside of the body. Writing about the link between allergies, asthma, and the environment, Swedish researcher Bengt Bjorksten recently noted:

> The high prevalence of allergies in industrialized countries is in contrast with the low prevalence of allergies in Eastern Europe, with a life style similar to that prevailing in Western Europe 40 years ago. The discussion of the impact of environmental changes on the incidence of asthma and other allergies has been limited mostly to the possible effects of a deteriorating air quality, poorly ventilated houses and an increased exposure to certain allergens, notably house dust mites. None of these factors can more than marginally explain the observed regional differences in the prevalence of allergic diseases. The concept of "life style" should therefore be expanded considerably. The mother is a significant "environmental factor" in early infancy. Recent studies indicate an imbalance in the gut flora of allergic, compared with non allergic infants, and in Swedish children compared with Estonian children. As the microbial flora drives the maturation of the immune system, changes in its composition may play a role for the higher prevalence of allergies and asthma.[2]

Why are children who have *more* access to modern Western medicine also more likely to have allergies? One major reason may be overuse of antibiotics and disinfectants, both of which kill not just harmful bacteria but also the good guys that keep the immune system and inner environment balanced. The end result in the gut is that yeast and other fungi start to overgrow—with subsequent changes in immune response throughout the body. Experiments with animals have shown that giving antibiotics produces yeast and mold growth in the bowel, which then triggers allergic responses in the lungs when they are exposed to mold spores.[3]

Have We Become Too Clean?

When we were growing up and one of us found a bug in our food, my dad used to say, "Don't tell anyone. They'll all want one." And when we dropped a piece of food in the dirt during a picnic, he wasn't overly concerned if we picked it up and ate it. He said, "Let the earth pass through you. Then you'll be immune to everything." The newest research suggests that he was on to something important. Compelling new evidence suggests that living in a too-clean environment may actually result in a weaker immune system. Exposure to low levels of dirt in childhood helps prevent later immune dysfunction. In fact, new clinical trials by Professor Graham Rook in London have shown that one can actually boost children's immune systems by injections of harmless microorganisms found in ordinary environmental dirt.

Increasingly, medical studies are documenting that there are long-term health benefits to making sure that children are exposed to germs, pollen, and animal dander early on, as well as making sure their own bodily flora aren't interrupted with antibiotics too often. In many countries, the prevalence of asthma has increased in parallel with improvement in hygiene and health standards and reduction in family size. As it turns out, children who are exposed to germs at day-care centers, have older siblings, have a rural lifestyle, reside on a farm with animals near the house, or have a dog in the house are protected against the later development of asthma.[4]

It is also well documented that having a baby by cesarean section increases the risk of asthma, as does bottle feeding instead of breast-feeding. A baby who comes through the birth canal is exposed to her mother's vaginal and bowel flora, thus helping establish the right microbial balance in her mucosal immune system. Coming through the birth canal also "tunes up" the lungs, wringing out excess fluid and getting them ready for their first moments of breathing. These first moments set the tone for the child's experience of breathing on her own. Breast-feeding also colonizes the gut with the beneficial bacteria that help program healthy immunity.

ASTHMA: A HOLISTIC APPROACH

While a full discussion of asthma is beyond the scope of this book, I'd like to explore how this illness points up the complexity of the forces involved in immune function and how little we still understand about such a common problem. It is also a very clear example of how emotions interact with both immune and lung function.

Asthma is a respiratory disorder characterized by an overreactive immune system that causes inflammation in the airways, so that they swell and tighten. The typical triad of symptoms that characterize asthma are shortness of breath (dyspnea), coughing, and wheezing. Some children have "cough-equivalent" asthma; they don't wheeze, but they go into coughing fits they can't stop. Though many asthma sufferers also have allergies and chronic nasal congestion, some don't. Asthma attacks are triggered when something in either a child's internal or external environment—or a combination of both—causes the muscles of the trachea and bronchial tree to become twitchy and hyperresponsive. Asthma is the most common reason children miss school, and despite an arsenal of medical treatments, both children and adults are dying from it in increasing numbers.

Common environmental triggers for an asthma attack are dust, tobacco smoke, animal hair, viruses, and cold weather. Even exercise can be a trigger. There is also a clear socioeconomic link. African-Americans have a 50 percent higher rate of severe asthma than the rest of the population and are hospitalized far more often than whites. Native Americans also have a comparatively high number of asthmatics among them.[5]

In addition, any situation in which a child has difficulty expressing her emotions fully can be an asthma cue. This is not surprising, given that the lungs are located in the fourth emotional center, or chakra. (The fourth chakra is related to our capacity to express ourselves fully, including the expression of joy, passion, sadness, anger, and grief.)

It's certainly possible that some asthma-related deaths could be avoided if everyone who had it understood how to approach the disease from a mind-body and nutritional perspective, using one's own power and resources, along with the best of medical science, to deal with it. At the very least, asthma sufferers could enjoy a much better quality of life, since asthma is a systemic disease that causes inflammation throughout the body. Therefore asthma sufferers often have fatigue and achiness as well as breathing problems.

A Smoke Screen for Emotions?

It's well documented that secondhand smoke increases the risk for childhood asthma, and respiratory infections of all kinds. What isn't generally appreciated is the link between difficult-to-experience emotions and smoking in the first place. Smokers smoke as a way to deal with and cover up difficult feelings. That means that parents who smoke are apt to be more out of touch with their feelings than those who don't. Children pick up on these unexpressed emotions and on the emotionally repressive environment that fosters them. This information goes right to their lungs and respiratory tracts—and is expressed in the form of asthma, bronchitis, and other respiratory illnesses. These patterns get handed down in families as surely as genes.

A Chemical Cascade

Regardless of the initial stimulus, the end result is the same—the release of inflammatory compounds, including histamine, bradykinins, leukotrienes, and prostaglandins.[6] These compounds cause leakiness in the lung's blood vessels, resulting in irritation and swelling of surrounding tissue. They also make bronchial-tube muscles contract and respiratory passages narrow. The airways then begin to secrete mucus, so they narrow and clog, which precipitates wheezing and difficulty breathing fully. Most attacks last only a few minutes to a few hours, after which the sufferer recovers quickly. But sometimes an asthma attack can escalate to the point where respiratory support in an intensive care unit is necessary. Over time, with continued asthma attacks, the nerve endings on the surface of the bronchial tubes become damaged. It takes smaller and smaller amounts of a trigger to produce a full-blown attack. The whole respiratory system is damaged and on red alert.

STAGES OF AN ASTHMA ATTACK

1. The child is exposed to an emotional or environmental trigger.
2. Her chest tightens and she develops a dry cough.
3. Breathing becomes harsh.
4. Wheezing develops during both inhaled and exhaled breaths.
5. Exhaling old air becomes increasingly difficult, leading to shortness of breath.
6. Shortness of breath triggers a feeling of panic, as well as increased heart rate and blood pressure.
7. The attack worsens. She must use her neck and shoulder muscles (accessory muscles) to take in a breath.
8. Breaking the chain of shortness of breath, wheezing, and coughing becomes nearly impossible.

Drugs Are a Bridge, Not the Whole Solution

The goal of drug treatment of asthma is to achieve stable periods without attacks so your child's body can heal. Many children now carry inhalers, but in more serious cases, daily drugs such as theophylline or even steroids may be necessary for symptomatic relief. The most common asthma drugs work by preventing leukotriene synthesis, thus interrupting the inflammatory cascade. But the suppression of these chemicals results in other problems, as most users of steroids can attest. In addition, researchers have found inflammation-promoting compounds in the lungs of individuals who don't get asthma attacks, which points to the fact that there are other factors involved in an asthma attack.

The Food-Immune Connection

A large body of research has shown that supplementing a child's (or an adult's) diet with foods containing essential fatty acids such as fish oil, DHA, and/or EPA has a very beneficial effect on asthma. These fats help prevent the synthesis of the inflammatory chemicals that trigger asthma. Given that the immune system triggers inflammatory changes that manifest differently in different areas of the body, they also help prevent eczema and other manifestations of allergy.

Ways to supplement with essential fats:

~ Put freshly ground flaxseed in oatmeal or cereal. Work up gradually to one tablespoon.

~ Serve wild sockeye salmon or sardines.

~ Use raw nuts and seeds (sunflower seeds, walnuts, pumpkin seeds, etc.).

~ Put one to three teaspoons of essential fatty acid oil in fruit juice, in oatmeal, or in a smoothie. I recommend OptOmega brand from USANA as an ideal blend of both omega-3 and omega-6 fats. (See Resources.)

In addition to making sure your child gets enough essential fats, I have observed that many children with asthma, allergies, or both, do much better when they follow a mostly whole-foods diet that doesn't contain dairy food, refined sugar products, hydrogenated oils (which interfere with essential fatty acid metabolism), or wheat. In addition, any child with allergies or asthma—or any child who has been on antibiotics—needs to have her bowel flora replenished with a good source of friendly probiotic bacteria. Some traditional foods that contain these are natto (made from fermented soybeans), miso, sauerkraut, yogurt, and some varieties of homemade pickles. You can also buy probiotics in capsule form and add them to a smoothie or other foods. Because they are living bacteria, they are destroyed by heat and light. (See Resources.)

Children also need a good multivitamin that helps optimize immune function. Anecdotally, I've seen kids with allergies and/or asthma enjoy a great deal of relief simply from vitamin supplementation alone. The reason for this is that the antioxidants in vitamins help prevent tissue inflammation. (See Resources.)

Many common foods contain proteins that cross-react with pollen, dust, and animal dander in a way that causes the immune system to overreact. The same is true for foods that contain additives and preservatives such as MSG (see Chapter 8). When you change a child's diet many symptoms of allergy, such as eczema, ear infections, and respiratory symptoms, go away on their own. Asthma also gets better. I personally know of dozens of kids who were spared the ordeal of ear tubes by these dietary changes.

The best way to avoid problems in the first place is to make sure your own diet is high in essential fats when you're pregnant, then breast-feed, or use a formula that contains essential fats and no hydrogenated fats. Then supplement your child's diet with a few drops of fish oil or flaxseed oil mixed into her food.

Don't expose young children to food additives, cow's milk, or wheat products for as long as possible. (You can't control this as much once they start school or day care.) By avoiding these common triggers, a child's immune system will be well functioning and able to handle foreign proteins in the future without overreacting.

How to Help Your Child Breathe Easier

Know your child's triggers and help her recognize them. It is possible for your child to decrease the frequency and severity of her asthma attacks, or even eliminate them. You and she first must find out which stimuli trigger her attacks and then help her work consciously with her internal and external environments to ameliorate the attack as soon as possible. Keeping an asthma journal will allow you to see patterns you might otherwise miss. Note the following: Where was your daughter when the attack occurred? What was she feeling? What was the environment like? Sometimes moldy environments such as damp cellars or garages can bring on an attack. Sometimes it's a trip to visit a relative or other family member. Some kids can't be anywhere near cats or tobacco smoke.

Let Your Child Get It off Her Chest

Encourage your child to talk about her feelings concerning stressful events in her life or about the things she is afraid of. This will bring emotions to the surface so they don't have to stay in her lungs.

No matter how hard it may be to listen to the emotional outbursts of young children, and no matter how unskillfully they may express themselves, a child needs to know that her emotions—all of them—exist for a reason. These emotions need to be validated and they need an appropriate outlet for expression. John Gottman, Ph.D., a research psychologist at the University of Washington in Seattle, writes, "Parents do enormous harm by invalidating a child's emotions, which causes children to doubt their own instincts."[7] This is also a setup for physical illness. The principle is to validate a child's experience. When the child complains, "My finger hurts," the best parental response is "A scratch can hurt," not "It couldn't hurt, it's just a scratch." Or when your child says, "I'm hot," a parent should answer, "It's hot in here for you," not "Don't be silly, it's freezing in here." Parents do not invalidate a child's perceptions and emotions out of malice, but they seem to believe it is their job to hold a mirror of "reality" up to the child. This well-intentioned invalidation, however, can do a great deal of harm.

The mind-body connection in asthma and other immune system diseases has been well documented. In one study, for example, 107 adults with mild to moderately severe asthma or rheumatoid arthritis were randomly assigned to write either about the most stressful event in their lives or about emotionally neutral topics. All patients wrote for twenty minutes on three consecutive days. The severity of their illnesses was then evaluated at two weeks, two months, and four months. Those who wrote about traumatic events—including the death of a loved one, problems in a relationship, or disturbing events from childhood—showed the greatest improvement. Asthma patients showed measurable improvements in lung function.[8] Other research has shown that this type of writing boosts immune function and reduces symptoms and medical visits in healthy, as well as chronically ill, patients.[9]

One of my patients found that her daughter seemed to be more susceptible to asthma attacks whenever she was visiting her grandmother, a woman who was emotionally cold and distant. The little girl eventually told her mother that she was afraid of Maw Maw. The connection made perfect sense because an emotional trigger such as fear or sadness will almost always exacerbate an environmental one

IMAGERY FOR BETTER LUNG AND IMMUNE FUNCTION

Simple imagery exercises can help a child learn how to relax her bronchioles consciously. (Healing imagery is especially powerful in children because they haven't yet developed their teenage and adult skepticism.) The following exercise is adapted from several in the book *Asthma Free in 21 Days,* by Kathryn Shafer, Ph.D., and Fran Greenfield, M.A. (See Resources.)

Golden Balloon Exercise

Intention: To strengthen and heal the respiratory system. To increase lung capacity.

Frequency: If the child is experiencing respiratory discomfort, use once every hour or two while awake, up to two minutes at a time. If breathing is normal, use once in the morning and once at night.

Say the following out loud to your child:

Close your eyes and breathe out three times. Imagine your lungs as a pair of golden balloons. As you breathe in, see, sense, and feel the balloons filling with white light and expanding. See and feel your chest expanding at the same time. As you exhale, see the balloons contracting forcibly, pushing out the used air through your nose. See this air being emitted as gray smoke and drifting away into the atmosphere. At the same time, see and sense your chest contracting. Now repeat this process up to five more times before opening your eyes. As you do this, know that your lungs are working rhythmically, filling you with energy and life. Then open your eyes and return.

such as cat dander. By allowing her daughter to express negative feelings about her grandmother, this mother provided a powerful "witness" function, thus helping validate her daughter's experience. Over
time, her daughter's body, feeling more secure with her feelings about
her grandmother, no longer had to get an asthma attack to express
her fear.

The Benefits of Nose Breathing

Mouth breathing is not a natural way to breathe. In fact, it triggers a stress response in the body, complete with all the fight-or-flight
hormones. Make sure your child breathes through her nose. This
alone can help prevent flare-ups of asthma, allergies, and sinusitis.
At a recent book signing, a young woman told me that she had heard
me recommend nose breathing at a previous lecture, and that it had
completely eliminated her asthma. She was thrilled.

Nose breathing helps ensure better development of the jaw and
facial bones. It also helps keep the rib cage flexible because it directs
the air to the bottom of the lungs, where there is more blood to be
oxygenated. Breathing into the lower lobes of the lungs expands the
rib cage with each breath, while mouth breathing expands only the
upper lobes. Taking full, deep breaths through the nose also warms
the air and filters it past the sinuses so that the mucosal immune system is more likely to be able to filter out dust and other particles.

Teach Your Child How to Stop an
Asthma Attack in the Early Stages

There is no question that a full-blown asthma attack can be terri-
fying. And that's why parents of asthmatic children often have a high
degree of vigilance. But once you understand how powerful the
mind-body connection is when it comes to immune and airway function, you can help your child learn to use her own resources to stop
an attack. This will strengthen her sense of safety and security, despite her condition. Many patients who had asthma as children have
told me that dealing with this condition actually taught them how to
assume responsibility for their health early on. As adults, they are far
healthier than their contemporaries who simply took their health for
granted.

Once your child understands what happens to her during a typical asthma attack, she'll learn to sense an impending episode and know how to avert it either with medication or by using imagery and breathing—or both—usually during stages one or two.

FEELING SAFE ON THE EARTH

Ultimately, immunizations, susceptibility to illness, use of antibiotics, diet, exercise, and one's emotional environment and beliefs are all interrelated. When a mother takes her children to the doctor frequently, wears a mask, freely encourages the use of inhalers and other medication, uses air purifiers, disinfectants, and nebulizers, she's giving her child the message that she is not safe in the world unless she takes complex precautions. All of these modalities have their place, of course. But it is the way in which the world is presented to the child that determines how her immune system will respond to the germs in the environment. Unless a child feels safe and secure in her family environment, and feels safe to express herself fully in a socially appropriate way, then all the immunizations, vitamins, and organic food in the world won't make a significant difference in a child's overall state of health.

You could raise your child in a sealed, air-conditioned house (to minimize pollen allergy), remove everything soft or fuzzy (to reduce dust allergies), vacuum the ductwork frequently (to get rid of mold), wash the cat once a month . . . or (sigh) get rid of him altogether. You could avoid wheat, dairy, eggs, chocolate, corn, and peanuts, and never eat out as a way to minimize food allergies. And though these measures would help initially, especially if you have an allergic or asthmatic child, sooner or later a child and her immune system are going to have to come to grips with living on planet Earth, dust mites and all!

A Word about Autoimmune Disease

At least 80 percent of all autoimmune diseases such as lupus, Graves' disease, rheumatoid arthritis, and multiple sclerosis occur in females. Though these diseases are associated with multiple genetic, environmental, and nutritional factors, they all have one thing in common: their symptoms are caused because the immune system of the sufferer is attacking her own tissue.

My clinical experience and a significant number of scientific studies suggest that the seeds of autoimmune illness are sown in childhood. One of the most common seeds is the belief that one is on some level unacceptable or unlovable. The immune system simply carries out that belief and attacks the body. A patient who had both Graves' disease and arthritis told me:

> When I was little, my mother was abusive. She told me that if I cried, she'd give me something to cry about by beating me more. So I learned to dissociate from my body and my feelings. Now my mother no longer beats me. But my immune system does. When I get upset for any reason, I get a sore throat and back pain within twenty-four hours.

Through therapy and dietary change, my patient has been able to develop a far more friendly immune system. But the original pattern is there inside her because the immune system memory is very long. Reprogramming it takes time and patience.

WISDOM CHALLENGE: *Should You Immunize Your Child?*

A recent article reported that they have just banned peanut butter in our local schools because of the increasing number of children who have severe peanut allergies.[10] And you can't get a peanut on an airplane anymore. This is an example of working at the wrong end of the problem! Instead of removing all peanuts from the environment, we need to be asking ourselves, "What is going wrong with the immune system of so many children today?"

I am concerned that bypassing the usual immune mechanism by vaccinating children for so many common illnesses, together with unhealthy changes in so many children's diet, upsets nature's balance and wisdom and helps explain why there's been such an increase in childhood allergies and asthma in the last generation—not to mention the growing number of kids with ADHD and autism.

My vaccination concerns are shared by many others. Here's a typical query from one of my newsletter subscribers:

> I'm having a great deal of difficulty with the whole vaccination issue for my baby. I'm using a group of somewhat conven-

tional pediatricians who follow the CDC [Centers for Disease Control] vaccination schedule for infants/children. Thus far, I have deferred giving her any vaccinations. What I am wondering is if you have any thoughts on the subject of a safer vaccine schedule, which may include giving vaccinations later on and eliminating certain ones altogether. I am in desperate need of someone I can trust who is a professional and who can help me assess the risk-benefit of all these vaccinations.

The issue of routine childhood immunizations has been something I've given careful thought to for over twenty years. I'll share my beliefs and personal experience here as a way to help others decide what makes the most sense for them and their children.

My Own Story: Ambivalence and Incomplete Immunizations

I remember taking my first daughter, Annie, to the pediatrician for her first shot. She weighed less than six pounds. Although Annie was full-term and healthy, she was still somewhat jaundiced because the bilirubin hadn't been fully cleared from her system. (Bilirubin, which can surge during birth, gives skin a yellowish color.) At the time, I had misgivings about immunizations after hearing Keith I. Block, M.D., speak about the issue at the East West Foundation in Boston in the early '80s. I also read the work of pediatrician Robert Mendelsohn, M.D. (who wrote *Confessions of a Medical Heretic*), and Richard Moskowitz, M.D. (a physician with an extensive background in immunization and homeopathy). These men, as well as Dr. Block, questioned the use of immunizations, citing data that showed that diseases like polio were on the decline at the time vaccines were introduced. And these same immunizations weren't without significant risk.

On the other hand, I had just completed eight years of rigorous training in Western medicine, which taught that childhood immunizations were safe and important, and I was married to a very conventional surgeon. Although I had doubts, I didn't want to look like a "bad" mother or push my agenda too far with my husband.

So I took Annie in, and despite her small size, the pediatrician gave her a full dose of DPT (diphtheria-pertussis-tetanus) in her buttock. Like many babies, she developed a high fever and was very irritable for several days. She also developed a red swelling the size of a half dollar at the injection site. It resulted in muscle necrosis (muscle cell destruction), which left a permanent indentation.

After that, I was reluctant to continue vaccinating her. I decided to postpone her immunizations for at least a few months. I felt comfortable relying on other ways to ensure her health. I knew that good nutrition created a healthy immunity. Since I was breast-feeding her, eating well myself, and taking supplements, I decided to put my faith in the wisdom of Nature rather than make her sick on purpose.

My husband didn't agree. So over the next five years, our differing approaches to the issue were played out with how and when our daughter got her shots. I insisted that if she was going to have a shot, she should get half the usual dose and also avoid the pertussis vaccine altogether. I wasn't alone in my concern over the pertussis vaccine. By then, the available form had come under increased scrutiny, due to its possible association with neurologic disorders. As a child, Annie never had another DPT shot. Instead, she got half the typical dose of DT—just once—and a polio shot. These were administered when she was three years old and I was away at a medical conference. Eventually, she got the minimum needed to enter school. And she never had another reaction to a shot.

Later, as a junior in high school, she got all the recommended shots before going to work at a mission in a remote area of Zimbabwe, Africa. At the time, I felt the risk from the vaccinations was significantly less than the risk of going into a Third World country unprotected.

When my second child, Kate, was born, I decided to forgo immunizations altogether. Kate was a very healthy child who never had a single immunization until she was sixteen. My husband was so busy with his practice that he didn't take her in to have shots when I was out of town. When she went to camp for the first time, the camp nurse and I compromised on a tetanus shot. Before going to college, she and I decided she might as well get the required shots—it was easier than taking on the college health service. Plus, I knew that her mature immune system was prepared to deal with the numerous viruses and toxins in the vaccines. She did well. But looking back now, I'm not sure I should have agreed so easily.

I'm glad that I minimized and delayed my children's immunizations. I also fully support those parents who choose to avoid immunizations altogether. The truth is, vaccines are neither 100 percent safe nor 100 percent effective. And their benefits come at a price. There's not a physician, public health official, or vaccine manufacturer anywhere who would disagree with these statements. Most public health authorities contend that the overall benefit of vaccines for the "herd" is worth the price that some individuals pay. When it comes to my own children, I don't agree.

Immunization Is a Classic First-Chakra Issue

Getting your child or yourself immunized is a culturally agreed-upon ritual, designed to shore up both aspects of first-chakra health. (The first chakra, or first emotional center, of our body controls our bones, joints, bone marrow, blood, and immune system.) The health of the first emotional center is directly dependent on two factors: our feelings of safety and security in the world, and our sense of belonging. This is the main reason it's so difficult to question the immunization issue. You fear losing the approval of the "tribe" or being made to feel that you're a bad mother if you don't immunize your child. A solid sense of personal safety and security, as well as information, is required to question what everyone else believes is best.

Vaccinations were created out of a sincere desire to eradicate deadly diseases like smallpox and polio. And they definitely have benefits. Many of us remember the summer polio epidemic following World War II, and the hero, Dr. Jonas Salk, who discovered the first polio vaccine. When I was a child, polio shots and later oral Sabin vaccines were given at our local school. As a result, we felt safer and more secure, though I hated getting the shots. And because of the triumph of the polio vaccine, the culture extended the same war-against-microbes approach to an increasing number of childhood illnesses, many of which, like chicken pox, are benign in the vast majority of children.

In the United States, there were eight new vaccines added to the approved Childhood Immunization Schedule between 1964 and 2002. This translated to a total of twenty-three doses, including: five doses of live virus polio; four doses of Hib (*Haemophilus influenzae* Type b, a form of meningitis); four doses of pneumococcal vaccine; three doses of hepatitis B vaccine; two doses of live MMR vaccine; and one dose of live virus varicella zoster (chicken pox) vaccine. Over the past forty years, the percentage of children being vaccinated has sky-rocketed. In 1967, the DPT, polio, and MMR vaccines were given to 60 to 80 percent of all American children. In 1996, DPT, polio, MMR, hepatitis B, and Hib vaccines were given to 80 to 95 percent. Since then, nearly 95 percent of all children entering kindergarten have received the vaccines prescribed by the CDC.

I am concerned by the sheer number of vaccines currently given to very young children. I intuitively feel that these are connected to the ever-increasing incidence of childhood asthma, allergies, diabetes, ADHD, autism, and possibly even cancer. I'm also concerned about our overreliance on vaccines as the primary way to prevent illnesses, while ignoring other aspects of immunity and health.

How to Legally Avoid Immunizing Your Child

Most states offer a religious, philosophical, or medical exception to "mandatory" shots. There are now at least thirteen states that have laws allowing parents to refuse immunizations for philosophical reasons. But the laws and procedures vary greatly from state to state, so you'll need to do some research. If you're not sure about this issue, become informed. Parents have a right to objective information prior to deciding whether to immunize their children. I've found that the most reliable information from an alternative point of view is from D.O. Joseph Mercola and D.O. Sherri Tenpenny. (See Resources.)

If you don't intend to immunize your child, or if you'd like to delay or reduce the number of immunizations your child receives, I recommend that you be proactive about your decision. Address the issue with your doctor or other health care provider on a nonemergency basis. Starting before your child is born is often necessary. Some pediatricians won't follow children who aren't immunized. In some states, day-care providers can also refuse to accept your child. So don't wait until your child gets sick or needs to see a doctor before setting up your team. To find out more on how to legally avoid vaccinations, go to *www.mercola.com/article/vaccines/legally_avoid_shots.htm*.

You want to be respectful of your doctor's views and training, but also find someone who will work in partnership with you. I didn't have any trouble with the schools because the state of Maine has a waiver form a parent can sign that says that you object to vaccines for religious reasons. Though I didn't object for religious reasons, I just decided to take the path of least resistance. It helped that I was a doctor, of course. The school officials assumed I knew what I was doing, wasn't neglecting my children, and was making an informed decision.

One of my friends, whom I'll call Shirley, is the mother of a two-month-old daughter. She really likes her new pediatrician, but she found herself up against the immunization issue when she went in for her first well-baby check. Luckily, her husband feels as strongly as she does about avoiding immunizations, so when the doctor made her disapproval clear, her husband went to bat for Shirley and his daughter. He looked right at the doctor, and said, "Shirley hates confrontations, so she won't discuss this with you. She'll just avoid the issue and avoid bringing our daughter in. Or she'll change doctors. So please don't bring this up again."

When Shirley called me for additional advice, I suggested that she and her husband tell the pediatrician how much they like her care, and also let her know they are willing to put their vaccination decision in writing for the baby's chart. That way they are sharing the presumed risk of not vaccinating. Generally, I've found that being openhearted and appreciative of the pediatrician's point of view can go a long way in getting the relationship you want.

After all, most pediatricians are not familiar with the research that shows the downside of vaccinations. And in their role as "protectors of children," they are doing what they've been trained to do. One of my pediatrician colleagues, a man who now gives seminars to parents on the dangers of immunizations, told me that he finished his training in 1983 and didn't even think to question immunizations until 1998. Initially, all of his information on immunizations came directly from the American Academy of Pediatrics. But after being in practice for a while and having seen some negative side effects, he began to do research on his own. And, as a result, he said, he can't in good conscience continue to recommend routine immunizations.

Dr. Mercola also suggests the following, which I agree with wholeheartedly: "In all your contacts with any member of the school, public health, or legal establishment, always remain calm, courteous, and humbly reverent toward their position. You are only asking of them that which the law dutifully binds them to give you. There is no reason, or advantage, to be gained by antagonizing them." Most officials believe they are discharging their trust, as outlined by law. If they are overstepping the law, then you must very diplomatically bring the true facts to their attention, but without attempting to belittle them. The more you can preserve their ego, the more easily and quickly you are likely to get what you desire—a waiver of immunization. So, as Dr. Mercola says, "Do not harass, belittle, or antagonize officials unnecessarily." The rest of his advice is equally succinct, respectful, and practical.

The Power of Natural Immunity

There's still a great deal we don't understand about living in harmony with nature and germs. The vast majority of the time, humans live peacefully with even the most deadly germs in their environments. Though we've been taught to fear germs, most documented infections don't even cause symptoms, let alone full-blown disease! It is well known, for example, that the vast majority of us live peaceably with pneumoccal pneumonia germs in our respiratory tracts—but rarely get pneumonia. In children deliberately exposed to cold viruses, only half get symptoms, even though cultures of their noses reveal that they have "caught" the virus.[11]

Richard Moskowitz, M.D., an expert on immunization and homeopathy, points out that the polio virus produces no illness at all in over 90 percent of those exposed to it. For others, it causes aches, pains, and GI upset, but little else. Though our culture is obsessed with the fact that diseases such as polio kill and maim several thousand victims per year, what we don't appreciate is the fact that millions of young people become infected by polio viruses each year and don't suffer *any* harmful consequences! Their immune systems protect them. And in the United States, the only cases of polio in recent years have been from the oral vaccine, which is now off the market.

In general, our culture teaches us to ignore the multiple ways our immune system keeps us healthy in spite of all the germs in our environment. Instead, we focus on the relatively infrequent times when the immune system is weakened, allowing germs to cause infection and illness.

It all goes back to the classic argument between scientist Louis Pasteur, who discovered the role of microbes in disease, and his contemporaries Claude Bernard and Antoine Bechamp. Bernard, who championed the concept of homeostasis in the body, and Bechamp, a physiologist, argued that germs can cause disease only when something in the environment allows it. Pasteur claimed that it was the germs themselves that were responsible for disease. On his deathbed, Louis Pasteur declared: "Claude Bernard was right . . . the microbe is nothing, the terrain is everything."[12]

Epidemiologist Leonard Sagan, M.D., points to evidence that, over time, a population develops a generalized level of resistance to diseases, and this level of resistance may be more important in controlling mortality than reducing exposure to the infectious agent. This helps explain why many of the childhood diseases we vaccinate for were on the decline even before the vaccines were introduced, including the post–WWII polio epidemic.[13] But it also explains why, when a population has had absolutely no collective immunologic "experience" with an infectious agent (as has occurred when native tribes were exposed to diseases borne by the first explorers) those populations were decimated.

Sagan points out that there is evidence suggesting that eradication of one infectious agent in a population may open the door for other equally virulent organisms in the environment, with one cause of death replacing another. AIDS is a stunning example.

Vaccines Are Not 100 Percent Effective

Vaccinations do not produce *true immunity*. This is the crux of the vaccination controversy for many parents and doctors. A vaccine is a "trick," meant to stimulate the immune system to recognize and fight the germ (introduced in the vaccine) if the body is exposed to it in the future. But this doesn't always happen. Plus, vaccines do not act merely by producing mild versions of the original disease they're meant to protect against. They commonly produce symptoms of their own. And in some children, these symptoms are very difficult to diagnose.

The truth is, there's never been a single, controlled clinical trial of a vaccine in which some children got it, others didn't, and then the health of both groups was studied to see how they compare. What we do have is conclusive evidence that the rates of diseases like measles are reduced in immunized populations. *However, the overall rates of illness and chronic diseases in children are actually higher than ever before, even though children today receive many more vaccines than in the past.* And in every outbreak of infectious disease, many of those who get the disease have been fully vaccinated.[14]

One of the main reasons for the difference between natural life-long immunity from bacteria or viruses and preventing an illness through injected vaccines may be rooted in the difference between the two main aspects of our immune systems. As I pointed out above, more than 80 percent of our total immune system activity is at the entry points of our bodies—on our skin and at the mucosal entryways of our mouth and nose, genital tract, and GI tract. When our immune system is working well, bacteria and viruses never make it into our bloodstreams. Giving vaccines by injection bypasses this system entirely.[15]

Vaccines Aren't 100 Percent Safe

It is well documented that individuals occasionally suffer a serious adverse reaction to immunization.[16] The reason for this is that the substances from which vaccines are made can cause reactions, depending upon a child's constitution. Vaccines are made either from live viruses that are attenuated (made less potent) by serial passage in tissue culture, or from bacteria or bacterial proteins that have been killed or denatured using substances like formaldehyde. You can't grow live viruses on healthy tissue—you need "sick" cells and disease-ridden environments to grow them. Vaccines are grown on pig blood, horse blood, rabbit brain, guinea pig cells, dog kidneys, and cow hearts, to name a few. All of these tissues can potentially harbor their own viruses and bacteria, which can be transmitted to susceptible humans through vaccines. To be effective, vaccines must also include substances known as adjuvants that cause tissue inflammation. This inflammation attracts immune system cells to the area so they can be "imprinted" by the attenuated germ or virus in the vaccine—and thus will recognize and destroy it in the future. But the adjuvants themselves can be quite toxic.

The Mercury Controversy

Preservatives used in vaccines, such as thimerosal, may also be toxic due to their high mercury content. Research in England reported an alarmingly high incidence of encephalopathy and severe convulsive disorders in British children traceable to thimerosal in the DPT vaccine.[17] Recently published studies have also linked the increasing risk of neurodevelopmental disorders in children, including autism, with increasing levels of mercury from childhood vaccinations.

In 1999, the American Academy of Pediatrics and the U.S. Public Health Service called for the removal of thimerosal from vaccines. But according to the April 2003 Director's Report from the American Association for Health Freedom, some of the manufacturers still haven't complied. The same report also states, "In another significant finding, the researchers . . . found that the mercury exposure of many vaccinated U.S. infants and children exceeded the maximum daily limits established by the Environmental Protection Agency (EPA)."[18]

The researchers concluded that their study "provides strong epidemiologic evidence for a link between increasing mercury from
thimerosal-containing childhood vaccines and neurodevelopmental
disorders and heart disease." In his discussion of this research, Dr.
Joseph Mercola wrote, "It is nearly incomprehensible that the well-
documented, toxic mercury is still in many vaccines, years after federal agencies have mandated that thimerosal be removed."

Despite these reports, there is still widespread controversy about
the role of mercury in vaccine-related problems. An independent
2001 review conducted by the Immunization Safety Review Committee, on behalf of the Institute of Medicine, concluded that the
evidence is inadequate to either accept or reject a causal relationship
between thimerosal-containing vaccine and neurodevelopmental
disorders.[19]

A Danish study, published in 2003, compared children vaccinated with a thimerosal-containing vaccine with children vaccinated with a thimerosal-free version of the same vaccine. It found
that the number of cases of autism and related neurologic conditions was no different in the two groups.[20] However, the researchers
did find a dramatic rise in autism and autistic-spectrum disorders in
both groups during the study period, similar to what has been observed in other countries. This leads to the possibility that there's
something else besides mercury in vaccines that is associated with
the problem.

THE BOTTOM LINE: Mercury is just one toxic substance in vaccines. Others include aluminum, yeast proteins, monosodium glutamate, gelatin, antibiotics, stray DNA and RNA, and other substances.
We do not know and have never attempted to discover what actually
becomes of these substances once they are inside the human body. I'd
rather not inject them into a young child—regardless of the current
data. It amazes me that we're concerned enough about the mercury
level in fish to warn pregnant women to avoid it, yet we inject it and
other toxins into infants shortly after birth!

I realize that the vast majority of data on vaccines in doctor's of-
fices and on the Internet is positive and very reassuring. But medicine
is full of instances in which conventionally accepted practice later
needed updating as new data became available. I'm always amazed
by how many people, including physician colleagues, share my concern once I bring it up. All parents owe it to themselves to look at the
other side of the issue. (See Resources.)

Increased Vulnerability Leads
to Adverse Vaccine Reactions

Many people have vaccinations with no problem at all. Again, as Drs. Antoine Bechamp and Claude Bernard pointed out more than a hundred years ago, it's the nature of the terrain, not the germs or toxins, that is the most important factor. Most healthy people can tolerate the toxins in vaccines. But if there's a weakness in the immune or nervous system to begin with, it's a different story.

When my friend and research colleague Mona Lisa Schulz, M.D., Ph.D., was defending her doctoral thesis, she felt both stressed and "under attack" by her thesis committee. Her sense of safety and security was fully taxed by the experience. The day after her oral thesis defense, she got a vaccine for hepatitis B, a requirement for all medical students at Boston University School of Medicine. The next day she woke up with swollen glands all over her body, and excruciating pain in all the joints of her hands and feet. A rheumatologist told her that she had classic "serum sickness" in which antibody/antigen complexes from the reaction to the vaccine had been deposited into all the joints in her body. Her doctor made sure she never got the second dose!

IF YOU DECIDE TO IMMUNIZE

Hold off on immunizing your baby for at least three months, and longer if possible. I question the wisdom of introducing foreign proteins and toxic substances from vaccines into a baby's body before age three months. During this time, a mother's body is basically regulating her child's immune system. And if she's fully present and breast-feeding, the baby will get antibodies from her milk that offer very specific protection against the germs that are in the child's environment. Why risk messing with nature's design at this critical stage?

There is science behind this. On his Web site, Dr. Mercola talks about studies done in Japan where DPT immunization was delayed until children were two years of age. Researchers found that these children experienced 85 to 90 percent fewer severe complications than babies who received the same vaccine at ages three to five months.

Appreciate biochemical individuality. Every child will react differently to the substances in vaccinations. Some may not have any reaction at all. I'd think twice before vaccinating a child if there is any family history of ADHD, autism, allergies, type 1 diabetes (autoimmune juvenile-onset), or asthma.

Limit the number of vaccinations given at one time. And know your shots. Some injections contain up to five different vaccines in one. And more of these combination vaccines are on the way. When you give them one at a time, you can monitor the effects of the vaccine more easily.

Avoid vaccines containing mercury. Before taking your child in for a vaccine, call ahead and ask your doctor to read the package insert to find out if the intended vaccine has mercury. If it does, ask for another type.

Don't immunize your child when she is already fighting an infection. Vaccines given at a time when a child isn't feeling well introduce foreign antigens into the baby's system that it must respond to, but at a time when that baby's immune system is already working overtime.

Be very selective about what vaccines your child gets. I don't believe that children should be vaccinated for chicken pox. The disease is very benign in children, but more severe in adulthood. By vaccinating all children, and preventing natural lifelong immunity, we may be setting up a situation in which even more adults get the disease, and at a time when its effects are most devastating. I also wouldn't recommend the MMR because many of my previously vaccinated patients had inadequate antibody protection against rubella in later years. I postponed vaccinating my daughters for rubella until puberty, when they were at possible risk for pregnancy. I also would never vaccinate a newborn for hepatitis B unless a parent or family member had active hepatitis B at the time the child was born.

Consider using the modalities available to detoxify possible side effects of the immunization. Note: I suggest detoxifying past vaccinations. It makes no sense to give a vaccine that you know is toxic and then try to detoxify it.

~ If you're breast-feeding, increase your intake of vitamin C to about 3 grams both before and after your child's immunization. This powerful antioxidant protects against tissue damage of all kinds.

~ A modality known as Nambudripad allergy elimination technique (NAET) is also very effective at ridding side effects from the system. (See Resources.)

~ Vibrational healing is another effective way to "clear" the toxins introduced by the immunization. Deena Spear has improved the health of many with this technique. (See Resources.)

WHAT I RECOMMEND TO HELP SHORE UP YOUR CHILD'S IMMUNITY

Every one of us wants to do everything we can to protect our child's health, whether or not immunizations are part of the plan. Happily, there are many ways to do this besides routine immunizations. Here's how:

Maintain a peaceful home that engenders hope and humane treatment of family members. The best way to protect your child's health and lifelong immunity is to maintain a peaceful and reliable home environment in which your child feels safe and loved. A truly massive body of research has now shown beyond a shadow of a doubt that the key to a healthy immune system and longevity is an upbringing that includes copious amounts of hope and happiness, and negligible amounts of despair, hopelessness, and helplessness. This is true after controlling for all other variables that we usually associate with health, including clean water, good nutrition, genetics, immunizations, and even education.[21]

Psychological stress of all kinds depresses immune function and leads to increased frequency of disease, particularly infections. That means that if you are living with an abusive spouse who threatens you around your children or threatens to harm the family pets, more damage is being done to your child's immune system than any and all immunizations can prevent!

Feed your child good nutritious food. Nutrition plays an undeniably important role in keeping children healthy. Let's examine the role of just one nutrient: vitamin A. In a randomized, double-blind controlled study of 189 children (median age ten months) in South Africa who were hospitalized with measles complications including pneumonia, diarrhea, and croup, researchers found that the children who were given vitamin A (a total dose of 400,000 IU retinyl palmitate) within five days of onset of the measles rash recovered much faster. The risk of major complications and death were cut in half too.[22] What was intriguing is that there was no evidence of vitamin A deficiency in these children.

(Note: Because of potential toxicity, high doses of vitamin A should not be taken except under medical supervision. The safest way to supplement vitamin A is to take beta carotene, which is converted to vitamin A in the body.)

Over fifty studies show that in almost every known infectious disease, whether bacterial, viral, or protozoan in origin, vitamin A deficiency is known to result in greater frequency, severity, and mortality.[23] In fact, vitamin A is sometimes referred to as the "anti-infective" vitamin.[24] Don't wait for the experts to agree. Make sure your child takes a high-quality multivitamin daily and eats as well as possible. Include probiotics or foods containing them. (Although, as I've said, a little junk food won't hurt them. They need to participate in some of our culture's rituals, and that includes an occasional french fry!)

Use immune-enhancing supplements. I recommend two herbal supplements for children: Kold Kare and Umcka. Kold Kare contains the Asian herb *Andrographis paniculata,* which has been shown to boost the immune system and decrease the number of colds per season in those who take it regularly. A child aged ten and up who is prone to colds, allergies, and sinusitis should take one or two Kold Kare tablets in the morning and one or two in the evening throughout the entire winter. Younger children can take Umcka.

Umcka is a well-studied and very effective herbal supplement containing an extract of the geranium *Pelargonium sidoides* that can help ward off colds, tonsillitis, ear infections, sore throats, and bronchitis. Take as directed on the bottle at the first sign of symptoms and continue for forty-eight hours after symptoms have subsided. (These supplements are available at your natural food store or through Emerson Ecologics. See Resources.)

Consider using homeopathy. Dr. Moskowitz suggests that parents familiarize themselves with the signs and symptoms of the most common childhood illnesses so they are prepared to intervene very early should the child get sick. He also points out that before vaccines, homeopathy was used very effectively during infectious disease epidemics to both treat and keep people healthy.

HOW TO APPROACH YOUR
DAUGHTER'S MEDICAL CARE

A woman who is in tune with her Mother Bear instincts knows when her child is fine and when she's not. Mothers who are well bonded with their children know better than any expert on the planet how their children are really doing.

On the other hand, mothers who do not have a good inner sense of safety and security themselves will often doubt their own judgment and defer to doctors and other experts in matters of health. Unfortunately, our culture participates in this at every turn, given our belief that there must be a "pill for every ill." Mothers who don't trust themselves are far more likely to overmedicalize their child by calling or running to the doctor every time the child gets a runny nose. This then sends the same message of insecurity and distrust on to her child. When a child has been taught that every symptom requires medical care, they grow up to rely more on experts than their own inner guidance.

A child needs to know that the body heals itself most of the time. When you cut yourself, it heals. Of course there are times when you'll need medical assistance—for instance for a deep cut. But it is well known that the children of physicians rarely get as much medical care as the physicians recommend to other patients!

I participated in only a couple of conventional "well-child" visits with my children because I knew they were healthy. When my younger girl was about seven, she said, "Mom, are we ever going to go to a doctor?" All her friends went to doctors, after all. I told her that she saw a doctor every day of her life—me and her father.

I did, however, occasionally take my kids in for acupuncture (using a laser, not needles) when they were sick. My older daughter had a truly wretched case of chicken pox when she was eleven, and acupuncture and herbs helped her sleep and heal. I also used classical osteopathy on occasion for general prevention.

Whatever modalities you choose, it's enormously reassuring to have a team of trusted health professionals you can turn to when you need to. This may include a pediatrician, a family doctor, and also a naturopath or practitioner of traditional Chinese medicine. My acupuncturist sees babies and children all the time—often after conventional medicine has failed to resolve ongoing problems. She has helped get rid of allergies, chronic stomach upset, and recurrent ear infections, among other ailments.

Thankfully, more and more physicians are holistically inclined these days. The main thing you want is someone who is a healer and believes in a child's ability to be healthy. This attitude is more healing and engenders more confidence and trust than any particular philosophy or mode of practice. One of my friends told me how important such a doctor had been to her:

> My pediatrician bolstered my confidence in myself and my child, which got off to a shaky start because of her birth defect. He had been a doctor in Romania before emigrating to the States, and he told me how the shepherds would come down from the mountains in the fall bringing the flocks and the new babies that had been born over the summer. He radiated faith in children's natural ability to thrive.

When Your Child Needs Medical Attention

Of course your child needs to see a doctor if she has been in an accident, suffers a serious illness, or needs a medical procedure of some kind. But at these times, your Mother Bear wisdom is especially crucial to your child's well-being.

Whenever there has been trauma of some kind, the human body pours out a huge amount of the stress hormones epinephrine and cortisol. This affects every function in the body, putting it on "red alert." In such a state, the reasoning part of the brain shuts down temporarily and consciousness turns inward, much as when a woman is in labor. This makes the child hypersuggestible. A mother or other caregiver has a golden opportunity to use this biologic state to implant "hope and healing" messages deep in the unconscious to be drawn on then and in the future.

The altered state associated with trauma can be thought of as fertile soil. You can plant healthy seeds that will help the person heal and replenish their emotional soil and healing capacity—or you can let torrents of fear erode the soil so that nothing grows except more fear. What you say to a child at this time can make a huge difference in that child's ability to heal.

This is one of the the messages of a wonderful book called *The Worst Is Over: What to Say When Every Moment Counts*, by Judith Acosta, L.C.S.W., and Judith Simon Prager, Ph.D. Acosta and Prager call this autonomic response to trauma "the healing zone." It's a time when a child (or an adult) is maximally open to the power of words, thoughts, and her environments—not unlike a state of hypnosis. When you say the right thing to a child during this time, such as, "I'm right here. I'll be with you. You're going to be just fine. Go inside and ask your body to stop the bleeding. I've called nine-one-one. They'll be here very soon," you will be connecting directly with the parts of her mind and nervous system that regulate healing functions. You are also providing the kind of outside authority that allows your child to relax and begin using her energy to start healing.

YOUR WORDS MAKE A DIFFERENCE

Here are some bodily functions that can be directly influenced with verbal first aid:

pain	sweating
heart rate	allergic responses
respiration	asthma
blood pressure	rate of healing
bleeding	dermatitis
inflammatory response	dryness of mouth
itching	immune response
contractions	glandular secretions
bowel motility	emotional reactions
smooth muscle tension	

HOW TO GIVE VERBAL FIRST AID

Center yourself. Do whatever you need to find that calm, sure center inside yourself. No matter how critical the situation, you always have time to do this. Say a prayer, take a deep full breath, tell yourself you have the ability to help—whatever works for you.

When I was an ob-gyn resident at St. Margaret's Hospital in Boston, I always centered myself before doing surgery by reading the prayer that was posted above the scrub sinks. I don't remember the precise words, but I know we asked that our hands would become the instruments through which the Great Physician could do His healing. It always made me feel much better and more up to the task ahead.

Understand your power to help. You are the ultimate authority in your child's life. When you take charge of the situation and give your child positive messages of support, you help her feel safe and protected. You can ask her to squeeze your hand or take some deep breaths. Whatever is appropriate. And her autonomic nervous system and bodily organs will respond dramatically. Don't worry about "getting it right." When you have the intent to use your words and presence for the ultimate good, you'll know what to say.

Communicate realistically. Though it's not helpful to be overly optimistic, there is a magic sentence that opens up rapport and allows the body to begin the recovery process in almost all acute situations. It is this: "The worst is over." In almost every situation, that is simply the truth. If you're not sure that it is, you can always say, "The worst is over for now." Your child has already had the accident, or the fall, or whatever. There are many physiologic benefits to that healing statement.

This same advice applies when you take your child to the doctor for a procedure that may be painful. Be honest but reassuring. If she asks, "Will this hurt?" say, "Yes, it will. But just for a moment"—or whatever is appropriate. Always convey your confidence in her ability to make it through the situation.

Work in partnership with your child's medical team. Consciously or unconsciously, your child will pick up any conflict between you and her caregivers. So do everything in your power to work cooperatively with your child's medical team. Sometimes you'll encounter a doctor or nurse who is rude, abrasive, or just not a healer. In that case, validate your child's feelings about the person, if appropriate, and find someone else as soon as possible. Letting your child know that you're not going to turn her over to an unskilled doctor or nurse will do a world of good for her sense of safety and security.

If your child is hospitalized, stay by her side as much as possible. Even if you're entirely happy with her medical care, your presence creates an island of normalcy in the midst of a strange and frightening environment. We've come a very long way as a culture since my sister Bonnie died in a hospital nursery untouched by my mother. Now parents can stay with their children and are encouraged to participate. What a relief!

Include your child in her healing. If possible, ask your daughter to help hold a bandage, or breathe slowly and deeply with you. Children love being included, and it helps them focus on something other than the pain or injury. Even a small choice like picking out a red or blue Band-Aid can help to restore a child's sense of control and dignity following the assault of pain and fear. Knowing that she is part of the process allows your daughter to tap in to her inner healing ability. And research bears this out. Pediatric oncologist Karen Olness, M.D., at Case Western Reserve University School of Medicine, has done extensive research on teaching children how to use self-regulation techniques such as imagery and hypnosis to help them deal with various treatments and to enhance immune function.[25]

Avoid blame and shame. If your child has fallen or hurt herself doing something you don't approve of, do not make things worse by saying, "Didn't I tell you never to do that?" or "I knew you'd hurt yourself." Reality has already taught your daughter a lesson. Now she needs your support and reassurance. Don't argue with your spouse about what the child should or shouldn't have been doing. You have to consciously censor these remarks, or they can interfere with the healing process. I'll bet you can recall several of these situations from childhood—where your original programming about illness comes from in the first place!

Intend to be a force for good and you will be. You will be most effective with helping your child (or anyone) when you exude confidence and show and feel concern. Loving intention is all that's necessary. Even if you don't get the words right, your genuine compassion and love will come through.

Confidence as a mother comes from knowing that you can help your child just by your presence and your words. So if you are the one who is first on the scene of an accident, just know that you're the one who is supposed to help. Both your child and you will, at this moment, enter a sacred space. I know. I've been there many times with my patients. It is a place where we share our common humanity and can truly be of service to each other.

10

Love Maps

How We Encode Mood, Sex, and Relationships

❁

T he vast majority of children are born with an innate sense of joy and happiness. This is one of their great gifts to us, and mothers are usually delighted to see the world afresh through their daughters' eyes. A friend recently told me me how her heart melted when she was carrying her sleeping three-year-old into the house after a car trip. It was dusk and the sun had just peeked out, lighting up all the rain droplets. Her daughter opened her eyes and exclaimed, "Look, Mommy! It's so sparkly!"

The mother who participates in her daughter's joyful emotions is actually helping to develop and reinforce the brain circuits that support healthy mood. However, the reverse is also true. Say, for example, that a sixteen-month-old is excitedly pointing to a monkey's antics in the zoo and trying to get her mother's attention. She wants to share her joy and win her mother's approval. But her mother may be too depressed or exhausted to respond, or she may simply be deeply absorbed in a conversation on her cell phone. Research has shown that at fifteen to sixteen months, a child is particularly vulnerable to what is known as the "danger of deflation"—caused by her mother's lack of interest or inability to mirror her child's excitement back to her.[1]

If her mother doesn't smile back at her when her child gets excited about something, then that child's mood deflates. When a child feels something, she naturally looks around to see if others mirror her feeling. If they don't, she feels ridiculous and ashamed of herself for feeling joyful. The inference the child makes is that her mood must be wrong. After all, her mother is bigger, more powerful, and in charge—she must be right! So the child starts to believe that something is wrong with her, and that joy is bad and must be hidden. Unfortunately, if a mother is usually preoccupied, if she is often in a difficult mood, or if she is dealing with serious conflicts in other parts of her life, she may unwittingly undermine her child's self-esteem.

The Roots of Self-esteem

Self-esteem is developed throughout one's life and will be discussed in detail in Chapter 12. In infancy and early childhood, self-esteem is all about reinforcement of a child's innate sense of joy and trust in herself. But positive reflection of her innate value is not enough to cement firm self-esteem as she gets older. Then she will need to accomplish goals and meet expectations—both those of others and those she has set for herself.

As a result of repeated experiences when her joy isn't reflected back to her, a child learns how to blunt her excitement and put a ceiling on her joy. After a while, she no longer gets excited and may feel that life is hopeless and that she is helpless to do anything about it. A feeling of futility and resignation gets wired into her body. This is then transmitted to her posture. Her head and eyes start to lower, and her exploration of both herself and her world becomes truncated. In short, the child becomes depressed.

TRYING TO WIN MOTHER'S LOVE: BIRTHING PERSONAS THAT REPLACE OUR TRUE SELVES

If a child comes to believe that she won't be lovable if she is true to her inner self, she may begin to develop a persona, a false personality that she creates in response to her perception of what others want her to be and do. This persona can start to take shape as early as age two and be firmly in place by age five. The number of possible personas is endless, but a very common one for girls is "the good girl" or the "helpful girl." I've also known my share of rebels. Wanda, one of my patients, told me the following:

> For as far back as I can remember, I've been driven to get my work done in a way that is pleasing to others. In kindergarten I remember that I cried when we had to draw a house with a classmate covering our eyes. I was frustrated that I wouldn't get it done right if I couldn't see what I was drawing. Once in fourth grade, I burst into tears because I couldn't figure out what 5 times 5 was on an achievement test. Though we hadn't even learned our times tables yet, I figured that if it was on a test, I should know the correct answer. But it wasn't just the correct answer that I craved. It was the positive adult attention that I would achieve because of it.
>
> Because my drive to achieve was not driven by the pure, positive desire to learn and to know, however, almost all of my achievements have been accompanied by a niggling sense of burden and struggle. I have never had a problem with will. It seems as though I was born with discipline, concentration, and the ability to stick to a schedule. But each morning when I arise I have this voice inside my head that insists that I must get up and get on with it, that there are things to do, obligations to be met. I love my work and it brings me great satisfaction. I am also self-employed and so have no boss but myself. I suspect that some of this sense of burden is simply the way I was born. And some is related to the environment in my home when I was between the ages of two and five.
>
> When I was age two, my younger sister was three months old and my older sister was six. To say that my mother had her hands full would be an understatement. I once had a psychic reading in which I was told that I used to run around the house shrieking in delight at the world. This was not okay with my mother (who could blame her?) and so I shut my voice down and became something much more acceptable: the classic good girl. My mother's best friend told me that I was her favorite child of the three of us because I sat in my high chair peacefully and didn't give anyone any trouble. I called my mother to ask her about this time period, and when I left the message on her answering machine, I suddenly found myself in tears.

Even without my mother's input, my body, through those tears, had given me the information I was seeking. Yes indeed, I knew that I had shut down my full capacity to experience everyday joy in life during this period and gave birth to a persona who did what she was told and tried at every turn to be acceptable by being pleasing to others and doing the right thing. Now at midlife I am finally ready to let go of my helpful persona and live once more from the inside out, enjoying every day to its fullest with trust and hope and joy, like the little two-year-old Wanda from long ago.

DEPRESSED MOTHERS, DEPRESSED CHILDREN

Depression in mothers can compromise a child's capacity to bond and form healthy, stable relationships throughout life. It may also set the stage for compromised immunity and other health problems. University of Washington psychologist Geraldine Dawson, Ph.D., has monitered the brain-wave patterns of infants age eleven to seventeen months whose mothers are depressed and has found markedly decreased activity in the frontal limbic areas of these children.[2] (The left frontal limbic area serves as the center for joy, compassion, contentment, and other positive social emotions.) Patterns of brain activity of these infants closely track the ups and downs of their mothers' depression. One of the most striking findings of Dawson's work is her discovery that by down-regulating their response to joy, infants also down-regulated their response to distress. In other words, there's reason to believe that a mother's depression decreases her baby's ability to feel emotions of *all* kinds fully, whether they be emotions of joy or emotions of sadness. They may grow up to have blunted emotions unless there's someone else in the family who is happy and joyful.

At the age of three, the children whose mothers were most severely depressed or whose depression lasted longer continued to show abnormally low readings on their brain activity. Mothers who were disengaged, impatient, and irritable tended to have babies with sad brains. It is not surprising that studies have shown that mental disorders tend to cluster around those individuals who have weak or insecure bonds to others because of problems such as abuse and maternal depression.[3] Parental substance abuse, divorce, and financial adversity also frequently characterize the childhoods of those who have difficulty forming healthy adult relationships. These adversities do not cause the problem; however, they tend to perpetuate it.[4]

A mother's depression needn't cause permanent damage in her children. Other studies have shown that depressed mothers who managed to rise above their own melancholy, lavishing their babies with attention and indulging in playful games, had children with more cheerful brain activity.

Other caregivers can also contribute greatly to a child's overall health and well-being when a mother can't be present, for whatever reason. One of my patients developed breast cancer when her daughters were two and four. She was often sick from her treatments and unavailable to her children. Her mother helped out with the children, and her husband was also very present for them. Though this wasn't an easy time for anyone, both girls are happy, healthy, and well adjusted as young adults. And their mom is also doing well.

ON CAREGIVERS

It is totally aberrant (and a very recent development) for a mother to stay at home, away from adult human contact, and meet all the needs of her young children by herself without the support of the rest of her "tribe." Raising children in isolation isn't good for either mothers or their children.

So you need to consider both your own and your child's mental and physical health needs when it comes to making your care choices. Whether you put your children in day care, have a baby-sitter, or stay at home with them yourself, the outcome will depend upon the quality of the care and the support it provides, not the type of care, per se.

I have a friend who runs an unlicensed day-care center near New York City. She has a long waiting list even though she refuses to follow "rules" such as avoiding picking up a child or cuddling her on her lap. She says, "I know what children need. And I give it to them. The children who go here are very, very happy. And so are their mothers—whatever the rules say." This woman is a godsend for both the mothers and the children she takes care of. She's a living, breathing "outer placenta." And we need many more like her!

THE BIOLOGY OF SADNESS AND DESPAIR

Darwin suggested from his observations that the emotions of adult human grief had much in common with the response of children separated from their mothers. And in fact, modern research has found that Darwin was correct. Hundreds of studies have documented that premature separation of a child from its mother results in physiologic changes in that child that depress immunity. And these changes may persist into adulthood.

Premature separation in early life may create the biology of sadness and despair in the body, and is a signal that the primary human need to belong to, feel supported by, and feel safe with a core group is not being met. As a result, the individual's overriding primal feeling is that the world is inescapably stressful because there is no one there to support, protect, and take care of her. In other words, there is a sense that "I don't belong here. I don't belong to anyone. No one is there for me. I'm doomed. Nobody cares." This early state of feeling hopeless and helpless may result in lowered resistance to loss in later life.

A child whose primal emotion is despair and sadness is apt to bond with people who are happy, and as a result will use another person's upbeat mood to regulate her own sadness. She may feel depressed and lonely unless there is someone around who pours energy into her. She may feel compelled to indiscriminately pursue companionship of any kind, whether it is healthy or not, so that she won't feel empty inside. On the other hand, she may find it next to impossible to enjoy a healthy, mutually beneficial relationship with equal give-and-take.

A woman who uses relationships to regulate her moods will often "hyperbond" to others. When such a hyperbonded relationship ends, the congenitally sad person's mood plummets. Her immune system perceives the loss as a fatal blow, which throws her back into her original state of biologic despair engendered by the premature loss of her mother.

In individuals whose temperaments run along independent lines, premature separation from their mothers may take a different tack. This woman may become an independent loner who feels she doesn't need anyone else, especially other women. Here is a poignant example, a letter I received from a forty-eight-year-old woman named Lynn who was one of my newsletter subscribers:

> My mother abandoned my brother and myself at a very young age. I wasn't yet a year old. We became wards of the

court, even though we have a father. But he wasn't granted cus-
tody. For the biggest part of my life, I didn't form any bonds
with females. There was no nurturing individual during my
early childhood and I was clueless in how to connect with a female. By the age of thirty, I had four children of my own. I could
no more leave one of them than cut off my arm. So I always
wondered how and why my mother had done what she had.
Later in life, when I met her, I didn't feel anything toward her.
And when I asked her why, her only explanation was that my
brother and I were "too young."

The point of all this is that I have survived, but not without
costs. Unfortunately, I feel that maybe my daughters will have to
pay some of the price. I know that I am a very strong woman
and that I can survive no matter what, but emotionally I have
many problems. I had no close relationships until I was thirty-
five. My main problem was not being able to trust and accept
that maybe someone could love me unconditionally and without strings, that I didn't have to be a superhuman being, that my
faults were acceptable, and that I had a lot to offer.

I look at my daughters, who are ages thirty and twenty-two,
and I see that they also have no female friends with whom they
can just pal around. I see a lot of restlessness in them. My older
daughter settles for less than she deserves and I can't help but
feel a little responsible for this. I don't know what I could have
changed, if anything. They all know that I love them more than
my life. They know that I have worked hard to provide for all of
us, and I know that they appreciate that. Though I'm alone, I'm
not lonely. But that doesn't necessarily work for them. So I guess
the legacy lives on. There will always be a sense of something
missing, and I don't quite understand the mother-daughter connection that I see some people at work have.

Lynn's story is filled with the legacy of loss. Her own Mother
Bear instinct is strong, but she has paid a high price for her stoicism
and the ability to "get it all done" without asking for help.

Happily, as adults, we have the ability to do this for ourselves.
But self-acceptance in adulthood never feels quite as nourishing in
the body as having had a mother or group of significant people in
early childhood who accepted us completely and unconditionally for
who we are. That's what's meant by the saying, "You can't go home
again." Countless women with inadequate bonding have found
peace and acceptance in adulthood. They enjoy a wide variety of

friends and have created a feeling of belonging and safety and security. After working so hard and having achieved such a hard-won
sense of self, they are usually surprised and upset by how a trip home
to visit their mother brings up old outdated feelings of inadequacy.

JUDY: Am I Worth Listening To?

Judy, another newsletter subscriber, realized that her adult relationship problems mirrored her earliest experiences with her mother. She
was fifty-three years old when she wrote me the following:

> All of my life, I have never thought my mother really lis-
> tened to me, or at least as far back as I can remember thinking
> about those things. I know when I would and do talk to her she
> would always be looking someplace else, doing something else,
> or change the subject in the middle of my talking. To this day,
> especially with my husband, if people do not act like they are re-
> ally listening to me, I get really insecure and will just shut down
> completely. When I talk to people (and I do have a very hard
> time talking), I try to say what I have to say very fast and short
> before I get cut off or bore people.
>
> I cannot really say that I have completely resolved this with
> my mother. Although I am aware of it and when she does it to
> me now sometimes I can stand up for myself with her. I cannot
> do this with others yet. My own daughter and I have a very
> close relationship. We talk easily and I try very hard to always
> support her whenever I can.

Another woman wrote:

> After years of introspection and some therapy on my part, I
> finally realized that my mother is quite emotionally blunted and
> probably always has been. To go to her with anything joyous,
> thrilling, or to share a sense of accomplishment was an exercise
> in disappointment. She'd say, "That's nice, dear." Or "I'm very
> proud of you," in a stoic, methodical way. Her words say one
> thing, but her body and facial expression say another.
>
> I've come to the conclusion that my mother is depressed
> and probably has been for years. It's as though there is a void
> inside her that is full only as long as someone is pumping their

energy into her. No wonder I feel tired and drained after talking with her.

Though I love my mother, I have never liked hugging her or being close to her physically. When she touches me, I want to withdraw immediately. I finally realized that I can trust my instincts about this. I'm not being a "bad daughter" by setting up healthy boundaries with her. She was never able to give me the emotional support I needed when I was a child.

ALICIA: Ordering Out When There's Nothing at Home

Alicia's mother was an alcoholic. She had some inherited family money and there were always nannies who took care of Alicia and her brothers and sisters. Though Alicia's home and family life appeared normal to the outside world, the children never knew whether their mother would be drunk or sober, whether she would be present for a family meal or outing, or whether she would even tuck them into bed at night. The nannies, who might have provided some consistency, never stayed very long because the household was too chaotic. Alicia's father dealt with the situation by traveling on business during the week.

Because of her temperament, Alicia learned very quickly how to get her natural need for positive attention met at school. She became a model student in kindergarten and remained so all the way through college. She later said to me, "When you don't get the love and regard you require automatically and unconditionally, you have to do something to earn them. Luckily, there are other places besides your family where you can get that love and respect." She quipped, "When you can't eat in, you order out!"

The problem for Alicia and millions like her, however, is that she is never really sure she is lovable and acceptable. When she buys one of her friends a gift or puts on a new dress, she often says, "You don't like it, do you?" before the friend has even had a chance to say anything! She has become so skillful at protecting herself from rejection that she actually rejects herself first. The problem with this form of "protection," however, is that it also prevents Alicia from being able to truly take in the genuine love and approval that are all around her in adulthood.

It's not surprising that Alicia has had a series of painful relationships with cold and indifferent women both professionally and personally. But over the years, as she has identified this pattern and learned how to change it, her life, and her health, have transformed for the better. She first had to learn how to identify the emptiness inside of herself that resulted from a cold and distant mother. Then she had to name her unconscious compulsion to fill her emptiness and sense of worthlessness by trying to win the love of women who were like her mother. Eventually, through therapy, dietary improvement, exercise, and positive affirmations, she has learned how to feel good about herself most of the time.

A Spiritual Home

It is also entirely possible for a child to have the kind of temperament and soul qualities that make it possible for her to get her emotional needs met, to some extent, through bonding with God or with the earth. Theologian Matthew Fox points out that every person he's ever met who had an abusive or neglectful childhood has found a place in nature that she went to, to find sustenance and peace.

FORMING BONDS WITH NATURE

Do you remember a special place you went for summer vacation as a child? Did you have a favorite rock or tree or a favorite bit of lakeshore that you saw as your very own soul place? This is how we make nature and the natural world our nurturing outer placenta. You know that the mountain, or the ocean, or the woods, will always be there for you. Children need time outside in nature in order to experience their bond to the earth directly. And that shores up their sense of safety and security in the world, because they're bonding to Mother Nature.

One of my patients is a deeply spiritual woman who said that on some level she realized in infancy that her mother wasn't going to be there for her, so she bonded with the Source itself, with God . . . something we all must ultimately do. This spiritual connection and her deep acceptance of all aspects of her life, including her history of physical abuse by her parents, has allowed her to maintain a phenomenally positive attitude that has helped her heal from a variety of very serious health problems, all related to immunity, blood problems, and joints, and all associated with her shaky start in life.

THE ROOTS OF SEXUALITY:
HEALTHY BODY IMAGE

Children are born with a natural love for and curiosity about their bodies. Knowing how many women struggle painfully with a poor body image, and how deadly the health consequences can be, I wanted my daughters to feel as good about their bodies as possible. When they were little, we had special "spa" nights, when I put on beautiful music and lit candles during their bath, and then followed it with a massage. I knew I couldn't protect my girls totally from negative cultural messages, but I wasn't prepared for the fact that the "keepers of the old rules and regulations" are everywhere. The only thing a mother can do is hold the torch of healthy body image as high as she can, work on her own body issues, and model for her daughter the skills to do the same thing.

I still remember that hot summer day at the beach when my older daughter was about two. As soon as we arrived, Annie tore out of the car and started running down to the water, flinging off her clothes as she went. By the time I caught up with her, she was naked at the water's edge, but her exuberance had evaporated. She looked unhappy and confused. Why? Because a group of older women, her grandmother's age, had shamed her about her nudity and asked her where her bathing suit was. In a split second, her innocent joy in the feeling of the sun and water on her naked body had been replaced with self-consciousness and her first experience of bodily shame. I was furious with those women. How could I have protected my daughter from that experience and the weight of the New England Puritan ethic about the inappropriateness of the body that fueled it? I couldn't. My convictions as a mother were no match for the judgment that oozed out from those self-proclaimed guardians of propriety. I told my daughter that her body was beautiful and fine, and that she didn't need a suit, whatever they said. But she never again approached the water so joyfully and so unself-consciously. The end of innocence.

On another occasion, when my daughters were two and four years old and visiting their grandparents, they wanted to go upstairs and take a bath after coming back from the beach. I went upstairs with them to draw the water and make sure they were safe, followed by their male cousin, then three years old, and a friend who was visiting, a boy who was four. I figured I'd divide the kids into groups once we got upstairs. But no sooner had we arrived at the top step when the mother of the four-year-old propelled herself into the bathroom in a state of near panic, because she thought that I would allow her son to bathe naked with my daughters. And guess what? I might have! Why? Because little children see naked bodies as normal and nothing to be ashamed of—until we adults teach them otherwise. I truly doubt that a tubful of little kids—with adult supervision—would have become involved in any lurid sex games. (Although we might have had a problem with water on the floor!)

When we make a big deal out of genital differences in young children and try to keep them from exploring their own bodies or seeing the bodies of the opposite sex, we run the risk of shaming them for their natural curiosity. Their natural desire to know the truth may become tainted with the parent's overlay of shame. My mother once mentioned that my father's mother had taught him that his penis was a "mustn't touch it." When she told me this, I was grateful that neither parent had passed this legacy of shame on to me.

I was pretty matter-of-fact when I taught my daughters what each of the three "holes" was that come out of their bottoms. One of my patients sometimes found her three-year-old in the bathroom with a mirror, taking a better look at the area. This is normal. We want our daughters to have a healthy sense of their anatomy—genitals included—from the youngest possible age.

YOUR LEGACY REGARDING BODY SHAME

~ How do you feel about other women seeing you naked? (For example, do you routinely wrap tightly in a towel whenever you are in a locker room with other women?)

~ What is your first memory about being uncomfortable with your nakedness?

~ What did you teach your daughter about her genital area? What were you taught?

~ What is (was) your family comfort zone around nudity?

~ What are your personal and cultural standards around nudity?

Girls, of course, face many more body prohibitions than boys, starting from a very early age. I've often felt that little girls' two-piece bathing suits are ridiculous because the bra tops so often end up around their necks! Why give a girl the idea that she has to cover her chest before she even has nipple budding? This kind of training is what begins to shut down the energy available to a whole area of our bodies—our chests and breasts!

Most children learn instinctively that there are some places where it's safe to be nude and other places where it is not. We can encourage their growing sense of inner guidance by mirroring appropriate behavior ourselves and also being honest about our own standards and comfort zone around nudity.

When my daughters were about eight and ten we went to visit my sister in New Mexico. One day we took a hike down to the Rio Grande in a remote area. It was hot, and we decided to take a swim even though we hadn't brought bathing suits. My daughters were perfectly at ease playing, dancing, and stretching nude in the water and on the shore. And my sister and I commented on how wonderful it was to have a few places on earth where we were still free to do this without feeling shame. However, it is very clear to me that my daughters and I would never have taken a nude swim in a group of strangers or even with some of the male members of our own families.

It is also clear that different families (and cultures) have different standards of behavior when it comes to nudity. There is nothing inherently right or wrong with any approach, *as long as it's based on respect, not repression and shaming*. Most of our behavior around nudity is just that: cultural, not biologic. Most European men and women are, for example, far freer with nudity at the beach than are most Americans.

There is a difference between healthy nudity and emotionally inappropriate nudity. One of my patients told me that her father used to routinely come into her bedroom and kiss her good night wearing only his shorts. She was always uncomfortable with this. I told her that her discomfort is the only information she needed about whether or not his behavior was appropriate. If a child is uncomfortable with something an adult is doing, it's because the adult's intent is not aboveboard. Many children get talked out of their healthy bodily responses, however, by adults whose intellectualizing confuses them and give them messages that are at odds with what their inner guidance is telling them.

It's fascinating that as children approach the "age of reason"—the next developmental stage—they often become naturally modest. This isn't because a child has been "shamed" in her family. It's because she has now internalized the norms of behavior in her culture. This phenomenon happens in concert with the ongoing development of the dorsolateral prefrontal cortex. A child now becomes actively aware of "what the other kids are doing" and she quite naturally is eager to fit in.

HOW A GIRL'S LOVE MAP DEVELOPS

Everyone has an internal love map—a model of what we believe love should look and feel like. Our love maps are laid down in our mind and body by our earliest relationships with our mothers or caregivers and are probably first mapped out by the hormone of attachment, oxytocin.[5]

A child's—and, later, an adult's—inner love map is determined by a wide variety of factors: her genetic inheritance, how she is nurtured at a critical stage of development, other early childhood experiences, her physical and cultural environment, her hormone levels, and also by the mystery of soul qualities.

Her love map may portray what she wants in an ideal partner. It may incline her to grow up heterosexual, homosexual, or bisexual. It may be programmed toward wanting a lot of sex, a moderate amount, or very little, or it may incline her to atypical sexual behavior. The environment can both trigger and reinforce a child's inner map, weaving the senses of smell, taste, hearing, sight, and touch powerfully into her later sexual responses.

Though many experts feel that once in place, love maps can't be changed or altered unless your brain changes physically, I've seen enough brain changes in myself and others to know that we probably have a broader range of love maps within us than we may think.

Erotic energy can also be attached to things other than an intimate love partner, which is why so many advertisements use sexual innuendo to sell products such as cars. I saw a recent rerun of the sitcom *Friends* in which the love map concept was humorously illustrated. The obsessive character Monica and her husband, Chandler, were visiting another couple who had been through infertility treatment and had finally adopted a baby. Monica and Chandler have themselves been agonizing about the adoption process. The wife of the couple they were visiting had created a carefully detailed, color coded, and indexed notebook to help other couples facing the adoption dilemma. They gave Monica the notebook and left the room to check on their son. Monica, who is known for her obsessively organized approach to life, leafed through the book and said to Chandler excitedly, "This notebook just gave me a little orgasm."

What Is a Normal Love and Sex Map?

What is "normal" is, for better or for worse, defined by the dominant culture, medical authorities, and increasingly, the creators of mass media that beam millions of sexual messages into our homes every day. For some, normal sex means that a man and a woman have vaginal intercourse in their own bed on Saturday night. "Normal," however, doesn't necessarily describe the range of sexual experiences a human can enjoy. The ideologic norm is frequently imposed by those in power, be it a parent, a peer, clergy, or the police.[6]

If a woman has experienced childhood sexual abuse, or some other major trauma, her love map may become distorted. She may fall in love with someone who has features of her perpetrator or she may have trouble with intimacy and sexual activity with anyone.

DOREEN and KATHY: Choosing a Model

As in every other area of our lives, we are influenced by our mother's and father's attitudes, spoken and unspoken, about sexuality and relationships. Here's an example:

Doreen and Kathy are sisters. Doreen, who is about six years older than Kathy, is a lawyer at a large, successful firm and has followed in the footsteps of her handsome, successful, entrepreneurial father and brother. Kathy, on the other hand, is a stay-at-home mom whose lifestyle and attitudes mirror those of her mother. Their mother, often described as a "good Christian woman," never worked outside of her home. She is the dutiful wife who does whatever her husband wants to do. She goes to church at least twice a week and prefers spending time at home with her grandchildren. Her husband, on the other hand, is constantly on the go, wanting to travel whenever possible. Though the family doesn't talk about it, it is well known that he has had a series of affairs with other women.

Doreen's inner love map is very much like that of her father. She is very attractive and always surrounded by men. She prefers "bad boy" types typified by the rock-and-roll stars of the 1970s and '80s. But a part of her also yearns for stability. A veteran traveler, she has had a series of tempestuous relationships with men who won't settle down. Currently, she is engaged to marry a very stable man whom she loves but considers somewhat "boring." Her sister, Kathy, on the other hand, dropped out of college to marry and have children. Kathy, like her mother, follows the lead of her husband, and goes along with his wishes. And like generations of women before her, including her mother, Kathy gets her needs met passively—by getting sick or by bursting into tears when she is disappointed and unhappy.

How Our Map Gets Laid Down by Sexual Rehearsals

Though a child's love map starts to be drawn in utero, she will keep imprinting its details about what love is and what it's not all during childhood—and for the rest of her life. Nearly all children go through "rehearsals" like "playing doctor" or "I'll show you mine, if you show me yours." This helps a child practice what is already biochemically encoded in her body and brain and also helps teach her how to figure out who she is and what she wants in love. As a child goes through her rehearsals she will be building the details of her love map, including how her body and the body of another responds. She may also learn about power relationships.

Research has shown that rhesus monkeys also must go through sex play with others when young or they will not be able to successfully mate in adulthood. They can't "assume the position," as it were, if they are reared alone without other young monkeys with whom to rehearse. Interestingly, if they are allowed a short amount of time with peers of the same age, they will do better, but still won't be as sexually functional as they would have been if they'd had normal amounts of uncontrolled time with other monkeys.

Though sexual rehearsals are normal for children, walking in on them can be challenging. One of my patients told me the following story:

> When my daughter was little, she adored dogs and sometimes pretended to be one. She often took baths with her two-year-old brother. I left the two of them in the tub while I walked out to answer the phone. When I came back in a moment later, my daughter was pretending to be a dog and was licking her brother's penis. He had an erection and was lying back with a smile on

his face from ear to ear. I calmed myself, and said, "Sweetie, please don't do that anymore." She replied, "But Mommy, he likes it."

Not wanting to shame her daughter or draw undue attention to the episode, this wise mother simply said, "I know, honey. But you can't do that anymore." She said to me, "I can't help but imagine that that little episode is going to be permanently encoded into my son's brain as an ideal scenario." She's probably right that it will be to some extent—although her calm handling of the situation is likely to have prevented the formation of a strong, emotionally charged memory in either her son or her daughter.

How Our Maps Become Distorted through Trauma or Boundary Violations

In order for a love map to develop normally, there have to be adequate boundaries between all family members, including parents and children. Love maps can get distorted if sex play or rehearsal occurs with people who aren't of an appropriate age and who violate society's norms concerning sexual contact. It is imperative that the individuals a child rehearses with (by playing house, playing doctor, or bathing) are the same age and that no power imbalance is involved.

If a child is the younger partner in a sexually abusive or exploitive situation, this situation can radically alter her love map. Example: If you are five and a seventeen-year-old boy routinely fondles you, that will affect who you are sexually attracted to and the details of what you find sexually arousing later in life. If a child is sixteen and has an incestuous relationship with her forty-year-old father, she will have a problem creating a fulfilling and mutually satisfying relationship with a peer later in life.

A child who has gone through this type of sexual experience may well repeat the pattern with a younger family member. For example, a ten-year-old boy who has had a sexually exploitive relationship with an older uncle may feel compelled to have sexual activity with a five-year-old cousin, thus perpetuating the family's aberrant love maps.

However, events that can distort an individual's love map do not necessarily have to be sexual in nature. They may include childhood illness, delayed puberty, witnessing abuse of one's mother, or some other type of emotional and physical trauma that rewires the child's brain.

The Burden of Secrecy and Shame

Imagine what happens to a girl if she finds herself forced into age-inappropriate sex play with someone who has power over her by virtue of his or her age and status. She knows that she will get into trouble if she tells her parents or another authority figure. But if she doesn't tell, she's also left holding on to a very uncomfortable secret and engaging in behavior that feels bad. To quit the activity brings rejection and ostracism from someone whom she may like, respect, fear—or all three! But if she doesn't quit, she runs the risk of being discovered by her parents or caregivers and blamed for her activity. Either way, she loses, and she inherently knows this. If she asks for help, she may experience both the threats of the perpetrator (who may be a family member) and her parents' wrath. This is why, in our culture, so few children actually talk about this stuff. I had a personal experience that bears this out.

> When I was about five years old, my sister and I decided to sleep out on the porch of a cabin we had down by our farm pond. My older brother and his friends were staying inside. As we were going to sleep, one of my brother's older friends, who was probably about ten, came out on the porch and told me to lift up my nightgown so he could show me something that I'd like. I remember doing this and feeling really uncomfortable about it. Just as my brother's friend was starting to lie down on top of me, my brother yelled out, "Get back in here and leave my sister alone." He did. But the next morning, he came up to me, grabbed me hard by the arm, and whispered viciously in my ear, "If you ever tell anyone about this, I'll kill you. Do you understand?" I nodded my understanding. And for all the reasons I've just mentioned above, I never told anyone about this until I was eighteen. I was too ashamed and frightened.

Though I had a mere brush with inappropriate sexual activity, I felt bad enough about it that I didn't say anything to anybody for years. Imagine what it is like for a child who is repeatedly sexually abused in some way who must keep silent. Not being able to talk about it is, in many cases, more traumatizing than the actual experience. The child's love map gets distorted not so much because of what was done but because of the silence and secrecy around it. The more intense the societal sanctions against what a child knows, the more intense the power of the unspeakable monster in that memory.

A common result of a distorted love map for a woman is that she becomes anorgasmic or simply doesn't want to have sex at all because her more acute sense of touch often becomes affected by sexual trauma. Some men, because of their own distorted love maps, require the intense and often exploitive imagery of pornography to become sexually aroused. A number of patients have told me how upsetting it is to them that their husbands needed to watch a pornographic movie or see a magazine in order to become aroused.

THE BOTTOM LINE: For a daughter to grow up with an inner love map that supports sustainable, nurturing relationships, she needs a healthy body image, an opportunity for safe same-age sexual rehearsals, and at least a few role models of loving couples whose healthy sexuality is part of that bond. (What she doesn't need is a daily diet of imagery and experience that teaches her that sexuality and commitment are two mutually exclusive areas of life.) Having these role models, even if they aren't her parents, will go a long way toward helping her develop a healthy love map.

NEGOTIATING RELATIONSHIP TRIANGLES

I was amazed and amused by the provocative behavior my daughters occasionally displayed with their father when they were about three or four years old. They'd sit on his lap, stroke his face, and generally bat their eyes at him. I'm convinced that in girls this behavior has less to do with sexuality per se than with wanting their father's undivided attention. Regardless of the intent behind the behavior, it was striking evidence of their innate hardwiring for getting male attention.

Traditional thinking about this behavior has been based on the original work of Sigmund Freud, who theorized that on their way to sexual maturity, all young children fall in love with one of their parents (usually the one of the opposite sex) and even desire a sexual relationship with them. The same-sex parent is the child's rival. This is the so-called Oedipal stage, named after the mythical Greek king who killed his father and married his mother. Freud coined the term to explain his observations about male development, and many have questioned how applicable it is to girls. We know from the work of psychologist Carol Gilligan and many others that most girls tend to be more focused on relationships than most boys. And dozens of studies have documented the differences between male and female sexuality, differences that begin in utero. I'm not denying that girls are hardwired from birth to express their sexuality, but I believe there's another way to look at the rivalries of this age.

The little girl has already learned to some extent to negotiate her needs and desires in her one-on-one relationships with care-givers and family. But now she is faced with a new challenge: how to negotiate the needs of three different individuals—the classic tri-angle. Her desire for exclusivity and her jealousy over the attention that her parents may give to each other or to other friends or sib-lings presents her with a moral and practical dilemma. How does she get her personal desires and drives for someone or something met when more than one person wants the same thing? Her de-mand for exclusivity conflicts with her growing understanding that she is not the center of the universe, and with her newfound sense of how her behavior impacts the feelings of those closest to her. This conflict helps wire in her consciousness of right from wrong in relationships.

Jacques Lusseyran, the blind author of *And There Was Light,* wrote:

> All of us, whether we are blind or not, are terribly greedy. We want things only for ourselves. Even without realizing it, we want the universe to be like us and give us all the room in it. But a blind child learns very quickly that this cannot be. He has to learn it, for every time he forgets that he is not alone in the world, he strikes against an object, hurts himself, and is called to order. But each time he remembers, he is rewarded, for every-thing comes his way.

It is no different for children who can see, except that the objects a child runs into are created by her own self-centeredness. If she remains self-centered and self-absorbed, she will be psychically "blind" to the needs and desires of others. She will remain in the dark about the richness of an interrelated universe, and paradoxi-cally never develop the skills and faith necessary to get the universe to work on her behalf. The objects she will run into are not solid, like furniture, but are instead the invisible, but nevertheless painful resistance or withheld affection of those the child needs the most.

Her task is to develop the skills necessary to "see" that her soul and the universe can help her meet her own needs even in the context of relationships with others.

The process often looks like this: A child becomes increasingly aware of the complex system of relationships around her, which include other people's emotions, thoughts, and feelings. As a result, she may, depending upon her soul qualities, become moody and irritable for a time as she learns how to integrate this new and often confusing information. One of my patients told me that her four-year-old daughter tried to flush her new baby brother down the toilet at this stage. On the other hand, if she's too selfless, she may become a child martyr, learning to sacrifice herself for the good of others. This is the little girl who becomes an angelic sweetheart when the new baby is brought home. Instead of playing outside, she shadows her mother, always wanting to help with the baby.

By the age of three or four, a child has a remarkable ability to know what is going on with more than two people. She can understand how others are feeling and knows how to respond to them. She begins to understand that her behavior will impact not only Mommy but also Daddy. And though she may want the exclusive attention of Daddy, she simultaneously knows that Mommy also may need and want his attention. Because she loves Mommy, she learns that she must temper her desire for the exclusive attention of Daddy with her need to fit in to the larger family system.

Of course, from time to time, we all find ourselves desiring that wonderful and deeply nourishing feeling that comes from having the exclusive attention of one other person focused on us. And like every three-year-old before and after us, each of us must learn how to move in and out of the light of another's focused attention, enjoying it while it lasts, and trusting in our ability to either attract it back to us when we desire it, while at the same time developing a connection with our inner self that is so nourishing that we are not overly reliant on relationships to fill us up.

Distorted Triangles: The Minuchin Child Syndrome

A patient once told me that she and her husband had lived all over the world, but that her husband's mother was "always in the trunk that they carried with them." What she was referring to, of course, was the fact that we tend to carry our nuclear family relationship patterns with us for our entire lives, at least until we become conscious of them and work to release the ones that no longer serve us.

When male and female energy come together, they create a third entity, a shared creation that is the fruit of that relationship, be it a business, a house, or a child. They will also bring to the relationship the inevitable unfinished business and incompleteness from their own childhoods. After a time, the couple begins to realize, consciously or unconsciously, that they have differences that cannot be resolved by expecting or demanding that one or the other change. They may then have a child as a way to deter and deflect conflict—again, either consciously or unconsciously. Back in the 1950s and '60s, couples were often counseled to have children as a way to cement the relationship. Later in life that same desire to deter conflict may take the form of moving (the "geographic cure") or building a new home.

A child born under these conditions will inherit the unfinished emotional business of her parents. Depending upon a child's temperament, she may well become a "conflict-deterring mechanism" for an entire family, which creates a real risk to her physical and emotional health. The term *Minuchin child* is borrowed from the work of Salvador Minuchin, M.D., a pioneering family systems therapist who posited that a child often behaves in a way that keeps the family together.[7]

STEPHANIE: The Canary in the Coal Mine

George frequently traveled on business and was away from home a great deal. Because he was so clearly married to his job, both his wife, Amanda, and young daughter, Stephanie, eventually became disengaged from him. To make up for the void in her life from her missing husband, Amanda became overly enmeshed with Stephanie. Now even when George came home, there was no emotional room for him: his wife and daughter were "married" to each other. However, when she was five years old, Stephanie developed recurrent abdominal pain, which worried both parents and brought them together to take care of their daughter. Medical testing revealed that Stephanie had gastritis.

Stephanie's illness was the canary in the coal mine, signaling the parents that something was wrong in their relationship. According to Minuchin's theory, the original problem was the disengagement of the parents. Stephanie's illness developed in response to this problem, in an unconscious attempt to repair their relationship. However, unless they do the real work required to repair their unfulfilled relationship,

Amanda will continue to look to Stephanie for the fulfillment that she isn't getting from her husband. And the child's "metaresponse" to this will be more illness—or accidents or disruptive behavior.

CHERYL: Another Minuchin Child

Gladys's husband developed a "bad back" when he was forty-two and did only odd jobs from then on. Gladys had always tried to "motivate" him, but now she couldn't seem to get him to do anything. Her response was to try to meet her achievement needs by funneling them through her daughters. One of her girls, Cheryl, was particularly emotionally sensitive. Whenever there was a conflict in the family, her body registered it, always in the form of some kind of cold or infection. Years later, her body and immune system still overreact (usually by breaking out in hives or getting a sore throat) if she feels a conflict at work or with one of her close friends.

"Mommy, I Save It All for You"

It's easier to manage the world if we divide it into simplistic notions of "good" versus "bad." But just as there's really no such thing as "good" versus "bad" cholesterol, in that both types are absolutely necessary to our health, almost all our life experience lands somewhere in the middle. Still, it appears to be human nature to focus on what we don't have rather than on what we do, and to make the thing we lack the "good" or most valued. This focus on what is missing and our tendency to good/bad thinking play out in our relationships from very early in life.

When one parent is absent more than the other, a child will cling to the parent who is present, while at the same time taking out on her (because it's usually the mother) the child's anger at the absent parent. This leaves the child free to fantasize about and value the absent parent. In essence, the missing parent carries the child's fantasy of the "good" parent, while the one who is actually caring for the child day to day bears the brunt of her child's anger and disappointment. This behavior is seen as early as age two, and it can cause enormous anguish for single moms whose ex-husbands show little or no interest in their children.

This split applies in other situations, as well. Anyone who has ever left her child with a caregiver will notice that when the child is first left, she will initially take out her anger on the caregiver. But then things settle down. However, the minute the mother walks in the door at the end of the day, her child runs to her full of complaints. The caregiver then says, "I don't understand this. She has been a perfect angel all day and we had a great time."

This used to happen to me all the time. When I'd walk in the door, my children would run to me and start to cry and complain. My husband, dumbfounded, would tell me that I was somehow eliciting this behavior because they had been fine until I came home! I felt invalidated. Many women have told me the same thing. A medical colleague of mine once asked her five-year-old why she did this. The child cried, "Mommy, I save it all for you!"

Here's the truth: Children reserve their worst behavior for their mothers almost from the beginning. This is because it's okay to be vulnerable around our mother. We know that she will love us despite our weaknesses. This pattern is likely to go on for our entire lives together. I once heard a Jungian analyst say that we project our insecurities on our mother. And we project our strengths and our power drives on our father. I believe that this is true to some extent. But sooner or later, a child has to realize that her mother isn't an emotional dumping ground. And the sooner the better.

From Emotional Vulnerability to Mother Blame

Because it's acceptable to be emotionally vulnerable around our mothers (which is partly biologically encoded), it becomes easier to blame them (or their surrogates) for the areas of our lives that aren't working rather than take responsibility for our own behavior and vulnerabilities. Thus the all-too-convenient excuse: "If my mother hadn't ignored me as a child, I wouldn't be treating you this way." Blaming mothers and expecting them to take whatever we dish out just perpetuates the cultural legacy that says a woman's job is to absorb and neutralize all the bad feelings around.

That said, I now find it endearing that my younger daughter routinely complains about her aches and pains only to me. I am proud of the competent young adult she has become, and I realize that when she does this, she simply needs extra comforting. Being able to admit your vulnerability on occasion is also a strength! I point this out to her so that she will learn how to care for herself more fully during the times I'm not available.

STEPS FOR HEALING THE LEGACY
OF EARLY CHILDHOOD

One. Acknowledge that any persistent beliefs and uncomfortable patterns that keep recurring in your life may well have their origins in decisions you made about life before the age of seven. Know that these decisions have probably shaped every major decision in your life from that point on.

Two. Bring gentle awareness to any area of your body that is speaking to you as you read this. Are your shoulders tight? Do you have butterflies in your stomach? Do you feel like throwing up? Just notice these things and bring compassion and awareness to the body areas that are involved.

Three. Keep breathing fully through your nose, with your shoulders relaxed, all the way down into the lower lobes of your lungs and all the way out through your nose or pursed lips. Breathing in this way will engage your parasympathetic nervous system and help calm you as disturbing and troubling emotions arise. As you keep breathing while remembering, you will be changing your body chemistry and lightening up as the memory goes through you.

Four. Take a walk or move around the room as you breathe. This doesn't need to be hard work. You aren't two years old any longer. You can take care of yourself now.

Five. Write down any personas you have adopted to win the love and approval or attention of others. Examples: good girl, efficient girl, saintly or angelic girl, hard worker, Miss Responsibility, overachiever, the frail or sickly child, bad girl, family clown, class clown, Daddy's little princess, Mommy's little helper, etc.

Six. Do a releasing and new-beginnings ceremony or ritual. You always have the power to change any old persistent patterns in your life, no matter when they started. The key factor is your willingness to name and release these patterns and then allow more freedom and joy into your life. A ritual simply offers a way to focus your intention to bring awareness to a situation; it also provides a safe container in which transformation and healing can naturally take place.

Using Ritual to Heal

There are dozens of ways to use ritual or ceremony to heal. I use them myself and have been recommending them to patients for almost twenty years because they are so powerful. One of the best guides I've seen is *The Joy of Ritual: Spiritual Recipes to Celebrate Milestones, Ease Transitions, and Make Every Day Sacred*, by Barbara Biziou.

The ritual I find myself using most frequently comes from my years of Proprioceptive Writing practice, a form of writing that integrates the imagination, intuition, and intellect. Proprioceptive Writing was simultaneously developed by Drs. Linda Trichter Metcalf and Tobin Simon (see Resources).

Here's what I do:

Light a candle, put on some classical music like Mozart, Boccherini, or Vivaldi, or other music that moves you deeply. Now ask your inner guidance to be with you. Take a few deep breaths, and then write down your dilemma and what you'd like to release. Also state exactly how you would like to feel. Today I wrote:

> I want to lay down my sense of being burdened. I want to feel lighter and more joyful. If life is eternal and we are co-creators with life, and if we'll never get it all done anyway, then what is this time pressure and sense of burden I carry about? What part of my childhood self am I needing to call on now? Burden—what do I mean by burden? Carrying a load, a backpack, weight—carrying one's own weight. Aha! I carry not only my own weight but other people's weight, as well. When did I start doing this? Age two. I got the idea that to be lovable I had to be helpful to my mother—a good girl—Mommy's little helper. Following my own instincts and joy was not okay. . . .

I kept writing for about twenty minutes, recording my thoughts and emotions as they arose, just noticing them and letting my witness self observe from the sidelines.

As you write, pay attention to how your body feels: Do you get a knot in your stomach or a headache when you write about something? Your emotions, particularly a lump in your throat or tears in your eyes, will let you know that you're on to something that is being released just by writing about it.

Room Two

Seven to Fourteen Years

11

The Age of Reason

Developing a Moral Compass

❀

As long ago as the Middle Ages, a child the age of seven was considered to have reached the age of reason. In English common law, a child was not considered capable of criminal intent before the age of seven. Rudolf Steiner, the visionary founder of the Waldorf education movement, believed that children were not developmentally ready to emerge from the world of imagination and storytelling until about age seven. He said that when a child's secondary teeth began to emerge, it was an indication that her brain had developed enough to take on the abstract and symbolic reasoning needed for reading.

In preindustrial societies, children could begin to serve as pages in courts at age eight. They could also begin to serve as apprentices. In the postindustrial world, school has taken the place of work. Until very recently, nursery and preschools were expected to provide mainly social preparation for later school experience, with some rudiments of numbers and letters as a foundation. Even though many children now spend years in day care and preschool before first grade, we still instinctively celebrate their entry into "real" school, the start of formal education.

The age of reason coincides with the beginning of the developmental stage known as latency. Latency refers to the fact that a child's early conflicts go underground and into a psychological time capsule, becoming hidden (or latent). Her energy is instead directed toward the outer world, where she develops mastery and skills that contribute to her sense of self-esteem and life purpose.

The interpersonal conflicts that were present earlier in childhood are still there, of course, but because the bulk of her energy is directed elsewhere by the demands of school and friends, they recede into the background. During puberty, the lid on the jar that holds earlier unresolved conflicts begins to loosen. A child's conflicts with self, parents, and authority resurface once again, now fueled by the hormonal and spiritual fires of her emerging sexuality.

Latency is really the golden age of childhood. It's when the vast majority of the experiences we later remember as "childhood" take place, even though, looking back, it's such a short time. During these years, most children are wonderful companions who are eager to cooperate and learn from you. And they really like to be with you!

THE DEVELOPING BRAIN

Prior to age seven, children have a relatively static and self-centered view of the world. They tend to live in the moment and are virtually incapable of abstract thought, since most haven't developed the frontal lobe circuitry necessary for it. One of my friends, who used to work as a counselor at a preschool day camp, gave me a classic example of the concrete thinking characteristic of young children.

At the beginning of the day, a five-year-old would give her two dimes and a nickel to hold until the canteen, which sold candy and other treats, opened in the afternoon. If she later gave the child a quarter back instead of her original two dimes and nickel, the child would start screaming that she had been cheated. After all, she had given her counselor three coins and was given back only one! Try as she might, my friend could not teach children this age the abstract notion that a quarter was exactly the same as two dimes and a nickel. If, on the other hand, she gave her kiddie campers twenty-five pennies in exchange for their two dimes and a nickel, they were thrilled. More and bigger were always better. A whole pile of the cheapest penny candy was more valuable to them than a single item that cost the same amount. By the same token, the biggest presents are always considered the best ones by little kids—because they "look" far more valuable than the smaller ones.

Just before age seven, however, a child's concrete view of the world begins to change as her brain develops the capacity for abstract thought. There is a spurt in brain maturation that opens up space to accommodate the increasing amount of experience and information that a child is exposed to every day. The brain attains 90 percent of its total weight by the age of seven. This growth spurt is so profound, and brain function is so versatile now, that even if a child had a stroke or severe head injury, she'd still be able to regain almost full function if the injury happened before puberty. This ability to accommodate is known as plasticity. It's also the reason why it's so much easier for a child to learn a language, pick up a musical instrument, or learn to ski before puberty than later in life.

The child's dorsolateral prefrontal cortex (DLPC) also continues to grow and develop, allowing her increasing control over her bodily functions and motor skills. By the age of seven, for example, most children have the concentration and fine motor coordination to begin to write cursively. This maturation is an ongoing process, however. So despite her enhanced physical control, it's not uncommon for a young school-age child to wet her pants now and again. But the older she gets, the less likely this is to happen, as her frontal lobes become more fully developed.

I remember a hilarious conversation we had at my house once. One of my daughters and her classmates were remembering the last time they had peed their pants at school. My daughter recalled an episode in the fifth grade, when she was ten years old. She was out on the school playground, having way too much fun to go inside, even though she had to "go." As she started down the slide, one of her playmates did something silly, and she laughed so hard she wet herself. She reminded me that I had brought dry clothes from home when the school called my office.

MORAL UNDERSTANDING:
HERE COMES THE JUDGE

The growth spurt of a child's brain at latency is accompanied by a change in her moral understanding. Before the age of seven, a child's moral world is concrete and can be divided into me versus you, right versus wrong, and black versus white. But now she has the capacity to understand not only abstract concepts—like the fact that twenty-five pennies is not better than a quarter—but also shades of gray between what is absolutely right and absolutely wrong. Now is the time for a child to develop an internally consistent moral structure so that she can successfully negotiate the many choices that she will be faced with in life.

A child's early bonding experiences set the stage for her later moral development, because morality is built upon the ability to bond with and have empathy for others. Without these qualities, individuals become amoral and sociopathic: they don't care about others and feel as though the rules don't apply to them.

Before she reaches the age of reason, a child needs concrete behavioral guidelines that let her know right from wrong. ("Don't hit your sister." "Don't run into the street.") And she needs consistent adverse consequences for breaking these rules—consequences that extinguish the behavior. Knowing what to expect and what the limits are actually helps a child to feel safe and secure, and therefore promotes health. However, morality isn't just about learning how to follow rules and regulations. In fact, the word *morality* is defined as "conforming to the rules of right conduct." The basis for all moral dilemmas has to do with who gets to determine what is "right conduct." The best person to determine this is, ultimately, the person herself. To be of maximum value to both herself and society, a child's morality must be built on a solid base of orbitofrontal development, so that it includes empathy and an ability to bond with others. The development of moral character in a child should involve both her brain and its connections to her body: she must know the rules in a given situation with her intellect and dorsolateral prefrontal cortex. And at the same time her orbitofrontal area must be engaged so that she is able to feel what is right behavior with her heart.

There are three predictable stages of moral development that correspond to the ongoing development of the dorsolateral prefrontal cortex. In describing these stages, I'm drawing partly on the work of Lawrence Kohlberg, Ph.D., a developmental psychologist at Harvard University. Note, however, that there's a wide range of moral development among individuals, and also in the age at which they reach a given stage. A person's morality will often depend upon her background and educational level. But some of it also depends on soul qualities. For example, one of my patients knew from the age of seven that she wanted to be a doctor. Learning and excelling at school became the most important things in her life. Her mother, on the other hand, told her that she was "selfish" and "self-centered" for not wanting to spend more time taking care of the house and their numerous relatives.

As you read through the different stages of moral development, you'll see why moral disagreements are so common.

First Stage: Preconventional Morality:
Ages Three Months to Four to Seven Years

The first stage of morality is egocentric. The child is focused on her own needs, period. She doesn't yet have the brain development necessary to appreciate both her own needs and those of another at the same time. The rights of others are irrelevant. In the later years of preconventional morality, a child may acknowledge that other people have interests too, but her own needs take precedence in almost any situation.

Children with brain development at the preconventional level are driven primarily by instinctual and emotional drives. They don't have enough frontal-lobe brain tone to inhibit their emotional response. They tend to be impulsive and to act from emotion unbalanced by reason. They can learn to follow clear black-and-white rules such as "Littering is bad. Throw the gum wrapper in a trash can, not on the ground." But a young child at this stage is not ready to learn the concept of sharing with another child—and shouldn't be expected to. To avoid some of the inevitable fights about a toy that two children want at the same time, parents or caregivers have to set up concrete external rules to govern behavior, for instance setting a timer and allowing each child to play with the item for ten minutes until it's the other child's turn. It's also important to make sure that each child in a group gets the same thing—or the same amount—to minimize fighting.

Discipline: The only rules the child follows at this stage are the ones that allow her to avoid punishment or disapproval. Rules are enforced through behavioral means, not by reasoning with the child. For example, if a young child is hitting her little sister, you remove her from the area and put her in another room alone where she has to sit by herself for a specific period of time. Don't reward her unskillful behavior by coddling her or overempathizing with her distress at no longer being the center of attention, or no longer being able to play with an item when it's time to go home, or time to let someone else have a turn. Doing so repeatedly could make her overly self-centered and difficult to be around. It's also a setup for running her parents ragged with her demands.

Second Stage: Conventional Morality:
Ages Four to Seven through Puberty

The child experiences "being good" as living up to what others expect of her. The highest level of conventional morality is embodied in the rules and regulations put forth by institutions such as the legal system, religious institutions, schools, and the government. These institutions create rules and regulations that are designed to ensure social order and decent conduct in the majority of people the majority of the time.

A child at the conventional stage will often be very vocal when she sees rules being broken. I remember once when my daughter Kate was nine. She and I drove with my friend Mona Lisa to the store. Mona Lisa entered the parking area through the "exit only" lane because it was more convenient. Kate exclaimed, "You can't do that!" There was nobody there and it really didn't make any difference. But Kate wasn't comfortable with bending the rules even when no one else would be hurt or inconvenienced in any way.

For some individuals, moral development doesn't progress beyond the conventional stage. Because they are unable (or unwilling) to feel what is right inside themselves, they rely instead on external authorities to decide for them. They trust these authorities more than themselves and often ignore that "still small voice" of doubt from within. So, for example, they follow the doctor's orders even when a part of them wonders about getting a second opinion. The prevalence of conventional morality is also one of the reasons it took so long before the whistle was blown on the decades of sexual abuse of children by a relatively small number of priests within the Catholic Church.

Discipline: The purpose of discipline is twofold: to enable an individual to fit into society and also to develop her will so that it becomes a strong inner "muscle," capable of directing her thoughts, emotions, and behaviors toward concrete, measurable goals that bring her a sense of accomplishment. Inner discipline and will are strengthened by first learning how to follow external rules and regulations. Over time, these become internalized in combination with a child's unique soul qualities. The optimal result is a solid inner moral compass that she can rely on to guide her through life. For this internalization process to be effective, a latency-age child requires some kind of consistent punishment or consequence for breaking a rule; for example, if she lies to her parents, she is not allowed to watch TV for a week. Instilling discipline also supports health, because a disciplined will is necessary to carry out regular self-care routines, such as exercising even when you'd rather not.

Third Stage: Postconventional Morality:
Ages Twelve to Fourteen into Adulthood

As a child leaves the innocence of middle childhood and nears puberty, her brain will increasingly be open to the shades of gray between absolute "right" and absolute "wrong" in a given situation. This is when she reaches the stage known as postconventional morality.

Individuals at this level will consider both moral and legal points of view in a given situation and recognize that these may be in conflict. They make their decision about what is right based on the principle of the greatest good for all concerned, and they are willing to make exceptions to the rules in individual cases. At this stage of development, their frontal executive brain function and orbitofrontal brains operate in partnership. Along with this comes mental flexibility: the capacity to know when to be conservatively law-abiding and when to be more liberal in applying a rule.

Young children often face dilemmas that offer them practice in moral decision making. One of my friends recalled that her mother had told her never to feed the stray cats that came around their house. But, feeling sorry for them, she always fed them, sneaking food behind her mother's back. When her mother asked if she was feeding them, she lied and said no. Her inner sense of what was right was stronger than her mother's rules. She knew she would be punished if her mother found out, but she said, "I didn't care. The risk was worth it." Another friend told me that she once stole money from her father's wallet to give to a kid at school who couldn't afford lunch.

Individuals who operate from postconventional morality realize that there are universal moral principles of justice and equality that may occasionally override man-made laws and rules. They can feel the distinction between what is moral and right and what is legal. Those with postconventional morality say, "I don't care what the law says, I will do what feels right in my heart." Breaking a rule for the higher good is altruistic. Breaking a rule for your own good only is characteristic of sociopathy.[1]

Discipline: Young teens and preteens often take every chance they get to push the envelope of parental authority as a way to test themselves and their inner sense of authority. And many have well-developed debating skills. They may be eager to defend their own actions with arguments that call on elements of postconventional morality. If you have a taste for these debates, they can certainly help to refine your daughter's thinking about the moral dilemmas she faces daily. However, school-age children and young adolescents still need, and often secretly long for, their parents' clear guidance on proper behavior. This is the time when a mother absolutely must assume her role as an authority who determines what is appropriate conduct for her daughter around thorny issues like dating, going out with friends, and the kind of experimentation with smoking, drugs, alcohol use, and sexuality that is now common in many middle schools.

You help your daughter when you stand firm in your Mother Bear energy, maintaining clear guidelines about right and wrong at a time when she is likely to be blasted with all kinds of peer and social pressure. Enforcing rules and setting limits from a place of fierce love serves an important protective function, providing your daughter with an external backbone as she is developing her own.

The Source of Most Moral Conflicts: A Disconnect between the Brain and the Heart

Interestingly, the way in which morality gets laid down in both the brain and body is heavily influenced by the extent of one's empathy and bonding circuits. If a child's bonding circuits aren't very well developed, every frontal-lobe task, including the development of morality, will be affected.

If an individual's morality stays in the conventional range beyond puberty, it tends to be focused on a rigid set of rules that are quite compartmentalized from a heart sense of what feels "right" inside. In these individuals, morality is a matter of frontal-lobe reasoning only. They don't question their choice of right or wrong. They simply pick a rule and stick with it. They don't understand that certain situations might require different thinking and behavior. They lack the mental flexibility required to balance the DLPC with the orbitofrontal, thus creating shades of gray around a rule. It can't be changed to suit the circumstances. Their concrete interpretation of what is wrong and what is right is an unwavering intellectual construct that never gets tested against how they feel inside their heart or gut. The rules are the rules. Period. They expect others to follow suit as well. Why? Because that's what society says is right and those who don't agree are wrong. Feelings about what is moral are considered irrelevant to the discussion. They are simply too messy and too complicated for what "should" be a black-and-white decision.

Since we tend to think of morality only in terms of what society deems important or politically relevant, many of the day-to-day issues that cause physical and emotional stress can seem trivial. I submit that they are often as morally relevant as the bigger issues. The test of right conduct applies whether we're talking about things like the death penalty and a woman's right to choose—or discussing whether or not it's okay to bring the family car home with no gas in it, or to put an empty milk container back into the refrigerator, or how much to tip the waitress. Ultimately, character and moral fiber are composed of one's actions in a variety of day-to-day situations, as in the following example.

JENNIFER: You Can't Eat That Cake

Jennifer is married to a man whose morality is very conventional. He is on the board of the local hospital, a role that involves regular socializing with the other board members and their spouses. As she dressed for one of these functions, Jennifer decided that she wanted to take her own dessert. She was following a special diet at the time that allowed her to have carbohydrates only during a one-hour period each day. This dietary approach was working very well for her and she had lost about ten pounds and lowered her cholesterol significantly. She knew that the desserts weren't very good at these hospital dinners and it was important to her that she get her one "treat" per day. So she packed a piece of chocolate cake to take with her. Her plan was to eat it very discreetly as part of her meal.

When her husband saw her with the cake, he said, "What are you doing?" She told him. He said, "You can't take that cake in there. I will not allow it. Our hospital has just hired a new cook, and we are obligated to eat what he serves. I am on the board." Jennifer's desire to eat the food that was right for her at that time was not a consideration. Her husband's need to follow his idea of "right versus wrong" was far more important to him than her feelings and her needs. End of discussion.

One small incident, perhaps. But over time, having her opinion and desires trivialized because her husband didn't think they were "important enough" is a health risk for Jennifer.

When there is a difference of opinion between a conventional and postconventional person, the postconventional person will usually be able to appreciate the point of view of the conventional person. The conventional person, however, often will not acknowledge the point of view of the postconventional person and will almost always attempt to make the postconventional person wrong and try to control her behavior. The person whose morality (and brain development) is at the conventional stage relies on a system of external control in order to feel safe. The postconventional person, on the other hand, has a far more solid, internalized system of control and empathy. She feels safe by virtue of this internalized system of adhering to what she feels to be the highest good and the highest truth for all concerned—including herself.

HOW THE INNER MORAL COMPASS DEVELOPS IN THE BRAIN

Frontal Executive	*Orbitofrontal/Temporal (Limbic)*
DLPC	Orbitofrontal cortex
Organizing	Spontaneous
Exclusive	Inclusive
Structuring	Expressing
Thinking	Feeling
Rational	Intuitive
What you think the world needs	What you feel the world needs

Note: The highest morality is when the two sides work together.

❀ WISDOM CHALLENGE: *A Daughter with Bonding Problems*

Individuals who have bonding problems may develop morality problems because their empathy circuits don't function well. In Chapter 7, I described differences in bonding patterns in terms of "Teflon" versus "Velcro." People with bonding problems are far out on the Teflon end of the spectrum. They're not particularly motivated by the love and approval of others and, consequently, the disapproval of parents or others isn't much of a deterrent.

These children are motivated far more by their own desires than by the need to please others. That's how they are born. They aren't "bad." But they may become "bad" if they are raised in an overly permissive atmosphere that lacks boundaries, expectations, rules, and regulations. In my experience mothers of such girls are often very empathic individuals. They have Velcro bonding circuits. And therein lies the dilemma. These mothers feel everything acutely—and automatically assume that their daughters do, too! Punishments that they would consider intolerable if directed at them—being left at home, a long time-out, having to miss a family outing, being yelled at, being grounded—don't even faze a kid with bonding challenges. As a result, an overly empathetic mother with a bonding-challenged kid can be easily manipulated. She's too afraid of hurting her child and making her unhappy. I recently heard of one such daughter whose mother found her in the bathroom "practicing" her crying at the age of five.

In order to rear a bonding-challenged child so that she develops good moral character, you must enforce rules and regulations consistently—even if your daughter tries to wear you down. She needs more structure, not less. And she will thrive when she knows exactly what is expected of her. For overempathetic mothers, the key to effective discipline is to be loving and playful when things are going well, and absolutely unmovable in requiring good behavior!

GENDER DIFFERENCES IN MORALITY

How morality gets laid down in a child's brain and body is heavily influenced by how secure her bonding and empathy circuits are. But there's another fascinating difference that is based on gender. Most women have brains that are physiologically less compartmentalized than most men's. One of the consequences is that they have more connectivity between the orbitofrontal region and the dorsolateral prefrontal cortex. This also means that their morality is more likely to fall into the postconventional realm.

The pioneering work of Carol Gilligan, Ph.D., the psychologist and author of *In a Different Voice,* showed that when school-age boys and girls were presented with the same moral dilemma, they made different choices about what was the "right" thing to do.[2] Here's one example:

> A man has a sick wife who needs medication. He has no money, so he steals the medicine from the pharmacy. When girls were asked about this situation, they tended to side with the husband who was caring for his wife in the best way he knew how. They did not consider his stealing wrong. In other words,

the moral value of caring took precedent over the law. Boys, on the other hand, tended to side with the pharmacist. They said that stealing was wrong regardless of the circumstances.

Gilligan was a research assistant for Lawrence Kohlberg at Harvard, and she was struck that most of the research of moral theorists such as Kohlberg and Erik Erikson had been done on boys and men. She pointed out that a psychology based on only one-half of the human race didn't serve anyone. Her own research helped to reframe psychology, and things have certainly changed since *In a Different Voice* was published in 1982.

For the first time in written history, a significant number of women lawmakers are beginning to leave the mark of their different moral understanding on our legal system. Over time, this contribution will create a more balanced society. We still have a way to go, of course, but we're making progress. Not so many generations ago, it was considered a husband's legal right to beat his wife as long as he used a stick no wider than his thumb. (That's where the expression *rule of thumb* came from.) Within my lifetime, unequal rights and arbitrary exclusion based on gender were taken for granted—and were perfectly legal. For example, my mother couldn't take out a loan in her own name at the time I entered medical school, in one of the first classes that had more than a few token women. Today, women residents in ob-gyn outnumber men—and they all have loans! It's important to remember that opportunities our daughters take for granted came about because individual women had the courage to follow their inner moral compasses instead of being "nice."

My Maternal Legacy: Challenging Church Authority

If we want our daughters to become who they really are, choose vocations that honor their inner wisdom, and keep their authentic voices during and after puberty, then we must support their perceptions and stand by them in the face of the inevitable challenges that come from the hierarchal institutions of our culture—whether they be our schools, our churches, or our own family members.

I personally inherited some of my ability to hold my ground with authority figures from my mother, Edna, and her mother, Ruth, my maternal grandmother. My mother had the courage to leave the Catholic Church in 1939, at a time when almost nobody questioned Church authority, let alone a thirteen-year-old girl. Here's what happened: My mother was working her way through Catholic school, doing cleaning at school to pay her tuition, because her family didn't have the money to send her. She didn't really fit in with the other girls, and they blamed her when one of them painted the toenails on the statue of the Blessed Virgin that sat on the altar. The priest tried to force my mother to confess her wrongdoing by having her kneel before the altar with outstretched arms for thirty minutes. But she hadn't painted the Virgin, so she didn't confess, even though the priest kept trying to extract a confession.

After a few days, the priest came to her home to confront her and her mother. My grandmother stood by my mother. She told the priest, "Edna is an honest child. If she said she didn't do it, I know she didn't." After about an hour of lecturing on the perils of burning in hell, the priest told my mother that he was going to excommunicate her and that she could never come back to church. (He didn't have the power to do this, but my mother didn't know that.) She came to her own conclusion: "If this is religion, I don't want anything to do with it."

The priest's behavior flew in the face of the very principles of honesty and integrity that my mother felt were an essential part of any religion she'd be interested in. She never returned to the Catholic Church. When she married my father, who was Episcopalian, she usually chose to avoid church on Sundays. She wasn't about to have anyone—or any denomination—tell her what she was supposed to believe. We children often went to church with my father. My mother said she was going to go to her "church," which was the woods behind our house.

My mother also challenged authority on her children's behalf. Though she generally took a hands-off approach to our day-to-day activities in school, if she sensed that one of us was being treated poorly, she didn't hesitate to take a stand. I remember a piano recital when I was about thirteen years old. My new teacher, the wife of an orchestra conductor, wasn't your average piano teacher. And she didn't give your average recital. In fact, unbeknownst to me, my mother, or my sister, she ran a recital like a master class. I played my piece and then my teacher asked Miriam, another student, to critique my playing. Miriam was clearly the apple of my teacher's eye and, though younger, was far more gifted than I. Miriam said, "I think she did very well." My teacher said, "I think Miriam is being very generous with you." Later, when we got into the car to go home, my mother turned to me and said, "You certainly don't ever have to come back here again." She knew that this kind of teaching style was abusive, especially in a child as perfectionistic, driven, and eager to please as I was. I later found another teacher.

Standing Up for Your Daughter's Highest Good Builds Her Sense of Right and Wrong

Because of my maternal legacy, I carried on this kind of Mother Bear mothering with my own daughters. Here's an example:

One evening when my daughter Kate was halfway through seventh grade I overheard her asking her father if she could drop an optional course she was taking entitled "Junior Great Books." The class was for gifted and talented seventh graders, and she had never said anything about it, one way or the other.

As I listened to her conversation with her father, I thought, *Uh-oh! She has just asked the wrong parent.* His reply to her was, "We can't just let you drop a course because you don't like it." I knew what was likely to come next. Kate ran up to her room and closed the door. I knocked gently and asked if I could come in. Through her sobs, she said yes. I sat down close to her and then held her as she cried as long as she needed to. Finally she drew in the kind of jagged breath that indicated she was almost ready to begin talking. I handed her some tissues and waited.

I suspected that my husband's response made her feel powerless to change something that was really bothering her, and that this was the driving force behind the tears—the hopeless-helpless feeling that there's no way out. I started our talk by suggesting that in the future she might want to come to me first about curriculum-related things. Then I asked her to tell me the whole story. (I know that parents are supposed to present a united front to their children. However, I often disagreed with my husband's more conventional moral positions, and it wouldn't have been honest for me to pretend otherwise.)

Kate told me that the teacher was boring and so was the topic. I knew that there had to be more to it than that, given the depth of her emotional response. So I asked her for a few examples. Then she told me what I needed to know. She said that the teacher made fun of some of the kids in the class and that it made her really uncomfortable and afraid to be there. Apparently things were getting worse, or else her tolerance for this kind of abuse had decreased since the beginning of the year. In any case, I knew my daughter well enough to know that if the class was making her that uncomfortable, we needed to do something to support her. So I told her that I would work with her to get her out of the class. She said that she needed a note from us the next day.

Later that evening I brought up the subject with my husband, telling him that Kate was very upset about this course and that I felt we should allow her to discontinue it, especially since it was optional. He said, "I don't want her to get the idea that she can drop a class anytime it doesn't suit her." I reminded him that our daughter was a straight-A student who wasn't in the habit of dropping anything or complaining about it either. He replied, "But I have no information here. She's not giving me any information."

The "information" he was looking for consisted of facts that could be processed by his DLPC area. The facts I was responding to came from my orbitofrontal bond with my daughter. Her emotional response was all the information I needed. It was then that I knew that I was right up against the primary difference between conventional and postconventional morality (which sometimes translates into the difference between male and female brains). My husband's concept of information was to gather data from other sources, as many as possible. My concept of information was built on an intimate knowledge of my daughter, her values, and her emotions. Her distress was enough information for me to excuse her from the class immediately.

My husband chose to gather more data by calling the parents of as many of the kids in that class as he could reach, much to my daughter's embarrassment. He discovered that the other kids hadn't said much to their parents either, but there was a vague sense that the class wasn't great. By bedtime, my husband and I had reached a compromise. He wanted to have a meeting with the school principal to go over his concerns. But I wanted to give Kate a note to get her out of the class the next day, because I felt that there was a risk of her being scapegoated by the teacher once the word got out that other students and parents were questioning the class. I convinced my husband that our daughter's well-being was my first concern, and that what was best for the community as a whole was an issue he could take on himself. He grudgingly agreed.

The next morning I gave Kate the note and left for an overnight speaking engagement, secure in the knowledge that my daughter could relax in school that day. When I called home later that night to find out what had happened, my husband told me that the entire course had been dropped! Apparently, once my daughter had had the guts to say something, other kids—and their parents—had done the same. Suddenly it became clear to the administration that something was "off" in that class, and swift action followed. I told Kate on several occasions how proud I was that she had had the courage to speak up for herself. I told her that she was heroic.

I had not intended to help the whole class by blowing the whistle on the teacher. My goal was to protect my own daughter. Period. My husband, whose perspective (and morality) was different, felt that there was a bigger issue at stake, and that it was best discussed with everybody involved.

Trusting What You Know and What You Feel

Self-trust is at the heart of health and is the essence of inner wisdom. My mother's unconventional interests, which were supported by my father, gave me the courage to trust my own inner wisdom, particularly in my career. As a result, I have been able to question the status quo in women's health care and also to help women throughout the world begin to trust their own inner wisdom more fully.

Many aspects of my career have been a laboratory for experiencing the difference between conventional (rule-bound) morality and postconventional morality (the combined wisdom of the intellect *and* the heart). Back in the early 1980s, my heart (limbic system) and my research (DLPC) told me to make sure all my pregnant patients—and all those who planned to become pregnant—supplemented their diets with folic acid to help prevent birth defects. At the time, this was not considered necessary by the authorities in my specialty because, though early studies supported the practice, "more research was needed." (This is the standard response of those with conventional morality. And that's perfectly understandable.) I knew that folic acid couldn't hurt and that it might well help. That's why I prescribed it. Doing otherwise felt morally wrong. But it took more than a decade for "the powers that be" to make folic acid supplementation the standard of care for pregnant women.

Likewise, my heart (limbic system) and my research (frontal lobe) strongly motivated me to support women in birthing their babies naturally at a time when nearly everyone in the hospital was given a spinal anesthetic to deaden feeling. I also delayed clamping the umbilical cord until it had stopped pulsating by itself. I intuitively knew that if the cord continued to pulsate, nature had a very good reason for it. Sure enough, I eventually came across the research of Dr. George Morley, who pointed out how elegantly Nature has designed the placenta and umbilical cord as a way for the newborn child to replenish its blood volume and establish oxygenation of the lungs right after birth. Attending birth in this way, as a natural event imbued with wisdom, was certainly not the conventional mind-set back in the 1970s when I was doing my training. But I did it anyway. Though I walked a fine line between the world of the intellect and the world of the heart, I knew deep within me that what I was doing was the right thing, though not always the popular or well-accepted thing, to do!

WOMEN AND GUILT

Guilt is the feeling of self-blame that arises in an individual with normal empathy and bonding circuits when she knows she has done something wrong or hasn't measured up to her own, her family's, or her society's standards for acceptable behavior. Guilt is a powerful signal of wrongdoing, the internalization of the painful feelings of shame we felt as young children. The reason moral standards work is that, when internalized and followed, they prevent most individuals from feeling the intolerable discomfort of shame and guilt. In most cases, social order is served, and our internal comfort is maintained. It is neither possible nor desirable to raise a daughter who never experiences guilt.

On the other hand, there's such a thing as feeling too much guilt. And in my experience, feeling too much guilt is very common in girls and women. Guilt and shame can be divided into two categories: justified and unjustified. One of the problems most women face—and pass on unwittingly to their daughters—is the problem of unjustified shame or guilt. Erica Jong once wrote, "Show me a woman who doesn't feel guilty and I'll show you a man." A more accurate statement is this: "Show me a woman (or a man) who doesn't feel guilty enough to change her behavior, and I'll show you someone who can't be controlled by the expectations of others." Either they don't feel shame or guilt in the way most people do (as in the case of sociopaths) or they have developed enough courage and self-trust to live their lives according to their own inner wisdom.

Women and girls are socialized from a young age to feel responsible for the happiness and comfort of those who are in a position of power. This is most often their father or other male figures, but it can also be a female authority figure. This is the norm in hierarchical societies of all kinds in which one's sense of safety and security depends upon knowing one's place and acting accordingly. (This is why Jennifer's husband got to decide whether or not she could eat her cake!) The problem with this model (and it is, after all, just one model of social organization) is the fact that happiness is ultimately an inside job. No one can make or keep another person happy, though it is a natural inclination for most of us to provide support and comfort to those we love.

On some level, we are all born knowing the essential truth that our primary job is to care for ourselves first, and then, from a place of empathy and love, offer our support to others who are doing the same. A child's innate (though usually unconscious) knowledge of this spiritual truth sets her up for a major moral dilemma: she wants to fit in and be liked by her family and others. But at the same time, she wants to develop her innate gifts and talents and to enjoy going after what she wants in the world. In latency, she reaches the developmental stage where her brain and body are primed for a huge amount of learning and mastery in the outer world. It is precisely at this time that many girls are given mixed messages about how to balance these two desires.

RACHEL: Don't Make Your Father Feel Bad

My friend Rachel was a superb chess player during grade school. Rachel always won, which frequently meant that she beat the boys. Her mother was proud and encouraging of this gift until Rachel started to beat her father. At that point, Rachel's mother told her that she should let her father win, because she was making him feel bad. Rachel found this very confusing. By the time she reached the sixth grade, Rachel also wanted to learn how to fix her bike herself so she wouldn't always have to ask her father to do it. But once again, Rachel's mother said to her, "Don't make your father feel bad. Let him fix your bike." Rachel also noticed that the others girls started to shun her whenever she beat the boys in chess. The joy went out of playing chess, and she eventually gave it up.

Rachel told me:

> Years later I finally realized that my mother (and society) were teaching me the most important unwritten rule that governs most women's lives—and leads to so much guilt and shame: "Be a good girl and keep everyone happy." What that meant is that I felt guilty whenever I won in chess and beat the

boys or my father. Somehow my mastery made them feel bad, instead of inspiring them to be better players. This didn't make sense to me. I got mad at my mother for trying to teach me something that I felt was just wrong. But she said that someday I'd understand. I didn't. But then I'd feel ashamed of myself for not being a "good" person because I was supposedly making my father feel bad about himself. After all, if I were truly a "good" girl, then serving my father and letting the boys win in chess would have made me feel good. But it didn't. It just made me angry. Then I'd feel ashamed for being angry!

Rachel's mother had also told her that it was her job to get up and serve her father at dinner each night, even though he didn't work outside the home and basically sat around the house and did very little. Her mother told her that if she had been a son she wouldn't be expected to serve her father. Then she'd have been assigned other tasks such as mowing the lawn—something Rachel actually wanted to do that her parents wouldn't allow her to do! Rachel continued:

> I couldn't imagine that my father's ego was so fragile that I actually had the power to make him feel bad about himself by beating him in chess or not letting him fix my bike. I also began to realize that my mother was training me to live a lie: "Pretend you're not as good as you are so that others will feel better about themselves." This felt wrong to me then and it feels wrong to me now.
>
> My mother always insisted that it's women who are the keepers of society's morals. I disagree. Women who teach their daughters to diminish themselves for the benefit of their fathers (or brothers) are doing just the opposite of what's moral and right. They're teaching their daughters that they must denigrate themselves in order to elevate others. And they're perpetuating the myth that men are fragile and weak, not strong and powerful. It seems to me that everyone eventually loses under this system.

"Good girl" training like Rachel's leads to a lifetime of unjustified guilt. One of my patients once told me, "I always feel as though everything is my fault. Even when I go into a public restroom, I keep thinking that it's my job to make it nicer for the next person. So I clean it up. But then I find myself feeling resentful." Another patient spent a couple of years working through the enormous guilt she felt about finally getting a divorce from a man who had been emotionally abusive for years and who refused to provide any support for their two children. She said to me, "I have this recurrent thought that if I just wrote to him and apologized for my shortcomings, that he'd somehow forgive me. And it would make life easier for our children."

THE COST OF SELF-ABANDONMENT

Believing that she's responsible for the happiness of others often puts a girl (and later, an adult woman) in the impossible situation of having to betray her true self. In the words of the famous physician Elisabeth Kübler-Ross, she is encouraged to become "a little prostitute." She learns not to trust her own inner moral compass—because her own passions and purposes are not deemed nearly as important as keeping "Daddy" (or his substitute) happy.

This double bind inevitably leads to unjustified guilt and shame. And these two emotions, if not relieved by changing one's thinking and behavior, eventually cause a great deal of wear and tear on the physical body. The long-term physical and emotional stress of shame and guilt in all their various forms (including remorse, grief, anxiety, and depression) can lead to addictions of all kinds. Used addictively, food, alcohol, sex, cigarettes, drugs, or work may temporarily numb the pain of abandoning one's true self, but at the price of contributing to everything from obesity to heart disease and breast cancer.

School-age children who have not yet reached puberty have a tendency to tell the truth. If they live in situations in which they cannot tell the truth, their bodies will do it for them. Whether or not a child becomes ill depends somewhat on her temperament and on her genetic tendencies. Sooner or later, however, the body presents its bill. And it never lies.

Given the amount of pain it causes to carry so much unjustified shame and guilt, why do women keep doing it—and then passing it on to their daughters? Because throughout recorded human history, aligning oneself with a man has given a woman more power, status, and influence than she would otherwise have had. If she hoped to survive herself, and create a good life for her children, she had better make some kind of alliance with a man—the more powerful, the better. This was portrayed brilliantly in the recent movie *Mystic River*. Annabeth (played by Laura Linney) knows that her husband, Jimmy (Sean Penn), has just murdered an innocent person. She knows that this is weighing on him. So she tells him that he's a king, and that sometimes kings have to make difficult decisions. As she begins to make love to him, she tells him in a hypnotic voice that he could "own" the whole neighborhood—that's how good a king he is. Turning a blind eye to her husband's crime, she uses his current dilemma to solidify her relationship with him, and thus ensure that she and their two daughters will be cared for and protected.

Because of the way in which girls and women are molded both by biology and by society, they are also far more susceptible than most men to being controlled by what other people think. A single woman has, until very recently, been seen as a loser. Having any man, no matter how unsuitable, was considered far better than being alone. I hadn't realized how powerful this social stigma was until I had to fill out an insurance form following my divorce. For twenty-five years, I had been able to pass muster by checking the "married" box, thereby winning the Good Housekeeping Seal of Approval. My inner dialogue went something like this: "I may be a doctor, but I'm also a wife and mother. So that makes me 'nice.'" Now I was faced with the distasteful and humiliating choice between "single" and "divorced." I chose "single."

Feeling that she's not good enough without a man puts a girl—and later a woman—at risk for all kinds of unskillful behavior in order to prove that she is desirable and worthy. This ranges from unprotected sex to getting into and staying in abusive relationships, or, at the very least, unfulfilling, deadening relationships. The truth is that for more than five thousand years, society has encouraged an internal split between values that are considered masculine (and match those of the DLPC) and those considered feminine (which most closely match those of the orbitofrontal brain area). As a result, girls project their masculine power drive onto boys and disown it in themselves. And boys project their vulnerability and tenderness onto girls. Neither gender develops true balance within herself or himself. And thus neither reaches their full potential for health and happiness. (Note: A great deal of research has documented the fact that egalitarian societies existed throughout Old Europe for over thirty thousand years. In geologic terms, our current patriarchal culture is relatively new. See Chapter 16.)

Though men and boys clearly have a capacity to feel guilt and shame, the context of this guilt and shame is far different. As John Wheeler wrote in his book *Touched with Fire*, "Femininity expresses the idea that there are things worth living for. Masculinity is the idea that there are things worth dying for." Men and boys are expected to put their lives on the line in the service of their country. They're socialized to fight others—physically if necessary—to prove a point or to establish their manhood. They're also expected to be aggressive sexually, while girls are socialized to resist if they want to appear "good." In order to behave as expected, boys learn early on to shut down their emotional vulnerability. Despite this, or perhaps because of it, boys are encouraged far more than girls to go after what they want in the world without having to worry about what others will think or about not being seen as "nice." Because every human being has both male and female energies, this kind of socialization encourages both girls and boys to behave in a way that is out of touch with their own inner guidance. That is a great loss—and a health risk—for both genders.

MODELING MORALITY: THE NEW COMMANDMENTS

A girl needs to learn where her moral responsibility begins and ends. And, as with everything else, she'll look first to her mother as a role model. School-age children can spot hypocrisy immediately. That means that a mother's behavior has to match what she says she believes. If she tells her daughter that she can be anything she wants to be, but continues to set aside her own goals in order to please others, then she isn't being morally consistent. Though her daughter may not be conscious of this now, or say anything if she is, it is this kind of gap between belief and behavior that sets the stage for mother-daughter conflict once puberty hits.

One: Thou shalt be guided by thine own moral compass. The most powerful lesson a mother can teach her daughter is that she has been given only one life that she can have absolute dominion over. That life is her own. She is born with a kind of personal morality, an inner sense of what is right and wrong for her. It's important to help her acknowledge and strengthen her faith in this inner knowing, even as she learns the rules and rights of others. A girl's own life, health, and happiness have to be her primary responsibility because no one else can create these things for her. When she takes her own life seriously, then she will be able to develop her own unique gifts and talents in such a way that they become a gift to the world.

Two: Thou shalt acknowledge thy unique inner spark. Every daughter needs to know that she has been born with a unique gift, a special expression of divinity that is unlike that of anyone who ever lived before or will ever live again. Her primary job is to remember that inner spark, fan it, discipline it, and develop it. A daughter can do this only by being true to herself, whether as a child prodigy chess player or a particularly empathic caregiver for animals. Her own inner moral compass will be her guide toward her Highest Good. A mother needs to help her daughter get clear about what she really wants in the world. If her clearest desire is for a home and family, then honor this desire. If it's to become a real-estate developer, then support her in that. If she wants to do both, let her know that all things are possible with faith, compromise, and persistence. Help her develop a strategy to go after what she wants.

Three: Thou shalt remain true to thine inner voice. A daughter can develop her inner wisdom and inner voice of authority when she is encouraged to be true to them and to recognize them. She needs role models who stand up for themselves and for her. She also needs to develop courage, integrity, and independence. This means that she must learn to balance standing up for herself with standing up for others. All of this will depend upon her level of self-esteem, a quality that is earned through skill building, discipline, and persistence. However, she won't be able to remain true to her inner voice if she's continually told, either verbally or nonverbally, that her primary responsibility is to serve and please her father, mother, brother, or husband at the expense of herself.

Four: Thou shalt not participate in manipulative or exploitive relationships. When a relationship begins to cause more pain than joy, and drain more energy than it replenishes, then it may be time to leave. This applies to friends in the fourth grade as much as it does to marriages. Every girl needs to learn when she's being manipulated to assume more than her share of the responsibility for a given situation. You can teach your daughter that whenever anyone says, "You made me [feel bad . . . lose my temper . . . break my promise . . . fill in the blank]," then she's being manipulated. And the other person is trying to get her to do something that will make them happy at her expense. She doesn't need to fall for this fundamental lie.

Let's face it, women and girls can also be champion manipulators of men (or boys) and other women (or girls). Only if a woman learns to speak her truth (New Commandment number three) will she be able to avoid underhanded ways of getting what she wants. A mother who lets her daughter get away with manipulation, or models manipulation, is participating in the immoral system.

Five: Thou shalt learn the skills of relating to others with integrity and mutuality. Relationships are meant to replenish and uplift us, not drain us. Healthy relationships are one of the primary joys of life. We shouldn't have to choose between being loved and also going after what we want. Self-development is, after all, far more fulfilling and lasting when it takes place in the context of relating to others.

Relating to others with integrity means that one acknowledges that everyone has her (or his) own inner Divine spark. A girl needs to learn that it's morally wrong to be jealous of the spark of another, or jealous of another's life or possessions. This is absolutely essential in our society of envy and one-upmanship. Though jealousy is a normal human emotion, it doesn't have to be fertilized. Instead, teach your daughter to use the good fortune of others as motivation for creating something better in her own life. Teach your daughter that it's possible to go after what she wants while also considering the needs and feelings of others. Point out role models that you think your daughter will relate to and ask her who her own role models are. These two aspects of life don't have to be mutually exclusive.

HAVING A SAY: FINDING YOUR VOICE

A girl's confidence in her own voice is usually at an all-time high just before puberty. This is the time of life when girls are most apt to be in touch with their personal truth. Unless she's been shut down for some reason, she'll have no problem telling you what she really believes. In fact, you may have trouble getting her to stop talking. Given our culture, a girl's inner voice isn't apt to reach this level of clarity or self-assurance again until she goes through menopause—which I like to describe as adolescence in reverse.

I recently saw a very funny television phone ad in which a latency-age girl is braiding her grandfather's hair and talking non-stop. She has already braided her grandmother's hair. Wearily the grandfather says that they have to listen to this for about two hours every night until the rates change and the girl can start calling her friends. Girls this age are known for processing every aspect of their lives and emotions—and those of their peers—by talking about them. This is normal and healthy. And given that communication is now easier than ever, via cell phones, e-mail, and instant messaging, it's a mother's job to simply observe this behavior and see it for what it is—a normal developmental stage. She may also have to set some boundaries, so that these conversations don't take precedence over schoolwork, chores, and family activities and meals.

Not all girls are allowed to freely express how they feel and what they think, however. And it is not unusual for a woman to struggle with a difficult maternal legacy in this area, with lasting health consequences. The following story from a newsletter reader is a beautiful example:

> When I was just three, my stepdad tried to strangle my mother during a fight and I had to intervene to stop him. Most of my childhood I felt I had to stand up for my mother, who was often quite ill and so shy that she had "no voice." In adulthood, I suffered from chronic throat infections and tension, especially when I felt I needed to stand up for myself or others who had "no voice." Now I am learning to let go and listen to my fifth chakra center, as it reminds me that I don't have to feel responsible for others and can have faith in Divine wisdom instead!

The fifth chakra, or emotional center, is the body area associated with the throat, tongue, mouth, neck, and thyroid. It is affected by issues relating to communication, will, and timing. The health of this area is shored up by knowing what to say, when to say it, how to say it, and being allowed to say it. Many women have thyroid and other problems (like canker sores in their mouth) when they have something to say but don't dare to say it, aren't allowed to say it, or repeatedly say it to the wrong person or to someone who can't or won't hear it.

The Impact of Gender

In families where men and boys are valued more than girls and women, girls lose their voices all too easily. Here's a case that was given to me by Mona Lisa Schulz, M.D., Ph.D.:

During my psychiatric rotation in medical school, I viewed a taped session of a single-parent family (mother only) consisting of two daughters and two sons who had come into family therapy. The reason for the therapy was that the six-year-old daughter had been playing with a family chemistry set in her mother's bedroom when her mother was at work. She had inadvertently set fire to the bedclothes. Her older brother had discovered her and the fire.

When the family came in and sat down, the mother sat with the two daughters to her right, and her older son sat on the other side of the room—opposite the girls. The younger boy, who was four, spent his time walking around the room and playing.

When the therapist asked what had happened, the older son immediately assumed the role of spokesperson. He had been the one to discover the fire, after all, and it was also clear from his demeanor that he considered himself the "knight" of the family and had assumed the role of the missing father. The six-year-old female "perpetrator" sat quietly with her hands folded in her lap—and so did her three-year-old sister. Compared to their brothers, they seemed deadened, as though their life force had left them.

Whenever the therapist asked another family member to speak, the older brother interrupted. The therapist had to continually ask that he hold his comments so that his mother or sister could speak. Interestingly, the therapist didn't address the three-year-old daughter even once.

Ultimately, the family resolved that the six-year-old would not play with the chemistry set again in an unsupervised fashion. Their primary goal was to make sure that the house didn't burn down—and who would disagree?

But when the film ended and the discussion began, I was left with the very unsettling feeling that a great deal was being missed in this situation—and that the girls in that family were likely to suffer in later life as a result. A series of questions rose in my mind: Did the six-year-old have a natural aptitude for science, or was she just trying to get her mother's attention? If her younger brother had set the fire by accident, would the family have reacted in the same way? Would this girl's potential interest in science be supported, even though she'd made a mistake, or would this incident successfully quell a budding scientific mind? If one of the girls had been running around and playing during the family session, as the younger brother had, would it have been tolerated by the mother and the therapist? If one of the girls had assumed the role of family spokesperson, would her insight have been tolerated and looked up to the same way as her older brother's was? If her older brother had set the fire and she had discovered it, would her account of the fire be believed and trusted in the same way his was? Would they even have come in for therapy about it? Or would it have fallen into the "boys will be boys" category of our cultural experience? If I were the younger girl in that family, would it matter to me that the therapist, an authority figure, had never asked for my opinion—or even my name?

Though it is impossible to know for sure what goes on in a family system from one therapy session, it was clear to me that the voice and will of the girls in this family had already been stifled.

Over the years, I've had literally hundreds of patients tell me stories about how their mothers kept their voices down while their fathers had the last word. And many others have told me that their brothers got all the support in the house for having the "right" answers or the worthy career goals. If a mother has a legacy such as this, she may well pass it down to her daughter unwittingly, thus silencing her daughter's voice and self-trust.

12

The Anatomy of Self-esteem

Seven Keys to Well-being

❁

Self-esteem is the cornerstone of health and of the behaviors that promote it. During the latency years, a child enters a new and crucial proving ground for self-esteem: the world outside her family. Some children, based on both temperament and early experiences, seem to race toward these new challenges with arms wide open. Others hang back and need a Mother Bear at their side who knows when to push and when to protect.

Parents and teachers talk a great deal about self-esteem, but they don't always agree on what it means. My definition is simple: Self-esteem is the amount of respect and positive regard an individual has for herself. It starts with the healthy bonding circuits laid down during early childhood. If the young girl has basked in her mother's loving attention, and if the connections between her orbitofrontal brain and her body are well established, it will be much easier for her to feel within herself what is right for her, and to know how to go after it. She will also have empathy for others. *Self-esteem without empathy equals self-centeredness or narcissism.*

Self-esteem is not based on a zero-sum model, the belief that there is only so much to go around, so that if your self-esteem is high, someone else's has to be low. Your self-esteem does not detract from mine, and I cannot raise my self-esteem by denigrating you. (At best, we enhance one another!) Self-esteem is multifaceted, not uniform. A girl (or an adult woman) can have high self-esteem in some areas and relatively low levels in others. For example, a girl may be a highly skilled athlete but have difficulty in one-on-one relationships. As a result, her self-esteem will be great on the playing field but her long-term emotional or even physical health may suffer later in life because of her relationship Achilles' heel. Similarly, a woman may have very high self-esteem in relationships but low self-esteem in areas concerning self-sufficiency. If she has never finished her education, has no in-depth intellectual interests, or has never learned how to earn or handle money, she is at risk for being overly dependent on others to take care of her.

Knowing that we are loved and respected by others is an essential ingredient in self-esteem, but ultimately self-esteem is an inside job. "Looking good" and putting a high polish on your self-presentation does *not* equal self-esteem. All the feel-good messages in the world can't give a child self-esteem if she does not experience herself as effective, competent, and true to herself. (The "do it myself" insistence of the toddler is a claim on self-esteem as well as on independence.) It's important that school-age girls be encouraged to develop areas of expertise and mastery that are recognized by the world beyond their immediate families. This sets up a positive self-esteem cycle. Each time she learns she can rely on herself, or relate effectively to others, or reach a personal goal, the more confidence she has for the next step in her development. And if she suffers a setback, the faster she is likely to recover and get moving forward again.

To capture the multifaceted nature of self-esteem, I've divided it into seven different areas. Of course, as you'll see in the discussion below, they intertwine in real life.

THE SEVEN AREAS OF SELF-ESTEEM

1. **Physical prowess:** Feeling confident in your body's ability to meet the demands of daily life through physical strength, endurance, and flexibility.

2. **Social skills and social comportment:** Knowing how to present yourself well and to act appropriately and graciously in a variety of social situations. Becoming someone others want to spend time with.

3. **Self-discipline:** Developing the ability to direct your will toward a desired goal in a sustained manner; to stay with a

task even when you're tired, distracted, discouraged, or no longer interested; to keep your promises.

4. Self-trust: Knowing how to tune in to and trust what you know and what you feel; to assess safety and danger; to act on your perceptions even when others may not agree with them.

5. Financial literacy: Developing your ability to spend, save, give, and invest wisely; to value your time and energy fairly; and to understand the laws of prosperity.

6. A place in the sun: Developing a special skill or innate talent for which you will be recognized and valued.

7. Positive self-image: Feeling secure and good about yourself, which includes a positive body image, and a positive relationship with self-adornment and personal style.

ONE: PHYSICAL PROWESS

Our bodies were designed to move throughout our lifetime. Joseph Pilates, the founder of the Pilates system of core strength, flexibility, and balance, said:

> Physical fitness is the first requisite of happiness. It is the attainment and maintenance of a uniformly developed body as well as a sound mind, fully capable of naturally, easily, and satisfactorily performing our many and varied daily tasks with spontaneous zest and pleasure.[1]

Physical prowess—the ability to feel strong and capable in her body—is an essential element of a child's sense of safety and security in the world. It also helps stabilize mood, preventing anxiety and depression through balancing the autonomic nervous system and producing neurochemicals such as endorphins that result in a natural "high." Exercise and breathing fresh air are like the nutrients in food. They help build independence and a sense of mastery. And they are a crucial investment in your daughter's future. Of all the lifestyle factors that have been studied, physical fitness is the best, most accurate predictor of a woman's longevity and health. To help your daughter enjoy moving her body is to give her primary prevention against osteoporosis, heart disease, cancer, obesity, and diabetes—all leading causes of premature death and disease in this country. Studies have also shown that girls who are physically fit have a more positive body image than those who aren't fit, regardless of how well their body aligns with the current cultural standard of beauty.

What researchers call "physical fitness" has three components: strength, endurance, and flexibility. While adult fitness programs may target these separately, a young child develops all three naturally if she engages in active exploration and play. As in all things, a girl's native temperament will determine her approach to physical prowess. Some children have an innate affinity for sports and easily learn the skills necessary to excel in them. For others, sports hold no interest at all. But they may well be interested in dance, yoga, or hiking. It's important that a daughter be encouraged to find her own unique way to stay physically fit, strong, and flexible.

It's not enough to talk about fitness to your kids. You have to model the behavior. Mothers who exercise and are fit have daughters who are far more likely to follow suit. The same is true with fathers. A recent study of nine-year-old girls done at Penn State University found that when neither parent promotes or supports exercise and athletics, just 30 percent of girls are physically active. When one parent gets involved, the figure rises to 50 percent. And when both parents get involved, 70 percent of girls report being very physically active.[2] Exercise habits, like eating patterns, get passed down from parent to child. So establishing these patterns needs to be a priority.

Physical Prowess Doesn't Have to Be Related to Competitive Sports

A girl's grade school experiences will set the tone for her relationship to fitness for the rest of her life. When I was growing up, physical fitness was synonymous with sports skills. This is still true in many schools. Sports are a great way to build physical prowess if a girl has natural skills and the desire to develop them. But if she is forced to play sports against her will, this can backfire and turn the child off to physical activity for years to come.

In his book *Body, Mind, and Sport*, John Doulliard, Ph.D., points out that 50 percent of middle school children have their first experience of failure and low self-esteem in school sports. The reason for this is that there's such a wide range of sports abilities among children—and also wide variation in the rate of development of these skills. If every child is expected to conform to the same standard, then some will inevitably fail. Some girls are natural athletes and others simply don't have these gifts. Some, like my daughter Kate, are born with enormous athletic talent but don't like competition. So no amount of pushing is going to get them to enjoy sports.

Our Cultural Legacy

The model of physical prowess I was brought up on had a distinct mind-body split built right into it. The coach (or gym teacher) was the mind and the players were the body. They weren't expected to think or feel at all. They were expected to carry out the instructions of the coach. Instead of listening to your body, you were encouraged to beat your body into the ground with running, push-ups, and so on. And taking time to stretch your muscles was just for sissies. Nobody had time to do that! This was certainly the training model that my sister learned with the U.S. Ski Team. It's little wonder that she sustained so many torn ligaments and had so many surgeries.

Then came the pioneering Jane Fonda exercise videos and the fitness centers of the 1970s. Though they weren't about sports, they were still all about "feeling the burn," not listening to your body. Still, despite their limitations, they got a generation of women to break a sweat at something and were, therefore, a giant step in the right direction!

My personal fitness program was based on the work of Kenneth Cooper, M.D., who introduced aerobics in the 1960s. Aerobics included any exercise that raised the heart rate enough to strengthen and tone the cardiovascular system and promote endurance through bringing oxygenated blood to the muscles more efficiently. When my parents started jogging regularly, I joined in. I liked the idea of choosing my own activities to get my heart rate up for an extended period of time. In college I stayed fit by running in place in my room, aiming for the number of aerobic "points" per week that were recommended. I also jumped rope sometimes. I never liked this much, but I knew it kept me healthy and also helped keep my weight under control. In medical school I had a boyfriend who did the decathlon. I took up running once again under his guidance and used running and also yoga as my primary forms of exercise throughout medical school and residency.

The entire fitness industry has continued to evolve since that time and so has our culture's approach to exercise. It's now easier than ever to find a fitness activity that suits one's temperament. We now know beyond any shadow of a doubt that the mind and body are profoundly connected, and that each of us must make a connection with our own body when it comes to exercise and fitness. Pilates and yoga, which are based on the unity of mind and body, have finally come into their own even though yoga, which heavily influenced Joseph Pilates, has been around since ancient times. It's very encouraging that the newest and most popular forms of exercise, like yoga, build flexibility, strength, and endurance at the same time. It's also encouraging that athletes of all kinds are also enjoying the benefits of these mind-body fitness approaches, and finding that they're helping them in their sports.

Passing on My Fitness Legacy

My life has been informed by my mother's physical prowess since birth. She has always been at her happiest when participating in sports or other outdoor activities. Sports were also the key to her leaving behind her original family circumstances. In 1941, when she was fifteen years old, she saw a movie called *Sun Valley Serenade* and became obsessed with the idea of skiing, even though she didn't know anyone who had ever skied. She took a train from Buffalo to nearby Ellicottville, where, as it happened, my father had introduced the sport of skiing to western New York State by putting a rope tow on a local hillside. The rest, as the saying goes, is history. This is a wonderful example of how when our soul is touched, our creative imagination begins to project us into a whole new life, drawing to us the people, places, and things that will make it a reality.

Though my temperament was ill-suited for competitive sports (and still is), my parents' emphasis on physical fitness made the development of a strong, healthy body a requisite for being part of the family. All those family hikes, skiing trips, and camping trips set me up for a lifetime of fitness. And that is a legacy I've been able to pass on to my daughters.

In my family, physical strength was expected, and we kids never questioned our ability to haul wood, clean out stalls in the barn, and shovel snow. These activities were simply part of life, whether you were a male or a female. Today, while I like the men in my life to pitch in and help out, and I appreciate having doors opened, I also like knowing that I am capable by myself. My daughters are the same way.

When my kids were little, we often went on family hikes to the beach, or to lakes and ponds in the area. The kids always enjoyed these outings and got plenty of exercise. They also participated in dance classes regularly starting at about the age of three and have continued these right up to the present. Only now they have also added yoga, Pilates, aerobics, and some weight training to the mix. Though we took them on ski trips occasionally, neither daughter took to this naturally. They didn't learn to ski until they were in their early teens and wanted to join their friends in the activity.

Now in their early twenties, my two daughters are both physically fit and exercise regularly, as do I. My mother's fitness legacy is alive and well in all of us, though in different forms. This past winter I took my mother, ski-champion sister, and younger daughter to a spa where I was lecturing. It was exhilarating to have three generations of us enjoying everything from dance classes to daily hikes. My fabulously fit seventy-eight-year-old mother was an inspiration for everyone there—a shining example of physical prowess at an age when the vast majority of women have bought the cultural programming that their bodies are supposed to be deteriorating.

TWO: SOCIAL SKILLS AND SOCIAL COMPORTMENT

In Room One, I pointed out that every child needs a sense of belonging to a place on the planet as well as to a group of people. Knowing that she belongs somewhere and that she fits in with others is a vital part of being comfortable in one's own skin, an essential building block of self-esteem. Feeling a sense of belonging and fitting in to one's immediate and extended family is the work of a girl's first seven years. The task of her second seven years is learning how to fit in to social situations that extend beyond her own family. Once a child goes to school, she quickly learns that belonging and fitting in aren't automatic. They depend, in part, upon learning social skills and diplomacy. Same-age friendships are so crucial to the growing girl that I've discussed them separately in Chapter 14. Here I want to focus on what we used to call manners.

Making a Good First Impression

Though there's some truth in the saying that you can't judge a book by its cover, any good publisher will tell you that a good cover goes a long way toward making a book attractive enough for someone to open it. It's the same with people. It takes only about fifteen seconds to form a first impression of a new person—usually before she has even opened her mouth to speak. This may not seem fair, but it's true. Since a girl has only one chance to make a first impression, it's very helpful if she learns how to do it skillfully—and in a variety of settings—not just at school where the standards required to "fit in" follow the dictates of peer pressure.

The Importance of a Good Handshake

When I was about nine years old or so, my mother and father sat all of us kids down and taught us how to greet new people. My parents dubbed themselves Mr. and Mrs. Peabody, a surname that cracked us up. We all had to practice being introduced to them, which included shaking their hands. "How do you do, Mrs. Peabody?" "Very well, thank you. And you?" The idea was to look them in the eye while smiling and shaking their right hand firmly and confidently.

That was my first formal lesson in social comportment. I remember my father demonstrating the "dead fish" handshake, or the "avoiding eye contact" greeting. He admonished us that it was important to have a firm, confident handshake accompanied by a warm smile and good eye contact. Both of these things said volumes about a person's character. And lack of them spoke volumes. It didn't take me long to realize that my father was correct. This small lesson in social comportment has served me well. I passed it on to my daughters when they were about eight or nine, too.

Hello and Good-bye: Greetings and Farewells

Acknowledging departures and reunions with the appropriate greeting binds us together in healthy and respectful ways that make us feel good. For that reason, it's very important that a child learns how to say hello and good-bye properly. This begins with greeting family members who are either coming home or leaving. It also involves taking the time to say good-bye when they (or you) leave. To this day, if one of my daughters is home and I have to leave the house before they wake up, I leave a note telling them good-bye and letting them know where I'll be. When they were younger, I went into their rooms to give them a kiss and a hug before leaving. I still do this if I'll be gone for a significant period of time. When they come home,

I also stop whatever I'm doing to greet them. When one of us doesn't take the time to do this, it feels as though there's a rent in the social fabric that requires repair. These small courtesies mean a great deal over the long haul.

Birthday Parties—A Social Laboratory

Children's birthday parties are the perfect place to teach early lessons in social comportment and gratitude. If your daughter is having the party, she can learn how to graciously greet her guests at the door and say a proper good-bye when they leave. She can also learn how to receive a gift graciously. In addition, being involved in planning a birthday party is a good introduction to the skills of initiating social contact. Some children are natural initiators—other kids just naturally follow their lead, play the games they suggest, and so on. Other children are almost entirely passive—they will go along, but they don't know how to "make it happen." This is clearly related to temperament, but it is also a learnable skill.

Thank-You Notes

You can always tell the children with "good breeding." They're the ones who acknowledge gifts with thank-you notes. Mothers are usually the ones who teach their children how to write thank-you notes. And birthday gift thank-yous are a good place to start. Teach your daughter that it's as important to thank family members and relatives as it is to thank friends and other acquaintances. I'm always thrilled and surprised when one of my daughters' friends sends me a little note or card after I've taken her out to dinner or had her as a guest in my home. It raises her value in my eyes. And those who don't do it lose status with me, no matter how great they are otherwise.

One of my friends told me that her grandmother used to send gifts and money to each of her grandchildren every Christmas and on their birthdays. In the last decade of her life, she stopped sending gifts to the grandchildren who had never thanked her. She also left them out of her will. My friend, who was one of the grandchildren who always thanked her, told me that her grandmother wasn't bitter about the lack of thanks. Instead she said, "I simply don't want to continue to reward ungrateful behavior. It will not help those children in life." She was right.

Children need to learn early on that we reap what we sow. Nothing—and I mean nothing—speaks louder about a girl's (or boy's) character than the fact that she (or he) takes the time to write a thank-you note. E-mails don't count as much, though they're better than nothing.

Offering to Help

Learning to help out in social settings also enhances a child's social standing and skill level. Most girls love to help with entertaining, whether by passing snacks to guests, setting the table, putting ice in the ice bucket, and so on. Helping should also include some of the cleanup. However, it's important to make sure that the boys and men in your family do their share. Otherwise, it's too easy to pass on the message that serving and cleaning up are the sole province of women.

THREE: SELF-DISCIPLINE

You've heard the old saying that success is 2 percent inspiration and 98 percent perspiration. Well, it's true. A lot of success in life—in any area—involves just showing up and putting one foot in front of the other to get the job done, whether or not you will be praised or recognized. That's why it's important that every girl learn how to direct her will toward a desired goal—without spending any energy trying to cut corners, defy authority, or in some other way avoid the necessary work. The old Nike ad "Just do it!" summarizes this quality perfectly. Self-discipline allows a daughter to access and then direct the reservoir of inner strength that all of us are born with. A child trains her will through repeated practice of a skill or performance of a task. In this way, her will becomes her servant—and her key to success, instead of a lifelong stumbling block that causes her to give up whenever the going gets tough, or boring, or she has a better offer.

Every girl needs to have some tasks that are simply expected of her on a regular basis. I grew up on a farm, and we had horses, cattle, and dogs. My siblings and I had to clean out the stalls regularly and also feed the horses and the dogs. In addition, we had to keep the wood box filled in the winter, which involved taking a toboggan up to the barn, loading it, and then sliding it down to the house—for several loads, often in snowstorms. (Ellicottville is in the snowbelt south of Buffalo.) Obviously I also learned a great deal of self-discipline from our family hikes and sporting outings.

With my daughters, I felt that self-discipline was best learned through schoolwork and extracurricular activities. They were expected to set and clear the table each night at dinner, but I didn't hold them to the kinds of chores I was raised with. Unlike my mother, I worked full-time outside our home, and I didn't want my limited time with my daughters to be spent monitoring household tasks. I also had household help when I was at work, so it would have been the nanny's job to make certain that the girls did their chores. I felt that it was inappropriate for a nanny to fulfill this parental role. And, to tell the truth, ever since medical school, a clean, orderly house had been very low on my priority list.

I had very high standards when it came to schoolwork, however. I regarded it as the girls' full-time job. They were expected to get good grades and get their homework done on time. I also expected them to do whatever was required for extracurricular activities that required practice, such as piano and voice lessons. Both daughters were highly disciplined in these areas and continued to do well in college. Yes, they've also learned the basics of cooking and cleaning. All three of us have finally come to appreciate the value of household order and organization after studying feng shui; we now understand how our environment reflects and profoundly affects us!

ON PRAISE AND BLAME

You help build your daughter's self-esteem when you bear witness to her accomplishments. Don't always wait for official occasions like recitals or report cards; let her know whenever you "catch" her doing well. We all still have that little kid inside who is saying, "Hey, Mom, look at me." So look at her frequently!

On the other hand, don't go overboard in a mistaken attempt to prop her up. Kids know full well when they've done their best and when they haven't. So don't praise your daughter for accomplishments that obviously fall short of what she's capable of, like handing a paper in late or doing a poor job of cleaning the kitchen. Resist wanting so much for your daughter to like you that you fail to enforce rules or standards of behavior.

Keep mistakes in perspective. I remember the day one of my daughters dropped something on a newly purchased rug. I noted it, realized it could be cleaned, and went back to watching television. She said, "Boy, am I glad you're my mother. Do you realize how many of my friend's mothers would have just flipped out about that? They would have gone ballistic!"

"Going ballistic" over garden-variety mistakes and messes tears down a child's sense of self. If she sees you acknowledging and cleaning up your own messes, she'll learn to handle hers responsibly without losing self-esteem.

FOUR: SELF-TRUST

The first day of school is a major rite of passage for mothers as well as children. Watching your daughter get on the school bus or walk into the classroom without you is a poignant exercise in letting go and trusting. This step is much easier if you've equipped your daughter with the sure knowledge that she was born with an inner guidance system that she can trust to help keep her safe. Every one of us was born with this ability. Inner guidance concerning safety and security comes through our physical bodies and is mediated through feelings in the solar-plexus area as well as those in the heart center.

Marcy, one of my newsletter subscribers, learned a powerful lesson about guidance from her mother, who was an orphan. And Marcy passed it on to her two daughters. I asked her to share this wisdom here because it's so practical and reassuring.

MARCY: Accessing Guidance

My mother was born to Italian immigrants in New York. She grew up in orphanages and foster homes during the early 1920s. Her mothering skills were self-taught as she did not have anyone to teach and nurture her while she was growing up.

I was an only child, and when I was young and would ask her about something, she would tell me to listen to my own Inner Guidance or Guardian Angels. She said they would always be there to guide me away from danger or bad situations. She would touch her solar-plexus area and tell me to "feel" the answers. As an orphan, she learned early on to listen to her Inner Wisdom, probably because that was the only thing she could trust.

When I had my own daughters and they began to venture out into the world, I started to teach them to listen to their Inner Guidance. It's difficult teaching a child in kindergarten on her way to her first sleepover how to listen to her own Guardian Angels. Divine Guidance is not easy to learn at any age and I wanted to teach both girls to know unquestionably when something was not right.

I sat down with them and took them through a guided meditation to show them exactly where in our bodies we feel the answers. I began to teach them how to listen and to interpret what our Guidance is telling us, and most importantly, not to question or look for the why or what. Just act on the Guidance, without question. Period.

I asked them to close their eyes and imagine a new puppy in their arms. The puppy is soft and smells nice. She is wiggling around in their arms trying to lick their face and wanting to play. The puppy is so soft, cuddly, and warm. We love this puppy and are so happy she is part of our family. When the girls were smiling and I knew they felt love for the puppy, I touched their hearts and told them this is the place that God fills with love. This is the place in our bodies that tells us we are safe, that the situation we are in is good. I asked them to describe the feeling in their hearts: warm, full, happy, light, and so on.

Then (still with their eyes closed) I asked them to imagine setting the puppy on the front lawn and watching the puppy run out into the street. They see a car coming down the street very fast and the puppy does not know she is in danger. They can't go into the street to get the puppy and the car is so close to running her over. . . .

I asked them to show me where they felt fear in their bodies. They touched their solar-plexus area. One daughter even started to cry. I explained to them that this is God's or our Guardian Angels' way of telling us there is danger and that something is not right. They understood the words "danger," "trouble," "frightened," "hurt." I showed them how we can touch the two places in our bodies (heart chakra and solar-plexus chakra) that guide us away from bad situations into the right situations or into safety.

Though my daughters were quite young when I taught them

this, they still use it all the time. Their skill in interpreting their Guidance has developed over the years, and they use the term "guidance" in normal conversation. My fifteen-year-old, Lauren, uses this skill to determine if she wants to get to know a boy. Megan, our thirteen-year-old, tells me when someone's house "feels wrong." Both of them have walked out of hair salons, restaurants, and movies, or called me from parties and sleep-overs to pick them up. They get it, and I am so thankful.

One of the challenges in teaching this to them was not to minimize their "feeling" for my convenience. There were a few times when they were "practicing" receiving Guidance that we would go somewhere and they would say, "I have the feeling," so we had to leave. Early on, I felt they would sometimes say to me, "My Angels are telling me this is not right, let's go," just to see my reaction. The challenge for me was never ever to ignore or disagree with them when they said it, no matter how trivial the situation. This was not always easy. But it was important, because it's all too easy to want to "think" our way out of a Guidance hit: "He looks so nice," or "They seem harmless," or "I told them I would be there." I always reinforce to them and to myself: Never think about it, just listen and act, without question. Now. Period.

By honoring their intuition, I feel that I have empowered them and helped to develop their self-esteem. They never have to justify their Guidance to anyone, for any reason.

I completely agree with Marcy, and I also honor her mother, who discovered her own guidance because she had no other choice. I've heard other people describe the solar-plexus area as our "inner siren." Letting your daughter know that she has this inner siren that she can trust is a far better strategy than telling your child "don't talk to strangers." The truth is, most strangers are trustworthy.

There's no question that this approach works. One of my friends told me the following story:

When I was about eleven years old, I had to take the late bus home from school because I was involved in band practice. When I got off the bus, I noticed this car parked near the bus stop. A man was sitting in the car. When I got off the bus, he got out of his car. I knew from the feeling in my gut that he was someone who wasn't safe. As I started to walk home, I noticed that he was following me. I was terrified. So I got down on the

road and actually hid underneath one of the other parked cars.
I saw his feet standing beside the car I was under. He clearly was
looking for me. But I just stayed there until he walked away.

Knowing What's Right for Your Body

One of the most potent ways a daughter learns to trust herself
and her own value, and thus internalize a strong sense of self-esteem,
is by experiencing her mother taking a stand on her behalf in the face
of outside authorities. I've already told the story of how my mother
provided this in spades. (It's certainly possible to trust yourself even
if you didn't have a mother who stood up for you—but it's not as
easy.) When a girl's mother stands up for her it becomes a part of her
emotional DNA, which she will then pass down to her daughter in a
seamless chain of maternal empowerment.

In contrast to the very positive legacy I received from my mother's
strong inner sense of right and wrong in the face of conventional
morality, there were other aspects of my maternal legacy that were a
source of pain and conflict. Ironically, my mother taught me to trust
my beliefs and convictions but not the feelings in my body that arose
from not wanting to participate in the family "religion" of sports, skiing, and vigorous outdoor activity. No wonder I ended up in the field
of mind-body medicine!

My mother's motto on our numerous hiking trips was, "Don't ask
for a lighter pack, ask for a stronger back." Every weekend morning,
we had to be at the ski lifts when they opened, even if the weather
was freezing rain. I didn't realize until I was about twelve that other
families spent weekends doing anything other than skiing and hiking.

As a child I had no choice but to go along with the program. My
mother and siblings thrived on this kind of activity and all were gifted
athletes. (In retrospect I have a feeling that my father would have enjoyed a warm-weather, nonheroic vacation once in while.) I stayed by
the fire and I buried myself in books and music whenever possible. I
tried to like sports, but I never could manage to convince my body
that I was having fun, except when it was sunny. In my family, that
put me into the ranks of the "fair-weather skiers," which was a term
of derision, not endearment. And like most children who are black
sheep in their families, I felt bad about my inability to measure up.

Over time I developed the ability to ignore my discomfort and to
push myself beyond my physical comfort zone for long periods of
time—ideal preparation for the surgical training that was in my fu-

ture. I also disconnected from the emotions of sadness and anger that were my natural response to feeling forced into activities for which I was ill suited! I didn't know this consciously, but my body sure did, and it presented the bill later.

Though I'm now grateful for my early training, which developed both my back and my will, I eventually found that living my life as though it were a mountain to be conquered no longer served me. This was a process, not an event. And it took me years to figure this out. After all, I had married a man who, like my mother, believed that outdoor activity, including winter camping, held the keys to the kingdom of heaven. And in the early years of our marriage, I tried as best I could to go along. Even though it "felt like home," it never really felt right either!

I remember the moment I truly realized that I could trust myself to decide what outdoor activity I should do. I was in my early forties. My daughters, husband, and I were on an eight-mile trail hike in the White Mountains. The day was hot and uncomfortable. My younger daughter Kate and I weren't having a very good time. So when we came to a fork in the trail, we decided that we wanted to go back. My husband and older daughter wanted to continue on to see the view. This time neither Kate nor I was about to be seduced by the "view will be worth it" line of reasoning. (I had been forcing myself to believe this for as long as I could remember.) Kate was way ahead of me in this regard because I had never forced her to go hiking. We figured that three more miles of misery just wasn't going to be worth it. What a revelation! I could say no. And my daughter could say it with me.

My mother and I can now laugh about the old days. She has changed, too. Although she still loves to climb mountains, play golf and tennis, and go hunting, she also likes to do Pilates, get massages, and come home to a warm place at the end of the day. This may seem like a small thing. To me it is a huge healing.

FIVE: FINANCIAL LITERACY

BASIC CONCEPTS OF FINANCIAL LITERACY

- Money is a universally agreed-upon form for giving and receiving value.
- One's relationship to money is heavily influenced by one's childhood experiences.

> ⁓ Money and prosperity are governed by universal "laws of prosperity"—for example, you can't get something for nothing.
>
> ⁓ Handling money responsibly is a skill that anyone can learn.

Childhood lessons about money and prosperity can influence a girl's health and wealth for a lifetime. These first lessons come from absorbing her parents' relationship with money and finances. The vast majority of girls are taught, either directly or indirectly, one or more of the following beliefs:

⁓ There's never enough money.

⁓ Money is difficult to get.

⁓ The best way to get money is to marry it.

⁓ Men are innately better at handling money than women.

These are the beliefs that manifest in the following grim statistics: Compared to men, women are 40 percent more likely to be poor. The older a woman gets, the greater the average gap between her income and that of a man the same age. In addition, single moms are twice as likely as single dads to be living in poverty.[3]

The subject of money, more than any other, lays bare people's core beliefs about life's possibilities. And changing their beliefs—and the behaviors that are an extension of them—may be the most challenging legacy that a girl faces. But it's worth it to discard beliefs that no longer serve us at any stage of life, starting as soon as possible. Most of the programming a child gets around money takes place during latency when her reasoning powers are newly awakened and her brain is primed for very rapid learning. These are the years when most girls become acutely aware of the economic differences between families, who has the "nice" house and the "best" clothes, what their parents can afford compared to others, and whether their parents fight about money.

The subject of money inevitably brings up humanity's collective fears of lack, poverty, and limitation—fears that are nearly universal. Poverty itself is everywhere associated with disease and chronic health problems. This is because money provides a safety net that offers some protection from the fallout of life's inevitable challenges such as a house fire or accident. Lack of it does just the opposite, eroding one's sense of safety and security in the world, thus adversely affecting immunity. Susceptibility to illness is the end result. A recent study by the Economic Policy Institute (EPI) found that in a given year about 30 percent of the poor experienced critical hardship, defined as being evicted, having utilities disconnected, doubling up in others' housing due to lack of funds, or not having enough food to eat; and that an additional 30 percent to 45 percent of the poor experienced other serious hardships.[4]

Although it's important to lend a hand to those who are suffering the very real effects of poverty, it's even more important to understand and eliminate the conditions that perpetuate it. Like every other aspect of our lives, financial health is heavily influenced by our thoughts, emotions, and behavior. Financial health is also affected by politics and social policy, neither of which take place in a vacuum. Social policies are the result of the thoughts, beliefs, and behaviors of an entire population. Thought patterns characterized by helplessness, hopelessness, and pessimism lead to depression, poor health, abusive relationships, and financial problems.

IMPOVERISHING BELIEFS

- Prepare for the worst—it's sure to come. *(pessimism)*

- It's impossible to ever get ahead of the bills. *(fatalism)*

- There's never enough money and never will be. *(fatalism)*

- The only way out of money worries is to win the lottery. *(magical thinking)*

- Prosperous people are selfish and/or nasty. *(envy)*

- It's more noble and holy to be poor than to be rich. *(martyrdom)*

- Someone else should provide you with money. *(entitlement)*

- There's only so much money to go around, so if someone is rich, others will have to suffer. *(persecution)*

Depressing, pessimistic, impoverished thoughts perpetuate poverty. Prosperous and rich thoughts perpetuate prosperity.

Antiprosperity Programming

A child is programmed against prosperity by being told things like, "Money is the root of all evil," or "Rich people can't be spiritual or good," or "Money doesn't grow on trees." What she is really being taught is that her very natural desire for the best life has to offer, materially and otherwise, is wrong or bad. The mother of one of my friends told her, "You can't even afford to look," whenever she looked into a store window at something she liked. When a daughter is raised this way, she learns to feel guilty for wanting things, even though this desire is inborn and is the basis for human progress and evolution. If a child is shamed regularly for wanting things that her family can't afford, she may eventually shut down her innate desires and aspirations and learn to settle for far less than she is capable of having. She learns that it's better to desire less than to risk repeated disappointment. Of course, in some kids, it also can breed a lifelong sense of "never enough" that drives them to be overly focused on accumulation of "stuff."

Shutting down desires and aspirations easily generalizes to other areas of life as well. In relationships, for instance, a persistent sense of limitation can influence what we feel we are "worth," and what we feel we deserve.

Instead of teaching our daughters to accept financial lack and limitation, we should be teaching them empowering ways to think about and behave concerning money and prosperity. Instead of stepping on their dreams and aspirations, we need to provide them with the tools of financial literacy so that they can be empowered to create heaven on earth in their own lives. The tools of financial literacy are twofold: you need to understand the universal laws of prosperity and how they work (see pages 346–347), and you need to know the nuts and bolts of money management to make the laws of prosperity grounded, real, and practical. But before you can teach these tools to your daughter, you need to get clear about your own financial history.

TAKE YOUR MONEY INVENTORY

~ How much do pessimism, depression, or a belief in lack filter into your beliefs and behavior? What form do they take?

~ Do you believe that it's possible for you to have true prosperity, i.e., health, wealth, and happiness?

~ Do you believe that it's more spiritual to struggle financially than to have enough money?

~ Do you know the basics of money management?

~ Who makes the major financial decisions in your family?

~ Do you know your net worth?

~ Do you have a financial plan for your future?

~ Do you have a will?

My Financial Legacy

Each of us has a particular relationship with money that is grounded in our personal history. Some women have been supported financially by their families or spouses for their entire lives, and don't even know where the money comes from. Others have been self-supporting since high school. It doesn't really matter what your family legacy is around money as long as you understand how your past is influencing your present. Once you do, you can change any beliefs and behaviors that need updating. I'll use my own story as an example.

Money was never discussed when I was growing up. We always seemed to have enough. We kids got a regular allowance that enabled us to go to the store and buy candy or gum about once a week. Other than that, my parents took care of providing us with all the essentials, including clothing. We often wore hand-me-downs and didn't think a thing of it. I don't remember ever hearing my parents argue or complain about money. As a girl who was in grade school in the 1950s and '60s, I wasn't interested in money. It wasn't an issue. My dad was a successful dentist in our small town and had taken over his father's practice. We seemed to have everything we needed.

My mother, on the other hand, had grown up during the Depression and remembers standing in breadlines as a girl. When she saw the movie *Seabiscuit,* it brought up many very unpleasant memories for her. When she married my father she upgraded her life circumstances considerably, much like a fairy tale. My father was thirty-six years old and successfully established in his father's dental practice.

My father's philosophy of life was to live it to the fullest, making every day count. (He told me his own father had been quite cheap; he wouldn't go on trips, even though his wife longed to travel. My father felt bad for his mother and identified with her, so he wasn't about to let pessimism control his approach to money.) One summer we rented a Winnebago and visited most of the western states. We were gone for nearly six weeks, which meant that there was no positive cash flow during that time because my dad wasn't seeing patients. I don't know how my parents managed this, because it wasn't discussed.

What I do remember is that there was a lot of tension every year at tax time when the accountant came to visit. (We kids weren't allowed in the room.) My parents sometimes had to borrow money to pay their income taxes and my mother worried about that. Still, my dad loved his work. And he figured that as long as he went to work each day, the money would always be there. The idea of "residual income" from a source other than his daily work never occurred to him. But it occurred to my brother, who, with my father's support, seemed to understand the laws of money and prosperity from an early age. He began to invest in land when he was in his early twenties while working construction jobs.

My vibrant and beloved father died suddenly of a ruptured cerebral aneurysm when he was sixty-eight, leaving my mother with no life insurance or other source of income. She was fifty-two at the time and in the prime of her life. Without the financial assistance of my brother, she would have had to sell the family farm. But because of my brother's prosperity consciousness and financial know-how, this didn't happen. And as a result, not only my mother but my children and our entire extended family have been able to enjoy my wonderful childhood home—our taproot into Earth.

Teaching My Daughters Prosperity Consciousness

By the time I was about twelve years old, I was fascinated not only with the connection between the mind and the body but also by the connection between one's thoughts and physical circumstances. Later I encountered Napoleon Hill's classic book *Think and Grow Rich,* in which he said that "thoughts have the peculiar quality of becoming their physical equivalents." By the time I had entered the workforce, I certainly saw evidence of this in my life and my practice. So when I had my children, I wanted them to know that the universe is a place of abundance, not limitation. I wanted them to take the experience of abundance right into the cells of their rapidly growing bodies so that they'd learn how to embrace abundance with their thoughts, not resist it or think it wasn't a possibility.

Like my parents before me, I never complained about prices and was careful to watch my own language about "having enough." Like mothers everywhere I also knocked myself out to make Christmases and birthdays special. When we walked past the first-class section in an airplane and my daughters asked why we couldn't sit up front in those big seats, I told them, "Someday you may well be able to—even if right now we can't manage it." After all, I wanted to sit there, too! I didn't want to resist first-class anything; I just didn't have a practical plan for getting there.

The problem with my early prosperity consciousness was that I was still missing the second tool of financial literacy: skills in money management. Like so many women, I wasn't involved with the major decisions about how our family spent, saved, and contributed our money. Despite the fact that I made an adequate living and did the actual bill paying for the household, I was convinced that the nitty-gritty of money management was far too complicated (not to mention boring) for me to bother with. So my prosperity consciousness stayed at a mental and emotional level, rather than being grounded in practical physical reality. I was mostly happy with this situation and glad that my husband wanted to take care of our major financial decisions.

My divorce was a wake-up call. I now had to go back to the latency stage of development in my own life to develop the skills I was missing. It wasn't enough to believe in prosperity consciousness. I also had to ground this consciousness in day-to-day money management. I put myself on a steep learning curve. I started with reading the first two Suze Orman books, *The Nine Steps to Financial Freedom* and *The Courage to Be Rich*. Then I moved on to David Bach's *Smart Women Finish Rich*. I redid my estate plan, hired a fee-only financial planner, and began the process of taking myself seriously when it came to money.

Then I read *Rich Dad, Poor Dad* by Robert Kiyosaki and Sharon Lechter. I learned that rich people don't think differently from the poor and the middle class. They think just the opposite! Intrigued by what I was learning, I purchased Kiyosaki's brilliant board game *Cash Flow* and played with my friends and daughters. The goal of the game is to get out of the rat race (living from paycheck to paycheck) and into the fast track—a switch that happens when you've replaced your paycheck income with residual income from real estate and investments. In addition to learning about the differences between different types of income, a player quickly realizes that it doesn't matter how big your paycheck is at the beginning of the game. A waitress or truck driver often gets out of the rat race sooner because their monthly expenses are so much lower than those of a doctor or pilot!

After playing *Cash Flow* regularly for several months, my thinking about money and business changed dramatically—and so did my behavior. I started to tithe 10 percent of my income and also started my first-ever investment account. I've continued to update my knowledge and skills ever since. This includes regularly affirming my ability to create prosperity through my thoughts, words, and behavior. I've passed this information on to my daughters.

THE RISKS OF OVERINDULGENCE

Programming prosperity does not mean buying your kids everything they want!

Marketing to teenagers is a $175 billion industry that is everywhere your kids are, including the Internet, television, and many school classrooms.[5] The average American child sees more than forty thousand commercials each year. This figure doesn't account for fast-food restaurants within schools, product placements in film and television, or corporate sponsorship of school sports and amateur and professional stadiums. The average kindergarten student has seen more than five thousand hours of television and has spent more time in front of the television than it takes to earn a bachelor's degree.[6]

Giving too much too soon and not being able to say no and stick with it puts kids at risk for both physical and mental problems. The research of Dr. Dan Kindlon, a child psychiatrist and author of *Too Much of a Good Thing: Raising Children of Character in an Indulgent Age,* and Juliet Schor, a consumer expert and author of *Born to Buy: The Commercialized Child and the New Consumer Culture* has shown that kids who are overindulged have an overblown sense of entitlement and trouble delaying gratification, expect to be the center of attention, and lack personal responsibility. Schor's research has also shown that overindulged kids suffer from depression, anxiety, low self-esteem, and psychosomatic complaints such as headaches and stomachaches. They are more apt to use drugs and alcohol because they have so little ability to tolerate discomfort. This makes sense. Media ads targeted to kids (and adults) are a setup because they give the false message that buying something is how you get and stay happy. Nothing could be further from the truth. Overindulged kids are also more apt to suffer from anxiety and depression as adults because they haven't learned important distress-tolerance skills. They enter the workplace with a profound sense of entitlement that sets them up for failure and further depression.

Here's what every mother needs to know:

~ Learn to tolerate your daughter's disappointment and distress when you say no. Failure to do so puts them at risk for future depression, anxiety, and social failure.

~ Understand that learning to delay gratification and deal with disappointment are as important to the developing psyche as coming into contact with germs is to the developing immune system. Distress tolerance enhances one's character and psychological hardiness.

~ Keep your sense of humor. When your daughter asks over and over for something that you're not going to buy her, say, "Nice job. Good try. I love your persistence. But the answer is still no."

Money and "stuff" themselves aren't the problem. The problem is the failure to set limits and boundaries. This cuts across all socioeconomic backgrounds. It took me a while to learn this, but better late than never. When my daughters were little, I was sometimes guilty of "buying their love." By the time they were teenagers, I had given them a set spending limit each month. They could spend the money as they pleased, but once they had spent it, that's all there was. I was amazed at how quickly they developed more critical shopping skills. Suddenly that "must have" pair of shoes wasn't so important.

There's Nothing Mysterious about Money Management

Though I'm certainly no financial expert, I've discovered that there isn't any big mystery associated with money management. I've learned I can trust my own inner wisdom around money just as I was teaching women how to trust their inner wisdom when it came to their bodies and their health. The same principles apply. In fact, when I met Suze Orman in the green room of the *Today* show, she told me that health problems show up in people's money first—as debt, cash flow problems, and so on—and then, sooner or later, manifest in the physical body. The reason for this is that our finances are part of our "extended body." And they accurately reflect our overall health. Suze said that it's much harder to hide money problems than health problems because money is so transparent: It's either there or it isn't. The physical body, on the other hand, is innately self-healing and is always working to stay that way. So it takes much longer for problems to show up in one's physical body than in one's financial "body." I have witnessed the truth of this repeatedly.

You Don't Have to Do This Alone

Kiyosaki and Lechter pointed out how important it is to have a team of professionals to help you create prosperity. To do so, of course, you have to get over your fear of finances and financial professionals.

The first thing I did was fire my broker—an individual who had spoken mostly to my husband about "our" finances for years. Suze Orman refuses to talk with just one member of a couple—even when the other partner says that she, or he, isn't interested. She clearly understands that both members have to be a team when it comes to money-management decisions. I couldn't agree more.

During the process of interviewing people for my new team, I realized that investment professionals, lawyers, and accountants are simply human, and that I was hiring them to work for me, not to judge me or be condescending.

At the beginning, I felt like a stupid little girl who wasn't worthy of the best advice available. I didn't think I had enough money to warrant the attention of money-management professionals. That attitude changed fast. I'll never forget the time an investment professional came to my office and, with incredible arrogance, started to question all of my business decisions. Because my income didn't come in a predictable, guaranteed way, he couldn't see how I could ever make ends meet—despite a very positive track record. (Like many women, I relied as much on my intuition when it came to my business as I did on the "facts.") I knew that he simply didn't understand this—we were coming from two different worlds. But I still felt two inches tall and very stupid when I was unable to answer his questions about expenses and cash flow. I realized that I never wanted to feel that way again.

So I removed my pension money from his firm and set about creating a more solid container for financial health, including a budget, a new bookkeeper, a skilled accountant, and an investment professional. I also came to see that I had unconsciously re-created my father's financial pattern. Like him, I loved my work and was always able to get money when needed, simply by going to work. But at midlife, I knew that trading dollars for hours was not the way I wanted to live for the rest of my life. Though I never intend to retire, I wanted the option of working less in the future. I needed a solid financial plan to create residual income.

Trusting Myself with Money

I had turned a corner. Never again would I allow a financial professional to treat me poorly. Never again would I allow a financial professional to think that she or he knew better than I how to deal with my money, or to pass judgment on my beliefs, how I ran my business or how I chose to spend my money.

I discovered that I had to make my own financial decisions, and that there wasn't a professional on earth who knew how to do that better than I. I learned that it is downright dangerous for a woman to leave all her financial decisions up to someone else, no matter how loving and well-meaning they might be. And if you happen to have someone in your life who is truly skilled with money, it's still important that they share their decisions with you and keep you informed about all aspects of your money, starting from the basics of where it is!

It's interesting to note that my loss of financial support from a spouse came at the same age as my mother's had, although her loss came through widowhood and mine from divorce. My mother's mother had gone through a divorce when my mother was in high school. Following this, my grandmother Ruth had to work nights as a waitress to support my mother and her sister. By marrying my father, my mother was able to improve not only her own destiny but also that of her own mother and that of her daughters. (My parents helped my grandmother move to our town, where she lived out her life in relative comfort.) Unlike my mother, however, I had been a practicing physician for over twenty years before my divorce. So I was able to rely on myself for financial support, though it wasn't easy. By taking my own maternal financial legacy to the next level, I have, in turn, improved the financial health of my own two daughters.

A FINANCIAL LITERACY PROGRAM FOR LATENCY-AGE GIRLS

Introduce your daughter to the concepts of saving, spending, and giving. Once a child is about seven or so and can handle abstract reasoning, she is ready to begin learning about money. Take her to the bank and open her first savings account—in her name. This way she'll feel comfortable in a financial institution from childhood onward. My daughter Kate told me that she'll never forget going to the bank and getting her first passbook savings account. She also got an ATM debit card so that she could deposit and withdraw her money conveniently. We made regular trips to the bank for depositing her allowance, birthday and Christmas gifts, and, as she grew older, babysitting money. She also withdrew her own money for gifts and special purchases. Now a college senior, she has been shocked to find that some of her classmates have never used an ATM.

EVEN SEVEN-YEAR-OLDS CAN LEARN TO MANAGE MONEY

An article in our local paper told how author Leslie Linfield, executive director of the Institute for Financial Literacy, used her seven-year-old son's first trip to overnight camp as an experiment in money management. The camp brochure said campers would need a minimum of three to five dollars per day for spending money. So she sat her son down and told him he would have twenty dollars for the five days of camp, and that whatever he didn't spend was his to keep. The only catch was that he had to keep a spending log in which he would record his purchases.

The week passed. Linfield wrote, "As he climbed off the bus, sunburned and bug-bitten, I figured the spending log was as forgotten as the sunblock and bug spray. Imagine my surprise when his first words were, 'I have my log and I think I have more than five dollars left, Mom.' " The two went over the log and the details of his spending decisions, including his purchase of an eight-dollar water bottle because it came with free soda refills for the entire week. He was clearly proud of his newfound skills. As Linfield concluded, "A seven-year-old on a fixed budget was able to set a financial goal, make intelligent purchasing decisions, and track his expenses. Those are the basic skills of personal finance, and they can be learned much earlier than we think, if only we teach them."[7] I couldn't agree more.

Teach your child (and yourself) the basics of cash flow management. As with all things, kids learn more from what you actually do in your own life than from what you say. Having a positive cash flow—more money coming in than is going out—is the nuts and bolts of prosperity. To accomplish positive cash flow, a child (or adult) needs to keep track of where her money comes from and where it's going. This involves making wise spending and saving decisions. It will also add to her growing arithmetic skills.

A girl should also be introduced to the discipline of investing or saving 10 percent of everything she earns (or gets from an allowance), if this is at all possible. When invested, this money begins to work for her. Once a child sees how this works, she's apt to become excited about it. Over time, she can be taught the joys of saving and investing versus spending. Both have their place, and both have to be kept in balance. If a child learns the basics of investing early on, she'll also see the possibility of creating enough positive cash flow that she won't have to spend her life living from one paycheck to the next.

The best teaching tool I've seen on the subject of money is *Cash Flow for Kids*. Robert Kiyosaki and his business partner, Sharon Lechter, have made this book and game (both a computer version and a board game) available free to teachers. I believe that financial literacy, including how to deal with credit cards, loans, banks, investments, and so forth should be a required course starting in grade school and continuing through high school. This would give all our children the tools that they need to create true prosperity in their lives. (See Resources.)

Teach your daughter the universal laws of prosperity and follow them yourself. The principles that govern prosperity are very similar to the principles that govern physical and emotional health: One's financial circumstances are seamlessly connected to one's thoughts and emotions. Once you begin to see how this works in your own life, you're on the path toward both financial freedom and improved health.

My all-time favorite prosperity author is Catherine Ponder, who was a minister of the Unity Church. Her books, which include *The Dynamic Laws of Prosperity, The Millionaires of Genesis,* and *The Prosperity Secrets of the Ages,* are loaded with helpful information that I use every day. I also love the work of Randy Gage, a man who was bankrupt and in poor health at the age of thirty, and who went on to become a multimillionaire through applying the laws of prosperity. His books *Accept Your Abundance* and *101 Keys to Prosperity* are very good summaries of the principles involved. (See Resources.) The brilliant economist Paul Zane Pilzer has also written a fascinating book, called *Unlimited Wealth: The Theory and Practice of Economic Alchemy,* that offers a new, far more prosperous way of thinking about economics and finance. Though a full explanation of the universal laws of prosperity is beyond the scope of this book, let me address a couple of them here.

~ **The Law of Circulation:** All health, whether physical or financial, requires circulation. It's very important to teach your daughter that all material stuff is just a manifestation of energy. It's meant to be used and enjoyed for as long as it's needed or wanted. Then it's time to let it go. Keep only the things that you absolutely love. When you no longer love them, let them go to someone else who will.

Hoarding and hanging on to more than you need creates congestion, stagnation, and ultimately, disease. (People whose garages, basements, closets, and attics are filled to overflowing with things they don't use but can't seem to let go of, often suffer from constipation!) When you freely circulate your money and let go of the stuff you no longer need or want, you're encouraging healthy circulation in your circumstances as well as in your physical body. Regularly clean out your closets and other storage areas and get rid of your excess. Help your daughter do the same. If her temperament is such that she tends to hold on, support her in learning how to release and let go.

~ **The Law of Giving:** The Bible teaches us to "cast our bread upon the waters." I don't believe that this was meant to be a guarantee about a fixed return on our "investment." Instead, it speaks to the power of faith in the abundant nature of the universe. Very often, in order to break up a holding pattern, we have to let go of something so that something else can come in. It's the same with money. Casting bread upon the waters is a symbolic way of saying that you get back what you give freely. Giving freely is part of creating prosperity.

I recommend tithing 10 percent of your income to whatever uplifts and inspires you. Tithing traditionally means giving 10 percent to God's work. For me, God is everywhere. And that means that I just trust my heart to tell me what to give to. If you can't give 10 percent (and there are times when this just isn't possible), then give what you can. I have learned to give financial gifts when I'm worried about money. Though it's scary, it always starts the flow in my direction once again.

~ **The Law of Attraction:** The Law of Attraction is the most basic law governing the flow of both energy and matter throughout the universe. It states that "like attracts like." The law of attraction also holds that thoughts held over time become their physical equivalents. To put it simply: Every thought has a characteristic vibration and effect on the body and the environment. Thoughts of love, happiness, and prosperity attract their physical equivalents. Thoughts of poverty, fear, and illness held over time produce their physical equivalents. When you concentrate on thinking prosperous, powerful thoughts, you begin to attract prosperous opportunities and circumstances into your life.

SIX: A PLACE IN THE SUN

Latency is the time of a girl's life when she is most apt to show signs of her true vocation, untainted by social and family pressures to be pleasing and nice, or to compete for the attention of boys. Her early vocational leanings will form the basis of her special "place in the sun."

I remember my father telling us that everyone, in order to be healthy and happy, needs to have their place in the sun, an area in which she shines. My parents' philosophy was that they would support whatever activity one of us wanted to do, as long as we did the work involved in further developing that skill or ability. This meant that if they were paying for piano lessons, you had to practice and make progress! My place in the sun was playing the piano and harp, and also doing well academically. I was the only one of my siblings who excelled in these areas. At the time, my academic and music skills seemed woefully insignificant compared to my sister Penny's place on the U.S. Ski Team. But eventually my own path worked out well. It just took a lot longer to manifest. Take-home message: Support your daughter in developing the skills she's naturally drawn to, whether or not you can see an immediate benefit or way to make a living from them.

For my daughter Annie, that special skill was writing, languages, and a flair for acting and singing that manifested during grade school. By the time she got to middle school, she was taking regular voice lessons and was also involved in a summer Shakespeare program. She eventually majored in English in college and is currently pursuing a career that combines writing, acting, and singing.

Her younger sister Kate was a dancer from the time she could walk. She spent the next couple of years of her life dressed in a pink tutu that finally fell apart from overuse. When family friends came over, the girls often danced around and sang for them. Though Kate plans to work in real estate and has a flare for finance, she is involved in two ethnic dance companies at college and also loves to go out dancing with her friends—a regular activity. As it turns out, neither of my daughters has a single competitive athletic bone in her body.

When a daughter is having problems in one area, like friendship, one of the best things you can do for her is to support her place in the sun, which is also where she is likely to meet her true peers. To have peers who are related by achievement and aspiration, as opposed to popularity and clothing style, is incredibly powerful for girls. One of my friends told me that she was kind of geeky in grade school, and not very popular. But she loved to dance and made several very solid friendships in dance class that lasted well into adolescence. Through finding her place in the sun, she also found her "tribe."

Having a place in the sun also involves being able to acknowledge someone else's place in the sun! The unbridled appreciation of the skills of another is one of the most powerful ways to create a lifetime of health and happiness. Appreciation is akin to love, and it has even been shown to balance the beat-to-beat variability of the heart, thus promoting overall health.[8] Taking kids to plays, musical performances, and sporting events to watch and appreciate others is a good way to engender this emotion.

SEVEN: POSITIVE SELF-IMAGE

Almost every school-age girl develops an internalized concept of an ideal self to which she aspires. This is an important developmental step, and it is made possible by the maturing dorsolateral prefrontal cortex. Her "ideal self" will be modeled on someone she respects and looks up to—usually, but not always, the parent with whom she most closely identifies. This may be her mother, or it may be her father if she takes after his side of the family in looks, demeanor, or general tendencies. She may also choose another nurturing role model who has been important in her life. A girl's self-concept and subsequent self-esteem are highly influenced by how well she believes she measures up to this internalized ideal self.

A mother's behavior models for her daughter what women are and what they do. It's important that she see her mother engaged in activities that bring her positive feedback and help her feel good about herself. It's also important that she see her mother interacting with both men and women in healthy, empowered ways. She incorporates these healthy patterns into her ideal self, and later finds herself naturally drawn to repeat them. Women who don't learn such patterns in childhood are sometimes mystified by how easy it seems for those who do. As a wise friend from a shaky background once said to me, "We have to do by art what others do by nature."

On the other hand, if a daughter routinely watches her mother being submissive and indecisive around men in general or her husband in particular, then she is apt to internalize this behavior instead of learning appropriate assertiveness skills. Her self-esteem in relationships will suffer. Like her mother, she may attract overbearing partners. Or she may do exactly the opposite—attract partners over whom she has total control. Either way, it will be difficult for her to form relationships with men where there's a balanced give-and-take.

Here's another example: Suppose your mother is a professional with two doctorates, a thin body, and a perfectly kept home. She is also emotionally controlled, cool, and somewhat aloof. However, she is at ease at social events like cocktail parties and always well-spoken and articulate. By age ten, it's clear that you are solid, not willowy like your mother. You take after your father's side of the family in looks, body build, and temperament. You're not comfortable speaking in public and you tend toward shyness in social situations. You are hard on yourself, but very artistically oriented. Keeping your room clean is not a priority. In school you get B minuses and C pluses.

If such a girl internalizes her mother as her ideal self, she will always fall short. Even though her temperament and approach to the world are inherently different from her mother's, she may spend a lifetime trying to live up to her legacy. She may, later in life, earn several advanced degrees, earn a huge income, get her body to its "ideal" weight, and still feel as though she doesn't measure up on some level.

Fortunately many girls have fathers with whom they identify and who help them shore up their sense of self. The father of a friend of mine taught her how to ride a motorcycle around the yard when she was ten. Later they went on bike trips together. They've always shared an interest in fast cars as well! Many girls connect with an aunt, a teacher, or another mentor. These are also the years in which girls get crushes on those who recognize them and reflect them in a positive light. I remember falling in love with my science teacher at about the age of twelve. Learning about the interior of a cell took on a whole new meaning that was tinged with romance!

Heroes and Idols: Imagining the Ideal Self

School-age girls are known for their tendency toward hero and teen idol worship. Through her idols, a girl explores ways of being in the world and experiments with her ideal self. Though these idols are far less potent than her own mother, they give her a variety of possible role models. The truth is that the qualities a girl admires in others are really inside her lying dormant. Watching those qualities in her idols is a safe way for her to imagine what her own life might one day look like. Though teen idols are real people, they actually function as living archetypes onto which girls can project unconscious parts of themselves and see these parts lived out before their eyes. This explains a girl's (and nearly everyone else's) fascination with celebrities whose job is to playact their way through life. Our culture pays them handsomely to live out our fantasies for us.

Our mass media are filled with many potential role models for girls, both positive and negative. My daughters loved She-Ra, Princess of Power, a cartoon series on television and also an action-figure doll. They also liked Jem and the Holograms. Jem was a cartoon rock star who fended off evil in each episode. As they got older and began to read more, their eyes were opened to the likes of Sojourner Truth, Maya Angelou, and Louisa May Alcott. At the same time, Madonna was all over television with her groundbreaking music and videos, including "Like a Virgin" and "Material Girl." As a friend with daughters the same age as mine once said, "It's fairly disconcerting to have your eight-year-old running around the house singing 'Like a Virgin.' " No kidding.

Happily, the American Girl doll collection, which was started by a schoolteacher, came out when my daughters were in grade school. They spent hours playing with Samantha and Kirsten, reading the books that chronicled their lives, and putting on plays with them as characters. When my younger daughter was twenty, she told me that she had learned and remembered more American history through the materials in the American Girl collection than in school! I applaud that company for creating such positive role models for girls and for their business success, although I realize that their products are out of the price range of many. Their popularity is a testament to the fact that not all girls spend all their time imitating the "flavor of the month" pop icon, whose real role is to market products to young girls.

When I was growing up, the mass media was a much less obvious presence than it is now. No family had more than one television and no one had a computer. And because the women's movement hadn't yet reached its second wave, there were also far fewer women role models in the media, apart from actresses such as Doris Day and Marilyn Monroe. I was a voracious reader, and I found my role models in books. Helen Keller was a role model for me because she went to Radcliffe and overcame astonishing adversity to become well educated. Elizabeth Blackwell was another role model, the first woman physician in the United States. I read her biography when I was about twelve, although I didn't consider becoming a doctor until after I finished college.

A mother or other female mentor can actively help her daughter find role models by being vocal about who she herself admires. One of my friends told me:

> I'll always remember the Sunday school teacher who loaned me a huge hardcover biography of Marie Curie to read when I was twelve or thirteen. I had a tough time lifting the book, much less understanding the scientific part of it! But I stayed with it anyway, because it came with the unspoken message that I should take myself seriously as a woman and aspire to make a difference in the world. Fifty years later, I still remember some of the pictures in that book.

Body Image: Feeling Comfortable in Your Own Skin

Of course I'd be lying if I told you that accepting one's body unconditionally is easy or that I have created a foolproof formula that you can follow so that your daughter will grow up loving her body and being entirely comfortable in her own skin. Given the influence of the air-brushed, breast-implanted "perfect" female bodies we see in the media, it's a very rare woman or girl who is happy with every aspect of her body.

Still, it's entirely possible to minimize the effect of the culture by starting with yourself. Never forget that each of us cocreates the "culture" around us. It's not somewhere "out there" doing it to us. You are a far more important influence in your daughter's life than the media will ever be! In fact, those girls who are overly influenced by the media are often making a misguided attempt to find some kind of guidance to follow. And this happens when their own maternal guidance is weak or absent altogether.

A daughter always picks up on her mother's attitudes about herself. If you make negative comments about your own body, your daughter will be much less likely to believe you when you tell her that hers is beautiful! So the sooner you learn to accept your body unconditionally, the better your daughter's chances for internalizing a healthy respect for her own body as well. Remember that you can love and accept your body unconditionally and still want to improve it through exercise, weight loss, or even plastic surgery.

The same goes for your daughter's father. Don't allow him to make negative comments about either your body or hers. This is abuse, plain and simple. If you put up with it, you'll be setting your daughter up for abusive relationships in the future. Her self-esteem will inevitably suffer. On the other hand, a father who compliments his daughter on her appearance or her clothing choices contributes immeasurably to his daughter's self-image and self-esteem.

I certainly brought my own share of baggage to this area. Still, I was at least conscious of the fact that I didn't want to pass on my own hang-ups to my daughters. I knew very early on that I was no "genetic celebrity." I was called "stocky" and "solid"—not exactly the physical assets that turn heads or get you full service at the gas station for self-serve prices. Like many girls in a similar position, I was forced to develop my inner resources instead.

So I encouraged my daughters to feel good about their bodies while also encouraging them to develop their inner resources: their intellect, their physical stamina, their compassion, their will, their self-discipline, their spirituality, and their sense of humor. No matter how good you look, relying mostly on your physical appearance to open doors of opportunity isn't a skill for the long haul. In the words of the famous Judge Judy, "Beauty fades. Dumb is forever." But that doesn't mean you shouldn't develop and appreciate the physical assets you were born with!

Developing a Personal Style

The development of a personal style in clothing, hair, and other aspects of body adornment is another area where mothers can really support their daughter's growing sense of herself. This is because how we dress and present ourselves to the world reflects our sense of self and self-esteem. One of my colleagues told me that her mother and her aunts seemed to grow more beautiful with the passing years, always dressing well and taking care with their appearance. As a result, she internalized the powerful belief that women get more attractive with age, and she has passed this on to her own daughter. On a recent family vacation with another family, she was horrified when her friend, the mother of a sixteen-year-old, told her daughter, "You better enjoy how you look now, 'cause it's all downhill from here!"

My Self-Adornment Legacy

Though I know that I was interested in clothing, makeup, and jewelry as a young girl, my mother took a "color me basic" approach. Her color palette for us as children, not to mention herself, was limited to navy blue, khaki, and green, with a little red thrown in now and then. Shopping meant a once-yearly expedition for school clothes. As a result, my budding fashion sense became truly latent, and I didn't think much about clothing or fashion (except when it came to ski wear) until I was in my thirties. When I got married, I was relieved to find that one of my relatives had a wedding dress that fit me well. I was in medical school, and shopping for a wedding gown loomed as an ordeal I didn't have time for!

I was also uneasy about what to wear to any event other than a casual social occasion. Luckily for me, this didn't come up very often once we moved to Maine. (In 1995, anyone who wanted to come was invited to former governor Angus King's inaugural ball—and people arrived in everything from tuxedos to flannel shirts and L.L.Bean boots.)

During the 1980s, one of my patients started giving seminars based on the popular book *Color Me Beautiful*. The idea was that women could be divided into different "seasons," depending on skin tone, each of which was associated with a specific color palette. When I first had my "colors" done at the age of thirty-four and found out that I was a natural autumn, the world of fashion and shopping opened up for me. I was no longer afraid to go into a store, feeling as though the salesperson either knew more than I or would try to foist something on me that was entirely wrong. I didn't realize that there were people who had a genius for helping out in this area. I also didn't know that we each have an instinctive sense of what looks best on us.

In the years since, learning to trust my own fashion sense has been a genuine healing for me. As my self-esteem and self-confidence have grown, these inner changes have resulted in more outward confidence in my clothing choices. Most importantly, my healing in this area has been passed on to my daughters, who love to get dressed up, and know exactly how to do it with confidence and ease.

I supported their growing sense of personal style by making sure that I didn't foist my own clothing choices on them, except when they needed guidance about what was appropriate to the occasion. (For example, I suggested to them that they not shop or travel in sweatpants or battered-looking old clothes, on the theory that they'd be treated better if they appeared attractive and stylish. They discovered that my theory held water when they took their first trips to the mall without me.)

Though I know that some latency-age girls couldn't care less about clothing, my daughters did care from the time they were very young. When Kate was in elementary school, she often asked me to come into her room to help her pick out her clothes for the day. I enjoyed being asked and always went in and gave her my opinion. And almost invariably, she'd go ahead and choose something else! It got to be a standing joke between us. She didn't know why she wanted me there, but somehow she felt it was important. In retrospect, I think that she was developing trust in her own taste and style and simply wanted me present to bless and approve of her process.

My maternal fashion legacy came full circle when my mother and a friend completed a book on the history of skiing in Ellicottville. The book was being launched with a large party at the Ellicottville Inn, and I wanted to help my mother look her best for the event. I took her shopping and taught her how to pull together a "look" that felt comfortable but also fashionable. We had a ball. She ended up with a new fall wardrobe full of vibrant colors and fabrics that looked great on her, but which she wouldn't even have tried on without some encouragement to push her fashion envelope. Since then she has cleaned out her closets and created a functional but more stylish and attractive wardrobe that more accurately reflects who she has become over the years.

HOW TO DOWNPLAY EARLY SEXUALIZATION IN CLOTHING

When I was growing up, there was no such thing as sexy underwear except in the tacky Frederick's of Hollywood catalogue that made us laugh. Our evening wear consisted of wool socks and flannel nightgowns or pajamas. Victoria's Secret, that updated and mainstream reincarnation of Frederick's, didn't yet exist, and neither did breast implants or Britney Spears. How our world has changed!

Now you'd have to live in a hole to avoid being deluged with overly sexualized images of young girls at every turn. If a girl is exposed to lots of mainstream media programming, she's bound to be influenced by the clothing styles and behavior seen in music videos and other television geared to teens and preteens. The entertainer Britney Spears pioneered the bare midriff, ushering in an era in which thousands of little girls tied up their T-shirts and rolled down their shorts in imitation. Clothing lines quickly followed, and fashion for girls has never been the same.

In a culture that's already pushing young girls into premature puberty on every level from diet to environment, it's important for mothers to downplay overly sexualized clothing choices in school-age girls. Here's what I suggest:

Limit the amount of time your child watches television. Choose the programs that you allow her to watch. This requires commitment on your part, but it's totally possible, especially during the early latency years.

When your daughter watches a "suggestive" TV show or movie, be there to supervise and provide commentary. I let my daughters watch *The Blue Lagoon* when they were about nine and eleven. The movie, with Brooke Shields, was a fairly innocent exploration of love and sexuality. I also took them to see *Dirty Dancing* because I just loved the movie. They loved it, too. They only recalled the dance sequences, not the sexual undertones. Of course, sexualized content has increased dramatically since that time. But sooner or later, a girl has to learn about sexuality—the good, the bad, and the ugly. Trying to completely protect her from it doesn't work. Depending upon her temperament, it may just make her more interested in illicit material.

Teach your daughter about the kinds of messages clothing styles send. If your daughter is drawn to overly sexualized styles, point out that these tend to "cheapen" her image and send the message that others can't take her seriously. Let her know that this might not seem fair, but it is, unfortunately, the way things are. Though your own style is ultimately more powerful than anything you say, this isn't always the case during the years when peer influence is so strong. Remember that you don't have to buy clothing that makes your daughter into a mini-sexpot, even if she wants you to. But resign yourself to limited control; girls may just borrow their friend's clothes when you're not available to supervise.

Don't overreact. Forbidding her to tie up her T-shirt or otherwise experiment can add fuel to the fire. Just downplay the whole thing. And set a standard about the kinds of clothing she can wear to school. School uniforms or dress codes are helpful because they eliminate much of the hassle over clothing choices. They also help girls focus more on their education than on the fashion fad of the day.

Enlist the help of like-minded mothers. Girls who resist your opinions are often more open to what their friends' mothers have to say. Meet with the mothers of your daughter's closest friends in an informal way and talk about the kinds of values you hold for your daughters as a group. You'll probably find that the other mothers feel the same way you do. They can become powerful allies in helping you instill appropriate values in your daughter—both when it comes to clothing and in other areas as well.

13

Eating for Life

Food, Weight, and Health

❀

Childhood food experiences will set the tone for your daughter's relationship to food and health for a lifetime. With her willingness to help out in the kitchen and her thirst for knowledge, this is the ideal time to teach a girl about the basics of food preparation, shopping, and enjoying family meals. She now has the brain development necessary to learn how to identify a ripe versus a green melon, and she's usually beyond the "I'll only eat chicken fingers" stage.

Family meals are an ideal way to share love and information simultaneously, thus shoring up the health of the first chakra. What you put on the table, how you serve it, and how it's enjoyed continue to program the gastrointestinal system as surely as infant feeding did earlier on. These are also the years when a girl is most likely to internalize the body image that she will have for the rest of her life. Many mothers have concerns about their daughter's weight at this time and want to be sure they are helping them to maintain a healthy body composition.

In order to help her daughter learn to eat for health on all levels, every mother needs to realize what she's bringing to the table from her personal weight and food history. I'm going to discuss my own food legacy in some detail because most of it applies in one form or another to approximately 75 percent of the population—those of us who have an ongoing struggle with our weight.

MY FOOD LEGACY:
WHOLE FOODS AND ADDICTIVE CARBS

My food legacy is really two different stories, both seamlessly intertwined.

One is the story of being brought up on natural whole foods, a result of my father's knowledge and enthusiasm about the subject. My family ate seven-grain cereal, took vitamin supplements, and ate homemade yogurt years before any of these things were mainstream. We also enjoyed fresh produce that was locally grown and seasonal: asparagus from our garden, strawberries and blueberries, Great Lakes peaches, and juicy northern spy apples. My physician aunt and uncle called us health nuts.

Then there was the other story: we really liked sweets and the types of carbohydrates that tend to raise blood sugar quickly—and addictively. Luckily, because most of our diet was healthy and we also exercised a lot, none of us was ever fat. But we weren't what you'd call svelte either. My mother sometimes used Metrecal, one of the first diet drinks on the market back in the 1960s, in order to control her weight. Mostly she kept fit through sports. We kids weren't allowed to have candy more than once a week. But we indulged our collective sweet tooth with regular ice cream sundaes while watching television at night. We also adored my mother's home-baked pies, cakes, and cookies, which were sometimes made with whole grain or unbleached white flour, but still loaded with fats and calories.

I continued my whole foods legacy when I had my own children—and advanced it a bit. At the time, the emerging scientific literature convinced me, along with many nutrition experts, that the key to health was to eat more whole grains, fiber, and vegetables, and far less meat. While I was a resident at New England Medical Center, I met Michio Kushi, the Japanese-born pioneer of the health and nutrition philosophy known as macrobiotics. I sat in on many of his consultations with people suffering from health problems. As with many women, my first pregnancy was the occasion for reevaluating my diet, and Kushi's approach was the one I adopted. I took cooking classes and cleared our cupboards of any canned and packaged foods. I raised my children on brown rice, miso soup, sea vegetables, beans, and some fish. We didn't consume meat or dairy products at all.

Despite this whole-grain-based, organically produced, low-fat, nearly vegetarian diet, I found that I still craved sweets. I consumed these in the form of whole grain cookies, rice cakes with peanut butter and maple syrup, and a variety of breads. My family and I also had pies, cakes, and cookies when we went out to eat—after all, I reasoned, they were vegetarian. We weren't alone in this. My sister Penny lived in the midst of the macrobiotic community in Boston at around the same time, and she told me that many "hard core" vegetarians often drove to Dunkin' Donuts under cover of darkness to get their sugar "fix."

In retrospect, I see that I was carrying on the two intertwined legacies of my childhood: wholesome natural foods consumed alongside ample quantities of foods that spiked blood sugar and led to sugar cravings—as well as increasing the risk of a whole host of other diseases, as I'll discuss below. I also came to see that the individuals who were most prone to sugar cravings had characteristic body types, like mine.

Little Mack Truck

When I was about four or five, I was playing on the rug in our kitchen one day while my mother and father talked with visiting friends. I heard my mother remark, "She's built like a M-A-C-K truck," spelling out the word "Mack" so I wouldn't know what she was saying. I knew what a truck was, of course, and I wasn't particularly thrilled to be compared to one. A few years later when I could read, I remember seeing my first Mack truck, complete with its solid bulldog hood ornament. In that moment it all came together for me—and helped cement into place a negative body image that I would spend the next forty years coming to terms with.

Though I was never really overweight as a child, I was certainly at the upper limit of what was considered normal for my height and weight. I was born with a large bone structure and lots of lean muscle mass. When they called out my weight in gym class in the seventh grade, I was one of the heaviest in my class at 125 pounds. At that time, normal weight was measured simply as a function of height, and at five feet two inches, I was supposed to weigh 115 pounds or less. I reached that weight only once in college when I truly starved myself. Even then, I was only able to maintain it for about two weeks, after which my food cravings, along with the fact that I constantly felt weak and cold, overcame my willpower. (When you're not keeping your blood sugar stable and your brain chemistry balanced, cravings always win.)

Early-Onset Dieting

At age twelve I went on the first of countless diets, all of them designed to keep me from ballooning into the size my body would have quickly reached had I eaten whatever I wanted. And what I wanted always included bread, potatoes, pastries, cookies, and ice cream. This path eventually led to an "up close and personal" understanding of weight gain and loss, and the biochemistry associated with them. Nothing I learned about diet and health in my medical training has been nearly as useful to me, either as a mother or a physician, as having to learn what is necessary to control a potential weight problem.

Looking back now, I see that much of my motivation for studying nutrition, cooking, and food—from macrobiotics to Atkins—has been a personal search for the Holy Grail of permanent weight control. I eventually found it, but it took me many years. In essence: Control your blood sugar and insulin levels (even if you're not diabetic) and weight control follows. I wish I had known this when my children were small. I would have cut back on the grains, increased the lean protein, and added more fruits. But at that time, very few scientists understood the endocrinology of food consumption and how each choice affects blood sugar and body fat. Nor did we appreciate the genetic differences in individuals that are a setup for sugar cravings and weight gain.

The Many Faces of Sugar Addiction

I danced around my sugar addiction for years, and controlled my weight primarily by exercising regularly and limiting my consumption of desserts and bread through sheer force of will.

Of course I was no stranger to the fact that food and mood are intimately connected. Food has enormous, well-documented effects on brain chemistry, including levels of the stress hormone norepinephrine and feel-good neurochemicals such as serotonin, dopamine, and opiates. Consuming sugar in all its many forms, including refined starches, is a very common way to soothe emotional pain and elevate mood. I had worked for years on my emotional eating triggers, and I had addressed the aspects of my job and personal life that had, in the past, led to unabated stress that I medicated with refined carbohydrates. This was no longer an issue.

Luckily for me, I hate the taste of alcohol and always have, because alcoholism is nothing more—or less—than a form of sugar addiction. Although I didn't make the connection at the time, I knew personally that a number of individuals in the macrobiotic community were alcoholics. And Alcoholics Anonymous meetings are famous for their sugary treats.

Still, I didn't yet have the missing link about blood sugar and insulin that finally solved the metabolic riddle that puzzles so many. Nor did I realize that as long as I kept trying to figure out how to include "treats" in my diet, like cookies, most grain products, or ice cream, I was still setting up my metabolism for blood sugar and insulin spikes, and for battles with the "munchies" later that day or the next.

I now see that my refined-carbohydrate cravings and emotional eating patterns were simply biochemical reactions stemming from a combination of stress hormones, spikes in blood sugar, and subsequent spikes in insulin.[1] All of these create a vicious cycle in mind and body that naturally leads to more of the same.

THE MISSING LINK:
GLYCEMIC STRESS AND INSULIN RESISTANCE

Excess body fat is in fact a symptom of a much larger problem: glycemic stress and eventual insulin resistance. This was the crucial missing link that I learned from the work of Dr. Ray Strand, a family physician in South Dakota and the author of *Releasing Fat: Developing Healthy Lifestyles that Have a Side Effect of Permanent Fat Loss*. Though I had long known about the connection between excess blood sugar, insulin, diabetes, and obesity, I hadn't realized the degree to which these—and many other conditions such as PMS and menstrual cramps—stemmed from the food choices made in childhood.

Dr. Strand has cared for many people in his community for thirty years, seeing them year after year for physicals, blood work, and health concerns. In the process, he has documented the metabolic changes that lead—often twenty years later—to full-blown insulin resistance. His in-depth clinical research and thorough review of the medical literature are hard to ignore. And his work reflects what I have seen in my practice and in my own life. No controlled study can match the perspective that comes from seeing patients year after year, and documenting how simple things like changes in diet, moderate exercise, and micronutrient supplementation can halt and eventually reverse insulin resistance and the conditions associated with it.[2] After reading Dr. Strand's book, I finally understood why I had battled with my weight for my entire life, and why so many of my family members had died from cardiovascular disease, despite following what was considered a very healthy diet. I also discovered the root cause of the current pandemic of obesity and its associated diseases: among them, diabetes, heart disease, stroke, and certain forms of cancer.

CHILDHOOD AND ADOLESCENT OBESITY: THE SCOPE OF THE PROBLEM

Between 1976 and 2000, the prevalence of overweight children doubled among those six to eleven years of age and tripled among those twelve to seventeen years of age. Black, Hispanic, and Native American and Mexican-American children and adolescents are disproportionately affected. Childhood obesity that persists into adulthood is associated with more severe obesity in adulthood. An obese seven-year-old has about a 40 percent risk for being an obese adult. Obesity at the age of twelve increases the adult risk to 70 percent. Between 1979 and 1999 obesity-associated hospitalizations (e.g. for sleep apnea and gall bladder disease) tripled among children ages six to seventeen years old. Type 2 diabetes, formerly called adult-onset diabetes, was once considered a disease of the middle-aged and elderly. It is now estimated to account for anywhere between 8 and 45 percent of all new cases of diabetes in children.[3] The earlier onset of this disease means that children will face a lifetime dealing with its burdens and costs.

Insulin Resistance Begins in Childhood

What Dr. Strand and others have found is that the long march to insulin resistance (also known as syndrome X or metabolic syndrome) often begins in childhood. It starts out with what he calls insulin abuse, which comes from regularly eating foods like bagels, white bread, crackers, instant oatmeal, mashed potatoes, and desserts that spike your blood sugar. Though most individuals don't realize this, white bread, most so-called wheat breads, and many other starchy foods are quickly converted into sugar, and they raise blood sugar accordingly.

Foods differ widely in their effect on blood sugar. The *glycemic index* was introduced in 1981 by Dr. David Jenkins as a comparative tool.[4] Foods were assigned a value from 0 to 100, based on how fast a given number of grams of a food raised blood sugar compared to a baseline food, typically glucose or white bread. (Dr. Strand and I use the index based on glucose, with glucose assigned the value of 100.) The glycemic index research led to an even more useful measurement: *glycemic load,* which accounts for both a food's glycemic index and how much carbohydrate it delivers in a serving. For example, you may have heard that carrots have a high glycemic index, but their glycemic load, based on serving size, is low.

In fact, most complex carbohydrates, including fruits, vegetables, beans, and whole grains, have low glycemic loads—eating them triggers only a mild rise in blood sugar. On the other hand, refined, pulverized grain has a high glycemic load, while fruit squeezed into juice becomes the equivalent of sugar water. White potatoes are an exception to the healthy glycemic profile of most vegetables—and they are by far the most popular vegetable in the American diet today, most of them consumed in the form of fries.

Glycemic Loads of Common Foods			
(Based on the Glucose Scale)			
BAD CARBS (>20)		GOOD CARBS (<10)	
Macaroni & cheese	32	All bran cereal	9
White rice	30	Beans	7
Baked potato	26	Coarse barley bread	7
Bagel, white	25	Plum	7
Fanta orange soda	23	Apple	6
Cornflakes	24	Carrot	3
Instant cream of wheat	22	Almonds	0
White spaghetti	21	Broccoli	0

Source: *Going Beyond Atkins,* Walter Willett; and Patrick Skerrett, "Separating the Good Carbs from the Bad,"

Newsweek, January 19, 2004, p. 47; also Ray Strand, *Releasing Fat,* Health Concepts Publishing, 2004, pp. 255–266

Why do high-glycemic-load foods cause "insulin abuse"? Because they disrupt one of the most delicate and crucial balancing acts in the human body: the secretion of insulin in response to food intake.

Insulin, the Storage Hormone

Good health depends upon our body's ability to make and utilize just the right amount of insulin to keep our blood sugar at optimal levels and our metabolism working normally. Consumption of refined carbohydrates and alcohol results in an immediate surge in blood sugar. This triggers the pancreas to secrete large amounts of insulin to process the blood sugar. Every cell in the body has insulin receptors on the surface. These allow insulin to "open the door" so that the glucose can enter the cell and be burned as fuel. Any glucose not needed immediately is stored as fat, ready to be tapped if we skip a meal, work out at the gym, or run for the bus. However, high levels of insulin actually *block* fat burning. The more you eat high-glycemic foods, the more insulin you have—and the more difficult it becomes for the body to release the energy stored as fat! This is the reason why so many young girls continue to be fat even though they exercise.

But things get even more complex. Over time, when blood sugar levels continue to be too high, the insulin receptors actually lose their ability to respond to this metabolic burden. They become insensitive, and a condition known as insulin resistance develops, in which the pancreas pours out more and more insulin, to less and less effect. Eventually neither the body tissues nor the pancreas can keep up with the blood sugar load. This is what leads to type 2 diabetes in susceptible individuals, who require either insulin shots or drugs known as oral diabetic agents.

Virtually every cell in our bodies is affected by insulin abuse, which also results in the production of excess inflammatory chemicals in the cells. Known collectively as series 2 eiconsanoids, these chemicals include the cytokines, prostaglandins, and prostacyclines—all of which are implicated in the majority of the diseases that plague us today, including cancer, heart disease, diabetes, and arthritis. That is why eating a diet that keeps blood sugar stable is so effective as part of a treatment plan for everything from headaches to insomnia! It's also why so many of the best-selling drugs on the market are designed to block the effects of inflammatory factors.

Still another complication: It has recently been discovered that fat cells themselves produce these inflammatory chemicals, which is one of the reasons obesity is a risk factor for cancer. Body fat is also loaded with insulin receptors, so the fatter you get, the more insulin it takes to get blood sugar into the cells.

The good news is that this entire process is reversible—if you catch it early enough. Once you stop eating foods that raise blood sugar, insulin levels return to normal, and it becomes easier to lose weight. You stop the long march to insulin resistance and type 2 diabetes. In some individuals, type 2 diabetes even goes into remission.

SYMPTOMS AND SIGNS OF INSULIN ABUSE

- ⁓ Fatigue and possibly shaky weakness following a meal
- ⁓ Carbohydrate cravings and uncontrollable hunger (the munchies)
- ⁓ Emotional eating
- ⁓ Nighttime eating
- ⁓ Slowly expanding waistline
- ⁓ Increasing resistance to weight loss

From Insulin Abuse to Glycemic Stress: The Road to Insulin Resistance

Dr. Strand introduces a very useful new concept he calls glycemic stress. This refers to the inflammation that occurs in the lining of blood vessels (endothelium) following a high-glycemic meal. This inflammation is the result of the release of unstable oxygen molecules, known as free radicals, produced when blood sugar becomes elevated. The rapid movement that occurs when free radicals are released in the capillaries and arteries actually causes tissue damage and inflammation. As current research is revealing, the oxidative stress caused by free radicals is at the center of the disease and aging process wherever it occurs in the body. In the blood vessels it eventually results in endothelial dysfunction—a condition in which the lining of blood vessels thickens and constricts—starting in the skeletal muscles. Eventually, it affects the entire cardiovascular system, including the brain and every other organ. And this sets the stage for the development of atherosclerosis (hardening of the arteries) later in life. It's also the reason why insulin resistance is associated with heart disease and stroke even in individuals who don't get diabetes and who aren't obese. (It is also true that not all obese individuals have insulin resistance or signs of metabolic syndrome.)

Glycemic stress creates an actual physical barrier, making it more difficult for insulin to get out of the blood vessels and into the fluid around the cell. When this happens, sugar can't get into the cell to be burned as energy. This process begins long before the insulin receptors on fat cells become insensitive to the effects of insulin or the pancreas becomes exhausted.

A Genetic Setup

About 75 percent of the population has at least some inherited tendency toward insulin resistance, a tendency that has surfaced because of our modern fast-food, underactive lifestyle. During the millennia over which humans evolved, this genetic legacy, which is now such a problem for so many of us, gave us a distinct survival advantage because it made it easier to store up excess fat for the inevitable lean times. Now, in times of plenty, many individuals show a marked accumulation of intracellular fat buildup, in both their liver and muscle cells, many years before they actually manifest diabetes or other evidence of insulin resistance. This fat storage is due, in part, to the fact that the skeletal muscles of susceptible individuals don't metabolize glucose as fast as they do in those who aren't susceptible. In fact, the offspring of insulin-resistant parents with type 2 diabetes have been shown to have an inherited reduction in skeletal muscle mitochondria—the part of the muscle cell that burns glucose for energy. Given the interaction between genes and the environment, the tendency toward insulin resistance and obesity appears to be getting worse with each successive generation of children.

INSULIN RESISTANCE: THE SCOPE OF THE PROBLEM

Over the past twenty years, type 2 diabetes has increased over 500 percent. Over 90 percent of type 2 diabetes is the result of insulin resistance, and 75 percent of the population is prone to sugar addiction and subsequent glycemic stress. Currently, a staggering 25 percent of the population has already developed full-blown metabolic syndrome and hundreds of thousands more are on their way toward type 2 diabetes. It is estimated that if current trends hold, one in three children born today will develop type 2 diabetes during their lifetime. Even for those who don't get diabetes, the accelerated aging of the arteries—due to continual inflammation and thickening—eventually leads to cardiovascular disease.

THE BOTTOM LINE: Every time you indulge in a meal that raises blood sugar quickly, you're causing blood vessel inflammation, which will eventually lead to tissue damage, build-up of fat in the muscle, and insulin resistance. This process can take years. But in the children of insulin-resistant parents, it can happen much quicker!

Stages of Insulin Resistance

Insulin resistance typically develops in these stages:

Stage 1—Glycemic stress: This happens when you consume foods with a high glycemic index and load. Blood vessel inflammation begins and glycemic stress ensues, resulting in blood vessel damage from oxidative stress. At this stage, many individuals actually experience hypoglycemia—the effects of low blood sugar. They feel weak and shaky after a high glycemic meal or after drinking caffeine. The reason is that the caffeine or the candy bar actually produces a stress response in the body, increasing epinephrine levels. This in turn raises cortisol, which triggers insulin production. Blood sugar levels initially go up, and then plummet below where they were before you ingested the caffeine (or the candy bar). Now you're worse off than when you started. So you reach for another "hit" of sugar or caffeine to make you feel better. It's a vicious cycle. Over time, the swings in blood sugar lead to a thickening of the blood vessels in muscles first, then elsewhere. Next, insulin can't get across vessel walls to help the muscle cells utilize blood sugar. And fat builds up in the liver and muscles.

Stage 2—Beginning of insulin resistance: The body responds by stimulating the beta cells of the pancreas to produce more insulin. As a result, blood insulin levels begin to rise. Over time, the pancreas must produce more and more insulin to get it across the thickened blood vessel walls. Insulin levels become permanently elevated as the person develops hyperinsulinemia, the first sign of true insulin resistance. High insulin levels result in a cascade of metabolic and endocrine changes including elevated blood triglyceride levels, low HDL (good) cholesterol, high blood pressure, cardiovascular disease, and increased risk of diabetes in susceptible individuals.

Once insulin levels rise permanently, a chain reaction is triggered that can't be stopped without significant lifestyle changes. One of the

first things Dr. Strand sees in individuals moving toward insulin resistance is low blood levels of HDL. (When I was a macrobiotic vegetarian, my HDL cholesterol was only 35—a level that is definitely
associated with an increased risk for cardiovascular disease. In my
most recent lipid profile, my HDL is at an all-time high of 75. In
medical school, I was taught that exercise is the only thing you can
do to raise HDL—so much for conventional training.) Central obesity (fat in the abdomen) also sets in during stage 2 insulin resistance,
complete with an expanding waistline. This is why waist measurement is an indication of glycemic stress (see below). Before a person
becomes insulin resistant, the muscles take up 85 to 90 percent of the
glucose from our meals to utilize for energy. Dr. Strand says,
"Muscles actually become insulin resistant long before fat cells do.
So glucose gets redirected to your fat cells—primarily in your abdomen. Now your insulin levels (your storage hormone) are getting
higher, and your muscles are not able to take up the glucose normally. This means that more of the glucose or calories from a meal
go directly to your fat cells to be stored as fat, instead of to your
muscle to be utilized as energy."

SIGNS OF EARLY INSULIN RESISTANCE

- ~ Nighttime eating
- ~ Central weight gain (expanding waistline)
- ~ Slow weight gain without change in diet
- ~ Low HDL cholesterol
- ~ Increased triglycerides
- ~ Heartburn
- ~ Increasing fatigue following a high glycemic meal or snack
- ~ Menstrual irregularities
- ~ Hypoglycemia
- ~ Craving sugar and high glycemic carbohydrates

Stage 3—Full-blown metabolic syndrome: Over time, insulin resistance leads to more dramatic metabolic changes that result in high
blood pressure, abnormal cholesterol levels, increased fibrinogen (a
blood-clotting factor), cardiovascular disease, and diabetes.

INSULIN RESISTANCE (SYNDROME X OR
METABOLIC SYNDROME) CONTRIBUTES TO:

~ Type 2 diabetes

~ Increased levels of fibrinogen (increased blood clotting)

~ Obesity

~ High blood pressure

~ Abnormal cholesterol levels (dyslipidemia)

~ Cardiovascular disease, including stroke

~ Most forms of polycystic ovary syndrome

~ Heavy menstrual periods

~ Anovulation

~ Hirsutism (including excess facial hair growth)

~ Male pattern baldness

~ Breast, colon, and other cancers

~ Depression

~ Dementia

Is Your Doctor Looking for Signs?

Standard blood sugar readings taken in most yearly physicals may not be elevated even when insulin resistance is far along, because the pancreas is still pumping out enough insulin to compensate. It's only when the pancreas has exhausted itself that elevated blood sugar shows up on the glucose tests. And remember, you can have normal blood sugar but still be creating cardiovascular lesions and also the beginning stages of cancer—all triggered by diet.

Every adult should have a lipid profile every five years or so to monitor total cholesterol, triglycerides, HDL (good) and LDL (bad) cholesterol. (I recommend getting a baseline lipid profile at the age of twenty or twenty-one.) An elevated triglyceride level and low HDL level are among the first signs of glycemic stress. And they can be present for years in thin individuals with no sign of diabetes or heart disease. These levels respond beautifully to lifestyle changes, and it's very satisfying to watch them come back to normal. (See Resources.)

A TEST YOU CAN DO YOURSELF

For adults, waist measurement is the most accurate assessment of the health risk from glycemic stress. Take a measuring tape and measure one inch below your belly button all the way around. For women, this should be thirty-four inches or less, for men forty inches or less. If it's greater, you're beginning to get central obesity. Note: Fat on the thighs and hips is far less metabolically active and poses little or no health risk.

Research from Katherine Tucker, Ph.D., a nutritional epidemiologist at Tufts University, suggests that the pattern of weight gain may be determined, in part, by where one's calories come from. She found that calories from pasta, white bread, and other refined carbohydrates tended to add fat around the middle, whereas the same number of calories from low-glycemic foods such as vegetables, fruits, and beans, didn't change waist measurement. My clinical and personal experience bears this out![5]

DOLORES: Diabetes in the Family

Dolores was a patient of mine whose family originally came from Portugal. She had struggled with her weight since her teenage years. On one of her routine annual exams, I found that her HDL cholesterol was on the low side (about 40), while her total cholesterol was 230. Everything else was fine, although I was concerned about her addiction to Diet Coke. (She consumed a six-pack a day.) Dolores told me that her entire family had a tendency toward weight gain, especially after pregnancy. By the time they reached midlife, they all started to "spill sugar." She thought this was just a normal part of aging because it had happened to every member of her family, both male and female. In addition to that, they all developed high blood pressure.

None of these problems was in fact inevitable for Dolores. Once she started to exercise regularly and learned how to control her weight through restricting grains and sugars, she escaped her genetic heritage.

Changing My Cardiovascular Legacy

My family, like Dolores's, has a genetic tendency toward insulin re-sistance and sugar addiction, but my legacy played itself out in various forms of cardiovascular disease, ranging from strokes to heart attacks to heart failure. All four of my grandparents died of cardiovascular disease. When I was about sixteen, my dad told me, "Someday a blood vessel will burst in my head and I'll float out into the universe." And that's exactly what happened when, at the age of sixty-eight, in the prime of his life, he was out playing tennis with my mother.

I do not believe that these diseases are inevitable, even though my siblings and I, and one of my daughters, have the kind of "heredity" that leads to the cardiovascular component of insulin resistance. We have addressed this both through our daily food intake and through our antioxidant supplement program, which together dramatically reduce blood sugar and oxidative stress. Hardening of the arteries, as well as most of the aging process in general, is caused by too much oxidative stress—much of which is preventable. (See Chapter 18 for a supplement program that works for both daughters and mothers.)

Signs and Symptoms of Glycemic Stress through the Life Cycle

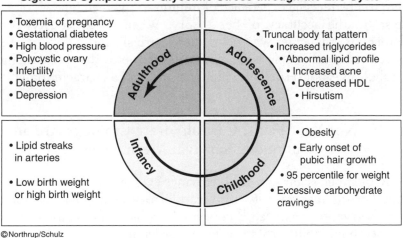

©Northrup/Schulz

Genetic Celebrities

About 25 percent of the population appears to be genetically re-sistant to the adverse effects of overproduction of insulin and insulin resistance. These individuals usually manage to stay slim no matter what they eat. For reasons that aren't entirely clear, they tend to burn up whatever calories they consume. The act of eating itself appears to speed up their metabolism: they get hot right after eating, and/or have increased gastrointestinal motility after a meal. They go into "burn and eliminate" mode, not the more common "hang on for dear life" mode that so many of us must contend with.

They also do not appear to have the same response to high glycemic foods as those who are genetically predisposed to obesity or insulin resistance. They can eat some, enjoy it, and then move on. Kathleen DesMaisons, Ph.D., author of *Potatoes, Not Prozac* and an expert on addictive nutrition, says that you can divide the population into two groups depending upon their memories of going out for ice cream as children. Those with a tendency toward glycemic stress and insulin resistance remember the ice cream itself as the most rewarding part of the experience. (That was me.) Those who aren't prone to weight problems remember other details, such as the ride in the car or the smell of the summer evening. In other words, the ice cream didn't "sing" to them in the same way.

DesMaisons posits that individuals to whom the ice cream "sings" are actually born with lower levels of endorphin receptors in their brains. They crave carbohydrates because sugar acts as a drug, making them feel better. The experience of millions of women (and alcoholics) attests to the accuracy of her theory. When a "genetic celebrity" mother has a daughter who never met a carb she didn't love, it can be a setup for conflict unless the mother understands that her daughter's metabolism is not related to willpower and isn't a character flaw!

It's Not Your Fault: Carbohydrate Cravings Are an Outmoded Survival Mechanism

Remember, sugar and grain cravings evolved as a survival mechanism. For the vast majority of human history, getting enough food to avoid starvation has been a continual problem. Humans developed the metabolic ability to store fat in order to get through times of famine. Unfortunately, this survival mechanism has now become the biggest health risk the developed world faces. Until you understand how to feed yourself the right amount of the right foods, you will be doomed to a lifetime of trying to use your will to fight cravings.

Understand that these cravings are a natural bodily response that won't be suppressed until you achieve the right metabolic balance and reverse glycemic stress. Of course these cravings can also be part of a person's inner wisdom, letting them know, through changes in their mood and anxiety levels, that something is out of balance in their lives. It's truly a vicious cycle. Dr. Strand writes, "Call it hunger, a craving, emotional eating, or an addiction; in the end, it leads to your downfall and forces you to do exactly the opposite of what you desire to do in the first place—eat less food." Does that sound familiar? If it does, then you'll want to address the problem so that you don't pass it down to your children.

Once you eliminate foods that spike your blood sugar, you'll never have to diet again because you'll have found a way to feed your body that will help you release excess fat and also prevent all the diseases associated with insulin resistance. You'll never have to count a calorie, a carb, or a fat gram again once you understand the principles. Yes, you will have to eliminate many of the foods you once craved. But take it from a veteran sugar addict, this isn't as hard as it sounds once you stabilize your blood sugar.

BEWARE THE HIGH-FAT ALTERNATIVE

For decades, nutrition experts told us that eating a low-fat diet was the key to preventing heart disease, obesity, and even cancer. The food industry responded by creating all kinds of packaged foods, from cookies and cakes to ice cream and chips, that were lower in fat but loaded with refined carbohydrates. Now the pendulum has swung in the opposite direction, and the supermarket shelves are full of products that are low in refined sugar and high-glycemic carbs but often very high in fat, such as low-carb chocolate and low-carb ice cream.

Too much fat (especially of the wrong kind) is just as unhealthy as too much refined carbohydrate. The right answer, as always, is *balance*.

Not all fat is bad. We need the right amount of the essential fatty acids found in seeds, nuts, fatty fish, and some oils. These are the omega-6 and omega-3 EFAs. No minimum daily requirement for these has been established, but most research (not all) suggests that the ratio between omega-6 and omega-3 fats should be about 3:1. Because the American diet is already quite high in omega-6 fats (from seed oils such as canola oil, peanut oil, etc.), it is far more important to get enough omega-3s from sources such as flaxseed, hemp seed, and wild salmon. Omega-3 fats are also available as supplements in capsule form. (See Resources; see also Chapter 3.) Their effect on the brain, the immune system, and virtually every cell in the body has been well established.

Saturated fat, the kind found in animal foods such as beef and eggs, can be a healthy addition to one's diet as long as the animals that supply it are organically raised with the right feed. For example, free-range hens produce eggs with higher omega-3 content. But in individuals who are genetically predisposed to high homocysteine levels, saturated fat is a risk factor for heart disease and stroke. However, this risk can be decreased dramatically by taking regular supplements of folic acid and vitamin B$_{12}$. Animal fat is also high in arachadonic acid, which can be a setup for the production of inflammatory eicosanoids in susceptible individuals. Those who have a history of arthritis should avoid animal fat for a couple of weeks and see if joint pain lessens. If pain returns when saturated fat is reintroduced, they should eliminate most of it permanently.

Partially hydrogenated fats (also called trans fats) are just plain dangerous. This type of fat isn't found in nature. It is created by blowing hydrogen into polyunsaturated fats at very high temperatures and pressures. This renders them solid at room temperature—as in margarine—and gives them a shelf life that seems to approach infinity. The problem is that these fake fats are metabolized into the membranes of virtually every cell in the body, including the fat-rich brain and nerve cells. Over time, they accumulate in the system and disrupt cell membrane function, contributing to the development of cancer, heart disease, and mood problems. Read labels and avoid buying foods that contain them. You'll be shocked to discover how many packaged foods do! But it will spur you to find healthier alternatives.

WISDOM CHALLENGE: *When You're Worried about Your Daughter's Weight*

My younger daughter Kate was, like me, a little overweight during latency, a condition that wasn't helped by the carbohydrate-rich vegetarian diet we followed in those days. But because of my own Mack truck legacy, I did everything I could to protect her from similar negative feedback. I downplayed her food choices because she was healthy and I didn't want to make an issue out of her weight. She eventually slimmed down during her adolescent growth spurt, but by that time I had also changed the family diet to one that included more protein, fruits, and vegetables, and far fewer grain products. (All farmers know that the way to fatten cattle is to feed them grain!) My own weight had gone up on our grain-based diet, and I was seeing exactly the same thing in my patients, along with adverse changes in their lipid profiles, hair, and nails. The research supporting the consumption of more protein and fewer carbs was also beginning to surface. I knew we needed to change.

I recently asked Kate how she had felt about her body image in grade school. She told me that at the age of nine, her best friend had said to her, "My mother thinks you're too fat." She also remembered a boy in her class calling her fat. She then added, "But you always told me that I was beautiful and that my body was fine, so I never really ended up feeling bad about myself. I'd just come home and know that I was okay." (Music to a mother's ears, let me tell you!)

I also asked her what would have happened if I had forbidden her to eat the carbohydrate-rich foods she invariably chose when we went out for breakfast on weekends. (Pancakes were her favorite, just as they had been mine when I was younger.) "I would have developed serious issues," she said. "You simply cannot overcontrol what a kid eats without creating major resistance."

I intuitively knew this. Once her paternal grandfather commented about Kate's weight to her father. So her father, being concerned, wondered if we should put her on a diet. I told him that if we did that, I was quite certain she'd end up with an eating disorder. Instead, I suggested he speak with my colleague, Marcelle Pick, R.N.C., at Women to Women who was (and is) very knowledgeable about eating disorders. She told him to back off and never mention Kate's weight or size in a derogatory way. He followed Marcelle's advice and we all came through this little glitch with flying colors. (See Resources.)

On the other hand, if our diet had contained lots of soda pop, cookies, and refined foods, the situation would have been much worse. Because most of our diet was good, we enjoyed family meals together, and both kids were involved in activities like dance and swimming, Kate's weight never really got out of control.

If you have an overweight daughter, you need to understand that you, more than any other person in her life, are in the best possible position to help her reach a healthy body composition. My daughter

Kate said, "It wasn't so much what you said about food, it was watching what you did, what you put on the table, that helped me learn to make healthy choices." Though you can't afford to be the "food police," you must assume parental authority and make sure that the food choices your daughter is exposed to are the ones that will support her health. That means that she may not like some of the foods you bring home. And if you remove some items that she really likes (like that old standby, prepackaged macaroni and cheese), she probably will protest. Tough. She can't drive yet and doesn't have the money to buy her own food. You're going to use this time to educate her taste buds! She'll appreciate it in the end.

Needless to say, healthy food choices should be a family affair. If your house is stocked with chips, soda, and snack foods for the rest of the family, your daughter would have to be a saint not to feel resentful, deprived—and, ultimately, rebellious.

PROMOTING HEALTHY EATING IN LATENCY

The seeds for all the diseases linked with glycemic stress are sown in childhood and fertilized and watered from then on by an individual's daily food and activity choices. This is why a child's early nutrition education and experience are so powerful for helping her create lifelong health. Here's what you can do to help:

Recognize your daughter's innate body composition. As children both Kate and I were at the top, and possibly over the top, of weight charts for our age. Overweight in children and adolescents is defined as a body-mass index at or above the 95th percentile for children of the same age and sex. Sometimes this is a health risk, and sometimes it's not. It depends upon how much of that weight is lean muscle mass and how much is fat. In general, body fat percentage should be between 18 and 26 percent in both girls and women. Men can be healthy at lower percentages of body fat than women.

Toward the end of latency, it is normal for body fat to increase in girls. This body fat is needed for proper hormonal functioning at puberty. So if your daughter looks a little pudgy just before puberty, don't worry. If she's eating mostly low-glycemic foods, she'll slim down once puberty hits.

Innate differences in body composition can have a significant impact on weight, even in completely healthy children. My own two daughters are very good examples of this. I gained exactly the same amount of weight in each of my two pregnancies: twenty-five pounds. My first daughter weighed five pounds eight ounces at birth. (She was born about a week and a half before her due date, but she was full term.) My second came right on her due date, and weighed eight pounds seven ounces. Their body compositions and metabolisms started out different and have stayed that way. My older daughter is about ten pounds lighter than her sister. Both of them have body fat percentages that are normal, around 19 to 22 percent. But the older has far less muscle mass than her sister, so the younger always looks more "buff."

Keep your house stocked with wholesome and delicious food, and follow the 80:20 rule. Aim to make about 80 percent of your child's daily food whole, healthy, and low glycemic. The other 20 percent can be the food she shares with her peers. Though she will no doubt eat her share of pizza and fries when she's with her friends, your daughter will eventually revert to the healthy and balanced eating that she was imprinted with in her home. I've seen this repeatedly with scores of young people—and my own two kids.

Don't bring it home. Keep junk food out of the house. Avoid soft drinks, candy, packaged snacks, and so on. Not only do these raise blood sugar too quickly, but sodas are also loaded with caffeine and chemicals that can cause side effects such as headaches—particularly if they contain the artificial sweetener aspartame. The phosphorous in sodas can also impair calcium and iron absorption and cause sleep problems.

Take your daughter food shopping with you, and prepare some meals together. Teach her how to choose a ripe melon, tomato, or pineapple. Shop the outer aisles of the grocery store. That's where the fresh "real" food tends to be. The prepackaged nutritionally poor choices tend to be in the middle aisles. It's always fun to try new recipes made with healthy ingredients. And you'll be amazed at how many fabulous recipes there are for fruits, vegetables, and protein-rich soy. Learning to cook can be a real boost to a latency-age daughter's sense of mastery and self-esteem.

Serve a breakfast that includes some protein. A good breakfast is the key to creating stable blood sugar—and a stable mood—for the

entire day. If breakfast contains some protein, some complex carbohydrate, and some healthy fat, then blood sugar will rise slowly and
remain normal throughout the morning. That means that you and
your daughter will have mental clarity and plenty of energy. There
are no good excuses for not eating breakfast. First of all, there are
now a variety of healthy shakes that can be made in the blender.
There are also a variety of bars that can be eaten on the run, if necessary. Though sitting down to a nutritious breakfast is ideal, a high-
quality bar with protein is better than going without eating at all.
(See Resources.)

If, on the other hand, you or your daughter gulp a bowl of refined
cereal with sugar on it, blood sugar spikes within an hour—and then
drops below what it was when you woke up. By 10:00 A.M., you're so
hungry you could eat the paper off the wall. (This is also what happens after a breakfast that consists of coffee and a bagel or pastry.)
You don't have a chance. By 4:00 P.M., blood sugar is so low that
when you come home from work (or school) you begin your evening
meal at the refrigerator—and it doesn't stop until you go to bed!

Eat regular family meals together. Research has shown that families
who sit down to meals together at least three times per week are
healthier and their children are better students. During the school
years, this can become a challenge. Don't allow everyone's erratic
schedules to be an excuse for missing this important family bonding
ritual. Nothing is more important. So make time for family meals,
even if that means meeting at a restaurant. More and more fast-food
places are offering healthier choices. Still, there's no substitute for a
home-cooked meal eaten around your own table.

*Avoid using the dinner hour to bring up an entire day's worth of
family conflicts and unfinished business.* This tends to link stress
with eating, and can set up a metabolic pattern that favors indigestion, at the very least. Dinner should not be a psychotherapy session.
(See "Dinner Table Diagnostics," on page 382.)

Serve smaller portions. In the last three decades, portion size has increased so dramatically that we no longer remember what a
"healthy" portion looks like. (I recently watched the movie *Miracle*,
about the Lake Placid Olympics in 1980, and I was stunned by how
tiny a cup of take-out coffee looked in one of the scenes.) Don't use
restaurant servings as a standard for what to serve at home.

Encourage your daughter to try everything at least once, but after that, do not force her to eat anything she doesn't want to eat. The dinner table is no place for control wars over food intake. My younger daughter didn't like greens. I tried to get her to eat them. But they always ended up in her napkin. Now she adores them!

Teach your child how to savor her food and stop when she is full. Most of the pleasure of eating comes from the interaction between the sense of smell and the sense of taste. To maximize this pleasure, you need to slow down and savor each bite. This also helps you extract the maximum benefit from the energetic components of the food—the life force, as it were. Remember, the only bite you can fully enjoy is the one that's in your mouth!

If your daughter bolts her food, try the raisin demonstration. Here are the instructions: Put one raisin in your mouth and hold it there briefly. Now chew it slightly, then press it between your tongue and the roof of your mouth. This will cause the maximum amount of flavor and taste to be released. Take the time to savor this flavor. Now go on to the next.

It takes about twenty minutes for the "I'm full" signal to reach the brain. So when family meal times are leisurely and pleasant, the actual experience of being well-fed registers fully in the body and mind. If you eat slowly, you'll almost always eat less, and you're far less likely to need to pick at snack foods the rest of the evening.

Don't offer desserts or high sugar foods as rewards. This will only add major emotional fuel to the fires of sugar addiction. If you want to serve dessert on occasion, then do so after a meal that contains some protein. This will automatically slow down the rate at which the dessert hits the bloodstream as sugar. When you're out with your daughter and a friend, consider splitting one dessert three ways. If you eat it slowly, savoring every bite, your body will get the "I feel well-fed" signal. And the message you convey will be enjoyment, not deprivation. (You can do the same thing with the fries at McDonald's.)

Avoid nighttime snacking. If there's one habit you want to avoid passing down to your children, it is nighttime eating, especially after 8:00 P.M. Studies have shown that if you eat most of your calories earlier in the day, you can maintain or even lose weight. But the same number of calories consumed at the evening meal or later will result in weight gain. When a family routinely snacks in front of the television at night, they are setting themselves up for a lifetime of health problems and obesity. Of course, breaking this habit is even harder because of the many TV ads for nutrient-poor junk food—all of which are designed to send you into the kitchen for something to munch on. So forewarned is forearmed. And if you must munch on something, make it fresh veggies such as carrot sticks and celery—without the fatty dip!

Some children, however need both an after-school snack and an evening snack, especially those who tend to be on the thin side. Make sure that snack is eaten consciously and served and enjoyed at the table. (Today's thin child too easily becomes tomorrow's over-weight adult.) Again, this snack should be healthy: Good choices would be apple slices with organic peanut butter, carrots with mild salsa, or organic yogurt and berries.

Help clean up the food environment at school. Once your daughter goes to school, you will no longer have the control over her dietary choices that you once had. Both public and private schools have frequent celebrations in which cookies, cakes, and candy are featured treats. Many teachers routinely offer candy to their students as a reward for academic progress or good behavior. Schools are finally waking up about this issue, in large part because the childhood obesity epidemic is too outrageous to ignore. Organize with other parents to get the vending machines out of the schools and to substitute healthy snacks for the usual "party fare." This change is going to take a while because sugar and refined foods are such a big part of our culture. So do the best you can, but don't make overly rigid rules about what a child can and can't eat at school, which can put the child at a social disadvantage.

Teach your daughter the connection between high-glycemic-index foods and emotional eating. Have her check in with how her body feels after eating high-glycemic-index foods. Ask her if she tends to overeat them and then feel bloated or have indigestion or heartburn. If she has a tendency to overeat, ask her to keep a journal of her feelings and food cravings. Help her connect the dots between her cravings, the type of food she's eating, and her emotions. The goal is for her to experience the fact that when blood sugar remains stable, emotional eating and having the munchies is very rare.

Encourage her to find pleasure in a variety of nonfood-related activities. Though it is true that eating refined carbohydrates is mood altering and relaxing, there are other, healthier ways to positively alter brain chemistry. These include exercise, listening to music, or participating in creative pursuits that bring you a sense of reward and recognition.

Make sure your daughter takes a regular vitamin-mineral supplement. Research has now shown beyond a shadow of a doubt that long-term vitamin and mineral supplementation helps prevent infection, cancer, heart disease, and boosts immunity. The quality of supplements is highly variable. In general, you get what you pay for. A quality supplement should be made with pharmaceutical-grade ingredients and have guaranteed potency. (See Chapter 18 for a full discussion of supplements.)

Encourage your daughter to remain physically fit. Regular exercise helps the muscles utilize glucose more effectively, and helps prevent insulin resistance. It is very well documented that girls who are physically fit and strong have a much more positive body image than those who are couch potatoes. It's best if you model physical prowess for your daughter yourself.

Teach your daughter to trust herself with food. I'll never forget a conversation I had in the early 1980s when my own two children were still very young. A female macrobiotic teacher, an expert in the healing effects of natural food, told me that she still had to prepare every bit of food for her daughters and be vigilant about their food choices. She said, "They obviously do not have any judgment when it comes to food. If it weren't for me they'd be out in the world eating junk." She assiduously kept her girls away from most common American foods and berated them if they ate peanut butter sandwiches. Her daughters were twelve and fourteen!

I remember thinking, *When will her girls develop their own judgment around food choices? And how will they ever develop it if she keeps setting up such rigid boundaries?* Until a child has reached the age of reason, what she eats is a parent's responsibility. But once she has, she is ready to learn how to make healthy food choices on her own without being controlled by a mother's disapproval.

Looking back, I've realized how my own judgments about food—like calling beef "dead cow"—did a real disservice to the self-esteem and growing inner guidance system of my younger daughter. She was naturally drawn to meat, and when she was nine, she announced that she wasn't going to be a vegetarian when she grew up.

As it turned out, her body wisdom was right on! Given her metabolism, she would indeed have done far better on more protein and fewer grain products.

I've since come to the conclusion that most people do better with some animal protein in their diets. I realize that vegans will disagree with this, and I understand and respect their position. Though I feel that many people would do well to cut back on the size of their meat portions, every indigenous tribe ever studied has had at least some animal protein in their diets. Most of the vegans I know simply aren't as healthy as they could be. (And many gain a lot of weight over time from insulin resistance.)

THE BOTTOM LINE: Health and weight control are ultimately about freedom. The freedom to know when you're hungry and when you've had enough. Freedom doesn't mean eating whenever and whatever you want. Like discipline, true freedom involves eating in a structured and conscious way. This is the gift you can give your daughter—and yourself.

DINNER TABLE DIAGNOSTICS:
FAMILY INTERACTIONS AFFECT HEALTH
AS MUCH AS FOOD DOES

Children's digestive systems are acutely sensitive to family stresses. It's worth repeating that the way a child is fed and the environment in which she is fed profoundly affect how her body assimilates her food. This starts in utero—a mother's emotions affect the amount of blood available to the baby—and continues to some degree throughout our lives. How a family deals with control issues, conflict, and all the emotions associated with them is often obvious around the family dinner table. In fact, what happens at your dinner table is a metaphor for the dynamics within your family system.

How does your family interact? There are two characteristic patterns of relating that can engender illness within a family. These are *enmeshment* and *disengagement*. Both are characterized by rigid, maladaptive interactions in which conflicts are never resolved.

Enmeshment: No Separation Allowed!

In enmeshed families, boundaries between individual members are weak or missing. A change in one family member or in the relationship between two members reverberates through the family system like sound in a one-room schoolhouse.

In Denise's family, her mother and father usually pass like two ships in the night, having grown apart emotionally. Her mother makes up for this by being overinvolved in her teenaged son's life. As dinner starts, mother and son are deep in conversation about who he should take to the senior prom. They discuss the pros and cons of a number of different girls. The son offers much more personal information than most adolescents would be willing to share. Denise, who is ten, listens in and desperately tries to take part, but she is definitely on the sidelines. Partway through the meal, her father walks in. After a perfunctory hello, her mother ignores him and continues talking to her son. Denise feels bad and pushes her plate away, having lost her appetite. Her body has picked up on the fact that her father is excluded. She gets up and brings him a plate of food, thus assuming the role of mother and wife and unconsciously carrying the responsibility for his care. When the son finishes eating, he announces that he has to get to basketball practice. As soon as he leaves, Denise's mother stands up and says to the father: "Can you believe who John is thinking of taking to the prom?" They then discuss their son's social life in vivid detail. Denise's brother is clearly the kingpin of the household, the person everyone talks about and centers their lives around. Denise feels left out but understands at some level that the only way to fit into her family is to worship her older brother as much as her mother and father do.

In enmeshed families, everyone knows everyone else's business. In healthier families, each member has his or her metaphorical room and is allowed and expected to close or open their door as needed. In enmeshed families, there's no privacy—either physically or psychologically. Anyone can barge in at any time. As a result, individual family members can't grow as individuals. When a personal boundary is crossed, a child may feel the need to act inappropriately parental toward one of her parents. This is exactly what happened to my patient Claire.

Starting at about age eight, Claire became the real-life Cinderella of her family—before the prince. Because her mother worked, she was expected to clean the house, prepare the family meals, and clean up afterward. Her older sister did next to nothing. Finally, her spine collapsed under the weight of this kind of responsibility, which was too much for any child. She developed very severe scoliosis and required surgery. Under normal circumstances, this would have separated her from her role in the family. However, separation in an enmeshed family isn't allowed. When a family member tries to individuate—or is forced to by illness—other family members can't deal with it. While Claire was in the hospital, her father lost weight. He wanted her to hurry up and come home so that she could cook and serve! Instead, because of the body cast and her mother's work schedule, she went to live with a relative for six months. She eventually healed and returned home, but the entire experience changed her profoundly. She was expected to go back to her usual role as though nothing had happened, but the unresolved conflicts, especially with her mother, began to erupt shortly thereafter—when Claire entered puberty.

TYPICAL PATTERNS IN ENMESHED FAMILIES

The royal "we." Your mother refers to family members as "we" or "the family" as though the family weren't composed of individuals. She avoids the word "I" and expects you to do so as well. ("But we always serve crown roast of pork on Christmas Eve.") Having an identity separate from the family is discouraged.

Recognition through serving the family. Female family members, in particular, get their sense of accomplishment and worth from serving the family in some way. Girls often strive for recognition by learning how to bake breads, cookies, and other high-glycemic carbs that the family loves.

Payback for individuation. If you choose to pursue an activity that is not approved by the family, you will experience a "payback" of some kind showing their disapproval. You're guilty when you follow your own heart and not the preapproved activities of the family. One of my friends became a vegetarian during college, letting her family know about her new preferences. But when she came home for vacation, her mother served a pot roast on the first night. And when my friend didn't eat it, her mother said angrily, "Well, I just don't know what you want anymore," and cleared the table abruptly.

Keeping it close to home. Everyone in your family lives within a small radius of each other. The vast majority of your social life revolves around family, such as birthdays, christenings, and anniversaries, and adult children are expected to turn up regularly for Sunday dinner at "home." If they don't live close by, they call each other every day.

The family loudspeaker system. When anything happens in your life, everyone in your family knows about it within a day. Family members often talk through another person. Mediating go-betweens are usually female, with the matriarch of the clan serving as harmonizer.

Abandon ship. Enmeshed families tend to have poor boundaries and weak alliances that are easily broken through triangulation. Let's say that a mother and daughter have decided that the girl should have a new outfit for the first day of school. It's expensive, but perfect. But then her father comes home, hears about the outfit, and decides that he can't afford it. Instantly the mother abandons her former alliance with the daughter and sides with the father. The girl is left feeling abandoned, but if she tries to protest, her mother says, "Why can't we all just get along?"

Decision through family polling. People in your family can't make a move or decision without running a family poll first. If you try to make a decision on your own, there's retribution.

The human smoother. You or your mother have been trained to be "smoothers" or "harmonizers" whose job is to get any potential conflict back under the rug as soon as possible. You use vague, non-specific language to avoid conflict while tangentially alluding to it. For example, your mother is having a conflict with your father, but she won't talk about this directly or even admit that the two of them are having a problem. Instead, she will say, "I'm just unhappy when there are fights in *the family*." Families who demonstrate this behavior tend to agree on things instantly and deny any conflict. When one member begins to individuate in any way, they make that person "the bad one" and then spend their time scheming about how to re-enfold the one who "got away."

Holidays on command. Neither you, your mother, nor other family members have ever spent major holidays away from home. If you don't arrive the day before the holiday, everyone has something to say about it. The holiday meal itself is a "command performance" that you skip at your peril. And you'd better overeat to show your appreciation, because Mom "put so much effort into it."

Parent as social organizer. Your mother orchestrates the social obligations of the family members and then, through guilt, coerces you to fulfill them. For example, you are expected to invite your parents' friends to your wedding, even if you don't know them. You're also expected to go to your parents' friends' funerals and other major life celebrations of people whom you don't know well or even care about.

The wounded puppy syndrome. Family members attempt to elicit nurturing, sympathy, or protection by acting meek, weak, or defenseless. Dragging a metaphoric wounded paw deters and avoids conflict. Example: You announce that you are going out with friends on Christmas Eve after the family goes to church. Your mother looks at you with tears in her eyes, and says, "Oh honey, I was so looking forward to sitting around the fire as a family this evening just like old times."

CONFLICT AVOIDANCE TECHNIQUES 101

You decide to bring a conflict out in the open, speaking at some length to describe in detail how you feel and what you want. The person you are addressing avoids the confrontation with one or a combination of the following tactics:

~ **Evasion.** He responds to your two or three paragraphs with two or three words: "I don't remember that," or "So what," or "That's your problem."

~ **Emotional collapse.** She bursts into tears and is unable to utter a word. This elicits your caregiving instincts, and you find yourself apologizing.

~ **Rationalizing or denying.** "You simply don't understand the problem," or "I didn't have time with everything I've had to do," or "What do you want me to do about it?"

~ **Joking.** Humor is a higher-order defense, but it's still a defense if it prevents you from settling the conflict.

These techniques apply in both enmeshed and disengaged families.

Disengagement: No Intimacy or Spontaneity Allowed!

Disengaged families are overly boundaried, the opposite of enmeshment. There is a lot of distance and privacy among family members, unbalanced by spontaneity or intimacy. Communication is guarded. Emphasis is placed on formal "rules." Conflict is suppressed or ignored.

Joan came from what she now refers to as a "sanitized" family. Her mother, a woman who was trained in 1950s-style home economics, prided herself on serving well-balanced and attractive meals, taking care to put the food on each plate "just so" before presenting it to her family. Second helpings were discouraged because Joan's mother believed in making "just enough." When Joan and her brother were little, they weren't allowed to have dinner with their parents. They were fed earlier in the evening, often before their father got home from work. When he did come home, the children were cautioned not to "bother" him because he worked so hard. They were expected to play quietly on their own while Joan's mother and father enjoyed a prolonged cocktail hour before dinner. This further separated the family members from each other by "medicating" them.

Joan remembers that when she was finally allowed to join her parents at dinner, she was often bursting with enthusiasm, longing to share the details of her day with her father. But she had to do this with restraint, and only after she was "called upon" to speak by her father. Her father routinely tapped her elbow with his knife to move it off the edge of the table. And he often said, "Is this the way you're going to eat if you're invited to the White House?" Dinner was served in courses, so Joan's mother spent most of the time going back and forth to the kitchen rather than participating.

TYPICAL PATTERNS IN DISENGAGED FAMILIES

Take a number. There's no such thing as a spontaneous dinner conversation. Family members have to talk "in turn," not all at once.

Keep your voice down. This type of family values order and control above all else. Therefore, singing or laughing out loud at the table is discouraged. Loud talking or animated discussion are also frowned upon.

Rigid rules. How one folds his or her napkin and uses silverware is far more important than family fun or interaction. The table is often set "just so." The serving bowls, platters, and utensils are deemed more important than the food itself.

No seconds allowed. The concept of abundance around food is lost on this type of family. Each member gets a small amount of each dish. There isn't enough for second helpings. In fact, second helpings are considered "excessive." On the other hand, you're also expected to "clean your plate."

Don't ask, don't tell. Members of overboundaried families don't ask each other how they're really feeling, nor do they share their true feelings with each other. Anything stronger than the midrange "I'm fine" type of feeling is considered too messy and difficult to control.

Feelings are dealt with through addictions. Disengaged families often use alcohol, food, or cigarettes to push down spontaneous, unacceptable emotions. The remarks and behavior that emerge under cover of alcohol are supposed to be forgotten or excused.

We've always done it that way. Disengaged families tend to follow the same holiday or birthday rituals year after year—going to the same places, having the same people over, cooking the same foods. Emotional security is gained by repeating the same "traditions" over and over again.

The cold shoulder. Because real emotions aren't discussed, rigid families have a host of physical signs that signal members not to "go there." They ignore emotional "outbursts" of any kind, and give those who engage in them the cold shoulder. This kind of passive-aggressive behavior guarantees that no conflict will even be addressed, let alone resolved. When asked a question they don't want to answer or address, parents often simply remain silent.

Here comes the judge. Rigid families think they're morally superior to others and convey this through a "nose in the air" attitude. Hearing a constant stream of disapproval of others' minor behavioral slips makes a child anxious. The whole world is booby-trapped with rules, but because they are unspoken, the child is left guessing at what is expected of her. If she inadvertently breaks one of these unspoken rules, she's reprimanded by being told, "You should have known that that would upset Daddy," and so on.

Taking hostages. If you don't conform to the rules and regulations, you are ignored, scapegoated, criticized, or belittled. For a child, attention is like oxygen. They need it to thrive. But in a rigid, controlling family, they must "de-self" themselves to get it. (For example, the father tells his daughter, "Your mother worked on this dinner all day. So you're going to eat it and like it.")

Shark-infested waters. Rigid family systems are often run on unexpressed anger that lurks right beneath the surface. Children are very intuitive and know this. So they will learn how to deflect this anger to make sure it doesn't get expressed directly or, worse, land on them. (For example, they work at being especially pleasing to Daddy or Mommy by saying "I love you," or by being the perfect little hostess who is always very helpful.)

There's No Such Thing as a Perfectly Functional Family—So Relax

Don't be surprised if you identify with a number of the patterns described above. There's no such thing as a "perfect" family that is completely free from unresolved emotional patterns. After all, some of these patterns have been handed down for generations! However, we're less likely to repeat them once we're conscious of them, so it's important to name your family's conflict-resolution patterns and resolve to heal them as best you can so that they are not passed on to your daughters. This is a lifelong process. Just do the best you can and then let the rest go.

14

The School of Friendship

Moving into the Larger World

❁

The lifelong dance between separation and intimacy begins in earnest in latency when a child begins to develop her own friendships and activities outside her home. The relationships school-age girls form with each other can be among the closest and most fulfilling of their lives, though they seldom last a lifetime. Grade school girlfriends tend to merge with each other and become inseparable. Nonetheless, these intense friendships—usually in the context of school, camp, sports, or other organized settings—have the advantage of being free from the emotional dynamics of one's family. They provide a girl with a much broader playing field in which she can develop two crucial and interrelated skills: 1) the ability to go after what she wants in the outer world, whether it be academic success, sports skills, or other forms of public recognition; and 2) the ability to form, nurture, and preserve relationships that are beneficial and supportive for all concerned.

Individuation during latency is a task for both mothers and daughters. As a daughter discovers her place in the larger world, her mother is going through her own developmental stage. Once her children are in school, many mothers pick up where they left off in their own lives in order to have children. They go back to work, back to school, or start a new business. Mother and fathers often find themselves at a new stage in their own relationship as well. Any relationship problems that went underground when the children were born will now resurface. On the other hand, their relationship may improve when they no longer have very young children to deal with.

Whatever she decides to do, a mother whose children are now in latency is at a crossroads in her life. She needs to find the balance between self-development and continuing to actively mother her children.

WHY FRIENDSHIP IS A LIFELONG HEALTH ISSUE

It is well documented that a woman's health is significantly benefitted by the quality of her female friendships throughout her life. For example, the much-publicized research by Professor Shelley E. Taylor, Ph.D., and her colleagues at UCLA has shown that women react to stressful situations by protecting and nurturing their young—which the researchers call a "tend" response—and also by seeking out social contact and support from others, especially women—the "befriend" response. Since social support enhances immunity and offers protection against heart disease, as well as other health problems, this "tend-and-befriend" pattern is a built-in female health enhancer.

Taylor based her conclusions on the analysis of hundreds of biological and behavioral studies of the stress responses of both humans and animals. She found that the "tend-and-befriend" response is characteristic of females of many species. It also differs from the usual response of males. When males are under stress, they tend to get aggressive or isolate themselves socially, the classic "fight-or-flight" response. Repeated fight-or-flight reactions are a distinct and very well documented health risk that is associated with hypertension, violence, and alcohol and drug abuse.[1]

The primary biologic basis for the health-enhancing tend-and-befriend response appears to be oxytocin, the bonding hormone. Taylor points out that both animals and people with high levels of oxytocin are calmer, more relaxed, more social, and less anxious. Oxytocin also leads to nurturing behavior and to seeking out social affiliation. Although males secrete oxytocin as well, its effect seems to be countered by male hormones, leaving women with the greater protective effect. Taylor concludes, "This biobehavioral pattern may provide insights into why women live an average of seven and a half years longer than men."[2]

Playing the Friendship Field

For many children, school is the most reliable and secure part of their social world. You can begin to see the loners versus the social butterflies on the playground right away. But in grade school, even the loners aren't really isolated because all the children share a common and very powerful bonding experience. The socialization process is built seamlessly into daily life, and peers become an increasingly important part of the child's "outer placenta." Friends offer companionship, recreation, the chance to share thoughts and possessions, and also the opportunity to serve as confidants. Friendships also teach important lessons about loyalty and social support in times of stress. Heated negotiations about playing by the rules, fairness, and who gets the window seat on the school bus help children internalize the conventional morality typical at this age, and even to begin to look beyond it.[3]

It's no wonder so many studies show that peer companionship and support are key determinants of social adjustment or maladjustment.[4] In fact, the quality of a child's friendships is one of the most reliable indicators of a child's overall emotional health, even in the face of other serious deficits.

Children with healthy bonding circuits and good self-esteem tend to do well in the friendship department, while those with shaky bonding or difficult temperaments face more challenges. Though it's easy to fall back on the "kids are rotten to one another" excuse if your daughter is having friendship problems, it's important that mothers not overlook these difficulties, simply hoping that she'll grow out of them. Although that is entirely possible, there are certain "red flag" signs that you need to be aware of (see "Friendship Red Flags" on page 397).

It's also important to realize that mothers who have lasting and nurturing friendships with other women, their sisters, and their own mothers are modeling a very powerful and health-promoting behavior for their own daughters.

❀ WISDOM CHALLENGE: *Time for Friends*

Women and girls now face major obstacles to cultivating and enjoying the health-enhancing benefits of female friendships. These obstacles are very recent in human history: working outside the home and the overscheduled lives of today's families. Many women who love their work and are proud of their ability to juggle their responsibilities are surprised to realize just how much they miss "girlfriend time." Professor Alice Domar, Ph.D., director of the Mind/Body Center for Women's Health at Mind/Body Medical Institute and Beth Israel Deaconess Medical Center at Harvard Medical School puts this beautifully:

> This subtle fraying of female bonds has bred a strangely unfeminist phenomenon: women looking to men to meet all their needs. In the old days, women's intellectual and creative needs were not met but their emotional needs often were—by other women in the home and community. More recently working women have so little down time—and so few strong ties with fellow workers—that they turn to their male partners to take up most of the slack. This puts too much pressure on partnerships, and women are often left hungry for the companionship of female confidantes.[5]

I highly recommend that all women make it a priority to spend time with friends. This needs to be scheduled into your calendar as regularly as getting a haircut. As one of my friends said, "The men come and the men go, but your good friends are with you for life." Amen.

Friendship Styles and Choices: as Unique as Your Fingerprint

There is no one right pattern of friendships. Each girl will be different depending upon her temperament. Children who are naturally outgoing may have an easier time initially and develop a wider circle of friends, but shy, slow-to-warm-up children also form intense bonds. Overall, it has been my experience that friendship is a quality, not a quantity, issue. If you have two or three good friends who've been with you in good times and bad, you're doing well.

One of my patients told me about her eleven-year-old daughter Emily, who was caught up in the classic preteen social whirl:

> Emily is always surrounded by her friends and much prefers to spend her time with her peers rather than me and my husband. If we didn't insist on it, we wouldn't even see her on the

weekends except for the time it takes to drive her to her friends' houses. Our home has turned into a preteen "call center." The phone is almost always for her, not us. Each morning, before school, at least one friend calls up to find out what Emily is going to be wearing to school that day. We finally got her her own phone number with a different ring from ours! We know that her friends are important, so we make sure that our home is the kind of place the kids want to come to. At least that way, we know there's a better chance of what we jokingly call a "sighting" of our daughter.

On the other hand, when I was in grade school and high school, my best friend was a girl whose family came to town to ski on weekends. During the school week, I was focused on academics. I did, however, have a steady boyfriend—the same guy—from the age of thirteen right through college. In retrospect, I see that my boyfriend took up the time that I might otherwise have spent with girlfriends. (I also had four siblings to play with.) I didn't form close ties with a group of female friends until I was about thirty-five!

In most cases, your role as a mother is to welcome your daughter's friends, and then to stand back and let it all happen. Friendships are valuable partly because they are *not* managed by parents. They help a girl to strengthen her voice by standing up for herself, to define the ways she is both like and unlike her parents and siblings, and to discover that other families have different values and lifestyles. It's when your daughter faces a friendship problem that you'll probably feel a tug to get more involved.

Though she had a wide range of friends from the time she first went to kindergarten, my daughter Kate always had one exclusive "best friend" as well. I still remember how devastated she was when one of those best friends moved away during first grade. It took her a while to find another best friend.

But loss of friends doesn't necessarily involve a physical move. Sometimes friendships end because a child closes her heart to another. A friend of mine has a seven-year-old daughter who broke down in tears when her mom picked her up at school after the first day of second grade. Her "best friend" had told her that she no longer wanted to be friends. Little Sophie was heartbroken.

That was just the beginning, because the girlfighting that is so common in middle school is now making its way down into the lower grades. This is, in part, because of cultural pressures to be sexy, cool, and popular—even before puberty. Sure enough, by the middle of the school year, Sophie's formerly friendly classmates had arranged themselves into a clique of "popular girls" who knew all the words to the Britney Spears songs that Sophie didn't know. Her family life doesn't revolve around popular culture or television. So Sophie no longer "fits in" even though she's a great student, a good soccer player, and has a good home life. Being left out is so painful that Sophie says she doesn't want to go to school anymore.

To tell the other side of the story, I remember vividly the day I drove Kate to her first day in sixth grade. She was eleven at the time. As I pulled into school her circle of friends were eagerly waiting for her. After she ran to join them, I noticed that a girl I'll call Jane was hovering on the outskirts of the circle, obviously trying to be a part of it. My daughter and her group were clearly shunning Jane. I watched Jane's face fall. She looked devastated. My heart went out to her. And I couldn't understand how my own daughter could be so unfeeling. Later, after school, I told my daughter that I knew how excited she had been to see her friends. But I also told her that it was not okay to rudely shut out another classmate, even if she didn't want to spend much time with her. I suggested that there are more socially skillful ways of moving away from a relationship that no longer works for you—for example, by slowly tapering your involvement and contact.

I'm quite certain that my observation didn't change anything in the short run. Years later, I asked Kate why she and her friends had done that to Jane. She said, "I'm not sure. She just didn't fit in. She was sort of geeky." Several years later, she apologized to Jane who, by then, had found her own circle of friends and activities.

Puberty is often a dividing line in girls' friendships. A girl who matures faster will often abandon her late-bloomer friend, whose brain and body have not yet experienced the effects of changing hormones. And the more mature one won't waste any time calling her former friend a "baby." Almost overnight, their regular forms of play together will seem too "childish" for the one whose body is maturing.

Rickie and Caroline, for example, had practically lived at each other's houses from third through sixth grade. They went to the same summer camp and roomed in the same cabin. Then something happened to Caroline over the summer before seventh grade. She developed breasts and got her period. It seemed to Rickie that Caroline had just dumped her without any explanation at all. When they started back to school, Caroline shunned Rickie and never returned her calls or her offers to hang out together. Instead, Caroline was only interested in boys. Rickie was heartbroken. Within one summer, she lost the most important friend of her life. And she was never able to talk about it with Caroline.

The Impact of Hurt Feelings

Research has shown that the pain of being left out registers in our brains in exactly the same way as physical pain. A recent study reported in the journal *Science* documented that the same areas of the brain that light up when a person feels physical pain also light up when a person's feelings are hurt through rejection or exclusion. Their study was innocuous enough. Thirteen student volunteers were encased in an MRI brain-scanning machine. The students played a simple video game where one of three players tosses a virtual ball to another. At first, the students watched as two players tossed the ball. Then their controls became active and they also played for a while. But soon, the two other players—computerized stooges really, played only with each other. As the students realized they were being left out, it hurt. The areas of their brains associated with pain lit up. In a news release about the study, one of the researchers commented: "There's something about exclusion from others that is perceived as being as harmful to our survival as something that can physically hurt us, and our body automatically knows this."[6]

Learning to deal with the pain of rejection and how to avoid it in the future is part of the process of growing up. Still, it's important to understand that the body and mind register this pain the same way they do physical blows! The pain needs to be validated and worked through. And every mother needs to take steps to stop this chain of pain when possible. (See "How to Help Your Daughter Negotiate Girlfighting" on page 418.)

FALLING OFF THE DEVELOPMENTAL CURVE

As hard as such rejections may be, they are usually part of the normal developmental process by which a girl learns to find her way in the world outside her family. However, there are some red flags that suggest she may be falling off the normal developmental curve.

Relationships: Your child becomes clingy with you or other adults and avoids contact with her peers.

Mood: She is often sullen, anxious, phobic, irritable, or suspicious; for instance, she gets angry when you try to help her find activities she might enjoy and finds fault with every one of them.

Attention: She's obsessed with one area of her life to the exclusion of others; for example, she worries about her appearance, makes lists, or focuses all her time on cleaning and organizing her room.

Memory: She ruminates about everything that happens at school, analyzing who said what and dissecting the faults of the other kids. She can talk about this sort of thing endlessly. She doesn't seem to notice the fun times or occasions when someone is nice to her.

Physical health: She's prone to small aches, pains, rashes, and other physical symptoms that are the result of emotional stress. Diagnostic tests fail to reveal any problems.

Nine-year-old Michelle was the daughter of another patient of mine. Her mother told me the following:

> Michelle has had trouble making friends and keeping them since the time she first entered elementary school. When she comes home at the end of the day, she complains about her classmates, always criticizing the other girls. She also seems jealous of some of her classmates, especially the ones who seem to be the most popular and good-looking. When she does have a friend home after school, she sometimes leaves her friend alone and wants to spend time with me and my husband. Michelle has always been a "little professor" and does very well in school. She prefers hanging around with adults rather than friends. I'm a little worried about her, but her teachers love her and tell me that she's doing fine.

Michelle may be showing signs of a developmental "ding" in the bonding and relationship areas. Michelle's mother, like mothers everywhere, knows that something isn't quite right with her daughter.

But she can't quite put her finger on it. And she's not getting any validation from the school system, even though she has asked her daughter's teachers about Michelle's friendship challenges.

If Michelle's relationship skills don't improve, her mother may end up being Michelle's primary nurturing relationship, and vice versa. It's easy to see how this can happen, given the strength of the biologic mother-daughter bond. When a mother senses that her daughter is no longer progressing normally along the developmental curve, she will automatically do everything she can to fix this. That "fixing" often includes donating her own time, energy, and resources to her daughter in a way that keeps both of them from moving forward in their lives.

ISABEL: Stuck in Latency

When I met her, Isabel was forty-eight years old and lived in a studio apartment in Boston. She had always been a good student but never had many friends. After college, Isabel went to Peru on a prestigious Fulbright scholarship and stayed there doing specialized research for several years. When she returned, she planned to write a book about her experiences and her research there. But all did not go as planned. She never finished her thesis. Her book deal also fell through. Apparently she was unable to get along with her editor or the staff at her publishing house. Her first job as a college teaching assistant ended within six months. According to Isabel, the job failed to use her gifts and talents, and was too boring. (Not to mention that her students complained about her teaching.)

Isabel eventually settled into a job as a secretary in the anthropology department of a local college. Although she had shown great promise in college, she was unable to create and sustain effective relationships outside the "parental" setting of the university. Her apartment was an altar to her past. And her life was characterized by an unchanging routine: every morning she bought fresh milk and eggs—just as she had done in Peru. Every night when she came home from work, she read *The New York Times*. She had a number of acquaintances from her college days with whom she occasionally went to a movie or a concert, but no close, ongoing friendships. She spent all of her vacations and many evenings with her widowed mother, who lived in a nearby suburb.

Isabel was developmentally stuck in latency. Her mother was her default relationship—the one she could count on as a safe harbor. Unfortunately, Isabel's mother had recently been diagnosed with breast cancer. The two of them were both heartsick with worry about the future.

No matter how hard they try, mothers cannot be all things to their children. Even the attempt to do so can cripple both a mother and her daughter. Regardless of a child's temperament, she won't be able to receive support and nurturing from others unless her own mother is flexible enough to allow this. Too many families "circle the wagons" and adopt an "us against the world" attitude that can put their health at risk later in life from lack of support.

MOTHERING PROGRAM FOR DAUGHTERS WITH DEVELOPMENTAL DINGS IN LATENCY

Mind the red flags. If a child wants to be mostly with her mother and not her friends, this is a red flag for future problems with individuation. Make sure that you're not your daughter's relationship default setting. If you notice that she always wants to hang around with you and your friends, tell her that you need time alone and also time with your own friends.

Don't become her social director. Though she may not like it, your daughter needs to figure out for herself how to spend her free time. (It may help to remind yourself that boredom is not an emergency or a fatal disease.) Between the ages of seven and ten, a child should be able to busy herself for two to three hours at a time. By the time she's fourteen, she should be able to spend most of her free time alone or with friends, and need only a couple of hours each day with her parents. Encourage her to pursue activities that interest her that she can do on her own.

Set healthy boundaries. Daughters with latency dings can take up a lot of space and seem to have endless problems they want their mothers to solve. Don't let your daughter monopolize the family conversation with her complaints about being victimized by her friends at school or camp. It may feel good to be needed, but you aren't doing yourself or your daughter any favors by being available for her relationship dramas (or, later, work dramas). If necessary, come up with a schedule that lists how much weekend or evening time you're willing to spend with her. Quality time with this kind of child is best spent in structured outings such as going to a movie, a museum, or out to dinner.

Encourage her to circulate socially. By age nine or ten, she should be able to call her schoolmates and make play dates for herself. You may need to rehearse such calls or set a time for her to make them; you also need to help her learn that this usually involves checking on the availability of the parents who drive! If she is repeatedly rejected even after reaching out, this may be very painful for you as well as for her. Repeated rejections are a warning sign that something needs to change. You and she may both need skilled help. (See below.)

Hold her accountable. Sometimes mothers of difficult daughters go overboard with feeling sorry for them. As a result, they let other things slide. This doesn't do a daughter any favors, because meeting expectations and feeling useful at home can actually shore up her self-esteem. Make sure your daughter pitches in and does regular chores around the house, even if she complains about this and is critical of you.

Focus on the positive. Every daughter, no matter how challenging, has aspects that are lovable and adorable. Focus on those whenever possible. This doesn't mean ignoring or downplaying the difficult stuff. But it will help you deal with this type of daughter much more effectively.

Be honest with yourself. If you find that you always want to spend your time with your daughter, instead of alone or with your husband or friends, you may have your own problems with separation. Seek help with a skilled counselor so that your neediness doesn't adversely affect your daughter.

Remember that you aren't a "village." Though a child needs at least one stable ongoing relationship she can count on, she also needs to be able to accept and receive nurturing from a number of different sources. Enlist others to help you care for your daughter—even if she only wants "Mommy." A teacher or neighbor can be a lifeline for this kind of girl.

Trust your gut. Many mothers who have children who are falling off the developmental curve are told that it's "just a phase," and that the child will grow out of it. Sometimes this is true. And sometimes it's not. A mother usually knows. Unfortunately, her instincts are often invalidated by others because our culture doesn't yet understand the impact and prevalence of bonding disorders.

Get professional support. Have your daughter evaluated by a mental health professional who is skilled in DBT (dialectic behavioral therapy). Though DBT was originally designed to treat people whose personalities became disordered by trauma, this type of cognitive behavioral therapy can help change the unskillful aspects of a girl's personality before she develops more severe problems down the road. A twelve-year-old probably doesn't need full DBT treatment, but a therapist who is well-versed in this approach will know which individual skills your daughter needs to learn to create sustainable relationships. The therapist will know how to help her to effectively change the thought patterns (and body responses) that are contributing to her problems in the first place. (See Resources.)

The maximum brain plasticity of a child of this age will make skills training far more effective now than waiting until after she is older and has experienced more social difficulties. Although it's never too late to learn new skills, our natural brain plasticity tends to decrease after the hormones of puberty come fully on board. And repeated rejection often sets up a pattern of avoidance that becomes entrenched over time.

Don't take it personally. Your daughter's bonding challenges are not always a reflection of you. Do your best to set a good example when it comes to relationship skills. After that, let it go. If your daughter's relationship problems persist, be realistic about her limitations and allow yourself to grieve. Ultimately, this is a matter between her and her soul.

HAVE YOU LOST YOUR INFLUENCE WITH YOUR DAUGHTER? REMEMBER THE CAT DISH SYNDROME

Many mothers of preteen girls face a different situation: they feel they are playing second fiddle to an array of friends who are quoted as authorities on everything from bedtimes to clothing allowances to how a sandwich should be cut. Yes, peer influence is very strong, but if this is your story, I invite you to consider what I call the cat dish syndrome.

I'm sure you've noticed that cats often completely ignore food that is in their dish until another cat starts to show some interest in what's in there. Then nothing will keep the formerly uninterested cat from going over to the formerly boring dish to make sure she isn't missing out on anything.

Well, humans are not so different—especially where mothers are involved. Once you recognize your ability to draw others to your "dish," you can use that attraction consciously to positively influence your own life and everyone else in your family.

Here's an example: When my daughters were about nine and eleven, I decided to decrease my dietary fat intake. I started to buy low-fat salad dressing for myself, even though it didn't taste as good as the regular kind. At meals, I put out several different bottles of dressing—regular as well as low-fat—so that my family could choose. No matter what I put on the table, the girls always went for my low-fat bottle. Meanwhile, several other bottles of once-popular dressing remained untouched except for their regular trip from the refrigerator to the dinner table and back each time we had a salad. I asked my older daughter why she was using the low-fat dressing. She said, "I don't know." So I experimented a bit and switched back to using the regular dressing. Sure enough, the low-fat stuff just sat there. The bottle I wanted for myself clearly held an almost magic charm for the rest of the family. (I have since discovered that this same principle applies to favorite items of clothing—and even to cars!)

In Chapter 2, I likened female energy or "yin" power to centripetal or "drawing-in" force—for example, the power of the female egg that sends out a signal to the sperm, then waits for the sperm to come to it. This drawing-in energy is the essence of mothering and nurturing. No wonder the dog is always in the efficiency triangle of the kitchen, and mothers of young children find it impossible to take a bath alone. After all, it is a mother's body that, on a physical level, has the wisdom to produce milk that has exactly the right proportion of macronutrients, micronutrients, and antibodies for her baby. The energy surrounding that same body can be equally nourishing. Millions of years of evolution and cellular memory have programmed us to trust that our mother's body has what we need, when we need it.

When your daughter is young, the effect of your centripetal energy on her (and your mate) will be easy to see. They will want every drop of nurture juice that you can produce. And during those early years, you'll probably have the feeling that you'll never have your life to yourself again. I certainly felt that way.

But as your daughter gets older, you'll experience a shift in the demands on your nurturing energy. This is natural and necessary. As you—for perhaps the first time in many years—understand your own need to individuate and care for yourself, your daughter will be going through a phase in which she'll want to spend more time with her own friends than she does with you. Now is the time to really monitor your "cat dish."

Given the degree of nurturance that your presence provides to your daughter, don't be surprised by what happens when you first decide it's time to step out to replenish your own dish instead of constantly refilling everybody else's. Just stand back and watch the cats start to circle.

Take a typical Saturday morning when my daughters were between ten and fourteen. The girls are still asleep, my husband has already started to work on his boat, and I want to get on with my own day. Still, almost as if it were biologically wired, I don't firm up my own plans until everyone has checked in. If the girls tell me they're going to be busy (as is increasingly common), then I might call a friend to go to a movie or to the beach.

Once I do, the cats invariably begin to notice that someone else is getting interested in the maternal cat dish. Doing chores around the house—or simply being home and potentially available—makes for a boring old cat dish that everyone ignores. But the minute I announce plans for having fun with a friend, you should see the cats run over to inspect the dish! Suddenly, their own plans seem to lose some of their glimmer. Why? Because Mom just started paying attention to her own dish.

Choosing to nurture yourself when your family suddenly feels threatened by your plans may be a real challenge for you. Why? Because you may be tempted to change your plans on their behalf—especially if they come up with a reason why they need you to be home later on, or to drive them somewhere. Stand firm, both around them and around their father. You want to model your right to a full life.

So prepare yourself for the inevitable cat dish syndrome. Name it when your children get old enough to understand it. Let them experience a mother who knows how to prepare a nourishing dish that not only attracts others but which she herself can enjoy. Revel in your ability to nourish yourself and others. And laugh when the cats start circling!

GETTING OVERLY ENMESHED
IN A DAUGHTER'S LIFE

Some mothers become overly enmeshed in their children's lives at this point. A woman runs the risk of missing her own chance for further personal development if she puts too much of her energy into running, micromanaging, and controlling her children and her mate in an attempt to make herself indispensable. Mothers who fall into this trap often have developmental potholes left over from their own latency. They feel good about themselves primarily through being of service to family members, even when their children no longer need their mothers in the same way as in the past. (We always need our mothers on some level, but we don't need them running our lives.) When a mother soothes her own fears of inadequacy by becoming overinvolved in the lives of her family members, she's at risk of truncating her own individuation process as well as her daughter's.

On the other hand, a mother who has gone through her own individuation process optimally during latency will be happy to back off and allow her daughter more autonomy, because she realizes that this means more freedom for both of them. Her day-to-day role will move from caregiving and feeding to a more supervisory one.

If, however, a mother clings to the old way of being with her children as they individuate, they will react with repulsion on some level because they will sense that her desire to be with them comes from her own neediness and incompletion. The child will know that her mother's motivation does not come from a pure place of wanting to share her child's company and wanting to support her daughter's highest interests.

ALICE: Separating from a Latency-Challenged Mother

It's noon on Saturday. Alice's sixth-grade friends are going out shopping and then stopping at McDonald's for lunch, and Alice has been invited. All of this has been arranged by the aunt of one of the other children, who will accompany them. But Alice's mother has been looking forward to spending some time with her daughter because her husband is away on one of his frequent business trips. Alice's mother isn't consciously aware of this. Instead, she communicates her desires by engaging in "mothering" behavior. She starts to prepare a nutritious lunch of soup and salad. She has also made some fresh bread. So when Alice reminds her about the McDonald's date,

Alice's mother points out that she has already started lunch and that fast food is unhealthy. She also looks crestfallen and dejected, even though she had originally approved the outing.

Alice has been looking forward all week to going out with her friends, but now she feels torn. She doesn't really process the message about nutrition, but her mother's face tells her how much her mother wants her to stay home.

Here's what's really going on: Alice's mother doesn't know how to nurture herself or get her needs met as an adult. When she was in college, she majored in liberal arts and put off thinking about a career. She married right after graduation and became pregnant within a year. When Alice was born, she felt as though she'd found what she had always been looking for. She became the quintessential homemaker, and as long as Alice and Alice's father and other relatives were around to enjoy her efforts, she felt fulfilled. She believed that she'd never again have to face the uncertainty and loneliness she had felt in high school and college. Alice's new independence threatens this comfortable assumption.

To Alice, her mother's behavior around the lunch feels repulsive, although she may not understand why. In fact, her mother is not acting like a parent, she is acting like a dependent child herself. This puts Alice in the unhealthy position of having to parent the very person who is supposed to be parenting her. The pressure to adjust her own needs and desires to take care of her mother's feelings is all the greater because she loves her mother.

Alice is trapped: If she chooses to be with her mother instead of her friends, she is losing out on a chance for individuation, not to mention fun. If she says yes to her friends, she has to feel her mother's disappointment. She may also have to endure "payback" behavior such as stony silence or sarcasm. Or when she comes home, her mother may start in with, "Your room is a mess," or "Is your homework done yet?" These comments simply deflect attention from the real problem: her mother's inability to let her daughter grow up.

Disengagement Is Also Unhealthy

Not all mothers with latency potholes become overinvolved with their school-age children. Instead, they may become hypercompetent in the outer world and throw themselves into the rigors of volunteer work or career—at the expense of their family life.

This type of mother is usually one who, by temperament, found the years of caring for little children extremely taxing. So when her daughter goes to school and she finds herself with more time on her hands, she may overreact to her newfound sense of freedom and overshoot this developmental step. She may become too disengaged from her daughter's need for consistent mothering and too focused on her own need for recognition and respect from the outer world.

DANIELLE: Dealing with Maternal Absence

Danielle was in her late twenties when she first came to see me. She had problems with menstrual cramps and obesity. She also suffered from hypothyroidism and frequent sore throats. Danielle told me that she had problems with feeling "worthy," even though she was a very skilled personal assistant for a successful businesswoman.

Noting that she had problems with both her self-esteem and also her personal "voice" (see "Having a Say," in Chapter 11), I asked her about her relationship with her mother. She told me:

> When I was about seven, my mother threw herself into volunteer work with our church and the local hospital. She was never home when I came home from school. I really don't know what she did. There was always something going on. I was expected to pick up my little brother from kindergarten and walk him home with me. I also had to make sure he had a snack. This went on for years. My mother didn't have to work outside the home. My father was a successful banker. To tell you the truth, I don't really know what she did all day, or even where she went.

It was obvious to me that Danielle could have used more mothering during latency. Instead, she was forced to take on the parental role with her younger brother prematurely. And this pattern had contributed to her feeling overly responsible for others—and also lacking self-esteem—during her adult life.

WISDOM CHALLENGE: *When a Girl Has a Difficult or Damaged Sibling*

When I was a child, I overheard a conversation between my parents and another couple that I have always remembered. They were discussing the effect that the birth of a retarded child had had on the family life of mutual friends. Over the years, I have had many patients who grew up with a sibling who was abnormal in one way or another, and I've realized that nearly every extended family has at least one severely troubled member, with problems including mental retardation, autism, borderline or other personality disorders, chronic illness, or hyperactivity. Though it's not a popular subject for discussion, having a difficult sibling can take an enormous toll on the normal children in a family, and the toll begins early on.

Donna, one of my patients, grew up with a mentally ill older sister whose emotional outbursts made her the center of attention. Donna's mother tried to keep the peace by keeping the older sister contained. Donna, the normal sibling, felt as though she had to be perfect to make up for the flaws of her sister. She became mature far earlier than is normal or healthy, her childhood needs becoming invisible. Her sister always "sucked all the air" out of the room and sapped everyone's energy. Donna told me:

> Because we never knew what would set my sister off, we walked on eggshells around her. And because her behavior was so erratic and upsetting, my mother never set limits with her. She wreaked havoc with my toys, my room, and my schoolwork. And I couldn't complain to my mother about it. I also never dared to have friends over because I didn't know what my sister would do. She embarrassed me. But I felt ashamed for feeling that way because my mother always took her side, and said, "She can't help it, Donna."

Another of my patients agonized over whether or not to invite her estranged and difficult sister to her daughter's wedding. Her daughter finally said, "No, Mom. Cory has wrecked every family gathering I can remember from childhood with her outbursts and drama fests. Please let me have a peaceful and beautiful wedding." The sister didn't come and the wedding was beautiful. But my patient still feels guilty about her decision because, like all of us, she longs for the Hallmark Card version of a family wedding complete with a reconciliation that can never happen.

In her eye-opening book *The Normal One: Life with a Difficult or Damaged Sibling,* Jeanne Safer, Ph.D., a psychologist who has a difficult brother, writes:

> The injury need not be catastrophic for a problem sibling to loom larger than a normal one; you still have to, in the words of an anorectic woman's sister, "arrange life around it." . . . Many siblings never even know a sibling's diagnosis, either because the condition is hard to categorize or because the parents choose not to find out. Ambiguity heightens their anxiety, and they grow up with an undercurrent of vague depression and nameless dread that must be kept to themselves. They learn to keep secrets.

If you have an abnormal child with normal siblings, you need to do everything in your power to make sure that the needs of the abnormal one don't take undue precedence over the needs of the normal one. The first thing I'd recommend is that you read Safer's book. You'll never look at this situation in the same way again. And it will provide you with the in-depth information you need to trust your instincts in a culture that tends to overly endorse the saintliness of those who care for abnormal individuals.

Intervene when the difficult sibling is getting out of control and violating the boundaries of the normal one. Defend the rights of the normal child. Don't make her overly responsible for the abnormal one. For example, if the troubled child doesn't have any friends, it's simply not fair to make the normal one take him or her along all the time. Don't expect your normal child or children to be caregivers on a regular basis. Get as much outside help as you can.

This isn't an easy situation for anyone, but a mother will make matters worse if she collapses herself into meeting the endless demands of the abnormal child at the expense of the other children in the family. This doesn't help anyone, including the difficult one. In fact, it just makes them more demanding and difficult, regardless of their diagnosis. Make a conscious effort to have time alone with your normal child, and make sure she knows that you will try to support her needs in every way possible.

Finding the Balance

When your kids start to push you away and prefer to be with their friends, you may well feel a tug in your heart or your abdomen. I certainly did, especially in late latency when my daughters made their weekend plans with friends and didn't even consider that I might want to spend time with them, too. I missed our weekend activities and knowing that they would always be up for going for a hike with my husband or me and going out to breakfast. On the other hand, I was delighted to see their interactions with their friends and teachers and to watch them blossoming into citizens of their larger communities, with friends and interests that had nothing to do with me.

It's natural to miss the special closeness that you once had with your children when they were little and thought you were the center of the universe. But now it is time to allow a different and more mature form of closeness and intimacy to develop.

Know that your daughter still needs you, but in a more advanced developmental way. It would be inappropriate for a mother bird to continue to put food in the mouths of her fledglings who are now capable of leaving the nest to get their own worms. If the mother bird kept force-feeding them, they wouldn't develop their own ability to feed themselves, much less learn how to fly on their own.

Trust in the process of life. Your daughter has everything she needs to become a whole, healthy, and self-assured adult. Your job is to be a model of what she is becoming and let her know that you trust that she can do it. Here's a great affirmation adapted from Louise Hay for this stage:

My daughter and I move forward as individuals with confidence and joy, knowing that all is well in the future.

ADOLESCENCE:
SURVIVAL OF THE MOST ADAPTABLE

Adolescence is a fiery time during which a girl's soul demands to be embodied and expressed in ways that support her unique passion and purpose. This is challenging in the face of a culture that encourages inauthenticity in girls, that denies them legitimate routes to power, and therefore encourages them to seek power by association rather than by achievement. Because our culture values boys more than girls, girls tend to undervalue themselves and their own time and energy. Instead, they fight among themselves, compete for boys, and put each other down—all signs of internalized oppression.

Being shunned by the popular clique of girls at school is a stressor for countless girls. But the way in which a girl interprets and responds to this event (often with her mother or father's guidance) is crucial to her future. If she decides that she's a "loser" and "ugly" and these perceptions don't change with time, then she's more likely to engage in addictions or other unskillful behaviors to make herself feel better and fit in with the "cool" crowd. On the other hand, she could choose to ignore those girls and turn her attention to mastery in other areas such as sports, academics, or music. She could also seek out friendships with other girls who aren't members of that clique.

Of course adolescence doesn't seem that simple when a girl is going through it. The pain felt by a girl who is being left out or actively attacked by other girls is intense, and very real. But this pain can be used as an impetus for personal growth. So girls should be encouraged to face it squarely and take steps to use their energy in more beneficial ways.

MEGAN: Cruelty as a Feedback Mechanism

Sometimes the response of a girl's peers, however cruel it may be, is actually delivering a message that needs to be heeded. One of my patients told me the following story about her daughter's experience in middle school:

> I'll never forget the time I drove my daughter Megan to a local pizza place to join her friends for dinner before a school dance. I watched as all of them left the restaurant without her, leaving her to finish her meal by herself, and then walk to the school alone, trailing after them. At the time, I was so furious that I had to squelch a very real urge to mow those girls down with my car! Megan told me stories about how her classmates sometimes got up from the lunch table and left as soon as she put her tray down. Though she was an excellent student, Megan seemed obsessed with the behavior of the other girls and just didn't seem to be able to make sustainable friendships.
>
> Worried about the way my daughter was being treated by

her peers, I met with her advisor to discuss the situation. And she told me that in her extensive experience in education, third-grade and middle-school girls were "the nastiest creatures on earth!" I was dismayed! At the time, I thought, *With this kind of thinking from a school authority figure, how will things ever change for the better?* Of course she told me that she would talk to the other girls about their hurtful behavior and also said that things would improve in high school. Frankly, this didn't comfort me much. It was hard for me to accept the idea that it was natural for girls to be this mean to each other!

Adolescents provide instant, unbridled, and often unkind feedback about how one is doing. Girls who are thrown into this milieu in middle school must learn to adapt in order to survive. In Megan's case, for example, it turned out that she was definitely contributing to the way her classmates treated her. Instead of expecting them to wait while she finished dinner, she should have been keyed in to the others and finished her meal on time. Her mother told me that Megan often kept others waiting for her. And she rarely pitched in to help with chores because she considered her activities and interests more important than fitting in with her family. Even as a child, she had been described by her friends as bossy. Her mother said,

> Throughout her childhood, Megan seemed very self-absorbed, never seeming to notice or care when it was time to get into the car to go to school, out to eat, or on a trip. When we were driving somewhere, she'd get lost in a book. When we arrived, she never had her shoes or coat on, so she'd make us wait once again. We always seemed to be waiting for her. Waiting while she finished getting dressed, getting her homework finished, etc. Once I drove her brother to school and left her behind because I was so tired of waiting for her!

Obviously Megan's peer group was not nearly as accepting as Megan's family was. And that's the crux of the matter. An adolescent's peer group won't let her get away with the kind of irritating behavior that her immediate family has grown used to. They're not yet codependent enough because their impulse control isn't yet fully laid down in their brains. And this can be a good thing! It helps prepare a girl for the way the world is, not the way she wishes it would be. It gives her instant and painful feedback.

Random Acts of Meanness: What's Really Going On?

At thirteen, Lisa was what her mother called a "late bloomer." The difference in physical development between her and the other girls was becoming more and more obvious. One weekend at a classmate's bat mitzvah party, she got into an argument with her friend Jamie. Jamie had started to attract a lot of attention from the boys, and she relished every bit of it. The argument built up until Jamie yelled down the table in front of their entire class, "Lisa, you're so flat, you make the walls jealous." Lisa felt all eyes on her chest, ran from the room in tears, and called her mom to come pick her up.

Your adolescent daughter could have the most amicable temperament in the world and still find the school social scene challenging. One of my girls went to a local private high school and one went to public school, both in a small town in Maine. The peer relationship issues were the same in both schools, and they were similar to news reports I was reading about adolescents in schools throughout the United States.

For example, I received the following announcement from the local high school principal when my younger daughter was a sophomore:

> We've been dealing with an issue here which is superficially about technology, but more deeply about core values, and I want to share it with you, hoping we can address it together.
>
> Students recently told us about a Web site called freevote.com that allows people to create voting "booths" on any topic. While this might sound like a good idea, some people have been creating very hurtful "booths," such as the "biggest loser at Yarmouth High School." And other even more mean-spirited booths which use language I don't want to repeat here. As you might imagine, this has been devastating for many of our adolescents who are very fragile anyway as they work to develop their own sense of self.
>
> Although we have made the site off-limits at school, and we are developing ways to address the deeper core values around using technology this way, we can't control what students do on computers outside of school. And students tell us that, thanks to the immediacy of instant messaging, the site and its impact are alive and well. So we ask that you talk with your sons and daughters about the responsible use of technology, and be aware

of how they are using Internet technology at home. Hopefully, together we can help our young people sort through the temptations offered by modern technology by using the Yarmouth core values as their filter.

And that was high school, which is often a welcome change after the madness of middle school. Quite frankly, I don't see how you can put a whole group of adolescents of both sexes together in the same classrooms for three or more years and expect things to go well. I've often said that our culture would be better served if we separated the girls and boys regularly and helped them channel their enormous energies into something useful. Trail maintenance on the Appalachian Trail is one of my favorite fantasies.

Adolescents Are Just Learning How to Censor Their True Emotions

Given my interest in improving women's health on all levels, I've struggled with the issue of adolescent nastiness and its negative impact on girls for many years. I finally found part of the answer to the dilemma when I learned about brain development. Here it is: The brain and hormonal changes that are part of adolescence bring up a variety of real, raw, uncensored emotions. An adolescent who is expressing anger or hostility toward another is really no different from an adult. The only difference is that the adult has learned how to censor the expression of those same feelings, often with addictive substances such as food, alcohol, or marijuana. Or those "unacceptable" feelings may have gone deep into the body to be expressed as illness. (In Chapter 15, I will discuss how that played out in my own body.)

The hugely popular reality television shows such as *Survivor, Fantasy Island, The Bachelorette,* and *American Idol,* in which the "entertainment" consists mostly of watching people being mistreated and publicly humiliated, are living proof that most adults still experience the same feelings they did in adolescence. The only difference is that they have learned how to hide those feelings, even from themselves.

Adolescence is a small window in time in which an entire peer group—all of whom are going through huge physical and emotional changes at slightly different rates—is thrown together in school to learn the social and vocational skills they will be applying throughout their lives. This process started in childhood, of course. But now, the addition of hormonal urges and sexuality make things much more intense. Because the effect of hormones on their frontal lobes is still new and incomplete, many adolescents are far less likely than adults to censor their deepest feelings or the expression of them. (Of course their impulsiveness affects other behavior as well, especially when substances such as alcohol are onboard—see Chapter 17.) If they don't like someone, if someone doesn't fit in somehow, adolescents, like animals in the wild, will pick on the person who is "different." Some of this is just biology—a kind of herd behavior designed to minimize the effect of difference. Some of it, however, is definitely attributable to the culture we live in.

THE IMPACT OF GENDER BIAS

One of the most compelling arguments for single-sex schools, at least for girls, is that girls in these environments are much less likely to base their self-worth on appearance than girls in coed environments. In addition, girls in single-sex environments are more likely to engage in activities or interests that are not necessarily considered "feminine," just as boys in single-sex environments are more likely to take art or dance.[7]

I believe adolescent female nastiness is a natural consequence of growing up in a patriarchal society in which a girl's needs for self-development have not been taken seriously until fairly recently. In hierarchical social structures like patriarchy, it has been observed that those with the lowest status tend to fight amongst themselves for the attention of those who have more power than they do. Alice Walker once remarked that the slaveowners knew very well how to keep the slaves in their places—just keep them fighting among themselves. Then their energies would be dissipated in petty squabbles while the social order that created their oppression was never challenged in an effective way.

Likewise, if we as mothers and women continue to believe that adolescent girls are just naturally nasty, moody, and difficult, then we cannot be of much help to them as they negotiate this critical entrance into the adult world of expanded self-expression and creativity.

And because the wounds of adolescence stay with so many women for so many years, their own unfinished business from this time frame in their own lives often gets triggered. If they haven't worked through their own stuff, they really cannot guide their daughters past the place where they too became stuck, and so the cycle continues, unbroken, passed from one generation to the next.

The research of Colby College professor Lyn Mikel Brown, and many others, indicates that girl fighting in middle and high school is largely a cultural phenomenon, not an innate character defect in girls. In an interview for her book *Girlfighting: Betrayal and Rejection Among Girls,* Brown said:

> I think a lot of it [girlfighting] comes from the way in which we pressure girls to show one side of themselves and hide another. When girls are angry or upset, there's a lot of prohibition to showing it directly. So to maintain their nice-girl reputations, girls find it less risky to take out their fears and anxieties on other girls in indirect ways—such as gossiping, backstabbing, and forming exclusive cliques—rather than challenging the way boys treat them, or the way our culture supports sexist practices. Girlfighting has long-term effects on girls, particularly if you're the one excluded.[8]

Relationship wars have been going on in the lives of girls for hundreds of years, just as they have with boys. The difference is that girls use words and emotional blackmail as weapons while boys use their fists. Louise Hay, the famous author and founder of Hay House, is now in her late seventies. She told me that she still remembers being shunned by her peers in school because she came from a poor family. She was not allowed to actually jump rope. She was only allowed to twirl the rope for the others. Just about every girl or woman I've ever met has at least one painful female friendship story from puberty. Though this is the norm, the warfare among girls clearly wouldn't be as intense if girls—and behavior that is considered feminine—were valued as much as boys (and behavior that's considered masculine).

Economic disparities, like those faced by Louise Hay, simply add fuel to the fire. In some schools, girls are practically pecked to death for wearing Wal-Mart jeans instead of Abercrombie & Fitch, or whatever the brand of the moment happens to be. In this respect, my girls were lucky to grow up in Maine. My younger daughter recently remarked, "I'm really glad that I didn't even know what a Tiffany's box looked like until I was seventeen." If I were a teacher in a class where status depended on conspicuous consumption, you can be sure I'd create a unit of study around it. I'd also teach kids about antiprosperity thinking, which this certainly is.

Lyn Mikel Brown contends that it isn't girls who need fixing, it's the culture. She's correct. My friends who have homeschooled their children have told me that this kind of fighting simply doesn't happen in the social settings in which their daughters get together with their peers. It is also far less common in all-girls schools.

Still, it's important to realize that "the culture" doesn't exist as an entity that is somehow separate from us. It is made up of individuals who keep a pattern going by participating blindly in it. Once an individual brings girl-fighting behavior to consciousness, she has a chance to stop her own participation in it. So the first step is naming specific negative behaviors: shunning girls who don't "fit in"; making fun of the "wrong" clothing or hair; fighting over boys; talking about girls behind their backs; betraying confidences; sending out hurtful e-mails, and so on. Then the pattern stops, one girl at a time. One mother at a time. One teacher at a time. One school at a time. That's how the culture changes.

A great deal of attention is now being given to girls' relationships in popular books and movies and through organizations such as the Ophelia Project, which started in the schools of Erie, Pennsylvania, and now offers workshops on relational aggression nationwide. Both mothers and daughters can benefit from reading Rachel Simmons's *Odd Girl Out: The Hidden Culture of Aggression in Girls* and Rosalind Wiseman's *Queen Bees & Wannabes: Helping Your Daughter Survive Cliques, Gossip, Boyfriends, and Other Realities of Adolescence*. Just being able to name that seemingly all-powerful girl a Queen Bee helps to take some of the sting out of her behavior. (See Resources.)

I might also mention that girls who have found their "place in the sun" and are working toward specific goals are far less likely to have problems with girlfighting. They simply don't have the time or inclination to get involved, although they might get sniped at now and again.

Taking a Stand

While it's impossible—and undesirable—to legislate every aspect of adolescents' relationships and communication style, we can still hold them accountable for unskillful behavior. We can also enlist our daughters' teachers and other mothers. You'd be amazed by what a few people can do to improve the atmosphere in school. A friend shared the following story about a strong teacher who intervened when her daughter, whom I'll call Sandy, got caught up in girlfighting.

SANDY: Lessons in Responsibility

Sandy, in cahoots with one of her friends, had circulated an anonymous e-mail around the school denigrating two other girls in their class. The e-mail had the desired effect. The girls felt embarrassed and humiliated and removed themselves from the lunch table where they had always sat with Sandy and her friends. One of Sandy's teachers knew very well who had sent the e-mail because she had overheard Sandy and a friend formulating it after class one day. She took quick action to nip the behavior in the bud.

First she called Sandy's mother and the mothers of the two targeted girls and let them know that she had an idea for how to stop the behavior. The mothers agreed. She then called Sandy and her friend into her room for a private meeting. She told them that their behavior was the obvious result of low self-esteem and a "loser" mentality, since no one who felt good about herself would be motivated to hurt others in that way. She also explained that indirect girlfighting was a sign of internalized oppression—and let them know how it hurt them and all girls in the end. Finally, she outlined the consequences:

First, Sandy and her friends would no longer be allowed to sit together in her class. Next, she assigned a project to Sandy and the two girls she had trashed. Together (victim and oppressor) they had to research the problem of girlfighting, come up with suggested solutions, and present their work to the entire class within two weeks. (Remember the teacher had already enlisted the support of the mothers, so the girls couldn't pit their mothers against the teacher, or against one another.) For research they had to view the movie *Mean Girls* and also read *Queen Bees & Wannabes*. They were allowed to work only with each other, not with other clique members.

Although this was a difficult time for Sandy, it taught her that her actions had consequences, and that she was responsible for them.

WISDOM CHALLENGE: *Stepping In, or Stepping Back*

If adolescence is when a girl is supposed to learn to stand up for herself and do what she knows is right, regardless of peer pressures, then what do you do when you see your daughter being victimized by the other girls—or being the victimizer?

One of my friends, the CEO of a major company, put it this way:

I didn't try to interfere much with my daughter's friendship dramas in grade school or beyond. Quite frankly, the same sorts of dramas I saw with her and her girlfriends go on every day in every company and with every group of adults I've ever worked with. I reasoned that the sooner my daughter learned how to deal with this on her own, the better.

To some extent I agree with her. After all, to be successful in the game of life, every girl must learn to negotiate being left out versus being part of a couple or a group. These fears don't ever really go away even though we become more adept at dealing with them. For example, a friend of mine who is a very accomplished literary professional told me that whenever she goes to a big convention, she still feels insecure about who to sit with at lunch. She told me, "Here I am, in my forties. And when I have my lunch tray and I look out over a sea of strangers, I keep looking for my coworkers so I don't have to sit alone, sit with someone who is boring, or worse yet, be rejected if I try to sit down next to a stranger who is saving a seat for someone else!" I can certainly relate. I experience the same feeling every time I go to a conference or medical meeting!

When you throw in the normal insecurities of young people who are trying to establish their identities, then add some peer pressure, you have a recipe for pain, drama, and exhilaration. All of this can be perplexing and painful for a mother to watch, especially if she herself hasn't healed her own wounds from adolescence.

However, if you can see that your daughter is really hurting, you may want to help her develop some skills for dealing with aggression and abuse. If you see her being hurtful to others (which may be much less obvious to you, as well as harder for you to acknowledge), then you may want to help her to find better ways of asserting herself and feeling good about herself. Most of the girls who indulge in that kind of behavior are doing it out of a sense of personal inadequacy, not because they're "bad" people.

HOW TO HELP YOUR DAUGHTER
NEGOTIATE GIRLFIGHTING

Validate your daughter's experience. Though it's usually not appropriate to interfere with a daughter's friendship dramas, it is important to validate her experience and her emotions—especially when she's the one who is being left out or picked on. These wounds are not trivial, although the situations that cause them may be, and you cannot expect your daughter to be "above it all" or to be reassured by being told "it will all be different in college."

Update your own views. Check out all the cultural assumptions you've inherited about girl fighting being "normal." If mothers continue to believe that adolescent girls are just naturally moody, nasty, and difficult, how can they offer an alternative? Stop participating blindly in the view that nastiness is biologically encoded on the genes that make us female, ready to manifest in all its ugliness at puberty.

Point out the real motivation behind the Queen Bees of the world. Teach her that cliques are designed to control the behavior of others for the benefit of the elite few. The only reason girls join cliques is because they feel inadequate and insecure on their own. Rosalind Wiseman's book can help you explain that Queen Bees maintain their power and influence by "sterilizing" the wannabes and drones around her, just as queen bees do in nature. The boys flock to her like the proverbial bees to honey, and she renders the other girls less desirable (sterilizes them) just by the power of her presence. Her "court" of wannabes exists to carry out her demands.

By acting the way she does, the Queen Bee will not learn skillful, authentic ways of being in the world—just the opposite. Her inner weakness is exposed by her need to be surrounded by a court to feel good about herself. Though your daughter may desperately want to be "seen" by the Queen, you can point out to her that being like the Queen is not a worthy goal, because the Queen is actually afraid that she is a loser. Real winners never need to put others down in order to feel good about themselves. Let your daughter know that this will become very clear toward the end of high school. Guaranteed. The Queen Bee will lose her power as her peers develop their personalities and self-esteem. And the boys will also drift away. I've seen it over and over again, and I'm sure you have too.

Accept your daughter's humanity and the fact that you may not be able to remove the influence of the Queen. Depending upon your daughter's temperament and self-esteem, she may feel compelled to win the favor of the Queen. Some girls are absolutely mesmerized by Queen Bees. They temporarily adopt them as an ideal self and are unable to see their flaws. If your daughter falls into this category, try to teach her that it is possible to relate to the Queen and her court without sacrificing one's integrity or values. Humor is often a very good way to do this. (See "How to Deal Effectively and Humorously with Peer Pressure" in Chapter 17.)

Don't allow your daughter to take it out on you! It's very common for adolescent girls to take their angst out on their mothers. When you allow your daughter to treat you disrespectfully, you are contributing to the problem. Don't put up with any withering looks or nasty behavior.

WHAT GOES AROUND COMES AROUND: REVIEW THE LAW OF ATTRACTION

This basic spiritual law applies to everything from money to happiness. (See "Financial Literacy" in Chapter 12.) The law of attraction can also be stated as "You reap what you sow" or "What goes around comes around." Let your daughter know that when she participates in backbiting, name-calling, or put-downs of other girls, she's actually doing it to herself. Sooner or later, it will come back to haunt her. This is also a good time to stress to her that her thoughts, emotions, and behavior are the way in which she creates the circumstances of her life! Thoughts of gratitude and appreciation produce beneficial circumstances. Thoughts of hatred, pettiness, and jealousy do just the opposite. Everyone is born with the power to choose what she gives her attention to and what she thinks about. And these choices ultimately shape our lives.

Keep talking and keep your ear to the ground. All daughters internalize their mother's voices inside their heads, even when they don't seem to be paying attention. That's why it's important to keep talking and keep commenting about the unskillful behavior of your daughter's friends. For example, one of the common behaviors I identified is called splitting—trying to destroy a bond of loyalty between two people by denigrating one to the other. Some of my daughters' friends would come to the house and whisper behind my back—criticizing me, my cooking, how I dressed, and so on. I intuitively knew when this was going on. And so when the offending girl left, I pointed out the behavior to my daughters and told them it was unacceptable. I also said, "I think the reason your friend does this is that she doesn't feel good about herself. Please understand where this behavior is coming from. And understand that it's not acceptable here in this house."

Be her mother, not her best friend. Unlike many of her peer group, it's important that a mother have the guts to take an unpopular stand—even if it makes her daughter angry. Let's say your daughter has told her friend Alice that she'll spend Friday night going over their school project together. But then the Queen Bee calls and invites your daughter to a party. At the same time she trashes Alice and calls her a "dorky loser." If you get wind of this, your job is to make sure your daughter follows through on her plans with Alice. You also have to let her know that it shows lack of integrity to gossip with the Queen Bee about Alice's clothes, shoes, and vocational choices, simply because they are different from what the clique deems acceptable. This is mob rule pure and simple. Instead, teach your daughter the importance of thinking critically regardless of social pressure.

Acknowledge and support your daughter's innate ability to deal with her own life. All of us are born with an inner radar that tells us what is safe and helpful and what is not. Your adolescent daughter is no exception, though she may override her inner radar from time to time depending upon how desperate she is for peer acceptance. Acknowledge this inner wisdom regularly. Let her know that you trust your own and that she can trust hers.

Here is another affirmation from Louise Hay to share with your daughter:

> *I express myself freely and joyously. I speak up for myself with ease. I express my creativity. I am willing to change and grow.*

15

Coming of Age

Body, Brain, and Soul at Puberty

❀

We are born with our soul qualities shining out through our eyes. Our orbitofrontal brain and body connections help us feel fully our hearts, our bodies, and our emotions. As latency ushers in the "age of reason," the strengthening dorsolateral prefrontal cortex enables us to censor part of ourselves, making us more palatable to our families and our society. This is a necessary developmental step, because it frees us to concentrate on mastery in the outside world. But then, at puberty, our hormones and the brain and body changes that are spurred on at this time reawaken our orbitofrontal emotionality. We are reconnected with our true selves and the full potential we were born with.

There's a good reason why all indigenous people on earth have provided their young people with specific rites of passage to signify their change in status from child to young adult. The explosive energies of individuation that are released at puberty require some kind of container in which they can be channeled constructively. Not only is your daughter's body changing from that of a girl to that of a sexually mature woman, her brain and emotions are also changing rapidly. In short, she is preparing to become a more independent member of her family and society. This is the time when her unique, inborn gifts and talents are ripe for recognition and in-depth development. It is also a time when the hormonal and brain changes of puberty loosen the lid on the jar marked "family conflict" that usually remains so neatly sealed during latency.

The degree to which we are supported to become who we really are by our families and social networks is the degree to which we will bloom at puberty and remain healthy. When we are not fully supported in becoming who we really are, however, we are at increased risk for developing illness or mood disorders at adolescence. Depending on our temperament, we may either suppress our individuality to fit in or individuate along lines that are foreign or unacceptable to our families in order to remain true to ourselves. Either path takes its toll both emotionally and physically.

COMING-OF-AGE RITES

~ The Nootka people of Canada had a big party right after a girl's first period. Then she underwent an endurance ritual in which she was taken far out to sea and left to make her way home by swimming back to land. When she arrived onshore, she was greeted by her entire village. After that, she was recognized as a woman who had demonstrated her capacity for patience and perseverance.[1]

~ Among the Dagara people of West Africa, the initiation of girls is performed once per year for all the girls who have started to menstruate in the preceding year. This ceremony is the beginning of a long period of mentoring that includes information about sex, intimacy, and the special healing powers of the menstruating woman.[2]

~ Many Navaho people still practice their puberty ritual for girls, the *kinaalda*. According to menstrual researcher Lara Owen, this is considered to be the most important of all their rituals because it brings new life to the tribe. In the month after a girl gets her first period, her entire extended family gathers together for a ceremony that takes place over four days. During this time the girl wears a traditional buckskin dress and her hair is braided in a special way. Each morning she gets up at sunrise and runs toward the rising sun. She is expected to run farther and faster each day. When she returns, an older female relative, taking the role of Ideal Woman, teaches her the Beauty Way, massages her body, and also instructs her in tribal wisdom about male-female relationships. Together the girl and her family, including the men, prepare an enormous corn cake, which they cook in an earth oven constructed especially for the occasion. Throughout the ceremony, the girl is expected to take on a new level of responsibility for herself and others. On the last night, all the people, led by their shaman, stay up all night praying for the girl and her family. The emphasis of this ritual is on both physical strength and character.[3]

These are just a few of many examples of indigenous cultures who had (or still have) positive coming-of-age rites, ranging from tattooing and changes in hairstyle and clothing, to ceremonies involving the entire tribal group, to solitary vision quests. In general, these rites are less physically challenging for girls than for boys, perhaps because every culture recognizes that men will never go through the arduous initiation represented by childbirth. However, all provide a clear boundary between childhood and adulthood, and represent the moment when the child assumes his or her responsibilities to the rest of the community.

Our own society's rites of passage seem superficial in comparison. Getting a driver's license, being able to vote, or consuming alcoholic beverages legally come too late chronologically to mark puberty, and they are not accompanied by the goodwill and instruction of the entire community. No matter how much our children look forward to them, they don't begin to acknowledge or honor the power available when your biology gives you a renewed brain, a new body, and new feelings! In the absence of culturally approved vision quests, meaningful coming-of-age ceremonies, or genuine tests of physical and psychological strength, too many young teens fill the void with drugs, alcohol, dangerous relationships, or compulsive consumerism.

DO GIRLS "LOSE THEMSELVES" AT PUBERTY?

A decade ago, the popular book *Reviving Ophelia* by clinical psychologist Mary Pipher, Ph.D., brought the nation's attention to the fact that many girls go "unconscious" at puberty, lose their voices, and fall prey to everything from eating disorders to depression, multiple body piercings, and exploitative sex. Pipher's work raised the consciousness of a generation of baby boom mothers like me by naming the experience of so many pubertal girls who seemed to turn into sullen, nasty people almost overnight. The result has been an ongoing cultural investigation into what happens to girls at puberty, why it happens, and how to prevent the all-too-common personality regression that so many girls go through just as they're supposed to be blossoming into young women.

Pushing Puberty

Though parents have complained about their adolescent children for all of written history, there is no doubt that adolescence was easier when the pace of life was slower, choices were fewer, gender roles were more rigidly defined, and the spell of the mass media was nonexistent.

We may long for a "simpler" time, but it's clear that those days are gone forever. Today the boundary between girlhood and womanhood has blurred significantly. Whether or not a girl has actually begun the physical process of puberty, the social pressures to behave in sexually mature ways have never been greater. These same pressures are also a major challenge for the mother-daughter relationship. Commercial interests frequently exploit the sexual sensibilities of adolescent girls at a time when they are trying to make sense of their stormy emotions and deeply felt longings and desires.

My older daughter took a course on female adolescence in college and wrote me the following:

> Today we analyzed teen magazines. It was really fun, and very interesting, though slightly disturbing. When you really look at what messages they are sending, it's scary. I did a writing exercise for class on an ad for Cover Girl cosmetics that said "Some girls take chemistry, some girls make chemistry." Agh!

The Cover Girl ad speaks to a deep and universal longing. On some level, we *all* want to make chemistry—whether or not we decide to take chemistry. Once a girl understands that she can have dominion over her own chemistry and learn how to make it for herself, she will be far less vulnerable to any cultural messages that could otherwise undermine her worth.

The information she needs starts with the transformation of her own body.

THE BODY AT PUBERTY

Puberty is a fascinating process that involves a series of hormonally mediated changes in a girl's body and brain. Although many people think of puberty as an event marked by the first menstrual period, the term in fact refers to the entire developmental sequence that leads to sexual and reproductive maturity. Its physical signs include accelerated growth, breast development, pubic and axillary (armpit) hair growth, and the body odor that results from the activation of apocrine glands in those areas (adrenarche). The first menstrual period (menarche) occurs near the end of this process. This entire sequence usually takes about four and a half years, although some girls go through it far more quickly than others. (The range is from a year and a half to six years.)

The changes of puberty begin in the brain. For about eight years, from early infancy until the beginning of the prepubertal period, two hormones known as gonadotropins—LH (luteinizing hormone) and FSH (follicle-stimulating hormone)—which stimulate the ovaries, are kept at very low levels in the body. By age ten or eleven, however, FSH and LH levels become elevated to the same high levels seen in a postmenopausal woman! The elevation of these hormones begins several months before the beginning of breast development, when the hypothalamus starts to release pulses of gonadotropin-releasing hormone.[4] This, in turn, signals the pituitary gland to release FSH and LH, which tell the ovarian follicles to begin developing and producing estrogen and testosterone. It is estrogen that stimulates breast development, bone growth, and female fat distribution, while testosterone stimulates sex drive and the increased sebaceous-gland secretions that can lead to acne.

It takes a while for regular ovulation to become established. In the meantime, a girl's periods are usually anovulatory and can be irregular or heavy. It's common for 25 to 50 percent of adolescent girls to still have some anovulatory periods four years after menarche.[5]

Many different factors affect hypothalamic and pituitary gland function, hence the timing of pubertal events. These factors can include strong emotions and beliefs, body composition and diet and family dynamics, in addition to genetic makeup. For the next forty years or so, a girl's, and later a woman's, menstrual and reproductive function will continue to be affected by these same factors, including her thoughts and emotions. As Mona Lisa Schulz, M.D., Ph.D., explains it:

The limbic system forwards emotional information directly to the hormonal "thermostat" of the body, the hypothalamus, which is located deep in the brain. The hypothalamus, in turn, forwards the information to every gland—the thyroid, ovaries, adrenals, pancreas, and so on. Signals are also sent to the autonomic nervous system. If a girl is very upset, the effect on her hormones will be substantial. If she's only slightly upset, the effect will be minimal.

Any woman whose period has come late, early, or not at all, during times of stress knows the truth of this in her own body.

There is a wide range of difference in how girls go through puberty. Some speed through the process quickly, while others seem to hang on to childhood as long as possible, then suddenly blossom at the age of sixteen, long after everyone else. Yet for all its twists and turns, puberty is a normal life process that seldom requires medical attention.

DAUGHTER AT PUBERTY, MOTHER AT MENOPAUSE

I've often said that menopause is puberty in reverse. During both stages, the brain experiences the same rapid changes in hormones. The rise in FSH and LH is one of the reasons why so many girls experience the same kinds of mood swings and temperature changes (hot flashes) as women going through menopause! During the several years it takes for regular ovulation to be established, estrogen, unbalanced by progesterone, may also produce the same brain irritability that estrogen dominance does during menopause.

Whether one's hormones are rising during puberty or falling during menopause, there's a two- to three-year period of hormonal instability and flux that is actually a biologically supported chance to clean up old unfinished business from the past. Though our culture leads us to believe that a girl's (or menopausal woman's) mood swings are simply the result of raging hormones and do not have anything to do with her life, there is solid evidence that significant conflicts due to relationships, siblings, parents, and so on that a girl feels powerless over or angry about are actually brought to conscious awareness by these hormonal changes. As I wrote in *The Wisdom of Menopause*:

Our brains actually begin to change at perimenopause. Like the rising heat in our bodies, our brains also become fired up! Sparked by the hormonal changes that are typical during the menopausal transition, a switch goes on that signals changes in our temporal lobes, the brain region associated with enhanced intuition. How this ultimately affects us depends to a large degree on how willing we are to make the changes in our lives that our hormones are urging us to make.

Like perimenopause, puberty is a "grow or die" time. The same longing for completion and fulfillment emerges. Most girls have their first erotic dreams starting at about age ten or eleven when their estrogen levels begin to rise. A girl has a hormonally mediated opportunity to connect with her soul's purpose, learn to listen to her intuition, and establish a strong sense of herself during the time when both her brain and body are blooming. Within a few short years, when her hormone levels are stable once more, she will have reached a new level of maturity and power. Once she reaches menopause, she'll be able to look back on the whole process and, once more, upgrade her beliefs and behaviors as she enters another "springtime"—the second half of her life.

Since the changes of perimenopause may precede menopause by as many as ten years, daughters often begin puberty around the same time their mothers begin perimenopause. This provides an enormous opportunity for healing at both ends of the mother-daughter spectrum.

Are Girls Maturing Earlier?

Environmental factors such as improved standards of living and better nutrition in mothers before and during pregnancy have played a significant role in producing taller and heavier children who mature earlier than they did one hundred years ago. At the beginning of the twentieth century, the average age of menarche in the United States was about 14.5 years. Now the median onset is 12.8 years, within a normal range from 9.1 to 17.7 years. Some research shows that the trend toward younger ages at menarche halted around

1960.[6] There's even data showing a slight upward trend, perhaps suggesting some environmental deterioration.[7]

These changes have affected boys as well as girls. One fascinating bit of data gleaned from historical records: In the 1700s, the mean age of voice change in the St. Thomas Boys' Choir in Leipzig, Germany (made famous by J. S. Bach), was 18; now it is 13.5 years.[8]

Periods Aren't Coming Earlier, Breasts Are!

Though the actual age at the first menstrual period hasn't changed in about forty years, what *has* changed is the age at which girls experience the other signs of puberty, such as pubic hair growth and breast budding. A study of seventeen thousand girls conducted by the American Academy of Pediatrics during the 1990s reported that a substantial number were showing signs of development (e.g., some pubic hair growth) six months to a year earlier than previously documented—in many cases, before the age of eight.[9] This falls within the range of normal, but a girl who shows any signs of pubertal development, such as breast budding or pubic hair, before the age of six needs a complete medical evaluation.

On average, black American girls begin showing signs of development between the ages of eight and nine; white American girls by the age of ten. North American girls as a group, regardless of race, begin to grow pubic hair and undergo breast budding about six months earlier than European girls. In general, those who live closest to the equator (or have genetic roots from those areas) go through puberty earlier than those in more northern climes. Daughters also tend to get their periods at about the same time as their mothers and sisters. The earlier the onset of puberty, the longer the duration of the process.[10]

Once a critical threshold of physical growth has been achieved, the central mechanism in the brain that controls the onset of puberty can be activated by the production of estrogen, regardless of its source. Since fat cells produce estrogen, girls who have a higher percentage of body fat usually begin the process of puberty earlier than the average. They also reach menarche earlier. (For reasons that are probably related to the secretion of melatonin, so do girls who are blind.)

In overweight girls, the early onset of pubic hair growth is often a sign of glycemic stress and insulin resistance. These are the girls who are most likely to develop later problems with irregular or heavy periods, polycystic ovary disease, and anovulation. They also tend to exhibit hyperandrogenism, meaning that the body is producing too much androgen, a class of sex steroids that includes testosterone. This occurs because the estrogen produced in body fat is easily converted into androgen, especially when there's too much insulin and cortisol in the system. As you've seen in Chapter 13, this is almost always the result of a diet that produces glycemic stress. Hyperandrogenism is associated with truncal obesity, acne, and excess facial hair growth, all of which resolve with dietary change in the vast majority of cases. (Note: Some facial hair growth is normal at puberty. In a girl of normal weight, it depends upon her genetic heritage. For example, Mediterranean women tend to have more dark facial hair than Scandinavian women.[11])

How Tall Will I Be?

My daughters, like many of their peers, wanted to be taller than they are. When my younger girl injured finger at about the age of twelve, her father, an orthopedic surgeon, took an X-ray to determine whether or not it was broken. It wasn't. But there was lots of talk about what her "bone age" was, and whether or not the epiphyses—the areas for growth on the end of the bone—showed promise of further growth or not. The answer wasn't definitive. What was, however, was the fact that both my daughters come from a long line of ancestors of relatively short stature. I'm five feet four inches, and my parents were about the same. And even though their father is six feet tall, his mother is only five feet two inches. My daughters took after the females on both sides, reaching their full height by about the age of fifteen.

Girls start their growth spurt earlier than boys, which is why so many of them tower over their seventh-grade male peers for a year or two. As the ovaries begin producing estrogen, the hypothalamus stimulates the pituitary gland to secrete growth hormone, which in turn enhances linear bone growth. In general, the earlier a girl gets her first period, the sooner her growth spurt stops. The opposite is also true. This is why so many tall, thin women say that they were gawky geeks in high school. While everyone else was getting breasts and attracting male interest, they were just getting taller and thinner—and waiting for the breast development that often came much later (and much less). Though most girls reach their maximum height before they have fully adult breasts, this isn't always the case. I told my daughters that they might be able to eke out another inch or so by the time they were in their late teens, as I did.

AGES OF PUBERTAL STAGES[12]

	Average Age (years)	Normal Range (years)
Breast budding	10.5	8–12.5
Onset of pubic hair	11.0	8–14
Maximal rate of growth	11.4	10–14.5
Menarche	12.8	9–17
Adult breast	14.6	12–18
Adult pubic hair	13.7	12–18

Body Composition Changes

In addition to breast budding and the growth of pubic hair, a girl's adolescent body goes through major changes in composition. Both her lean body mass and total body fat increase, and her body fat *percentage* also increases from its prepubertal level. This results in part from a complex change in the interaction between estrogen and leptin, a hormone produced by fat cells that helps regulate their metabolism. Much of this new fat goes to her buttocks and hips. In boys, on the other hand, lean body mass tends to increase while the percentage of body fat decreases. It's no wonder that so many adolescent girls begin their first diets at this time, while their male peers are able to consume entire quarts of milk and whole pizzas without gaining a pound! Boys go through their growth spurts on average between ages thirteen and sixteen, along with the increases in testosterone which result in facial hair, lean muscle growth, and deepening of the voice.[13]

Breast Changes

Breast budding is the first stage of breast development. One side often develops before the other, so girls are sometimes scared that they have a tumor. My older daughter called me to her room when she first a noticed a "lump" beneath one nipple, terrified that something was wrong with her. I reassured her that everything was normal, but she burst into tears when I told her that she was starting the changes of puberty. She was eleven at the time and, like many girls of that age, she was horrified by the idea of leaving childhood behind.

The nipples can become very sore during this time. Reassurance that this is normal will itself help to decrease the pain, as will following a good diet. I've never seen a single case of true pathology associated with this pain. Following breast budding, the areolae widen. Then the breast itself enlarges under the nipple area. Though one breast will always be slightly larger than the other, some girls have a marked asymmetry. It may take several years before the breasts are approximately the same size. It's possible for breast growth to continue until a girl is eighteen or so, though she usually reaches her adult breast size within a couple of years after menarche.

The First Menstrual Period

Getting your first period can either be a celebration or a trauma depending upon your age, whether you are the first of your peers to get it, and the circumstances under which it happens. My two daughters were night and day in their responses. Kate was only twelve, and she cried inconsolably for hours while I tried to reassure her that she'd get used to it over time and even come to appreciate this sign of her connection with the moon and the universe. Mostly I just held her and let her grieve. She quickly learned how to use every sanitary product she needed, and when one of her friends got her first period at our house, Kate simply took care of the details like a pro. The other girl's mother and I talked about this later, and she said, "I was kind of hoping that it would happen when I was around so that the two of us could have a mother-daughter moment over it. But Kate handled it beautifully. She knew exactly what to do!"

Her older sister, Annie, who was much leaner than Kate, didn't get her period until she was fourteen. So, in contrast to Kate, all her friends had already started their periods and she was eagerly awaiting hers. She got it at school and, as luck would have it, I was home. I drove over with a Native American amulet that I had bought for her in anticipation of this day. She loved it. I took her out of school and we spent a quiet day together because she had a few cramps. That night her father brought her flowers when he came home from work. But I still have the exquisite handmade symbolic coming-of-age doll that I meant to give Kate. It seemed inappropriate to celebrate such a painful memory. Maybe I'll save it for a granddaughter.

Even in the best of circumstances, some anxiety is normal. For example, in the months prior to their first period, it is common for girls to develop a vaginal discharge that is either clear, white, or slightly yellow. This discharge is the result of increased vaginal secretions stimulated by estrogen. A friend who hadn't known this recalled, "I was very frightened when I started to have a flow of colorless mucus, which happened before the 'bleeding' that I was well prepared for. I decided I had given myself cancer by masturbating! Where that guilt came from, I'll never know, since my mother was very liberal on such subjects and reassured me forthrightly when I shared my cancer fears."

Girls often feel heightened self-consciousness when they have their periods. Wondering if boys can "tell" has been a hot topic among middle-school peers for generations! Girls who are involved in sports have to learn how to deal with the bleeding while competing. It takes a while to get the basics down, particularly for swimmers.

WISDOM CHALLENGE: *What Sanitary Products Should Your Daughter Use?*

Sanitary products have come a very long way since the old belt and pad of my adolescence. However, I generally recommend that a girl use pads until her periods stabilize and become more regular. This is particularly true if her periods are heavy. Scented pads should be avoided because the chemicals in the scent can be quite irritating.

Some girls prefer tampons. These are fine on occasion, but I'd prefer that young girls avoid using them regularly. The reason is that the adolescent cervix undergoes fairly rapid growth and change in the area known as the transformation zone, where mucosal cells change into squamous cells in the acidic environment of the vagina. This is the area from which Pap smears are taken. Tampons can cause irritation here. (I've seen a number of cervical ulcers resulting from the use of scented tampons. In one case, the ulcers looked just like cervical cancer, and a biopsy was necessary to determine the diagnosis.) While there's absolutely no evidence that regular cotton tampons can cause cervical abnormalities, I believe that it's safer to allow the vagina and cervix to develop with minimal exposure to unnecessary environmental agents. That is also why I advise against douching, a practice that is absolutely unnecessary and just perpetuates the idea that the vagina is "dirty." Douching actually *increases* the risk of bacterial infection.

If a young girl does use tampons, she should make sure to change them at least every six hours. If a tampon is left in too long, it may become colonized with *Staphylococcus aureus,* a type of bacteria commonly found on the skin, which under the right circumstances grows out of control and produces a toxin that affects nearly every system in the body, resulting in toxic shock syndrome (TSS).

TSS first gained attention in the early 1980s when a national outbreak occurred in otherwise healthy menstruating women. It was associated with the use of a highly absorbent type of tampon that was immediately taken off the market. The number of cases declined rapidly, but TSS still occurs. TSS begins with relatively nonspecific flulike symptoms. In menstrual cases symptoms appear two to three days after the onset of menses and may include fever, low blood pressure, reddening of mucosal surfaces in the vagina and eyes, and skin rash. TSS can be dangerous if it's not recognized and treated appropriately. For this reason, I don't recommend superabsorbent tampons, which are more apt to be associated with staph bacterial overgrowth.

There have also been some reports to the effect that tampons contain dioxin as a result of chlorine bleaching, which might increase the risk of endometriosis. However, a study of tampons done at Georgetown University Hospital found only trivial amounts of dioxinlike contaminants, amounts at least six orders of magnitude lower than what we are routinely exposed to in our food supply.[14] Would this pose a risk for some individuals? Possibly, but it is very, very low. In the grand scheme of things, I can't bring myself to worry about it, especially when you compare it to the very real and known risks of alcohol, smoking, drugs, and a refined-food diet!

A number of menstrual educators recommend the use of environmentally friendly cloth menstrual pads that can be soaked, washed, and reused. Though I certainly can't argue with the environmental issue, and though it's absolutely true that the soaking water makes a fabulous fertilizer for plants, it's also true that most young girls already feel weird enough about getting their periods. Most are absolutely not going to use a reusable menstrual pad when everyone else is using mainstream products. Mothers who are drawn to eco-friendly menstrual products for health and philosophical reasons would be well advised to give their daughters a choice—and then wait until the daughters are older to reintroduce the cloth pad idea.

BRAIN CHANGES DURING ADOLESCENCE

During adolescence, the remarkable brain growth and transformation that characterized childhood begins to stabilize, preparing the child for adult responsibilities and productivity. On a physical level, it has been established through PET scans, MRIs, and EEGs that the cognitive changes of adolescence are accompanied by the elimination of cell-to-cell synapses, cell death, and subsequent thinning of the outer layer of the brain, known as the cortex. But even as the brain loses some of its childhood connections, new connections are being created. This dynamic remodeling of the brain begins to level off around age twenty, but it continues at a slower rate throughout our lives.

As at all important life stages, adolescence is a time when we must make choices about where we will concentrate our attention. As we prune our lives along the lines of our choosing, our brains are doing the same thing. The brain and nerve pathways that persist are the ones that are well traveled. But in choosing these, we eliminate a number of possibilities that were available to us during earlier childhood. Instead of having a virtually limitless choice of scenic byways, we now selectively choose and use a limited number of inner four-lane highways. Mastering a new skill like playing a musical instrument or speaking a foreign language may become somewhat more difficult. On the other hand, the resulting increase in speed and power—or competence in areas that an adolescent is good at—is often quite striking.

Brain plasticity is the quality that enables our brains to recover after injury or easily learn new things. Before puberty, a child who suffers from a stroke or other brain injury has the capacity to undergo remarkable recovery because so much of her brain is not yet committed to established pathways. A twenty-year-old who suffers the same injury is not statistically as likely to recover as much brain and body function as the eight-year-old does. Despite this decline in plasticity, research has shown that our brains have the ability to grow new cells and make new connections throughout our lives; we continue to be able to learn and heal.

The Dance of Commitment Versus the Dance of Plasticity

The brain changes that a child undergoes at adolescence are a biologic reflection of the challenge we face throughout our lives: balancing free creative expression, expansiveness, fluidity, and freedom with structure, rules, and regulations. In adolescence a girl searches for identities to which she can commit, just as her brain searches for patterns to which it can commit. Consciously or unconsciously, she is preparing for crucial adult choices: choosing a mate and choosing a career that reflect who she really is and wants to be. To a girl who is leaving the relative freedom and seemingly unlimited possibilities of childhood behind, this process may feel frightening as she comes face-to-face with having to make choices and assume greater responsibility for them. It's normal for a girl to undergo some suffering and struggle during this stage, including mood swings, but the degree of this suffering depends both upon her temperament and upon the availability of role models who can support her emerging sense of self.

At puberty, a girl begins to search in earnest for outside validation for her innermost hopes and dreams for herself as a young woman. When she doesn't find what she's looking for, or when she sees women making compromises that the males in her family or society are not asked to make, she quite naturally becomes angry, frightened, or disappointed. That's part of the reason for adolescent rebellion. It's a natural consequence when a girl's longings and sense of unlimited possibilities run headlong into the limitations and compromises she sees in the lives of her parents and other adults. Her unbridled passions are not yet tempered by a fully developed DLPC, nor has she had to deal with the realities of adult burdens and responsibility.

If her emotions aren't validated and redirected in a positive way, her disappointment, anger, and anxiety may take any of the following routes, depending upon her innate temperament:

~ They turn inward as depression, moodiness, or physical illness.

~ They become a setup for self-destructive behavior of all kinds, including substance abuse, getting involved in destructive relationships, or engaging in multiple body piercing and tattoos.

~ They turn outward as hostility toward peers, parents, or other authority figures.

Most girls, however, reach a new emotional set point and calm down toward the middle to end of high school.

My Coming-of-Age Legacy

One of the gifts of writing this book has been coming to terms with the ways in which all these forces played out in my own life, over several generations.

My mother was a consummate tomboy whose happiest hours of

childhood were spent playing ball with the neighborhood boys. When she got her period, she was no longer allowed to play with them. She was expected to assume a woman's role in society. And looking around in the late 1930s, that role didn't seem very appealing to her. Devastated, she begged her mother to take her to the hospital and get her "fixed." Clearly she was not in a position to celebrate her budding womanhood.

This legacy lived on in me, but it manifested in an entirely different way. When I was in my twenties and thirties, I honestly believed that I had escaped the trials of puberty without a scratch! I couldn't understand what all the moaning and groaning was about. It was only after I learned about the mind-body connection in health that I saw clearly how I had stuffed my pubertal angst into my body instead of feeling it. It manifested in physical illness.

I developed astigmatism and myopia and had to get glasses, even though no one else in the family had any vision problems. I developed classic migraine headaches so severe that I was hospitalized for a week in Boston to rule out a brain tumor. I felt tired all the time. I also developed plantar fasciitis, a very painful inflammation of the connective tissue on the soles of the feet, a condition related to fibromyalgia. Once I started my period, my cramps were so bad that I often had to leave school. Though the cramps and migraines eventually resolved completely, my eyes never recovered. I still wear glasses and contacts.

Back then, I, like millions of other adolescent baby boomer girls, had no socially acceptable way to express my emotions, especially my anger. If you had asked me if was angry, I would have denied it. Anger wasn't an emotion we were encouraged to feel or deal with in my family. We did joy and happiness. Sadness was also allowed and so was empathy. But anger, uh-uh.

The first major issue of puberty for me was being forced into precocious motherhood by my own mother's absence. By the time I was twelve years old, the resources in my family were being shunted into my sister's skiing career. My mother drove her all over the Northeast to ski races, and Penny eventually became a member of the U.S. Alpine Ski Team. As the oldest daughter, I was expected to cook dinner for my father and siblings and also keep the house neat. (My brothers weren't expected to do any of the extra caretaking.) I resented this, but any resentment I felt quickly went underground. Expressing it simply wasn't safe.

Another major issue was not getting recognition for who I was. Once when I was about thirteen, I told my parents that I needed a quiet place in the house to study or practice my music. I pointed out that in many families being a good student meant a lot. My dad shot back that the family was sick of hearing me play the theme from *Exodus* on the piano over and over again. And besides, the family didn't exist to fulfill my needs. He also said that when I got to college I'd learn that nobody would care about my need for quiet. (He was right.) At the time, I remember crying uncontrollably and saying how much his comments hurt. But I was ignored. My mother said nothing.

So I learned to keep quiet, study in the midst of chaos, and get my recognition needs met by my teachers. I learned to translate Caesar's *Commentaries on the Gallic War* from the original Latin to the background of the *Red Skelton Show* on television or my younger sister's accordion practice. I developed the ability to shut out the world and concentrate. Of course I had feelings about this. Years later, when I became familiar with traditional Chinese medicine, I realized that every illness I experienced at that time was related to the liver meridian, the primary emotion of which is anger. My weight struggles, starting with that first diet at age twelve, also resulted in part from trying to prove my worthiness by nurturing and caring for others. (Those who don't feel worthy often give to others what they themselves would really like to receive. This pattern leads to "carrying the weight" for them. This isn't healthy for either party!)

Up until midlife, I had had no idea that I was still holding this childhood anger and resentment inside me. But there was no doubt about it. When I first started to write about my adolescent health problems, I developed a bright red, flaky rash on my throat, chest, ears, scalp, and back of my neck that went on for many months. Steroid cream worked temporarily, but the rash came back, and I decided I didn't want to keep suppressing whatever was trying to get my attention. So I just let it work its way out, all the while remaining open to the message it had for me. Skin rashes are the body's way of trying to build up "armor" or protection. They also represent irritation and anger just below the surface. The location of the rash was also telling. The throat is related to self-expression, speaking one's truth, and having one's say. It took me a while to find the words to express what my body was telling me about my mother-daughter legacy.

Around the same time, I also started to have the eye symptoms that were the prodrome for my migraines—something I hadn't experienced in many years. Though a visit to my acupuncturist stopped these symptoms before they became a full-blown migraine, it was obvious to me that my usual defenses were weak, and that my old anger was right beneath the surface.

In the months that followed, I experienced firsthand the kind of midlife healing I described at the beginning of this chapter. As I explored my anger and felt it fully, I rediscovered the intensity of those teenage years. I felt in my bones how much a child thrives on recognition and will do whatever is necessary to get it. But I also began to see the rest of my family with a wider vision.

Ironically, my sister Penny, the former world-class skier and mother of three sons, told me recently, "There was no way I could compete with how smart you were in school. So I chose skiing because I was good at it. And Mom fully supported it." She thought I was the "winner" with whom she couldn't compete, even though she was the one with the roomful of trophies and press clippings!

I also realized that my mother would rather have been skiing or hunting than ironing, keeping house, and preparing meals in the classic 1950s housewife role. It's no wonder that she was willing to drive my sister all over the Northeast for so many years. I see now that I simply picked up her burden and carried it forward in my own way. This never works, of course. But that doesn't mean we don't try.

Looking back, I believe that my daughter Kate was to some degree affected by this maternal legacy, given her initial reaction to menarche. However, by allowing her to simply feel all of what she was feeling and not trying to make the experience "better," I believe that the negative legacy lost a lot of its steam. Neither of my daughters ever developed the menstrual cramps, eye problems, migraines, or other physical problems that I had at puberty.

CONSCIOUS MOTHERS, CONSCIOUS DAUGHTERS

Whenever I encounter the widely held societal belief that boys are easier to raise than girls, or that teenage girls are inherently nasty, I inevitably feel an impassioned response rise up from deep within me. I've finally realized why. As young women, we may incorporate the messages of our society into the DLPC of our brains in such a way that our orbitofrontal brain-body connections go to sleep and their vital messages become censored. This is when Ophelia truly goes unconscious. But keep in mind that the brain synapses that result in this cultural "anesthesia" are primed at home! The very idea that one gender should be easier to deal with than the other—on any issue—is so obviously the result of unexamined patriarchal bias that it's amazing to me that we still buy into it. As mothers of daughters, each of us must learn how to recognize this bias when we run into it, and also recognize it within ourselves so that we don't pass this female-paralyzing belief on to our daughters or granddaughters.

Significant numbers of people still believe that it's possible to have a perfectly behaved, angelic daughter who suddenly turns into an uncontrollable bitch because of "hormones." Nothing could be further from the truth. She's simply expressing the conflicts that have always been there just below the surface—conflicts such as the inequity between male and female roles that she can see so clearly right in her own home and school with the fresh vision of puberty. Any conflicts that a daughter feels, whether within herself, her family, or her culture, will now be fanned by the hormonal fires of puberty. And those hormonal fires are all about self-actualization, self-development, and self-expression.

Reviving Ophelia was published just as my own daughters were reaching puberty. They, and many of their classmates, read it. I recently asked one of them what she thought of it, and she said, "At that point, I was looking for any reason why I was feeling the way I was feeling. I found it helpful." The book documented the grim realities of adolescence for many girls: it rang true with what I had seen and heard in my medical practice. Nonetheless, I remember thinking, *Why should Ophelia need reviving? Couldn't we do something different as mothers and as a society so that fewer girls would fall into this adolescent coma?* It didn't make sense to me then or now that perfectly healthy, well-adjusted girls would suddenly fall off a cliff at puberty, a normal life stage.

Books such as *Reviving Ophelia, Saving Beauty from the Beast, Queen Bees & Wannabes, Odd Girl Out,* and *Girlfighting* have elucidated the cultural context that puts so many adolescent girls at risk. But that's only one part of the story. Daughters don't become "unconscious" in the areas in which their mothers are fully conscious. Ophelia won't need reviving if her mother has already been resuscitated—or never needed resuscitation in the first place. Beauty is less likely to fall for the Beast if her self-esteem is high and if her mother has taught her how to be in touch with her instincts.

Each of us must take responsibility for the ways in which we keep "the culture" going up close and personal in our own homes and in our own lives. This is infinitely harder than blaming the culture. It is also a far more rewarding and powerful way to change the conditions of our lives—one mother and daughter at a time.

How Hormones, Personality, and Archetypal Energies Align at Puberty

The physiologic brain and hormone changes of puberty coincide beautifully with the universal archetypal rhythms that shape our souls. In the midst of the inevitable conflicts, I find it comforting and practical to think about major life transitions in this objective, "big picture" way.

"I Know What I Want": Early Creative Release and Self-awareness

Ten- to eleven-year-old girls are very clear about what they like and don't like. They'll tell you what's on their minds. This is when children often find and commit to art, poetry, sports, dance, or other creative outlets that hold the key to their future vocation. The rules of society have now been internalized (though they're not necessarily obeyed), which frees the child to concentrate on creative tasks. The ego grows strong and life takes on a blissful "summer-lasts-forever" quality.

What were you like at ages ten and eleven? If you can't remember, ask your mother. This age always holds significant keys to a girl's soul qualities. I spent hours sitting up in trees reading books or acting out fairy tales in the lilac bushes with paper-doll fairies I had drawn and cut out. I also loved to wander along the edge of our farm pond, catching salamanders and gathering wildflowers, seedpods, and other natural objects. Little wonder that I ended up majoring in biology.

"I Know What I Want, but Sometimes I Have to Wait": Growing with Limitations and Structure

When my daughter Kate was at this stage, she actually knew more people in our town than I did and her social calendar was always full. I recall how amazed I was that she had accomplished this without any help from me at all! At this age, a girl's intellectual growth accelerates and she may form strong beliefs that are different from those of her family. (If her family or social group has very strong feelings about what one should believe, then her maturing insights and perceptions may be suppressed and judged as "bad" or "wrong" or "sinful.") Similarly, if a child is interested in computers or music but comes from a family that has produced generations of doctors, she will do best if she is supported in the endeavors she's drawn to even if they go against the family grain.

The blossoming of sexual desire and interest is also perfectly natural at this stage. And so is masturbation. But if a child has been taught that sexual feelings are dirty or shameful, she may interpret this to mean that she herself is bad or shameful, simply because she has feelings that are as natural as grass growing green in the spring!

A child this age often feels the tension between wanting to remain a child yet knowing she must assume more responsibility to the family and society. The blissful, carefree days of childhood that seemed to last forever are now fading as the child moves into the harsher realities of impending adulthood.

"Can We Agree to Disagree?": Confrontation with Authority versus Defining Yourself against Authority

By about the age of fourteen, the inner tension between childhood and adult responsibility often manifests as confrontation with authority. This is when even the most mild-mannered, cooperative child may become moody and withdrawn or belligerent and rebellious.

This creates a problem in families like mine growing up, where if you came downstairs in the morning with a less-than-happy countenance, you were sent back upstairs so that you could redo your entrance in a more positive manner. I do not recall emotional outbursts of any kind. We did have lots of joy and laughter, however. On the surface, this appears delightful. But, as I've mentioned, I learned early on to suppress my so-called "negative" emotions such as anger and sadness instead of understanding that these were an important and very valid part of my own inner guidance system. As a result, I was also terrified of the expressed anger of others, since I had no experience with it. I eventually learned how to disagree diplomatically, but this skill has taken decades to master. As one of my colleagues says, "Diplomacy becomes avoidance or manipulation if one hasn't first squarely confronted the genuine differences involved." It's important for a girl to begin to trust her own inner authority. We may use that power unskillfully at first, even offensively, but it's worse if we never assert it at all.

MOTHERING AT PUBERTY:
NINE WAYS TO HELP YOUR DAUGHTER THRIVE

The following guidelines will help you and your daughter negotiate her coming of age with maximum access to the power and possibilities inherent in this important time.

One: Get Your Own History Straight

Every one of us has baggage from our past that we're not aware of. It's just the way it is. The unresolved pain from your past will be unwittingly passed on to your daughter. Do the best you can and don't worry about it. Remember, she picked you as her mother and part of her soul's journey is to work with the material she was given. Be as honest as possible with both yourself and your daughter about your own experiences at puberty and be compassionate with yourself. If you suffer from conditions such as PMS, menstrual cramps, fibroids, or endometriosis, then your body is carrying unfinished business from the past, and/or something else (like diet) needs adjusting. Remember, the biggest gift you can give your daughter is your own healed self.

One of my newsletter subscribers, Joan Morais, is the author of *A Time to Celebrate: A Celebration of a Girl's First Menstrual Period*. She sent me a very moving letter about how her book was born out of a desire to introduce her three daughters to their first period in a meaningful way—in contrast to her own mother's perfunctory remark, "You're a woman now," which meant nothing to her. She wrote, "Going on this deep inward journey and learning why it is so important to celebrate and honor my menstruation, my entire life changed. I no longer suffered from intense PMS, I changed a deep cultural view of hiding menstruation and did not pass it on to my daughters, and I learned to love my female body."

Though most young adolescents aren't yet ready to digest a mind-body approach to menstruation, their souls are longing for some acknowledgment of the true power of this rite of passage. And if you, like Joan, have embraced this power yourself, you'll make it much easier for them. To help get you started, I recommend that you read the chapter on the menstrual cycle in *Women's Bodies, Women's Wisdom* and also *Honoring Menstruation: A Time of Self-Renewal* by Lara Owen. (See also Chapter 16 of this book.)

When my daughters were adolescents, I was not aware of the suppressed anger and resentment I described above or of its effect on my body. But I did know that they needed to be given permission to feel their emotions fully in a safe way that didn't hold others hostage or blame them. And I also knew that those emotions weren't "just hormones." Stormy emotions almost always carry a message, but girls at puberty simply don't yet know how to communicate that message skillfully. The storms of early adolescence are often like the tantrums that erupt when a toddler is overtired or frustrated. The Fast-Food Rule still applies. (See Chapter 7.) So when your daughter is upset, make sure you "take her order" and repeat it back to her right from your heart: "Karen, I can see that you are upset right now. So just do what you need to do to make yourself feel better. If you want to talk, I'm available."

Don't get me wrong. It's never healthy to dwell on and marinate in negative emotions. But as my own body taught me, suppressing, ignoring, or criticizing them isn't healthy either. The happy medium involves acknowledging and feeling the emotion fully, naming its function, and then letting it go.

THE FIRST BRA

Many mothers, having healed the wounds of their past, are eager to celebrate their daughter's coming of age with special events such as helping their daughter buy her first bra. Some girls can't wait for this rite of passage and others are horrified. Even if they've gotten their first period, many girls this age are very self-conscious about their new bodies and the attention they are getting. Buying anything but the most utilitarian bra or undershirt may seem too sexually charged regardless of the girl's breast size. Many simply don't feel comfortable looking "sexy" until they are older (for some that's at least fifteen).

One of my newsletter subscribers described how her daughter tried to hide her breasts with her long hair, refusing to get a bra even when she needed one. Her peers were into tank tops and undershirts. She said, "It was painful to watch her dribbling down the basketball court while trying to hide her breasts. But there was nothing I could do. Luckily this phase passed." On the other hand, there's the woman who told me she couldn't wait to get her first bra when she was

in seventh grade, even though she didn't have anything to put
into it.

So give it time. It takes a while for a girl's emotional development to catch up with her reproductive development.
And that can create a few awkward years in which they are
little girls who want to sit on your lap one minute, and fully
grown-up young women who don't want anything to do
with you the next. The important thing is to see your daughter as an individual and honor her choices and where she is
in her emotional development.

Two: Learn to Create Your Own Happiness

If you want your daughter to be healthy and happy, your job is to
be healthy and happy yourself so you can model this for her. (By the
way, it is not her job to make you happy by doing everything you
want her to do. It is not your mother's job to make you happy either.)

Your own balance and happiness have to be more important
than your child's. Otherwise you have nothing to give her. A mother
who is willing to give up every ounce of her own happiness and joy
to her children becomes a martyr.

If you have a daughter who is difficult, it may well be easier to
relate to her from a place of despair. Your vibration will be a better
match for hers. But that will leave you both in greater despair.
Remember this quote: "Dimming your own light to make another's
appear brighter makes the whole world darker."

Three: Revise Your Expectations for Family Time

Young adolescents need parents around. But they need them at
odd hours. Routine family time doesn't work the way it did during latency. The golden moments of quality time are often when you're driving them to school or to an event. It's a way to tune in to their lives
that you wouldn't otherwise have. You need to make an effort to be
home when they're popping in between social events. There's a special
value in simply being there and staying within earshot in a way that is
entirely different from the early grade school years, when they tended
to love you and your company and really wanted you around. Now
they don't—but they do. It's approach-withdrawal-approach all over

again, just like when they were two. By being available, you'll be there when they really need to talk.

It's also important to schedule special times together. Your interactions with your puberty-age daughter shouldn't be limited to driving her to and from activities—although those drives are very important times to check in. An example is "movie night" when a daughter gets to pick a PG-13 or R-rated movie that her mother might not be totally comfortable with. Watching together is a way to "detox" some of the adverse but powerful cultural messages that our daughters are bombarded with. You're there to put in your own two cents! This was one of my favorite activities with my girls.

Family outings and trips often become subject to negotiation. Give your daughter leeway not to participate some of the time. At age thirteen, I had just fallen in love with my first boyfriend when my family left for a monthlong trip to the national parks and Alaska. I pined for him the entire time, breathlessly awaiting his letters. But I also had fun with my family, and, looking back, I'm glad I didn't miss the trip. Later that year, however, I often spent the day with him while my family went skiing. We'd go to movies, make pizza, and generally hang out together. If my family had tried to force me to go skiing every weekend, I'd have done everything in my power to be with my boyfriend. Luckily, it never came to that.

Four: Support Your Daughter's Sense of the Sacred

Given their growing sense of identity and search for an authentic self, it's not surprising that so many ten- to thirteen-year-old girls become fascinated by metaphysical subjects such as astrology, angels, or tarot cards. Of course, this same urge can also be channeled into one's religion. Starting at about age thirteen, I used to play the organ at my church, and I recall how fervently I participated in the rituals and ceremonies associated with the Episcopal Church year. I felt the sacredness of the hymns and scriptures in those days with an acuity that I've never experienced since. Whether through religion, metaphysical studies, or simply listening to their inner voice, writing down their dreams, or keeping a journal, adolescent girls are instinctively drawn to areas that are alive with meaning and possibility. This is a time when one's soul is connecting with its true passion and purpose, and your daughter's interest in spiritual things will help her find meaning in the inevitable trials associated with becoming an adult.

A Spiritual Mentor

When I was about twelve, I baby-sat one evening for the grandchildren of a family friend. Once the children had gone to sleep, I picked up a book called *Natives of Eternity*, written by Flower Newhouse, a Christian minister and mystic who could see and communicate with angels. Reading about the angels of birth, death, music, fire, and more and seeing paintings of their faces moved me deeply. It felt like proof that what I had always hoped was real. I was elated, and I went home and shared my discovery with my mother. She in turn called her friend Gretchen and told her of my enthusiasm. Gretchen had a copy of the book sent to me and also invited me to have breakfast at her home to discuss angels and other mystical subjects. She had studied metaphysics for years and had been to the Christward Ministry run by the Reverend Newhouse on several occasions. This breakfast grew into a series of uplifting and delightful visits that continued throughout my high school and college years. Gretchen was one of my early spiritual mentors.

One of the ways you can support your daughter is by teaching her about the feminine face of God. The book *Moon Mother, Moon Daughter*, by Janet Lucy and Terri Allison, includes many myths, such as that of Kwan Yin, the Chinese goddess of compassion. The authors gathered these beautiful teaching stories while working with a group of ten- to twelve-year-old girls. Reading them together with your daughter will introduce her to the feminine face of divinity that is present in every culture. This is also a way to reclaim our historic past: the many thousands of years when Goddess-centered religions, which were egalitarian and peaceful, existed in most of Old Europe. In these religions, the female body and its processes were seen as sacred. This history is very empowering for young women to know.

My daughter Annie recently reminded me that during the week of her first period I gave her a copy of a special book about the spiritual power of coming of age. Though I had forgotten about it, she hadn't, because she loved reading it. The book was *Flowering Woman: Moontime for Kory*, by Mary Dillon with Shinan Barclay. I also recommend *The Seven Sacred Rites of Menarche: The Spiritual Journey of the Adolescent Girl*, by Kristi Meisenbach Boylan.

Five: Create a Coming-of-Age Ceremony

If your daughter agrees and is enthusiastic about it, I recommend some kind of planned coming-of-age celebration for her. Remember, however, that adolescents are acutely sensitive to the dominant culture and its negative messages about the female body. So some won't want this coming-of-age ceremony to have anything to do with menarche. Don't push your daughter to have a ceremony that you really want to heal your own coming of age. (Quite frankly, I think that many of us baby boomers are using our fiftieth birthdays to accomplish this!)

You don't have to wait until your daughter gets her first period. Instead, you can plan this ceremony—or a special mother-daughter trip or event—anytime between the ages of eleven and fourteen. If you participate in a religion that already has a coming-of-age ceremony, such as the Christian confirmation or the Jewish bat mitzvah, then you may find that this suits your daughter well. But others will want to create a more female-focused ceremony that might include more Goddess energy. A collaborative known as the Red Web has put together a number of resources to teach women and girls the importance of reclaiming the wisdom of their menstrual cycles and menopause. (See Resources.)

COMING-OF-AGE CELEBRATIONS

When I asked my newsletter readers for coming-of-age memories, the responses I received were a wonderful testament to the mother-daughter bond at menarche. Here are just a few:

~ When my older daughter (now sixteen) turned eleven, I started thinking about how we would punctuate her coming of age. I remembered my own first period as traumatic, coming the day before entering a new school in a new state, so I wanted Molly's to be far more natural and uplifting. I wrote to my circle of female friends and family, asking them each to help me celebrate Molly from afar by sending a card, note, or reading that they would want to share with her whenever the day came. I planned to keep them all in a special envelope or booklet and wait for the time to share them.

These women, including my college roommate, sisters-in-law, and childhood friend, all seized the opportunity to do something very special. What came back over the next few months were boxes filled with gifts, books, writings. I found a beautiful storage box covered in a floral fabric in which I would present these gifts, rather than the planned envelope or scrapbook. The box was filled with a series of butterfly objects—a butterfly necklace, trinket box, and hairclips to signify her transformation; a Celtic plaque depicting the maiden, mother, and crone to educate her about the cycles of life; photos of one of her aunts in "stylish" cat-eye glasses at the age she first menstruated; a book of teen wisdom; a big box of gourmet chocolates from a grown cousin who said this would always make her feel better at "that time of the month." And there were many, many written words of wisdom and memory from these wonderful women, including an awkward note from her grandmother (my mom), who simply didn't know what to say to acknowledge an event that was so very private when she was a girl.

The day Molly got her period, she was very matter-of-fact, as she often is about life. Before she got into bed, I took her into our guest room and pulled out the celebration box. She first read the card from me, which explained what she was about to receive, and then together we opened the large fabric box and all the beautifully wrapped gifts from her "sisters" inside. For that hour, it was as if all of the women we knew were right there in the room with us, a circle of women drawn together across distance and time. Together we shared what women are all about—memories, advice, and deeply held feelings.

~ Getting your first period was a big day in our house. It was the only time my mom allowed me and my two sisters to take the day off of school. We would start out with a special morning together at the house, lounging around and taking our time getting ready. We then went out to lunch to a fancy restaurant and proceeded to an afternoon of shopping to buy a new outfit for the new young woman. (Again, this was a luxury, as we weren't the type of family to buy everything we wanted.) What I cherish most about the day, though, was spending time with my mom and her talking about how this was a special time that should be celebrated.

~ Before Marina's first period arrived, I contacted all the people who cared deeply for her and requested that they write a few sentences about what they wished they had known at her age. What ideas, attitudes, beliefs, and awarenesses could have made a big difference to their adolescence? What tools and strategies had they learned from life? The outpouring of loving, gentle, wise advice was immensely touching.

I printed and bound these treasures into a book, which I presented to Marina in a small ceremony with her best friend and her best friend's mom. Not only did we mark her transition with meaning but she now has a valuable resource to help guide her during times of challenge. She also has the experience of a deep, loving support network—so rare for a teen to know and realize.

Six: Teach Emotional Literacy to Your Daughter and Model It Yourself

The stormy emotions associated with adolescence can be weathered far more effectively if you realize that all emotions are simply messages from our inner guidance system. Each has a function. Each is telling us something we need to know. Each should be felt fully and then released. It's that simple. If this doesn't happen, or if any emotion is put down or suppressed, it can cause illness.

If your daughter becomes moody or "mouthy," give her a lot of space and don't try to cheer her up or "fix" her emotions. Let her discover the inner guidance that will help her reach her own solutions. However, she also needs to realize that her feelings affect others. If she says "I don't want to talk about it" when you query her obvious sadness, tell her it's okay to feel sad, but that she needs to figure out how to solve her problem in a way that doesn't negatively impact everyone else in the family. Let her know you're available if she wants to talk about whatever is troubling her, but that it's not okay for her to sit sullenly at the dinner table without saying a word. This is an example of holding everyone else hostage. You might demonstrate how that feels by doing it yourself—ever so briefly—and see how she likes it. It's better to have her leave the table and figure things out on her own.

Do not, under any circumstances, allow yourself to be your daughter's personal trash compactor. It's never okay to let your daughter abuse you in any way. That means that when she rolls her eyes at you, or suggests that you are "stupid" or "uncool," just stop her right there. When my daughters (or their friends) started in with this, I got right up on my high horse, and told them: "If you persist in that behavior, you are contributing to the degradation of women that has been going on for the last five thousand years. I will not allow that in my home because this is the way it gets perpetuated in the culture. If you persist, I will come into your school and give a lecture about this to your class." That pretty much nipped the behavior in the bud!

You must, on the other hand, let your daughter know that any anger or sadness she may feel has a valid message for her. (And she might get very angry with you for preventing her from doing everything she wants to do. That has to be okay with you. You cannot try to be her friend all the time.) You might suggest that she write in a journal or start a meditation practice so she can learn what that message is and what to do about it. The intuitive "hit" about what the emotion means usually comes only after you've fully felt the emotion.

This approach models healthy emotional boundaries. You are not being overly enmeshed or overly disengaged. She knows that you care from a place of respect and that her emotions are valid. But you aren't about to allow yourself or other family members to be manipulated by them.

Seven: Validate Your Daughter's Inner Wisdom

Despite the pervasive influence of the mass media and mass culture, our daughters can learn that their own inner wisdom and intuitive voice are far more potent guides to a life of fulfillment, health, and joy than anything outside themselves. Once they learn to identify and trust this voice, they will be far less apt to get caught up, at least for long, in the emptiness of meaningless relationships, frantic consumerism, or using addictive substances and processes whose purpose is simply to numb pain and awareness.

Eight: Let Someone Else's Mother Tell Her

Daughters need as many "mothers" as possible. When they're not willing to listen to you, chances are that they'll listen to someone else's mother. I have been that "other mother" for a lot of girls, and it's a very empowering and fulfilling role. But I've also relied on other mothers when it came to my own daughters.

About the time that my own daughters came of age I began a series of discussions with my younger daughter's seventh-grade teacher, who was also the mother of one of her longtime friends. Our daughters went through both elementary and high school together. Knowing the perils of adolescence, we decided to be proactive.

Together we held several meetings with the seventh-grade girls (no boys were present), including our daughters, in which I talked to the girls about their fertility and creativity cycles, their sexuality, and their changing bodies. I managed to make sure that my own daughter got to "overhear" the stuff that I knew every girl needs to know, but in a way that she could take in at her own pace. We told the girls how their bodies, hearts, and spirits were growing and changing in preparation for womanhood. In addition to giving the girls a positive perspective on the physical processes of puberty, we also wanted to create a safe place in which they could speak freely about what was on their minds and in their hearts. We talked about menstrual cramps, breast size, boys, and everything else they wanted to discuss, including their grief over the end of some of their friendships, as people began to change and grow apart.

During our sessions together, I witnessed the acute pain that girls often feel when leaving childhood and developing womanly bodies. Whether consciously or not, most know that their bodies may be objectified by others as sex objects instead of being seen as the temples that house their souls. Mostly we kept open the lines of communication between mothers and daughters at a time when they often shut down. The feedback we got from the parents of the other girls was very gratifying. I know we made a difference.

The other small miracle occurred when I took Kate to New York City to see a play. We asked friends of ours to get tickets for whatever they thought would be good. And that is how we happened to attend the premiere of the The Vagina Monologues, which is based on Eve Ensler's interviews with women of all ages and backgrounds. I thought I had died and gone to heaven as I sat in an audience full of celebrities with my thirteen-year-old, not-too-happy-with-puberty daughter, experiencing these hilarious, deeply moving, and utterly engaging women's stories read and performed by the likes of Whoopi Goldberg, Calista Flockhart, Glenn Close, Marisa Tomei, Gloria Steinem, and Shirley Knight. It was an evening of women's empowerment that I will never forget. Talk about letting someone else's mother get the message across to your daughter!

This particular performance also kicked off a series of annual V-Day celebrations on Valentine's Day, dedicated to ending violence against girls and women worldwide. And the cultural consciousness-raising has continued. Seven years later, when my daughter Annie performed in a college production of *The Vagina Monologues,* Kate and I sat together, enthralled, in the front row. We'd all come a long way.

Nine: Give Up Your Illusion of Control

Our daughters are individual souls who come into this life fully equipped to influence their own environment, starting from the moment of birth. They also have the ability to learn and respond according to their inborn temperament. What this means is that we mothers aren't as responsible for how our daughters turn out as we've been led to believe. Though we certainly do influence our children profoundly, we are not their Higher Powers. They have their own. It's ultimately not our responsibility to create a perfect childhood or adolescence for our daughters. It is our job to be supportive when doing so doesn't detract from our own health and happiness. As a mother, I take comfort in the fact that I had exactly the kind of adolescence I needed, migraines and all, in order to do my life's work. I wouldn't change a thing. I hope that one day my daughters will feel the same. But they probably won't realize this fully until midlife. So lighten up and enjoy your daughter's coming of age. Know that she is here to carry her maternal heritage to the next level in her own unique way and in her own time.

Room Three

Fourteen to Twenty-one Years

16

Aphrodite Rising

Channeling the Energy of Sexuality

❖

There are times in everyone's life when the potential to become someone new and different and better is particularly apparent. Adolescence is one of these times. This is when many an ugly duckling discovers she is becoming a swan; when a young girl starts to intuit the feminine power and wisdom within herself; when she sees new possibilities at every turn. If the rising life force associated with this time is nurtured, protected, and fertilized, the bloom that results is a blessing and a thrill to behold.

I remember watching this stage with wonder when my younger daughter was fourteen. Kate had developed a svelte new figure, and the self-confidence that often goes with such outer changes. One day as the school year was ending she said to me, "This summer I'm going to be strong and rich!" Kate had gone through a lot of grieving when she got her first period at the age of twelve. Unlike Annie, who didn't start her period until she was fourteen and had gone through the physical and emotional changes of adolescence much more gradually and without any major personality changes, Kate had experienced puberty as something sudden, something she wished weren't happening, and her previously always-sunny personality became somewhat moody and subdued for a couple of years. Since she had had such a difficult period of adjustment, I was particularly happy to see her come alive once again. At that time, I wrote:

Kate has changed. I can feel life and celebration and Aphrodite flowing through her very strongly. She is mowing the lawn without being told. She is interested in yoga and doing her ab exercises every night. She is interested in dresses for the first time. (Kate had lived in overalls for most of her grade-school years and almost never wore a dress.)

She's also talking about learning to sail around Casco Bay. The kundalini is rising quickly in this one.

As a mother, I feel like a gardener who has been fertilizing and aerating this soil for years. Now something strong is coming through this child that is far bigger than I am. But I must continue to water and feed this force so that it can grow straight and tall—and not bend and break before it has even had a chance to develop bark on the tender areas.

Watching Kate brought back to me so vividly that time of life when you always have the feeling that something good is about to happen. For me that feeling started to surge when I was around age thirteen. Suddenly I felt that I was physically powerful, that I could do or be or have anything I wanted. And one of the things I wanted to become was a good tennis player. I was so determined and had so much drive that I shoveled the cow manure off the concrete slab in the back of the barn and drove practice shots against the wall for hours. Talk about sublimation!

LOVE, LONGING, AND LIBIDO

The same rising life force that changes a girl's body, mind, and spirit at puberty also makes her fertile and capable of becoming pregnant. In ancient Greek mythology, Aphrodite was the name given to the goddess of sex and love. Aphrodite is the embodiment of female fertility, sexuality, and love. She first manifests in a girl's life at adolescence, appearing in the form of desire and longing. Like all forces of nature, a young woman's libido must be consciously honored and acknowledged. Only then can she learn how to channel this potentially explosive energy in constructive and healthy ways.

It's important that an adolescent girl understand the true nature of sexuality early on, especially if, like so many girls that age, she has problems with her sense of self-worth. Then she is apt to put the needs of others, including their sexual needs, before her own. And this can lead to sexual relationships that are unfulfilling at best, exploitative and even abusive at worst.

Adolescent girls are often overcome with a sense of longing, yearning for connection with a boyfriend or significant other. They fall in love with love, as it were. This feeling is not just about sex, nor is it experienced only by girls. In fact, in a study on this kind of falling in love, an experience to which she gives the name "limerance," psychologist Dorothy Tennov, Ph.D., found that 95 percent of the women and 92 percent of the men rejected the statement, "The best thing about love is sex."[1]

CULTURE AND SEXUALITY

It is politically correct to imagine that girls get horny in the same way as guys and would take the same approach to sex if it weren't for the fact that they would be considered "sluts" if they did. And certainly it is true, as Naomi Wolf says in *Promiscuities: The Secret Struggle for Womanhood,* that "the honest facts about female sexual development in adolescence—especially the facts of girls' desire—have sustained a long history of active censorship." No kidding. While male writers generally talk with pride about their first sexual experiences, female writers—and girls everywhere—tend to hide the facts of their past sexual experiences for fear of how others will think of them. As a gynecologist, I was often the only person in a patient's life who knew all the details of her sexual history, complete with abortions and sexually transmitted diseases.

But the culture's beliefs about gender can have an even more profound influence, going beyond secrecy and shame to the very core of sexual experience. Wolf writes that anthropologist Margaret Mead concluded in 1948, after observing seven ethnic groups in the Pacific Islands, that the value a given culture ascribes to female sexuality affects a woman's capacity to achieve sexual fulfillment. For a woman to view her sexuality in a positive light, Mead believed that she must live in a culture that:

~ recognizes and honors female desire

~ allows her to understand her sexual anatomy

~ teaches the lovemaking skills that give women orgasms.[2]

Despite the fact that orgasm is a normal bodily function that one doesn't need "training" to experience—even priests and nuns have orgasms during their dreams, as Masters and Johnson documented—the frontal-lobe circuits in the dorsolateral prefrontal cortex can be trained to inhibit the orgasmic response. We're hardwired for sexual pleasure, but it's fairly easy to mess with the way the wires are connected. And that's where culture and upbringing come in.

There's no way to discuss female sexuality separately from the culture in which it gets expressed. Though it is true that there have been cultures in which men and women have enjoyed equal power and autonomy, in sexual and other areas of life, we don't currently live in one. So it is nearly impossible to know what part of a girl's libidinal impulses are really an expression of sexual desire, what part are simply an expression of her urge to be accepted and valued by the gender that has historically had more clout.

Living in a culture that does not extend them full equality, girls must learn how to claim their right to sexual satisfaction, and also learn how to do so in a way that enhances their health. I see this as the central challenge of adolescent female sexuality. That said, there are girls who've managed to find sexual fulfillment in the context of a caring relationship. I remember meeting a fifteen-year-old girl and her sixteen-year-old boyfriend at one of my book signings. They were in a committed sexual relationship and she had brought him to my lecture because he was interested in learning about her body, particularly the wisdom associated with her menstrual cycle. I'll never forget the two of them. Precious. On the other hand, many girls wait for years to find the right partner—if they ever do. Without knowing that their sexuality is a gift to be shared only with someone who honors and values them, they may fall into relationships in which they don't get much satisfaction, sexually or emotionally. Ruth is a good example.

Ruth had her first sexual experience in the back of her boyfriend's car when she was sixteen following an evening of drinking. She allowed it to happen because she thought it was the only way to hold on to her boyfriend. Although they did continue to see each other through high school, their relationship never went much beyond the sex. When she got to college, Ruth had a series of sexual relationships that were similarly unfulfilling. Even though she currently has a steady boyfriend, she doesn't really enjoy sex that much and has never had an orgasm. She has, however, learned how to fake it so that he'll think he's a good lover. She told me that "lots of my friends do this." Though she doesn't have much in common with her boyfriend, he is "good-looking and a decent guy" (as she put it). She stays in the relationship because she's afraid of being alone and not having a date. Ruth's high need for approval from boys and authority figures, low self-esteem about her abilities (she was a C student in high school and barely made it through her final exams), and difficulty being alone have, unfortunately, set her up for a lifetime of unfulfilling sexual experiences.

Too many young women like Ruth give up on themselves out of a lack of self-worth. One way out of this dead end is through the hard work that leads to a feeling of accomplishment. The more skills a young woman can master, whether in school or a job situation, the more choices she will feel she has—including choices about her relationships.

All girls need to know that there's an alternative to Ruth's approach to sex that is far more fulfilling and life-enhancing. It involves understanding that when love, desire, and self-respect are combined, sexuality can be a conduit to the Divine.

Celeste, another of my patients, had a first sexual experience that stands in sharp contrast to Ruth's.

> I don't know why, but as far back as I can remember, I've known that there is something sacred and special about sex. When I was eleven, I remember a very vivid dream in which I was in an aqua pool of water. And this gorgeous angelic creature came and kissed me. And I just melted into that kiss. I always knew that I wasn't going to share my body with just anybody. I had to love him and know that he loved me in return. I was willing to wait until I knew that I had met the right guy. I felt very secure about this. And I had spontaneously learned how to masturbate when I was twelve. So I didn't need a boy to feel an orgasm.
>
> Once, when I was in college, a guy I had dated for a while couldn't understand why I wouldn't have sex with him. I replied, "Because I can't imagine it would add anything to our relationship." He couldn't believe it. After all, at that time (the late '60s), everyone was sleeping with everyone else. It was a sexual free-for-all. Though I didn't judge those who experimented sexually with lots of partners, I always knew it wasn't right for me. Soon after college, I met the man who would become my husband. I'll never forget it. Looking at him made my knees shake. I knew within three days of meeting him that he was "the one." And when we first made love, I just melted into

him. It was truly a spiritual experience. It felt as though our bodies disappeared and we became one. I found myself floating in a blissful state that seemed to go on and on. . . . As though I were riding a wave of energy that has always been there but which you can only feel in a state of love and surrender. Obviously I've never regretted my decision. And of course I'm also so grateful that my inner conviction saved me from having to worry about getting herpes, genital warts, and worse. A lot of my friends got these conditions and I felt very badly for them. Their sexual experiences gave them sexually transmitted diseases—not the love they really wanted.

Celeste is very lucky to have had such an understanding of what makes for joyous, loving sex. She always felt as though her libido was "something good," not something to be ashamed of. And because she understood how valuable it was, she also knew she had to be discerning about sharing it. Healthy sex, like eating well, is based on self-esteem, self-respect, and a belief that your body is a gift that has tremendous worth and should be shared only with someone who will give something in return. Except for charity, one wouldn't willingly give something of value to anyone who didn't appreciate it and reciprocate. Why give your body to someone with whom there is no reciprocity? Perhaps Celeste found a model for a loving relationship in her parents, or in someone else she knew or read about. But wherever she found it, she knew in her soul that sexuality is to be honored as part of the very life force of the universe.

I had the same feeling, from very early on. When I was a teenager, I knew that I could never be physically intimate with anyone I didn't care about. I always brought my whole self to a relationship. If I kissed someone, I was present during that kiss. I lost myself in the bliss of it, the total sensuousness of it. And I was never able to do this unless I respected the whole person I was kissing. I never had a split between my sexuality and my spirituality.

I know, however, that my own dating history is atypical—I think partly because I've always hated the taste of alcohol and so have never been drunk. This made it a lot easier not to do stupid things or to give in to pressure from boys who weren't right for me. When I was twelve, I fell in love with one of my older brother's friends, who was fourteen at the time. I still remember the "mushiness" that I felt in my heart whenever I saw him. We shared books, music, and everything that happened to us in our hometown and our school life. This relationship, like every important relationship I have had since then, was solidly grounded in my orbitofrontal brain-body connection. I'm a major "bonder" and have never been capable of sharing myself physically with someone unless there was also a sincere sharing of our hearts. My body simply won't let me.

I stayed with the same boyfriend right through the first year of medical school. (I went out on a few dates with other guys in college. I even fell head over heels with one. But when I went to visit him at his parents' house, he just wanted to watch soap operas on television with his mother—big red flag!) After that, I had another boyfriend who was part of my medical school class for two years. Then I met the man who became my husband, who was my surgical intern. I knew immediately that this was the real thing and married him nine months later at the age of twenty-five. We stayed happily married for twenty-four years, until my midlife growth spurt hit and it became clear that we were no longer on the same wavelength.

I was very fortunate that all my relationships with boys and men were loving ones. When sex is limited to a transaction to get something you want, you have to be able to disconnect your bonding circuits and your heart from the rest of your body—including your spirituality. Your body will eventually send you the bill for this. (The entire field of gynecological diseases is nothing more than a description of these various bills.)

THE SPIRITUAL CORE OF SEXUALITY

On the subatomic level, sex is everywhere. It is the mysterious binding energy that keeps the electrons spinning around the nucleus. It is the energy of God and spirit expressing itself in ever-changing, ever-evolving physical form. It is the life force that results in flowers blossoming in the spring and bringing forth fruit in the fall. It is the attracting energy that binds every part of the universe. In the mineral world, it is the force that binds elements together to form compounds. In humans, it's the desire and longing that attracts two people together to create something new. Mona Lisa Schulz, M.D., Ph.D., points out that the areas of the brain that are important for sex drive are the same ones that are involved in spirituality. Like every other aspect of the natural world, sex operates according to certain basic laws of the universe. This is stated brilliantly above the main door of the Mary Frances Searles Science Building at Bowdoin College: "Nature's Laws Are God's Thoughts." Sex also goes beyond physical procreation, as evidenced by the fact that humans continue to experience the sex drive long after their reproductive capacity is over. The older one gets, the more sex takes on a spiritual dimension, though that dimension is available at any stage of life. Sexual energy is the force behind creativity, sharing, and self-expression on all levels.

In an article entitled "Spiritual Sex: Beyond the Physical" that was published in my April 2004 e-letter (see www.drnorthrup.com, e-letters), sex researcher and author Linda Savage, Ph.D., author of *Reclaiming Goddess Sexuality,* wrote:

> Spiritual sex encompasses sexual energy that goes beyond physical sensations of pleasure, genital orgasms and even the loving connection of sexual communion. It is unlike the common view of sex, which is genital stimulation and the release of tension through orgasm. When it is consciously practiced, there is a quality of "mindfulness," which is heightened awareness and expanded consciousness. The more cosmic experiences utilizing sexual energy are most likely to occur in ecstatic states. The essence of spiritual sex is enhanced awareness, extraordinary inspiration, and a sense of merging with the life force.

In the broadest sense, sex is spirit seeking expression in physical form. That's why sexuality is so profoundly linked with spirituality—an idea that is familiar in many other cultures. In countless ancient temples throughout Southeast Asia, for example, there are carvings of divine beings locked in sexual embrace—a form of spiritual communion. And in India there is a rich tradition of temple priestesses that goes back thousands of years. These women were trained from girlhood to consecrate their bodies and sexuality to God. Though men came to the temples to have sex with them as a sacrament of spiritual cleansing, their sexuality could not be owned by any man.[3]

Imagine living in a culture where sex was a sacrament rather than a sin! In the Western world, however, there has long been a culturally embedded split between sexuality and spirituality. But now there's growing interest in naming and healing that schism. Dr. Savage continues, "It may seem outrageous to view sexuality in such lofty terms. Yet, it no longer makes sense to deny the spiritual dimension of our sexuality, as if we had 'lower' physical urges and 'higher' spiritual functions, disconnected from the body. Sexual energy is the source of our connection to the life force. . . ."

Sexual love is one of the most profound aspects of our roman-

tic lives—the physical act that allows us to make a reality of the longing for wholeness we all feel. A deep desire to unite with our beloved
is an essential part of being in love. Writing about sexual desire in
their book, *The Sacrament of Sexuality,* Morton Kelsey, an Episcopal
priest, and his wife, Barbara, say, "In this desire we can see the longing for union with the hidden parts of ourselves, with our souls, and
with God." When sex is truly an act of making love rather than taking from or exploiting another person, we feel whole because the
union we experience with the loved one puts us in touch with our
very soul. This is an opening to the Divine—an act that may culmi-
nate in our seeing our beloved as an expression of the Divine.

DISTORTED LOVE MAPS: A CULTURAL EPIDEMIC

It has been said that you can't heal a sexually repressed culture
by taking off its clothes. Our culture is the perfect example of this.
Although there is more explicit sex on television and in the movies
than ever before, the kind of sex we are exposed to is typical of a repressive culture—mechanistic, exploitative, demeaning to women.

When sexuality is divorced from spirituality and emotion, women are particularly susceptible to being hurt. It is, after all, a rare
woman who can regularly go out to bars, hook up with casual
strangers to have sex, and find it fulfilling. Given the hormonally
primed bonding and emotional circuits in most women's brains,
most will begin to form a bond after such an encounter and will ultimately be left feeling empty. Many women have told me they feel
far more lonely having a pseudorelationship with someone they're
not truly connected to than they do being by themselves.

Yet if we look at the media images of sexuality and love that are
beamed into our homes daily, what we see is a cultural love map dis-
tortion. These images normalize what is, in truth, a damaging approach to sexual behavior—the separation of love and caring from
sexuality. And they also devalue the female body by depicting an
ideal that almost no woman can live up to. Thanks to the media, we
have raised an entire generation of young men and women who have
unrealistic and impossible-to-fulfill ideas about what makes a
woman sexually attractive. Young men almost universally desire
semi-anorectic women with large breasts, a body type that is rare to
nonexistent in nature; and young women almost uniformly wish to
conform to that body type—except in the African-American community, whose men tend to like their women much more generously

endowed. Though one could argue that it's not really the media that are at fault here, I disagree. It is very well documented that both the content of TV programs and the amount of time spent watching can and does adversely affect the behavior of individuals, as I discuss below.

How Love and Sex Pathways Are Laid Down in the Brain and Body

From infancy on we are forming ideas about what sexual love between people looks and feels like. Our relationships with our mothers and fathers, their relationship with each other, what we see in the media and watch going on among the people who live in the world around us—all of these, for better or worse, have emotional and biological effects on an individual's inner love map. Usually a girl who has been raised by people who love and respect each other, and her, will know intuitively that love and sex go together. But depending on innate temperament and/or environment, a girl who has been heavily influenced by the mechanistic, soulless portrayals of sex in the media or on the Internet may experience a disconnect between her orbitofrontal bonding areas and her sex drive. In other words, she will find it difficult to truly feel the kind of loving bond with another that enhances sexual desire naturally.

We live in a culture that encourages this kind of disconnect. From the big-breasted, willowy bodies of the Victoria's Secret lingerie models (many of whom I'm sure have implants) to the hypersexualized (albeit funny and entertaining) content of such popular TV shows as *Sex and the City, Friends,* and *Will & Grace,* and the ubiquity of porn on the Internet, our culture is so saturated with unrealistic and often exploitative pictures of sexuality that it cannot help but affect our children's minds.

Unfortunately, no matter how hard we try, there's almost no way to prevent a daughter from being exposed to overly sexualized media content, because it is as common as dandelions. A study on the effects of the media by the American Academy of Pediatrics, for example, showed that the average young television viewer is exposed to greater than fourteen thousand sexual references each year.[4] This exposure has an effect. A recent prospective study by Rebecca Collins, Ph.D., of the Rand Corporation found that youth age twelve to seventeen who watched the most sex or sexual innuendo on TV—it didn't matter whether the show had explicit dialogue about sex or showed actual physical contact—were twice as likely to have sexual intercourse as those who didn't watch sexual content. And the sex was likely to be unprotected. Black youth who watched sexual content, however, were less likely to begin having intercourse, which is intriguing. According to this study, 46 percent of high school students had had sexual intercourse, which helps explain why the United States has one of the highest teen pregnancy rates in the industrialized world. And for every four sexually active teens, one is diagnosed with a sexually transmitted disease.[5] Yet popular television shows rarely show the adverse consequences of irresponsible sexual behavior such as AIDS and other sexually transmitted diseases like herpes, or unintended pregnancy.

Speaking Up about Pornography

Sexual addiction to online pornography Web sites is now a major problem that is eroding relationships and families. The Internet was not up and running until my children were in their middle teens, so this was something I never had to deal with. Now little kids are surfing the Net almost by the time they can sit up on their own! It's been estimated that about 40 percent of the Internet is devoted to pornography. Sooner or later, no matter what a parent does, a child is going to be exposed to sexually explicit material. It's important to be prepared for this.

How a daughter will be affected depends in part upon what her parents do, and in part on her own temperament. One of my patients remembers the first time she saw pornography. She was a very empathetic child and remembers feeling really bad for the women in the porno scenes. She said she could pick up on the women's sadness. She didn't want to look any further. Other people are attracted to pornography, even from a very early age. The daughter of one of my friends, who is only seven years old, managed to log on to a live video of a woman performing oral sex on a man. She wanted to know what would happen if he "had to go to the bathroom." She was obviously fascinated by the site and wanted to keep watching it. Although some children just seem to be drawn to sexually explicit material like moths to a flame, I would also say that this family's Internet controls weren't working well.

Parents have to monitor their children's media exposure and Internet use (especially young children's) and speak up about material that they think is inappropriate. My daughters used to love *Sex and the City*. Though it was well written and smart, I loathed it. And whenever I was in earshot of it, I kept up a running commentary on why I found it offensive.

When a parent talks to her child honestly about material that she finds offensive, explaining what is objectionable about it, whether it's a show that seems to her to undermine the beauty of sex by portraying it as exploitative and loveless or content that is downright pornographic, she will be arming her with helpful information. Do the best you can: know what your daughter is watching on TV and what sites she is visiting on the Internet, be aware of where she is in her free time and with whom—and speak your mind when you think she is out of bounds. She needs to know not just where you stand but that you are willing to *take* a stand when she is watching or doing something that you think will be harmful to her. This is part of Mother Bear wisdom.

One of my patients told me the following story about her daughter:

> When Sissy was fourteen, she had an online encounter with a sexually inappropriate individual. She was in a chat room on the Internet. Some guy asked what her measurements were. She responded by asking him how long his penis was. He told her that it was eleven inches long. She stayed in the chat room for a while longer, even though it was clear that he was a loser with nothing better to do than have exchanges like that with girls on the Internet. The reason I know this is because she told me. I couldn't understand why Sissy continued talking to him. I also didn't understand why she wanted to draw me into a conversation about him. I would have ignored him and signed off right away. But Sissy didn't. I don't understand it. And to tell you the truth, I'm a little worried about her.

Sissy's mother should be more than a little worried. This kind of behavior should alert a mother to the fact that her daughter's love and sex map is distorted. Her bonding circuits are being wired to respond to sexually provocative input, and she may end up engaging in risk-seeking sexual encounters far worse than mere chat-room exchanges. Sissy's mother needs to tell her daughter, in no uncertain terms, that she never wants this to happen again. Sissy must be made to understand that what she is doing is not only wrong but dangerous. Internet predators often prey on a young girl's needs for male interest and approval.

It's always best to talk openly and honestly about sexual content or sexual encounters that you consider inappropriate. If you clam up out of embarrassment, or declare that it is too disgusting even to discuss, you'll just shame and confuse your daughter—or stimulate even greater interest. Patrick Carnes, Ph.D., an expert on sexual addiction who cowrote *In the Shadows of the Net,* says that the epidemic of Internet porn addiction will finally force our society to get clear about sex.

I hope he's right. But to really realign our ideas about sex, we have to be honest with ourselves about our own experience.

GETTING YOUR SEXUAL HISTORY STRAIGHT

As I've said, I have spent much of my career on the front lines of women's health, dealing with what happens to women's bodies, minds, and spirits as a result of their sexual beliefs and behaviors. And a lot of it is just plain painful. I've seen countless women with herpes or warts that they caught from a sexual partner who wasn't truthful about his own sexual history (or didn't even know he was contagious). I've also seen several tragic cases in which teenage girls developed pelvic inflammatory disease from sexually transmitted disease with a resulting loss of fertility. And then there's the unwanted pregnancies. The list goes on and on—much of it related to the culture of secrecy and shame that surrounds sex in our culture.

No mother is under any obligation to share her sexual past with her daughter, of course. This is especially true when doing so would serve no purpose. What she is obligated to do, however, is make sure that she has confronted, to the best of her ability, any past sexual trauma or disappointment that may influence the legacy she passes on to her daughter. In my experience, it is not a mother's history of abuse or promiscuity that is the problem in a mother-daughter legacy; it is the fact that it is taboo that destines it to be repeated in subsequent generations, until the pattern is brought to consciousness and healed.

When I was a resident at St. Margaret's Hospital for Women in Dorchester, Massachusetts, it was connected with St. Mary's Home for Unwed Mothers. (Both institutions are now closed.) A social worker who had worked at St. Mary's for twenty years and had helped arrange dozens of adoptions for the babies of these unwed mothers told me that she would never adopt a baby herself. When I asked her why, she said, "Because I've seen a repeated pattern here that is very troubling. You can't imagine how many of these babies

who are given up for adoption seem to then get pregnant themselves—at exactly the same age that their mothers did with them. It's
uncanny. And these babies were all placed in good, loving homes!" I
don't think it's the fact of adoption itself that was the problem, or
anything in the genetic legacy of the birth mother—rather it is the secrecy that used to surround the adoption process, and the failure to
level with adopted children about the facts surrounding their birth.
Today's emphasis on more honesty and openness about adoptions is
a step in the right direction.

SEX IS NATURAL, NOT SHAMEFUL

Life itself is sexually transmitted! So when we reduce our discussion
of sex to the mechanics of it—how to avoid pregnancy and sexually
transmitted diseases, and how to minimize the discomforts of menstruation—we do a grave disservice to young people. Trying to teach an
adolescent the basics of reproductive health and well-being without
also celebrating the link between sex, love, creativity, and spirituality is
like trying to explain the beauty of a Beethoven symphony by teaching
someone how to take apart the radio on which the music is playing!

At puberty, a girl's body begins to awaken to and participate in
the magnificent rhythms of the universal life force seeking expression
through her. As a result, she is, quite naturally, filled with longing and
desire. Libido infuses the whole world around her with its associated
emotions and sensations, heightening the beauty and drama of everything in her environment. That's why adolescents are certain that
they're the first ones to have discovered and truly appreciated the
glory of a full moon or the delight of walking on a beach at sunset.

Though sex has been called sinful and shameful by many religious leaders, sexual desire is a natural, normal part of life. From
birth to death, this life force courses through our bodies, demanding
expression and fulfillment. Unity minister Catherine Ponder put it
this way: "The only forbidding (and forbidden!) thing about sex is
man's gross misunderstanding and consequent misuse of this great
life force."[6] I couldn't agree more.

When a young woman accepts her physical desires as a manifestation of the universe's creative energy, she learns to trust and respect her
body and her sexuality at the most fundamental level. She knows her
sexuality is about much more than physical gratification, just as religion and spirituality are about far more than listening to a minister in
a church. She grows up unashamed of her innate sexuality, knowing

that it is an aspect of her spirituality expressing itself through her body, and that the erotic can be holy. As a result of honoring this aspect of herself, she can learn to express and share her sexuality with discretion and in ways that enhance her self-esteem and self-worth.

A good first step in helping your daughter understand the way in which her sexual being is ultimately an expression of the divine life force is through a discussion of her menstrual cycle. By the age of fourteen most girls will be quite familiar with the mechanics of the cycle—though it's always good to review it with them, for example when in the cycle do they ovulate, for how long do they remain fertile, and so forth. But beyond the mechanics, you need to make sure they know something about the meaning of the menstrual cycle.

Tamara Slayton, founder of the Menstrual Health Foundation, points the way to this larger vision of women's cyclical rhythms:

> It has been suggested that the movement and preparation of the female egg for possible fertilization is a recapitulation of the coming into being of the earth and humanity—that stored within a woman's monthly cycle is an ancient memory of the evolution of spirit into matter. To find our way to this memory of cosmic origins is our task as women preparing for the future.

THE MENSTRUAL CYCLE, CREATIVITY, AND SEXUALITY

The life force that governs the menstrual cycle is the same life force that governs the waxing and the waning of the moon and the ebb and flow of the tides. Girls need to know that their bodies and cycles are part of this miraculous process. All human beings are here on Earth thanks to this cycle! Likewise, the accompanying sex drive and the natural release of orgasm are not only completely normal and natural, they are hardwired into the species as powerful incentives to keep the species going by engaging in the joy of the physical act of creation. Trying to deny, ignore, or denigrate this powerful urge is like trying to stop the earth from turning. It's not possible. The sex drive, like the element of fire, can be either destructive or regenerative depending upon how it is channeled. And with the rewiring of the frontal-lobe circuitry that occurs at puberty, young adults are beginning to have the neurologic ability to control and channel their appetites. Without such control and discipline, no real freedom is possible.

The menstrual cycle governs the flow not only of bodily fluids but also of mood and creativity. Encourage your daughter to observe how she feels at different times during her cycle, emotionally and spiritually as well as physically. For example, she may notice that her energy, creativity, and libido are full speed ahead at ovulation. And she may notice that she becomes far more inward and introspective just before her period is due. Help her to understand that the reason these changes occur is because the menstrual cycle mirrors the creative process. There are times when you get lots of creative insights and have the energy to act on them. And then there are times when you have to leave a project and "put it on the back burner" to simmer. When a young woman learns how to work consciously with the universal energies of her cycle, she develops a deep trust in and respect for her body. As a result, she is far less likely to share it with someone who doesn't also respect her. I hope the following description of menstrual wisdom will help a girl see her menstrual cycle in a completely new way.

The Extroverted Phase: Onset of Period to Ovulation

From the onset of a period until ovulation, the body is ripening an egg—and, symbolically at least, preparing to give birth to someone or something else. This is known as the follicular phase, the time when a girl's energy is most likely to be high and to be focused on the world around her—relationships with friends and family, schoolwork, extracurricular projects and activities. Estrogen, which favors "outer focus," is rising now. It is common for a girl to feel filled with enthusiasm and new ideas. This is a good time to initiate new projects.

The Receptive Phase: Ovulation

At midcycle, a girl ovulates. An egg is released and the cervical mucus provides a virtual superhighway for sperm to get to the newly ripened egg for conception. Ovulation is accompanied by the same attracting energy that electrons exert within each atom of matter. The increasing estrogen levels that build toward ovulation are now accompanied by a rise in testosterone, which intensifies a girl's sexual feelings, and by an abrupt rise of the neuropeptides FSH (follicle-stimulating hormone) and LH (luteininizing hormone), which help orchestrate ovulation, and also heighten her sexual receptiveness. At the same time that the girl is experiencing the intensified sexual feelings created by all this hormonal activity, she secretes specific pheromones that make her more attractive to others. If she has a boyfriend, the three days or so surrounding ovulation are the time when he is most likely to push for sexual expression in some form. In other words, he "won't be able to keep his hands off her."

But fertility has a meaning beyond the sexual. During ovulation, a girl is fertile in many other ways, making her naturally more receptive to others and to new ideas. I call this being ripe for cross-pollination of all kinds.

The first two weeks of the cycle are all about doing and acting, mingling one's energy with others and being available to them on many different levels. Our society values women's outer focus and sexual receptiveness as "good," and as a result, girls internalize this value and come to see these first two stages of their cycle as "the best times of the month."

The Reflective Phase: Ovulation to Onset of Period

The second half of the cycle, which begins once ovulation is over, is known as the luteal phase. Estrogen levels remain constant at this phase, and progesterone levels rise at this time, because the egg that ovulated leaves behind a small area in the ovary that changes into what is known as corpus luteum, a small area that produces progesterone. Progesterone has a calming and introspective effect and helps a girl turn her attention inward toward herself, especially during the first couple of days of her period. This is the time for a girl to look back on what she's been doing, to evaluate what is working in her life and what isn't, and to think about how she is going to respond and change. She may need to adjust her diet, her friendships, her study habits, and so on. Her more inward focus during this phase of her cycle is perfect for writing in a journal, meditating, taking long walks, and other introspective activities.

Many girls feel slowed down and moody during this time and may beat themselves up for what they see as their lethargy. Tell your daughter that she's not meant to be upbeat and outgoing all the time. What she is feeling is a natural part of the creative process. The right hemisphere of the brain, which is the more intuitive part of the brain, is particularly active now. That makes the last days of the luteal phase an ideal time for accessing inner guidance. (If she doesn't pay attention and heed this guidance, the result could be PMS and other symptoms—crying louder to get her attention!)

The Resting Phase: Menstrual Period

Menstrual bleeding begins when estrogen and progesterone levels reach their lowest point. The flow of blood can be thought of as a monthly "clean out" of not only the body but also the mind and spirit. It's no wonder that so many girls feel less energy on the first day or two of their period. Many also feel a little crampy. Mild cramps can be relieved by a hot bath, heating pad, or simply by slowing down and breathing deeply through the nose. The body naturally wants to slow down a little. That doesn't mean a girl can't play sports or go about her normal activities if she feels like it. What it does mean is that she needs to be more caring, compassionate, and generous with herself. Her "skin" is thinner during this phase. This is a perfect time to spend more time at home, sorting through closets or drawers, going through old papers, or in some other way working consciously with the body's "letting go" and "cleaning out" energy.

However, because our culture is overly focused on incessant activity and productivity, girls are often reluctant to get the rest they need. Let your daughter know that this is her monthly "gift." In

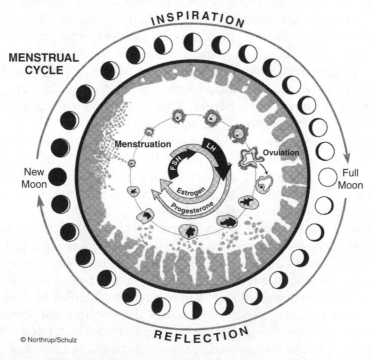

THE MENSTRUAL CYCLE AND LUNAR WISDOM

many cultures, women and girls went to moon lodges when they were menstruating. Their meals were prepared and brought to them by others, and they simply enjoyed a monthly retreat. One of the most inspiring accounts of women taking this kind of time for themselves comes from the Yurok people of Northern California, who believe that a menstruating woman should isolate herself from mundane duties during her period because this is the time when she is at the height of her powers. Rather than wasting her energy on household chores, she is supposed to devote herself to concentrated meditation in order to find out the purpose of her life, and to accumulate spiritual energy. She knows that she can use this energy to purify herself for spiritual accomplishment.[7]

Assure your daughter that the way she feels is an authentic expression of what her body really needs, and that she should do what she can to meet those needs—resting, reflecting, staying close to home if that's what feels good to her. She can have a little "moon lodge" celebration in the privacy of her own mind. (See Resources.)

In summary, the menstrual cycle is a monthly opportunity to work consciously with our creativity, transform difficulties, and begin anew. All girls need to know that their cycle can help connect them to their feminine wisdom once they learn to respect it and work consciously with it.

ACKNOWLEDGING AND CHANNELING ADOLESCENT LIBIDO

Girls feel the sex drive in their bodies long before they are psychologically ready to commit to marriage and the demands of a mature relationship. That's why some indigenous cultures have sanctioned sexual experimentation among young people so they can "get it out of their systems" early on.

But regardless of whether or not a culture has or used to have a way to allow adolescents to learn about sexuality directly from each other, it's clear that girls in these societies marry far earlier than they do in Western industrialized society. It's also clear that girls in times past were quite different biologically from those today. Our modern lifestyle with its ample food supplies, artificial light, and decreased physical activity, as well as the explosion of sexually provocative material in the mass media, has resulted in earlier puberty, more regular ovulation, and greater sexual receptivity and fertility than in the past.

The bottom line is this: The average time between the onset of puberty and the formation of a committed, mutually respectful sexual relationship with an appropriate partner is longer now than it has ever been in recorded human history. That's a lot of years to be expected to "just say no" to something as strong as the normal human sex drive. More than ever before, girls need to know healthy ways to deal with their sexuality. But our simultaneously sex-obsessed and sexually repressed culture offers them very little guidance on how to do this.

How to Consciously Direct Sexual Desire and Longing

Sex is a dynamic force that encompasses far more than just physical desire. It is the creative desire for positive expression in every aspect of life. In the words of Unity minister Catherine Ponder: "The grand secret about sex is that it can be transmuted and directed through your thoughts, attitudes, and actions to benefit every phase of your world!"[8] It's far better for girls to learn how to channel their libido constructively rather than risk abusive or unsatisfactory relationships of any kind. But channeling libido does not mean trying to suppress it. Nor should girls be taught to feel guilty about sexual desire or longings. Instead, they should understand that it's possible to consciously direct libido and to express it in nonharmful ways. They should also understand that it's normal to have sexual dreams and thoughts, some of which may seem inappropriate or downright immoral. This is just part of being human.

SELF-PLEASURING UNTIL THE RIGHT ONE COMES ALONG

Though achieving orgasmic release through masturbation is certainly not the same as the profound fulfillment one feels in a mutually committed and loving sexual relationship, it is a very effective and normal way for an adolescent girl to deal with her sexual energy. One of my patients, who learned to masturbate only when she was in her thirties, described her experience this way:

> Discovering the pleasures of a vibrator was liberating for me. I couldn't believe that something this good could be free. It was like discovering Disney World right in my own body. Up until that time, I had gotten myself in some

> pretty awful relationships because my sex drive is really high. But as soon as I discovered that I was able to take care of this energy myself, I found that I no longer felt as though I had to compromise myself in relationships just to get the sexual release I needed. My relationships since that time have been far healthier as a result.

All of us have the capacity to express our sexual energy on three different levels: physically, mentally and emotionally, and spiritually.

1. Physically: The life force that finds expression through orgasm is actually the basis for one's bodily energy, health, and vitality. One of the reasons why athletes are sometimes cautioned against having sex before athletic competitions is so that they won't dissipate too much of that vital energy.

2. Mentally and Emotionally: The life force finds expression not just in physical ways but through the use of one's ideas and talents, one's intellectual and emotional urgings, one's ideas and intuitive insights. Art, music, literature, movies, books, scientific break-throughs—all are examples of consciously channeling the emotional and mental aspects of vital life force.

3. Spiritually: The life force finds an outlet through our desire to know the true nature of God and the universe. It is the thirst for knowledge, spiritual insight, and understanding. When an individual consciously does good work either by herself or as part of a group, she is expressing life force on the spiritual level. Whenever you care deeply for another being and love that person unconditionally, you are channeling the spiritual as well as the emotional aspects of the life force. Something as simple as a walk in the woods, the act of taking in the sights and sounds and smells of nature, can also be a spiritual transaction.

ESSENTIAL SEX EDUCATION FOR TEENAGERS

If I ruled the world, I'd make sure that all teens knew about both male and female sexual anatomy, including how their bodies respond sexually, how one gets pregnant, when, and why. I'd also give out information on how they can protect themselves from pregnancy, and from the risk of sexually transmitted diseases. Because the subject of sex arouses such heated emotions, I'd teach girls and boys separately in an environment where they felt safe and able to ask whatever questions they needed to get answered. And I would teach them about more than the mere mechanics of sex. I'd let them know the whole truth—that young men and women are capable of using their sex drive consciously, respectfully, and responsibly if they choose to.

WHAT ALL ADOLESCENT GIRLS NEED TO KNOW ABOUT SEX

⁓ How to value themselves and their bodies, including their capacity for pleasure

⁓ The sexuality-spirituality connection

⁓ The facts about both male and female sexual anatomy

⁓ The facts about how to prevent pregnancy and protect oneself against sexually transmitted disease. (This information has never been shown to increase the likelihood of a teenager's having sex.)

Principle One: Making love is different from having sex.

There's a crucial difference, both biochemically and neurologically, between making love as an extension of one's emotional bond with someone and having "casual" sex with someone you don't really care about. The current term *hooking up* is only too accurate a description for the kind of loveless, uncommitted sexual relationships that are now commonly depicted in the mainstream media.

That kind of casual coupling may work for some, depending upon temperament. The writers of *Sex and the City* made it seem as though it worked for Samantha for quite some time (I don't believe it). But by program's end even Samantha had succumbed to the love of a good man! It may have taken breast cancer to get her to that place (very telling) but she, like all the other women on the show, eventually found true love. In fact, the entire last season of *Sex and the City* seemed to be dedicated to putting love and sex back together.

For most women, as Carrie and her friends seem to have concluded, there's a problem with having sex outside of a loving relationship. If a woman is having sex without love, the biochemistry isn't the same. She may have to use pot or alcohol in order to loosen up. Casual sex may be exciting at first, but in order to keep it stimulating over time, a woman will have to ramp up her arousal circuits through artificial means. (That must have been why Samantha was such an expert on props!) If no emotional bond is present or if anger, disappointment, or other unfinished emotional business is clogging those circuits, then it's much, much harder to get sexually aroused.

In contrast, if you're kissing or making love with the right person for the right reasons, the relationship itself is intoxicating enough. The solid, loving connection causes the brain's orbitofrontal bonding circuits to supply the hormones that keep desire coursing through one's veins. When the physical act of sex is combined with a meeting of the mind, emotions, and spirit, sex becomes a deeply rewarding, health-giving act for both participants. In relationships in which a couple truly loves and appreciates each other, it doesn't much matter what kind of "technique" they use. Though they may employ a wide range of fantasies and props for the fun of it, ultimately the sex is satisfying because of the attractive force of their mutual love and appreciation for each other.

Principle Two: Not everyone is "doing it."

In sharp contrast to the sexual revolution of the 1960s and '70s, there's now a growing trend among teens to abstain from intercourse, despite the fact that the television shows geared toward teens would have you believe that everyone is "doing it." According to the Centers for Disease Control, the number of high school students who say they've never had sexual intercourse rose by 10 percent from 1991 to 2001. Young people attributed their decision to remain abstinent to caring parents, a desire to gain more control over their own lives before having sex, and a sense of unreadiness. I've certainly met a lot of young women in both my practice and my daughters' circles of friends who have felt this way and stayed virgins—at least until college.

Principle Three: Oral sex is sex.

Although intercourse among teens may be on the decline, oral sex seems definitely to be on the increase. A recent study of 212 tenth graders showed that they were much more likely to engage in oral sex than sexual intercourse. And most (70 percent) didn't use protection, such as condoms, during oral sex. Forty percent of the boys and girls surveyed said they had engaged in oral sex within the past year and over 25 percent of those who had had oral sex said that they'd had three or more sexual partners in the past year.[9]

Many teens define sex only as intercourse. But no matter what anyone says, oral sex *is* sex. And as practiced by most teenagers, it's a particularly degrading form of sex for girls, since it is not usually reciprocal. Instead, oral sex is a "service" that girls provide for boys without getting anything in return—except the fleeting attention of a boy and an increased risk of sexually transmitted diseases.

ORAL SEX AND STDs

There's been a recent rise in sexually transmitted disease among teenagers, in part due to oral sex practices. Three million American teenagers become infected with one or more STDs each year, including bacterial infections like chlamydia, gonorrhea, and viral infections, including HIV and AIDS. Though the risk of getting an STD through oral sex is lower than with intercourse, it is definitely possible to become infected with STDs during oral sex.

Engaging in oral sex does, of course, provide sexual release for the boy without the risk of pregnancy for the girl. But a girl's self-esteem has to be pretty poor to allow her mouth to be used as a vehicle for a guy to relieve his sexual tension. There's not a chance that this could ever be considered a spiritual experience, let alone one based on mutual respect and love (unless the couple is monogamous and the girl's sexual pleasure matters as much as the boy's does).

Perhaps what the girls think they're getting out of the experience is "popularity." In a study by Mitchell Prinstein, Ph.D., sexually active teens were viewed as more popular by their peers.[10] Here's a story that a friend of mine just related:

> One day I picked up the phone and was horrified to hear my fourteen-year-old daughter talking to a boy about giving him a blow job. I was shocked, to say the least. I immediately interrupted the call, telling the two of them that I had overheard everything and that if they ever talked about this again or acted

on it I would immediately call his parents and alert the school. Afterward, when I asked my daughter to tell me what was going on, she confessed that she had fallen in with a clique at school and was trying to earn their respect and loyalty. They had apparently "dared" her to call this guy and offer oral sex. She told me she had no intention of following through with it. It was just a prank. Prank or no prank, I told her that any further instances of this behavior would result in her being taken out of school and sent to an all-girls academy that was nearby. To impress upon her the potential seriousness of the situation, I also asked a friend who worked at Planned Parenthood to come over to the house and show my daughter graphic textbook pictures of girls with venereal warts and herpetic sores on their tongues and lips—all the result of giving "blow jobs."

For teenage girls to be providing oral sex to boys as a way to earn popularity is certainly one of the more saddening aspects of our culture's double standard when it comes to sexuality and the status of women.

Principle Four: The double standard is alive and well.

One of the ongoing challenges adolescent girls face is the fact that Western culture applies a double standard to male and female sexuality, with the sexual needs of males being viewed as far more important than the needs of females. Our culture focuses on a male dominator archetype of sexuality where the size of erections and the number of sexual conquests are what is most important, not true intimacy. It's little wonder that so many men must resort to Viagra for sexual performance: they haven't learned how to connect their penises to their hearts. This type of male sexuality (which is also degrading to the spiritual side of men) has been glorified, while female sexuality has been vilified and controlled at every turn.

The historical and archeologic research of Riane Eisler, Ph.D., author of *The Chalice and the Blade;* Merlin Stone, author of *When God Was a Woman;* and archeologist Marija Gimbutas, Ph.D., has documented that this patriarchal arrangement hasn't always been the norm on planet Earth. For at least thirty thousand years, egalitarian cultures that worshiped the feminine aspect of God, and celebrated female sexuality, lived peacefully in Old Europe, the Middle East, and the Indus Valley. Anthropologist Helen Fisher, Ph.D., also provides evidence of indigenous tribes in Canada, Africa, and Australia that had far more egalitarian arrangements as recently as the late 1800s. Unfortunately, European influence eventually lowered the status of women even in these places. After becoming indoctrinated by colonial Europeans, the tribes in Africa and Canada began beating women for the first time![11]

Though it's encouraging to think that there is nothing inevitable about the patriarchal model of sexuality and that we can someday change it, the fact remains that even in the wake of the very powerful feminist movement of the 1960s and '70s, the double standard is still determining many of our attitudes. For example, very few girls come of age feeling proud of their bodies and knowing that their sexuality is as strong and vital and in need of expression as a boy's. In her book *Promiscuities,* Naomi Wolf recounts stories of adolescent girls who were initially fascinated by their changing bodies, but who were put down by other girls when they dared admire themselves in the mirror or celebrate themselves in any way. Because of such attitudes, few girls know that when female sexuality is honored, it is a force that can enhance their entire lives.

A boy is expected to have sexual experiences as part of his birthright, though these experiences are apt to be termed *getting laid,* not *making love.* In other words, there's not supposed to be anything spiritual or loving about them. A boy's reputation for being a "stud" and a "player" is all that is at stake, not his heart or his soul. However, a girl who engages in anywhere close to the same behavior as a boy is considered "loose" or, in today's parlance, a "ho."

Girls may think they're proving themselves the equals of boys by emulating them in their sexual behavior, but aside from the question of whether that behavior is good for either a boy or a girl, there's the simple fact that this culture values males more highly than females. Because most boys have more social clout than most girls, male attention confers status and is considered highly desirable. That's why girls who lack good self-esteem are vulnerable to being pressured into having intercourse or providing oral sex to boys who don't care about or respect them. From their standpoint, male attention, regardless of how fleeting, is worth the price they pay.

A girl needs to understand that her self-worth cannot be enhanced in any sustainable way by engaging in sexual activity with a partner who has only a physical connection with her. As many a girl has learned to her great regret, giving herself so freely may in fact do just the opposite, both because of the way it makes her feel and because of the way people—including the boy whom she "serviced"—are likely to talk about her and look down on her.

Principle Five: Your body is your own.

Thanks in part to the pervasive influence of the media, now much aided and abetted by the Internet, many young girls feel pressured to have sex long before they want to. The younger they are when they first have sex, the more they regret it later. A 1998 public opinion poll of sexually active youths ages twelve to fourteen showed that 81 percent of them (both female and male) said they wished they had waited longer. This study showed that 14 to 20 percent of girls have had sex by the age of fourteen, often under the influence of alcohol. In fact, there's a direct relationship between a girl's use of alcohol and the likelihood of her having sex—and not using contraception.[12]

Regret is common in older teens as well. A survey of young men and women age twenty to twenty-one in New Zealand found that 54 percent of the women who had lost their virginity wish they had waited longer to have their first sexual experience. Here are some other highlights from this recent survey:

> The average age at first sexual intercourse was sixteen for women and seventeen for men.
>
> Curiosity was the main reason for virginity loss in 27 percent of women and 35 percent of men.
>
> Seven percent of women felt forced into their first experience.
>
> Only 15 percent of the women were in love at the time.
>
> Ten percent of women and men admitted to being a *little* drunk at the time.
>
> Thirty percent of women said the act was "on the spur of the moment."[13]

Mothers who can help their daughters to understand that they should never feel coerced into doing anything they don't want to do are providing them with an excellent tool for resisting peer pressure. Sometimes, as a parent, you actually have a chance to witness your children reaping the benefits of such advice. One night my daughter Annie had a party at our house with both boys and girls present. It was late at night when about six of them went out into the hot tub on our back deck. From my bedroom, where they assumed I was asleep, I overheard one of the girls suggest that they should all take off their clothes because clothes are simply a stupid convention of society. From the way the other kids responded, this remark clearly made most of them somewhat uncomfortable, probably because none of them had been drinking. (We didn't allow alcohol, marijuana, or smoking at our daughters' gatherings. And since neither of my daughters liked the behavior of those who have used these mood-altering substances, they preferred that their friends not come to their gatherings already prelubricated with alcohol.) Just then I heard my daughter come up with a perfect reply for the situation: "I don't think that's a good idea," she said, "because then, when the time comes that you might want to see someone naked for the first time, the initial thrill would be gone." One of the boys chimed in that he completely agreed, and added, "Undressing a girl for the first time is one of the biggest turn-ons there is." Though I have no idea whether he'd ever experienced that personally, I loved the way both he and my daughter saved face while also staying in their comfort zones and keeping their bathing suits on! And I was really impressed, because even in adulthood I've sometimes found it difficult to stand up for myself in comparable circumstances.

For example, once after a long day of medical meetings held at a beautiful private home, a group of my mostly male colleagues went out onto the back deck and were soaking nude in the hot tub. Some were drinking scotch and others were smoking cigars. They boisterously yelled for me to take off my clothes and join them. Joining them felt truly uncomfortable. Every cell in my body told me that this was the last activity on the planet that would help me relax or enjoy myself. So I smiled and told them that I was going to pass. They persisted, but I resisted. Later, I worried that these individuals, some newfound colleagues, would think that I was an uptight New Englander. I was about thirty-one at the time and eager to be accepted. So I found myself going over the situation repeatedly in my head and second-guessing my own inner wisdom. Was I a prude? Did I have issues about my body and nakedness?

Eventually I came to the simple conclusion that what this group thought about me didn't matter. Their activity simply didn't feel safe or appealing to me at that time, even though I had enjoyed a productive day of medical meetings with the same individuals. Now, with the meetings over, I simply did not feel called to open myself to their energy by getting into a hot tub naked with them. I have subsequently discovered that my feelings about nudity in a group are entirely dependent on the intent of the group. When there is a sense of respect and no hidden agenda, nudity is not a problem.

Sometimes nudity can be sexually abusive. One of my patients said that when she was a young teen her father routinely walked by her room naked and with a full erection. Though he never came in, this behavior made her very uncomfortable. I call this emotional incest. My experience is that anytime you feel uncomfortable with nudity in any context, you are responding to another person's lack of respect for your boundaries, at best, or to a hidden agenda, at worst.

Principle Six: Knowledge is power, always.

All teens need a solid sex education. Sex is a virtually inevitable part of adult life. Though I feel strongly that education about the advantages of abstinence should be offered, I'm also convinced that teens need to be taught everything from how to use a condom to all the different forms of birth control and how to use them. They also need to know about the female fertility cycle and when pregnancy is most likely to occur. In addition, they need to know how to protect themselves from sexual predators, STDs, and unwanted pregnancy. There's absolutely no evidence that teaching girls about safe sex and birth control will promote sexual activity, despite the opinions of a vocal minority.

As the children of a gynecologist, my daughters were brought up with pelvic models that they played with in my office. They also knew all about condoms and birth control from the time they were in elementary school. I remember once at dinner, we were talking about donor insemination, a procedure I did regularly at the office. My older daughter, who was eight years old at the time, said, "You can get AIDS from that." Of course she was correct. Another time she was baited on the school bus by a group of older girls who asked her if she knew what a condom was. She replied, "Yes, it's something you use when you don't want to get pregnant." Anne said, "They backed away from me real fast, because I was obviously not a good target for their little game."

WISDOM CHALLENGE: *Making Sure Your Daughter Is Protected*

Like it or not, some girls are going to have sex when they are teenagers. They need to be protected. Over the years, I've seen many young women who were brought by their mothers to obtain birth control and others who came to my office alone to ask for it. My philosophy has always been that it is my job to assist the girl or woman who is my patient. And that is why I have always provided girls with both the information and the birth control options that are most appropriate for them—whether or not their mothers have been present. Though it's always ideal to have the mother involved, sometimes circumstances mitigate against this.

Every girl who is sexually active needs a yearly pelvic exam and Pap smear. And of course she also needs to know how to protect herself from both STDs and pregnancy. I believe that if a mother wants to make sure her daughter gets what she needs but isn't sure her daughter will admit to her that she is having sex, she should give her doctor written permission to supply her daughter with the necessary information and protection whenever she asks for it.

One of my e-letter subscribers wrote that soon after her daughter started getting her period, she let her know what was required of her now that she was entering into the world of grown-ups:

> I told her that the onset of adulthood means taking on certain responsibilities as well as certain freedoms. One of the so-called "freedoms" is to respond to the sex urge. Along with the pleasures of a sexual relationship there are also many pitfalls—unwanted pregnancy, sexually transmitted diseases, etc. And while her father and I were raising her with a certain set of mores, which we hoped she would abide by as she continued to mature, she also needed to understand that we would always love her and be supportive of her. We talked about unplanned pregnancies and abortion. We talked about sexually transmitted diseases, which I admitted to not having enough knowledge about. (We went to Planned Parenthood to get the information.)
>
> When my daughter was ready to leave for college, I sat with her and we talked about perhaps getting her birth control pills. I was the proactive person in that discussion. My viewpoint was that I did not want her to get herself into a situation by accident

and not be prepared. At first she declined. A few days later she came back to me and said she had given my conversation much thought and, while she would not actually start to use them, she would also feel better having them at her disposal. I do not know exactly when she became sexually active. What I do know is that she entered into that relationship fully prepared, with full knowledge of all possible pitfalls, and a full understanding of all the pros and cons.

Now, that's a good mother!

BOY-GIRL DYNAMICS

Learning How to Act Around Boys

All girls need the opportunity to interact with boys in a normal, developmentally appropriate way. It's not possible or helpful to try to protect a daughter from the world of boys and men. She needs exposure to that world in order to learn discernment about who to trust and who not to trust; who is worthy of her time and attention and who isn't; who will support and respect her and who won't. Adolescent dating and socializing is the container in which she will learn these things directly.

A mother (or father) who forbids a daughter to date or tells her that boys only want one thing, will, depending upon the temperament of the child, stifle a daughter's budding sexuality and sense of self-esteem—or catalyze a full-scale rebellion. One of my friends remembers that her mother reduced the entire discussion about boys and dating to the following refrain: "Don't shame us. Don't come home pregnant." My patient said that she barely knew what pregnancy was at that time.

Another told me that her mother wouldn't let her go out with boys when she was in high school. "We'll have none of that" was her mother's blanket statement about dating. The only place Mary was able to interact with boys her own age was at the YMCA where she taught swimming. After all, she said, "Since the Y was the Young Men's *Christian* Association, my mother couldn't very well object to my activities there." To break free from those and other unreasonable restrictions, Mary went away to college and never looked back. At college, she had sex for the first time and enjoyed a close relationship with her boyfriend for a couple years. She also dated a few other young men and eventually married a man whom she has been very happy with.

Mary's older sister, Sherry, however, adhered completely to the family tribal programming. She never dated, and because her parents believed that daughters should live at home until marriage, she stayed under their roof throughout her college years. She met the man who would become her husband in her senior year. He was the first man Sherry had ever dated, and she married him soon after her college graduation. The marriage turned out to be a disaster. Sherry had been attracted to her husband because he was good-looking, but she didn't have enough experience to have any discernment about men, and he turned out to be a person who was more interested in skiing and biking than in getting a job or helping to support the family that Sherry wanted. Because she had never individuated from her parents enough to leave them behind when she got married, Sherry didn't go far from home—she made sure that she and her husband found a house in the same neighborhood that her parents lived in. And she turned to her father, not her husband, for help with everything from household repairs to car trouble. The marriage lasted less than a year. And a second marriage also ended in divorce about five years later.

Fathers, Daughters, and Dating

A girl's father and his attitudes about women create an indelible imprint upon her psyche about her own worth and also about what to expect from a man. If he is warm, loving, and attentive, then she's apt to choose a man who is similar. If, on the other hand, her father is cold, distant, abusive, or possessive, this will also influence a daughter.

Once, when I was about fourteen and my boyfriend had broken up with me for a few months, I was feeling distraught and very depressed. My father gave me a hug and made me feel valuable and attractive despite my lack of a boyfriend. He said, "There are many other fishes in the sea. Right now you can't see that. But believe me, you are blue chip stock. Don't sell yourself short or spend much time pining over that guy. There will be lots of others in your future." I am very grateful to have had a father like that. But even the most loving fathers can instill in their daughters a sense of unease about relations with the opposite sex. My father let me know that I was valuable with or without validation from a boyfriend, but he did it without trying to scare me off from men. Not all fathers are able to do this. For example, a patient told me about a conversation she had had with her husband and two teenage daughters:

> Recently we were having a family brunch at a local restaurant. The girls hadn't received their allowance for a while and we were discussing their monetary needs. My older girl, who is fifteen, asked us what sort of allowance each of us had had in high school and college. My husband, John, said that at the time he was in college in the late '60s, the boy still paid for everything on a date. So his parents supplied him with about $120 a month, to cover car upkeep, dating expenses, clothes, etc. But he told our daughters that when they started to date, he wanted them to pay their share of the expenses rather than letting the boy treat them. I asked my husband why he thought the girls should pay. He said, "Because when the guy pays for dinner and a movie or a show, then he may feel that the girl owes him something more." I asked him to elaborate. He said, "Well, at least a good-night kiss." I said, "Even if she doesn't like him?" He didn't want to go on, but made it clear to our daughters that boys feel that if a date pays for everything, there is an automatic power imbalance in the relationship and the girl "owes" something in return for his investment.

Obviously men in our culture can be quite ambivalent when it comes to their daughters and their relationships with men. My personal financial planner told me that in the course of her work she's never yet met a man who felt that his son-in-law was capable of taking care of his daughter! Before we were married and before we had even decided if we were going to have children, I remember my husband saying something like, "If we ever have a daughter, I'm going to build a fence around the house when she turns thirteen." Remember, he didn't even know if we were going to have children. Yet the very thought of having a daughter brought up his instinct to protect them from other men.

Beauty Tries to Save the Beast: The Danger of "Love Addiction"

One of the recurring archetypes in our Western culture is that of the bad boy in the black leather jacket riding a motorcycle. He is James Dean, Danny in *Grease,* Marlon Brando in *On the*

Waterfront. He lives on the edge—and he operates outside the boundaries of her parents' world. To many a girl, he represents a passport to individuation. And also the perfect chance to "stick it" to her parents, whose authority she is apt to be testing. This type of guy can be magnetically attractive to women, offering them both the chance to "save" him with their goodness and also the possibility of sexual pleasure. He becomes a personal project. Note the word *project*—because that's exactly what he is. He is a blank screen onto which a girl projects all of the sexual and spiritual energy that she has not consciously identified as her own. This type of guy is narcissistic and needs her love and attention to "complete" him. And while he's feeding on this love, he will give her all of his attention and make her feel special because "she is the only person who understands him." Narcissistic and empty inside, he can also be dangerous because once he has "hooked" a girl, he will do whatever it takes to keep her attention focused on him. If a girl is using drugs or alcohol or in some other ways has blunted her inner guidance system, she may get taken for a dangerous ride.

I'll never forget the time I took my seventeen- and nineteen-year-old daughters out to dinner at a beautiful restaurant in the city where my older daughter was going to college. We were sitting in a window and when I looked across the street, I saw a very stylish, beautiful young blond woman sitting down at an outdoor café with a man who didn't look right to me. He was handsome and muscular and had on what is popularly known as a "wife beater" T-shirt. He also had an "edge"—a sneer on his face, and an obvious chip on his shoulder. Frankly he scared me. He looked angry and belligerent, as though he opposed all social convention and rules. My older daughter pointed out that the girl (whom I'll call Leslie) had been in a musical with her. They knew each other. I remembered seeing Leslie in that play. She was very talented and seemed to have a successful career ahead of her. I then asked my daughter who the guy was. She said she wasn't really sure. She did know that he hadn't gone to college. Apparently he and Leslie had been living together for the last two years of her college career.

Then I asked why Leslie would pick a guy like this. Both of my daughters, awash in the political correctness that comes with a liberal education, jumped all over me for being "elitist"—as though the fact that he wasn't in college was my objection to him. It was the guy's "edge" that made me so uncomfortable, not his educational credentials, but I'll admit that I didn't know how to articu-

late my discomfort. I told them that I just felt there was something
"off" about this couple. Anyway, I voiced my opinion and then
dropped it because neither daughter seemed to get my point.

About a year later, just a month before my daughter graduated
college, she told me that Leslie had been shot and killed by that same
boyfriend. Her career had been taking off in New York City and she
had broken up with him. Her mother had come to help her move out
of her apartment in preparation for a move to NYC. While Leslie ran
out to do an errand, her mother began packing. When Leslie returned, her old boyfriend slipped out from the shadows, put a gun
to her head, and killed her—and then killed himself. Her mother
heard the whole thing.

I was stunned at this loss. And I grieved for her parents. I also
wasted no time reminding my daughter about our dinner conversation a year earlier, and my puzzlement over why Leslie had chosen
such a boyfriend. When someone is under the spell of a "bad boy," it's
like having an addiction. In fact, it is an addiction, if you think of addiction as continued "use" despite adverse consequences, which is one
of the definitions. A girl literally "loses herself" in the relationship.
And that is what happens when you have any kind of addiction—
whether to a substance such as alcohol, or a person. All addictions
serve to numb us to what we know and what we feel, disabling our
inner guidance system. Bottom line: Beauty can't save the Beast, and
she can't save a bad boy who is going nowhere. If she tries, things can
get ugly pretty fast.

WISDOM CHALLENGE: *Sending the Right Warning Signs*

If your daughter is in a relationship that you suspect is not good for
her, it's hard to know what to do, but you really have to trust your
Mother Bear wisdom. You don't want to risk overreacting lest you
drive her away from you and into his arms! On the other hand, you
can't just pretend that everything is okay. She is looking to you to see
your reaction, even if she doesn't seem to want your advice. Tell her
how you feel about the guy and then drop it. Truly, nothing is more
powerful than having a mother share with her daughter how she really feels. Even if the daughter disagrees with her, her mother's words
will register on some level.

On the other hand, if your gut is telling you that the guy could actually be dangerous, you have to stand right up on your Mother Bear hind legs, bare your claws and fangs, and growl as deeply as you know how! Your daughter is in peril and your gut knows it. Chances are that if you have a relationship of mutual trust she'll listen to you.

If your daughter refuses to stop seeing him, however, then you may have to take stronger measures. If she is under eighteen, you are legally responsible for her welfare. That means that you have every right to physically remove your daughter from harm's way. Depending upon your circumstances, you may need to take her out of school, send her to camp, or even send her out of the country for a while. Better safe than sorry. And it's far better to know that your daughter is safe even if she accuses you of "ruining her life." Deep down, she will know you care. She may even welcome your intervention, especially if she doesn't have the skills to know how to get out of a bad relationship herself, which is often the case with girls that age.

My parents gave me some great preventive advice about how to recognize a bad relationship. They said, "If a guy tells you he needs you and can't live without you, run the other way!" This actually happened once. I immediately thought, *Oh my! This is what my parents were talking about,* and ended the relationship!

Self-Esteem and Dating

Good self-esteem sets the stage for healthy relationships with boys—and everyone else! I didn't want my daughters to waste their time with boys who didn't respect them. And I knew that self-confidence and self-acceptance were the keys to helping them avoid such encounters. By the law of attraction, the more you like yourself and what you have to offer, the more likely you are to attract a man whose attributes will match your own. The good men I know all want women they can be proud of.

Mothers can go a long way in helping their daughters take themselves and their lives seriously enough not to waste their time on men who aren't worthy of them. I believe my own sense of how to behave with men was cemented into place by my mother's attitude. She was never a "girly girl" who required male attention to be happy. Although she liked men and, being very athletic, enjoyed hunting, fishing, and playing sports right alongside them, I never saw her flirt with men or do anything else just to get their attention. So I learned that I was okay with or without a boyfriend, and that I should always expect to be treated as an equal.

Mera, one of my e-letter subscribers, recently wrote about the impact of her mother on her self-esteem.

> At about age ten, Mother asked me what I wanted to do with my life. Whom would I emulate? I suggested Ruth in the Bible, Whither thou goeth, etc.
>
> No, she replied, tell me three women alive *today*! Immediately, Helen Keller, Mrs. Roosevelt, Madame Chiang Kai-shek came to mind. Within a week we had tea in the White House, within a month I was interviewing Helen Keller for my school newspaper. And finally twenty years later, when I was working as a professional reporter, I was able to interview Madame Chiang Kai-shek—who died only last year at age a hundred and three!

Mera is now a gerontologist.

The most important thing a girl needs to know is that she has to have her own life and her own interests. She shouldn't expect a man to fulfill her and make her life worth living. If she (or her mother) truly feels that she is nothing without a man on her arm, then she's likely to attract a man who will treat her poorly—the same way she is treating herself!

When the Mother Heals Her Own Relationship Patterns, She Creates a Healthier Template for Her Daughter

Though I started out with a fairly decent sense of self-worth, I had a pattern of losing myself in relationships. I didn't know this until midlife when my career success gave me a boost in my self-esteem—a boost that gave me enough courage to want a change in the dynamics of my closest relationships. I was still the peacemaker, "the sun will come out tomorrow" codependent person who put most of the gas in the tank called relationships. That story is well documented in *The Wisdom of Menopause*. It's a common story. And it culminated in the end of my twenty-four-year marriage.

During the soul-searching that was part of this painful life change, I had to wade through mountains of guilt. After all, wasn't it a mother's job to keep the peace at any price, soothe her husband's anger, do whatever it took to keep him happy, put his and her children's needs for a stable family before her own? Wasn't it her job to keep her voice down, and make sure that home was a safe and comfortable place? Wasn't a mother supposed to cheerfully arrange her life around their schedules? The needs of mothers come last—after everyone else's. I call this the "chicken wing syndrome": the mother gets the wings that are left over after she serves everyone the choice pieces. Why mess that up and create so much pain and suffering for everyone else? Why rock the boat? Why not just go along?

Those were the patterns I had to face and change within myself. They were rooted very, very deeply in my mind and body and fertilized regularly by our culture, which has made motherhood and martyrdom nearly synonymous.

I don't want to leave you with the impression that I was some saintly maternal figure during my twenty-plus years of married life. I wanted my daughters to have a role model of a mother who didn't shrink from disagreements with their father. So I pushed the envelope as far as I thought it could go. But there were still a lot of evenings when I held my tongue and worked hard to shape the conversation at the dinner table so that it would make everybody feel better, particularly if my husband seemed to be harried or in a bad mood.

Ultimately, I came to see that the price of soothing everyone else's emotions was too high. But in order to change the pattern, I also had to acknowledge another part of my legacy. I did most of the nurturing in our house because it never occurred to me that I deserved true partnership within my home. I wasn't sure I was worthy of more, especially in the husband department. A part of me felt that I had to prove myself by overgiving in order to be loved.

At midlife, those patterns began to change as a strong inner voice began to emerge that refused to be silenced. It was shocking to realize that even with all my outward success, I still lost myself at home.

The good news is that whenever a mother has the courage to heal the unhealthy patterns in her own life, her daughter is likely to benefit as well. What it may have taken a mother half a lifetime to become conscious of, her daughter may learn in a much shorter period of time. The following story from one of my patients is a great example.

GEORGIA: Breaking Up and Breaking the Pattern

Approximately nine months after my husband and I separated, my seventeen-year-old daughter Georgia started dating a boy named Jim, with whom she had been friends since the eighth grade. Georgia and Jim seemed happy together. They both liked the same sports and the same kinds of music. And both were superior students who shared many of the same classes in high school. But after about a month, I noticed that Georgia seemed a bit agitated and I asked her what was going on. She told me that Jim always interrupted her and didn't seem to give her credit for knowing anything. He always seemed depressed and negative, and was constantly down on the crass commercialism of the culture—for example, he once called a can of Diet Coke that Georgia took out of the refrigerator "a can of carcinogens"—while participating fully in it himself. Georgia was quick to point this out to him, but he couldn't hear it. Eventually, Georgia decided it was time to share with Jim how distressing she found his constant interruptions and put-downs. His response was to tell her that he felt they were just too different from each other and he didn't want to work on keeping the relationship going. In essence he broke up with Georgia the minute that she asked him to step up to the plate and make a positive change.

Georgia was both angry and hurt and couldn't understand why a guy who was so intelligent and had so much going for him could be so unwilling to look at his own relationship patterns. Jim had had a series of girlfriends who did all the work of calling him, asking him out, and even deciding where they would go and what they would do. When he first invited Georgia on a date, he admitted that he had no respect for these girls but said that he had now matured enough to be with a girl like her—someone with self-respect and intelligence.

It became pretty clear to me that Jim had many of the same characteristics as Georgia's father. He was handsome, talented, and intelligent, but he was also depressed and controlling. We had separated because I was no longer willing to let him control my behavior and also make all the major decisions without my input. I wanted a true partner instead of a man whose emotions I was always trying to take responsibility for soothing.

Georgia was devastated when Jim broke up with her. And boy could I relate! I understood right down to my bone marrow how frustrating it is to see someone with so much potential who is so unwilling to do what is necessary to become a happy and productive human being. Georgia said to me, "I keep thinking that I should be pointing out to him when he's being controlling and depressing. After all, we've been friends for years." What had been even more confusing to her was the fact that boys like Jim (and my husband) appear to be open to feedback and even to ask for it. But then they aren't willing to do the hard work of making changes in their behavior. I told Georgia that one of the very hardest things to do in a relationship is to let go of trying to change the other person. Here's the advice I gave her: "Honey, you need to get on with your life and accept that Jim will never change. . . . Ever. Believe me, it's not worth spending any more of your time thinking about him. . . . I know that you're hurting and that you think that something is wrong with you. But the problem is his. There's nothing wrong with you."

My patient told me that it took Georgia a couple years to get over her relationship with Jim. But one day when she was home from college during summer vacation, she ran into him. He was more depressed than ever, was using drugs, and, as usual, had a girl with him whom she virtually ignored. Georgia was grateful that she had seen him because she realized how far she'd come. He was no longer interesting to her in the least.

Men like Jim have bonding problems, pure and simple. They hide their vulnerability behind arrogance and the need to control others, particularly women. And far too often, they find vulnerable women who are entirely willing to sacrifice themselves and their dignity in order to stay in relationships with these guys.

Given our society, most girls have a long way to go in the self-esteem department when it comes to relationships, and no wonder. Regardless of their age, males seem to have far less difficulty finding a mate than do women who are of equal status and success. I have come to believe that this is a necessary stage in our evolution toward a more egalitarian society. The only way to get there is for girls to develop self-esteem on all levels, including their desirability as women.

Orbitofrontal Love:
Love That Sets Your Heart on Fire

The kind of romantic relationship that most people, male and female, long for is one characterized by mutuality on all levels. Neither individual has the upper hand or more worth. Body, mind, and spirit are all connected in the expression of love. And the feelings the two people have for each other are based on unconditional love and acceptance, not the needs of the ego. Ideally, your mother's relationship with you and with your father modeled all these qualities, and you in turn are able to model them for your daughter.

Right now our culture is changing rapidly when it comes to relationships. The bar marked "fulfillment" has been set higher than ever because women no longer have to marry simply for economic reasons. They have more financial clout and more choices. But that doesn't mean they don't still want to have love in their lives. However they choose to express it, the need for human love and closeness is universal, and it's here to stay. Everyone I know, including me, wants to have that special someone in our lives who represents, in the words of Dr. Phil, "a soft place to land."

I have faith that our daughters will take up where we mothers have left off—and having learned from our mistakes will love more consciously and unconditionally than ever.

17

Addictions

Escaping Painful Emotions

❁

You can't take care of yourself if you don't understand the concept of responsibility. As a girl moves through her teens toward adulthood, she must come to grips with and take responsibility for more and more of her own choices, whether it's a matter of her relationships with boys, her commitment to her schoolwork, her decisions about college, or the wide range of issues that have the potential to affect her health. The stakes are very high at this age. In terms of her health, everything from the food she eats to the exercise she gets to the dangerously addictive mood-altering substances she may ingest can have lifelong consequences.

Knowing this, many women find it very difficult to step back and let their daughters make choices—and mistakes. But every woman has to find her own balance between sheltering her daughter completely from the potential consequences of bad decisions and giving her enough freedom to learn from experience. After all, adolescence is the time when a girl should be learning some of her most important life lessons, under the guidance but not the control of her parents. Her daughter's adolescence is a critical time for a mother to model for her daughter the proper balance between taking care of oneself and taking care of others. If she is either overly enmeshed or overly detached from her daughter's life, neither mother nor daughter will benefit.

One of my patients told me what a revelation it had been for her when she came to see me for her first pelvic exam at the age of sixteen. Oddly enough, the part of the experience that had registered as a wake-up call was that, while examining her throat, I asked this young woman if she flossed regularly. It was in that moment that she realized that she, not her mother, was now responsible for the proper care and feeding of her body.

Another of my patients recounted what happened to her when she developed a severe neurologic problem that forced her to drop out of college. Describing her response after her doctors finally told her that there was nothing more they could do for her, she said, "In a strange way, this was very freeing. I realized that I was alone with my problem and that my survival depended upon being willing to take complete responsibility for my life and health. Knowing that I was (and am) responsible for my health and life made me feel both peaceful and empowered. But believing that my health was in the hands of my parents, my doctors, or my genes—now there's a thought that really terrified me and made me feel powerless." She eventually healed herself through lifestyle changes, affirmations, and a strong inner drive.

Though my patient's is an extreme example, it illustrates an essential truth: to live well, we all have to take responsibility for our lives and our health. And the sooner the better. Few things are more empowering than understanding that you have the potential to influence and direct your life through taking responsibility for yourself and your choices.

Because adolescence is when a girl gets birthed into adulthood, it is an ideal time to establish a philosophy and practice of self-care and healthy behaviors that will serve her well for the rest of her life. A girl's changing body and newly awakened sexual interests will, quite naturally, fuel her self-care efforts. However, they may also sometimes derail her, for the emotional turbulence that often results from these inner and outer changes can seem overwhelming. When that happens, self-destructive impulses may win out over the self-affirming ones that inform a young girl's willingness to begin taking responsibility for her well-being. Your job is to recognize when normal emotional upheaval is moving over into the realm of pathology.

Moodiness and anxiety run rampant at this age, and rare is the young woman who escapes them entirely. But there is a difference between major and minor depression, and between anxiety and anxiety disorders, hard as it may sometimes be to distinguish between them.

DEPRESSION AND ANXIETY

In adolescence, a variety of factors may predispose certain girls to develop emotional problems. One such factor is certainly hormonal. The dramatic elevation in estrogen and other hormones that characterizes this life stage acts as a stimulant on key frontal- and temporal-lobe centers for emotion and behavior, so that even the most well-adjusted girls are likely to experience occasional bouts of moodiness and impulsivity. There's not too much you can do about these mood swings except try to ride them out—and put up some boundaries so that your daughter doesn't feel free to take out her emotions on you.

Another factor is the many new stresses that adolescents are suddenly confronting. Huda Akil, Ph.D., the codirector of the University of Michigan's Mental Health Research Institute, has researched the links between stress, brain circuitry, and depression, and found that "the best way to activate the stress system is with social situations."[1] Middle school, high school, and college students face so many new kinds of social situations that it's no wonder some of them develop emotional disorders. When she started her senior year in college, my younger daughter, finally comfortable and happy both socially and academically, said, "I look at all those freshman coming in and I feel so bad for them. I'm so glad I don't have to go through all that again! It makes me sick to my stomach just thinking about it." Yet Kate, like most girls, made it through the emotional storms of adolescence relatively unscathed.

For some girls, however, the normal pruning and reshaping of brain circuitry that occurs at this age may unmask a tendency toward mood and personality disorders that was dormant during latency.[2] It's important to remember that such problems don't just leap out of the closet and land on a girl. They are triggered by a combination of genetic, environmental, nutritional, and experiential as well as hormonal factors. And there's also the fact of temperament. Some girls just have greater innate hardiness in response to stress.

Having said that, it's clear that some girls will need outside help. Over and above the factors just cited, their emotional state may also have been affected by drugs and/or alcohol, or even by factors as basic as the lack of adequate sleep. If you think your daughter is genuinely troubled, you'll want to seek professional help. But when you do, you must remember that psychiatry, more than any other branch of medicine, is an art rather than an exact science. Despite the advent of MRI and neuropsychology personality assessments, there is no scan or blood test that can give anyone a definitive psychiatric diagnosis of depression, anxiety disorder, panic disorder, or bipolar disorder (not to mention the more severe psychiatric diagnoses of schizophrenia and autism/Asperger's syndrome). Accurate diagnosis and appropriate treatment are very much a matter of the practitioner's intuition, skill, and experience. And I would add that they also require a certain amount of common sense.

It used to be the case that being diagnosed with any kind of mental disorder cast a real stigma over a family. Now the pendulum has swung in the opposite direction and diagnoses for depression, bipolar disorder (and the newer, more controversial bipolar II, III, and IV), and anxiety disorders are handed out only too freely—along with the latest medications believed to be effective in treating them. For example, Mallory, the daughter of one of my friends, was always high-strung and afraid of the dark. After her parents divorced when she was fourteen, she started to get panicky, moody, and irritable. Her mother took her to a mental health professional, who diagnosed her with bipolar II and put her on an antidepressant and mood stabilizer. After six months of trying different medications, none of which really seemed to make a difference, my friend decided that this route wasn't helping and wasn't worth it for her daughter. Instead, she got Mallory involved in a support group for teens of divorced parents, and also helped her improve her diet and get off sugar and caffeine. This approach worked well. Mallory was able to talk about her difficult feelings with her peers and eventually recovered without medication or further psychotherapy.

Given the ambiguities of diagnosis and the unreliability of reporting, we don't really know how prevalent frank disorders are during either adolescence or adulthood. Some studies suggest that the incidence of problems in mood, thought, and behavior that are serious enough to adversely affect relationships and vocational and societal adjustment may be as high as 30 percent in teens and 16 percent in adults. But as they get more secure in their identity, and the turbulent social adjustment challenges of adolescence subside, half the girls with such problems are able to get over their emotional ups and downs on their own.[3] So when a mother says, "She's just going through a stage. She'll get over it," she may well be right!

However, just being female in this culture increases our risk of mood and personality disorders. Girls are twice as likely as boys to experience depression in adolescence, for example, although their rates are about equal up to age 11.[4] Studies have also shown that 20 to 30 percent of all women, as opposed to only 10 to 15 percent of men, will, at least sometime in their life, develop a clinically significant problem such as depression or anxiety.[5]

It is well beyond the scope of this book, and my expertise, to discuss diagnosis or treatment of the entire range of emotional problems a teen can have. Diagnosis is complicated not only by the normal volatility of adolescence but by the fact that such disorders are often complex combinations of problems. For example, though most people tend to think of depression as a discrete disorder, about 50 percent of all depressed teens also have problems with anxiety.[6] However, as with latency, there are a number of red flags that may signal trouble. Neuropsychiatrist Mona Lisa Schulz lists a number of key indicators that can help a mother decide whether her daughter may need outside help.

If any of the following descriptions apply to your daughter on a daily basis, or often enough and to a degree of severity that they interfere with her capacity to have relationships outside of her family, to succeed in school, and to eventually survive and thrive on her own, you may wish to seek an expert mental health opinion.

RED FLAGS FOR EMOTIONAL PROBLEMS

Physical symptoms: Fatigue; slowed thoughts, speech and movement; excessive sleeping or insomnia; repeated nightmares; major fluctuations in weight; constant complaining of aches and pains; jumpiness; agitation

Mental symptoms: Incessant brooding, worrying, thoughts associated with hopelessness, suicide, despair

Mood: Down in the dumps, nervous, irritable, anxious about leaving home to go to school or other peer events, loss of interest in activities

Behavior: Rage attacks; compulsive behaviors like washing, checking, or ritually controlling her environment; refusing to go to school or participate in other usual activities

Perceptual problems: Hallucinations, hearing voices

If you do end up deciding that your daughter needs profesional help, you may want to consider whether she would also benefit from other kinds of interventions. A large body of research has shown that using nutritional supplements and/or herbs, in addition to or instead of prescription medications, can be very effective. For example, it's well documented that the herb St. John's wort is as effective as an SSRI (serotonin reuptake inhibitor to increase serotonin) for mild to moderate depression. And in some studies, exercise was able to cure 50 percent of mild to moderate depression. Every parent owes it to her daughter to make sure her daughter is getting the best that both conventional and complementary medicine has to offer.

You also need to be vigilant about what is being offered. If a doctor simply hands out a prescription for an SSRI such as Prozac, Zoloft, or Celexa, do educate yourself on the potential dangers of these drugs. Antidepressants may well be dangerous for adolescents (and children). In the United Kingdom, the Committee on Safety of Medicines (CSM), which is the equivalent of our FDA, in 2004 banned the use of all SSRIs for treating depression in children and adolescents because of the increased risk of suicidal behavior that was noted shortly after the drugs were begun.[7] In our own country, similar concerns have led the FDA to appoint two advisory panels to call attention to the need for more caution in prescribing antidepressants and also to create new labels warning of the dangers.[8] It's too early to tell how much of an effect this will have on the number of prescriptions written. But I certainly hope it will reverse what I consider a very disturbing trend toward the overuse of medication and provide the impetus for parents to seek out safer, more effective long-term solutions.

Antidepressant use among children and adolescents grew three- to tenfold between 1987 and 1996. And between 1998 and 2002, there was a 50 percent rise in prescriptions, despite the fact that clinical trials have failed to prove that they work.[9] I'm very concerned not just about the immediate effects of these drugs, which include the suicidal tendencies noted in the U.K. as well as in many U.S. studies, but about the long-term, yet unknown, side effects of giving teens psychoactive drugs during a time of rapid brain development.

Every young girl, including those with a tendency toward depression and/or anxiety, needs to learn emotional literacy whether or not she takes medication. She should learn her mind-body's way of expressing fear, anger, sadness, love, and joy. If she doesn't learn how to skillfully listen to her thoughts and emotions and use them as the fuel for change and growth, she is far more likely to develop significant depression, panic, personality disorder, and problems with physical health. Merely giving Prozac or Celexa or some other "pill" for depression and anxiety without also supporting a girl nutritionally, cognitively, and socially isn't going to give your daughter the tools she needs for a lifetime of mental and physical health. It's like blowing air into a balloon with a hole in it.

WHEN THE GOING GETS TOUGH:
ADDICTIONS AS A WAY TO ESCAPE
PAINFUL EMOTIONS AND RESPONSIBILITY

Though troubled teenagers may be particularly vulnerable to the temptations of mind-altering substances like alcohol and drugs, plenty of young people who are simply going through the normal ups and downs of adolescence find themselves succcumbing to their lure as well. But I'm convinced that the enormous health risks associated with the use of alcohol, cigarettes, drugs, and other addictive substances can be minimized for our daughters. To do this we will have to fearlessly address our own personal and family legacies around addiction. The work begins with understanding what purposes are served by addictive behaviors and substances in the first place.

Addictive substances are all a form of self-medication that results in changes in mood (hence the terms *mind-* or *mood-altering substances*). They "medicate" the DLPC and orbitofrontal pathways for emotion and thought, thus quieting the anxiety associated with "shoulds" and "oughts," so that instead of doing something constructive in response to an emotion, the individual simply becomes numb.

Some people seem to be more prone to such self-medication than others, and we can speculate why this is so, based on some interesting research that has been done on animals. Studies have found that dominant animals have fewer stress-hormone receptor sites in their hippocampal areas than do subordinate, more timid animals. Experts feel that differences in the number of stress hormone receptor sites in the brain may also be associated with tendencies toward dominance and submission in people, and may help to explain differences in their susceptibility to drug use too. Adventurous people tend to drive fast, participate in sexual experimentation, and try drugs just to see what the experience feels like. More timid people, on the other hand, may use alcohol and other substances to self-medicate.[10]

Though our culture likes to focus on the drama of drug addiction and lethal drug overdoses among teenagers, the fact is that these deaths are relatively rare. In 1993, for example, only ten children and twelve teens died from drug abuse in Southern California compared to 1,996 adults aged twenty or over. The vast majority of deaths from drug overdose are in middle-aged men, not teens.[11] I have never encountered a single teen drug death in all my years of practice. Alcohol is much more deadly to teenagers, yet we do not take it nearly as seriously.

But over and above alcohol, drugs, and cigarettes, there are many other forms of addictions, which are not limited to the intake of substances. These include a wide variety of behavioral addictions, including sex, gambling, work, and exercise, which, when practiced compulsively, can create biochemical changes in the brain and body similar to taking a drink or shooting up with heroin. There are also emotional addictions: some people have an addictive need to feel the excitement that comes from being the center of attention (narcissism); others always need to be in a relationship in which they feel needed—they are dependent upon the dependency of others, i.e., codependent. Some can only feel the rush through gambling, engaging in dangerous activities, or having love affairs with married men.

Whatever the "drug" of choice, it is used in order to make us feel better by numbing us to feelings such as anger, fear, grief, anxiety, or boredom—feelings that may seem too overwhelming to handle. These emotions, uncomfortable as they may be, have a purpose— which is to get us to change something in our lives that isn't working. They are part of our inner guidance system. If we don't allow ourselves to feel these emotions fully and then heed their messages, then we're not motivated to change and grow. On some level, we know this, which is why we feel the need to lie about or minimize the fact of our addictions. Otherwise we would have to own up to the necessity to make changes.

Because addictions help us to avoid taking responsibility for ourselves, our habitual thought patterns, and our emotions, they interfere with our ability to work, study, and have relationships. In short, habitual use of addictive substances or behaviors keeps us from fulfilling our work and family responsibilities, and ultimately prevents us from living lives that are as productive and fulfilling as they could be.

Telling the Truth about Mood-Altering Substances

Our culture is more awash in addictive substances than ever before, partly because of the influence of the media and advertising, which offer drugs, cars, alcohol, or other consumer goods as quick fixes for social discomfort and uneasiness. But all cultures throughout recorded history have used mood-altering substances to one degree or another. Even animals sometimes use mood-altering substances, for example birds get drunk on fermented berries, and goats get high on berries that contain caffeine.

Addictive substances can be divided into two categories: those that are socially—and legally—acceptable, and those that aren't. Socially acceptable addictive substances in our own culture include caffeine, sugar, tobacco, refined carbohydrates, and alcohol. Socially prohibited addictive substances include marijuana, LSD, cocaine, heroin, and a wide variety of other drugs that are mood altering. (Many perfectly legal prescription drugs necessary for pain relief are, of course, addictive if taken for too long or under the wrong circumstances.) Whether or not a given substance is considered socially acceptable depends upon the time, the place, and the culture. In his book *From Morphine to Chocolate*, Andrew Weil, M.D., points out that the ingestion of coffee and chocolate have both been banned at one time or another and under various circumstances.

Mothers would do well to admit, right from the start, that almost all of us partake of the mood-altering effect of one or more addictive substances from time to time. Whether your thing is chocolate or wine, you use it to elevate your mood, even if you are not truly addicted to it.

Why Cool Is Dangerous

Teenagers use drugs and alcohol for the same reasons their parents do—to feel better, to avoid difficult feelings, to avoid taking responsibility for some aspect of their lives. When a teen feels awkward or insecure, she will often turn to drugs or alcohol to appear "cool" (just as there are many adults who can't be in a room of strangers without a wineglass and/or a cigarette in hand). But looking cool is a health risk—not just because of the physically damaging effects of the substance itself. The whole point of looking cool is to disconnect one's facial expression from one's emotions, and one's mind from one's body. Drugs and alcohol help wire that disconnection into place—and that's a setup for health problems. A college friend of one of my daughters made a very interesting observation on the subject: "So many students here go around living in their heads all week. When the weekend comes, they want desperately to reconnect with their bodies or at least temporarily forget the discomforts of their daily lives. So they drink too much and have illicit sex all weekend—only to wake up on Monday morning and escape back into their heads."

ALCOHOL

Alcohol and Brain Development

Our laws indicate that twenty-one is a safe age at which to begin drinking, since that's when drinking is legal. Many adolescents, of course, start drinking far earlier than that—long before the frontal-lobe circuits of the brain are able to handle it and still maintain some semblance of reason. During the teens and early twenties, many frontal-lobe circuits that are necessary for organization, planning, socialization, empathy, and morality are still being molded, shaped, and fine-tuned. If these brain circuits are immersed in a weekly alcohol bath, their long-term development is adversely affected. That's why every year that a teen delays consuming alcohol decreases the potential damage alcohol can do to her brain development, as well as her social and educational development.

Adolescents and young adults between the ages of eighteen and twenty-four who engage in binge drinking (consuming five or more drinks in a row with a drink being defined as a standard bottle or can of beer, a six-ounce serving of wine, or one ounce of hard liquor)[12] on a regular basis have been shown statistically to do more poorly in employment, education, and taking financial responsibility for themselves or family members.

Binge drinking between the ages of fourteen and twenty-one decreases the size of key memory areas in the brain, namely the hippocampus, by 10 percent. No one knows whether or not this brain shrinkage is reversible. But we do know that adolescent binge drinkers have lower intellectual abilities, as evidenced by the fact that they score lower on the vocabulary and memory portions of standard neuropsychological tests.

In animal models, alcohol interferes with acetylcholine, the brain chemical necessary for learning. Low doses—the equivalent of one drink—that had no effect on mature animals seriously impaired the ability of younger animals to learn.

Alcohol does more than acutely impair thought, problem solving, learning, memory, and coordination. In adolescents in particular it may also have long-term effects on the brain areas that are necessary for these same functions.[13] This is because these are the years when the brain is still especially well primed to learn in response to experience, a brain state known as plasticity. Though we can continue to learn later on in adulthood, plasticity decreases with age, and earlier behaviors and thought patterns tend to get wired in.

Cynthia Kuhn, Ph.D.; Scott Swartzwelder, Ph.D.; and Wilkie Wilson, Ph.D., professors of pharmacology and psychology at Duke University Medical Center and authors of the book *Just Say Know,* put it this way, "Since the young brain is in the process of making permanent connections between nerve cells, the presence of any chemical during this period could change that 'wiring' in unpredictable ways for the rest of a person's life." The brain also changes in response to repeated use of a drug by adapting and modifying itself to reduce sensitivity. The authors of *Just Say Know* state, "We have very little information about how well the brain 'adapts' to repeated alcohol exposure during adolescence. Experience with other drugs suggests that it might even be *less* tolerant, which means the brain could be *more* affected over the long run."[14]

TEEN ALCOHOL USE: SCOPE OF PROBLEM

Alcohol is the drug of choice in our culture. During the *Animal House* years, the large number of kids who regularly get drunk—at weekend parties, in hidden suburban "living room pubs," in fraternity and sorority houses—are increasing their tendency for developing a lifelong addiction to alcohol. The key word here is *regularly.* The daughter of a friend of mine has a college roommate who routinely "premedicates" herself with shots of liquor before leaving her room on weekends. She then continues to drink the rest of the evening. She is all too typical of many college students.

Despite the fact that it is illegal for them to drink, alcohol is easily available to most teenagers. Many parents underestimate the number of teens who drink, as well as the frequency and the levels of consumption. The latest data from the University of Michigan's "Monitoring the Future" project show how common alcohol use in teens really is:

	8th graders	10th graders	12th graders
Used during the past year	43%	65%	73%
Used in past 30 days	22%	41%	50%
Been drunk in past year	19%	42%	53%
Been drunk in past 30 days	8%	24%	32%
5+ drinks in a row, past two weeks	15%	25%	31%

Note: 5 drinks in a row is definition of binge drinking[15]

Why the Legal Drinking Age Is Twenty-one

Drinking is legally permitted at twenty-one, the age at which society concurs that most people have enough judgment to handle alcohol—and specifically to know when to drive and when not to after imbibing. Research compiled by Mothers Against Drunk Driving (MADD) showed that in the late 1960s and early '70s, when a number of states lowered their drinking age from twenty-one to eighteen, there was a significant increase in highway deaths among teens in the eighteen to twenty-one age bracket. In 1982, for example, when many of the states still had a minimum drinking age of eighteen, 55 percent of all fatal crashes involving youth drivers also involved alcohol. So, in the early 1980s a movement began to change the drinking age back to twenty-one. Many states passed such laws, and a number of them were then monitored to check the difference in highway fatalities. Researchers found that teenage deaths involving car crashes dropped considerably—in some cases up to 28 percent—after the drinking age was increased to twenty-one. In fact, the alcohol-related traffic fatality rate has been cut in half since 1982! One study estimates that from 1975 to 2002, a period that encompasses the years immediately before the drinking age was raised and the approximately twenty years since, more than 21,000 lives have been saved.[16] Though this is good news, we still have a very long way to go when it comes to the adverse effects of alcohol on driving—and on many other aspects of public health. According to the National Highway Traffic Safety Administration FARS data, 6,390 young people age fifteen to twenty were killed in alcohol-related traffic accidents in 2000. (Not all 6,390 of those killed were driving; some were simply going along for the ride.)

Alcohol and Brain Function in Teenagers: The Need for an "External Frontal Cortex"

As the driving statistics indicate, we need to be concerned about not just the long-term but the immediate effects of alcohol on a young person's brain. The former are relatively slow and insidious, while the latter are fast and sometimes deadly. Adolescents get drunk on lower doses of alcohol, and with less awareness on the part of the drinker, than adults over the age of twenty-four. In fact, adults have to drink twice the amount a teen does to experience comparable memory, cognitive, judgment, and motor-coordination effects.

Although adolescents get drunk much faster than adults do, they are much slower to "feel the buzz," and to experience the effects of alcohol on their motor coordination and their ability to remain conscious. In comparison to adults who drink a similar dose, teens are less likely to fall down and pass out. That means that teens are liable to keep drinking, and engaging in potentially dangerous activities—like driving—all the while thinking that they're okay. In sum, even though they don't feel it, alcohol has far more potent effects on the brains of young adults than on the brains of older people.

Not only does alcohol go to their heads faster, but the vast majority of teenagers don't yet have the frontal-lobe circuitry for good judgment firmly enough wired into place to offset the effects of alcohol. By the time they do "get the buzz," not only are they likely to have drunk more than an older person to achieve a comparable effect but their judgment about such matters as drinking and driving is likely to be even more impaired. (Not that the average drunk adult is a model of rational thinking!) That's why teenagers are involved in so many drunk driving episodes.

A recent article on teenagers and the latest findings of neuroscience points out that "the human brain, once thought to be fully developed by about age twelve, continues to grow and mature into the early or mid twenties. And the last part to mature is the frontal lobes, or prefrontal cortex, responsible for all the hallmarks of adult behavior—impulse control, the regulation of emotions and moral reasoning." Asked how most teenagers manage to get through adolescence without doing lasting harm to either themselves or others, developmental neuroscientist Abigail Baird, Ph.D., attributed their survival to good parenting, which she likened to having "an external frontal cortex."[17]

The Social Use of Alcohol

Alcohol use is completely normalized in nearly all social situations, including those involving the medical profession. I've never been to a medical meeting that didn't serve alcohol, an activity that's often jokingly referred to as liver rounds. And I've worked with several alcoholic doctors. The denial around this is striking. I believe that our culture's love affair with alcohol is one of the reasons why so many medical studies continue to be done trying to document the "heart healthy" effects of wine, when, in fact, you can get this same beneficial effect from the antioxidants found in grape juice or by taking antioxidant vitamins.

The roots of this love affair often go back to the teen years, when the use of alcohol to lubricate the social gears is particularly tempting. Teens who spend their high school years with a glass of alcohol in their hands at every party they go to never really learn the social skills necessary for relationships and healthy bonding without alcohol on board to smooth the way. Instead of learning techniques for dealing with the discomfort of a social situation, they simply blunt the feeling to make it go away. Yes, social situations can be very uncomfortable and awkward during adolescence—and also in adulthood! On some level, few of us ever really leave the eighth grade when it comes to our feelings about entering new social situations. But medicating this anxiety with alcohol doesn't serve teens (or anyone else) over the long term.

Later, when a teen leaves home for college and lives on her own, social demands and relationships get even more complex. That's one of the reasons why alcohol and drug use tend to accelerate during this period of time. Chances are good that the young adult who participates in regular drinking and drug use never learned in high school how to deal with social pressure and anxiety without these crutches.

One of my friends recently decided to stop drinking altogether after one too many drinks resulted in a DUI conviction. Since she made that decision, she reports, "I've found that parties aren't as much fun anymore if I'm not drinking. I had no idea how great an effect alcohol had on my ability to enjoy myself in a social situation. What an eye-opener." My friend has a ten-year-old daughter who, she vows, will learn social skills that will make it unnecessary for her to use alcohol to have a good time.

Why It's So Hard to Acknowledge the Adverse Effects of Alcohol

Alcohol is our society's oldest and most well-accepted drug. It's part of the very fabric of our society. Going out with friends and "getting hammered" or "getting a buzz on" is a tried-and-true rite of passage. Because so many parents have gotten drunk as teens and now seem to be functioning well as adults, they don't see a problem with their children drinking, even though it's not legal.

Let's look at this logically. It is no secret that alcohol has critical effects on a baby's rapidly developing brain and that pregnant women should therefore avoid it. We also know that it has adverse effects on the rapidly developing brain of a child. As we have been discussing, the adolescent brain is also still growing and developing, and will continue to do so well into the twenties. Our culture insists that young people wear helmets when riding a bike or skiing, to protect them from possible head injury. But more brain cells are killed annually by alcohol than all the head injuries from accidents combined!

Alcohol is a neurotoxin, plain and simple. It kills brain cells in a dose-dependent fashion. So do other addictive substances such as nicotine and caffeine.

The Effects of Alcohol on Women's Health

Because a teenager's behavior with alcohol sets up her relationship with it for the rest of her life, it's crucial that she and her mother understand the health risks. As little as one drink a day has been shown to increase the risk of breast cancer by 9 percent. Each time you add another daily drink, it increases your risk of breast cancer more. Five drinks a day increases your risk of breast cancer by 41 percent. The reason for this is that alcohol is metabolized by the liver, the same place that estrogen is metabolized. As a result, women who drink have higher circulating estrogen levels, which, over time, favor the growth of breast cancer. Women worry about the genetic risk of breast cancer and are also more than willing to "run for the cure." The fact is, they also have to be willing to put down the bottle![18] Also keep in mind that alcohol is a refined carbohydrate, so it wreaks havoc with blood sugar and contributes to unwanted weight gain. I've seen many a teenage girl pack on the pounds, especially around her abdomen, when she has taken up regular drinking.

What to Tell Your Daughter about Drinking

As a general rule, you should educate your teenage children about what alcohol does to the developing brain. If you yourself drank as a teenager, tell them that if you had known then what you know now, you would have delayed drinking. Encourage your kids to delay drinking alcohol as long as possible.

If there is any family legacy of alcoholism, be sure they know about it and understand the implications for their own lives. The general statistics are that 40 percent of adult children of alcoholics will become alcoholics themselves. And 25 percent of adult grandchildren of alcoholics will become alcoholics.

Talk to them about how alcohol is used as a social lubricant—which doesn't actually do a very good job. Suggest to them that they become scientific observers of human behavior around alcohol. Once they start watching, they'll see that alcohol doesn't improve socialization. It actually does the opposite. It can make people behave inappropriately and inhibit their capacity for true social bonding. One of my friends put it this way: "When a guy comes up to you at a party, is flirting with you, and seems interested in getting to know you better, it's hard to take him seriously if he's been drinking. You don't know if it's him or the alcohol that's doing the talking." Alcohol acts like a tranquilizer on the brain, much like Valium. So it's an anxiolytic. It "loosens" people up and disinhibits them—often in ways they won't feel so good about the next day. One of my college-student patients said, "I finally decided to get rid of the beer in my refrigerator. It's wonderful to wake up feeling refreshed in the morning instead of hungover."

Tell your kids to have enough self-confidence and courage to be true to themselves without alcohol. One of my daughters had a good friend who didn't smoke or drink because, as he said, "I'm committed to the idea of having fun and expressing myself without chemical assistance." That's a worthy goal for everyone! Teach your children that it is possible to enjoy their peers without drinking, even when others around them are indulging. The key is a sense of humor and a nonjudgmental attitude. It also helps to just hold a glass of something nonalcoholic in your hand all night so it looks like you fit in. (See "How to deal effectively and humorously with peer pressure," page 527.)

Finally, in talking to your children, remember that it's your duty to uphold the law. Underage drinking is illegal, pure and simple, and your children need to know that you will not tolerate their participation in illegal activities.

TERRY and TED: Sobering Up About Alcohol

The following story, a composite based on people from my personal and professional life, illustrates how parents who are ignorant of the effects of alcohol on the teenage brain, and seemingly indifferent to the laws regarding alcohol and teenagers, can unwittingly set in motion a chain of events with the potential for real tragedy.

Terry and Ted have two teenage children, John and Jacqueline. Terry, age fifty-one, was brought up in a family in which alcohol was consumed at every family event. Whether it was a baptism, graduation, wedding, funeral, or just hanging around after dinner watching TV, beer and wine were always available, and the teenagers were welcome to imbibe along with the adults, so long as the drinking was moderate. Even though the legal drinking age is twenty-one, Terry had grown up with alcohol use in her home her entire life, so she didn't really follow the twenty-one rule in her own home. Terry and Ted always felt that if they didn't make a big deal about alcohol, their kids wouldn't go berserk at parties or drink and drive. They weren't negative about alcohol and let their kids have occasional sips of wine when they were growing up, and drank beer with them once they were teenagers. Neither parent drank to excess and both felt that their relationship with alcohol was normal.

Both John and Jacqueline were good students, on the honor roll, and involved in many after-school activities. When John and Jacqueline had friends over, neither Terry nor Ted felt that it was a big deal if they allowed the kids to have an occasional beer while watching a football game on TV or participating in a game of pool. Both parents enjoyed their reputation of being "cool" parents who were not like other "uptight" parents.

When Jacqueline was a senior in high school, Terry and Ted decided to go away on a long weekend to ski. They had a stern and honest talk with their kids, asking them to use good judgment and common sense if they invited any of their friends to the house.

On Sunday evening when they returned, Terry and Ted were horrified to find that someone had driven erratically across their front lawn, leaving tire marks all over it. The house smelled of disinfectant and had obviously just been cleaned. There were several garbage bags filled with empty beer cans and hard liquor bottles. Both of their children appeared exhausted and nervous.

Under questioning, John and Jacqueline revealed that on Saturday night there had been a small party at the house which, unfortunately, got out of control and became a much bigger party, with people they didn't even know coming over from adjacent towns. Neither of them had known what to do when the situation got out of control. One of the "guests" had tried to dive into the hot tub headfirst. A couple of kids found their way onto the roof. Another was driving "doughnuts" in the circular driveway. Jacqueline walked in on two of her friends having sex upstairs in her parents' bedroom.

As the kids drank more and more, things got even more out of control. Two boys got in a fight and one broke a beer bottle over the other's head, causing him to lose consciousness. Everyone was terrified. If they took him to the hospital or called 911, they could all get arrested for underage drinking, and John and Jacqueline's parents, would be implicated and legally responsible for what went on at their house. Besides, who would drive to the ER? This incident ended the party. Some people cleaned up the mess while others stood around and waited for the unconscious kid to regain consciousness, which he fortunately did, with no apparent ill effects.

Both Terry and Ted were understandably very upset by this incident. They thought that their children knew how to use alcohol wisely. What had gone wrong?

Terry and Ted are like a lot of parents. They simply didn't know what alcohol does to the still-developing brain of a teenager. If they did, they would have been in a much better position to anticipate the consequences of allowing their children and their children's friends to drink in their house. And they would never have put their children at risk of being involved in a real tragedy.

WISDOM CHALLENGE: *Where to Draw the Line on Underage Drinking*

There's nothing ambiguous about teens and drug or alcohol use. It's illegal and it's dangerous. Period. And we know numerous facts about *why* it is dangerous and therefore *should* be illegal before the age of twenty-one. We know that if the growing brain is exposed to it regularly, it has an adverse effect. We know that alcohol is a neurotoxin that has been shown to impair learning in both adolescents and young adults after as little as one drink. One drink can cause a teen to fail a breathalyzer test.[19] Yes, one drink. We know that alcohol impairs judgment, coordination, and speech. And we know that teen drinking can lead to troubles with alcohol later on: a 1998 study by the National Institute on Alcohol Abuse and Alcoholism reports that if a teen starts to drink regularly at the age of fifteen or earlier, she has a 40 percent chance of alcohol abuse as an adult!

Still, alcohol is everywhere in our culture. So how absolute do you want to be in your ban on alcohol for underage children? Your own attitude and behavior will do more to influence your daughter than any other factor, but you truly must educate yourself about the risks.

When my daughter Kate was a high school senior and was going on a one-week class trip to Spain with her Spanish class, I recall a prolonged discussion with other parents at her school about whether or not our children should be allowed to have a glass of wine or sangria with their host families if it was served at a family dinner. My response was, "When in Rome, do as the Romans do." In other words, if my daughter wanted to partake of some wine with her host family in Spain, why not? Similarly, when a generous aunt took my daughters at ages sixteen and eighteen on a trip to Paris, they decided that they liked drinking wine with dinner, as is the custom there, and that was fine with me. At the time of this writing, my daughters are twenty-one and twenty-three. Both have a healthy relationship with alcohol, enjoying a drink only occasionally but not needing one to enjoy a social activity, alter their mood, or get to sleep.

You have to decide what your personal truth is about alcohol. Those who've had to deal with alcoholic family members will feel differently from those who haven't. Your own drinking habits will also influence your decision.

When I was growing up, my dad had a glass of sherry when he came home from work about three times per week. He also enjoyed having wine or beer at social events on weekends. I never saw him drunk, though my mother said it occasionally happened, especially when he was visiting an old friend from WWII and they stayed up reminiscing. My mother didn't drink at all because she didn't like the taste—a disinclination that was passed on to me. When the girls were growing up, my dislike for the taste of alcohol set the tone in our family. Although we always had wine and some hard liquor around (much of it given to us as gifts), the bottles often gathered dust because my husband had only an occasional drink and we didn't entertain much given our on-call schedules. Never having experienced alcohol as a problem among family members either when I was growing up or in my adult life, I don't object to it in moderation, even though I don't personally drink. And I certainly don't want to make others uncomfortable when they have a drink in my presence. But if your own experience has been more negative, you may feel much stronger than I do about prohibiting your children from even the very occasional indulgence.

TOBACCO

Although buying cigarettes is illegal in most states until you are eighteen or older, this is a law that is probably even more readily broken by teenagers than the laws about alcohol—and that's a real shame. As Dr. Andrew Weil points out, smoking a cigarette is like injecting heroin directly into the brain, and it is possible to get addicted from smoking only a single cigarette. Of all the addictive substances out there, cigarettes are the least forgiving when it comes to experimentation!

Here's an example from my own upbringing: When I was about eleven, my father and mother sat all of us down in the kitchen and put a pack of cigarettes on the table in front of us. They said, "Rather than have you sneak around experimenting with smoking and trying to look cool, we thought that we'd give you a chance to smoke right here at home." My father lit up a cigarette and passed it around. I hated it immediately and got a bloody nose. Several of my siblings got sick. My oldest brother, however, who was about fifteen and was probably already smoking, continued for another twenty-five years, and didn't quit until he was in his late thirties.

At that time we didn't really know how dangerous smoking was. By now, however, pretty much everyone is clear about the risks associated with smoking cigarettes. When it comes to women's health, the list is very extensive. Cigarettes and the substances in them contribute to cervical cancer, poisoning of the ovaries, premature aging of the skin, infertility, miscarriage, low birth weight babies, breast cancer, and, of course, lung cancer. Every year, cancer of the lung affects 80,000 women in the U.S. and 93,000 men. It accounts for 25 percent of all cancer deaths in women.[20] These statistics are particularly alarming given that girls are now smoking more than boys, partly because nicotine is an appetite suppressant that allows them to remain slim.

Whether or not a teenager begins to smoke is heavily influenced by the mass media. This makes sense, since this is the age group that is most susceptible to pressure to "fit in." And the media is a powerful messenger of what it takes to fit in. It's interesting to note the amount of tobacco smoking in the media recently, especially among young women. A concrete example of how powerfully advertising can influence smoking is the following: The number of American teens who took up smoking jumped 73 percent, from 708,000 to 1.2 million, between 1988 and 1996, and the rate at which teens became smokers also increased, climbing 50 percent, from 51 per 1,000 in 1988 to 77 per 1,000 in 1996, according to estimates from the CDC—1988 being the year that RJ Reynolds introduced Joe Camel in a very successful advertising campaign, and 1996 being the year the FDA outlawed the use of Joe Camel in advertising.[21]

Of course advertising can also influence people in positive ways. In Maine an aggressive media campaign that has included very clever ads on the adverse effects of smoking has helped decrease the rate of teen smoking by 47 percent since 1997—another proof of the power of marketing, but this time it was marketing with a conscience.

Although the media (and peer pressure) are powerful, parents can be more powerful still. A recent study from Dartmouth Medical School documented that *those adolescents who perceived strong parental disapproval of smoking were less than half as likely to become smokers compared to their peers, even if they had a sibling who smoked or a parent who smoked!* Additionally, peer pressure to smoke was strongly negated by strong expectations of parental punishment of such behavior![22]

Another aspect of this study showed the value of consistency: when an adolescent perceives that her parents are becoming more lenient about smoking over time, she is more likely to take up the habit. On the other hand, if parents are perceived as staying strict or becoming even stricter about their disapproval of smoking over time, this serves to prevent their adolescents from using tobacco. Since the vast majority of women who smoke started the habit before the age of eighteen, it's critical that parents play a very proactive rule in discouraging this devastating and difficult-to-break addiction.

Tobacco is one drug that I have zero tolerance for. Though I certainly have some beloved friends who smoke, I forbid smoking in my house, my car, or anywhere around me. I can't stand the smell or the way it clings to my hair and clothing.

While hating smoking, I don't judge smokers. I know how hard it is to quit. My maternal grandmother was a smoker and that certainly contributed to her death from a heart attack at the age of sixty-eight, which occurred after shoveling snow off her driveway. Smoking shuts down feeling and the energy of the heart, so my response to women who smoke is compassion for whatever it is in their lives that demands numbing. If they want to quit, I refer them to acupuncture, which has been helpful to many of my patients and friends.

MARIJUANA (CANNABIS)

A vast number of people use marijuana regularly, just as millions use alcohol regularly. It is readily available to adolescents. My older daughter once told me, "Mom, everybody at my school smokes pot." Marijuana, like alcohol, can take the edge off life for a while. After smoking it, people feel relaxed and dreamy. They feel more at ease with the people who are around them (socialization through chemical assistance). Over time, however, it will take more and more of the addictive substance to get the same effect.

Another of the attractions of marijuana comes from its being il-legal, which means there's a tremendous sense of social camaraderie and ritual around "scoring" it and then getting together to smoke. The culture of dope is steeped in the thrill of "getting away with something," which is very appealing to an adolescent's need to indi-viduate from her parents or other authority figures.

GOOD NEWS ABOUT MARIJUANA USE

Though millions of teenagers use marijuana, its use seems to be declining recently, according to the ongoing Monitoring the Future project, begun in 1975, which follows the behav-iors, attitudes, and values of American secondary school stu-dents, college students, and young adults. Each year, the study surveys a total of some fifty thousand eighth-, tenth-, and twelfth-graders about their substance use, including marijuana, heroine, cocaine, marijuana, Ecstasy, and so on. This vast research project has found a very gradual decline in drug use between 2002 and 2003. In addition to the de-clines in use, fewer young people in each grade say they've ever used an illicit drug. The authors state, "Because mari-juana is by far the most widely used of the illicit drugs, trends in its use tend to drive the index of any illicit drug use. In 2003, marijuana use exhibited its second year of de-cline in the upper grades and its seventh year of decline among eighth-graders. Its use has now fallen by three-tenths among eighth-graders since their peak in 1996 and by about two-tenths and one-tenth, respectively, among the tenth- and twelfth-graders since their recent peaks in 1997. In 2003, 13 percent, 28 percent, and 35 percent of the eighth-, tenth-, and twelfth-graders indicated having smoked mari-juana in the prior twelve months." Interestingly, the stu-dents in all three of these grades had an increased level of awareness about the risks of marijuana compared to previ-ous years.

Given the power of the media, "it's quite possible that the National Youth Anti-Drug Media Campaign by the Office of National Drug Control Policy and the Partnership for a Drug-Free America, which communicates the dangers of marijuana use, has had its intended effect," states researcher L. D. Johnston, Ph.D.[23]

CANNABIS AND THE BRAIN

As with alcohol, marijuana has a wide range of effects on the brain, both immediate and over the long term.

The THC effect. Marijuana impairs brain functioning far longer than the actual "high" lasts. The subjective feeling of being high lasts for several hours after smoking marijuana. But because it takes so long for the active ingredient in marijuana (tetrahydrocannabis—THC) to be eliminated from the body, the effects on brain function can last for several days to a month. THC is fat soluble and stays in the body's tissues for weeks, which is why urine tests can detect it for weeks after actual use.

Learning problems. Marijuana has an adverse effect on learning, memory, and cognitive processing speed. The persistence of THC and its byproducts affect the brain's ability to learn and remember. THC has a direct effect on the acetylcholine levels in the hippocampus, the part of the brain that encodes and lays down new memory. A study of pilots using flight simulators showed that their cognitive function for learning and memory—and also for motor skills (see below)—was impaired for at least twenty-four hours following a modest use of marijuana. One of the problems, however, is that the user doesn't recognize this impairment. If an adolescent uses marijuana daily, her learning ability will be hindered, and she may develop increasing emotional and psychological dependence on the drug. Dedicated cannabis users who use marijuana daily over many years suffer from learning, memory, and attention difficulties. (If you've ever been around an old "druggy," you know exactly what this is like. It's as though part of the person is off in space somewhere. The character Mitch, one of the folk singers in the movie *A Mighty Wind,* is a perfect—albeit exaggerated—example.)

The severity of cognitive deficits is related to the number of years of use. The more years you use marijuana, the more problem you have focusing your attention and the higher your distractibility. This helps to explain why individuals who use marijuana for many years are likely to undermine their chances of achieving their life and career goals.

Physical function. Marijuana affects the brain's ability to process fine motor movement, thus affecting physical performance in sports, playing an instrument, driving, and so on.

Addictiveness. Marijuana is addictive in some individuals. Some, though not all, individuals who use marijuana become emotionally and psychologically dependent upon it. When they stop using it, they experience sleep problems, irritability, anxiety, and depression. As with cigarettes and alcohol, other individuals can use these drugs occasionally without any obvious adverse effects.

OTHER EFFECTS OF CANNABIS

Apathy syndrome. Over time, chronic marijuana use leads to apathy, aimlessness, the loss of motivation to achieve, lack of long-range planning, and decreased productivity. Although Andrew Weil, M.D., who has done research on marijuana use, argues that these traits are more likely to be present in the first place in those who use marijuana, I believe that marijuana users are more prone to apathy because marijuana, like most psychologically addictive substances, decreases anxiety—which blunts the very emotion that is necessary to mobilize us to deal with conflicts, create forward movement, and achieve mastery in life. Remember, emotions always affect cognition, and cognition influences one's behavior. When an adolescent (or adult) smokes a joint to relieve anxiety instead of learning how to deal skillfully with the situation that is causing anxiety, she is setting herself up for apathy.

Lung damage. Smoking marijuana causes lung damage the same way that cigarettes do; for example, emphysema-like changes in the alveoli of the lungs where oxygen is picked up by the blood. This effect can be seen after a year of daily use and may be picked up on pulmonary function tests, chest X-rays, or MRIs.[24]

Hormonal problems. Finally, some studies show that marijuana affects hormones in such a way that it decreases sperm counts, testosterone levels, and other reproductive hormones.[25] Mona Lisa Schulz, M.D., Ph.D., calls this the testicular shrinkage syndrome. Marijuana may also increase the ratio of female hormones to male in the body, thus causing males to have gynecomastia or breast development. I've personally observed this in a number of male long-term pot smokers.

TAKE YOUR OWN
SUBSTANCE-ABUSE INVENTORY

When you talk to your children about the hazards of alcohol, cigarette smoking, marijuana, and other drugs, it helps if you are clear in your mind about your own drug use. Kids can smell deceit very quickly. So make sure that you are as honest with yourself as you would want them to be with you. Ask yourself the following questions:

~ What is your past or present relationship with mood-altering substances?

~ Do you still use any of them? How often? Under what circumstances?

~ Are you ever tempted to lie about your use of any of these or keep it a secret?

~ What is (or was) your reason for using these substances?
To have fun?
To fit in?
Because you were uncomfortable in a social situation?
To lift depression?
To feel better about yourself?
To escape feelings of pain, separation, loneliness, or awkwardness?

~ What is your family legacy with any of these substances?

~ Are you willing to discuss your present use of mood-altering substances with your daughter?

~ Are you willing to discuss your past use of any of these with your daughter?

Note: Regardless of your past, you can help your daughter stay off drugs. For more information and advice, go to www.theanti drug.com.

TERRY and TED: Taking Inventory

Ted and Terry, the parents of the teenagers described earlier whose party spun out of control under the influence of alcohol, were so upset about what had happened that they decided to stop drinking themselves, in order to set a better example for their kids.

However, they soon realized that this was more difficult for them than they imagined it would be. They noticed that on the nights they didn't drink, they got short-tempered, on edge, and had trouble sleeping. They literally didn't know what to say, and felt self-conscious with each other and with their kids when they didn't have a beer or a cocktail to smooth the way.

Soon they found that they were sneaking a beer or two when the kids were out and hiding the cans. After a few weeks of this, Terry realized that she and her husband had a problem that they needed to deal with. She and Ted sat down with their children and admitted that they were concerned about their alcohol use. They named themselves alcoholics. (Remember, most alcoholics are successful executives, pilots, and doctors, not skid-row bums!) John and Jacqueline were stunned and also filled with respect. They realized that their parents were really cool now because they weren't doing what all the other antidrug and antialcohol parents were doing—telling their kids "Do as I say, not as I do."

Terry and her husband both attended the one-week addiction-treatment program at the Caron Foundation, while their children stayed with relatives. Eventually the kids joined their parents at some family meetings and became educated about how alcohol had affected their family and their social development. Today, neither Terry nor Ted drinks and both teens have decided, because of their family history, to delay alcohol use, at least until they have developed enough social confidence to get by without the need to drug themselves with alcohol or another recreational chemical.

AN ALCOHOL-SPECIFIC INVENTORY: CAGE SCREEN FOR DIAGNOSIS OF ALCOHOLISM

Alcohol abuse is described as any "harmful use" of alcohol. The following CAGE screen is the one that doctors typically use to diagnose alcoholism:

Have you ever:

C Thought you should CUT back on your drinking?
A Felt ANNOYED by people criticizing your drinking?
G Felt GUILTY or bad about your drinking?
E Had a morning EYE-OPENER to relieve hangover or nerves?

Two or three positive responses equals a high index of suspicion for alcoholism. Four positive responses is considered diagnostic. [26]

Though different researchers use different terms to define problems with alcohol, these different terms themselves speak volumes
about the denial that is the hallmark of the disease. When it comes
to alcohol, *harmful use, alcoholism, alcohol abuse,* and *alcohol dependency* are all variations on the same theme. They all indicate a
problem with alcohol. One of my friends, a longtime member of AA,
puts it this way: "It's not the amount of alcohol you drink that defines whether or not you've got a problem. It's your psychological
and physiologic dependence on it. If you can't get through the day
without a drink, then you're an alcoholic. Plain and simple. Anyone
who splits hairs over the definition is probably participating in what
we in AA call stinkin' thinkin'." I agree with her.

THE BOTTOM LINE: If you are concerned about your use of alcohol, get help. Talk to your doctor, or go to your nearest AA meeting,
or call your local hospital or mental health center to find a good
drug and alcohol counselor. If you feel that your daughter has a
problem, then get professional help to set up a formal intervention.

HOW TO HELP YOUR DAUGHTER
DEAL WITH DIFFICULT EMOTIONS WITHOUT
CHEMICAL ASSISTANCE

*Do not condone the use of drugs, cigarettes, or alcohol in your home
or elsewhere even if your position is unpopular.* This is crucial for
young and middle teens.

Be realistic and compassionate. Don't teach your daughter that
those who use drugs such as marijuana are bad. Many of those who
use drugs and alcohol are good people who are functioning members
of society. The thing to get across is this: Given the adverse affects of
addictive substances, how much healthier, happier, and more effective could these individuals be if they weren't using these substances?

*Teach your daughter how to build emotional mastery and develop
balanced biochemistry in her brain without addictive substances.
Do the same thing yourself.* One of the reasons that addictive substances are addictive is that they produce a chemical "high" in the
brain that feels good. In other words, they induce euphoria quickly
and numb pain of all kinds—emotional as well as physical. The
problem is that continued use is associated with what's known as ha-

bituation, meaning that it takes more and more of the substance to produce the desired result.

Happily, there are healthy ways to produce the same chemical reward in the brain without resorting to addictive substances. Raising your brain levels of endorphins, serotonin, and other "reward chemicals" can be done through a variety of natural means. The tried-and-true methods for doing this are meditation; exercise; developing sports, academic, musical, and interpersonal skills; and finding a purpose in life. All of these will enhance self-esteem and the brain chemistry of "reward." In other words, it feels good to engage in activities that are useful to both you and your community. Eating a good diet with sufficient quantities of protein, low-glycemic-load carbohydrates, and healthy fats like omega-3s also helps produce these feel-good brain chemicals. (See "Diet" section.)

Dare to be "uncool!" Don't fall into the trap of trying to be a cool friend to your daughter or her peers by joining with or condoning their adolescent behavior and acting as though using drugs, cigarettes, or alcohol is okay. You are the parent. You need to act like one.

All of us want our daughters and their friends to like us. And when teens gather in groups, that group mind has a way of making us feel as though we are the geeks of the century. You know what I'm talking about. Your teenage daughter looks at you disapprovingly, and says, "Mom, you're not wearing *that*, are you?" She acts embarrassed to be with you. She tries to make you feel stupid. She sneers at you if you dare to talk straight about your disapproval of her "cool" friends who use alcohol and drugs.

When adolescents try to make you feel stupid and uncool, they're really just projecting their own intense insecurity on you. And it's apt to bring up all your own unresolved issues from adolescence. Acknowledge this to yourself but have the courage to stand your ground. What teens are really looking to you for is boundaries and rules. (Remember the need for an "external frontal cortex"—that's you.) It takes enormous courage to stand up to exactly the same kind of peer pressure feeling that may have toppled you when you were fourteen. Now's your chance!

Walk your talk. Be a role model. Be the change that you are seeking. Kids can smell hypocrisy a mile away. Your behavior is much more influential than your words. So if you yourself regularly use alcohol, cigarettes, marijuana (or your work) as an escape, then your daughter is much more likely to do the same—especially if you use these substances to wind down and relax. As the study cited above shows, it is possible to be a smoker and still influence your kids away from smoking if you strongly disapprove of smoking. But to do this effectively, you'd have to be very honest about your own addiction to tobacco (or any other substance)—and let your kids know that you can't seem to stop and don't want the same thing to happen to them.

Let your daughter know what you think about her friends who use cigarettes, drugs, and/or alcohol. When my daughters brought home friends who used any of these substances, I always told them how sorry I felt for these friends because kids don't become addicted to substances unless they feel significant unresolved stress from some area in which they feel bad about themselves or their lives. In other words, they use mood-altering substances for the same reason that adults do: to keep from feeling something they don't want to feel! Social anxiety about fitting in is relieved by substances that lower one's inhibitions. The drinking behavior that one sees at an adolescent party, though less polished, is not much different from the drinking and drug use that occur socially among adults.

Adolescence is obviously a stressful time, when being accepted by one's peers is of enormous importance to most teens. But medicating their awkwardness with substances is a poor substitute for developing true mastery in social, educational, and work situations.

Let your kids know you're there for them. Tell your daughter that she can always count on you when she's not sure what to do or gets scared. Obviously we can't protect our daughters from all the scrapes and bruises associated with growing up. What we can do is let them know that they can talk to us about anything that concerns them without our being overly critical and judgmental.

When I was a teenager and started going out at night with my friends, my parents said that no matter what happened, I could call them and they would come and get me, at any time and any place, and no questions asked. So I always knew that if I was at a party or on a date and things started to get scary or out of control, all I had to do was call my parents, and wait for them to pick me up. I told my daughters the same thing.

Teach your daughter how to face daily responsibilities. All adolescents need to learn how to be responsible for something other than their own gratification. One of the best ways to instill a sense of responsibility in your teenager—and also help her shore up the health of the organs and functions of her third emotional center (stomach, digestion, liver, gall bladder)—is to require her to get a job. This can be a job outside of the home for pay or a task in the home that she must do on a regular basis. Regardless of whether it is for pay or not, the key is that it be a job that has to be done day-in and day-out. And there must be consequences for not doing the job. If the dog isn't fed, the table isn't set, the laundry isn't done, the floors aren't washed, or whatever the job is, privileges will be taken away. The ability to stick with a task—even when it's boring or difficult—is crucial to developing one's sense of responsibility and truly learning how to "show up" for life. And it helps a teenager to feel good about herself. This is one of the reasons why working is so helpful to individuals with all kinds of problems, including depression and chronic pain. The movie *Life as a House,* which showed the healing effect of work on a troubled young boy, is a stunning example of this. The main character, a sullen, moody, drug-addicted adolescent, improved all aspects of his life by learning the skills and discipline necessary to tear down and rebuild a house, in partnership with his father.

Teach your daughter how to deal effectively and humorously with peer pressure. My parents told me all about peer pressure and how to resist it, advice that really got through to me and proved enormously helpful. Explain to your daughter that pressure from peers to participate in an activity such as smoking, drinking, or eating foods that you'd rather avoid is always motivated by a lack of self-esteem on the part of the person (or group) who is doing the pressuring. On some level, these individuals feel insecure about their behavior, so they try to make themselves feel better by getting other people to participate, too! Hence, peer pressure. Knowing this is the key to dealing effectively with peer pressure, at any age, and also being able to fit in and be cool. The best thing for your daughter to do when confronted with such pressure is to put her peers at ease, accept them, approach them with self-deprecating humor—but not give in.

The following suggestions might help your daughter put this approach into practice. Tell her to:

~ join with them in spirit, but not in the activity. For example, if you're offered a drink, just take the drink. You don't have to drink it. My daughters used this tactic all the time. They'd stand around with a glass in their hand all night long, pretending they were participating.

~ plead a medical problem. If you're offered a cigarette or pot, you just say, "Oh gosh. I'm sorry, but the last time I did that, I got an allergic reaction and had to be taken to the hospital."

~ never act "holier than thou." By calling her friends on their behavior or giving them a lecture on the dangers of what they're doing, your daughter will only risk being ostracized. I knew an adolescent who once reported her peers for smoking in the school bathroom. As you might imagine, after that she had difficulty making and keeping friends!

~ use humor. If you can get them to laugh, you have instant acceptance and everyone's guard comes down. My friend Mona Lisa Schulz used to tell friends, "I'm sorry, I can't join you. Last time I tried that stuff I got psychotic. I thought I was a bat and bit someone. Otherwise I'd love to join you guys." This works every time.

Let go and let God. Finally, when it comes to the behavior of your children, it's important to do what you can and then let it go—especially once they've graduated from high school. You have to release your illusion of control. It's possible to do everything right as a parent and still have a daughter who ends up smoking or drinking or using other harmful substances. If that happens, don't beat yourself up. Realize that your daughter has her own Higher Power, and you are not it. She may well come around when she hits her late twenties or early thirties.

18
Self-care Basics
A Tool Kit for Good Health

On the most basic level, self-care is a question of what a girl does with her body and what she puts into it. Self-care involves everything from her daily food choices and behaviors to her exercise activities and the types of health-care professionals she chooses to see (probably with a lot of input from you). The quality of her self-care contributes dramatically to her state of health and happiness. How well she takes care of herself depends in part on how much she understands about the relationship between the choices she makes and the ways she feels—and looks.

SELF-CARE AND SELF-ESTEEM: THE SEAMLESS LINK

Good self-care is also based on a foundation of self-esteem. If a girl feels good about herself, she will want to take care of herself. If she doesn't, she is much more apt to indulge in self-destructive behaviors that are a reflection of her lack of self-worth. It's that simple. One of my patients told me that she never wears a seat belt when she's feeling bad about herself, and I think that sums it up.

Self-esteem and self-care are also seamlessly linked with a healthy sense of responsibility. Adolescence is the time when a girl will be making more and more of her own choices. But it is a time when a mother should still be active in guiding her daughter to make good choices. Chances are, you know a lot more than your daughter about the factors that will help her live a long and healthy life. Below I've chosen to focus on a number of the key issues that come up during adolescence—some that a teenage girl is likely to take very seriously without any prompting from you (like skin care) and some that you are more likely to take seriously because you understand their long-term consequences (like eating disorders). Be there to give her guidance on both.

SKIN CARE

The skin is a kind of "external" nervous system that is derived from the same embryonic layer as the brain and central nervous system. This helps to explain why the skin is affected by every thought you think, as well as every food you eat.

The effects of aging on the skin begin in earnest during the teen years but the damage may not show up until years later—as wrinkles, age spots, and fine lines. The teen years are an ideal time to implement a solid skin-care program that will reward your daughter with a glowing complexion for life. Here's what every teenage girl needs to know:

Diet and the Skin. The key to a great complexion throughout life starts on the inside—with a sound diet. Your diet shows all over your face. Foods that stabilize blood sugar and insulin help keep skin clear and unblemished. Foods that raise blood sugar and insulin levels—sugar and most refined grains, especially the refined carbohydrates we call "white" foods—contribute to acne and breakouts. That's because a diet that raises blood sugar also raises androgen levels so that the balance between androgens and estrogens is disrupted. The resulting hormonal imbalance affects the oil ducts in the skin in a way that leads to acne. (See Chapter 13 for guidelines for keeping blood sugar under control.)

Vitamin and Mineral Supplements and the Skin. The skin is nourished by anything that increases circulation, balances hormones, and fights free radicals. A wide variety of nutrients helps with this process, including the B vitamins, which are necessary to metabolize hormones; omega-3 fats, which are necessary for healthy cell membranes; and antioxidant vitamins, including vitamin C, which not only fight the free radicals that damage the skin but help maintain healthy collagen, the substance that gives skin its elasticity. (See "Supplementation Plan for Adolescent Girls".)

Cleansing and Moisturizing Regime and the Skin. Every adolescent girl should begin a good skin-care regimen that includes proper cleansing day and night with a cleanser that is pH balanced for the skin. (Most soaps are too alkaline.) She should also start moisturizing morning and night with products that contain antioxidants such as vitamin E and coenzyme Q10. Research on the effects of antioxidants on the skin has revolutionized skin care, with the result that many moisturizers now contain antioxidants. So check the labels to make sure they're included. Antioxidants also enhance the protection of the collagen layer of the skin to prevent later wrinkling and skin cancer. The sooner your daughter starts to take good care of her skin, the better she'll look years later!

Stress and the Skin. No matter how good a diet a young girl eats, stress can have an adverse effect on sensitive skin, especially during the hormonal swings of puberty. This can come out as an increased tendency to get pimples, as well as rashes and hives—yet another reason to give your daughter techniques for dealing with stress.

Sunlight (and Sunscreen) and the Skin. Although we all need exposure to sunlight for health (see "Sunlight: An Essential Nutrient" in Chapter 8), there is still no doubt that excessive ultraviolet radiation from the sun is the number one cause of premature skin aging. The effects are cumulative with time, so even young girls should be using sunscreen or sunblock on the face, neck, shoulders, and chest.

I never leave the house during the day without at least 15 SPF on my face, neck, and shoulders, and neither do my daughters. On the other hand, we try to get regular mild sun exposure on other areas of our bodies for the health and vitamin D effects.

Rx for Skin Breakouts. My favorite treatment for skin breakouts is tea tree oil. Because of its antiseptic and antifungal properties, it is an ideal topical application. Tea tree oil makes pimples go away faster, particularly the ones under the skin that haven't come to a head yet.

Diet and Unwanted Hair Growth. Most adolescent girls are disturbed by the hormonally stimulated hair growth that occurs during puberty, which may include dark hairs around their nipples, on their lower abdomens, and especially on their faces. Some of this hair growth is simply genetic and is more common in those of Middle Eastern, Eastern European, Greek, Asian, and African descent. But regardless of one's genetic tendencies, eating a diet that keeps blood sugar and insulin levels under control can help curb unwanted hair growth, just as it helps prevent acne. This is because the disruption

of the balance between androgens and estrogen that results from elevated blood sugar and insulin acts not only on the oil ducts in the
skin, causing acne (as discussed above) but on the hair follicles, promoting excessive hair growth. Early insulin resistance and glycemic
stress are the main driving forces behind the premature appearance
of pubic, axillary, and facial hair in so many young girls. Because
glycemic stress is a risk factor for this and for so many other adolescent and adult health problems, every effort must be made to eat an
insulin-normalizing diet like the kind I described in Chapter 13,
which will definitely help minimize unwanted hair growth.

Nondietary Treatments for Unwanted Hair. Fortunately, there is
more that can be done for excess hair growth now than ever before.
Laser hair removal is improving all the time and can be used on the
face and also the bikini line. It's expensive, but compared to years of
embarrassment, it's worth it. There is also a wide variety of waxing,
bleaching, and shaving approaches to unwanted hair. My suggestion
would be to consult a state-of-the-art dermatology or plastic surgery
center run by board-certified professionals who specialize in the use
of cosmetic laser procedures.

MENSTRUAL CRAMPS

Menstrual cramps affect about 60 percent of teenage girls in this
country. I suffered from severe cramps from the onset of my period
until my late thirties, when I finally discovered acupuncture and herbs
and got rid of them for good. Until then, cramps were a major life disruption for me. I had to leave school on many occasions, and even
had to scrub out of surgery a couple times because the cramps were
so bad. Given my experience, it has certainly been a pleasure to see
that this is one legacy that I addressed so thoroughly that it didn't get
passed down to my daughters. Though my older daughter occasionally got cramps in high school and college, she has been able to stop
them almost completely with the kinds of treatments I describe below.

No girl should have to suffer from menstrual cramps for years on
end. There are so many things that can help.

Diet. Again, the same diet that helps keep skin clear and weight
under control also prevents excess production of prostaglandins, the
hormones released when the lining of the uterus is shed, which produce cramping of the uterine wall. Another possible dietary consideration is the arachidonic acid contained in eggs, red meat, and dairy
products. Girls who are very sensitive to these foods may be able to

eliminate cramping by avoiding these foods for the two weeks prior to the menstrual period.

Supplements. Calcium and magnesium are especially helpful in preventing cramping because both of these minerals have a relaxing effect on muscle contraction. The B vitamins and vitamin C are also helpful. The Supplementation Plan below contains adequate amounts of all these vitamins and minerals. In addition, if a girl is not eating a diet with adequate amounts of omega-3 fats relative to omega-6 fats, as described in Chapter 13, she should take a daily omega-3 supplement, and/or one to two tablespoons of flaxseed oil, or a 400 DHA supplement, or one to four tablespoons of ground-up flaxseed. (See Resources.)

Topical Treatments. Menastil, an over-the-counter product whose active ingredient is calendula oil, can be rubbed on the skin over the lower abdomen. The oil is absorbed into the skin and has a homeopathic effect on the uterus that stops cramping. I have used this with several patients and with my daughters with great success.

Antiinflammatory Drugs. Over-the-counter antiinflammatory drugs such as Advil and Anaprox work extremely well for menstrual cramps. The key is to take the drugs *before* the cramping begins in order to lower the levels of the prostaglandins before they become high enough to cause cramps. Since cramping generally begins for most girls within a couple hours of the onset of bleeding, that means taking them as soon as possible after the period has started.

Acupuncture and Herbs. For those who do not get sufficient relief from cramps by following the suggestions above, I strongly recommend acupuncture and Chinese herbs, performed and prescribed by a practitioner of traditional Chinese medicine (TCM). TCM has very well-documented success in treating gynecological problems of all kinds, including irregular periods, infertility, heavy bleeding, and so on. Research has shown that most individuals will need about ten treatments, after which the cramps will be significantly relieved. The Chinese herb bupleurum (Xiao Yao Wan) is also very effective when taken as directed. (See Resources.)

Heat and Rest. The fact that so many girls have cramps speaks volumes about our culture's love affair with incessant productivity and activity at the expense of adequate periods of rest. Menstrual cramps are a sure sign that the sympathetic nervous system stress hormones associated with "fight or flight" are out of balance with the parasympathetic chemicals of "rest and restore." That's why cramps are often relieved by simply resting with a hot water bottle on the lower abdomen, or taking a relaxing hot bath.

SLEEP

"Sleep is as important to our overall health as exercise and a healthy diet," says Dr. Carl Hunt, director of the government's National Center on Sleep Disorders Research. But it has been well documented that high school students don't get enough sleep. A study of 3,100 teenagers in Providence, Rhode Island, for example, found that 26 percent reported getting six and a half hours of sleep per night or less.[1] And sleep deprivation among young people is getting worse. Seventy-one percent of college students reported sleep complaints in 2000, up from 24 percent in 1978.[2] Unfortunately, the bad sleep habits that are often established during these years can contribute to a lifetime of sleep disorders.

While the need for sleep, like all things pertaining to health, is different for each person (for example, I've read that Albert Einstein needed ten hours a night), research suggests that adolescents need at least eight hours per night, and many do better with nine or even ten hours. Since this is a time when their brains are forming new nerve connections and neural networks at an extremely rapid pace, literally rewiring their brains, it is critical that they get enough sleep to support these developments. And since they are in school and trying to learn new material every day, they are in particular need of the brain-regulating effect of the REM sleep stage, when the acetylcholine that helps reconstitute memory circuits is replenished.

The Culture That Never Sleeps

Many people in Western industrialized society are sleep deprived because they are overscheduled, overworked, and overstimulated. The existence of artificial lighting, our 24/7 addiction to mass media, and the constant pressure to keep moving, keep producing, have created a very "sleep macho" culture in which those anomalous individuals who, by some quirk of biology, don't need more than four to five hours of sleep per night, are held up as the gold standard for everyone else. Applying this standard to an adult, let alone a teenager, truly does a disservice.

Unfortunately, teenagers on average need more sleep than adults, and face even greater challenges to getting it. Most high schools have an early start time, while the typical teenager likes to stay up late and sleep late. Many spend the after-school hours doing sports, extracurricular activities, working at jobs, or hanging out with friends. Consequently, they don't begin their homework until late at night. Social pressures play a role in sleep deprivation too. As sleep expert William Dement, M.D., Ph.D., says in his book *The Promise of Sleep,* for today's teenagers "staying up late becomes a coming-of-age emblem . . . ," which further exacerbates the problem of getting enough sleep.

Teenagers didn't always stay up late, of course. There's no doubt that over the millions of years of human evolution teenagers went to sleep when night fell, just as everyone else did. But all of this pressure to stay up late and be a night owl has created a biologic shift in the circadian sleep rhythms. No wonder teenagers today are sleep deprived. Their sleep patterns have been so disrupted that their entire bodies are affected. According to Mona Lisa Schulz, M.D., Ph.D., the mechanism by which social pressures have had such an impact on their biological clocks has to do with the hypothalamus, which is the area of the brain that is the hub for receiving emotional and social information and transducing it into bodily reactions. The hypothalamus is also the area of the brain that controls sleep and wakefulness cycles. This doesn't mean that teenagers are doomed to be sleep deprived, because as Dr. Schulz also points out, human beings have frontal-lobe executive control over our actions—if we choose to employ it. Learning how to get enough sleep is just another part of a teenager's growing up and becoming responsible for her own life and health. No one knows this better than I. Ob-gyn training is a study in sleep deprivation and learning how to get around it. I don't pretend that this is easy, but I think it's critically important!

Why? Because sleep deprivation leads to reduced productivity, poor performance in school, moodiness, and, because it's associated with increased cortisol levels, may even contribute to weight gain and the other medical problems associated with higher than normal stress hormone levels, including reduced resistance to bacteria and viruses. Sleep deprivation is also believed to lead to drug use among teenagers, as well as violent and aggressive behaviors, and the likelihood of developing sleep disorders that become chronic.

When the brain runs on too little sleep, it malfunctions in a wide variety of areas:

~ Reaction time slows.

~ Attention span suffers and concentration is impaired. This is in part due to what scientists call microsleeps, repeated periods lasting one to ten seconds when the sleepy brain just zones out and doesn't process information.

~ Driving is adversely affected. Though I could find no data specific to teenagers vis-à-vis lack of sleep and auto accidents, in adults at least 100,000 auto crashes and 1,550 traffic deaths a year are caused by falling asleep at the wheel.[3] Because teens have driving skills that are still being formed, it makes sense that they'd be even more likely than adults to have accidents when sleep deprived. According to the American Academy of Pediatrics (AAP), "Youngsters aged sixteen through nineteen make up just one in twenty motorists, yet they are behind the wheel in one in seven accidents that kill either the driver or passengers"—very sobering statistics.[4]

~ Ability to learn is undermined. A sleep-deprived brain is low on acetylcholine, a substance generated during the REM phase of sleep (associated with dreaming), which helps reconstitute the memory circuits each night. Low acetylocholine levels make it harder for the brain to store information.

~ Creativity and problem-solving abilities suffer. This is why it's good advice to tell someone who has reached an impasse in her work to "sleep on it." Whether she's trying to write the next line of her poem or solve the next part of a complicated calculus problem, the balm of sleep will help her brain neurons make the necessary connections.

~ Mood is negatively affected. Sleep deprivation can lead to an increased risk of anxiety and depression, especially if drugs and alcohol are part of the pattern.[5]

DEALING WITH SLEEP DEPRIVATION

Teens need to train themselves to adapt their sleeping and waking cycles to the society they live in so that they get an adequate amount of sleep during this critical developmental period. They also need to learn strategies for getting by on too little sleep for those times when there just isn't a realistic alternative. For example, my daughter Ann was involved in a professional production of *Romeo and Juliet* when she was a junior in high school. She'd come home from performances at 10:30 P.M., do several hours of homework, and then get up at 6:30 A.M. to go to school. Because she was so motivated and stimulated, she actually managed to get through that particular academic period without suffering any adverse effects from exhaustion. In fact, she was in a great mood and had high energy the whole time. But no one can keep up this kind of schedule indefinitely without paying a price. So here's what I recommend for your sleep-deprived daughter (or anyone else suffering from lack of sleep):

Keep active. Move around as much as possible to stay awake.

Don't drive. Don't ever get behind the wheel on too little sleep. It has been suggested that driving while sleep deprived is as dangerous as drinking and driving. This is especially true in teens whose driving skills are not yet well developed. Trying to compensate for sleep deprivation with caffeine creates an artificial sense of competence. No one can drive safely on too little sleep, least of all teenagers.

Eliminate caffeine. Avoid drinking coffee, tea, or other caffeinated beverages like colas, since they interfere with sleep. In many young women, even one cup of coffee in the morning interferes with sleep later that night!

Nap. Take cat naps of at least ten minutes whenever possible—they can be surprisingly restorative.

Create a sleep schedule. Make up the "sleep debt" on weekends or whenever possible, but only as a temporary measure. Both Dr. Mona Lisa Schulz and Dr. William Dement point out that it's better to keep to a regular sleep schedule, going to bed and waking up at the same time each day. This is known as "sleep hygiene." Allowing a teen to sleep hours later every weekend further disrupts her sleep/wakefulness cycle. Given how overbooked the average teenager is, it will require considerable time-management and prioritization skills to maintain good sleep hygiene. But these skills will stand her in good stead for the rest of her life.

Reduce stimulation. Don't watch television, listen to loud music, or do any activities on the computer that aren't related to homework for at least an hour before bedtime, to cut down on overstimulation. I recommend not allowing your daughter to have a television or computer in her room.

Get regular exercise. This will make it easier for your daughter to fall asleep once she finally gets to bed.

In general, you should do what you can to discourage activities that require your daughter to miss the sleep she needs. I know how hard that is, since during high school both my daughters were involved in theater productions with nighttime rehearsals and performances that really cut into their sleep. They were passionate about these activities, and I didn't feel I could deny them the opportunity to take part. But for the rest of the school year, I insisted that they be home during weeknights and in bed by 11:00 P.M.

Set the tone for a healthy relationship with sleep. Make sure your daughter understands the connection between sleep and all the other aspects of her life—health, mood, and the ability to function well at school, behind the wheel, on the job, in every sport activity. Give your daughter a bedtime, and then make sure she sticks to it. We set bedtimes for younger children, but give teens more leeway. I think this is a mistake. You don't need to be heavy-handed about bedtime. Most girls really want their mothers to encourage them to get enough sleep. There's nothing like a little trip up to their bedrooms to "check in" and suggest that they hang it up for the night.

EXERCISE

If I had to choose just one thing that helps a girl's self-esteem and health on all levels for a lifetime, it would be regular exercise. The human body was designed to move, stretch, lift, run, twist, and turn. Exercise can take the form of dance, yoga, Pilates, running, walking, or any sport. The main thing is that whatever a girl chooses to do, she should do it regularly. Women who exercise regularly have dramatically decreased risks for their biggest health challenges—heart disease, cancer, diabetes, and osteoporosis. Exercise also has wonderful cosmetic benefits, including permanent weight control, enhanced muscle tone, and clear skin. It's no accident that a female athlete like Venus Williams is considered a sex symbol.

Girls who are on sporting teams get their exercise needs met automatically, but very few girls will continue to play soccer or basketball after high school. That's why it's crucial for girls to establish exercise habits that will last a lifetime, whether or not they play on a team.

NOSE BREATHING

Exercise can be revolutionized by learning how to breathe through your nose while you're doing it. Yes—revolutionized! Regardless of what type of exercise a girl does, her ability to develop and maintain maximum endurance and lung capacity, as well as to prevent respiratory illnesses and sinusitis and other sinus infections, will be vastly improved by breathing through the nose. This is the way humans were designed to breathe. Mouth breathing is a sign of stress. It automatically tells the body that there's an emergency.

Following is just a partial listing of the advantages of nose breathing:

~ Makes exercise much easier because it restores sympathetic/parasympathetic balance so that you finish a workout energized, not exhausted.

~ Stimulates the vagus nerve in the upper abdomen, allowing you to exercise more strenuously at a lower heart rate.

~ Keeps the rib cage flexible. As a result, lung capacity is optimized and you can oxygenate your body and brain more efficiently.

~ Minimizes occurrence of colds and sinus infections, because air that is breathed into your lungs through the nose has been warmed and filtered by the cilia in your nasal passages.

~ Improves metabolism because the better aeration of the lungs oxygenates the blood and burns calories more efficiently. I liken nose breathing while exercising to a woodstove in which the wood is dry and banked properly for efficient burning and heat production. On the other hand, breathing through the mouth while exercising is like burning paper. It burns quickly, producing very little heat or light![6]

DIET

As already discussed, a girl's adolescence is characterized by a relative increase in both lean body mass and body fat. Adolescence, like the prenatal period and the adiposity "rebound" period of young childhood, is the third well-documented "critical period" for the development of obesity, and that has serious implications for the future. Studies suggest that up to 80 percent of individuals who are overweight in adolescence will become overweight adults.[7]

The number one risk factor for excessive body fat, particularly abdominal fat, is eating too many processed foods, especially processed foods that are also rich in additives such as MSG (monosodium glutamate), since they interact with the satiety centers in the brain and promote overeating. Refined grains and other refined carbohydrates, including alcohol, are also big contributors to overweight and specifically to abdominal fat, because of their influence on blood sugar and insulin levels.

The ideal diet for an adolescent girl is the same one I described in Chapter 13 for latency-age girls. Regardless of how much a girl weighs at adolescence, no dieting is necessary if she eats foods that result in stable blood sugar and insulin levels and also gets regular exercise. Her diet should consist mostly of fruits, vegetables, low-fat dairy foods, lean meats and fish, and a limited amount of grain or grain products. She also needs a healthy source of fats in her diet, which can come from eggs, fish, flaxseed, or supplements such as DHA. (See Resources.) Of course I'd be lying if I told you that most adolescent girls follow this approach to diet! (See "Disordered Eating," below.)

VITAMIN AND MINERAL SUPPLEMENTATION

I believe that every teenager should take supplemental vitamins and minerals. Eighty percent of American children and adolescents (not to mention 68 percent of adults) do not eat the recommended five portions of fruits and vegetables per day. Though it's not difficult to include these in the diet if a child is eating at home or at good restaurants, the average teen diet of fast foods simply lacks the nutrient density necessary to reach one's biologic potential. But even for those who follow a healthy diet, including lots of fruits and vegetables, it's still a good idea to supplement the diet with vitamins and minerals.

I've come to this conclusion based on both my many years as a medical practitioner and on my personal experience. I am now convinced that high-quality vitamins and minerals can significantly affect our well-being. Vitamins and minerals help minimize DNA damage, improve health, and prolong healthy lifespan.[8]

A deficiency of any of the key micronutrients—folic acid, vitamin B_{12}, vitamin B_6, niacin, vitamin C, vitamin E, iron, or zinc— mimics radiation damage, causing DNA and gene breakage and setting the stage for various cancers. According to Bruce Ames,

Ph.D., a leading expert on molecular toxicology and nutrition at UC Berkeley, the evidence suggests that even small vitamin and mineral deficiencies result in more cancer-causing damage than radiation and chemicals.[9] Micronutrient deficiency may explain, in good part, why the quarter of the population that eats the fewest fruits and vegetables has about double the cancer rate for most types of cancer when compared with the quarter with the highest intake.

Even if the average adolescent did eat the five helpings of fruits and vegetables needed to meet the vitamin and mineral requirements that are considered adequate, that would by no means be an optimal diet. The RDA is simply a figure that was set by a committee of nutritional experts in order to ensure that a population (not a given individual) is protected from gross deficiency diseases such as scurvy and beriberi. But there is a big difference between taking enough of a nutrient to prevent a gross deficiency disease and taking enough to create optimal health! Moreover, there are a number of essential nutrients for which an RDA has not yet been established. Bottom line: your daughter should be supplementing her diet, even if you feel she eats a reasonably healthy diet.

Supplementation Plan for Adolescent Girls

The following nutrient ranges are optimal for adolescent girls. I know of no "one-a-day" vitamin tablets that contain enough of the right amount of vitamins and minerals for optimal health. Several pills will be necessary. They should be taken in divided doses with meals in the morning and at night. (Note: Some people are so sensitive to the energizing effects of the B vitamins that they should only take B's in the morning, so that their ability to sleep is not affected.)

Vitamin A (as beta carotene)	9,000–15,000 IU
Vitamin C	500–1,500 mg
Vitamin D (as cholecalciferol)	400–2,000 IU
Vitamin E	200–450 IU
Vitamin K	40–60 mcg
Thiamine (B_1)	9–100 mg
Riboflavin (B_2)	9–50 mg
Niacin (B_3)	15–100 mg
Vitamin B_6	10–100 mg
Folate (as folic acid)	800–1,000 mcg
Vitamin B_{12} (as cyanocobalamin)	30–250 mcg
Biotin	100–500 mcg

Pantothenic acid (B$_5$)	30–400 mcg
Calcium	800–1,200 mg
Iodine (as potassium iodide)	150 mcg
Magnesium (chelate)	400–1,000 mg
Zinc	12–50 mg
Selenium (as amino acid complex)	80–120 mcg
Copper	1–2 mg
Manganese	1–15 mg
Chromium (as chromium polynicotinate)	100–400 mcg
Molybdenum	45–60 mcg
Choline	45–100 mg
Inositol	30–500 mg
N-acetyl L-cysteine	30–65 mg
Vanadium (as vanadyl sulfate)	30–100 mcg
Boron	1–3 mg
Iron	30 mg
Trace minerals	1 mg

DISORDERED EATING: OBESITY, BULEMIA, ANOREXIA, AND EVERYTHING IN BETWEEN

Though it may not seem obvious on the surface, obesity is as much an eating disorder as bulimia and anorexia. In fact, state-of-the-art research in this area now approaches them as different aspects of the same thing: disordered eating. And obesity has just been named a disease by the American Medical Association.

A combination of factors conspires to put the majority of adolescent girls at risk for at least some form of disordered eating. The ubiquitous media messages that suggest that an unrealistically thin body is essential for attractiveness to boys, the desire to fit in, the prevalence of high-calorie, nutrient-poor junk food, and an increased tendency to store body fat all collide at adolescence and land squarely on the bodies of adolescent girls. Many young women who are overweight begin their first of a lifelong series of diets during adolescence. At any one time, it is estimated that 77 percent of girls and women 21 and under are "on a diet."[10] Typically a girl starts dieting, which often leads to binge eating in reaction to the feelings of deprivation, which in turn triggers compensatory behaviors such as excessive exercise, use of laxatives, diet pills, diuretics, smoking, caffeine, diet colas, or vomiting to avoid gaining the weight lost while dieting. Disordered eating begun in adolescence tends to follow women right through adulthood. Here's how one woman, whom I'll call Peggy, described the pattern—one I'm sure you'll recognize:

> Since I was a teenager, I've found that no matter what I do, I can't lose weight and keep it off. Though I was a little overweight in high school, I really began to "derail" in college when I gained the "freshman fifteen" and then some. I have been on every diet you can imagine . . . the grapefruit diet, the protein diet, the carbohydrate addicts diet . . . you name it, I've been on it! As soon as the diet begins to work, and I lose weight, I always end up sabotaging the diet and binge eating. I've tried everything to lose weight. I used to drink a lot more than I do now . . . until I realized that beer can really put on the weight too. Oh yes, I also smoke . . . I am almost embarrassed to admit this, but I do. Every time I try to quit, I gain at least ten pounds. Help! Sometimes I feel as though I'm hopelessly destined to be overweight for life.

A great deal of evidence from clinical and epidemiologic studies has shown, beyond any doubt, that dieting and a slim body ideal are, *in themselves,* risk factors for the development of eating disorders! In an extensive study of 36,320 public school students, dieting frequency was related strongly to poor body image, fear of being unable to control eating, and a history of binge eating.[11] You can't diagnose an eating disorder based on a girl's appearance or weight. Most bulimics, for example, are of normal weight.[12] Like the prevalence of heavy social drinking, which actually constitutes alcohol abuse, disordered eating is so common that it's often not recognized as such. Television shows and movies that depict women and girls turning to ice cream or other sugary foods and refined carbs when they are upset normalizes this behavior, tacitly endorsing it.

Disordered eating has significant health consequences. Those who maintain a healthy body weight and healthy body-fat index through moderate exercise and good food choices are much more likely to enjoy good hormonal balance and regular periods. Those who engage in disordered eating experience changes in the hypothalamic areas of their brain that may, depending upon severity, result in anovulation, amenorrhea, heavy or irregular periods, polycystic ovarian disease, depression, and eventually, fertility problems and osteoporosis. Of course, there's a vast difference between the immediate life-threatening effects of anorexia and the long-term toll taken on health and life expectancy by obesity, and between either of those and being fifteen or twenty pounds overweight and going on the occasional brief diet. But they're all on the same spectrum of disordered eating, which also includes yo-yo dieting, bingeing, bulimia, and so forth.

Given our culture's obsession with thinness, and the fact that the majority of people are now clinically overweight, it's clear that we are in the middle of an epidemic of disordered eating. Although it has gotten much worse in very recent times, it's also a legacy that is being passed on by mothers who have struggled with their weight for years and given their daughters unhealthy messages about what an ideal body looks like, and how to keep weight under control. Overweight and obesity often "run in the family." But if mother and daughter commit to changing the mind-set and behavior patterns that have locked that tendency into place, there's nothing inevitable or "in the genes" about packing on those pounds.

Disordered Eating and the Diet Mind-set

Though dieting is not one of the criteria for diagnosis of an eating disorder, as mentioned above it is a risk factor for developing an eating disorder. I believe that the diet mentality has contributed significantly to disordered eating by being a setup for failure, because being "on a diet" implies that you will be coming "off the diet" once you reach your goal, after which you think you can eat all you want of whatever you want once again! This approach can never work. As Oprah Winfrey has so eloquently demonstrated to millions, eating healthfully is a way of life—day in, day out. There are no shortcuts or miracle diets.

I have worked in the area of nutrition, weight control, and exercise with thousands of women and girls for over twenty years. I have also spent a lifetime working hard to control my own weight, doing everything from fasting to exercise to dieting (see Chapter 13, "Personal History"). I know what works and what doesn't. Dieting doesn't work. It's a law of the universe that for every restrictive diet there will be an equal and opposite binge. When you say to a girl, "You can't eat cookies," all her subconscious mind hears is "Eat cookies." As a result, a very powerful urge to eat cookies is set into motion. And it will be satisfied one way or another. The key to long-term weight control, and eating disorder prevention, for both yourself and your daughter, is to stop your own dieting and teach your daughter how to approach food healthfully and with self-esteem.

We need to teach our daughters how to identify actual physical hunger and how to feed it optimally. (See "How to Tell the Difference between Physical and Emotional Hunger," below.) We also need to show them how to soothe their moods with things other than food or substances like sugar or caffeine. (See "How to Boost Mood Without Food".) And we need to demonstrate, in our own lives, the connection between healthy eating and self-esteem. Eating well (which may mean learning to eat less food than you want) to maintain a healthy weight is life affirming and stems from self-respect. Overeating, habitually starving yourself, or throwing up several times a day is exactly the opposite.

How to Tell the Difference between Physical and Emotional Hunger

~ Physical hunger often feels like actual pain or "gnawing" in the stomach area.

~ Physical hunger can be signaled by fatigue, drowsiness, inattention, light-headedness.

~ If it's not mealtime and you can't tell whether the hunger you want to feed is emotional or physical, try this simple experiment: Don't eat for fifteen minutes. Instead, walk around, exercise, or otherwise distract yourself. If you are still hungry, have a healthy snack that has balanced amounts of protein, fat, and carbohydrate.

~ Drink enough water. Many people think they're hungry when they are actually thirsty. This is particularly true in the afternoon, when dehydration can cause a midday slump easily mistaken for a need to eat something as a pick-me-up. Before eating, drink eight to fourteen ounces of water and then wait about fifteen minutes before eating.

~ Keep your blood sugar stable by making sure you eat a breakfast that contains some protein, fat, and carbohydrate. It's impossible to tell the difference between physical and emotional hunger when your blood sugar is low from disordered eating!

~ Be patient with yourself. If it were easy to separate emotional from physical hunger, the majority of the population wouldn't be overweight! Food and love are very intimately connected. Learn how to love yourself without expressing that love through food "treats."

The Fat–Stress Connection

Cortisol, the so-called stress hormone, is released in higher than usual levels when you are under stress. Excess cortisol causes the body to produce insulin, a hormone that enhances the storage of fat. Excess cortisol also results in an almost insatiable appetite for sugar, alcohol, and refined carbohydrates such as pasta, potato chips, pretzels, and so on. The more stress, the more cortisol; the more cortisol, the more insulin; the more insulin, the more carb cravings, and the more storage as fat! It's a vicious cycle that only stops once a person commits to changing all the triggers, both dietary and emotional, that cause it![13]

One particularly difficult trigger to overcome is the legacy of past abuse. Research has shown that adult survivors of childhood physical, emotional, or sexual abuse are at high risk for obesity,[14] and one of the mechanisms by which that risk factor operates is cortisol. Abuse of any kind is obviously stressful, and many survivors of abuse have classic PTSD (post-traumatic stress disorder), with brains and bodies that continue to oversecrete stress hormones even when there is no longer a threat.

We've learned a lot about the connection between abuse and obesity from the huge 1998 ACE (Adverse Childhood Experiences) study of seventeen thousand people, which documented the dramatic adult health consequences of childhood abuse and dysfunction. The ACE study was initially begun in response to observations made in the mid 1980s during an obesity program at the Kaiser Permanente San Diego Department of Preventive Medicine.[15] This program had a very high dropout rate. Surprisingly, many of the people dropping out were successfully losing weight, which turned out to be *why* they were dropping out. Detailed life interviews with almost two hundred such individuals unexpectedly revealed that childhood and adolescent abuse was remarkably common among them, and antedated the onset of their obesity. Once the program had taught them how to break the vicious cycle of cortisol/insulin/overeating by controlling their intake of refined carbohydrates, including alcohol, the emotions associated with the abuse began to arise—because they were no longer using these substances to soothe their emotions. Moreover, obesity turned out not to have been the problem for them but rather the solution. Excess weight was their protective insulation against being sexually attractive once again. Once they lost weight and ran the risk of attracting attention, the pain of the sexual abuse they had endured in the past began to resurface. For example, a woman who gained one hundred and five pounds in the year after being raped said, "Overweight is overlooked. And that is exactly what I need to be." The underlying belief of these people was that "being thin is not safe"—hence the high dropout rate.

In reflecting on the enormity of all this, researcher Vincent Felitti, M.D., wrote:

> If the treatment implications of what we found in the ACE study are far-reaching, the prevention aspects are positively daunting. The very nature of the material is such as to make one uncomfortable. Why would one want to leave the relative comfort of traditional organic disease and enter this area of threatening uncertainty that none of us has been trained to deal with?[16]

There is absolutely no question that individuals with a painful history of abuse use food, cigarettes, and alcohol consumption as a way to soothe uncomfortable emotions associated with a sense of vulnerability and/or violation. People under much lesser forms of stress do the same, with the inevitable result being weight gain. And as Dr. Felitti says, it's much easier to deal only with the so-called organic aspects of the problem—to lose weight by going on a diet, taking a diet pill, even undergoing weight-reduction surgery—rather than delve into the emotions and beliefs that are causing an individual to engage in health-eroding behavior in the first place. In the end, however, I have found that it's far more satisfying and helpful if a mother (or a physician) is willing to acknowledge the existence of the "tough stuff." Only then can she support her daughter in tapping in to the inner wisdom that will help her deal with her problems and heal them—with appropriate professional intervention, if necessary.

There's Always Hope

Studies show that up to 15 percent of teenage girls are now obese.[17] In many cases, so are their mothers. Though it is not easy to change eating habits, I offer the following story from one of my physician colleagues, whom I'll call Irene, as inspiration that it is possible. She puts it this way: "Fat is dreams in storage. Once you take steps to realize your dreams and face the fears that are holding you back, the fat is free to leave."

Irene was morbidly obese as a teenager. Her mother was schizophrenic and she, the oldest daughter, had to care for her younger siblings while her father was on duty in Vietnam. She said that the refrigerator was her most trusted friend. And though she was taken to doctor after doctor, she knew in her heart that she wasn't going to lose the weight until she graduated high school and got out of the house. Once she went to college, she joined a Weight Watchers group and started an exercise program. Over the course of the next couple years, she was able to lose the weight and has kept it off. This wasn't quick or easy. She also spent a considerable amount of time in therapy to learn how to feel her emotions fully. She called me once during the process, and said, "Now I know why so few people manage to keep weight off. Feeling all of my emotions about my mother—and also facing my fear that I will become just like her—has been the most painful thing I've ever had to do. But the end result has been worth it." Having gone through this herself, she now has a job in which she runs groups for obese patients—letting them know, by her example, that weight loss is completely possible if they're willing to do the work involved in freeing themselves from the past.

HOW TO BOOST MOOD WITHOUT FOOD

There are a number of tried-and-true ways to soothe one's mood other than by eating. Here are a few:

~ Aerobic exercise increases endorphins, the "opiates" of the brain. It also decreases excess cortisol and helps offset food cravings.

~ Meditation also enhances opiate levels in the brain and decreases stress effects. Ten to twenty minutes per day is adequate.

~ Breathing deeply through the nose into the lower chest and abdomen decreases stress hormones and enhances mood.

~ Napping is another strategy for mood enhancement—especially in the sleep deprived.

A PLAN FOR DEALING WITH DISORDERED EATING

Understand the food-mood connection. You won't be able to establish healthy eating patterns if you continue to eat junk food or food that is addictive. Sugar, alcohol, caffeine, and food additives such as MSG can have profound effects on satiety, appetite, and mood.

Stop dieting. For every food restriction you subject yourself to now, there will be a binge that is equal to or greater than the deprivation, until you acknowledge and take care of the emotions that are driving the eating in the first place. Sometimes a structured food plan is necessary for a time in order to learn the basics of healthy eating. But the mind-set should always be that you are following a "healthy eating plan for life," not a diet that you get to "go off" once you reach your goal.

Know thyself. Girls and women with disordered eating tend to work around food. They become cooks, bakers, waitresses, and nutritionists. This is a good example of how the intellect, through knowledge, tries to heal the wounds of the heart. But intellectual knowledge can't heal the wound at the heart of disordered eating. The only thing that can is feeling your emotions fully and letting them go. You can know the RDA of all the vitamins and minerals, the calorie or fat-gram count of every food known to humanity, and how much exercise is necessary to burn off the calories in an M&M. But you'll still feel inadequate until you deal with the emotions you are trying to medicate away. They're trying to tell you something, to get you to change. Your job is to heed their message, not silence it.

Get inspired. It's very inspiring and helpful to read first-person accounts from those women and girls who have "been there" and made it through. I particularly like all of Geneen Roth's books, including *When Food Is Love.* No one has ever written more eloquently or helpfully on the subject of eating and emotions.

I also recommend *It Was Food vs. Me . . . and I Won,* by Nancy Goodman. She is funny and extraordinarily honest about what it takes to face your feelings and learn to live a life beyond food.

Access the power of community. One of the reasons why Weight Watchers, Curves, OA, and other groups work (as long as you keep going) is that you are part of a community of others who are supporting you. You meet new people and get support for your new way of being. We all need support for major life changes. And changing one's approach to food is major! OA (Overeaters Anonymous) is a free twelve-step program (based on AA) that has helped millions throughout the world overcome emotionally triggered eating so that they can create healthy eating patterns and richer lives.

Take action. In her brilliant memoir about recovering from food addiction, Episcopal priest Margaret Bullitt-Jonas put it this way:

> The first step in the long process of recovery, and the foundation of a food addict's subsequent well-being, is putting down the fork, putting down the food, one day at a time. No insight into self, however subtle, no analysis of the dynamics of addiction, however accurate, no understanding of the nature of desire, however sophisticated or enlightening—none of these fine things can substitute for action. The healing of addiction depends, first and foremost, not on what we know, nor on what we feel, but on what we do. . . .[18]

Bullitt-Jonas's insights about addiction are as relevant for cigarettes or alcohol as they are for food.

Cognitive Behavioral Therapy for Eating Disorders

If you feel that your daughter has an eating disorder that is potentially dangerous or life-threatening, go to your nearest mental health center, preferably one connected with a medical school. Enroll your daughter in a program that uses cognitive behavioral therapy specifically for eating disorders. Life Skills Training (dialectical behavioral therapy [DBT]/ the Marsha Linehan Model) is a form of cognitive behavioral therapy that teaches you how to recognize an emotion you're feeling (fear, anger, sadness), identify why you're feeling the way you do, and learn how to soothe your distress before it becomes physicalized in your body.

Life Skills Training is not standard psychotherapy. It's taught in a classroom format by a coach who focuses on acquiring certain skills.

Dialectical behavioral therapy and other forms of behavioral therapy are my first choice when therapy is required—not just for eating disorders, but for many other problems. These therapies help people change their thoughts and therefore their behaviors, and both my clinical experience and the research data show that they are effective at improving quality of life and health. (For more information about the research, Google "cognitive behavioral therapy.") Though there is a place for "talk" therapy, there are no long-term outcome studies that prove that it works. I've seen far too many women and girls "regress" and become less skillful at dealing with their emotions rather than more when "supportive" psychotherapy goes on for too long. Talking about one's "wounds" for too long can simply reinforce one's feelings of victimhood at the expense of feelings of mastery and competence.

To find a DBT or cognitive behavioral therapy counselor in your area, call your local mental health center or contact the following: DBT Training Group, 4556 University Way NE, Suite 200, Seattle, WA 98105, or on the Web at www.behavioraltech.org.

ASPARTAME

Many teenage girls (and their mothers) are addicted to diet colas—and I do mean addicted, as I'll discuss below. I've had patients who start every day with a diet cola and end up drinking a couple of liters daily as a substitute for eating food, and as a way to keep their mood up and their weight down. This concerns me greatly, because most diet colas contain aspartame, an artificial sweetener, and many of them also contain caffeine. Each of these by itself can be damaging to health, and together they are even more so.

Aspartame and Nerve-Cell Death

Aspartame is a combination of two naturally occuring amino acids, aspartic acid and glutamic acid. Both of these are neurotransmitters that play an active role in the central nervous system, being utilized by 75 percent of all nerve cells in the spinal cord and brain. Together these two create what is essentially a neurotoxin in susceptible individuals. This is because aspartic acid and glutamic acid are excitotoxins—that is, they excite nerve cells to fire. Some excitement in the form of nerve-cell firing is necessary for alertness and paying attention. But too much is not good for anyone—including nerve cells. Nature has provided a cleanup crew for the excess excitotoxins in the form of glial cells, which wrap around nerve cells and absorb and process excitotoxins like little sponges. But if the excitotoxin levels get too high, the glial cells can't keep up, and the nerve cells get overstimulated as a result. When this happens, nerve cells swell and the genetic material within them clumps and releases free radicals. Since the body's antioxidants can't handle the increased levels of free radicals, brain cells die.

Just about every nerve cell in the body has receptor sites for both glutamic and aspartic acids—*which means they are capable of becoming overexcited to the point of cell death* (apoptosis). That's the definition of an excitotoxin. It can stimulate a cell to death!

Aspartame, Caffeine, Mood, and Behavior

Nerve-cell death isn't the only problem caused by excessive amounts of caffeinated diet colas containing aspartame. Caffeine increases the stress response via increasing norepinephrine and epinephrine, which results in decreased levels of serotonin, the neurotransmitter that's important for mood stabilization, planning, and impulse control.

Norepinephrine and epinephrine provide a short-term jolt of energy and alertness that is often followed by depression, increased insulin production, low blood sugar, and all the biochemical effects of stress that, over time, increase carb cravings and also increase the risk of just about every disease there is.[19]

Diet Cola Addiction

Of all the diet products on the market, diet colas are, in my experience, the most harmful. This is because aspartame and caffeine both have so many negative effects, and because the two of them in combination are particularly addictive. There's a certain irresistible "buzz" that many people get from diet cola. This kind of addiction does not seem to occur with diet ginger ale, for example, because even though it too contains aspartame, it does not have caffeine. Nor does it occur with Diet Rite colas, which can contain caffeine but are sweetened with saccharin, not aspartame.

Aspartame consumption, particularly in the form of diet colas, has been linked with multiple sclerosis–like symptoms in many individuals. These symptoms include headache, blurry vision, slurred speech, or memory loss.

Who Should Avoid Aspartame

Though I certainly recommend that everyone try to minimize aspartame consumption, there are some individuals who are particularly susceptible to its harmful effects. Because of its impact on the central nervous system, people with the following conditions, or with family histories of these conditions, should completely avoid aspartame:

- Neuropsychiatric problems such as depression, anxiety attacks, obsessive-compulsive symptoms, manic-depressive illness, schizophrenia

- History of head injury

- Blurred vision

- Memory loss

- Chronic fatigue syndrome, fibromyalgia

- Tinnitus (ringing in ears)

- Spasms, shooting pains, numbness

- Attention deficit disorder or hyperactivity disorder

- Spinal-cord injury

- Multiple sclerosis

- Lou Gehrig's disease

- Migraine headaches

- Spinal disc problems

- Parkinson's disease

- Alzheimer's disease

CAFFEINE

Caffeine has powerful stimulant effects on the central nervous system, and our hyperactive culture runs on it. But caffeine is a drug, pure and simple. It is also a neurotoxin. Excessive amounts can cause seizures. Even as little as one cup in the morning can lead to panic, anxiety, and insomnia in susceptible individuals. In my practice, I've "cured" many cases of caffeine-induced insomnia simply by prescribing "caffeine cessation."

Caffeine-containing colas are a very common, yet underrecognized, cause of headache in both children and adolescents. In one study, children in a headache clinic were found to be consuming at least 1.5 liters of cola per day with an average of 11 liters—1,415 mg of caffeine—per week. When they stopped consuming caffeine, their headaches went away.[20]

Caffeine is the most commonly used psychoactive substance in our culture, by young people and adults alike. In one study, young teens consumed an average of 63 mg of caffeine per day, the amount found in about half a cup of brewed coffee. However, some consumed as much as 800 mg per day, the equivalent of almost seven cups of coffee.[21]

Caffeine can increase blood pressure in adolescents (as well as adults) and can also adversely affect the heart, causing heart palpitations and irregular heartbeat.[22] Caffeine can also cause or exacerbate GI symptoms such as irritable bowel syndrome, ulcers, heartburn, acid reflux, and hiatal hernia. Caffeine can also lead to urinary frequency and bladder and urethral irritation.

As with alcohol, children and adolescents are more susceptible to the effects of caffeine than are adults. One 12-ounce can of cola in an adolescent has been found to have the same effect as about four cups of coffee in an adult.[23]

Caffeine consumption leads to mood alteration, and to physical dependency that is serious enough to result in withdrawal symptoms if it is stopped. Regular caffeine consumption also leads to habituation, or tolerance, meaning that the more you take in, the more you need to achieve the same effects. As with alcohol, it's best for an adolescent to avoid it as much as possible so that her growing brain does not become habituated to it.

Many people love the effects of caffeine: it increases mental alertness, decreases reaction time, and can improve verbal memory. However, it does all of this by stimulating epinephrine release in the brain and body. This is the "fight or flight" hormone that prepares you for danger by increasing blood pressure, respiration rate, and kidney function (which is why caffeine results in increased urination). I recall that one of my nephews had a Jolt party when he was an adolescent. The idea was to consume as much of this caffeinated soda as possible, until everyone was bouncing off the walls.

AMOUNTS OF CAFFEINE IN COMMON BEVERAGES[24]

Food	Caffeine
Coca-Cola—12 oz	45 mg
Diet Pepsi—12 oz	36 mg
Mountain Dew—12 oz	54 mg
Jolt—12 oz	110 mg
Percolated coffee—6 oz (note—this is a very small cup)	110 mg
Drip coffee—6 oz	150 mg
Grande Starbucks coffee—16 oz	550 mg
Tea brewed 5 minutes—6 oz	45 mg
Chocolate bar (small)	30 mg

Caffeine and Females

About 75 percent of the research on caffeine has been done on men. Yet males and females don't react to caffeine in the same way. Women pay a higher price for the caffeine "buzz" than men do.

~ Caffeine is more difficult for the female body to break down into substances that are no longer psychoactive in their body. For a man, the effects of a cup of coffee or can of Coke last two and a half to four and a half hours. For a women, these effects can last anywhere from four to seven hours.

~ Caffeine detox is menstrual-cycle-dependent. In the second half of the cycle (the luteal phase), it can take up to two hours longer to eliminate caffeine from her system than in the first half of her cycle. Women on the Pill or other hormones take twice as long to detox caffeine (and alcohol too).

~ Caffeine is a bladder irritant in women and can cause urinary frequency and burning to the point where a woman feels she may have a bladder infection.

~ Caffeine promotes excessive urinary excretion of magnesium, calcium, sodium, and potassium because it increases urination. This puts women at increased risk for osteoporosis later.

⁓ Caffeine can cause iron deficiency, because it appears to oxidize the available iron in foods and supplements and convert it to a form that is far less bioavailable. A single cup of coffee can reduce iron absorption by 39 percent. (Some people with anemia do not recover until they eliminate caffeine from their diets.)[25] Females are particularly prone to anemia because of the blood loss during menstruation.

⁓ Caffeine can trigger migraine headaches, especially in women.

⁓ Caffeine can cause breast tenderness and other symptoms such as cystic breasts.

⁓ Caffeine increases PMS symptoms.

⁓ Caffeine increases the rate of miscarriage and low-birth-weight babies.

For all the reasons listed above, I recommend that a girl avoid caffeine entirely if she has any tendency toward anxiety, irritability, insomnia, moodiness, low blood sugar, urinary tract infections or urinary frequency, or an eating disorder (caffeine is an appetite suppressant).

Make sure that you don't have cola available in your home. If you must have something, make it noncola diet drinks.

Fortunately, caffeine detox takes only three days—during which you have a headache, feel irritable, and are also very tired. But then it's over.

CREATING A LEGACY OF HEALTH

Guiding your daughter toward good health and lifestyle choices can be very challenging. Perhaps she is insisting on her morning cup of coffee, or she doesn't see why she can't drink diet colas throughout the day, or she's got much more interesting things to do with her life than sleep, or she thinks it's weird that she has to take all these pills when there's nothing wrong with her, and her best friend just lost ten pounds on the latest diet craze and looks absolutely fabulous in her bikini. She'll be out of the house and out from under your watchful eye soon enough, and then she'll be making all these choices for herself. But while she's still at home, do what you can to promote good habits, because many of the habits she establishes now are likely to remain with her for a lifetime. Help pass down a legacy of health. She'll thank you for it for the rest of her life.

19

The Real World

Becoming the Author of Your Own Life

❊

The terrain of adolescence, with all its challenges and complications, is the testing ground against which your daughter must prove herself before she is ready for full independence. Although she needs this testing, she also needs your help. More than ever, you must stand tall and give her the benefit of your fierce, tough-love Mother Bear wisdom. Otherwise, you may raise a "cub" who doesn't have what it takes to make it on her own, much less manifest the life of her dreams.

Because adolescence is the passage to adulthood, it is the time when a girl must learn the skills necessary to survive—and eventually thrive—on her own. Her soul qualities, combined with her passion and purpose, provide the fuel to get her safely through this passage. Her mother can help provide the impetus, letting her know that if she decides what she wants and goes after it, she will very often get it. I believe that we are goal-seeking creatures by nature. The best way to realize dreams is to name them and take concrete, actionable steps toward realizing them.

SETTING GOALS: A FAMILY TRADITION

I taught my daughters to write down their goals every year on New Year's Eve, beginning when they were each about twelve years old. Eventually it became a family ritual that all four of us—my husband, daughters, and I—looked forward to and participated in. We'd sit on pillows in a circle on the floor, around a little "altar" of sacred space that I created, using a round piece of satin cloth on which I placed flowers, candles, and other meaningful objects such as stones, shells, and crystals. Each of us also put a favorite object of our own into the center. Then I put on some uplifting music, lit the three candles on the altar—one for the past, one for the present, and one for the future—and opened the journal in which we had recorded our goals the year before. We'd go around the circle, each of us reading aloud what we had written in the journal the previous year, and we'd discuss and celebrate each other's accomplishments. Next we took little pieces of paper and wrote down anything we wanted to release from the prior year. Keeping the contents of these notes secret, we burned the papers, releasing the negative energy we didn't want to carry into the New Year.

After that, each of us in turn talked about and then wrote down what we wanted to accomplish the following year. Then, holding hands, we'd bless our little ceremony and blow out the candles. Every year we repeated this ceremony, reading what we had written, seeing how far we had come, celebrating the goals we had achieved, and discussing how we might overcome obstacles to the remaining goals, if they still seemed worthwhile. We'd also make adjustments where necessary. Goals continually change as we grow and develop.

By the law of attraction, we attract what we give our attention to. And when we write down our goals and read them over often, we're far more apt to accomplish them. Our job as thinking, conscious humans is to create the best lives we can. We do this by having goals and working to manifest them. Living your life without goals is like sailing a boat without any way to steer it. You're at the mercy of the winds and the tides instead of using them to get you where you want to go. Having concrete goals is like having your sail up and your rudder in the water at the same time.

MERGE VERSUS SURGE: CLAIMING WHAT'S HERS

For many a young girl—and many women too!—the drive to go after what she wants in the world (for example, grades, college acceptance, a raise, recognition, material possessions, success, status, popularity) seems to conflict with the need to be loved and accepted. Although these drives are not mutually exclusive, it is often difficult to negotiate the ever-shifting boundary between self and selflessness. For girls and women there is an inclination to defer to the needs and opinions of others, a tendency reinforced by what I call the hormonal "veil" that falls over reproductive-age women, rendering them more receptive to the compromises involved in finding a mate and raising a family. This is fine as long as a girl doesn't completely lose herself in acquiescing to the demands of relationships.

Where exactly a girl locates the boundary between self and others will change as she moves from infancy to childhood to adolescence and adulthood, until finally it becomes embedded, quite literally, in the functioning of her immune, endocrine, and nervous systems. Similarly, her sense of what is socially acceptable and desirable, which will affect her capacity to nurture and satisfy herself while at the same time fitting into society, will be programmed with ever-greater fixity during these years, the wiring for that sense being laid down in the DLPC of her brain. As discussed earlier, the closer one gets to adulthood, the less "plastic" or flexible the neural pathways between brain and body.

Self-Sacrifice Programming

When the program for womanhood that gets laid down in adolescence is overly focused on taking care of the needs of others while ignoring one's own, there is a high price to be paid. In all but bona fide saints, the programming of self-sacrifice leads inevitably to guilt, resentment, envy, anger, martyrdom—emotions that are associated with elevated levels of the stress hormones cortisol and epinephrine, which increase insulin levels, ultimately resulting in cellular inflammation in the body. Vast amounts of research have now shown that cellular inflammation is the root cause of almost all diseases, including the most common ones in women: cardiovascular problems (including high blood pressure and stroke), autoimmune diseases, cancer, chronic fatigue, menstrual cramps, PMS, and even depression. In other words, too much self-sacrifice makes us sick. Various studies bear this out. For example, people who neglect their own health for the sake of caring for others have been found to be more apt to smoke and to abuse alcohol, and to be at increased risk for depression, heart disease, and chronic stress. When they themselves get sick, their survival rates are lower.[1] Stress, which is generally linked with self-sacrificing behaviors, has also been shown to increase the risk for breast cancer.[2]

Self-sacrifice goes against what our souls know to be true: our highest and most important value *must* be our own happiness and fulfillment. But ours is not a culture that has acknowledged that this is true for women as well as for men. Self-sacrifice programming in all its many guises is the "chain of pain" that many mothers have, understandably, passed down to their daughters for generations. It has helped them fit in to a society that hasn't valued women as much as men; and it's a form of "payback" to a mother for the self-sacrifice *she* has made. (Men in our culture are also programmed with self-sacrifice messages, but theirs have traditionally had to do with laying down their lives in war, and, of course, until recently, when the responsibility began more and more to be shared, with doing all the work of supporting their families.)

Self-sacrifice in women is the chain of pain that not only makes us sick but keeps so many stuck in dead-end relationships, jobs, and lives. It's why women don't ask for or receive the same promotions in business that men do.[3] Self-sacrifice (as well as its opposite—self-centeredness or narcissism) inevitably has an adverse effect on immune, endocrine, and nervous systems functions over time. After years and years of treating thousands of patients suffering from headaches, chronic fatigue, menstrual cramps, unwanted pregnancies, fertility problems, addictions, and depression as well as cancer, chronic pain, fibromyalgia, back pain, and other stress-related disorders, I am convinced that the degree to which a girl has internalized self-sacrifice programming and is carrying it out in her life is the degree to which she is apt to have health problems. And of course I have seen this enacted in my own life—the skin rashes, eye problems, and headaches that I described earlier—and in the lives of my daughters.

The Urge to Merge: Being Miss Congeniality

When Kate was fourteen, she desperately wanted a part in the high school play. She practiced and practiced. She wanted it so badly, and I identified with her so strongly, that I felt as though I would be personally devastated if she didn't get a part. I coached her with her singing and told her that she had to be convincing. At the same time, I also knew that her success in this endeavor was really out of my hands. Watching her go through this process, I wrote:

> Her challenge in this regard is that even though she is bright and very talented, she tends to defer to the opinions and needs of others—and doesn't really want to put herself "out there" too much lest others not like her. I've told her that sometimes, to get what you want in life, you have to abdicate the throne of Miss Congeniality. That's difficult for Kate.

I was thrilled when she got a part. Later, when a few extra speaking lines were given out, she didn't get one. She had been passed over for kids who were far less talented. Once again, I told her that she had to make sure that she put herself out there as a serious contender. She thought about this over the weekend in her very inward way. (She processes deeply and internally and rarely uses words.)

On Monday morning, she awakened with a stomachache and pain just below her rib cage. She didn't feel much like eating and she decided to stay home. She didn't have a fever. Her illness was similar to the illnesses she had always gotten. They go right to her gut. She can manifest a fever, nausea, and vomiting more quickly than anyone I've ever seen. And her illnesses are very real.

Kate's conflict at that age—the desire for success in the outer world of competition versus the need for love and acceptance—is a conflict that troubles many women long past adolescence, sometimes for their entire lives. It's no wonder that the conflict hit Kate right where she felt trapped—in the middle of her body, the third chakra. This is the area of the body that is either strengthened or weakened by the degree to which a girl is able to balance her dueling drives in ways that make her feel good about herself, thus shoring up her self-esteem and sense of personal power.

The conflict between self and others continued to be a problem for Kate, and got expressed in a variety of ways, behaviorally and physically. Though she is a gifted athlete and student, she spent her middle and early high school years choosing friendships over accomplishments in both of those fields of endeavor. She participated in a variety of sports in middle school, including soccer and tennis, but she played them for the sake of being with her peers, not scoring against them. In the seventh grade she played in her first big all-school tennis tournament, which meant that she had to play against her teammates as well as those of other schools. She won her first set 6–0. But then she had to play against one of her best friends. She was terrified and felt sick to her stomach. (At the same time that I was worried about how Kate was going to cope with this conflict, I overheard one of the boys saying how upset he was that he had to play against one of his own teammates. I was glad to have overheard this, as I had been under the impression that only girls found this kind of inner struggle difficult.)

Kate won one game against her friend and lost the others. When she got into the car after the match, she hit her head on the doorjamb. Though she hadn't hit her head very hard, the physical "trauma" broke an emotional dam inside her. She started sobbing. They were tears of anger at herself for losing points that she knew she didn't need to lose—and also tears of release from the tension she had felt at having to play under pressure in a major public forum. The friend she had lost to, a girl with less innate athletic ability but a fierce competitive spirit, went on to win the championship.

There was never any use pushing Kate to participate in athletics (or anything else) once she had made up her mind that she was no longer interested. She and her sister both have strong wills, which I have, of course, encouraged. No matter how many sports she tried, none of them "stuck." And though she has always been a straight-A student, she's not a competitive scholar either. On the other hand, she was always drawn to dance like a moth to a flame. She started taking dance classes when she was three, and she has been dancing and eventually performing in dance companies ever since. Dance is a constant and ever-present source of joy and inspiration to her, and to those who watch her. And being part of an ensemble allows her to excel without doing so at anyone else's expense.

How to Help Your Daughter Deal with Disappointment and Other Stormy Emotions

Young girls (and many adults too) need to learn how to identify their emotions and the purpose they serve. And they need to learn how to connect the dots between a belief, a thought, and a subsequent feeling. They also need a safe and effective way to process their difficult emotions, so that they don't hold other family members "hostage" to them.

The first thing your daughter should understand is that all emotions are normal. They are just "energy" that moves us. Emotions that feel good mean that the thoughts and beliefs associated with them are moving us in the direction of health and happiness. Emotions that feel bad mean that we're holding thoughts and beliefs that are leading us away from happiness and fulfillment. But getting back on track requires that we first process the difficult emotion.

Example: Your daughter doesn't make the cheerleading squad. She becomes angry, sad, or disappointed. That's natural and normal. She needs to be able to express her disappointment fully in order to get over it healthfully. This may take anywhere from a couple hours to a couple days, depending upon how much making the squad means to her. At the same time, she also needs to be encouraged to turn her thoughts in a different direction, one that makes her feel better. For instance, "Okay, I didn't make the squad. That means that I'll have enough time to pursue photography and music instead of having to go to all those games every weekend."

One of the most immediately effective ways to process negative emotions is through exercise, which generates endorphins, and lowers the stress hormones cortisol and epinephrine. Running and lifting weights are particularly good for anger. Sadness and depression are often helped by yoga.

THE BOTTOM LINE: Emotions are our inner guidance system, letting us know what direction we're going toward—happiness or the opposite. Understanding the message behind the emotion and doing something about it is where our power lies—always.

The Urge to Surge: Going for the Gold

During Kate's junior year, she spent the winter in what's known as the Maine Coast semester, a program in which she lived in a wood-heated cabin on the coast of Maine with a small group of other juniors from schools across the country. Together they studied ecology, turned compost, worked with livestock, and helped prepare and clean up after meals. They also had to fulfill a rigorous academic program. Separated from her schoolmates and family and their expectations of her, Kate finally realized that she had something to say and that others wanted to hear it. This was a turning point.

By the time Kate reached her senior year in high school, she had far more confidence in herself and no longer needed the approval of her peers nearly as much as she had earlier. In fact, she spent a lot of her senior year doing preapproved independent-study courses that often didn't require her presence at school. She had truly found her own voice. And interestingly, by the time she got to college, she had no problem getting great parts in a couple of musicals, even though the competition for parts was far more rigorous than anything she had faced in her small high school.

THE COMPETITIVE SPIRIT

Throughout our lives, we must face the reality of competition and learn how to deal with it effectively. A good athletic coach (or teacher) knows that she will be most effective at her job if she can inspire her students by evoking their love and respect. When the students "play their hearts out" it's often because they crave the approval of such a coach. That was certainly part of my motivation when I was in middle and high school. Of course, if competing to win is simply another way of pleasing others at your own expense—for example, playing soccer competitively because your older sister was good at it and your mother has pushed you to do it too, even though you'd rather concentrate on the arts—then it's not healthy. But if the spirit of competition comes from the soul, as it did for me, it can be very meaningful. I was born wanting to achieve in school and I put enormous pressure on myself to do so from the day I entered kindergarten. In the eighth grade I set myself the goal of becoming valedictorian of my high school class, and I achieved it. I always knew that academic success would be crucial to fulfilling my life's purpose, even though for a long time I did not know what that purpose would be.

Learning how to deal with competition builds the health of both the second and third chakras and the organs associated with these centers. Every girl needs to learn to deal effectively with the stress of competition by using it in alignment with her soul's unique purpose.

The Effect of Competition on Female Biology

Competition has a profound effect on biology, and biology affects competition. For example, it is well documented in monkeys that the proximity of a dominant female, one who has either won a fight or frightened or displaced others, may inhibit ovulation in subordinate females. In fact, lion, wolf, and baboon females vary sharply in their reproductive success depending upon their dominance relationship within the group. Harassment in family settings appears to cause anovulatory cycles in baboons and monkeys. These cycles are associated with high levels of prolactin and cortisol, hormones that respectively inhibit libido and help the body cope with stress.

The same thing happens in humans, but we have the ability to consciously influence our biology through self-reflection. What this means is that we can reframe our perceptions about competition in ways that create health, not distress. We do this by moving beyond the winner-versus-loser dichotomy and using competition as the energy it takes to hone our skills and to get clear about our life's purpose. Research supporting this view of competition has shown that its effect on us does not depend on the outcome of the event but on how we feel about the experience of participating in it. In a study of male and female students ages eighteen to twenty-one, University of Rochester researchers found that when the focus of competition is on winning at all costs, competition has a negative effect on an individual's motivation to keep improving. But when both the participants and the observers focus more on good performance than on winning, the effect on the motivation of competitors is enhanced— regardless of whether they win or lose.[4]

Many Ways to Win: Our Advantage over the Apes

Evolutionarily speaking, a female mammal's reproductive success depends upon her ability to attract a strong, healthy male who will provide her with offspring and protect her against marauders. That's one of the reasons why girls who are "genetic celebrities"—

who attract the attention of adolescent boys because of their physical attributes—have such success in high school. But in my experience, these early bloomers may peak very early and then "go to seed" relatively quickly. Because their genetic celebrity was not something they had to strive for, they often fail to develop the skills necessary to build on their early success. Once high school is over, they tend to fall off the achievement and success curve, because we no longer live in the kind of world where the qualities that go into "reproductive success" are necessarily predictive or indicative of other kinds of success. Unlike the monkeys, we've evolved different ways of "winning," which is why high school reunions can be so worthwhile for those who weren't very popular early on. These are often people who got off to a slow start but picked up speed and an abundance of skills in later life. One of my patients put it this way:

> Since my breasts didn't stand out, I knew I was going to have to use my brain. And like girls everywhere, I learned that if you don't have the right kind of body to create a secure place for yourself in the world, you had better develop another attribute that is attractive, unique, and outstanding. Since I've reached midlife, I've learned that sooner or later, everyone needs to learn this lesson. I've watched some of my former "prom queen" friends become devastated when they turned forty— right when I really began to hit my stride! I think Judge Judy has summed it up correctly: "Beauty fades. Dumb is forever." Ultimately, I came to see that my happiness and self-fulfillment were more important than clinging to adolescent notions of what attractive meant.

Regardless of the nature of our inner blueprints, everyone is affected by competition one way or another. For example, like many people who've been driven to succeed academically, I used to have recurrent nightmares about trying to find the room where the final exam was being given, terrified that I would miss it. Over the years, as I've found my own unique path in life, those dreams have receded. Part of the reason is that I've discovered how to live healthfully with competition.

All mothers can help their daughters learn the skills necessary for success and can also nurture their daughters' desire to excel. Encouraging your daughter to ask for and go after what she wants in the world, whether it's a place on the soccer team, a promotion, or acceptance to the college of her dreams, is one of the most powerful ways for you to heal and update your own legacy. To do so, you may have to reframe your ideas about competition and the role it plays in life.

Appreciating the Benefits of Competition

When I asked my sister Penny to reflect on how her athletic career had helped her as an adult, she had this to say:

> During my teens and early twenties, being on the ski team gave me a wonderful sense of purpose, a chance to do something I was good at and felt a real passion for. When I look back at my many years of competition from my present vantage point, I see that they gave me a very healthy dose of self-trust and confidence in my body. I had the stamina to raise three healthy boys. I know that I can stick with a task and complete it even when I'm tired and would rather be doing something else. My ski team experience also gave me the skills necessary to be both a team player and a competitor. I now run a home-based business that I have been growing (with my husband) for nearly a decade. My tenacity and ability to work well with others has contributed a great deal to my success. Failure has simply never been an option. I do what it takes.

The increasing visibility and success of female athletes is a change that many girls are enjoying to the hilt. It's a wonderful fact of modern life that girls and women now have more chances than ever before to compete and to win acclaim, and not just in the world of sports but in business, law, medicine, science, and the arts. The world is opening up to us in so many ways! But we have to make sure that our daughters take full advantage of these opportunities, and not just pay lip service to them.

Using Competition to Zero In on Gifts and Talents

Let your daughter know that competition can help her channel her best energies to those areas that mean the most to her, and where she has the most to offer. This doesn't mean opting out of other activities. Yes, it's always potentially embarrassing to get up on the dance floor when you don't know the steps, or to do anything else new—but that's how you keep adding new brain cells! Besides, people who won't do anything unless they can excel at it miss out on a lot of fun. But your daughter has to figure out what she's meant to excel at and what she should simply enjoy. Here's an example from my own life:

When I got to medical school, I quickly realized that no matter how long or hard I studied, I simply wasn't going to be at the top of my class. Some of my classmates had photographic memories and managed to get straight A's without any study at all. In comparison to them, I had to work very hard. So I realized right away that I had a choice: I could make myself sick and miserable by putting in more and more hours in a futile attempt to compete for the same grades. Or I could study enough to get acceptable grades and still have a relatively balanced life. I chose having a life. I hiked, I skied. I went to concerts. And I also played my harp in the Dartmouth Symphony—a move my adviser (who played the bass behind me) didn't approve of! He thought I should be spending all my time in the library. I knew he was wrong.

By the time I started to see patients in the clinic, I began to come into my own. I was really good at listening, and realized early on that this skill would provide me with crucial information about how to tailor medical treatments to each person's situation in practical, real-life ways. This became the basis for my entire approach to women's health, and has opened up my career in ways I never dreamed possible back in my medical school days.

Overcoming the Zero-sum Model Mind-set

Self-destructive competition (the kind that undermines health) is based on the same zero-sum model that also rules the conventional approach to money: in other words, "There's only so much to go around. If you have more, then there will be less for me. If I win, then you are a loser." For many people, the combination of innate temperament and environmental influences ensures that the voice of the zero-sum model gets internalized at a very young age. We can learn to say no to that voice if we understand that in the overall game of life we can all be winners.

Sometimes losing something in one area also ends up creating success in another, leading us down paths we couldn't possibly have foreseen. For example, when my friend Mona Lisa was a sophomore at Brown University, she developed narcolepsy and epilepsy and her grade point average fell to 2.2. Sleeping eighteen hours a day, she had to drop out of college, unable to compete in her premed courses. She was told that she would never be able to get into medical school, a dream she'd had since the age of seven. Since conventional medicine was unable to help her, and she was determined not to be sidelined by her illness, she turned to Chinese medicine, acupuncture, and affirmations, and eventually was able to heal herself. This gave her an appreciation for healing modalities outside the confines of Western medicine, which has informed her work and her beliefs ever since. The experience of overcoming such great obstacles gave her a drive to succeed that was even stronger than it had been before, and she ended up graduating from Brown and eventually getting into not just medical school but into a combined M.D.-Ph.D. program, something her advisers had deemed impossible. And this she did even though her illness had taken such a toll that it was nearly impossible for her to read and write. To complete her Ph.D. thesis, she had to go to a remedial reading instructor, where she had the humiliating experience of sitting in a classroom with child-size desks and chairs. Talk about being made to feel small! Even this loss had a silver lining. It forced her to develop other parts of her brain, mainly her intuition, which is a large part of her practice and gift to the world.

Accepting and Overcoming Insecurities— Everyone Has Them!

I heard Barbra Streisand interviewed on *Inside the Actors Studio* the other night. A student asked her how she managed to be so self-assured. She said, "Don't make the mistake of thinking that my self-assurance means that I don't have insecurities. I do." Yes, even Barbra Streisand, successful as she is, has her moments of doubt. The key is to move forward in spite of one's insecurities. Tell your daughter the only way to do this is to make sure she's on her own path— not a path that someone else (not even you!) wants her to be on. Then no matter how rocky the road, she will be going in the direction that will eventually take her to the place that is right for her.

Aligning the Competitive Spirit with the Life Force

Anyone who has ever strived to be her very best in any field of endeavor has a voice inside her head that tells her she could do better if only she tried harder. The inner competitive drive is like a force of nature—and, like nature, it can sometimes become overwhelming. Tell your daughter to make friends with it, to appreciate the fact that it's urging her on to better things. But she must heed its message skillfully. She must not let it become punitive or destructive. If what she hears is any kind of negative message about her innate value or worth, she is using the voice to flog herself, not to encourage her to be the best that she can be. While it is not possible to rid ourselves of this inner critic, it is possible to live in peaceful coexistence with it. The way I do this is to practice what author and spiritual teacher Walter Starcke, author of *The Third Appearance: The Crisis of Perception,* calls "double think." I acknowledge that I am completely human and fallible. And at the same time, I also know that my soul is perfection itself, always guiding me toward greater fulfillment and happiness.

Succeeding on Her Own Terms

Sooner or later your daughter will learn that there will always be someone who is more talented than she is, smarter, richer, prettier, with a slimmer body, bigger breasts, and more awards. If this bothers her, she will never be at peace with herself (or have normal levels of stress hormones). The only real success is in learning how to use her innate gifts and talents to their fullest, and letting them guide her to the life she is meant to have. Doing so will uplift everyone around her.

Do I Have to Give Up Me to Be Loved by You? When Love Is Competitive

Of course sometimes people want you to be smaller than you could be. This happens when one person is made to feel that she has to lower her own voltage in order to create the illusion that the other person is shining more brightly than she is, and it is particularly common in male-female relationships. Many women do this because they've been led to believe that the male ego is fragile—a belief that I feel is not only a health risk to women but terribly degrading to the dignity of men. In the popular movie *Mean Girls* (based on Rosalind Wiseman's book *Queen Bees & Wannabes*), actress Lindsay Lohan's character pretends that she doesn't understand math so that she can win the favor of the cute guy who sits behind her in class—such a typical scenario!

The same belief system can play out in other kinds of relationships too, including lesbian relationships, as the following story illustrates.

DOTTIE: Asthma and Palpitations

Dottie came to see me because of heart palpitations and asthma attacks—two symptoms that often indicate unresolved emotional issues. When I asked her what was going on in her life, she told me that she and her partner were having some problems. Dottie had just finished getting her Ph.D. in cell biology at an excellent school, and her partner was a lab tech in the same institution. But now that Dottie had an advanced degree and many career opportunities, her partner was feeling threatened and told Dottie that she was afraid that Dottie would leave her. On the night before her visit with me, Dottie had the following dream: She got up to go running and tried to put on black Reebok sneakers (a type of shoe, she explained, that was symbolic, for her, of the type of footwear worn in her group of friends). But no matter how hard she tried she simply couldn't get them to fit her feet. The insoles were all wrong. As she continued to try to put them on, the actress Mariel Hemingway came into the room, and told her, "I know what's wrong with you. I can fix it." And Mariel proceeded to sit on Dottie's chest, both suffocating and frightening her.

When Dottie told me about this dream, she said, "I keep getting into relationships with people with whom I initially feel really good because we have so much in common. But my pattern is that I always become more successful in the outer world than they are, and then they become threatened and want to control me and my behavior. And then I feel suffocated and have no choice but to leave. I did the same thing with my mother. Before puberty I was my mother's shadow, and she thought I was just like her. When I reached puberty, however, she kept trying to control everything I did and everywhere I went if these activities took me away from her either physically or emotionally. I eventually had to leave home for good in order to live a healthy and sane life. Unfortunately, I seem to keep repeating the pattern by choosing partners who become my mother. I guess that my dream is telling me what I need to do."

Dottie understood from her dream and our visit that her heart palpitations and lung problem were related to her needs for both closeness and separateness in her relationship. And right now her relationship had moved too far in the closeness direction. It was smothering her. When she went home and discussed this with her partner, however, she was met with stony silence. Eventually she had to leave the relationship rather than participate in the merged relationship that her partner desired.

If Dottie's former partner refuses to grow (which is a common scenario), she will undoubtedly find herself with another individual who wants to collapse her life and dreams into one neat package. We've all seen these couples. They are the ones who, after a decade or so of living together, begin to look and sound like each other, regardless of their gender. Though this kind of relationship may soothe the fears of each member, it also stifles the ongoing creativity and growth that true partnership can be a catalyst for. Here's the moral of this story: When you dim your light so that someone else shines more brightly, the whole world becomes darker! Dimming your light for another is also a distinct health hazard.

DOING IT HERSELF:
WHO IS RESPONSIBLE FOR WHAT?

When children are very young, they start expressing their desire for autonomy by refusing to hold your hand. How many times did you hear "Me do it" during the toddler years, even though your daughter didn't have the physical, emotional, or cognitive skills to do whatever it was she was trying to do? Adolescence, like toddlerhood, is another developmental stage during which your daughter's desire for independence may exceed her skills, especially those skills that go into what we have agreed to call judgment. Still, this is a time when she must be given enough rope that she can explore the world on her own—though not so much that she can hang herself. Adolescents need limits, even though they're always knocking up against those limits and trying to get you to remove them.

When bear cubs reach adolescence, Mother Bears need to walk a fine line between allowing their cubs to roam freely through the forest and letting them fall prey to the dangers that lurk there. Because each cub is different, the Mother Bear also needs to trust her instincts about what is right for hers. Only you can know if your daughter has become responsible and skillful enough in her approach to life to keep herself safe in her forays away from home and out from under your protective gaze. But one thing is for sure: the more responsibility you give her in her formative years, the more competent she is likely to become.

I don't underestimate the difficulty of getting an adolescent daughter to start taking responsibility for her own life. She knows that if someone else assumes the responsibility, she can always sit back and criticize if things don't turn out the way she wanted. Making choices and decisions about life is always a risk, because if she says yes to something, she's automatically saying no to something (or someone) else. What if she makes the wrong choice? What if she makes a mistake? Reluctant as she may be (and you may be as well!), you owe it to your daughter to give her lots of practice in decision making and responsibility taking.

Taking Responsibility: Kate, Stage One

My experience has been that children take responsibility only when you require them to do so. As a lifelong member of the "taking too much responsibility for others" club, it took me a while to figure this out, but gradually I saw that I was doing nobody any real favors—not myself and not my daughters either—by trying to take responsibility for everything. Once I began shifting some of that responsibility onto the shoulders where it belonged, I found my daughters very capable. They weren't too happy about it at first, but they did the job. Here's an example:

When Kate was about twelve, I planned to take her to Florida during school vacation the following spring. This was part of a family tradition—I would take Kate on vacation while my husband took Annie, since the two girls went to different schools with different vacation schedules. Kate and I would have to make our plans well in advance, so that I could schedule my work around her vacation, but I was happy to do this because it was a time of being together that both of us always looked forward to. This year, however, because her friends had become so important to her, I decided to offer to pay all expenses for her to bring a friend, too. She seemed excited about the idea, but she kept changing her mind about the time, the place, the friend, and so on. Finally, I said to her, "Okay, we're running out of time. I'll make all the arrangements, but only after you've made the choices. And once I do, there will be no changing your mind."

She said, "You're making me paranoid. Why is there such pressure?" I replied, "Because I'm not getting a clear signal from you about what you want. And you need to know that if I provide the time, the money, and the wherewithal to go somewhere nice, you can't come to me in three months and say, 'Oh gee, can you change the reservation? I forgot that I have a concert, or a rehearsal'—or whatever. You must take full responsibility for making this commitment."

She seemed resentful of my expecting her to take any responsibility. The trip suddenly seemed to be getting very difficult. And I didn't know why until it came out that her real discomfort was coming from the fact that if she asked just one of her friends, some of the others might be hurt. She didn't want to leave anyone out by making a choice because she'd have to deal with the consequences of hurt feelings.

As I began to help her with this dilemma as well, I suddenly realized I was doing far too much work and being overly responsible for everything involved: I was willing to take my daughter and her friend on a great trip, to pay for everything, and to make all the reservations and plans. And now, I was even about to spend an hour with my daughter helping her make a decision about whom she should take and how to deal with the potential emotional fallout from those who were left behind. I was taking responsibility for everything, including my daughter's feelings, and the feelings of all of her friends. No wonder I had weight problems!

A healthy sense of boundaries—knowing "who's responsible for what," in other words—is absolutely essential for the optimal health of the third chakra, which includes the midback area, the kidneys, the adrenals, and the digestive organs including the liver, stomach, pancreas, and small intestine. All issues of weight, whether it's carrying too much or too little, are related to the health of the third emotional center. Mothers can't possibly take responsibility for all the choices and feelings of their adolescent daughters and still remain healthy and at a healthy weight.

I realized that I needed to pass some of the responsibility to my daughter. (Not all, of course, because she was still only twelve years old.) As soon as I talked to Kate about it, she understood. She realized that she was now responsible for choosing a friend and for dealing with any potential fallout, and she rose to the task. She made her choice, the trip went well, and she didn't lose any friends over the situation.

Taking Responsibility: Kate, Stage Two

Adolescents don't learn to take responsibility immediately. There's a growth curve. The most important thing a mother can do is resist the urge to pick up the responsibility she is trying to let go of. Let it just sit there until the real owner comes along and claims it.

Another year went by during which I repeatedly asked Kate to tell me what her schedule looked like, whether she wanted to go on vacation in February or April, and whether or not she wanted to bring someone, and if so, should it be her cousin or a friend. She needed to decide, and she needed to decide soon. She kept putting this off, caught up in the immediacy of her schoolwork and social life. One night at dinner, Kate said, "Well, when are we going to Anguilla?"

I said, "Kate, I don't think we should go. I've asked you numerous times to tell me your school schedule and find out which vacation week you want to go. And I've also asked you whether you want to invite a friend or your cousin. Planning a vacation takes time and effort. And I can't do it without your help and guidance.

"I know that you want me to call the school and your various advisers, call your cousin and her parents, coordinate everyone's schedules, book the plane tickets, and then, once everything is arranged, get on the plane with you and make sure you have a great time. But you are no longer at a stage in your life where that can happen. You and your sister have too many things going on that only you can make decisions about. I know that in the past I've made all these arrangements. But I'm unwilling to do that any longer because as soon as I do, you'll tell me why you can't go on that particular day because of a scheduling conflict. So you go ahead and do the legwork, and when you have a plan, present it to me and we can work from there."

As soon as I had had my say, Kate got the message. She started to think out loud and confirm all of what I had just told her. Since she still hadn't decided about the ski team, she didn't know if her February break would work. She wasn't sure about her April break because she might be in tennis practice then. And of course there was also the one-act play competition—she didn't know when that would be. That was just the question of timing! On top of that, we also had the friend-versus-cousin dilemma. Whom should she take? If she chose her cousin, we didn't know whether or not her cousin's parents would let her take off a few days from school. Enough said.

The good news was that once again I had put the ball back in her responsibility court. In the end, she figured out her schedule priorities, and when she found out that her cousin couldn't go, she invited her friend Ellen. We had a blast.

Taking Responsibility: Kate—Liftoff!

By the time she was fifteen, Kate had made lots of progress in the responsibility department. For example, one summer day, she and her friends decided at the last minute that they wanted to attend that night's performance of *A Midsummer Night's Dream* in which Ann had the role of Titania. I asked Kate to make arrangements. She and a friend did everything. She called her friends, got a head count, and then let each of the friends know that they had to have something to eat before they went. She also arranged rides for everyone. Another milestone on the road to responsibility. And now, when we take vacations together, she gets right back to me about the details, and also helps with reservations and planning.

Learning to Read Her Own Signals: Ann's Progress

When your daughter has to make hard choices, it's very tempting to step in and make them for her; after all, you have a lot more life experience than she does. But what you don't have is *her* life experience, and therefore sometimes you may really not be the best judge. If at all possible, it's better to step back. Let her know that she has the ability deep within herself to make decisions that are health enhancing for her. Tell her that her body will give her a signal that will let her know. Her job is to listen to how she feels.

When my daughter Ann was a junior in high school, she won a part with a local professional theater (in the production of *Romeo and Juliet* I mentoned earlier). Rehearsals and performances were going to cut right into the main part of her fall semester, at a time when she was taking several advanced-placement courses that required about three to four hours of homework each night. With college coming up so soon, my husband and I were concerned that she not let her grades suffer. It seemed to us, as well as to Ann's teachers, that she was going to have a very hard time managing her schoolwork along with what amounted to a full-time job in the theater. In fact, the principal at her school told her that he recommended that she turn down the part and concentrate on her studies. Still, Ann was certain that being in the play was the right thing for her. Given that she'd been involved in theater from middle school onward, I decided to support her.

Ann surprised all of us that fall. She was far more organized, focused, and disciplined about her time than ever before. As a result, she had the highest grades of her high school career, and also an unforgettable experience. I was reminded that each of us has enormous inner resources available to us when we're truly following our heart's path and not some societally determined program that someone else has created for us.

WISDOM CHALLENGE: *Who's Responsible for Getting Your Daughter into College?*

This is a bit of a misnomer, because of course ultimately your daughter must be responsible for getting herself into college—that is, getting the grades that will create her record, filling out the applications, taking the SATs, making a good impression at interviews. Even if I could have done part of that process myself, for example, by writing some of the essays on those applications, I would never have done such a thing. It's dishonest, and would have taken away from my daughters' feeling of achievement and sense of integrity. They could never have felt that they "owned" their place in college.

On the other hand, I certainly worked hard at supporting (and pushing) both my girls during the process. To be perfectly honest, I don't think that either of them would have gotten into the colleges they ended up attending without my help—and yes, coercion!

Although there were many other areas of my daughters' lives that I expected them to take full responsibility for once they had reached junior or senior year of high school, I didn't feel that either of them had a full enough sense of her potential to aim as high as I thought she should in her college choices. Nor did I feel that they, or practically any teenager, could understand how much planning, organization, discipline, and just plain hard work was required to fill out the applications in a timely and optimal fashion. Given that I felt that the question of what college they would attend had important implications for the rest of their lives, I was not willing to just step back and let them sink or swim.

I certainly don't mean to say that if either of my daughters had not gotten into a top Ivy League school, that I think she would have "sunk." As it happens, both daughters did end up going to excellent schools. If they hadn't gotten in to them, their lives would have turned out fine, of that I am sure. But my fear was that they would sell themselves short by not trying for the best schools possible, or by not giving it their absolute best if they did try. I saw it as my job in my Mother Bear capacity to growl and swat and nip until they threw themselves into the task of applying to college with all their heart, soul, and mind.

Other mothers I know have put more of the onus on their children. Where a mother draws the line with this, as with so many other decisions during the course of her child's development, is something only she can decide.

Behind the Scenes of the College Application Process

I was no expert on filling out college applications, taking SATs, or finessing entrance interviews, but I did realize early on that the whole process amounts to practically a full-time job—and that it comes at a time when the average teenager already has more activities and academic work than she can deal with. I can't imagine a teenager getting through the process without a lot of parental support and guidance. Though my daughters had excellent high school guidance teachers who certainly did their part, the teachers have many students whom they are responsible for. A mother can devote much more time to the task, if she thinks that's the right thing to do—which I did.

Both of my daughters were good students with good SAT scores, so there was never any question that they'd get into college. But I wanted to encourage both girls to apply to the colleges of their dreams. I felt that regardless of whether they got in or not, participating in this kind of competition was another way for them to align themselves with the life force and realize themselves most completely. So along with my friend Mona Lisa, I went to work to help them. Mona Lisa told both girls the following: Getting accepted at the college of your choice is basically sales and marketing. Imagine a committee of ten very bored, tired college professionals who have to read hundreds of essays and applications. Your job is to get them to wake up and be amused or intrigued with what you have to say. You want your application to sparkle.

My older daughter had been convinced, by a combination of temperament and advice from school, that the likelihood of her getting into a top college was slim to none. I didn't agree. As Mona Lisa said, "You can't score the goal if you don't shoot the puck." Besides, Ann is a real scholar and a born student. Though she argued with both of us, we still made sure she filled out applications to eight schools, all of which were very highly competitive. At one point, to get her organized and into the right mind-set for writing her essays, Mona Lisa set a timer at her house and had Ann write nonstop about a subject of her choice for fifteen minutes. This process got repeated until Ann got it right. (I was glad to have a friend help out with this because mothers and daughters can get into real power struggles at times like these.) During the application process, her dad and I split up the task of taking her around to visit different schools. This was a major project in itself, taking more time, money, and energy than I could have imagined. In the end, Ann was accepted by a fabulous college and all of us were thrilled. Once there she made friends for life and received a wonderful education.

When my younger daughter, Kate, began to think about college, I knew that the question of where she would go was even more important to her self-esteem, because her academic flame had always appeared dimmer in comparison to her sister's. (This is the kind of Mother Bear wisdom that mothers always have.) So, once again, Mona Lisa and I geared up. Although Kate is very bright and has always gotten straight A's, she just doesn't like academics very much and never will, which meant that she didn't have the drive to try for a first-rate school. Still, because I knew she had it in her, I really put the pressure on. She initially presented us with some less-than-great essays for her college applications. Mona Lisa asked her if it was her best work. She admitted that it wasn't. Mona Lisa said, "Why would you show me less than your best?" Kate rewrote them until they were great. At one point during the application process, she burst into tears, and said, "Nobody puts as much pressure on their kids as you and Mona Lisa!" And then, between sniffles, she cried, "But I wouldn't have it any other way!" She got into her first-choice school, early decision. I nearly burst with pride and relief. And the experience was just what the doctor ordered. She now looks back on the whole process and agrees that it was well worth the effort.

WISDOM CHALLENGE: *When Your Daughter Fails to Get into the "Right" College*

What do you do if your daughter opens her college acceptance letters and finds out that she has been rejected by her first or even second or third college choices? This can be really painful to witness, especially if her friends are celebrating their acceptances. You're hurting in your heart, yet this is when you, as a mother, have to stand firm in your faith that, no matter what, everything will turn out all right. You must not expect your daughter to be able to have that kind of faith, however—not at first. First she will have to grieve her loss. This can take a while. During this time, do not rush in with platitudes like "When God closes a door, he always opens a window." Though this platitude is absolutely true, your daughter needs to feel her feelings fully before she is ready to see the possibility of a silver lining in her personal cloud. She will eventually get to this place with your support.

If she is still mourning her bad fortune after a few weeks, she needs an extra push to get her to that place, so she doesn't bog down in chronic resentment, disappointment, or anger. You might point her in the direction of some good inspirational literature, or tell her a story that reminds her that the path toward fulfillment is rarely a straight line. One of my own favorites concerns my sister Penny. When she was on the U.S. Ski Team and training for the Sapporo Olympics, Penny developed a pilonidal cyst, which required surgery. Instead of simply draining the cyst, her surgeon removed her entire tailbone! (I'll never understand why.) Because her recovery was so prolonged, she missed her lifetime goal of going to the Sapporo Olympics. The process of coming to grips with this forced her to evaluate what she really wanted out of her life. She came to the realization that she wanted a home and a family—something she hadn't given a thought to while training! During this process, she met and married the man of her dreams, a man with whom she has happily shared the last thirty years of her life. As Penny discovered and as each of us knows from our own experience, there are all kinds of detours that bring us blessings we can only appreciate in retrospect.

After giving your daughter a pep talk, ask her to make some decisions. There may be other ways to go to the college of her dreams. Would she like to take a year off and reapply? Would she consider transferring for her sophomore or junior year? Help her to use the energy of rejection to get clear about what's really important in the long run.

When I was at Dartmouth Medical School, the administration hired a wonderful and insightful psychiatrist to sit in the laundry room of the med school dorm every Tuesday. That way, when you were folding your laundry, you could chat with him about any potential problems without actually having to admit you needed a "shrink." I once talked with him about my fear of not getting a good internship placement. He said, "In the long run, where you go to college and where you do your internship never matters. It's how well you do when you're there. There are great opportunities and great people at every college in the country." He himself had gone to a college I had never heard of, and did his internship at a small community hospital I had never heard of either. He said, "Life keeps presenting you with endless opportunities, so don't sweat something as insignificant as where you go for your internship." Looking back with the wisdom of hindsight, I see how absolutely right he was.

Money Matters: The Means to Do It Yourself

Adolescence is when many girls will have their first paying jobs, which can be anything from baby-sitting to yard work. Some may even start business ventures, such as selling craft items that they make or providing tutoring services. A girl's first lessons in providing value to others are learned rapidly in a job setting. My daughters both did baby-sitting in middle school. I remember that Kate once put in well over eight hours and was given only twenty-five dollars for her time—far less than I would have made at the same job over thirty years earlier. She was furious with the woman who had hired her and even called her afterward to complain. I don't remember the outcome. What I do remember is that this was an important, though not pleasant, lesson for my daughter. She learned that she had to state her rates right up front and stick to them. She also learned that she could pick and choose her clients. She never baby-sat for that family again, but developed relationships with a few favorites who paid her well and whose children adored her. In other words, she learned that work can be both emotionally fulfilling and financially rewarding.

It's important that a girl update her financial knowledge at this stage in whatever way is appropriate for her situation. For example, if you haven't done so already, this is a good time to set up a brokerage account to help your daughter learn the basics of investing and saving. My husband and I had set up brokerage accounts for our daughters for college, but they weren't involved in these. I didn't include our daughters nearly enough in the basics of finance because, until my divorce, I left all such matters to my husband. Though common enough, this approach sends girls the mistaken message that boys and men are better with money matters than girls. This, in turn, establishes a precedent for relationships that can keep a woman trapped in her "golden handcuffs."

❁ WISDOM CHALLENGE: *Who's Responsible for Paying for College?*

Many girls have their first encounter with financial reality when they start filling out college applications, particularly the ones for financial aid. For many families, the choice about where a daughter will go to college is based on what the family can afford and how much debt the young woman is willing to shoulder in the postgraduation years. Some girls work their way through college while others don't have to. I can certainly appreciate the advantages of both scenarios. It's axiomatic that we tend not to appreciate what is simply handed to us. Thus, a girl who must work her way through college is more apt to "own" her education and take advantage of all her college has to offer, compared to someone whose parents are paying for everything. Our family was able to afford college tuition to the colleges our daughters chose, so I didn't ask them to work. I already knew that they could hold down a job and be of service to others, and I wanted them to be able to focus as much time as needed on their studies. However, I didn't use the "I'm paying for it" line to pressure them to get straight A's. I felt that by this time, the motivation for good grades really had to come from within, not from my harping on it.

Every family has its own approach to the question of who pays for what. My parents agreed to put me through college, but no further. I paid for medical school myself. When it came to my daughters, my husband and I started putting money away for them for college when they were still in grade school. We also took advantage of the various college tuition tax credits that are available. As a result, we were able to pay for them in full, and neither of them will have to worry about repaying college loans. That plus the fact that I have decided to help support each of them for the first few years after college means that they will have a lot of freedom to explore various career options during that critical postgraduation life passage.

Whatever decision a family makes about paying for college, parents should be as honest as possible with their children about what kind of financial support they can expect. If a daughter is going to have to share in the financial burden, she should know this ahead of time—years ahead of time, ideally, so that she can start saving and thinking about how she is going to earn the money she will need.

College is, after all, a gateway into the real world of adult life. For some girls the gateway turns into an expressway—they have to start dealing with reality much sooner than others. But I've never

met a student who had to work her way through college who resented the experience or suffered unduly as a result of it. Having to
work is nothing to be ashamed of, and it may actually jump-start a
girl's career by helping her learn valuable skills and make important
contacts. For example, both my daughters had college friends whose
summer jobs helped them land very lucrative jobs in law and finance
in New York City after college.

Money Matters: The Will to Do It Yourself

Sometimes parents use the money they pay for tuition as a means
of controlling their daughter, and this kind of coercive parental control can become so uncomfortable that it forces a girl to do whatever
it takes to become financially self-sufficient. This situation is more
common than you might think. Dealing with it head-on is both
frightening and empowering. Here's an example:

The parents of one of my friends refused to pay their share of the
college she had been accepted to and wanted to attend—an amount
calculated by the college after looking at the financial aid forms she
had submitted, which stated her parents' income. They wanted her
to live at home and go to a local college, rather than the more prestigious, and expensive, college that she had selected.

She decided that it was worth it to her to pay her own way, because she saw the school she had chosen as crucial to her career aspirations. For two years this very determined young woman worked
twenty to thirty hours per week, in addition to taking a full load of
courses, in order to pay for school and to officially establish her financial independence. Once she could prove that she was self-supporting, she became eligible for a financial aid package calculated on
the basis of her own modest income, not that of her parents, which
was much larger. She was then able to get more loans, grants, and
scholarships. Though she finished college with a lot of debt, she got
the education she wanted and also broke free from the legacy of
parental control, which she felt was stifling her.

BEGINNING THE PROCESS OF LETTING GO

It's true that some mothers try to exercise too much control over
their daughters. But on some level, all mothers dread their daughters'
coming of age. Like all major life transitions, adolescence and the

inevitable separation that will occur as the girl begins to claim her own life, is associated with loss. The daughter will no longer have the constant nourishing presence of her mother to guide and protect her, and the mother has to step back and watch her daughter make her own way, complete with all the mistakes that mark these passages. Preparation for this stage begins with the cutting of the cord after birth, and continues with various symbolic cuttings of the cord throughout the rest of the daughter's childhood and adolescence, until one day (if all goes as it is supposed to) she's out the door—to college, or to a job and her own apartment, or to a relationship with a significant other. Someone once said that the love between parents and child is the only one that is considered successful if it ends in separation. If you do it right, she leaves!

The early years of adolescence are a time when many mothers may feel the pangs of this impending separation with particular poignance. Here's what I wrote when my daughter Kate was fourteen:

> Tonight Kate and I are at home alone. She has, as usual, spent the better part of the evening on the phone with one of her friends. She hardly gives me the time of day either in the morning when she leaves for school or in the afternoon when she arrives home. She is almost totally preoccupied with her friends and her social life in general. It's amazing to watch this child—who once used to get physically sick when I left the house for longer than a day—now virtually ignore me . . . even when I've been gone for a few days.
>
> Yesterday I returned home from a weekend conference. I hadn't seen Kate since the previous Friday morning when she gave me a quick hug on her way out the door—a good-bye that I had insisted upon . . . otherwise she would have left for school without giving my absence another thought. And on Sunday afternoon when I arrived home, she didn't even say hello or "Nice to have you back" until I reminded her that I had been away and told her that I wanted a hug.
>
> Here I am, a midlife woman doing work in the world that I love. In the words of one of my friends, "You are living the life of my fantasies." And I know that and I am deeply fulfilled by it. But I still miss my daughter's need for me in the old way. Me, the woman who thought that the toddler years would never end. The woman who never thought she'd get enough sleep again. Now I'm mourning the loss of my daughter's companion-

ship. Her need to be with her friends takes precedence over her need to be with me.

She needs me, of course. But it's not the same. She still wants me to tuck her in at night and take her shopping. And some evenings she likes to come into my bedroom and ask me questions about her diet and her body. But she used to want to spend the night on a futon in my bedroom or, when my husband was out of town, sleep with me. I also notice that, when she is finished talking with her friends at night (which is at bedtime), she will sometimes hang around in the same room with me for a few minutes . . . as though she is somehow "charging up her batteries."

I enjoy my children . . . and I want them to want to spend time with me . . . and they do. But I'm not their first priority anymore . . . nor should I be. But knowing this doesn't make my grief any less acute.

Mononucleosis: Unconscious Conflict about Separation

The ambivalence about separation can be a two-way street. As much as your daughter may long to strike out on her own, especially as she gets older and is about to graduate high school or has started college, she may also feel frightened, lonely, or just plain homesick. And sometimes those feelings manifest in a physical way that offers the opportunity to return to the nest and get some more mothering, as in the case of mononucleosis and other stress-related disorders.

Mononucleosis is an infectious disease caused by the Epstein-Barr virus, which is common throughout the world. It occurs very frequently in childhood, when it is characterized by mild, nonspecific symptoms or none at all. Approximately 50 percent of the people in industrialized countries will have experienced a primary infection with EBV by adolescence. It occurs much earlier in developing countries. Mono has sometimes been called the kissing disease because the Epstein-Barr virus is transmitted primarily through saliva.

By adulthood, almost everyone will test positive for signs of EBV in the blood, even if there has never been any apparent infection.[5] The bottom line is that EBV is everywhere, all the time. But the individuals who get acutely sick from it as young adults are the ones who have compromised immune systems. And those who get chronically sick from EBV are the ones who somaticize their stress and need better skills for coping with it. (See "Hardy Girls" below.)

Acute mono infection is diagnosed by the clinical triad of fever, enlarged lymph nodes, and sore throat, in the presence of a positive monospot blood test and atypical numbers of white blood cells knows as lymphocytes. The most persistent symptoms are malaise and fatigue, although some people develop enlarged spleens. In the vast majority of cases, acute mono is a self-limited disease, meaning that it goes away with supportive care. Most patients are well enough to return to work or school within three to four weeks. But occasional patients will remain exhausted, have difficulty concentrating, and be unable to return to full activities for months. Some have chronic relapses continuing for years.

CAROL: The Immune-System–First-Chakra Connection

Carol was a patient of mine who came to see me off and on during her early twenties. She had been diagnosed with acute mononucleosis during her second year in college and had to drop out for a year and move back home. She never fully recovered from her first bout with mono and her illness became chronic, forcing her to decrease her course load and to delay graduation until several years after her classmates. When she did finally graduate, she moved back home and went to work as a receptionist in her father's firm, but she missed many days of work because she was so fatigued. Although none of the many doctors she consulted could find anything wrong with her, an alternative practitioner told her she was suffering from fibromyalgia/chronic fatigue, caused by the Epstein-Barr virus that had remained in her system after she had mono.

Carol eventually stopped working and, now twenty-six, is still living at home with her parents. Her parents are worried that she doesn't seem to be getting any better, or any closer to being able to be independent.

Although virtually everyone has been exposed to EBV and has antibodies to it, the vast majority of people do not have the symptoms that Carol—and many others—suffer from, such as lack of initiative and motivation, low libido, aches and pains in the joints, and trigger-point tenderness. These symptoms are not due to the presence of EBV. They are, instead, the result of a complex interaction between a person's brain and immune system. In my experience, many of the young women who develop these conditions, especially when they become long-lasting and debilitating, are experiencing conflicts about separating from their families of origin and going out into the world. In Carol's case, she didn't yet have the skills she needed, either emotionally or vocationally, to find her place in the outer world away from her parents. Similarly, her parents were having trouble distancing themselves enough from their daughter's distress to see that she needed professional help. This is another instance of the kind of problem that cognitive behavioral therapy can help. Cognitive behavioral therapy has been shown to work very well for chronic fatigue/fibromyalgia and other conditions that have a strong mind-body component, such as chronic Lyme disease.

A girl's late teens and early twenties are all about having one foot in her original home and one foot teetering on the edge of a new life that is not yet firm or solid. Creating a safety net of people, places, and activities to support this new life takes time and patience. No one can be expected to figure out how to do it overnight. In the meantime, a girl who is feeling overwhelmed by the changes she is anticipating or experiencing may find that seemingly random "twists of fate" in the form of illnesses such as mono or accidents or other crises have provided her with the the perfect out for retreating to her home—from college, or even just from the pressures and stresses of high school life. When this happens, a fearless first-chakra inventory is in order. It's time for the girl to sort out her thoughts, beliefs, and emotional responses concerning her ability to feel safe in the world, and issues relating to belonging versus standing alone, dependence versus independence. She may very well need professional help doing this.

Hardy Girls

Mothers of daughters with mono, chronic fatigue, chronic Lyme disease, irritable bowel syndrome, homesickness, or other symptoms affecting their ability to leave the nest successfully should of course be sympathetic to the possibility that their daughters are reacting to life changes that have undermined their sense of safety and security. But contrary to popular belief, it is not the stress of those changes that leads to illness. It is the way in which a person deals with stress that is most predictive of illness.

Let me explain further because this information is crucial to lifelong health. Thirty years ago, two U.S. Navy medical researchers came up with the original Holmes-Rahe Social Readjustment Scale as a way to document and quantify the relationship between specific stresses and the risk of getting sick; for instance, death of a spouse was worth 100 points, beginning or ending of school was worth about 25 points, change in residence 20 points, and so on. (Many of the stresses listed on the Holmes-Rahe scale, such as changes in school, residence, living conditions, social activities, and sleep habits, are apt to be experienced by college students.) The Holmes-Rahe scale predicted that anyone with 300 or more points in a year would be likely to get sick.

But follow-up studies have actually shown that there is very *little* correlation between the specific stresses experienced by an individual and her likelihood of illness! In other words, it is not the stress itself that causes illness. It is the individual's response to that stress. For example, the research of Suzanne Kobasa, Ph.D., a psychologist at the University of Chicago who followed a number of AT&T executives over an eight-year period during the original breakup of the company, found that many of those with the highest stress scores didn't get sick. And some with much lower scores did. She termed the ones who stayed well "hardy," a concept that has been validated by work done by a number of other researchers.[6] (See Resources for more information on dealing with stress-exacerbated illnesses.)

The following hardiness factors, often expressed in terms of the three C's, are what predict one's response to a given stress:

Commitment—having a sense of purpose in life, experiencing life as meaningful

Control—feeling that one can make a difference, can influence one's own destiny

Challenge—viewing obstacles as challenges rather than as threats

Those with the strongest hardiness factors had the best chance of resisting illness in times of stress. You can help build and reinforce your daughter's hardiness factors, beginning in her earliest years. Encourage her to set goals; help her to identify her strengths; work with her on developing a plan for getting back on her feet whenever she stumbles; give her support for participating in activities that have meaning for her. She must also establish good self-care rituals (see Chapter 18) and address any substance-abuse issues (see Chapter 17) as part of the process of creating an inner as well as outer sense of strength and well-being. But there is probably nothing that will help your daughter develop a sense of control and empowerment as much

as the habit of setting goals, establishing priorities, and then reviewing them to assess progress—in other words, creating a life plan.

Mother Bear Wisdom—Redux

I have read that when a young bear reaches adolescence, its
mother, having taught it everything it needs to know to survive, will
simply walk away. If her offspring tries to reconnect with her, she
will swat her away. The time has come for the adolescent bear cub
to make it on her own. The mother instinctively knows that further
direct mothering will be counterproductive.

We human mothers must acknowledge the same, despite the fact
that every cell in our bodies may long to rescue our daughters from
the consequences of their own choices and actions. By the time a
daughter is in her late teens, we simply must step back and let her
figure out a lot of things for herself—while still being there to give
advice, when it is requested. We don't want to rob our daughter of
one of the most freeing and satisfying aspects of life: the sure knowledge that she has what it takes to make it on her own. This sometimes means kicking a reluctant daughter out of the nest, or simply
turning away and keeping our mouth shut when she makes obvious
mistakes. A mother has to know how to truly support her daughter
in a way that strengthens her, and doesn't enable her to stay stuck.
That's what the late teens and twenties are all about.

Avoiding Mother-Daughter Sabotage

This stage of your daughter's life is also about *your* not getting
stuck. Some mothers, sensing their daughters moving away from
them into their own lives, try to live out their frustrated ambitions
through their daughters. When a daughter is truly ready to leave the
nest, a mother may feel an unconscious need to have her fulfill the
expectations and dreams that were denied her. This was what I saw
happening with my patient Jane and her daughter Felicia.

Felicia was a very gifted skater. Jane had dedicated her life to
Felicia's skating career, and dreamed of Olympic glory for her child.
But by the time Felicia turned eighteen, she had fallen in love and
wanted to retire from the rigors of skating competition so that she
could spend more time with her boyfriend, and give their relationship a chance to grow into something permanent. Jane was furious

because she had spent so much time, money, and energy supporting her daughter's Olympic ambitions. But at this stage there began to be a real question about whose ambitions these were. Interestingly, Jane herself had always wanted to be a professional dancer, but early marriage and motherhood had put a stop to those ambitions. Now she saw her daughter possibly headed down the same road and it seemed to her like a waste. To Felicia it felt as though she was being controlled by her mother, who only found her lovable if she was skating in competitions. Soon she began experiencing repeated orthopedic injuries, which left her off the rink for months at a time, and eventually put an end to the skating career her mother had nurtured so carefully.

When Mom Is Jealous

To understand why a mother's jealousy feels so bad, you have only to remember why a mother's approval feels so good. Our mother's loving gaze when we were infants is what wired our brains for relationships. It was our first experience of love and bonding. Maternal attention and love is a lifelong nutrient that we all crave— and that's as true when a daughter is leaving for college as it is when she was a toddler taking her first steps.

To feel really happy and sure of her choices, a daughter will always at some level crave her mother's support and blessings, especially when she's perched on the brink of a significant developmental milestone (a birth canal, as it were) in her life; for instance, progressing from one "room" to the next, going off to college, taking a big trip, moving to a new city, starting a new job or a new career, getting married, having a baby.

What our mother says to us at these times gives us confidence in ourselves. Like the toddler learning to walk, we constantly look to her for a sense of how well we're doing. For example, one of my friends went off to Paris to get a job in the fashion industry following a very short-lived marriage. Her mother really shored up her confidence when she said, "When I was your age, I never would have had the courage to do what you're doing. I'm so proud of you." Another mother went to visit her newlywed daughter and showed her respect for her daughter's new role when they were making dinner together. She asked, "Do you want the tomatoes cut in slices or wedges?" Even a gesture as modest as this can offer tremendous validation to a young woman.

On the other hand, a mother who has unresolved envy and resentment about her own lot in life may withhold her love and support just when her daughter is approaching one of those developmental milestones and needs her mother the most, particularly if the mother sees her daughter moving toward the kind of freedom and happiness she feels cut off from herself. Instead of supporting her daughter, such a woman may begrudge her what she has achieved. "Must be nice to be going off to Paris after making such a mess of your marriage," she will say, instead of what my friend's mother told her. Or "Wish I could have had someone hand me an all-expenses-paid ticket to a fancy college when I was your age." Or she may just give her daughter the cold, silent treatment.

What a Resentful Mother Wants:
Become a Martyr like Me

Mothers with unresolved resentment and envy often hope their daughters will take up the same burdens they see themselves as having shouldered, giving them the message that this is part of the job of motherhood, or the lot of womankind. If the daughter agrees, the two of them can become "loving partners in martyrdom"—the only two people who can truly understand how tough it is and how much you have to suffer in this world.

If, however, a daughter refuses to pick up the burden, her mother may become resentful and withhold her love and approval. The message is: If you don't stay here and stay stuck, just like me, you're a bad person and a bad daughter. When a mother withholds her love and approval it feels awful—like our life-blood is being clamped off. Hence the saying "When Mama ain't happy, ain't nobody happy." The daughter is now in a no-win situation. If she says no to her mother, she feels bad about herself. But if she says yes, she inevitably feels angry and resents her mother. This is a mother-daughter relationship based on guilt and obligation, not love and compassion— another link in the mother-daughter chain of pain. Until the daughter breaks the stranglehold of this chain, she and her mother will be locked in a pattern of behavior that may adversely affect not just the two of them but subsequent generations as well. Factors that may have helped forge the chain of pain beginning in the daughter's childhood years include alcoholism in the mother, a history of mental illness or abuse, narcissism, or an innately difficult personality. A mother who for any of these reasons was unable to show her love for her daughter, or to be there for her, may produce a daughter who believes that she is unworthy, and that she must be responsible for her mother's happiness as a way of redeeming herself.

Truth: Everyone, including mothers, was born with the inalienable right to life, liberty, and the pursuit of happiness. Being taken for granted and working without adequate support almost always leads to resentment, grief, envy, or martyrlike messages and behavior: "If you really loved me, you would . . ." Or "I give and I give and I give, and this is what I get in return?" Or "You'll be sorry when I'm dead and gone." But that doesn't mean it's the daughter's job to make up for what her mother didn't have.

When Mom Is Ambivalent

Some mothers are so sensitive to the impending separation from their daughters that they may encourage them to stay around home for a while longer to "think things over and figure out what they want to do." A mother may do this in any of a number of different ways—by making home life very comfortable, almost too comfortable to leave (redoing her daughter's room, giving her separate living quarters in the basement or attic or annex, cooking all of her meals for her and even doing her laundry); by offering financial assistance that is conditional upon her staying at home; or worst of all by making her daughter feel guilty for leaving—perhaps even getting sick to hold on to her for a while longer. The problem here is not the daughter who is leaving but the mother who is terrified about stepping into the next part of her own life. Empty-nest syndrome is all about having to figure out who you are and what your purpose and value is, once your child no longer needs you in the same way. (A child's departure can also be threatening if she has been a buffer between the parents at times of marital conflict.)

The truth is, no matter how happy and fulfilled we may be in our own lives, all mothers feel ambivalent when our daughters leave home. Just like the fetal cells that have been documented to persist in a mother's circulation for up to twenty-seven years, our feeling that our daughter is part of our very being will also persist—for far longer than twenty-seven years! This is why we often hold on to her childhood "stuff" in our basement for so long.

There's an old saying that "once your kids are fit to live with, they're living with someone else." And there's a lot of truth to that. If you've done your job well, you often find that your kids become your favorite people in the whole world. You naturally want to spend time with them. The good news is this: If you let them go and find their way—while still shining love on them and giving them however much practical support is consistent with your own values—then they really never leave.

PARENTING AT A DISTANCE

If you have given your daughter increasing amounts of developmentally appropriate responsibility at home, she will be well prepared for college. She will have internalized a consistent moral code of conduct that will see her through the challenges of college and beyond. In other words, a level-headed high school senior will not suddenly turn into a wild party animal with failing grades once she goes off to college. On the other hand, if a girl has been raised without expectations and responsibilities, or in an overly strict manner that she feels the need to rebel against, she may indeed fall apart at college. Here's the deal: College is the first time in most kids' lives when nobody is monitoring their behavior on any level. They're free to come and go as they please, eat what they want, when they want, and even stay up all night drinking if they want. (Binge drinking is a ubiquitous fact of life on many college campuses even though many administrations have been taking steps to curb its dangers, even closing down fraternities when necessary.)

A college student must learn to deal effectively with deadlines, schedules, sleep, eating, sex, dating, drugs—basically everything that is out there in the real world. In both my own and my daughters' experiences, many college students don't yet have the skills for self-management that are required for success in life. If they're still in rebellion mode, or "Mom or Dad will clean up after me" mode, or "I don't know why I'm here" mode, then they may well end up being put on academic probation, going on drinking binges, or dropping out of school. Dropping out is sometimes the best thing a young woman can do, actually, providing her with a year or two off during which she can get some work experience under her belt and prepare herself to settle down and get the most out of her college experience when she returns.

Some college students fall off the "growth curve" because of difficulties at home that cause them to lose, temporarily, their internal compass and sense of purpose. If there is a serious illness or death in the family, if the parents divorce or move away from the home where their daughter had grown up, such events can shake up the first chakra of a college freshman or sophomore, effectively pulling the rug out from under her just at the moment when she is trying to figure out how to live independently for the first time, and is maximally vulnerable. Parents may be undergoing their own changes once their children leave home, prompting midlife reevaluations that may end not just in divorce but in remarriage and sometimes a fresh start on family life. (It's not uncommon to see college students pushing a new half sibling in a baby stroller at parents' weekend or graduation.) Depending on temperament as well as those hardiness factors discussed above, a young woman's immune system may react strongly to the ripple effect of these changes.

I got divorced in the year that my older daughter first went off to college. Knowing that such a major life change could have an adverse effect on both my daughters, I made sure that I stayed in the house in which they were raised and tried to keep their lives as stable and "recognizable" as possible. Despite this, they each had a couple of fender-benders while driving that year. And so did I—energetic evidence of our newly shaky first chakras. But it could have been far worse.

My advice is this: As much as parents might be tempted to make big changes in their lives once a child goes off to college, consider holding off on the optional ones (like selling the house), at least until your daughter completes her sophomore year. It's very comforting to college students to know that they can go home to their old room. It helps give them a taproot into the earth at a time when everything is changing. By the time she's a junior or senior, your daughter will have her feet much more securely on the ground and will be better able to handle changes in her home environment.

Though this may be hard to believe, the truth is that your daughter needs you during her first two years in college, just as much as she needed you in high school. Although most colleges bend over backward to make sure that incoming freshmen have plenty of support to get them through this life passage, it's still a big one. And sophomore year may be harder still, because this is when things suddenly get "real." There's no freshman orientation period to structure and guide the students' social interactions, no cushion. A daughter has to create her own schedule and social life and make choices about how to spend her time.

My daughters routinely called me during college to ask for my advice about everything from what I recommended about their friends' various illnesses to what I thought about the courses they were taking to financial matters—for example, how much spending money they could count on. I was fortunate that both my daughters chose colleges within a day's driving distance, because I drove down to visit them far more than I thought I would—sometimes to see them perform in a play or other events, sometimes just to take them to lunch, bring little gifts, try to cheer them up when they were down. Kate had a particularly difficult time during sophomore year. (That dreaded sophomore slump is very real for many—it was for me too.) I had to intervene with the Dean of Residential Life to help get her a single room after she had gone through all the proper channels and still wasn't getting anywhere. It was the only time that I ever dealt directly with college officials on behalf of either of my daughters. In general, college is a time when parents need to let their kids make their own way, their own decisions (and mistakes).

Still, I didn't hesitate to overrule my daughters when they were making decisions that seemed to me to put them at risk. A mother's role in helping her daughter negotiate the choices on her path can be likened to the corrugated borders in the breakdown lanes of major highways that make a loud noise when you go too far off the road on either side. Your daughter is learning to drive and you can't do that for her. But you must let her know when she's veering too far off the main drag. When necessary, I've been a loud road border for both my daughters. For example, the summer after her freshman year in college, Ann wanted to live in New York City for a month and participate in a theatrical production there. I felt strongly that she lacked the skills needed to find a place to stay and to negotiate the complexities of such a big city. She was veering off track and I let her know it. I insisted that she come home that summer and get a job. The job she found was working the graveyard shift at Denny's. She actually loved the experience and learned a great deal about "the real world." The experience also improved her self-esteem and her mood, and helped her get subsequent jobs.

The following summer Ann lived with roommates in an apartment in the city where she was attending college, and spent the summer working in a clothing store. By the time she graduated from college, she had mastered the skills of living on her own, and moved to New York—just as she had wanted to do several years before. She now negotiates city living far better than I ever could. And she is well on her way to becoming totally self-supporting while also pursuing a career in the arts. She has the courage to put herself on the line by auditioning for plays—part of her understanding that every day is an "audition" in the game of life. She and I both agree that working those summer jobs gave her important skills that she now uses every day. There is nothing like the feeling of knowing that she really can "do it herself"!

The Cafeteria Is Closed (or about to Close)

By the time a daughter reaches the age of twenty-one, she is considered an adult. She can vote and she can drink alcohol legally. Interestingly, she won't be able to rent a car until she is twenty-five because the insurance companies apparently know something that many young people don't: the frontal lobe circuits for judgment and impulse control still haven't reached maturity, a fact reflected in the poorer driving records and higher rate of accidents of people in their early twenties compared with those in their later twenties. The experiences that the average twenty-something faces as she moves into the "real" world of adult responsibility and individual accountability are a very sobering way to cement those circuits into more adult patterns.

Every mother wants to know that she has raised a daughter who has the skills to make it on her own. But this is a time when those skills will be tested to their maximum—and sometimes the daughter doesn't do such a great job of her first attempts at independent life.

Learn to Watch Your Daughter
Fail without Intervening

Her twenties are the time when a daughter is supposed to move out into the world and make it on her own. One of the most challenging aspects of mothering a child this age is knowing how to support her, yet not give her so much support that she becomes overly dependent or overly entitled. Here's an example from one of my patients:

> My daughter Donna moved to L.A. after she graduated from college. Her dream was to become a musician. But she was also good at math and she ended up majoring in music with a math minor. When she first moved to Los Angeles, she took a job clerking at an architectural law firm. The job paid well and she had good benefits. But after about six months, her boss told her that she didn't appear to have the skills for the job and she

was fired. She told her father and me that she was fired not because she couldn't do the work but because the work was not her passion. She really didn't like it. Her father and I realized that the real problem was that Donna didn't want to work for a living and be responsible for her own financial survival.

After all, Donna had been going to school from the age of three to the age of twenty-two. Someone else had always prepared the curriculum for her and made sure she didn't fail. And she had always been a brilliant student. She spent her summers in music camps and other related activities that her father and I paid for. Because she had never had to work, she never needed to develop the skills necessary for self-reliance. Now for the first time in her life, Donna was facing the "real world" without a preset curriculum or a ready-made support system (her father and me) all lined up to pick up the pieces and carry them for her.

I was angry with Donna for getting herself fired in less than a year. Her father had stuck his neck out to get her the job. It also paid well—far better than the jobs that Donna's friends had. My husband told Donna that he hadn't liked being a legal clerk either but it was good training. She retorted, "Yes, but you knew you wanted to be a lawyer." Though that was true, it still bothered me that my daughter had gotten herself fired passively. That's entirely different from deciding to leave a job proactively and on good terms to find another way of supporting yourself that is more in line with your desires.

But when I told Donna how I felt, she became angry with me, and said, "Please don't give me any more advice. I already hear your voice in my head more than I want to. I have to make my own decisions and live my life on my own terms." I knew then and there that I had to back off and stop supporting Donna financially. Though it made her angry, I told her that the first step to living life on your own terms was to learn how to put a roof over your head and food on the table. Learning how to do this while also pursuing your passion doesn't usually happen overnight. But if you're committed, you can still manifest your dreams.

Like Donna and her mother, some mothers and daughters will have to have a blowup of sorts at this life stage. Painful as these ruptures are, they can ultimately be very healthy for both mother and daughter. The love that is inevitably there below the surface is powerful enough to withstand some truth-telling. And this is far preferable to keeping your feelings about your daughter's choices to yourself—while still supporting her. This is a definite health risk for a mother.

One of my patients scrimped and saved to help support her daughter until she was twenty-seven years old. During that time, her daughter lived with a boyfriend and didn't make much of an effort to pursue any goals or dreams. My patient pined and grieved over her daughter's failure to "step up to the plate" and take responsibility for her own life, until finally her sadness turned into anger when her daughter failed to send her a Mother's Day card or even call her. That was it. She told her daughter she was cutting her off, because it was time she learned to support herself. Though her daughter was initially furious, a couple years later she told her mother how grateful she was for the experience. Once she had had to make it on her own, she figured out how. She went back for further job training and now has the skills she needs to make a living. This was a huge boost to her self-esteem, and led to a genuine healing of the mother-daughter relationship.

CLAMPING THE FINANCIAL CORD

Every mother has to decide for herself how much and for how long she's going to support her daughter financially. There is no one formula, though personally I feel that most young women should be totally self-supporting by the age of twenty-eight, unless they're in professional school full-time. I do know that there are enormous cultural differences when it comes to this issue. For example, my acupuncturist tells me that Chinese people often support their children until they are married, and beyond. The same goes for many other ethnic groups.

My parents paid for college and that was it, but I have deviated from this formula. I paid for college and then paid my daughter Ann's rent and health insurance for several years while she got herself settled in New York. I plan to do the same for Kate. After those first few years they'll be entirely on their own. I would never let either of them starve or go without necessary medical care, of course. Both of them know there will be a kind of safety net beneath them in emergency situations.

THE BOTTOM LINE: No matter how much you want to support your daughter, chances are very good that you will die long before she does. If she has never learned to survive without you, you won't be doing her any favors.

But here are some favors you *can* do for her, which will help launch her into her own life:

Show her how to put together a good financial team. To help your daughter negotiate knowledgeably in the real world, she'll need to learn how to find and work with the right people. These may include an accountant, a lawyer, a broker, and so on. Both my daughters are learning about tax planning with the guidance of a skilled accountant and both have their own investment accounts. When Ann was twenty-one and Kate was nineteen, I arranged for them to meet with my lawyer to go over my estate plan. I've set things up so that in the event that anything happens to me they'll have immediate money to pay expenses and won't be saddled with lots of red tape to wade through. They also know where to find my will and other important documents.

Consider a mother-daughter business venture. One scenario that is increasingly common is the mother-daughter business venture. We've all grown up with the Joe Smith and Sons business model, and now we're finally seeing the Josephine Smith and Daughter enterprises. Most women don't have generations of business savvy to fall back on, so many are making it up as they go along—and bringing their much-needed relationship-centered skills to the table. The major challenge for women-run businesses, whether they are mother-daughter or not, is the same one that applies to mothering in general: the tendency of women to keep the peace at any price, not ask for what they want, and put their own needs last. If this pattern isn't acknowledged and changed right up front, it leads to anger, resentment, sadness, and the inevitable illness that follows when these emotions fester too long.

Several years ago, I encouraged both of my daughters to get involved in a company whose products I've used and recommended for years. This has become something that the three of us now do together, along with my mother, sister, and other extended family members. We have all learned a great deal while having a lot of fun. And we've also taught others how to do the same. (To learn more about this, go to www.drnorthrup.com, click on Women's Health and go to the Prosperity Center.)

One of the reasons I like the business my daughters and I are in is that while success depends upon creating sustainable relationships with others, the model precludes codependence. In other words, no matter how much you want to, you can't make another person successful unless she (or he) also puts forth her own effort.

Tell your daughter you know she can do better than simply survive. Barbara Ehrenrich's book *Nickel and Dimed: On (Not) Getting By in America* documents the enormous financial difficulties faced by women who work in minimum-wage jobs. For those with children, things are even worse. In an ideal world, no woman would have children without first finding adequate means to support both herself and her children. Unfortunately, we don't live in such a world. It's just the opposite. Studies have shown that it is the poorest and least well educated young women who tend to get pregnant the youngest—and at a time in their lives when their financial resources are apt to be the most lean.

Having worked with large numbers of pregnant teens and women in minimum-wage jobs, I can tell you this: The ones who get out of the cycle of poverty are the ones who manage to connect with their own Higher Power and inner wisdom. They engage their spirits and their wills in the direction that they want to go, and don't spend much time complaining about where they are.

One of my friends who was saddled with enormous debts was homeless right after college. To make ends meet, she worked two jobs and lived in a church until she was discovered one night by the pastor. He had compassion for her dilemma and helped her find affordable housing. Her life is an illuminating illustration of how consciousness creates circumstances—not the other way around. If she had had more financial support from her parents, she wouldn't have had to go through such a grueling experience. On the other hand, she wouldn't have become the successful and resilient person she is today—a woman who is as grounded in the reality of God and the power of faith as anyone you'll ever meet.

The world is full of both angels and devils, and periods of success alternating with periods of adversity. You have to focus on the angels and have faith that you have what it takes to make a better future for yourself and/or your children. You will be able to do this only if you learn how to listen to and heed your inner guidance. It also helps to consciously direct your thoughts.

If you get down on your knees and truly ask for help and guidance, you will get it. It's that simple. My maternal grandmother is an example. She raised my mother and my aunt by herself, working as a waitress and bringing food home to her children after hours. Though she had only an eighth-grade education, my grandmother had a lot of common sense, a great sense of humor, and a basic faith in the goodness of life. She never felt sorry for herself and always made the best of what she had. Though my mother had to do all the housework as a child, she understood that this was what was necessary. Going to the movies provided her with a vision of a better life. She once told me, "I used to sit on the back step and look up at the stars. I knew that there was something more for me than the life I was living."

Help your daughter understand the paradox of wealth. I've worked with many women and men over the years who have inherited money or have trust funds. Some bring their own unique passion and purpose to this legacy and enhance it. But for others, this kind of money legacy doesn't end up helping them create health and happiness. Often just the opposite. That's because the inheritance these individuals receive isn't just money. They also receive the legacy of having been given something without having had to spend any of their own life energy in exchange. This can lead to feelings of guilt and inadequacy because on some deep level, they have not had to tap in to their own creativity and ability to create abundance. Someone else did it for them. They will never feel the true exhilaration that comes from creating something out of nothing all by themselves using their own gifts and talents. Any good philanthropist will tell you that this is why it's so difficult to give a good grant—a grant that gives people a chance but doesn't do the work for them. If they don't have to work for it and they know there's always more where that came from, there's the danger that they won't tap in to the Source of abundance within themselves.

Never forget that the essence of abundance is not just material wealth. Having a grateful heart and an appreciation for life itself— for what we have made of our lives, as well as what we have been given—is the most blessed of all forms of abundance.

When a Mother Feels as though Her Daughter's Problems Are Her Fault

When I was in medical school, one of my professors took a group of us to a nearby state-run facility for adults and children with severe physical and mental disabilities. Many of the residents at the school had been placed there by parents who were unable to care for them at home. As my professor walked around the wards, pointing out various genetic disorders, he also told us that one of the first things he did after he began working at the institution, no matter how long ago the child had been placed there (some had been at the school for years), was to call the parents of each resident. He did this as an act of kindness and mercy, explaining to the parents that most of these genetic disorders or other problems were unavoidable and had nothing to do with anything the mother had done or not done during her pregnancy. Many of these mothers hadn't known this. And lacking up-to-date genetic information, they had blamed themselves for their children's disabilities. For example, one mother whose child had a rare genetic disorder that causes tumors on nerves (neurofibromatosis) and thus severe mental retardation had spent years thinking she was responsible. She had gone swimming in the ocean while pregnant even though her doctor had told her not to, and she assumed this had caused the problem.

To a person, every mother that my professor contacted had spent years feeling guilty about what had happened to her child—even though none of them were in any way to blame. Most of the children had extremely rare genetic problems that were well beyond their control. What my professor said to the mothers changed their lives. They knew they could finally stop feeling guilty. I'll never forget how healing such information was.

Although the problems these women had felt responsible for are different from the kind of life-passage problems that can crop up when a young woman is just setting out on her own, the same principle applies: mothers have to accept that, at a certain point, their daughters' problems are their own!

My Life Is Up to Me

No matter what a daughter or mother's situation, one thing is very clear. By the time a daughter is in her twenties, the motor for her own life must be fully engaged, no matter what has or hasn't happened with her mother. She must assume responsibility for her own life, her own choices, and her own happiness.

Being responsible for herself doesn't mean that mother and daughter will be disengaged from each other. Most women and their mothers will be friends for a lifetime, even if the friendship goes through periods of being strained. Like all relationships, it will have its ups and downs.

The quality of their friendship will be most truly life- and health-sustaining once both of them have learned how to enjoy their own lives on their own terms. For both of them, this will involve an inevitable process of letting go. I myself am feeling this very poignantly right now. As I write, my younger daughter, Kate, is a senior in college and will be graduating this spring. Even though she eventually wants to move back to Maine, she first plans to live in New York City for a few years. (She tells me she wants a *Friends*-type experience.) I want her to be happy and fulfilled. But like so many mothers, I wish she could find that fulfillment living closer to home. She recently told me that she'd like me to keep her room as it is for a few years. But after that, I can do what I want with it. The very thought of that hurts my heart!

Meanwhile, Ann, my older daughter—who was meant from birth to live in New York City—is happily making her way on her own. She tells me she's not sure she'll be able to come home for either Thanksgiving or Christmas this year because of work. I understand. But that doesn't mean I'm happy about it.

Once again, I'm perched on the edge of another developmental stage, my "nest" becoming more empty of my daughters' day-to-day presence than ever before. And once again, I'm ambivalent. I want my daughters to have full, rich lives of accomplishment just as I want the same for myself. But I also want them to be here with me . . . always. I wish we could all live together, like one of those extended families that used to be so commonplace and are now disappearing. But that is not on our paths. I take comfort in knowing that, on some level, my daughters are always with me and I am always with them. We are and always will be bound together by love, and by, as Adrienne Rich put it, "the knowledge flowing between two alike bodies, one of which has spent nine months inside the other."[7]

Epilogue

20

The Legacy Continues

Mother-Daughter Wisdom through the Generations

Throughout this book, I have focused on the seven-year cycles of growth and development that launch a daughter into adulthood. But the mother-daughter relationship certainly doesn't end when a daughter leaves home. Whatever our age, life continues to offer us opportunities to shore up our mother-daughter bond and heal our maternal legacy.

There are three key times when the energy of birth, renewal, and healing is particularly concentrated:

Birth: When we are born, give birth to a child, or adopt a child, the energies of creation flow through us. The same is true when our daughters themselves become mothers. One of my friends has just become a grandmother. She is clearly "in love" and looks ten years younger.

Menopause: Hormonal changes trigger the need to shed our old skin and reinvent ourselves. This often involves coming to peace with our mothers and with the unfinished business of the first half of our lives.

Death: Death is the final birth canal back into nonphysical life. The light available during this transition is truly powerful.

Each of these life stages is a stairway in the house of life that I described in Chapter 2. Because each contains the wisdom, energy, and potential of our original birth, each is an unparalleled opportunity to heal our mother-daughter legacy and be reborn ourselves.

MOTHER AS NORTH STAR

Going through each of these birth experiences, whether metaphoric or literal, forces us to enter unknown territory. We must let go of the past, shed our old familiar skins, grieve our losses, and create ourselves anew. Our bodies and souls know this, so we naturally desire the guidance and support of someone who has been there before and can show us the way. Someone who has been with us from the beginning: our mother. If she is standing firmly in her wisdom and power at the top of the stairway of her life, she is like the North Star—a beacon of strength and guidance. Looking up to her, we know what comes next. We can move forward with confidence, knowing that we'll be okay.

Patricia is the fifty-five-year-old sister of one of my friends. She traveled to Maine this summer with her eighty-five-year-old mother, Catherine, who was here to visit the friends and family of her childhood—for what she felt was probably the last time. Catherine and Patricia have lived together since Catherine suffered a severe heart attack two years ago. Until then, Catherine had worked part-time as a receptionist at a fitness center and lived in her own home. Although she didn't want to move in with her daughter and son-in-law after her heart attack, Patricia, who is a nurse, urged her to do so. Catherine finally agreed, but she told her daughter, "Now, honey, please consider me a boarder. You and your husband need to have dinner together without me when you both come home in the evening. It's important to your marriage." Of course they don't consider her a boarder, but everyone appreciates her sensitivity to their needs. Catherine is the kind of mother and grandmother whom everyone enjoys being around. She has a great sense of humor and a wise perspective on life. Her grandsons often tell her their problems before they tell their own parents. She shines brightly—a North Star—at the top of her life staircase.

If your mother is approaching the end of her life and you, like Patricia, have always had a close and comfortable relationship with her, then any care she needs may not seem overly burdensome (although you may still need support and help). One of my friends, a sixty-year-old real-estate broker, has had her ninety-five-year-old mother living with her for the past several years. This woman has been a North Star for hundreds of people. She was a professional musician until she tripped over her dog and broke her hip at the age of ninety-four. Though she is physically frail, she is still self-contained, feisty, and able to spend time alone without lots of attention. Rather than being a burden, this wise woman has more company than she can deal with! All of her former students want to be a part of her life and help her out. She still teaches occasionally. And her radiant and timeless soul shines brightly through her eyes.

My mother has been a shining North Star to all of her children and grandchildren. She has also inspired thousands of others. Watching her glide down a ski slope, climb a mountain, or maneuver her RV into a parking space effortlessly, all at the age of seventy-eight, turns the stereotypes about aging on their heads. She's not on any prescription medications, seldom visits a doctor, and is vitally healthy. My mother's North Star influence is a large part of the reason I feel that I won't begin to reach my peak until at least age sixty-five.

DEBORAH: When the Daughter Becomes the Mother

Not all mothers shine so brightly when they get to the rooftop of their lives. Shortly after giving a lecture on adult daughters and their mothers, I received the following e-mail from a midlife woman (I'll call her Deborah) who is facing this kind of challenge.

> I found your talk perfect for my life situation. One question: my mother is eighty-one and refuses to be in the room she belongs in at this stage of her life. I am the oldest child and she is trying to put me in the position of parent. Needless to say, this drives me nuts.
>
> I am fifty-four, mother of two, recently divorced, and starting a career as a life coach. I'm also busy volunteering, working out, traveling, etc. My father died five years ago and as Mom's health has deteriorated, things have gotten worse. We were never close, so now it is very hard for me to be at her beck and call.
>
> Any suggestions? I have a twenty-year-old daughter who had an eating disorder seven years ago but who is now doing well. I want to pass on a healthy legacy to her.

Deborah's situation is shared by thousands (if not millions) of midlife women, who are themselves on the stairway of menopause while their mother is approaching the rooftop of her life. They often have young adult daughters as well. Here's what they need to know: The challenge they are facing, though difficult, is a huge opportunity for healing and updating their legacies. If they can truly make peace with their mothers now, they can stop a chain of pain that may have been going on for generations. And the health benefits are enormous for both themselves and their daughters.

Deborah's mother, like many of her generation, is likely to have spent her life meeting the emotional needs of her husband. Her passion and purpose was keeping him happy. Now he is gone, and she hasn't yet developed the skills necessary to undertake the developmental tasks that are appropriate for her life stage. I've known many women like Deborah's mother. They have often stopped driving long distances by the time they're fifty, relying on their husband to do it. When he dies, they won't drive more than a few blocks, and never at night. They also lack financial literacy and don't know where the money is or whether they have enough to live on. Unable to rely on themselves, they expect their daughters to become both their mothers and their husbands. And for daughters who are going through their own midlife rebirths, the timing couldn't be worse.

Coercion through Aches and Pains

Many older mothers seek care and validation from their daughters through minor physical complaints. Their doctors often can't find anything wrong. In my profession, we have a name for this condition: "the dwindles." Like a kid who doesn't want to go to school and gets a stomachache, a mother who has the dwindles may be reluctant to do the work of letting go and moving on to the final stage of life.

It's not uncommon to watch an elderly mother "enjoy" ill health for years while her midlife daughter runs herself ragged trying to please her. Mom's physical complaints become the focus of their time together. These daughters often battle with the excess weight that comes, in part, from carrying the responsibility for their mothers' health and happiness while sacrificing their own. They may also smoke and drink alcohol as a way to soothe their stress. If these daughters take a break, they feel guilty, as though they're letting their mothers down. At the same time, they may also feel resentment, anger, and grief, emotions that result in too many stress hormones and subsequent tissue inflammation. Over time, this adversely affects the heart, breasts, lungs, and bones, setting the stage for the diseases that claim the lives of most women: heart disease, cancer, and osteoporosis.

I have a friend whose eighty-two-year-old mother is in perfect health, yet complains constantly about her bunions, spots on her skin, and other minor ailments. She phones her daughter twice a day and gets angry if her daughter won't take her calls immediately. My friend is fifty-six, manages her own business, and is constantly running in circles for her mother, taking her to doctors, renewing her house insurance at a better rate, and then fielding her complaints—most recently, because her new, cheaper insurance policy has a higher deductible. My friend doesn't dare say no to her mother because if she did, she'd have to endure her mother's anger. And that would bring up unresolved guilt about her self-worth that stems from childhood. She is the middle child, and her mother always referred to her as "the weed between my two roses." The "roses" are her brothers. My friend quiets her anxiety by smoking and has developed a chronic cough. I worry that if something doesn't change, she will become ill and perhaps die before her mother.

Though it's tempting to become your mother's mother, it doesn't serve either of you. Unless she's truly incapacitated, resist the urge to be at her beck and call. Doing so when you don't really want to simply reinforces the outmoded belief that you're a bad daughter if you don't do what your mother wants you to do. And it will cause her to regress and become overly dependent at a time when she needs to be strengthening her connection with her soul. Doing too much for her actually weakens her ability to move to the rooftop of her life with joy and clarity.

Know that you cannot heal a lifetime of difficulty with your mother by sacrificing your quality of life for her in her later years. It will just exhaust you. And it won't change her. When it comes to caring for your mother, you need to know your limits. You can't do it all alone any more than the mother of a newborn can meet all of her child's needs without an "outer placenta" to support her.

Set Up Healthy Boundaries

Come up with a schedule of the times when you can willingly be available to your mother. Choose activities that are fun for you both, like going out to lunch or to a movie. Let her know in advance that this is when you'll be available. Other than that, you have your own life to live.

If your mother *is* truly ill or needs extensive care, get help. Get your siblings involved. All too often, it's the oldest daughter, the single daughter, or the one who no longer has children at home or a man in her life who is pressed into duty. The other siblings get let off the hook. If they live at a distance, figure out what your time with Mom is worth, including driving, making meals, and shopping. Then call a family meeting and suggest that your siblings pay you, or else hire outside help.

Remember, every time you give in to your mother's demands or feel unjustified guilt or shame about your own needs or your desire for happiness, you put your health at risk. And that sends a loud and clear message to your own daughter about a woman's worth. When you can't be available to your mother or you have to say no to one of her requests, then learn to let it be okay that your mother doesn't like it. You absolutely must let her anger or her disappointment be hers and not take it on as evidence that you are a bad daughter. Don't wallow in resentment either. Remember, she wouldn't be able to "hook" you if you didn't have a part of you that feels that she might be right.

Instead, use your thoughts to affirm a better reality, remembering that thoughts, over time, become their physical equivalents. Here are some affirmations for this situation that I've adapted from Catherine Ponder's *Dynamic Laws of Healing*:

> *I now rejoice in the sure knowledge that my mother has her own Higher Power and I am not it.*

> *I give thanks that Divine Love is revealing the truth about this situation now.*

> *I rejoice in the sure knowledge that all is well and that Divine Love is healing this situation now.*

The Gate Swings Both Ways

It's not always the aging mother who is stuck. Sometimes it's her midlife daughter. Many midlife women are tempted to use their mother's failing health as an excuse for withdrawing from living their own lives. If you're facing the challenge of divorce or widowhood, a job change, or the empty nest, you need to reinvent yourself.

You must resist the urge to put your mother in the middle of a conflict in order to prevent yourself from solving it. Catch yourself saying things like "If it weren't for my mother, I would:

~ get remarried

~ go back to work

~ complete my education . . . and so on

Mona Lisa Schulz, M.D., Ph.D., was recently consulted by a midlife woman with a number of health problems. The woman mentioned that she had an opportunity to move into a career she had always wanted, but that "the time just wasn't right." Instead, she explained, she was taking a year off to take care of her mother. Dr. Schulz asked her a key question: "If the man of your dreams showed up with a plane ticket to take you traveling around the world, would you go? Would your mother understand?" The answer to the first question was yes and the answer to the second was no. I rest my case.

WE BECOME WHAT WE RESIST

How many times have you heard a woman say, "Oh no, I'm becoming just like my mother"? A friend of one of my daughters told me, "In my family, we call it HTN—Heading Toward Nana." Of course, most women who are worried about becoming their mothers are really talking about the negative aspects of their mothers. (No one is worried about being called "gorgeous and accomplished, just like your mother"!) The three major birth canals offer an opportunity to observe what we don't like in our mothers, so we can stop resisting and struggling with it. In a tug-of-war, the way to win is just to let go of the rope. When you refuse to react when your mother pushes your buttons, you're on your way to a new legacy of health and freedom.

One of my patients had a mother who was controlling, manipulative, and cheap. When my patient was young, her mother found fault with everything and everyone, never wanting to pay full price for goods or services. Whenever they'd go into a restaurant, her mother found something wrong with the food. Then she'd demand an adjustment on her bill. At department stores she'd always demand to speak to the manager so she could get a discount on an item of clothing she found a flaw in.

This was enormously embarrassing to my patient growing up. So she has overcompensated in the opposite direction. And 180 degrees from abnormal is not normal. She accepts shoddy workmanship, allows herself to be overcharged, and settles for substandard treatment. Of course, she always manages to attract women (or men) into her life who take advantage of her and try to get the upper hand. For example, she hired a housekeeper who always came in late and stole money from her. But she was afraid to say anything, fearing that the woman would be angry with her—just like her mother! My patient has spent her life being overly accommodating and unwilling to speak up for herself, lest she be "just like Mom."

When It's Hard to Let Go

No matter how old your mother is, and no matter what your history is together, it can be hard to let her go. As a doctor, I've seen many daughters who infantilize their elderly mothers, treating them as though they were irresponsible toddlers who will run out into the street and get run over by a car. Or they worry incessantly about their mother's diet or medication. Quite frankly, what difference does it make if your eighty-five-year-old diabetic mother has a piece of chocolate cake or forgets a dose of medication? Yes, it's possible that one of these days she may die! But you cannot prevent the inevitable. Trying to do so just makes life miserable for everyone concerned. The belief that we can and should thwart death at every turn, especially when a woman is clearly on the stairway to the rooftop of her life, is reflected in the fact that nearly 90 percent of Medicare dollars are spent in the final weeks of life. Sooner or later, we have to let our mothers go, just as they had to let us go when we became adults.

HEALING INTO DEATH

It's no coincidence that so many labor and delivery nurses and midwives become hospice volunteers later in life. They are naturally drawn to both the beginning and the end of life. They know that the two processes are very much the same. The only difference is who is waiting on the other side to greet us. Because mothers and their daughters have been through the birth process together, it is quite natural for a daughter to midwife her mother back to her spiritual home. That's another reason why a mother's conscious death, with her daughter as her midwife, can help heal the mother-daughter legacy. Here's what Marie, the newsletter subscriber I quoted in Chapter 1, wrote about caring for her mother at the end of life:

> I would be wrong to give the impression that I had a perfect relationship with my mom. I did not. We were often at odds, and many times unable to really talk to each other, yet there was never any doubt that we loved each other.
>
> I had the privilege of caring for her through a difficult illness for eight intense months before she died. I had just been laid off my job of twenty-five years shortly before she got really ill. I truly believe that everything happens in my life for a reason. Though it was one of the most difficult times in my life, I also had some of the most beautiful moments with my mom.

I've said earlier that a woman labors as she lives. She also dies as she has lived. Another newsletter subscriber realized that she was not going to be able to heal her relationship with her mother even at the time of her mother's death. Here's what she wrote:

> When my mother was dying after a year of dancing with cancer, I asked her if she wanted me to stay with her in New Jersey (I live in California). I was fifty-five, she was eighty. Her response was, "No, I wasn't with you when you were born, you don't need to be with me when I die. Go home."
>
> I was not adopted so I puzzled over this for months. Eventually I understood: she used to brag about the fact that she was "not there" for three days—the day before and two days after my birth—because of twilight sleep [a form of anesthesia]. That insight helped me understand why she and I had never really bonded. Perhaps that is why I insisted on natural

deliveries with my own three children (forty-nine, forty-seven, and forty-four years ago) with whom I am really closely bonded. My husband of fifty years (their father) and I often "double date" with them. So my mother's distance from me motivated me to mother my own children differently—and in a better way.

This is a painful example of how our mothers often become our most profound teachers about what's important, a lesson they sometimes teach by withholding the very quality we crave. In this case, the mother's parting gift was a recognition of how important it is to be fully present.

Our culture's fear of the birth process is reflected in our fear of death. Whether we're coming or going, we're taught to be afraid. We're also taught that it's not possible to negotiate either of these birth canals consciously without being numbed or drugged into a modern version of twilight sleep.

Over the years, I've learned enough about near-death experiences to realize that the process of dying is not the dread thing we've been lead to believe it is. Just the opposite. Those who have "crossed over" and then come back are transformed and uplifted by the experience, often losing all fear of death.[1] If births in our society were more courageous and conscious, then our final passage through the birth canal out of earthly life would be the same. We wouldn't have to experience either one hooked up to a series of tubes and monitors. The spiritual teacher known as Abraham has a great mantra for all of us to consider: "Happy, healthy, dead."[2] This underscores the fact that it is not necessary to linger painfully at the end of life.

The daughter of the ninety-five-year-old musician I mentioned earlier told me that her mother spoke openly about her own death. "Don't worry about me, Pam," her mother said. "When I'm ready to go, I'll just roll over, face the wall, and be gone. I close doors. I don't look back." This attitude of living in the present is what has allowed this woman to live so healthfully and well for so many years! She doesn't hang on to the past and is willing to face the unknown future with courage and trust.

Having spent more than twenty years attending women giving birth, and having gone through my own rebirth at midlife, I am utterly certain that we can trust the process of life and its complement, the process of death. Both are perfectly safe, natural processes that our bodies know how to do. Neither was designed by our Creator as a medical event. We need only surrender to the guidance available from our souls, our inner wisdom, and our connection to the Source or the Divine Mother in all her many guises. The key to both a healthy birth and a healthy death is to learn how to let go, and, as I will discuss below, the best preparation for letting go is the process of forgiveness.

If Your Mother Has Died

Motherless daughters of all ages talk about lacking a kind of internal compass once they have reached and then exceeded the age at which their own mother died. Without their personal North Star to show them the way, they don't know what to expect.

Daughters who lose their mothers in childhood or early adulthood are forced to internalize the maternal function early on. They are also forced to connect with their souls and with the archetype of the Divine Mother sooner than most of us. As difficult as this is, they may develop true wisdom at a far younger age than do women whose mothers are still living.

Motherless daughters know that though no one can replace one's biological mother, the world is full of surrogate mothers who can step in and provide nurturing and assistance when necessary. The best way to find one is to state your need clearly to the Universe. Then allow the law of attraction to bring one to you. I've seen my share of husbands who are nurturing companions and advisors—and who even cook, clean, and shop! They perform the mother role beautifully for their wives. I've also known many older women who consciously mentor the young women in their lives, thereby filling the mothering role that is missing.

Most importantly, women who have lost their mothers at any age need to know that they're not really motherless. On a soul level, their mothers are always with them. Marie, the newsletter subscriber I quoted above, was forty-nine when her mother died. Her poignant letter continues:

> One of the most painful things I realized when my mom died was that I would never again be loved as unconditionally (in this life) as a mother loves. Yet I often still feel that wonderful love today. I have experienced my mother touching my life after death. (See the wonderful book *Feathers Brush My Heart*, by Sinclair Browning.) My mother used to say, "A penny for your thoughts," when she sensed there was something bothering me, or that I

needed to talk about. After she died, I would find a penny (a single penny) in the oddest places or at the oddest times. I knew it was her way of letting me know she still loved me. It still happens and just touches me to the core each time. Often now it is when I am feeling alone, or dealing with something difficult or hard . . . and I know it is her way of hugging me.

Another reader writes:

It's been twenty years since my mother died, but our relationship continues to grow and change. This has been a big surprise to me. Although our bond went very deep, things were difficult between us in the years leading up to her death. Today that old hurt and anger are gone, and now I feel her with me every day in all the things she taught me to love. When I plan an adventurous trip, she comes along. When I visit a museum or listen to music, she is looking and listening with me. When I finally made vice president, I dedicated it to her, because she modeled hard work. And when my sister and I get together for a meal, we'll often say, "What do you think Mom would be cooking now?" because unlike her meat-and-potatoes friends, she was always trying new tastes, new recipes. I don't have a daughter, but both my sons are terrific cooks. When I see one of them in the kitchen chopping a big pile of garlic, I know where that came from, and I silently say "Hi, Mom."

THE MEDICINE OF FORGIVENESS

Whatever has happened or is happening between you and your mother, you can heal it and yourself through the power of forgiveness. Forgiveness is the true key to letting go. It frees you from the past and gives you back your own life.

Contrary to popular belief, forgiveness is a gift you give to yourself. It is not something you do for someone else. Holding a grudge, blaming your mother (or yourself) for the problems of your life is like taking poison and waiting for someone else (or yourself) to die. Fred Luskin, Ph.D., director of the Stanford Forgiveness Project, has written that the basis for not being able to let go of a past hurt is that, at the time you were hurt—whether by betrayal, shaming, disapproval, or abandonment of any kind—you lacked the skills to handle the emotional pain. None of us were born with these skills. In fact, we often don't realize until years later that we have old resentments that are adversely affecting us. The first step toward freeing yourself of these difficult feelings is to admit that you have them and to allow yourself to feel them fully. Emotional pain from the past must be acknowledged and validated before we can let it go. But then we must let it go, because holding on to anger, grief, or resentment long after the painful event is over is a real health risk.[3] Forgiveness is a powerful way to update our legacies. It takes time, patience, and willingness. And it's worth all the effort it takes.

An Affirmation for Forgiveness

To help yourself forgive, say to yourself regularly:

Mom, I forgive you. I release you and let you go. I now go free into greater and greater joy and fulfillment. I release you to do the same. I know that your spirit is strong and that you have everything you need to connect with your spirit directly. I release you to do what you need to do next in your own life. Only you know what that is. Whatever your choice, I support that choice. I honor myself enough to create healthy boundaries between you and me. As I connect with my Source energy, I release you to do the same. I now connect with the Divine Mother who is always there for me. I trust that the Divine Mother, working through me, will show me what I need to do in my life now. I know she will do the same for you. I entrust you to her care. I entrust myself to her care.

Taking Responsibility for Forgiveness

Forgiveness is the peace that emerges when you take a hurt less personally and when you take responsibility for your feelings. The past is not responsible for how you feel now. Forgiveness means becoming a hero instead of a victim in the story you tell about your mother. For example, a woman whose mother clearly favored her brother is now sick and in need of care. She turns to her daughter.

Instead of resenting this, her daughter chooses to see the situation in a new way. She says to herself, "I've never been able to say no to Mom because I haven't felt really good about myself. Now I have a wonderful opportunity to learn those skills, set up healthy boundaries, and really forgive and accept myself. I know that I have the inner wisdom to do this. Though the details aren't worked out yet, I know that I can learn how to do it without sacrificing my health and my happiness. I've also discovered that the person I really needed to release and forgive is not my mother, it's me!"

When we're willing to take responsibility for our own lives and our own happiness, forgive ourselves—and allow our mothers to do the same—our world changes. So much pain comes from the erroneous notion that it's our job to make our adult children or our mothers happy. This simply isn't possible. Living a healthy and happy life is really a choice. You do it by using your own power to choose thoughts, behaviors, and beliefs that feel good. This is a process that takes time and effort. It means being willing to look for and find beauty and joy in every day. You have to consciously look for thoughts and things that make you feel better. This becomes easier with time.

One of my newsletter subscribers wrote a poem that conveys this beautifully:

THEN AND NOW

I was so involved in
Protecting your feelings
That I didn't honor mine.
I was so involved in
Trying to make you happy
That I couldn't find
My own happiness.
I was so involved in seeking your acceptance
That I didn't accept myself.
I was so involved
In trying to look pretty for you
That I lost my sense of inner beauty.
I was so involved in taking care of you
That I didn't take care of myself.
I was so involved in nurturing you
That I didn't nurture myself.

I was so involved in loving you
That I didn't love myself.

I honor my feeling today.
Now I can empathize with yours.
I have found my own sense of happiness today.
Now I can share in yours.

I accept myself today.
Now I accept you, unconditionally.
I see the inner beauty in myself today.
Now I see the beauty in you.
I take time to nurture myself daily.
Now I can nurture you.
I love myself today.
Now I can return your love.

—NAME WITHHELD BY REQUEST

Sacrifice, Guilt, Martyrdom:
Catch Yourself in the Act and *Stop*

One day as I neared the end of writing this book, a woman over-heard me describing it to a friend. She came up to me, and said, "You're not going to tell me I have to visit my mother, are you?" I re-assured her that I was not. Going to visit your mother when you don't want to will not heal you or her. When we sacrifice our lives for the perceived good of others without including our own needs, we are participating in behavior that makes and keeps us sick. This doesn't help anyone. It is antilife, antihuman, and antiwoman. Do you really want to continue this legacy and pass it on to your children?

You heal your maternal legacy at the very moment when you stop participating in martyrdom, self-sacrifice, guilt, or resentment. When you change your habitual response to your mother, the legacy of pain stops. That's all that is necessary. Healing your legacy doesn't mean that your mother will change. And it doesn't mean that she will stop trying to push your buttons. It means that you stop your habitual response to her.

Be willing to accept whatever your mother does or doesn't do. (The same goes for your adult daughter, if you have one.) Be willing to accept whatever she feels or thinks about you. Know that it isn't about you and you can't change it. Let her behavior and beliefs be about her. Stop trying to control her. It's so freeing to just let your mother (or your daughter) feel whatever she's going to feel about you. Let it be okay with you—whatever it is. This is not easy but it's possible with practice. You just sit with "what is." Meditate on it. Don't try to change it. You'll notice that your emotions will change automatically. Know that you have the ability to handle whatever your mother thinks or does about your behavior. Let her response be okay with you. You are doing what it takes to heal your legacy even though it's uncomfortable at first. Labor usually is. But the reward, the new "baby," is worth it. You are worth the effort that it takes to be reborn and renewed.

FORGIVENESS DOES NOT MEAN . . .

~ that whatever your mother did to you was all right;

~ that you should spend more time with your mother, or that your relationship will necessarily improve;

~ that you should do what she wants you to do when it doesn't serve you, or sacrifice your own health or happiness for her. This just re-creates the same pattern you are working to forgive;

~ that you should allow your siblings or your father to tell you what you "owe" your mother.

Do the best you can. The mother wound is bigger than each of us. The poet Adrienne Rich put it this way: "The woman I needed to call my mother was silenced before I was born."

Although the work of my generation has been to awaken those women's voices from silence, we still have a ways to go. It is our job to become the change we are seeking. That is the only way it will actually manifest in our lives.

One final thing: True forgiveness includes physical release, which often comes only after you've allowed yourself to feel the anger, rage, or sadness that have been buried for years. The letting go of forgiveness heals every cell in your body. In the case of my friend Angie, whom you first met in Chapter 6, this process actually reversed infertility.

ANGIE: Healing into Life

Angie was nineteen when she left her home in a working-class English city to travel around the world, working at odd jobs wherever she went. She eventually came to the United States to work as a nanny and, after several years, met and married a wonderful man. Getting married and then settling down in her own home was like a dream come true except that she was continually worried about her health, always fearing that she'd get cancer or some other disease. She also couldn't seem to get pregnant, even though there was no medical reason for her infertility.

During this time, she and her husband flew back to England to attend a family wedding. After the festivities, her mother criticized Angie, suggesting that she was not showing appropriate gratitude for a gift she had been given by a family member. Angie told me:

> Even though the incident was fairly trivial, my mother's criticism made something in me snap. I got so mad at her that I wanted to choke her! And I would have too, except that my husband stepped in to calm me down.
>
> We flew back to the States and I couldn't bring myself to speak with my mother or her sister for six months. I was too angry. I realized that I had gone halfway around the world to get away from her negative influence, but it was still there inside of me. She was a single mom (she got pregnant during a one-night stand) who lied to me about my father, whom I never knew, and called me a devil child. She said that I had wrecked her life. When people asked her if I was her only child, she'd answer, "Yes, and she's worse than ten."
>
> My mother's disappointment about her own life felt like a burden from which I couldn't escape. And so I carried this burden around with me for years, unaware that it was affecting every cell in my body. When I finally let myself feel the full force of my anger at my mother for foisting this on me, something deep within me took a deep breath and healed. I released her. I lost weight. And within four months, I was pregnant and had a healthy pregnancy and birth.
>
> Having my baby—my mother's only grandchild—then created profound healing between me and my mother.
>
> When she came to visit after my son was born, my mother taught me how to take care of him. And I was so grateful. She also shared with me the truth about her own life and how

ill-equipped she had been to take care of me. Her mother had taken care of me during the day so she could go to work. But then my grandmother died suddenly and she was left with the burden of my care all by herself. She didn't have the skills to handle it. And I, too little to understand what was going on, thought I was the reason for her unhappiness.

I finally felt compassion for myself—and for her. And I also know that the reason I was unable to get pregnant was that I was afraid of becoming like my mother—and passing down the same burden of guilt to my child that my mother had unconsciously passed down to me. Feeling my rage and releasing it allowed me to get pregnant. And it was also the first step toward healing my mother-daughter legacy.

On Angie's fortieth birthday, her mother, unable to come to the United States, sent her the following divinely inspired letter—a beautiful testimony to a healed legacy and to mother-daughter wisdom.

Know this, my child,

As a parent there is not a more genuine or important message I have to offer. I love you and have always loved you. I've tried to show you by my words and actions this love but I realize that I may have fallen short at times. To the best of my ability, with the work of my body, the limits of my mind, and the strength of my soul, I have tried to give you love, shelter, and food. I have tried to give you as much of my time as possible in this hectic, hurried world. I have tried to give you fun and laughter. I have tried to give you safety and protection that you have a right to and I have an obligation to give. I have tried to let you know about life's unpleasantries without scaring you too much. I have tried to give you as much trust as possible in an apparently untrusting world. In all my breaths, my true intention has never been to hurt you or bring you any unnecessary pain. I have tried to be to you the best parent I could with the tools given to me. I want you to know that for any times I have hurt you, disappointed you, or let you down, knowingly or unknowingly, I'm sorry. I'm sorry for my shortcomings and the mistakes I made that caused you any pain, for this I ask your forgiveness. Thank you for the pleasures and treasures you have given me, both deserved and not. There has never been anything that you have done that has taken away my unconditional love for you. Always and now in my eyes, heart, and soul, you are to me the most beautiful bud, the loveliest bloom, and the most perfect flower. I've loved you from the day you were born. I love you with every breath you take. I will love you forever.

Love,
Mum

When Angie shared her mother's letter with me, I wept. There is truly nothing sweeter or more poignant than a mother who has the courage to admit her vulnerability and her humanity, and then to risk asking her daughter to forgive her for what she didn't yet know. This simple heartfelt act is all it takes to heal a lifetime of hurt, pain, and misunderstanding.

MY CLOSING PRAYER

My closing prayer for mothers and daughters everywhere is that each of us be willing to support each other as we birth the highest and best lives possible. That we learn to honor and respect each other without requiring undue sacrifice. That we become willing to forgive each other for the pain and hurt we may have unwittingly caused each other. That we honor each other as powerful teachers. That we know our Mother Bear wisdom lives in every cell of our bodies and is always available even when our own mothers are not. That we know we can call on our grandmothers for guidance whenever we need it. And finally, that the mother-daughter relationships of the future become so steadfast and supportive that when a woman says, "I'm becoming just like my mother," she will beam with pride. And her friends and family will proclaim, "Well done!"

Notes

THE FOUNDATION OF MOTHER-DAUGHTER HEALTH

Chapter 3: The Miracle of Conception

1. Dillard, A. (1974). *Pilgrim at Tinker Creek.* (New York: Harper's Magazine Press), 183.
2. Forrest, J. D. (1994). Epidemiology of unintended pregnancy and contraceptive use. *Am J Obstet Gynecol, 170* (5 Pt 2), 1485–89.
3. Speroff, L., R. Glass, and N. Kase. (1999). *Clinical gynecologic endocrinology and infertility,* 6th ed. (Philadelphia: Lippincott, Williams, and Wilkins), 112–17.
4. Johnson, J., et al. (2004). Germline stem cells and follicular renewal in the postnatal mammalian ovary. *Nature, 428* (6979), 145–50.
5. Birch, E. E., et al. (2000). A randomized controlled trial of early dietary supply of long-chain polyunsaturated fatty acids and mental development in term infants. *Developmental Medicine & Neurology, 42* (3), 174–81.
6. Barnes, B., and S. G. Bradley. (1994). *Planning for a healthy baby: essential preparation for pregnancy.* (London: Vermillion Publishing).

Chapter 4: Pregnancy

1. Giles, R. E., H. Blanc, H. M. Cann, and D. C. Wallace. (1980). Maternal inheritance of human DNA. *Proc Natl Acad Sci USA, 77* (11), 6715–19.
2. Birky, C. W., Jr. (1983). Relaxed cellular controls and organelle heredity. *Science, 222* (4623), 468–75; Davidson, E. H., B. R. Hough-Evans, and R. J. Britten. (1982). Molecular biology of the sea urchin embryo. *Science, 217* (4554), 17–26.
3. Elia, I. (1985). *The female animal.* (Oxford, England: Oxford University Press), 4.

4. Personal communication from a colleague. Biologist's name not known.

5. Casey, M. L., and P. C. MacDonald. (1994). Human parturition. In J. P. Bruner (ed.), Endocrinology of pregnancy, 5 (4), of *Infertility and reproductive medicine clinics of North America*. (Philadelphia: W. B. Saunders); Liggins, G. C., P. C. Kennedy, and L. W. Holm. (1967). Failure of initiation of parturition after electrocoagulation of the pituitary of the fetal lamb. *Am J Obstet Gynecol, 98* (8), 1080–86; Condon, J. C., et al. (2003). A decline in the levels of progesterone receptor coactivators in the pregnant uterus at term may antagonize progesterone receptor function and contribute to the initiation of parturition. *Proc Natl Acad Sci, 100* (16), 9518–23.

6. Geschwind, N., and A. M. Galaburda. (1985). Cerebral lateralization: biological mechanisms, associations, and pathology. *Archiv Neurol, 4* (5), 428–59.

7. For further documentation, see pregnancy chapters, *Women's bodies, women's wisdom*, rev. ed., (New York: Bantam Books, 1998).

8. Gelles, R. J. (1988). Violence and pregnancy: are pregnant women at greater risk of abuse? *J Marriage Fam, 50*, 841–47.

9. King, A., and Y. W. Loke. (1991). On the nature and function of human uterine granular lymphocytes. *Immunology Today, 12*, 432–35.

10. Bianchi, D. W., G. K. Zickwolf, G. J. Weil, S. Sylvester, and M. A. DeMaria. (1996). Male fetal progenitor cells persist in maternal blood for as long as 27 years postpartum. *Proc Natl Acad Sci USA, 93* (2), 705–708.

11. Berga, S. (1998). Commentary: identification of fetal DNA and cells in skin lesions from women with systemic sclerosis. *Ob/Gyn Clinical Alert, 15* (2), 12.

12. Kolata, G. Stem cells: promise, in search of results. *The New York Times* (Aug. 24, 2004).

13. American Academy of Pediatrics, American College of Obstetricians and Gynecologists. (2002). *Guidelines for perinatal care*, 5th ed. (Elk Grove Village, IL: AAP and Washington, DC: ACOG), 96.

14. Dossey, L. (2003). Taking note: music, mind, and nature. *Altern Ther Health Med, 9* (4), 10–14.

15. Durham, L., and M. Collins. (1986). The effect of music as a conditioning aid in prepared childhood education. *Journal of Obstetric, Gynecologic, and Neonatal Nursing, 15* (3), 268–70; Kershner, J., and V. Schenck. (1991). Music therapy-assisted childbirth. *Int J Childbirth Educ, 6* (3), 32–33; Caine, J. (1991). The effects of music on the selected stress behaviors, weight, caloric and formula intake, and length of hospital stay of premature and low birth weight neonates in a newborn intensive care unit. *J of Music Therapy, 28* (4), 180–92.

16. From "If I had my life to live over again," by Erma Bombeck—a popular article sent to me via the internet. Original source unknown.

17. Gabbe, S. G., et al. (2003). Duty hours and pregnancy outcome among residents in obstetrics and gynecology. *Obstet Gynecol, 102* (5 Pt 1), 948–51.

18. Testimony. (May 12, 2004). Statement by Eve Lackritz, M.D., Chief, Maternal and Infant Health Branch, Division of Reproductive Health, National Center for Chronic Disease Prevention and Health Promotion, Centers for Disease Control and Prevention, Dept. of Health and Human Services on Meeting the Challenges of Prematurity: CDC Prevention Efforts, before the Subcommittee on Children and Families, Committee on Health Education, Labor and Pensions, U.S. Senate.

19. McGregor, J. A., K. G. Allen, M. A. Harris, M. Reece, M. Wheeler, J. French, J. Morrison. (May 2001). The omega-3 story: nutritional prevention of preterm birth and other adverse pregnancy outcomes. *Obstet Gynecol Surv, 56* (5 Suppl 1), S1–13; Allen, K. G., and M. A. Harris. (2001). The role of n-3 fatty acids in gestation and parturition. *Experimental Biology and Medicine, 226* (6), 498–506.

20. Da Fonseca E. B., R. E. Bittar, M. H. Carvalho, M. Zugaib. (Feb. 2003). Prophylactic administration of progesterone by vaginal suppository to reduce the incidence of spontaneous preterm birth in women at increased risk: a randomized placebo-controlled double-blind study. *Am J Obstet Gynecol, 188* (2), 419–24; Meis, P. J., M. Klebanoff, E. Thom, M. P. Dombrowski, B. Sibai, A. H. Moawad, C. Y. Spong, J. C. Hauth, M. Miodovnik, M. W. Varner, K. J. Leveno, S. N. Caritis, J. D. Iams, R. J. Wapner, D. Conway, M. J. O'Sullivan, M. Carpenter, B. Mercer, S. M. Ramin, J. M. Thorp, A. M. Peaceman, S. Gabbe. National Institute of Child Health and Human Development Maternal-Fetal Medicine Units Network. (June 12, 2003). Prevention of recurrent preterm delivery by 17 alpha-hydroxyprogesterone caproate. *N Engl J Med, 348* (24) 2379–85.

21. Mamelle, N., M. Segueilla, F. Munoz, and M. Berland. (1997). Prevention of preterm birth in patients with symptoms of preterm labor—the benefits of psychologic support. *Am J Obstet Gynecol, 177* (4), 947–52.

Chapter 5: Labor and Birth

1. Wing, D. A. (1999). A labor induction with misoprostol. *Am J Obstet Gynecol, 181* (2), 339–45; Ventura, S. J., et al. (1995). Advance report of final natality statistics, 1993, monthly vital statistics report, 44 (3 supplement). (Hyattsville: MD, Public Health Service, Centers for Disease Control and Prevention, National Center for Health Statistics, 44 (3 supplement)),1–88; American College of Obstetricians and Gynecologists. Induction of labor. *ACOG Practice Bulletin No. 10.* (Nov. 1999). (Washington, DC: ACOG).

2. Weber, A. M., and L. Meyn. (2002). Episiotomy use in the United States,

1979–1997. *Obstet Gynecol, 100* (6), 1177–82; Goldberg, J., et al. (2002). Has the use of routine episiotomy rates decreased? Examination of episiotomy rates from 1983 to 2000. *Obstet Gynecol, 99* (3), 395–400.

3. Menstrual extraction is an actual procedure that has been used as a way to prevent pregnancy. And the new birth control pill known as Seasonale, which markedly reduces the number of periods a woman has, is marketed to women both for "convenience" and with trumped-up attempts to convince women that their monthly cycles are "dangerous" to health!

4. Fletcher, H. M., et al. (July 1993). Intravaginal misoprostol as a cervical ripening agent. *Br J Obstet Gynaecol, 100* (7), 641–44; Wing, D. A., et al. (1995). A comparison of misoprostol and prostaglandin E2 gel for preinduction cervical ripening and labor induction. *Am J Obstet Gynecol, 172* (6), 1804–10; Mundle, W. R., and D. C. Young. (1996). Vaginal misoprostol for induction of labor: a randomized controlled trial. *Obstet Gynecol, 88* (4 Pt 1), 521–25; Wing, D. A., and R. H. Paul. (1996). A comparison of differing dosing regimens of vaginally administered misoprostol for preinduction cervical ripening and labor induction. *Am J Obstet Gynecol, 175* (1), 158–64; Surbek, D. V., et al. (1997). A double-blind comparison of the safety and efficacy of intravaginal misoprostol and prostaglandin E2 to induce labor. *Am J Obstet Gynecol, 177* (5), 1018–23.

5. Klaus, M. H., and J. H. Kennell. (1976). *Maternal-infant bonding: the impact of early separation or loss on family development.* (St. Louis, MO: C. V. Mosby).

6. Hall, M. H. (Aug. 1990). Commentary: confidential enquiry into maternal death. *Br J Obstet Gynaecol, 97* (8), 752–53.

7. Schuitemaker, N., et al. (1997). Maternal mortality after cesarean section in the Netherlands. *Acta Obstet Gynecol Scand, 76* (4), 332–34.

8. Shearer E. L. (1993). Cesarean section: medical benefits and costs. *Soc Sci Med, 37* (10), 1223–31.

9. American College of Obstetricians and Gynecologists, Task Force on Cesarean Delivery Rates. (2000). Evaluation of cesarean delivery. (Washington, DC: ACOG).

10. Miovich, S. M., et al. (1994). Major concerns of women after cesarean delivery. *J Obstet Gynecol Neonatal Nurs, 23* (1), 53–59.

11. Declercq, E. R., C. Sakala, M. P. Corry, S. Applebaum, and P. Risher, (Oct. 2002). *Listening to mothers: report of the first national U.S. survey of women's childbearing experiences.* (New York: Maternity Center Association/Harris Interactive Inc.).

12. Lydon-Rochelle, M., et al. (2000). Association between method of delivery and maternal rehospitalization. *JAMA, 283* (18), 2411–16.

13. Jolly, J., J. Walker, and K. Bhabra. (1999). Subsequent obstetric performance related to primary mode of delivery. *Br J Obstet Gynaecol, 106* (3), 227–32.

14. Crane, J. M., M. C. van den Hof, L. Dodds, B. A. Armson, R. Liston. (1999). Neonatal outcomes with placenta previa. *Obstet Gynecol, 93,* (4), 541–44.
15. March of Dimes. Medical references: preterm birth. http://www.march ofdimes.com/printableArticles/681_1157.asp?printable=true
16. Van Ham, M. A., P. W. van Dongen, J. Mulder. (1997). Maternal consequences of caesarean section. A retrospective study of intra-operative and postoperative maternal complications of caesarean section during a 10-year period. *Eur J Obstet Gynecol Reprod Biol, 74* (1), 1–6.
17. Annibale, D. J., et al. (1995). Comparative neonatal morbidity of abdominal and vaginal deliveries after uncomplicated pregnancies. *Arch Pediatr Adolesc Med, 149* (8), 862–67.
18. Levine, E. M., et al. (2001). Mode of delivery and risk of respiratory diseases in newborns. *Obstet Gynecol, 97* (3), 439–42.
19. Goldberg, R. *Delivery mode is the main determinant of stress urinary incontinence after childbirth: analysis of 288 identical twins.* Presented at the 2004 Joint Meeting of the International Continence Society and the International Urogynecology Association, August 23–27, 2004, in Paris.
20. Moran, M. A. (1997). *Pleasurable husband/wife childbirth: the real consummation of married love.* (Fairfax, VA: Terra Publishing).
21. Carter, C. S., and M. Altemus. (1997). Integrative functions of lactational hormones in social behavior and stress management. *Ann NY Acad Sci, 807,* 164–74.
22. Ackermann-Liebrich, U., T. Voegeli, K. Gunter-Witt, I. Kunz, M. Zullig, C. Schindler, and M. Maurer. (1996). Home versus hospital deliveries: follow-up study of matched pairs for procedures and outcome. Zurich Study Team. *BMJ, 313* (7068), 1313–18; Davies, J., E. Hey, W. Reid, and G. Young. (1996). Prospective regional study of planned home births. Home Birth Study Steering Group. *BMJ, 313* (7068), 1302–6; Northern Region Perinatal Mortality Survey Coordinating Group (1996). Collaborative survey of perinatal loss in planned and unplanned home births. *BMJ, 313* (7068), 1306–9; N. P. Springer, and C. Van Weel. (1996). Home birth. *BMJ, 313* (7068), 1276–77; Wiegers, T. A., M. J. Keirse, J. van der Zee, and G. A. Berghs. (1996). Outcome of planned home and planned hospital births in low risk pregnancies: prospective study in midwifery practices in the Netherlands, *BMJ, 313* (7068), 1309–13.
23. Gaskin, I. M. (2003). Appendix A: the farm: outcomes of 2,028 pregnancies: 1970–2000. In *Ina May's guide to childbirth.* (New York: Bantam Books), 321–22.
24. Klaus, M. H., and J. H. Kennell. (1976). Maternal-infant bonding: the impact of early separation or loss on family development. (St. Louis, MO: C. V. Mosby).

25. Landry, S. H., et al. (1998). Presented at the meeting of the Pediatric Academic Societies of America, New Orleans, LA.
26. Wood, S. (Dec.–Jan. 2003). Childbirth today. *Parenting*, 96–102.
27. Morley, G. M. (1998). Cord closure: can hasty clamping injure the newborn? *OBG Management, 10* (7), 29–36; Kinmond, S., T. C. Aitchison, B. M. Holland, J. G. Jones, T. L. Turner, and C. A. Wardrop. (1993). Umbilical cord clamping and preterm infants: a randomised trial. *BMJ, 306* (6871), 172–75.
28. Clement, S. (2001). Psychological aspects of cesarean section. *Best Pract Res Clin Obstet Gynaecol, 15* (1), 109–26; Gathwala, G., and I. Narayanan. (1991). Influence of cesarean section on mother-baby interaction. *Indian Pediatr, 28* (1), 45–50; Trowell, J. (1982). Possible effects of emergency caesarian section on the mother-child relationship. *Early Hum Dev, 7* (1), 41–51.

Chapter 6: The Fourth Trimester

1. Bostock, J. (1962). Evolutional approach to infant care. *Lancet, 1*, 1033–35. Also cited in: Schore, A. N. (1994). *Affect regulation and the origin of the self: the neurobiology of emotional development*, (Hillsdale, NJ: Lawrence Erlbaum Assoc.), 432.
2. Almroth, S. G. (1978). Water requirements of breast-fed infants in a hot climate. *Am J Clin Nutr, 31* (7), 1154–57; Gillin, F. D., D. S. Reiner, and C. S. Wang. (1983). Human milk kills parasitic intestinal protozoa. *Science, 221* (4617), 1290–92; Schwartz, G. G., and L. A. Rosenblum. (1983). Allometric influences on primate mothers and infants. In L. A. Rosenblum, and H. Moltz, (eds.). *Symbiosis in parent-offspring interactions*. (New York: Plenum Press); Tronick, E. Z., et al. (1985). Multiple caretaking in the context of human evolution: why don't the Efé know the western prescription for childcare? In M. Reite and T. Field (eds.), *The psychobiology of attachment and separation*. (Orlando, FL: Academic Press), 293–322.
3. Blalock, J. E. (1989). A molecular basis for bidirectional communication between the immune and neuroendocrine systems. *Physiol Rev, 69* (1), 1–32.
   Infancy represents a critical period during which bidirectional communication occurs between the neurological system, the endocrine system, and the immune system. So what's going on is, the mother-daughter relationship sets down all the wires between the neurological system, the endocrine system, and the immune system.
4. Tucker, D. M. (1992). Developing emotions and cortical networks. In M. R. Gunnar and C. A. Nelson (eds.), Developmental behavioral neuroscience: the Minnesota symposia on child psychology, vol. 24. (Hillsdale, NJ: Lawrence Erlbaum Associates), 75–128.

5. Goodwin, D. W., F. Schulsinger, J. Knop, S. Mednick, and S. B. Guze. (1977). Alcoholism and depression in adopted-out daughters of alcoholics. *Arch Gen Psychiatry, 34* (7), 751–55; Moore, J., and E. Fombonne. (1999). Psychopathology in adopted and nonadopted children: a clinical sample. *Am J Orthopsychiatry, 69* (3), 403–9.

6. Shelov, S. P., et al. (2004). *Caring for your baby and young child, birth to age 5.* (New York: Bantam Books).

7. Field, T. M. (1986). Interventions for premature infants. *J Pediatr 109,* 183–91; see also Montagu, A. (1986). *Touching: the human significance of the skin,* 3rd ed. (New York: Perennial Library).

8. Raymond, L. N., E. Reyes, S. Tokuda, and B. C. Jones. (1986). Differential immune response in two handled inbred strains of mice. *Physiol Behav, 37* (2), 295–97.

9. Laudenslager, M. L., M. Reite, and R. J. Harbeck. (1982). Suppressed immune response in infant monkeys associated with maternal separation. *Behav Neural Biol, 36* (1), 40–48.

10. Solomon, G. F., S. Levine, and J. K. Kraft. (1968). Early experience and immunity. *Nature, 220* (169), 821–22.

11. Garber, A. (Aug. 16, 1997). Police gather details on gun that killed 12-year-old. *Portland Press Herald,* 6.

12. Wilson, A. C., J. S. Forsyth, S. A. Greene, L. Irvine, C. Hau, and P. W. Howie. (1998). Relation of infant diet to childhood health: seven-year follow-up of cohort of children in Dundee infant feeding study. *BMJ, 316* (7124), 21–25.

13. Horwood, L. J., and D. M. Fergusson. (1998). Breastfeeding and later cognitive and academic outcomes. *Pediatrics, 101* (1), E9.

14. Hechtel, S. (Jan. 31, 2000). Bilirubin acts as antioxidant in the brain. Reuters Health.

15. Ryan, A. S. (1997). The resurgence of breastfeeding in the United States. *Pediatrics, 99* (4), E12; American Academy of Pediatrics, Work Group on Breastfeeding. (1997). Breastfeeding and the use of human milk. *Pediatrics, 100* (6), 1035–39.

16. Smith, T. R. (1997). *Socio-cultural aspects of the infant feeding decision.* Doctoral thesis, Department of Sociology, University of Florida, Gainesville, Florida.

17. Tian, Q. (Oct. 17, 2003). Women kept in dark about safety of silicone implants. *USA Today,* 13A.

18. Cohen, S., et al. (1997). Social ties and susceptibility to the common cold, *JAMA, 277,* (24), 1940–44.

19. Ruberman, W., E. Weinblatt, J. D. Goldberg, and B. S. Chaudhary. (1984). Psychosocial influences on mortality after myocardial infarction. *N Engl J Med, 311* (9), 552–59; Russek, L. G., G. E. Schwartz, I. R. Bell, and C. M. Baldwin. (1998). Positive perceptions of parental caring are associated with reduced psychiatric and somatic symptoms. *Psychosom Med, 60* (5),

654–57; Russek, L. G., and G. E. Schwartz. (1997). Perceptions of parental caring predict health status in midlife: a 35-year follow-up of the Harvard Mastery of Stress Study. *Psychosom. Med., 59* (2), 144–49; Russek, L.G., and G. E. Schwartz, (1996). Narrative descriptions of parental love and caring predict health status in midlife: A 35-year follow-up of the Harvard Mastery of Stress Study. *Altern Ther Health Med, 2* (6), 55–62; Russek, L. G., S. H. King, S. J. Russek, and H. I. Russek. (1990). The Harvard Mastery of Stress Study 35-year follow-up: prognostic significance of patterns of psychophysiological arousal and adaptation. *Psychosom Med, 52* (3), 271–85.

20. Zuckerman, B., H. Bauchner, S. Parker, and H. Cabral. (1990). Maternal depressive symptoms during pregnancy, and newborn irritability. *J Dev Behav Pediatr, 11* (4), 190–94; Winslow, J. T., N. Hastings, C. S. Carter, C. R. Harbaugh, and T. R. Insel. (1993). A role for central vasopressin in pair bonding in monogamous prairie voles. *Nature, 365* (6446), 545–48.

21. Hofer, M. A. (1984). Relationships as regulators: a psychobiologic perspective on bereavement. *Psychosom Med, 46* (3), 183–97.

22. This area grows very rapidly in this early developmental period of 10 to 12 and 16 to 18 months. The frontal pole is larger in the human right hemisphere, perhaps reflecting how critical this wiring is to emotional health and happiness.

    Weinberger, D. R., et al. (1982). Asymmetrical volumes of the right and left frontal and occipital regions of the human brain. *Ann Neurol, 11* (1), 97–100; Weis, S., et al. (1989). The cerebral dominances: quantitative morphology of the human cerebral cortex. *Int J Neurosci, 47* (1–2), 165–68.

23. Mona Lisa Schulz, M.D., Ph.D., notes that the mother-child bond, especially postpartum, is actually a model for how one person can know what is going on in another person's body. This ability is the basis for medical intuition.

24. Modahl, C., L. Green, D. Fein, M. Morris, L. Waterhouse, C. Feinstein, and H. Levin. (1998). Plasma oxytocin levels in autistic children. *Biol Psychiatry, 43* (4), 270–77.

25. Huffman, L. C., Y. E. Bryan, R. del Carmen, F. A. Pedersen, J. A. Doussard-Roosevelt, and S. W. Porges. (1998). Infant temperament and cardiac vagal tone: assessments at twelve weeks of age. *Child Dev, 69* (3), 624–35; Porges, S.W., J. A. Doussard-Roosevelt, A. L. Portales, and P. E. Suess, (1994). Cardiac vagal tone: stability and relation to difficultness in infants and 3-year-olds. *Dev Psychobiol, 27* (5), 289–300; Doussard-Roosevelt, J. A., B. D. McClenny, and S. W. Porges. (2001). Neonatal cardiac vagal tone and school-age developmental outcome in very low birth weight infants. *Dev Psychobiol, 38* (1), 56–66.

26. Beebe, B., et al. (1982). Rhythmic communication in the mother-infant

dyad. In M. Davis (ed.), *Interaction rhythms: periodicity in communicative behavior.* (New York: Human Sciences Press); Brazelton, T. B., et al. (1974). The origins of reciprocity: the early mother-infant interaction. In M. Lewis, and L. A. Rosenblum, (comp.), *The effect of the infant on its caregiver* (New York: John Wiley & Sons), 49–76.

27. Breen, D. (1975). *The birth of a first child: towards an understanding of femininity.* (London: Tavistock Publications, Ltd.), 176–77.

28. Elia, I. (1985). *The female animal.* (Oxford, England: Oxford University Press).

29. O'Hara, M. W. (1995). *Postpartum depression: causes and consequences.* (New York: Springer-Verlag).

30. Kendell, R. E., D. Rennie, J. A. Clarke, and C. Dean. (1981). The social and obstetric correlates of psychiatric admission in the puerperium. *Psychol Med 11* (2), 341–50. See also: Thurtle, V. (1995). Post-natal depression: the relevance of sociological approaches. *J Adv Nurs, 22* (3), 416–24; Kendell, R. E., S. Wainwright, A. Hailey, and B. Shannon. (1976). The influence of childbirth on psychiatric morbidity. *Psychol Med, 6* (2), 297–302.

31. Steiner, M. (1990). Postpartum psychiatric disorders. *Can J Psychiatry, 35* (1), 89–95.

32. Williams, K. (1996). Antepartum screening questionnaire. *Medical Tribune, 3* (6), 5. Reported at annual meeting of the North American Society for Psychosocial Obstetrics and Gynecology, Santa Fe, New Mexico.

33. Dalton, K. (1985). Progesterone prophylaxis used successfully in post-natal depression. *The Practitioner, 229* (1404), 507–8.

34. Sichel, D. A., L. S. Cohen, L. M. Robertson, A. Ruttenberg, and J. F. Rosenbaum. (1995). Prophylactic estrogen in recurrent postpartum affective disorder. *Biol Psychiatry, 38* (12), 814–18.

ROOM ONE: THREE MONTHS TO SEVEN YEARS

Chapter 7: The Emotional Brain

1. Hubel, D. H., and T. N. Wiesel. (1965). Binocular interaction in striate cortex of kittens reared with artificial squint. *J Neurophysiol, 28* (6), 1041–59.

2. Mayberg, H. S. (1997). Limbic-cortical dysregulation: a proposed model of depression. *J Neuropsychiatry Clin Neurosci, 9* (3), 471–81; Pandya, D. N., and E. H. Yeterian. (2001). The anatomical substrates of emotional behavior: the role of the cerebral cortex. In G. Gainotti (ed.), *Handbook of Neuropsychology, vol. 5,* 2nd ed. (New York: Elsevier), 49–87.

3. Weinberger, D. R., D. J. Luchins, J. Morihisa, and R. J. Wyatt. (1982).

Asymmetrical volumes of the right and left frontal and occipital regions of the human brain. *Ann Neurol, 11* (1), 97–100.

4. Schulz, M. L. (1998). *Awakening intuition.* (New York: Harmony Books).

5. Hellige, J. B. (1990). Hemispheric asymmetry. *Annu Rev Psychol, 41,* 55–80; Wittling, W., and M. Pfluger. (1990). Neuroendocrine hemisphere asymmetries: salivary cortisol secretion during lateralized viewing of emotion-related and neutral films. *Brain Cogn, 14* (2), 243–65; Davidson, R. J., et al. (1990). Approach-withdrawal and cerebral asymmetry: emotional expression and brain. *J Pers Soc Psychol, 58* (2), 330–41.

6. Tulkin, S. R., and J. Kagan. (1972). Mother-child interaction in the first year of life. *Child Dev, 43* (1), 31–41.

7. Amsterdam, B. K., and M. Levitt. (1980). Consciousness of self and painful self-consciousness. *Psychoanal Study Child, 35,* 67–83; Broucek, F. J. (1982). Shame and its relationship to early narcissistic developments. *Int J Psychoanal, 63* (Pt 3), 369–78.

8. West, M. J., and A. P. King. (1987). Settling nature and nurture into an ontogenetic niche. *Dev Psychobiol, 20* (5), 549–62; Tulkin, S. R., and S. Kagan. (1972). Mother-child interaction in the first year of life. *Child Dev, 43* (1), 31–41; Fagot, B. I., and K. Kavanagh. (1993). Parenting during the second year: effects of children's age, sex, and attachment classification. *Child Dev, 64* (1), 258–71; Strachey, J. (ed. and transl.) (Original work published in 1905). *The standard edition of the complete psychological works of Sigmund Freud.* (London: Hogarth Press: Institute of Psycho-Analysis).

9. Power, T. G., and M. L. Chapieski. (1986). Childrearing and impulse control in toddlers: a naturalistic investigation. *Developmental Psychology, 22* (2), 271–75.

10. Random House. (1993). *Random House Unabridged Dictionary,* 2nd ed. (New York: Random House).

11. Kohut, H. (1971). *The analysis of the self: a systematic approach to the psychoanalytic treatment of narcissistic personality disorders.* (New York: International Universities Press); Nathanson, D. L. (1987). A timetable for shame. In D. L. Nathanson (ed.), *The many faces of shame.* (New York: Guilford Press), 1–63.; Malatesta-Magai, C. (1991). Emotional socialization: its role in personality and developmental psychopathology. In D. Cicchetti, and S. L. Toth (eds.), *Internalizing and externalizing expressions of dysfunction: Rochester symposium on developmental psychopathology,* vol. 2. (Hillsdale, NJ: Lawrence Erlbaum Associates), 203–24.

12. Mahler, M. S. (1979). Notes on the development of basic moods: the depressive affect. In *The selected papers of Margaret S. Mahler, M.D.* (New York: Jason Aronson), 59–75.

13. Felitti, V. J., R. F. Anda, D. Nordenberg, et al. (1998). Relationship of childhood abuse and household dysfunction to many of the leading

causes of death in adults. The Adverse Childhood Experiences (ACE) Study. *Am J Prev Med, 14* (4), 245–58.

14. Lynd, H. M. (1958). *On shame and the search for identity*. (New York: Harcourt, Brace).
15. Kohut, H. (1978). Thoughts on narcissism and narcissistic rage. In P. Ornstein (ed.), *The search for the self: selected writings of Heinz Kohut, 1950–1978*. (New York: International Universities Press).
16. Mahler, M. S. (1979), op. cit.

Chapter 8: Mouth and Gut Wisdom

1. Dodman, N. (1997). Lucky the wool-sucking cat. In *The cat who cried for help: attitudes, emotions, and the psychology of cats*. (New York: Bantam Books), 171–84.
2. Norris, J. M., et al. (2003). Timing of initial cereal exposure in infancy and risk of islet autoimmunity. *JAMA, 290* (13), 1713–20.
3. Osler, M., et al. (1995). Maternal smoking during childhood and increased risk of smoking in young adulthood. *Int J Epidemiol, 24* (4), 710–14.
4. Mennella, J. A., G. K. Beauchamp. (1998). Smoking and the flavor of breast milk. Correspondence, *N Engl J Med, 339*, (21), 1559–60.
5. Bhargava, S. K., et al. (2004). Relation of serial changes in childhood body-mass index to impaired glucose tolerance in young adulthood. *N Engl J Med, 350* (9), 865–75; Soothill, P. W., et al. (1987). Prenatal asphyxia, hyperlacticaemia, hypoglycaemia and erythroblastosis in growth retarded fetuses. *BMJ (Clin Res Ed), 294* (6579) 1051–53; Economides, D. L., et al. (1990). Hypertriglyceridemia and hypoxemia in small-for-gestational-age fetuses. *Am J Obstet Gynecol, 162* (2), 382–86; Strauss, R. S., W. H. Dietz. (1998). Growth and development of term children born with low birth weight: effects of genetic and environmental factors. *J Pediatr, 133* (1), 67–72.
6. Pilzer, P. Z. (2002). *The wellness revolution: how to make a fortune in the next trillion dollar industry*. (New York: Wiley & Sons), 83.
7. Feskanisch, D., et al. (1997). Milk, dietary calcium, and bone fractures in women; a 12-year prospective study. *Am J Public Health, 87* (6), 992–97.
8. Cumming, R. G. (1994). Case-control study of risk factors for hip fractures in the elderly. *Am J Epidemiol, 139* (5), 493–503.
9. Altered food is very big business and the dairy industry receives $7 billion a year in government subsidies. There are other factors involved too. Monsanto Pharmaceuticals (now known as Monsanto Co.), manufacturers of bovine growth hormone, puts a great deal of pressure on dairy farmers. The company sued the family-owned Oakhurst Dairy here in Maine a couple years ago because the dairy advertised that none

of its dairy farmers used bovine growth hormone. Monsanto argued that this was misleading for the consumer since, according to them, there's no difference between milk produced with or without BGH. Eventually a compromise was reached when Oakhurst dairy agreed to say that there is no evidence of a difference below their label that reads "produced without artificial growth hormone."

10. Hypponen, E., et al. (2001). Intake of vitamin D and risk of type 1 diabetes: a birth-cohort study. *Lancet, 358* (9292), 1500–3.
11. Vasquez, A., G. Manso, and J. Cannell. (2004). The clinical importance of vitamin D (cholecalciferol): a paradigm shift with implications for all healthcare providers, *Altern Ther Health Med, 10* (5), 28–36.
12. Nelson, M. E. (2000). *Strong women, strong bones: everything you need to know to prevent, treat and beat osteoporosis.* (New York: G. P. Putnam's Sons).
13. Painter, K. (Aug. 25, 1998). Parents no longer rush to flush toddlers' diapers. *USA Today,* 7D.
14. Iacono, G., et al. (1998). Intolerance of cow's milk and chronic constipation in children. *N Engl J Med, 339* (16), 1100–4; Loening-Baucke, V., (1998). Constipation in children. *N Engl J Med, 339* (16) 1155–56.

Chapter 9: The Immune System

1. Maier, Steven F., M.D., Ph.D., a neuroscientist at University of Colorado at Boulder.
2. Bjorksten, B. (Aug. 1999). Environment and infant immunity. *Proc Nutr Soc, 58* (3), 729–32.
3. "Are antibiotics to blame for many allergies?" Study: bugs in the gut may cause symptoms felt in the head. MSNBC Aug. 25, 2004.
4. Christiansen, S. C. (2004). Day care, siblings, and asthma—please, sneeze on my child. *N Engl J Med, 343* (8), 574–75; Ball, T. M., et al. (2000). Siblings, day-care attendance, and the risk of asthma and wheezing during childhood. *N Engl J Med, 343* (8), 538–43.
5. Shafer, K. C., and F. Greenfield. (2000). Asthma free in 21 days: the breakthrough mind-body healing program. (San Francisco: Harper San Francisco), 25.
6. Ziboh, V. A. S. Naguwa, K. Vang, J. Wineinger, B. M. Morrissey, M. Watnik, M. E. Gershwin. (March 2004). Suppression of leukotriene B4 generation by ex-vivo neutrophils isolated from asthma patients on dietary supplementation with gammalinolenic acid-containing borage oil: possible implication in asthma. *Clin Dev Immunol, 11* (1), 13–21; Carey, M. A., D. R. Germolec, R. Langenbach, D. C. Zeldin. (2003). Cyclooxygenase enzymes in allergic inflammation and asthma. *Prostaglandins Leukot Essent Fatty Acids, 69* (2–3), 157–62; Review; Wenzel, S. E. (2003). The role of leukotrienes in asthma. *Prostaglandins Leukot Essent Fatty Acids, 69* (2–3),

145–55; Review; Surette, M. E., I. L. Koumenis, M. B. Edens, K.M. Tramposch, B. Clayton, D. Bowton, F. H. Chilton (2003). Inhibition of leukotriene biosynthesis by a novel dietary fatty acid formulation in patients with atopic asthma: a randomized, placebo-controlled, parallel-group, prospective trial. *Clin Ther, 25* (3), 972–79.

7. Gottman, J. (2001). Meta-emotion, children's emotional intelligence, and buffering children from marital conflict. In C. D. Ryff and B. H. Singer (eds.), *Emotion, social relationships, and health.* (Oxford, England: Oxford University Press), 29.

8. Smyth, J. M., et al. (1999). Effects of writing about stressful experiences on symptom reduction in patients with asthma or rheumatoid arthritis: a randomized trial. *JAMA, 281* (14),1304–9.

9. Ibid.

10. Bell, T. (Sept. 15, 2003). Schools ban peanuts as precaution. *Portland Press Herald,* 1A.

11. Naclerios, R. M., et al. (1988). Is histamine responsible for the following symptoms of rhinovirus colds? A look at the inflammatory mediators following infection. *Pediatr Inf Dis J 7* (3), 218–22.

12. Delhoume, L. (1939). De Claude Bernard a d'Arsonval. (Paris: J. B. Baillière et fils).

13. Sagan, L. (1987). The health of nations: true causes of sickness and well-being. (New York: Basic Books), 68.

14. Gustafson T. L., et al. (1987). Measles outbreak in a fully immunized secondary-school population. *N Engl J Med, 316* (13): 771–74.

15. Halperin, S. A., et al. (1989). Persistence of pertussis in an immunised population: results of the Nova Scotia enhanced pertussis surveillance program. *J Pediatr 115* (5 Pt 1), 686–93; Ward, J., et al. (1990). Limited efficacy of a haemophilus influenza type b conjugate vaccine in Alaska native infants. *N Engl J Med, 323* (20), 1393–1401; Christie, C., et al. (1994). The 1993 epidemic of pertussis in Cincinnati. Resurgence of disease in a highly immunized population of children. *N Engl J Med, 331* (1), 16–21; Poland, G. A., and R. M. Jacobson. Failure to reach the goal of measles elimination: apparent paradox of measles infections in immunised persons. *Arch Intern Med, 154* (16), 1815–20; (1966). Measles outbreak among school-aged children—Juneau, Alaska. *Morb Mortal Wkly Rep, 45* (36), 777–80; Lemon, S. M., D. L. Thomas, (1997). Vaccines to prevent viral hepatitis. *N Eng J Med 336* (3), 196–204.

16. (1959). Immunisation in childhood. *Brit Med J,* 1, 1342–46; Miller, D. L., et al. (1982). Whooping cough and whooping cough vaccine: the risks and benefits debate. *Epidem Rev, 4,* 1–24; Hinman, A. R. (1984). The pertussis vaccine controversy. *Pub Health Rep, 99* (3), 255–59; Pollock, T. M., et al. (1984). Symptoms after primary immunisation with DTP and with DT vaccine. *Lancet, 2* (8395), 146–49; Peltola, H., and O. P. Heinonen. (1986). Frequency of true adverse reactions to measles-mumps-rubella

vaccine. A double-blind placebo-controlled trial in twins. *Lancet, 1* (8487), 939–42; Miller, D., et al. (1993). Pertussis immunisation and serious acute neurological illnesses in children. *Brit Med J, 307* (6913), 1171–76; Honkanen, P. O., et al. (1996). Reactions following administration of influenza vaccine alone or with pneumococcal vaccine to the elderly. *Arch Intern Med, 156* (2), 205–8; Nichol, K. L., et al. (1996). Side effects associated with influenza vaccination in healthy working adults. A randomized, placebo-controlled trial. *Arch Intern Med, 156* (14), 1546–50; (1997). Paralytic Poliomyelitis–United States, 1980–94. *Morb Mortal Wkly Rep, 46* (4), 79–83.

17. Bierman, C. W., and D. S. Pearlman, (eds.) *Allergic diseases of infancy, childhood, and adolescence*. (Philadelphia: W. B. Saunders Co), 27–35.

18. Cosmos, C. (April 2003). Director's Report. (Great Falls, VA: American Association for Health Freedom), 8.

19. Stratton, K., A. Gable, M. C. McCormick (eds.). (2001). Immunization safety review: thimersol-containing vaccines and neurodevelopmental disorders. (Washington, DC: National Academy Press).

20. Hviid, A., et al. (2003). Association between thimersol-containing vaccine and autism. *JAMA, 290* (13), 1763–66.

21. Felitti, V. J., et al. (1998). Relationship of childhood abuse and household dysfunction to many of the leading causes of death in adults. The Adverse Childhood Experiences (ACE) Study. *Am J Prev Med. 14*, (4), 245–58; Foege, W. H. (1998). Adverse childhood experiences. A public health perspective. *Am J Prev Med, 14* (4), 354–55.

22. Hussey, G. D., and M. Klein. (1990). A randomized, controlled trial of vitamin A in children with severe measles. *N Engl J Med., 323,* (3), 160–64.

23. Scrimshaw, N. S., et al. (1968). Interactions of nutrition and infection. WHO monograph series no. 57. (Geneva: World Health Organization).

24. Green, H. N., and E. Mellanby. (1928). Vitamin A as an anti-infective agent. *Brit Med J, 2,* 691–96.

25. Olness, K., and D. P. Kohen. (1996). *Hypnosis and hypnotherapy with children*. (New York: Guilford Press).

Chapter 10: Love Maps

1. Mahler, M. S. (1979). Notes on the development of basic moods: the depressive affect. In *The selected papers of Margaret S. Mahler, M.D.* (New York: Jason Aronson), 59–75; Izard, C. E. (1990). Facial expressions and the regulation of emotions. *J Pers Soc Psychol, 58* (3), 487–88; Izard, C. E. (1991). *The psychology of emotions*. (New York: Plenum Press).

2. The study authors, Kristin D. Mickelson, Ph.D., and Ronald C. Kessler, Ph.D., of the Harvard Medical School in Boston, suggest that this is because insecure attachments may predispose some people to develop

psychological conditions. Conversely, having a mental disorder may hamper the ability to form secure relationships. (See reference 18 for citation.)

3. (Nov. 15, 1997). U.S. survey explores relationship styles. *Science News*, 152 (20), 309.

4. Dawson, G., et al. (1992). Frontal lobe activity and affective behavior of infants of mothers with depressive symptoms. *Child Dev, 63*, (3), 725–37.

5. Insel, T. R. (1992). Oxytocin—a neuropeptide for affiliation: evidence from behavioral, receptor autoradiographic, and comparative studies. *Psychoneuroendocrinology, 17* (1), 3–35.

6. Money, J., and G. F. Pranzarone. (1993). Precursors of paraphilia in childhood and adolescence. *The Child and Adolescent Psychiatric Clinics of North America: Sexual and Gender Identity Disorders, 2* (3).

7. Minuchin, S., et al. (1978). *Psychosomatic families.* (Cambridge, MA: Harvard University Press), 23–50.

ROOM TWO: SEVEN TO FOURTEEN YEARS

Chapter 11: The Age of Reason

1. Colby, A., L. Kohlberg, et al. (1987). *The measurement of moral judgment, vol. 1.* (Cambridge, England: Cambridge University Press).

2. Gilligan, C. (1982). *In a different voice.* (Cambridge, MA: Harvard University Press).

Chapter 12: The Anatomy of Self-Esteem

1. Gallagher, S. P., and R. Kryzanowska (eds.). (2000). The Joseph H. Pilates Archive Collection: Photographs, Writings, Designs. (Philadelphia: BainBridgeBooks).

2. Krahnstoever-Davison, K., T. M. Cutting, and L. L. Birch. (Sept. 2003). Parents' activity-related parenting practices predict girls' physical activity. *Med Sci Sports Exerc, 35* (9), 1589–95.

3. Proctor, B. D., and J. Dalaker. (2003). U.S. Census Bureau, current population reports, poverty in the United States: 2002. (Washington, DC: U.S. Government Printing Office), 60–222.

4. Pressman, S. (Sept. 2000). *Explaining the gender poverty gap in developed and transitional economies.* Luxembourg Income Study Working Paper No. 243. (Syracuse, NY: Maxwell School of Citizenship and Public Affairs, Syracuse University).

5. Zollo, P. (2004). *Getting wiser to teens: more insights into marketing to teenagers.* (Ithaca, NY: New Strategist Publications).

6. Walters, Amye, and CWK Network, Inc. (Sept. 29, 2004). Tipsheets for *Parents Can't Say No.* http://www.connectwithkids.com/tipsheet/

2004/196_sept29/say.html and (Sept. 1, 2004) *Model Reading*, www.conectwithkids.com/tipsheet/2004/192 sept1/model.html

7. Linfield, L. (Aug. 30, 2004). Even 7-year-olds can learn to manage money. *Portland Press Herald*, A9.

8. McCraty, R., et al. (1998). The impact of a new emotional self-management program on stress, emotions, heart rate variability, DHEA and cortisol. *Integr Physiol Behav Sci, 33* (2), 151–70.

Chapter 13: Eating for Life

1. Underwood, A., and J. Adler. (Aug. 23, 2004). What you don't know about fat. *Newsweek*, 46.

2. Ames, B. N. (Apr. 18, 2001). DNA damage from micronutrient deficiencies is likely to be a major cause of cancer. *Mutat Res, 475* (1–2), 7–20.

3. Dietz, W. H. (Feb. 26, 2004). Overweight in childhood and adolescence. *N Engl J Med, 350* (9), 855–57.

4. *Newsweek*, August 23, 2004.

5. Ibid.

Chapter 14: The School of Friendship

1. Taylor, S. E., L. C. Klein, B. P. Lewis, T. L. Gruenewald, R. A. Gurung, and J. A. Updegraff. (2000). Biobehavioral responses to stress in females: tend-and-befriend, not fight-or-flight. *Psychol Rev, 107* (3), 411–29.

2. "UCLA researchers identify key behavioral pattern used by women to manage stress," College of Letters and Science, UCLA, online news release, http://www.college.ucla.edu/stress.htm.

3. Clarkin, A. J. (1997–1998). Peer relationships. In Chapter 11: transformation of interpersonal relationships. In J. Noshpitz (ed. in chief), S. Greenspan, S. Wieder, and J. Osofsky (eds.), *Handbook of child and adolescent psychiatry, vol. 2, the grade-school child: development and syndromes*. (New York: Wiley & Sons), 88.

4. Ibid, 89.

5. Domar, A. D., and H. Dreher. (2000). *Self-nurture: learning to care for yourself as effectively as you care for everyone else*. (New York: Viking), 210.

6. Eisenberger, N. I., M. D. Lieberman, and K. D. Williams. (Oct. 10, 2003). Does rejection hurt? An FMRI study of social exclusion. *Science, 302* (5643), 290–92.

7. "Would single-sex education benefit your child? Some research suggests that students in 'all-girls' or 'all-boys' schools out perform those in non-gender specific programs." (Feb. 26, 2004). *Today Show*, MSNBC Interactive. www.zaret.msnbc.com/id/4387854

8. Ricks, S. (Jan. 19, 2004). Never easy, being a girl is harder than ever. *Portland Press Herald*, 10B.

Chapter 15: Coming of Age

1. Cameron, A. (1981). *Daughters of copper woman.* (Vancouver, BC: Press Gang Publishers).
2. Owen, L. (1998). *Honoring menstruation: a time of self-renewal.* (Freedom, CA: Crossing Press), 35.
3. Ibid, 33–34.
4. Apter, D., et al. (1993). Gonadotropin-releasing hormone pulse generator activity during pubertal transition in girls: pulsatile and diurnal patterns of circulating gonadotropins. *J Clin Endocrinol Metab, 76* (4), 940–49.
5. Read, G. F., D. W. Wilson, I. A. Hughes, K. Griffiths. (August 1984). The use of salivary progesterone assays in the assessment of ovarian function in postmenarcheal girls. *J Endocrinol, 102* (2), 265–68; Vuorento, T., and I. Huhtaniemi. (October 1992). Daily levels of salivary progesterone during menstrual cycle in adolescent girls. *Fertil Steril, 58* (4), 685–90.
6. Zacharias, L., W. M. Rand, and R. J. Wurtman. (1976). A prospective study of sexual development and growth in American girls: the statistics of menarche. *Obstet Gynecol Surv, 31* (4), 325–37.
7. Dann, T. C., and D. F. Roberts. (October 1993). Menarcheal age in University of Warwick young women. *J Biosoc Sci, 25* (4), 531–38.
8. Speroff, L., R. Glass, and N. Kase. (1999). Abnormal puberty and growth problems. In *Clinical gynecologic endocrinology and infertility,* 6th ed. (Philadelphia: Lippincott Williams and Wilkins), 390.
9. Herman-Giddens, M. E., et al. (1997). Secondary sexual characteristics and menses in young girls seen in office practice: a study from the Pediatric Research in Office Settings network. *Pediatrics, 99* (4), 505–12.
10. Marti-Henneberg, C., and B. Vizmanos. (1997). The duration of puberty in girls is related to the timing of its onset. *J Pediatr, 131* (4), 618–21.
11. Ibanez, L., N. Potau, R. Virdis, M. Zampolli, C. Terzi, M. Gussinye, A. Carrascosa, and E. Vicens-Calvet. (1993). Postpubertal outcome in girls diagnosed of premature pubarche during childhood: increased frequency of functional ovarian hyperandrogenism. *J Clin Endocrinol Metab, 76* (6), 1599–1603; Ibanez, L., N. Potau, N. Georgopoulos, N. Prat, M. Gussinye, A. Carrascosa. (1995). Growth hormone, insulin-like growth factor-I axis, and insulin secretion in hyperandrogenic adolescents. *Fertil Steril, 64* (6), 1113–19.
12. Speroff, L., R. Glass, and N. Kase (1999). *Clinical Gynecologic Endocrinology and Infertility,* 6th ed. (Philadelphia, PA: Williams and Wilkins), 387; Herman-Giddens, M. E., op. cit.
13. Marshall, W. A., and J. M. Tanner. (1970). Variations in the pattern of pubertal changes in boys. *Arch Dis Child, 45* (239), 13–23.
14. Scialli, A. R. (May–June 2001). Tampons, dioxins, and endometriosis. *Reprod Toxicol, 15* (3), 231–38.

ROOM THREE: FOURTEEN TO TWENTY-ONE YEARS

Chapter 16: Aphrodite Rising

1. Tennov, D. (1979). *Love and limerence: the experience of being in love.* (New York: Stein and Day).
2. Wolf, N. (1997). *Promiscuities: the secret struggle for womanhood.* New York: (Random House).
3. Bonheim, J. (1997). Aphrodite's daughters: women's sexual stories and the journey of the soul. (New York: Simon and Schuster).
4. American Academy of Pediatrics, Committee on Public Education. (1999). Media education. *Pediatrics, 104* (2 Pt 1), 341–43.
5. Collins, R. L., et al. (Sept. 2004) Watching sex on television predicts adolescent initiation of sexual behavior. *Pediatrics, 114* (3), 280–89.
6. Ponder, C. (1964). *The prosperity secret of the ages: how to channel a golden river of riches into your life.* (Englewood Cliffs, NJ: Prentice-Hall), 304.
7. Buckley, T. (1998). Menstruation and the power of Yurok women. In T. Buckley and A. Gottlieb (eds.). *Blood magic: the anthropology of menstruation.* (Berkeley, CA: University of California Press), 190.
8. Ponder, C.
9. Prinstein, M. J., C. S. Meade, and G. L. Cohen. (2003). Adolescent oral sex, peer popularity, and perceptions of best friends' sexual behavior. *J Pediatr Psychol, 28* (4), 243–49.
10. Ibid.
11. Fisher, H. E. (1992). *Anatomy of love: the natural history of monogamy, adultery, and divorce.* (New York: Norton).
12. Moore, K. A., A. Driscoll, and L. D. Lindberg. (1998). *A statistical portrait of adolescent sex, contraception, and childbearing.* (Washington, DC: National Campaign to Prevent Teen Pregnancy).
13. Dickson, N., C. Paul, P. Herbison, and P. Silva. (1998). First sexual intercourse: age, coercion, and later regrets reported by a birth cohort. *BMJ, 316* (7124), 29–33.

Chapter 17: Addictions

1. Voelker, R. (2004). Stress, sleep loss, and substance abuse create potent recipe for college depression. *JAMA, 291* (18), 2177–79.
2. Weinberger, D. R. (1996). On the plausibility of "the neurodevelopmental hypothesis" of schizophrenia. *Neuropsychopharmacology, 14* (3 Suppl), 1S–11S.
3. Kovacs, M., et al. (1984). Depressive disorders in childhood. I. A longitudinal prospective study of characteristics and recovery. *Arch Gen Psychiatry, 41* (3), 229–37.

4. Ibid.

5. Ibid.

6. Lake, J. (2004). The integrative management of depressed mood. *Integrative Medicine, 3* (3), 34–43; Muskin, P. R. (ed.). (2000). *Complementary and alternative medicine and psychiatry.* (Washington, DC: American Psychiatric Press).

7. Jureidini, J. N., et al. (2004). Efficacy and safety of antidepressants for children and adolescents. *BMJ, 328* (7444), 879–83.

8. Edelson, E. (Sept. 17, 2004). FDA backs warnings on antidepressants for children. *Health Day News.*

9. Jureidini, J. N., et al. (2004). Op. cit.

10. Voelker, R. (2004). Op. cit.

11. Unpublished analysis of data from the California Center for Health Statistics, Microcomputer Injury Surveillance System. (Sacramento: California Department of Health Services, 1985–98), by sociologist Mike Males, Ph.D., University of California at Santa Cruz, Dept. of Sociology.

12. Kuhn, C., S. Swartzwelder, and W. Wilson. (2002). *Just say know: talking with kids about drugs and alcohol.* (New York: W. W. Norton and Co.), 65.

13. Yakovlev, P. I., and A. R. Lecours. (1967). The myelogenetic cycles of regional maturation of the brain. In A. Minkowski (ed.), *Regional development of the brain in early life.* (Oxford, England: Blackwell Scientific), 3–70; Yakovlev, P. I. (1962). Morphological criteria of growth and maturation of the nervous system in man. *Res Publ Assoc Res Nerv Ment Dis, 39,* 3–46; Swartzwelder, H. S., W. A. Wilson, and M. I. Tayyeb. (1995). Age-dependent inhibition of long-term potentiation by ethanol in immature versus mature hippocampus. *Alcohol Clin Exp Res, 19* (6), 1480–85.

14. Kuhn, C., S. Swartzwelder, and W. Wilson. (2002). Op. Cit.

15. Johnston, L. D., P. M. O'Malley, J. G. Bachman, and J. E. Schulenberg. (2004). *Monitoring the future: national results on adolescent drug use: overview of key findings, 2003.* NIH Publication No. 04–5506. (Bethesda, MD: National Institute on Drug Abuse).

16. Mothers Against Drunk Driving (MADD). "Why 21?" Fact sheet. www.madd.org/stats/1,1056,4846,00.html

17. Raeburn, P. (Oct. 17, 2004). Too immature for the death penalty? *New York Times Magazine.*

18. Collaborative Group on Hormonal Factors in Breast Cancer. (2002). Alcohol, tobacco and breast cancer-collaborative reanalysis of individual data from 53 epidemiological studies, including 58,515 women with breast cancer and 95,067 women without the disease. *Br J Cancer, 87* (11), 1234–45;Thun, M. J., et al. (1997). Alcohol consumption and mortality among middle-aged and elderly U.S. adults. *N Engl J Med, 337* (24), 1705–14.; Britton, A., and K. McPherson. (2001). Mortality

in England and Wales attributable to current alcohol consumption. *J Epidemiol Community Health, 55* (6), 383–88.

19. www.safeyouth.org/scripts/teens/alcohol.asp

20. Minna, J. D. (2005). Neoplasms of the lung. In D. L. Kasper et al. (eds.). *Harrison's principles of internal medicine,* 16th ed. (New York: McGraw Hill), 506.

21. Associated Press. (Oct. 9, 1998). Teen smoking rises in Joe Camel years. *Portland Press Herald,* 9A.

22. Sargent, J. D., and M. Dalton. (2001). Does parental disapproval of smoking prevent adolescents from becoming established smokers? *Pediatrics, 108* (6), 1256–62.

23. Johnston, L. D., P. M. O'Malley, J. G. Bachman, and J. E. Schulenberg. (December 19, 2003). Ecstasy use falls for second year in a row, overall teen drug use drops. (Ann Arbor: University of Michigan News and Information Services).

24. Tashkin, D. P., B. J. Shapiro, L. Ramanna, G. V. Taplin, Y. E. Lee, and C. E. Harper. (1976). Chronic effects of heavy marihuana smoking on pulmonary function in healthy young males. In M. C. Braude and S. Szara (eds.), *The pharmacology of marihuana.* (New York: Raven Press), 291–95.

25. Hembree, W. C., 3rd, G. G. Nahas, P. Zeidenberg, H. F. Huang. (1978). Changes in human spermatozoa associated with high dose marijuana smoking. *Adv Biosci, 22–23,* 429–39.

26. Ewing, J. A. (1984). Detecting alcoholism. The CAGE questionnaire. *JAMA, 252,* (14), 1905–7.

Chapter 18: Self-care Basics

1. Wolfson, A. R., and M. A. Carskadon. (1998). Sleep schedules and daytime functioning in adolescents. *Child Dev, 69* (4), 875–87.

2. Hicks, R. A., C. Fernandez, R. J. Pellegrini. (2001). Striking changes in the sleep satisfaction of university students over the last two decades. *Percept Mot Skills, 93* (3), 660; Tsai, L. L., and S. P. Li. (Feb. 2004). Sleep patterns in college students: gender and grade differences. *J Psychosom Res, 56* (2), 231–37.

3. Ritter, M. (Feb. 21, 2004). Scientists study how to keep brain awake. The Associated Press.

4. Greydanus, D.E. (ed.), and P. Bashe (writer). (2003). The American Academy of Pediatrics, caring for your teenager: the complete and authoritative guide. (New York: Bantam Books).

5. Voelker, R. (2004). Stress, sleep loss, and substance abuse create potent recipe for college depression. *JAMA, 291* (18), 2177–79.

6. Saibene, F., et al. (Dec. 15, 1978). Oronasal breathing during exercise. *Pflugers Arch., 378* (1), 65–69.; Petruson, B., and T. Bjuro. (1990). The

importance of nose-breathing for the systolic blood pressure rise during exercise. *Acta Otolaryngol, 109* (5–6), 461–66; Lorig, T. S., and G. E. Schwartz. (Sept. 1998). Brain and odor: I. Alteration of human EEG by odor administration. *Psychobiology, 16* (3), 281–84; Hirsch, J. A., and B. Bishop. (1981). Respiratory sinus arrhythmia in humans: how breathing pattern modulates heart rate. *Am J Physiol, 241* (4), H620–29.

7. Dietz, W. H. (2004). Overweight in childhood and adolescence. *N Engl J Med, 350* (9), 855–57.

8. Dobson, A., J. DaVanzo, M. Consunji, et al. (January 2004). A study of the cost effects of daily multivitamins for older adults, prepared by the Lewin Group for Wyeth Consumer Healthcare.

    For an extensive data base on the role of nutritional supplementation in preventing disease, see Dr. Ray Strand's Web site www.bio nutrition.org

9. Ames, B. N. (1999). Micronutrient deficiencies. A major cause of DNA damage. *Ann N Y Acad Sci, 889,* 87–106; Ames, B. N. (Apr. 18, 2001). DNA damage from micronutrient deficiencies is likely to be a major cause of cancer. *Mutat Res, 475* (1–2), 7–20.

10. French, S. A., et al. (1994). Food preferences, eating patterns, and physical activity among adolescents: correlates of eating disorders symptoms. *J Adolesc Health, 15* (4), 286–94.

11. French, S. A., et al. (1995). Frequent dieting among adolescents: psychosocial and health behavior correlates. *Am J Public Health, 85* (5), 695–701.

12. Brewerton, T. D. (April 2002). Bulimia in children and adolescents. *Child and adolescent psychiatry clinics of North America, 11* (2), 237–56.

13. Teicher, M. H., et al. (1997). Preliminary evidence for abnormal cortical development in physically and sexually abused children using EEG coherence and MRI. *Ann NY Acad Sci, 821,* 160–75.

14. Gustafson, T. B., and D. B. Sarwer. (Aug. 2004). Childhood sexual abuse and obesity. *Obes Rev, 5* (3), 129–35.

15. Felitti, V. J., R. F. Anda, D. Nordenberg, et al. (1998). Relationship of childhood abuse and household dysfunction to many of the leading causes of death in adults. The Adverse Childhood Experiences (ACE) Study. *Am J Prev Med, 14* (4), 245–58; Felitti, V. J. (1993). Childhood sexual abuse, depression, and family dysfunction in adult obese patients: a case control study. *South Med J, 86* (7), 732–36.

16. Felitti, V. J. (2002). [The relationship of adverse childhood experiences to adult health: turning gold into lead]. *Z Psychosom Med Psychother, 48* (4), 359–69. German.

17. Dietz, W. H. (2004). Overweight in childhood and adolescence. *N Engl J Med, 350* (9), 855–57.

18. Bullitt-Jonas, M. (1999). *Holy hunger: a memoir of desire.* (New York: A. A. Knopf).

19. Maher, T. J., and R. J. Wurtman, (1987). Possible neurologic effects of aspartame, a widely used food additive. *Environ Health Perspect, 75,* 53–57; Wurtman, R. J. (1983). Neurochemical changes following high-dose aspartame with dietary carbohydrates. *N Engl J Med, 309* (7), 429–30; Staton, P. C., and D. R. Bristow. (1997). The dietary excitotoxins beta-N-Methylamino-Alanine (BMAA) and beta-N-Oxalylamino-L-Alanine (BOAA) induce necrotic- and apoptotic-like death of rat cerebellar granule cells. *J. Neurochem, 69,* 1508–18.

20. Hering-Hani, R., and N. Gadoth. (June 2003). Caffeine-induced headache in children and adolescents. *Cephalalgia, 23* (5), 332–35.

21. Pollak, C. P., and D. Bright. (2003). Caffeine consumption and weekly sleep patterns in U.S. seventh-, eighth-, and ninth-graders. *Pediatrics, 111* (1), 42–46.

22. Savoca, M. R., et al. (2004). The association of caffeinated beverages with blood pressure in adolescents. *Arch Pediatr Adolesc Med, 158* (5), 473–77.

23. *Caffeine: A Healthy Habit?* (June 2003). Patient education brochure published by Washington State University Health and Wellness Services, Pullman, WA, also available online at www.hws.wsu.edu/brochures/caffeine.htm).

24. Ibid.

25. Hindi-Alexander, M. C., et al. (1985). Theophylline and fibrocystic breast disease. *J Allergy Clin Immunol, 75* (6), 709–15; Gabrielli, G. B., and G. De Sandre. (Nov–Dec 1995). Excessive tea consumption can inhibit the efficacy of oral iron treatment in iron-deficiency anemia. *Haematologica, 80* (6), 518–20; Feldman, R. S., et al. (1997). Principles of neuropsychopharmacology. (Sunderland, MA: Sinauer Associates, Inc.), 611–16; Rossignol, A. M. (1985). Caffeine-containing beverages and premenstrual syndrome in young women. *Am J Public Health, 75* (11), 1335–37; Rossignol, A. M., and H. Bonnlander. (1990). Caffeine-containing beverages, total fluid consumption, and premenstrual syndrome. *Am J Public Health, 80* (9), 1106–10.

Chapter 19: The Real World

1. Shuler, R. (Fall 2000). The cost of kindness: self-sacrifice can cripple caregivers. *UAB Magazine, 20* (2).

2. Chen, C. C., A. S. David, H. Nunnerley, M. Michell, J. L. Dawson, H. Berry, J. Dobbs, T. Fahy. (1995). Adverse life events and breast cancer: case-control study. *BMJ, 311* (7019), 1527–30; Bahnson, C. B. (1981). Stress and cancer: the state of the art. Part 2. *Psychosomatics, 22* (3), 207–20; Bremond, A., G. A. Kune, and C. B. Bahnson. (June 1986). Psychosomatic factors in breast cancer patients: results of a case control study. *J Psychosomatic Obstetrics and Gynaecology, 5* (2), 127–36; Levy, S. M., R. B. Herberman, T. Whiteside, K. Sanzo, J. Lee, J.

Kirkwood. (1990). Perceived social support and tumor estrogen/progesterone receptor status as predictors of natural killer cell activity in breast cancer patients. *Psychosom Med, 52* (1), 73–85; Levy, S., R. Herberman, M. Lippman, T. d'Angelo. (1987). Correlation of stress factors with sustained depression of natural killer cell activity and predicted prognosis in patients with breast cancer. *J Clin Oncol, 5* (3), 348–53.

3. Frankel, L. P. (2004). Nice girls don't get the corner office: 101 unconscious mistakes women make that sabotage their careers. (New York: Warner Business Books).

4. Vansteenkiste, M., and E. L. Deci. (2003). Competitively contingent rewards and intrinsic motivation: can losers remain motivated? *Motivation and Emotion, 27* (4), 273–99; Vallerand, R. J., and G. F. Losier. (1999). An integrative analysis of intrinsic and extrinsic motivation in sport. *Journal of Applied Sport Psychology, 11* (1), 142–69.

5. Schooley, R. (1994). Epstein-Barr virus infections, including infectious mononucleosis. In K. J. Isselbacher, et al. (eds.), *Harrison's principles of internal medicine, vol. 1*, 13th ed. (New York: McGraw Hill), 790–93.

6. Kobasa, S. C. (1979). Personality and resistance to illness. *Am J Community Psychol, 7* (4), 413–23; Kobasa, S. C. (1979). Stressful life events, personality, and health: an inquiry into hardiness. *J Pers Soc Psychol, 307* (1), 1–11; Friedman, R., D. Sobel, P. Myers, M. Caudill, and H. Benson. (1995). Behavioral medicine, clinical health psychology, and cost offset. *Health Psychol, 14* (6), 509–18; Funk, S. C. (1992). Hardiness: a review of theory and research. *Health Psychol, 11* (5), 335–45; Hellman, C. J., M. Budd, J. Borysenko, D. C. McClelland, and H. Benson. (1990). A study of the effectiveness of two group behavioral medicine interventions for patients with psychosomatic complaints. *Behav Med, 16* (4), 165–73.

7. Rich, A. (1986). *Of woman born: motherhood as experience and institution*. (New York: Norton).

Chapter 20: The Legacy Continues

1. For an extensive bibliography of medical studies on near-death experiences, see M. Morse (1992), *Transformed by the light: the powerful effect of near-death experiences on people's lives*. (New York: Villard Books).

2. Hicks, E., and J. Hicks. (2004). *Ask and it is given: learning to manifest your desires*. (Carlsbad, CA: Hay House).

3. Luskin, F. (2002). *Forgive for good: a proven prescription for health and happiness*. (San Francisco: HarperSanFrancisco).

Resources

THE FOUNDATION OF MOTHER-DAUGHTER HEALTH

Chapter 3: The Miracle of Conception: Igniting New Life

Recommended Reading

Carista Luminare-Rosen, Ph.D., *Parenting Begins Before Conception: A Guide to Preparing Body, Mind, and Spirit for You and Your Future Child* (Healing Arts Press, 2000); www.creativeparenting.com.

Dr. Luminare-Rosen, co-director of the Center for Creative Parenting, offers an invaluable guide for parents preparing for a new baby, with information about how they can optimize their child-to-be's physical, mental, emotional, and spiritual health (including working consciously with your baby's soul before conception). This holistic guide blends both ancient wisdom and the latest medical knowledge about prenatal health.

Jeannine Parvati Baker, Frederick Baker, and Tamara Slayton, *Conscious Conception: An Elemental Journey Through the Labyrinth of Sexuality* (Freestone Publishing Co., 1986).

This book is a comprehensive reference guide for fertility awareness and natural family planning, teaching couples how they can experience fertility in a way that will enhance their sexuality instead of inhibit it.

Rick Hanson, Ph.D., Jan Hanson, L.Ac., and Ricki Pollycove, M.D., *Mother Nurture: A Mother's Guide to Health in Body, Mind, and Intimate Relationships* (Penguin Books, 2002).

The key to creating a healthy, happy society is to make sure that mothers are happy and healthy. *Mother Nurture* is a treasure trove of information to help accomplish this crucial goal, written by a psychologist, acupuncturist, nutritionist, and an obstetrician-gynecologist. Everyone who is a mother or loves a mother should read this book.

Susun S. Weed, *Wise Woman Herbal for the Childbearing Years* (Ash Tree Pub., 1985).

The definitive herbal guide to the childbearing years, this book is packed with excellent advice and wise comfort for those undergoing the changes associated with conception, pregnancy, and parturition. It also serves as an excellent resource for hands-on professional herbalists and health educators alike. The book includes a section on fertility awareness for men and women; lists of teratogenic agents; foods and herbs to avoid; helpful illustrations; and detailed instructions for prescriptions ranging from a simple raspberry leaf infusion to complex remedies for every eventuality.

Full-Spectrum Lighting

Most artificial light, including both regular incandescent and standard fluorescent lighting, lacks the full and balanced wavelength spectrum found in sunlight, which in the proper amounts is considered a nutrient. Using natural lighting in your home optimizes your health in many ways, most notably enhancing mood and fertility. Sources of products for natural lighting include:

Light for Health
P.O. Box 1760
Lyons, CO 80540
Phone: 800-468-1104
Web site: www.lightforhealth.com

Natural Lighting
1939 Richvale
Houston, TX 77062
Phone: 888-900-6830
Web site: www.naturallighting.com

Ott-Lite Technology
P.O. Box 172425
Tampa, FL 33672-0425
Phone: 800-842-8848
Web site: www.ottlite.com/wtb.asp

To Find Your Body Mass Index (BMI)

The National Institutes of Health offers a quick and easy BMI calculator on its Web site. Type in your height and weight, and you instantly see your BMI. The default is set to inches and pounds, but you can click a tab to use the calculator in metric measurements instead. The page also gives information on what your BMI means—what is healthy, overweight, or obese. The link is: http://nhlbisupport.com/bmi/bmicalc.htm.

Avoiding Toxic Chemicals:

The Children's Health Environmental Coalition (CHEC) Web site includes a detailed list of hazardous chemicals commonly found in households. The site grades each toxin on its level of danger as well as lists where it is found, what the health effects of exposure are, and what some safer alternatives may be. Although the chart is meant for children, it's also good advice for adults, especially women considering pregnancy. The link is: www.checnet. org/healthehouse/chemicals/chemicals.asp.

The Pregnancy Exposure Hotline (781-466-8474 or 800-322-5014 in Massachusetts) is supported by the Genesis Fund, with funding from the National Birth Defects Center. It provides confidential and nonjudgmental counseling based on currently available medical information for pregnant women exposed to potential teratogens (chemicals that could cause malformations or genetic mutations in a developing child). The organization's Web site (www.thegenesisfund.org/pehservices.htm) answers many questions and also contains a link that can help you find similar services in your area.

Recommended Reading on Avoiding Toxic Chemicals

Susan M. Barlow and Frank M. Sullivan, *Reproductive Hazards of Industrial Chemicals: An Evaluation of Animal and Human Data* (Academic Press, 1982).

Sources for Omega-3 Fats

The main sources of omega-3 essential fatty acids (EFAs) in our diets are fatty fish, eggs, nuts, seeds, sea vegetables, and green leafy vegetables such as spinach, broccoli, cabbage, collards, and kale. Unprocessed vegetable oils—especially flaxseed oil—are also rich sources of EFAs, although the refining process used for many commercial oils (including soybean and canola oils) removes nearly all the essential omega-3 fatty acids. Some sources of these essential fats that I particularly recommend include:

Vital Choice Seafood's "Dr. Northrup's Healthy Mom and Baby" salmon combination packages. Wild Alaskan salmon is a rich source of omega-3 fatty acids (particularly important for optimum brain and neurological system function). The Vital Choice Company now offers a variety of its salmon product combinations designed specifically for new mothers. All Vital Choice salmon is naturally organic and free of antibiotics, growth hormones, and artificial coloring. It comes vacuum-packed and frozen. Some "Healthy Mom and Baby" combinations also include Vital Choice's Alaskan sockeye salmon oil capsules. Vital Choice also sells salmon fillets and salmon burgers separately. For more information, contact:

Vital Choice Seafood
605 30th Street
Anacortes, WA 98221
Phone: 800-608-4825
Web site: www.vitalchoice.com

USANA's OptOmega essential fatty acid oil: Contains an ideal ratio of the two essential fatty acids known as alpha-linoleic acid (an omega-3 fatty acid) and linoleic acid (an omega-6 fatty acid) that are important to cardiovascular health. In addition, these fatty acids also promote healthy immunity, mental sharpness, and healthy skin. Some children diagnosed with ADD have shown positive results after taking essential fatty acid supplements. This all-natural vegetarian product is produced from certified organic, unrefined cold-pressed flaxseed, sunflower seed, pumpkin seed, and extra-virgin olive oils and contains no trans fatty acids. For more information, contact:

> USANA
> 3838 West Parkway Boulevard
> Salt Lake City, UT 84120
> Phone: 888-950-9595
> Web site: www.usana.com

USANA's BiOmega-3: These capsules contain 1,000 mg of cold-water-fish oil, including the important omega-3 fatty acids EPA and DHA, in a natural form that is easily absorbed by the body. For more information, contact USANA.

Neuromins from Nature's Way: These gelcaps contain a vegetable source of DHA that closely matches the DHA in human breast milk and is specially formulated for maternal nutrition. For more information, contact:

> Emerson Ecologics, Inc.
> 7 Commerce Drive
> Bedford, NH 03110
> Phone: 800-654-4432
> Web site: www.emersonecologics.com

Vital Choice Seafood's Alaskan Sockeye Salmon Oil Capsules: This product is made according to pharmaceutical standards from pure wild Alaskan salmon. Each 1,000 mg softgel provides 150 mg of EPA and DHA. This 100 percent natural supplement is the only oil supplement certified by the Marine Stewardship Council as originating from 100 percent sustainably harvested fish. For more information, contact Vital Choice Seafood.

Whole Flax Seed from Cathy's Country Store is organically grown in North Dakota and has an especially nutty and delicious flavor. For more information, contact Emerson Ecologics.

FiProFLAX (ground flax) is cold milled by Health from the Sun from premium quality flax with a high oil content. Alternatively, you can take certified organic flaxseed oil from a bottle (although the shelf life is short, so keep it in your refrigerator for maximum longevity) or in gel capsules. For more information, contact Emerson Ecologics.

Omega Smart Bars: This totally organic vegan product not only delivers a healthy dose of omega-3s but it's also high in fiber and has a low glycemic index. The ingredients (which are all organic) include ground flaxseed, figs, agave nectar, a number of dried fruits, soy flour, toasted soy nuts, and either almonds or walnuts, plus a little cinnamon and other organic spices. This product contains no artificial flavorings, dairy or whey, hydrogenated oils, processed sugar, wheat, synthetic vitamins, eggs, predigested hydrolyzed or soy protein isolates or caseinates. For more information, contact Emerson Ecologics.

Nutiva's Hempseed Bars: Hempseed is another good source of EFAs and contains a perfect balance of omega-3, omega-6, and gamma-linoleic acids (GLAs). This great-tasting snack from Nutiva offers a combination of hempseeds and flaxseeds, as well as sunflower seeds, pumpkin seeds, and honey. These bars are made from the finest organic ingredients, grown without pesticides or herbicides, and they're loaded with protein and vitamin E. They come in three varieties—regular organic flax, flax and chocolate, and flax and raisin (with almonds). For more information, contact Emerson Ecologics.

Nutiva's Organic Hemp Protein Powder: This product is 100 percent raw certified organic hemp protein powder and contains no hexane, gluten, dairy, lactose, or sweeteners. It's 37 percent protein, 43 percent fiber, and 9 percent beneficial fats. Add it to shakes and smoothies for a healthy breakfast or afternoon snack. For more information, contact Emerson Ecologics.

Silk's Enhanced Soymilk: This soymilk tastes just like regular Silk soymilk, but it's been fortified with omega-3 fatty acids from flax oil. It's also enhanced with calcium carbonate, vitamin C, vitamin E, vitamin A, vitamin D, and vitamins B_2, B_6, and B_{12}. If you can't find it at your supermarket, look for it at health food stores or whole-foods supermarkets (such as Whole Foods or Wild Oats) that carry a wider range of the Silk products.

Information on DHA

Docosahexaenoic acid (DHA) is an omega-3 fatty acid essential to human brain and eye development and function. Most of us don't get nearly enough of this vital nutrient (the National Institutes of Health recommends consuming 300 mg a day), which is particularly worrisome for women who are pregnant or breast-feeding. The best sources of DHA include eggs from chickens raised on DHA-rich food, wild (not farm raised) cold-water fish such as salmon and sardines, and supplements made from algae. Sources of information on DHA include:

Healthwell, a Web site operated by New Hope Natural Media (the leading publisher of natural products magazines and producer of natural products trade shows and conferences in the U.S.), offers an excellent and detailed article about DHA at the following link: www.healthwell.com/hnbreak throughs/may99/fattyacids.cfm.

Martek Biosciences Corporation (888-OK-BRAIN; www.dhadepot.com), a manufacturer of microalgae products, operates a site called DHA Depot with lots of detailed information about this nutrient, including its importance for pregnant and lactating women and infants. The site also features a calculator that allows you to figure out how much DHA you get in a typical day's meals and snacks.

Daily Supplemental Vitamins and Minerals

Daily vitamin and mineral supplements are vital at any time, but especially so when you're trying to conceive. Make sure your supplements are guaranteed potency and manufactured according to GMP (Good Manufacturing Processes) standards, a term that denotes high quality. I recommend:

USANA's Essentials: Actually two different high-potency supplements, USANA's Mega Antioxidant Vitamin supplements and USANA's Chelated Mineral supplements, taken together as a daily regimen. These products provide optimal, balanced amounts of the essential vitamins and minerals, along with fifteen potent antioxidants (including olivol, or olive fruit extract, a recent addition). For information, contact:

> USANA
> 3838 West Parkway Boulevard
> Salt Lake City, UT 84120
> Phone: 888-950-9595
> Web site: www.usana.com

Verified Quality's Super Multi-Complex: This daily supplement has twenty-eight vitamins and minerals, but contains no coatings, binders, or fillers. It's also free of dairy, wheat, eggs, soy, yeast, commercial sugars, starch, preservatives, and hydrogenated oil. For information, contact Emerson Ecologics.

For Information on the Glycemic Index

The glycemic index ranks carbohydrates based on how quickly they elevate blood sugar levels. Those foods that break down quickly during digestion and raise blood sugar quickly have the highest glycemic indexes. Those that break down slowly, gradually releasing glucose into the bloodstream, have low glycemic indexes. For more information: The Glycemic Index Web site allows you to type in a food and get its glycemic index as well as its glycemic load (determined by considering both the glycemic index of a food and the amount of the food you eat). It also provides lists of low-glycemic-index and high-glycemic-index foods and answers common questions about the glycemic index and loads. The link is www.glycemicindex.com.

Recommended Reading on the Glycemic Index

Jennie Brand-Miller, Ph.D., Thomas M. S. Wolever, M.D., Ph.D., Kaye Foster-Powell, M.Nutr. and Diet, and Stephen Colagiuri, M.D., *The New Glucose Revolution: The Authoritative Guide to the Glycemic Index—The Dietary Solution for Lifelong Health* (Marlowe & Co., 2003).

The authors are the leading authorities in the world on the effects of glucose on the blood and the glucose index. This revised and expanded edition not only thoroughly explains both glycemic index and load but also includes tables listing glycemic values of various foods and healthy low-glycemic-index recipes.

Source for Agave Nectar (A Low-Glycemic-Index Sweetener)

Nekutli Agave Nectar: A 100 percent organic syrup from the agave plant (found in Mexico), yielding a high-fructose sweetener that is sweeter than sugar but rated as a low-glycemic food (with a glycemic index of 46, lower than honey). It dissolves quickly, even in cold beverages. For more information contact:

The Colibree Company, Inc.
P.O. Box 1727
925 Gibson Avenue
Aspen, CO 81612
Phone: 866-NEKUTLI (866-635-8854)
Web site: www.agavenectar.com/product.html

Information on Monosodium Glutamate (MSG)

MSGtruth.org is a Web site written by professionals trained in food science, food processing, and biology who no longer work for the food industry. The site shares independent research conducted on MSG, and includes listings of foods commonly containing MSG (www.msgtruth.org/avoid.htm) as well as listings of foods commonly considered free of MSG (www.msgtruth.org/eatwhat.htm).

Foresight Preconception Care Program

Foresight, the Association for the Promotion of Preconceptual Care, is a nonprofit organization based in Surrey, England, founded to promote the importance of good health and optimum nutrition in both parents before a child is conceived. Foresight's goal is to provide prospective parents with sensible, easy-to-follow advice for achieving this goal. For detailed information about the Foresight preconception program, including publications that can be downloaded from the organization's Web site, contact:

Foresight
28 The Paddock
Godalming
Surrey, GU7 1XD
United Kingdom
Phone: 011-44-1483-427839
Web site: www.foresight-preconception.org.uk

To Pinpoint Your Fertile Periods

Ovusoft's fertility software is an FDA-cleared conception aid and fertility-awareness program that can help you gain insight into your body's cyclical cues and signs. And Ovusoft helps you conceive more quickly, cutting the time from an average of six months down to about two to three months. The software relies on the Fertility Awareness Method (FAM), a natural method of determining your fertile time by observing and tracking certain simple body signs. The product comes with the book *Taking Charge of Your Fertility: The Definitive Guide to Natural Birth Control, Pregnancy Achievement, and Reproductive Health* (HarperCollins, 2002) by Toni Weschler, which provides an in-depth explanation of the Fertility Awareness Method. Ovusoft offers a fifteen-day trial version you can download from the company's Web site. For more information, contact:

Ovusoft
120 West Queens Way, Suite 202
Hampton, VA 23669
Phone: 757-722-0991
Web site: www.ovusoft.com

Ovulook Ovulation Tester: This simple and empowering tool allows women to learn about and take charge of their own fertility. By taking a saliva sample and applying it to a slide, you can then view and record your saliva patterns to easily determine when you are ovulating. Unlike other saliva samplers, Ovulook also allows you to create your own individual fertility calendar to see when you are ovulating. Ovulook is 98 percent accurate. I recommend it highly. For more information, contact:

Ovulook
P.O. Box 1011
Kapaau, HI 96755
Phone: 866-688-5284
Web site: www.ovulook.com

Chapter 4: Pregnancy: Trusting the Process of Life

Recommended Reading

Holly Roberts, D.O., *Your Vegetarian Pregnancy: A Month-by-Month Guide to Health and Nutrition* (Simon & Schuster, 2003).

This book by my friend and colleague Dr. Holly Roberts, a board-certified ob-gyn physician and a longtime vegetarian, is full of vital information for all pregnant women following a vegetarian approach. I myself followed a macrobiotic diet when pregnant with my two children, though I now include more fish and some meat in my diet.

Shari Maser, *Blessingways: A Guide to Mother-Centered Baby Showers Celebrating Pregnancy, Birth, and Motherhood* (Moondance Press, to be published in May 2005); www.blessingway.net.

Shari Maser is a Certified Childbirth Educator and mother of two who shares her ideas about how to help pregnant and adoptive women celebrate their transition into motherhood. Her book includes a step-by-step guide to planning a personalized "mother shower," complete with creative suggestions for including men and children in the event. She also shares plenty of stories and comments from women who have participated in Blessingways.

Recommended Reading for Infertility

Niravi B. Payne and Brenda Lain Richardson, *The Whole Person Fertility Program: A Revolutionary Mind-Body Process to Help You Conceive* (Three Rivers Press, 1997); www.niravi.com.

Niravi Payne is a therapist who has devoted her professional life to helping couples conceive through her Whole Person Fertility Program. Her view of current fertility problems is both enlightening and empowering. If fertility is an issue that concerns you, I highly recommend that you read the entire program in this book and go through all of the exercises. Your responses will be an invaluable guide on your journey toward healing your fertility.

Randine A. Lewis, *The Infertility Cure: The Ancient Chinese Wellness Program for Getting Pregnant and Having Healthy Babies* (Little, Brown, 2004).

Randine Lewis, Ph.D., M.S. (in Oriental medicine), shows how to blend traditional Chinese medicine with Western fertility treatments to help women conceive. *The Infertility Cure* gives women an effective, natural means of supporting their efforts to get pregnant that includes diet, acupressure, and Chinese herbs. The purpose of this program is to help women increase their overall health and well-being, strengthen the organs and systems vital to reproduction, heal specific conditions that may affect fertility, and even support Western-based reproductive technology (such as IVF and hormone therapy).

Julia Indichova, *Inconceivable: A Woman's Triumph over Despair and Statistics* (Broadway Books, 2001), foreword by Christiane Northrup, M.D.

If you are considering assisted reproductive measures but feel uncomfortable forcing your body, read this book. Julia Indichova tells her own story, as a forty-three-year-old woman who was told she'd never get pregnant without assisted technology. Very inspiring and medically accurate.

Omega-3 Fats and Daily Supplemental Vitamins and Minerals

(See Chapter 3 Resources.)

Chic Maternity Clothes

Bella Blu (888-678-0034; www.bellablumaternity.com) is an online pregnancy boutique with truly beautiful maternity clothes and accessories— everything from jeans to formal wear, sleepwear to swimwear, and outerwear and underwear for the mother-to-be.

Ginger That Works for Morning Sickness

Nature's Way Ginger Root Capsules: Each of these capsules contains 550 mg of Chinese ginger root *(Zingiber officinale)*, with a guaranteed potency of 1.5 percent essential oils, principally gingerol and shogaol. For more information, contact:

Emerson Ecologics, Inc.
7 Commerce Drive
Bedford, NH 03110
Phone: 800-654-4432
Web site: www.emersonecologics.com

Down Syndrome Information

The National Down Syndrome Society is an education, research, and advocacy organization devoted to enhancing the quality of life for those who have Down Syndrome. The organization's Web site is amazingly comprehensive, including not only background information, current research findings, and other resources but also a growing "family and friends" section that tailors advice to specific groups—parents, siblings, grandparents, and friends. For more information, contact:

National Down Syndrome Society
666 Broadway
New York, NY 10012
Phone: 800-221-4602
Web site: www.ndss.org

Down Syndrome Quarterly is an interdisciplinary journal devoted to encouraging and sharing research on Down syndrome. It's available by subscription, although its Web site also posts several useful articles and other information that anyone can access. For more information, see the following link: www.denison.edu/collaborations/dsq/.

Recommended Reading on Down Syndrome

Martha Beck, *Expecting Adam: A True Story of Birth, Rebirth, and Everyday Magic* (Times Books, 1999).

This poignant but at times downright funny book tells the extraordinary story of the parents of a Down's baby and how his birth not only changed their lives but also stretched their views of the world and what is possible within it. Inspirational reading for all mothers-to-be.

Sources of Information on Genetic Screening

Kids Health (www.kidshealth.org), a comprehensive parenting Web site, offers a link to an exhaustive article on all the different types of prenatal screening available, who should have them, and what the results might mean. The link is:

http://kidshealth.org/parent/system/medical/prenatal_tests.html

Family therapist Gayle Peterson, M.S.S.W., L.C.S.W., Ph.D., specializes in prenatal and family development. She's the author of *An Easier Childbirth, Birthing Normally,* and her latest book, *Making Healthy Families.* Her Web site (www.askdrgayle.com) contains a wealth of information for families, including an article on whether or not prenatal testing may be right for you. The link is: www.askdrgayle.com/recent6.htm.

Positive Affirmations, Meditations, and Guided Imagery for Pregnancy and Childbirth

The Pocket Midwife, by my friend and nurse-midwife colleague Susan Fekety, C.N.M., is a small spiral-bound book designed to stand up by itself, making it easy to do your affirmations while you cook, brush your hair, or go about your day. To order, visit www.pocketmidwife.com.

Body-Centered Hypnosis for Pregnancy, Bonding, and Childbirth audiotape from Gayle Peterson, M.S.S.W., L.C.S.W., Ph.D., contains exercises designed to decrease anxiety and increase confidence and a sense of well-being. Designed to be used throughout your pregnancy, this tape also includes a section with birth visualizations. To order, contact your local bookstore or order online at www.amazon.com.

Opening the Way is a meditation tape series designed by the Monroe Institute, the nonprofit research and education institute that pioneered products using the binaural beat phenomenon to attain unusually deep states of meditation. This eight-tape Hemi-Sync series from Monroe Products contains exercises on general relaxation, the father's support, the health of mother and baby, birthing, postpartum well-being, and even contacting the baby's soul before birth. To order, visit www.hemi-sync.com or call 800-541-2488.

Resources for Grief Following Miscarriage or Losing a Child

The following Web sites offer a wide range of support options and resources for further information geared to women who have lost a child:

Empty Cradles (www.empty-cradles.com) provides an online support network for mothers who have suffered miscarriage, a stillborn birth, the loss of an infant in utero, or the death of an infant from SIDS. The site offers background information as well as advice for what to expect and how to cope. You are also invited to create a star for your child that will shine in a cyber-galaxy memorial to lost children.

Silent Grief (www.silentgrief.com) offers healing, support, and hope to women who have lost a child. The site offers a forum for sharing, essays from women, and articles on miscarriage and other early child losses.

ObGyn.net's "Maternal Grief" page offers information about online support group meetings as well as links to other Web pages offering different types of support to grieving mothers. The link is: www.obgyn.net/women/women.asp?page=women/loss/loss.htm/.

Recommended Reading for Miscarriage or Losing a Child

Lorraine Ash, *Life Touches Life: A Mother's Story of Stillbirth and Healing* (NewSage, 2004). Foreword by Christiane Northrup, M.D.

After a trouble-free pregnancy, Lorraine Ash delivered a little girl who had died in utero. Shocked and distraught, she searched for answers that could help her understand what she had been through and how she could heal from the devastating experience. While on this journey, she began to see that the bond between mother and child transcends death. From this discovery, she was able to find solace, which ultimately helped transform her grief into joy. Lorraine Ash's story has universal appeal for anyone who is suffering from loss and grief, whether or not it's from pregnancy loss.

Maria Housden, *Hannah's Gift: Lessons from a Life Fully Lived* (Bantam Books, 2002).

Maria Housden's stunningly beautiful and moving testament to the wisdom and grace of her terminally ill child helps readers grieve the past and simultaneously open their arms to the future. In addition to being a godsend for anyone whose child is seriously ill, it's a very good read. I urge all of you to read it and be as touched, moved, and inspired as I was.

Cynthia Kuhn Beischel, editor, *From Eulogy to Joy: A Heartfelt Anthology* (Capital Books, 2002).

This wonderfully wise compilation of a hundred thirty essays is by and for those who are grieving the loss of a loved one (children as well as others). The book shows what a wide range of reactions are normal and appropriate, and shares not how to get over the loss but how to get through it and grow in the process.

Chapter 5: Labor and Birth: Accessing Your Feminine Power

Recommended Reading

Ina May Gaskin, *Ina May's Guide to Childbirth* (Bantam, 2003); www.ina may.com.

This book by one of the best-known pioneers of midwifery offers good, solid, detailed information about prenatal care and labor, and it's filled with uplifting and empowering birth stories that you can use to imprint yourself with the right words and affirmations about childbirth. It's also chock-full of national resources for the midwives, doulas, and birth centers that will provide you with the right atmosphere to birth normally. My most fervent prayer for all pregnant women is that they read Ina May's book and heed its wisdom, because the information in this book truly can change the world.

Sheri Menelli, *Journey into Motherhood: Inspiring Stories of Natural Birth* (White Heart Publishing, 2004); www.journeyintomotherhood.com.

All women and girls need to hear the stories in this fabulous book and know, really know, that natural birth is full of magnificent, life-changing wisdom. In this inspiring book, childbirth educator Sheri Menelli shares stories and advice from forty-eight women who gave birth at home, in the hospital, and even outdoors. Menelli teaches women that labor can in fact be painless, and she includes information on incorporating options such as yoga, hypnosis, and water birth into labor and delivery.

Marshall H. Klaus, M.D., John H. Kennell, M.D., and Phyllis H. Klaus, C.S.W., *Bonding: Building the Foundations of Secure Attachment and Independence* (Addison-Wesley Publishing, 1995).

Renowned bonding experts Klaus, Kennell, and Klaus are neonatologists and child researchers who share information on how to effectively bond with your newborn (starting during pregnancy and including information for creating an optimal birth experience). This is essential reading for parents-to-be, because research shows that the first few hours of a baby's life are critical to the bonding process that continues throughout infanthood.

Gayle Peterson, M.S.S.W., L.C.S.W., Ph.D., *Birthing Normally: A Personal Growth Approach to Childbirth* (Mindbody Press, 1981).

Childbirth educator and reform pioneer Gayle Peterson discusses the journey of personal growth that mothers take during pregnancy. The book also shares holistic principles for prenatal care, including practical and even technical information that is helpful for mothers-to-be as well as the professionals who attend them. Peterson has also written *An Easier Childbirth: A Mother's Workbook for Health and Emotional Well-Being During Pregnancy and Delivery* (J. P. Tarcher, 1991) and *Making Healthy Families: With Notes from the Web* (Shadow and Light Publications, 2000).

Marilyn Moran, *Pleasurable Husband/Wife Childbirth: The Real Consummation of Married Love* (Terra Publishing, 1997); www.unassistedhome birth.com

Home-birthing expert and lay researcher Marilyn Moran had her first nine babies in a hospital before birthing her tenth at home attended by her husband. Through the experience, she became a tireless supporter of home birth, and with this book she shares quotes from other mothers who have birthed at home as well as scientific research supporting the benefits of giving birth in this uniquely personal and spiritual way.

Paulina Perez and Cheryl Snedeker, *Special Women: The Role of the Professional Labor Assistant* (Cutting Edge Press, 2000).

Paulina (Polly) Perez, R.N., B.S.N., is an internationally known expert on labor support who consults with hospitals and birth centers throughout the United States to help them set up comprehensive labor support programs. She also operates a regional doula referral service in the northeastern U.S. I highly recommend her books, which also include *The Nurturing Touch at Birth: The Labor Support Handbook* (Cutting Edge Press, 1997). To order directly from Cutting Edge (Perez's office), call 802-635-2142.

General Resources for Childbirth

Childbirth.org (www.childbirth.org) was founded by childbirth educator and doula Robin Elise Weiss. The site is a source of comprehensive information on pregnancy and childbirth run by a group of childbirth experts, including doulas, midwives, baby nurses, lactation consultants, and others.

Birthworks (www.birthworks.com; 800-862-4784) believes in empowering women by developing their self-confidence, trust, and faith in their own ability to give birth. They give classes in birthing nationwide and also serve as a resource for birth information.

Maternity Center Association (MCA), a nonprofit organization dedicated to improving maternity care and the conductor of the study *Listening to Mothers: Report of the First National U.S. Survey of Women's Childbearing Experiences* (October 2002). The Listening to Mothers project is part of MCA's ongoing initiative to regularly monitor trends in maternity care, keep key audiences informed, and develop innovative and responsible programs to improve maternity care and better meet women's needs. For more information, contact:

Maternity Center Association (MCA)
281 Park Avenue South, 5th Floor
New York, NY 10010
Phone: 212-777-5000
Web site: www.maternitywise.org

Coalition for Improving Maternity Service (CIMS) is a collaborative effort of numerous individuals and more than fifty organizations representing over ninety thousand members. CIMS aims to promote a wellness model of maternity care that will improve birth outcomes and substantially reduce costs. The organization's Web site includes a wonderful article called "Having a Baby? Ten Questions to Ask." The link for the article is www.motherfriendly.org/resources/10Q/. For more information, contact:

Coalition for Improving Maternity Service (CIMS)
P.O. Box 2346
Ponte Vedra Beach, FL 32004
Phone: 888-282-CIMS (888-282-2467)
Web site: www.motherfriendly.org

Holistic Moms Network generates awareness, education, and support for holistic parenting nationwide. The organization facilitates grassroots community building by helping moms start local chapters that create a sense of community, where parents (and even grandparents) can share experiences and resources. For more information, contact:

Holistic Moms Network
P.O. Box 408
Caldwell, NJ 07006
Phone: 877-HOL-MOMS
Web site: www.holisticmoms.org

Teresa Robertson, birth intuitive, registered nurse, and certified nurse midwife, is a real pioneer. I consider her work to be the obstetrics of the future, which involves connecting with your baby intuitively before it is born, working in partnership with the baby's consciousness. Her work also includes maximizing women's fertility (her techniques have been shown to improve conception and birth rates by 30 percent) and helping to heal pregnancy losses. She also helps women connect and bond with their future adoptive children. A big part of the beauty of her work is that it empowers women, helping them reinforce their trust in their own inner wisdom. She consults by phone as well as in person. For more information, contact:

Teresa Robertson
3011 Broadway, Suite 32
Boulder, CO 80302
Phone: 303-258-3904
Web site: www.birthintuitive.com

Resources for Giving Birth in Water

Birth Balance is a resource center for water birth. The director, water birth pioneer Judith Elaine Halek, is a certified hypnotherapist and birth counselor as well as a specialist in pre/postnatal fitness and massage. The Web site contains lots of information on water birth resources and personal experiences of women who have chosen this childbirth option. For information, contact:

> Birth Balance
> Planetarium Station, P.O. Box 947
> New York, NY 10024-0947
> Phone: 212-222-4349
> Web site: www.birthbalance.com

Waterbirth International Research, Resource and Referral Service is a project of the nonprofit public benefit corporation Global Maternal/Child Health Association. Founded in 1988 by Barbara Harper, Waterbirth promotes laboring and birthing in water as a safe and gentle alternative to today's standard high-tech birthing style. Waterbirth shows women that the use of water in labor is easily integrated into any hospital standard of care and results in better outcomes, fewer cesareans, and a more satisfying birth experience for the whole family. For more information, contact:

> Waterbirth International
> P.O. Box 1400
> Wilsonville, OR 97070
> Phone: 800-641-2229.
> Web site: www.waterbirth.org

Information about Doulas and Birth Assistants

Birth assistants come in several different varieties—doulas physically and emotionally support the mother during birth itself, monitrices (most of whom are nurses) are doulas who have clinical skills to assess fetal and maternal well-being during childbirth, and midwives do all of this plus provide prenatal care. The following organizations provide information about birth assistants, as well as referrals for birth assistants in your area:

Doulas of North America (DONA): an international association of more than four thousand doulas nationwide who are trained to provide the highest quality emotional, physical, and educational support to women and their families during childbirth and postpartum. Founded in 1992 by Marshall Klaus, M.D., Phyllis Klaus, C.S.W., John Kennell, M.D., Penny Simkin, and Annie Kennedy, DONA also certifies doulas. For information, contact:

Doulas of North America (DONA)
P.O. Box 626
Jasper, IN 47547
Phone: 888-788-DONA (888-788-3662)
Web site: www.DONA.org

Association of Labor Assistants and Childbirth Educators (ALACE) began as an association of midwives and expanded later to include doulas. ALACE provides training and certification. For more information, contact:

Association of Labor Assistants and Childbirth Educators (ALACE)
P.O. Box 390436
Cambridge, MA 02139
Phone: 888-222-5223
Web site: www.alace.org

International Childbirth Education Association (ICEA) was established in 1960 and has more than six thousand professional members from forty-two countries. Focusing on family-centered maternity care, this organization serves as a resource of information for the public, publishes the quarterly journal *International Journal of Childbirth Education,* and both trains and certifies doulas, childbirth educators, postnatal educators, and perinatal fitness educators. For more information, contact:

International Childbirth Education Association (ICEA)
P.O. Box 20048
Minneapolis, MN 55420
Phone: 952-854-8660
Web site: www.icea.org

Childbirth and Postpartum Professional Association (CAPPA) involves caring for women before, during, and after birth through education and support. This nonprofit organization was founded relatively recently (in 1998) and has become the fastest-growing doula and childbirth organization in the world. CAPPA trains childbirth educators, lactation educators, labor doulas, antepartum doulas, and postpartum doulas. For more information, contact:

Childbirth and Postpartum Professional Association (CAPPA)
P.O. Box 491448
Lawrenceville, GA 30049
Phone: 888-MY-CAPPA (888-692-2772)
Web site: www.cappa.net

Association of Nurse Advocates for Childbirth Solutions (ANACS) is dedicated to helping nurses improve maternity birthing practices and promoting a mother-friendly nursing philosophy. For more information, contact ANACS by phone (301-434-5546) or through its Web site (www.anacs.org).

Recommended Reading on Doulas and Birth Assistants

Marshall Klaus, M.D., John Kennell, M.D., and Phyllis Klaus, C.S.W., *The Doula Book: How a Trained Labor Companion Can Help You Have a Shorter, Easier, and Healthier Birth* (Addison-Wesley, 1993).

No woman should be without support during labor, and a doula is the ideal embodiment of women's wisdom. The doula's traditional role as a practiced caregiver to women (beginning in ancient Greece) benefits the entire budding family. Formerly titled *Mothering the Mother,* here is the revised, definitive, and well-documented guide to the many practical, physical, and psychosocial benefits of engaging the services of a doula.

Information about Cord Clamping

Cordclamping.com (www.cordclamping.com) is devoted to sharing information (including scientific studies) with both parents and birthing professionals about the normal function of the placenta during and after birth and the harmful effects of early cord clamping.

Resources for Vaginal Birth after Cesarean

VBAC.com (www.vbac.com) shares scientific studies, professional guidelines, and government reports about having a successful vaginal birth after a cesarean. The group provides referrals to quality VBAC programs across the country.

Positive Affirmations, Meditations, and Guided Imagery for Pregnancy and Childbirth

(See Chapter 4 Resources, page 661.)

Chapter 6: The Fourth Trimester: Creating the Outer Placenta

Recommended Reading

Nancy London, M.S.W, *Hot Flashes, Warm Bottles: First-Time Mothers Over Forty* (Celestial Arts, 2001).

If you or someone close to you has become a first-time mom later in life, you will want to read about the special challenges faced by "menopausal moms," as chronicled here by Nancy London.

Life After Childbirth: Making It Work for You, written and published by The Vermont Postpartum Task Force. This booklet, last updated in 2002, is full of information and resources addressing what new mothers can expect physically and emotionally after childbirth—including the warning signs of postpartum stress and ways to minimize its effects. The authors, all mothers themselves, include a childbirth educator, a mental health counselor, two labor and delivery nurses, and a postpartum support group coordinator. For more information, contact:

The Vermont Postpartum Task Force
P.O. Box 522
Hinesburg, VT 05461
Web site: vermontpostpartumtaskforce.org

Information on Touch and Touch Research

The Touch Research Institutes are dedicated to studying the effects of touch therapy at all stages of life, including its effects on newborns. When the first institute was founded in 1992 at the University of Miami School of Medicine by director Tiffany Field, Ph.D., it was the first center in the world devoted solely to the study of touch and how it can be applied in science and medicine. Since then, more TRIs have opened in the Philippines (where studies have shown massage therapy helps preterm infants gain weight more quickly) and in Paris. For more information, contact:

Touch Research Institutes
University of Miami School of Medicine
P.O. Box 016820
Miami, FL 33101
Phone: 305-243-6781
Web site: www.miami.edu/touch-research

Sources for Breast-feeding Information

La Leche League International is the leading breast-feeding organization in the world, offering a wealth of support to breast-feeding mothers. Founded in 1956 by seven women who had learned about successful breast-feeding while nursing their own babies, La Leche League now has three thousand local groups in the United States alone. Telephone counseling is available twenty-four hours a day, along with access to an extensive library of breast-feeding literature. The Web site even has a catalogue selling breast-feeding equipment of all kinds. For more information, contact:

La Leche League International
1400 North Meacham Road
Schaumburg, IL 60173-4808
Phone: 847-519-7730
Web site: www.lalecheleague.org

Breastfeeding.com (www.breastfeeding.com) is a resource for everything you could ever want to know about breast-feeding, including equipment and products, nursing clothing, professional advice, message boards and chat rooms for nursing moms, a nationwide lactation consultant directory, various articles on breast-feeding and its benefits, and much, much more.

Medela, one of the most popular breast-pump companies, offers an extensive library of information on its Web site. The site covers every possible breast-feeding challenge and its solution, including breast-feeding adopted babies, babies with various physical challenges, information on going back to work while breast-feeding, and more. The link is: www.medela.com/NewFiles/bfdginfo.html.

Medela also offers a very informative and detailed page on breast-milk collection and storage guidelines (including specific pumping and storage guidelines, general nursing information, feeding tips, storage and freezing information) at this link: www.medela.com/NewFiles/coll_store.html.

Jack Newman, M.D., is a pediatrician practicing in Canada. Dr. Newman is an outspoken proponent of breast-feeding and started the first hospital-based breast-feeding clinic in Canada in 1984 at Toronto's Hospital for Sick Children. He offers numerous articles and other resources on breast-feeding at the following link: www.bflrc.com/newman/articles.htm.

Taking Medications When Breast-feeding

The American Academy of Family Physicians maintains a Web page that discusses breast-feeding while taking medication. It also lists medications considered safe for breast-feeding mothers, as well as a list of medications that are not recommended during breast-feeding. The link is: www.aafp.org/afp/20010701/119.html.

Information on Breast-feeding and Returning to Work

ProMom (a nonprofit organization dedicated to increasing public awareness and acceptance of breast-feeding) has a Web page devoted to practical and detailed information on continuing to breast-feed after returning to work. The link is: www.promom.org/bf_info/bf_work.html.

ProMom also offers an inspiring Web page called "101 Reasons to Breast-feed" at this link: www.promom.org/101.

Sources for Nursing Clothes

Motherwear sells beautiful, stylish, and functional tops, dresses, sweaters, and loungewear for breast-feeding mothers with a 100 percent guarantee. You'll also find breast pads and other supplies, as well as books and other breast-feeding resources. For more information, contact:

> Motherwear International, Inc.
> 320 Riverside Drive, Suite C
> Florence, MA 01062
> Phone: 800-950-2500
> Web site: www.motherwear.com

Recommended Nipples and Pacifiers

For those times when your baby does take a bottle (whether you're feeding her formula or your own expressed breast milk), use a physiologically designed nipple that's as close to nature as you can get. Standard bottle nipples don't make the infant "work" to get milk. Babies can just use their lips to suck the tip of the nipple instead of their whole mouths, the way they do on the breast. Also, standard nipple holes are larger than the numerous smaller openings on the breast, so milk flows much easier and faster and sometimes infants end up rejecting the breast in favor of this easier route. If you instead use some of these more natural-shaped nipples with flow control that imitate a mother's nipple in shape and design, your baby will find it easier to switch back and forth between the two with no problem. For an excellent discussion of this issue, see the following link on the Breast-feeding after Reduction Information and Support Web site (which has plenty of helpful information about why the right nipples are important when supplementing with bottles, even if you have not had a breast reduction): www.bfar.org/nipples.shtml. Here are some good examples:

Avent Newborn Slow-Flow silicone nipples: This broad, soft, and long nipple is similar to a human nipple when a baby is sucking on it. It's designed to allow a baby to suckle with a wide-open mouth, using her tongue and lips to latch on, similar to breast-feeding. The length of the nipple means the tip will be in the same place in the back of the mouth as it is during breast-feeding, eliciting the swallowing reflex.

Playtex's NaturaLatch Newborn Slow-Flow Nipples: The silicone version of this product has been clinically proven to support breast-feeding by encouraging proper latch-on because the nipple has a raised, textured area that is similar to a mother's nipple. Its slow-flow design is another plus.

Evenflo Ultra nipples: These wider silicone nipples also imitate the breast, and they come in three flow speeds—slow (recommended for newborns up to age three months), medium (for three months to six months), or fast (for six months and up).

The best pacifiers are also those with more natural nipples. Here are two good options:

The NUK nipple by Gerber is the most recommended orthodontic pacifier because it allows the baby's tongue, palate, and jaw to develop naturally.

Evenflo's Natural Comfort pacifier with keep-away shield not only has a wider base to imitate the breast but its shield keeps the baby's face from pressing against the pacifier, reducing irritations, redness, and rashes.

Recommended Formula (When Not Breast-feeding)

If you choose to use infant formula, choose one that is supplemented with docosahexaenoic acid (DHA), which is important for brain function and vision development. A good brand is Enfamil Lipil, which contains the highest levels of DHA and arachidonic acid (ARA, another essential fatty acid that promotes healthy growth of organs and tissues) found in baby formulas. It comes in several varieties—iron fortified, lactose free, soy formula, and a thicker formula designed for babies who spit up frequently.

Goats' milk is a good choice for babies who can't tolerate either cow's milk or soy milk formulas. Meyerberg goat milk (available in health food stores) contains no preservatives and is free of antibiotics and bovine growth hormones. It also contains more calcium, vitamin A, vitamin B6, and potassium than cow's milk. However, an infant drinking goat's milk formula exclusively should also receive a multivitamin with iron supplement prescribed by her doctor. For a discussion about the use of goat's milk, along with links for formula recipes, see the "Got Goat's Milk?" page on the AskDrSears Web site. The link is: www.askdrsears.com/html/3/T032400.asp.

Sources for Lambskins for Infants

Lambskins keep babies cool in summer and warm in winter and feel soft and comforting to the touch. Because air easily circulates through the fibers, there's no danger of suffocation. Some options include:

Winganna Lambskins, imported from England, are soft, dense, and resilient. The wool has been sheared and then combed to eliminate any loose fibers. These skins are machine washable and can even be tumble dried. Products include baby fleeces, mattress covers, car-seat and stroller covers, and even incubator pads. For more information, contact:

> Winganna Lambskins, Inc.
> 540 Wallace Road NW, #122
> Salem, OR 97304
> Phone: 800-849-7512
> Web site: www.winganna.com

The Carrying Kind is a British company that offers merino organic lambskins from merino/corriedale lambs, known for their extremely fine and soft wool. The lambs are organically reared, so the skins are guaranteed free from chemical residue. The company can ship anywhere in the world. For more information, contact:

> The Carrying Kind
> P.O. Box 211
> Hertford, SG13 7ZF
> United Kingdom
> Phone: 011-44-1992-554045
> Web site: www.thecarryingkind.com

Co-sleeping Products

Arm's Reach Co-Sleeper: This special type of three-sided criblike bassinet attaches to the side of your bed so you and your baby have your own separate sleeping spaces, yet your infant remains within easy reach. Wonderful for mom-baby bonding as well as easy middle-of-the-night breast-feeding. The units are made to fit most bed heights and come in a variety of finishes. In addition to the bassinet, most units also convert to a playard and changing table. The company also makes a mini-co-sleeper on wheels and a fancier sleigh-bed model that converts to a changing table and a love seat (creating a cozy reading or cuddling space for toddlers). Arm's Reach products are recommended by prominent pediatrician William Sears, M.D. For more information, contact:

> Arm's Reach Concepts, Inc.
> 2081 North Oxnard Boulevard, PMB #187
> Oxnard, CA 93030
> Phone: 800-954-9353 or 805-278-2559
> Web site: www.armsreach.com

Help Getting Your Baby to Sleep

White noise—so-called because like white light, it contains all frequencies— not only masks other sounds but also provides a soothing environment that will help your baby get to sleep. The following companies make white-noise/nature-sound machines or CDs:

Sleep Well Baby sells a wide variety of nature-sound and white-noise machines made by Marpac, the industry leader. For information contact:

> Sleep Well Baby
> 217 Country Club Park, PMB#403
> Birmingham, AL 35213
> Phone: 866-873-3026
> Web site: www.sleepwellbaby.com

Pure White Noise sells a wide variety of white-noise CDs, including both nature sounds (such as wind, waves, and rain) and household sounds (vacuum, air conditioner, fan). For information contact:

> Pure White Noise
> 6219 Whittondale Drive
> Tallahassee, FL 32312
> Web site: www.purewhitenoise.com

The Hush Baby CD contains three tracks of white noise that play simultaneously blended with a gently rhythmic digital wave pattern. For information contact:

Hush Baby Products
P.O. Box 8047
Chicago, IL 60680
Web site: www.hush-baby.com

Many kinds of music are also conducive to settling your baby down to sleep, and I especially recommend the soothing flute music of Maria Kostelas. Maria's *Mother's Melody/One Heart* CD is a favorite of neonatal wards; nurses have found that this CD calms newborns instantly, and it reduces stress for the nurses too! This collection of five tranquil flute melodies was also designed to enhance bonding between mothers and their babies. *Mother's Melody* includes the music of Native American, South American, Irish, and classical flutes along with guitar, harp, violin, cello, and piano music. Maria suggests that moms-to-be listen to the music before their babies are born, as well. For more information, contact:

Flutes of the World
513 Wilshire Boulevard, Suite 221
Santa Monica, CA 90401
Phone: 310-393-1211
Web site: www.flutesofthe world.com

Postpartum Doulas

(See doula information in Chapter 5 Resources, page 666.)

Postpartum Depression (PPD) Information

Depression After Delivery, Inc., is a national nonprofit organization that provides support for women suffering from depression during pregnancy or after delivery. Its focus includes education, information, support groups, telephone support, and professional referral for women and their families (including names of local support groups for PPD). For more information, contact:

Depression After Delivery (D.A.D.)
Box 1282
Morrisville, PA 19067
Phone: 800-944-4773
Web site: www.depressionafterdelivery.com

Postpartum Support International is an educational, referral, and advocacy group devoted to increasing awareness about and discussion of postpartum depression. Its Web site has lots of background information, as well as a bookstore, Internet forums and chat rooms, links to local support groups across the country, and a self-assessment test. For more information, contact:

Postpartum Support International
927 North Kellogg Avenue
Santa Barbara, CA 93111
Phone: 805-967-7636
Web site: www.postpartum.net

Emerita's ProGest Body Cream is a 3 percent natural progesterone formula
that delivers 20 mg of progesterone per one-quarter teaspoon (the recommended application). It's very useful helping tame postpartum depression
(PPD). ProGest was the first transdermal progesterone cream available
commercially and is still the leading brand. It has a long history of clinical
use and physician satisfaction. This product comes in a tube or in a box of
single-use packets and is available online or over the counter in most health
food stores. For more information, visit Emerita's Web site at www.pro
gest.com or contact Emerson Ecologics.

Cognitive Behavioral Therapy

The National Association of Cognitive-Behavioral Therapists is an organization dedicated solely to the teaching and practice of cognitive-behavioral
psychotherapy, which holds that our own thoughts cause our feelings and
behaviors (as opposed to external things like other people or situations).
CBT therapists teach patients that even if they can't change a situation, they
can change the way they think about it, helping them to become calmer and
at peace with life's challenges. The organization's Web site not only has an
extensive description of this type of therapy, it also has a search page that
provides names of certified CBT therapists in your area. For more information, contact:

The National Association of Cognitive-Behavioral Therapists
P.O. Box 2195
Weirton, WV 26062
Phone: 800-853-1135
Web site: www.nacbt.org

Lesbian Mother Issues

The Lesbian Mother Support Society (LMSS) was a Canadian group that
provided peer support for lesbian parents and their children, as well as les-
bians considering parenthood. While the society no longer exists, a group
still maintains a wonderful Web page called simply Lesbian Mothers
Support that continues to share extensive information on and resources for
the unique issues lesbian parents face. The volunteers who run the Web site
have continued to answer e-mails and phone calls. For more information,
contact:

Lesbian Mothers Support
c/o Calgary Gay and Lesbian Community Services Association
205a -223-12 Avenue SW
Calgary, AB T2R 0G9
Canada
Phone: 403-265-6433
Web site: www.lesbian.org/lesbian-moms

ROOM ONE

Chapter 7: The Emotional Brain: Empathy, Will, and Shame

Recommended Reading

Mona Lisa Schulz, M.D., Ph.D., *Awakening Intuition: Using Your Mind-Body Network for Insight and Healing* (Harmony Books, 1998); www.drmonalisa.com.

Written by my close friend and colleague, this book is the definitive work on how and where emotional patterns affect our physical bodies. In this groundbreaking, major work on intuition, well-being, and brain science, Dr. Schulz reveals innovative, fresh, and exciting ways to tap in to intuition that has the power to improve your health and save your life. A neuropsychiatrist, neuroscientist, and medical intuitive in Yarmouth, Maine., Dr. Schulz teaches that intuition is not some mystical talent but instead as natural a sense as our other five. This book is well researched, funny, and life changing. Dr. Schulz is also the author of *The New Feminine Brain: How Women Can Develop Their Unique Genius and Intuitive Style* (to be published by Free Press in August 2005).

Harvey Karp, M.D. (with Paula Spencer), *The Happiest Toddler on the Block: The New Way to Stop the Daily Battle of Wills and Raise a Secure and Well-Behaved One- to Four-Year-Old* (Bantam Books, 2004).

Dr. Karp, a pediatrician and child development expert, says the key to communicating with toddlers is to think of them not as pintsize humans, but as a pintsize cavemen with their own primitive language. He then outlines the rules of this language, including the use of short phrases, repetition, a dramatic tone of voice and body language. Dr. Karp is also the author of *The Happiest Baby on the Block: The New Way to Calm Crying and Help Your Baby Sleep Longer* (Bantam Books, 2002).

Paul Schenk, Psy.D., *Great Ways to Sabotage a Good Conversation* (Standard Press, 2002); www.drpaulschenk.com

In this helpful book, written with a sharp sense of humor, Dr. Schenk (a clinical psychologist in private practice in Atlanta) outlines how we often fall into language traps while talking with children, mates, friends, coworkers, and others who sabotage what we mean to say. By shifting our choice of words, he explains, we will not only boost our communication skills but greatly improve our relationships.

Dialectic Behavioral Therapy (DBT)

Described as "an eclectic mix of cognitive-behavioral techniques, skills training, Zen, and existentialism," DBT can be extremely helpful for anyone dealing with extreme emotional reactions (which, when left unaddressed, can lead to a number of serious mental and physical health problems). I believe that everyone with somatic illness of any kind, particularly a chronic illness, can benefit from the skills discussed in the Linehan approach even though they were designed for those suffering from a mental health diagnosis. Most major mental health centers now offer DBT groups.

Recommended Reading on DBT

Marsha M. Linehan, Ph.D., *Skills Training Manual for Treating Borderline Personality Disorder* (Guilford Press,1993); www.behavioraltech.com and http://faculty.washington.edu/linehan.

Dr. Linehan is a professor of psychology and an adjunct professor of psychiatry and behavioral sciences at the University of Washington, Seattle, WA. She is also director of the Behavioral Research and Therapy Clinics.

Scott E. Spradlin, *Don't Let Your Emotions Run Your Life: How Dialectical Behavior Therapy Can Put You in Control* (New Harbinger Publications, 2003); www.ksdbt.com.

Spradlin is a DBT therapist and certified counselor in Wichita, Kansas.

Chapter 8: Mouth and Gut Wisdom: The Roots of Self-Care

Recommended Reading

Paul Zane Pilzer, *The Wellness Revolution: How to Make a Fortune in the Next Trillion Dollar Industry* (Wiley & Sons, 2002); www.paul zanepilzer.com.

The best-selling author of this book, a step-by-step guide for entrepreneurs in the wellness industry, shares some fascinating information and statistics about the booming health and wellness industry. Pilzer is not only a world-renowned economist and multimillionaire software entrepreneur but also a lay rabbi and an adjunct college professor.

Fereydoon Batmanghelidj, M.D., *Your Body's Many Cries for Water: You Are Not Sick, You Are Thirsty!* (Global Health Solutions 1992);www.wat tercure.com.

Many common health problems (everything from asthma and arthritis to migraines and autoimmune diseases) are actually caused by chronic dehydration, according to Dr. B (as Dr. Batmanghelidj is nicknamed). Decades ago, while serving time as a political prisoner in an Iranian jail, Dr. B successfully treated three thousand fellow prisoners suffering from stress-induced peptic ulcer disease with water—the only "medicine" he had. He has since focused his career on researching the link between pain and disease and chronic dehydration.

Taro Gomi, *Everyone Poops* (Kane/Miller Book Publishers, 1993); www.everyonepoops.com.

This simple children's picture book (along with another favorite by the same publisher, *The Gas We Pass* by Shinta Cho) explores the generally taboo subject of bowel movements in humans and animals with brief, blunt, and informative narration that's a scream to read with your kids—even the illustrations are funny.

For Grinding Your Own Baby Food

The KidCo Food Mill (long known as the classic Happy Baby Food Grinder) strains and purees as well as separates seeds, bone, and skin. It's simple to use and requires no batteries or electricity—it works solely on mom-power. It's also lightweight, portable, and dishwasher safe—and incredibly affordable. For more information and to find an dealer in your area, contact:

KidCo, Inc.
1013 Technology Way
Libertyville, IL 60048
Phone: 800-553-5529
Web site: www.kidco.com

Multivitamins for Children

USANA's Usanimals: USANA's vitamin and mineral supplements include this chewable product designed for children containing an antioxidant phytonutrient blend of blackberry, cranberry, raspberry, and wild blueberry fruit powders. It also contains large doses of the powerful antioxidants vitamins C and E. For more information, contact:
USANA
3838 West Parkway Boulevard
Salt Lake City, UT 84120
Phone: 888-950-9595
Web site: www.usana.com

Pioneer's Chewable MVM: In addition to dozens of vitamins and minerals, this high-quality children's supplement (for ages three and up) contains a blend of twenty-five whole-food fruits and vegetables. Getting your kids to eat brussels sprouts has never been this easy. For more information, contact:

Emerson Ecologics, Inc.
7 Commerce Drive
Bedford, NH 03110
Phone: 800-654-4432
Web site: www.emersonecologics.com

Cod Liver Oil for Vitamin D

TwinLab Norwegian Cod Liver Oil: Cod Liver Oil is a good source of vitamin D as well as vitamin A and the omega-3 class fatty acids EPA (eicosaspentænoic acid) and DHA (docosahexænoic acid). TwinLab's product also contains natural cherry flavoring, so children won't mind the taste. For information, contact Emerson Ecologics.

To Treat Vulvar Irritation

Resinol Medicated Ointment: Made by U.S. Dermatologics, Inc., in Lawrenceville, NJ, this ointment is available at your local drugstore or supermarket. For further information, call 877-USDERM2 or visit www.us derm.com.

Preventing and Treating Sunburn

USANA's Daytime Protective Emulsion (SPF 15): A gentle, nongreasy sunscreen that protects against both UVA and UVB rays while it moisturizes and repairs sun-damaged skin.

USANA's Night Renewal Cream: Contains a host of natural ingredients that not only boost moisture levels but also help sun damaged skin.

For more information contact:

USANA
3838 West Parkway Boulevard
Salt Lake City, UT 84120
Phone: 888-950-9595
Web site: www.usana.com

Trienelle's Daily Renewal Crème: Contains a healthy dose of tocotrienols (a recently discovered high-potency form of vitamin E that's much better at quelling free-radical damage from the sun than regular vitamin D, known as D-alpha tocopherol). Trienelle also contains a wide variety of other skin-specific antioxidants such as coenzyme Q10 (CoQ10), alpha hydroxy acids, procyanadins, and a clinically proven collagen-supporting ingredient known as microcollagen pentapeptides. Trienelle also contains sunscreen and is nonirritating, making it ideal for daily use. Trienelle was formulated by a physician with years of experience in the benefits of nutritional medicine for the body, who wanted to make these benefits available to the skin, as well.

Trienelle Nightly Restoration Formula contains twice the tocotrienol content as the Daily Renewal Crème and is an excellent moisturizer to use following too much sun exposure.

For more information, contact:

> Aspen Benefits Group
> 7600 Mineral Drive, Suite 700
> Coeur d'Alene, ID 83815
> Phone: 800-539-5195
> Web site: www.trienelle.com

Chapter 9: The Immune System: A Mirror on the Mind and Environment

Recommended Reading

Kathryn C. Shafer, Ph.D., and Fran Greenfield, *Asthma Free in 21 Days: The Breakthrough Mind-Body Healing Program* (Harper San Francisco, 2000); www.asthmafree.org.

A must-read for anyone affected by asthma. In this groundbreaking and life-saving book, Dr. Shafer and mind/body therapist Fran Greenfield share a step-by-step process clinically proven to decrease asthma attacks and help people either eliminate or greatly decrease asthma medication. The key is a series of exercises that will help you tap your creative potential, learn how to identify and express your emotions fully, and use your dreams for guidance. The authors also provide readers with practical information, including breathing instruction.

Robert Mendelsohn, M.D., *Confessions of a Medical Heretic* (Contemporary Books, 1979).

A best-selling book detailing many examples of how Western medicine sets out to help but often ends up harming patients. The late Dr. Mendelsohn is also the author of *How to Raise a Healthy Child . . . in Spite of Your Doctor* (Contemporary Books, 1984).

John Gottman, Ph.D., *Raising an Emotionally Intelligent Child: The Heart of Parenting* (Simon & Schuster, 1998); www.gottman.com.

Dr. Gottman—a researcher and psychologist who cofounded the Gottman Institute in Seattle with his wife, Dr. Julie Schwartz Gottman—explains how parents can teach their children to understand and regulate their emotions with his five-step emotional coaching process, which involves validating children's feelings as well as helping them come up with more appropriate ways to solve problems.

Judith Acosta, L.C.S.W., and Judith Simon Prager, Ph.D., *The Worst Is Over: What to Say When Every Moment Counts* (Jodere Group, 2002); www.theworstisover.com

This book is like an answer to a prayer. It gives everyone, from parent to firefighter, the knowledge and courage to say exactly the right thing at the right time in a way that is healing, uplifting—and often even life-saving. The book gives sample scripts for what the authors (both therapists) call verbal first aid, both in emergency and nonemergency scenarios—including what to say to children.

Gary F. Fleischman, O.M.D., and Charles Stein, *Acupuncture: Everything You Ever Wanted to Know* (Barrytown, Ltd., 1998); www.Acupuncture NewHaven.com.

This easy-to-read guide is useful for patients and medical professionals alike, discussing the fundamentals of traditional Chinese medicine as well as sharing information on how TCM is used to treat various conditions. Dr. Fleischman is a board-certified acupuncturist practicing in New Haven, CT, who earned his degree from the China Institute of Acupuncture and the Guangdong Provincial Hospital of Traditional Chinese Medicine in Guangzhou, China.

Ruth Kidson, M.Sc., M.B., B.S., *Acupuncture for Everyone: What It Is, Why It Works, and How It Can Help You* (Healing Arts Press, 2000).

If you have ever wondered how and why acupuncture works, this book by a British doctor is an excellent place to begin your reading. Dr. Kidson demonstrates how an acupuncturist makes a diagnosis and how the patient is then treated. For the person drawn to this modality yet wary of the experience, this text makes going to an acupuncturist much less intimidating.

Sources for Omega-3 Supplements

(See Resources for Chapter 3.)

To Find a Practitioner of Traditional Chinese Medicine (Acupuncture)

Traditional Chinese medicine (TCM), a three-thousand-year-old health and wellness system, is based on the idea that all illness stems from imbalances of chi, or life energy, in the body. Its primary focus is prevention, although its therapies (including acupuncture as well as the use of Chinese herbs and bodywork) also treat pain, illness, and disease. It's ideal to get a referral to an acupuncturist or TCM practitioner from your health-care practitioner, but if you can't find one this way, contact:

> The National Certification Commission
>   for Acupuncture and Oriental Medicine
> 11 Canal Center Plaza, Suite 300
> Alexandria, VA 22314
> Phone: 703-548-9004
> Web site: www.nccaom.org

To Find a Naturopathic Pediatrician

Naturopathic doctors (N.D.s) are physicians who rely mostly on natural methods to help the body heal itself. They focus on the underlying cause of illness instead of relying mainly on the treatment of symptoms. They usually incorporate a variety of types of alternative or complementary medicine in their practice, although they may also use conventional medicine, depending on the individual patient. For more information on naturopathic physicians or to find one in your area who specializes in pediatrics, contact:

> The American Association of Naturopathic Physicians
> 3201 New Mexico Avenue NW, Suite 350
> Washington, DC 20016
> Phone: 866-538-2267 or 202-895-1392
> Web site: www.naturopathic.org

Information on Homeopathy

Homeopathy is a practice that uses minute doses of extremely diluted plant, mineral, and animal substances that produce the same symptoms the patient is suffering from in order to help the body stimulate the immune system against those very symptoms. The term comes from the Greek words for "similar" and "suffering," and it's based on the principle of "like cures like." For more information and to find a homeopathic practitioner, contact:

> The National Center for Homeopathy
> 801 North Fairfax Street, Suite 306
> Alexandria, VA 22314
> Phone: 703-548-7790
> Web site: www.homeopathic.org

Recommended Reading on Homeopathy

Richard Moskowitz, M.D., *Resonance: The Homeopathic Point of View* (Xlibris Corporation, 2001); http://members.aol.com/doctorrmosk.

Dr. Moskowitz is a highly respected practitioner of classic homeopathy in Watertown, MA, who has practiced the specialty since 1974 and written extensively on the subject.

For Information on How to Legally Avoid Having Your Child Vaccinated

Joseph Mercola, D.O, "How to Legally Avoid Unwanted Immunizations of All Kinds," www.mercola.com/article/vaccines/legally_avoid_shots.htm.

Dr. Mercola's Web site, www.mercola.com, also contains articles sharing research on a wide variety of health and wellness issues.

For Information on Nambudripad Allergy Elimination Technique (NAET)

Nambudripad's Allergy Elimination Techniques were developed in 1983 by Devi S. Nambudripad, M.D., D.C., L.Ac., Ph.D., a California acupuncturist, chiropractor, and kinesiologist. NAET is a noninvasive, drug-free, completely natural method of eliminating allergies of all types using a blend of selective energy balancing, testing, and treatments used in acupuncture/acupressure, chiropractic and allopathic medicine, and kinesiology. For more information or to find a NAET practitioner in your area, contact:

NAET
6714 Beach Boulevard
Buena Park, CA 90621
Phone: 714-523-8900
Web site: www.naet.com

For Information on Vibrational Healing (Including Helping to Clear Toxic Side Effects of Immunizations)

Deena Zalkind Spear is a vibrational and acoustical healer with a degree in neurobiology from Cornell University who combines twenty-nine years of experience as a violin maker with her training as an energy healer from the Barbara Brennan School of Healing. Her book, *Ears of the Angels: Healing the Sounds—Heard and Unheard—of Humans and Animals* (Hay House, 2003), is a delightful and humorous account of her healer's journey. I have referred many friends and family members to Deena. For more information on Deena and her methods, contact:

Singing Woods
P.O. Box 6562
Ithaca, NY 14851
Phone: 607-387-7787
Web site: www.singingwoods.org

Cold Medication for Children

Kold Kare (formerly sold as Kan Jang), made by Kare-N-Herbs (formerly known as the Swedish Herbal Institute): this product contains the potent Asian herb *Andrographis paniculata*. Kold Kare has been awarded Product of the Year for the past twelve years by the Swedish Health Council because of its immune-enhancing qualities during cold and flu season. Although this product is recommended only for children ages twelve and up, the company is currently developing a liquid form for younger children. For more information, contact:

Emerson Ecologics, Inc.
7 Commerce Drive
Bedford, NH 03110
Phone: 800-654-4432
Web site: www.emersonecologics.com

Umcka ColdCare Alcohol Free Drops and Umcka ColdCare Cherry Syrup: These products made by Nature's Way contain a homeopathic tincture of *Pelargonium sidoides,* a species of geranium shown to relieve cold and sore-throat symptoms and speed recovery from colds, flu, sinus infections, and sore throat. For more information, contact Emerson Ecologics.

Probiotics

Antibiotics not only get rid of unwanted bacteria that make us sick, they unfortunately also eliminate the beneficial bacteria naturally occurring in our digestive tract that are essential for the optimal absorption of nutrients from the food we eat. (Our intestines typically carry up to four hundred different strains of bacteria!) Probiotics, on the other hand, help restore our natural intestinal balance, improving nutrient absorption and aiding digestion, by providing the type of environment in which these beneficial flora need to thrive. Some good examples of these products include:

NutriCology's Gastro Flora: These capsules contain four different probiotic bacteria, including *Lactobacillus acidophilus, L. rhamnosus, L. casei,* and *Bifidobacterium longum.* Gastro Flora contains no milk, grains, yeast, soy, or other common allergens. For more information, contact:

Emerson Ecologics, Inc.
7 Commerce Drive
Bedford, NH 03110
Phone: 800-654-4432
Web site: www.emersonecologics.com

Bio-Botanical Research's ProFlora: These drops, formulated from the highest quality botanicals, contain *Lactobacillus salivarius, L. acidophilus,* bifido-bacteria complex, and botanical cofactors, including aloe vera. Unlike other probiotics, it requires no refrigeration. For more information, contact Emerson Ecologics.

Gaia Herbs' Swedish Bitters Elixir: a traditional European herbal tonic manufactured from organic and wild-crafted herbs (including turmeric rhizome, gentian root, calamus root, milk thistle seed, wild yam root, cardamom seed, fennel seed, ginger rhizome, Indian gooseberry, bitter orange essential oil, anise seed essential oil, and sea vegetation blend) in a base of alcohol and spring water. This product is very helpful for mild indigestion. For more information, contact Emerson Ecologics.

For the Latest Information on Autism

The National Autism Association serves to advocate for, educate, and empower those with autism and their families. The organization raises public and professional awareness of autism spectrum disorders. For more information, contact:

National Autism Association
P.O. Box 1547
Marion, SC 29571
Phone: 877-622-2884
Web site: www.nationalautismassociation.org

The Center for the Study of Autism (CSA) provides information about autism to parents and professionals and conducts research on the efficacy of various therapeutic interventions. For more information, contact:

Center for the Study of Autism
P.O. Box 4538
Salem, OR 97302
Web site: www.autism.org

Chapter 10: Love Maps

Recommended Reading

Barbara Biziou, *The Joy of Ritual: Spiritual Recipes to Celebrate Milestones, Ease Transitions, and Make Every Day Sacred* (Golden Books, 1999); www.joyofritual.com.

Biziou, a teacher of what she terms "practical spirituality," describes simple but meaningful ceremonies for everyday routines as well as rites of passage that you can design to fit your own circumstances and beliefs, with an emphasis on celebration and healing—even for sad events such as miscarriage. Biziou is also the author of *The Joy of Family Rituals: Recipes for Everyday Living* (Golden Books, 2000).

Proprioceptive Writing (PW)

This technique, developed by Linda Trichter Metcalf, Ph.D., and Tobin Simon, Ph.D., helps you explore your psyche and improve your mental, emotional, physical, and spiritual health through writing. It facilitates self-expression and creative breakthroughs, as well as spiritual growth. PW uses a process defined as inner hearing to train people to listen to their thoughts with empathy and curiosity and then to reflect on them in writing. Drs. Metcalf and Simon developed PW after a decade of teaching writing to college students. I personally worked with them privately and in group settings for seven years. For more information, contact:

The Proprioceptive Writing Center
88 Lexington Avenue, Mezzanine D
New York, NY 10016
Phone: 212-213-5402
Web site: www.pwriting.org

Recommended Reading on PW

Linda Trichter Metcalf, Ph.D., and Tobin Simon, Ph.D., *Writing the Mind Alive: The Proprioceptive Method for Finding Your Authentic Voice* (Ballantine Books, 2002).

Drs. Trichter and Simon founded the PW Center in 1982 and are now codirectors of the center. Dr. Trichter also teaches PW at institutions including the New School University, Esalen Institute, Omega, and the New York Open Center.

ROOM TWO

Chapter 11: The Age of Reason

Recommended Reading

Carol Gilligan, Ph.D., *In a Different Voice: Psychological Theory and Women's Development* (Harvard University Press, revised edition, 1993).

Dr. Gilligan, a psychologist and professor at the New York University School of Law, is a specialist on gender issues. This classic, first published more than twenty years ago when Dr. Gilligan was on the faculty at Harvard, challenged the field of psychology to look at women in a radically new way. In this revised edition, Dr. Gilligan shares her thoughts on the changes this book has made in the field.

Coping with Guilt

Coping.org (www.coping.org) offers on-site manuals that teach tools for personal growth in coping with a variety of life stressors. The authors—James J. Messina, Ph.D., and Constance M. Messina, Ph.D.—are therapists practicing in Tampa, FL.

The manual on guilt (www.coping.org/growth/guilt.htm) includes information on the effects guilt has on us and how others may play on our sense of guilt as well as a step-by-step process for overcoming guilt.

The Doctors Messina offer similar detailed online manuals dedicated to self-esteem (www.coping.org/growth/esteem.htm), trust (www.coping.org/growth/trust.htm), self-affirmations (www.coping.org/growth/affirm.htm), and even perfectionism (www.coping.org/growth/perfect.htm). For a full list of their Tools for Personal Growth online manuals, see this link: www.coping.org/growth/content.htm.

Chapter 12: The Anatomy of Self-esteem

Recommended Reading on Fitness

John Douillard, Ph.D., *Body, Mind, and Sport: The Mind-Body Guide to Lifelong Fitness and Your Personal Best* (Harmony Books, 1994; revised edition, Three Rivers Press, 2001); www.lifespa.com.

Dr. Douillard is a former professional athlete who applies mind/body principles to fitness in this book, designed to help readers determine which sport (and so which diet and exercise program) they are is best suited for, depending on their individual nature. The suggested fitness programs include plans for the competitive athlete as well as plans for the rest of us. The revised edition includes forewords by tennis stars Billie Jean King and Martina Navratilova. Since I discovered John Douillard's work I have approached all sports and exercise this way, and it has enhanced my enjoyment of physical activity immeasurably.

Mari Winsor, *The Pilates Powerhouse: The Perfect Method of Body Conditioning for Strength, Flexibility, and the Shape You Have Always Wanted in Less Than an Hour a Day* (Perseus Books, 1999).

Pilates is an excellent way to strengthen your core muscles and also increase flexibility because it engages your mind, muscles, breathing, and stretching all at once. Pilates has influenced and improved the way I perform every other activity, including walking!

To keep track of your Pilates workouts, I also recommend Mari Winsor's *The Pilates Workout Journal* (Perseus Books, 2001).

Brooke Siler, *The Pilates Body: The Ultimate At-Home Guide to Strengthening, Lengthening, and Toning Your Body—Without Machines* (Broadway Books, 2000).

Brooke Siler is one of the most sought-after Pilates instructors in the country, and for good reason. Extremely well-organized and easy to use, this book is great for at-home practice as well as travel, whether you are just starting out or a seasoned Pilates practitioner. All you need to go with this book is a mat and the desire to strengthen, lengthen, and tone your body.

Miriam E. Nelson, Ph.D., *Strong Women Stay Young* (Bantam, revised edition, 2000); www.strongwomen.com.

This book is great for learning the basics of strength training. Dr. Nelson's program is scientifically proven to build muscle and bone mass in midlife women. The Strong Women Stay Young program consists of two forty-minute weight-training sessions per week in which you work opposite muscle groups together, which not only builds strength but improves balance (something women start to lose in their forties). It's simple; you can do it at home or in the gym; and, regardless of your current fitness level, you'll obtain results quickly. In one study, Dr. Nelson found that the elderly patients who participated in her program significantly improved their strength and decreased their falls in just a few weeks.

Peggy W. Brill, P.T., *The Core Program: 15 Minutes a Day That Can Change Your Life* (Bantam Books, 2001).

Over the years, scores of women have complained to me about their aching backs, sore necks, hip pain, shoulder pain, and so on. Though stretching and exercise usually help alleviate most common aches and pain, not all methods help all people. Finally, I've found a simple fitness routine developed expressly for women that works regardless of your age, shape, or starting point. Because it takes only fifteen minutes per day, just about everyone can benefit. I urge you to incorporate the Peggy Brill's Core Program into your life right now. It's a brilliant and refreshing way to create health daily.

Recommended Reading for Parenting Issues

Dan Kindlon, Ph.D., *Too Much of a Good Thing: Raising Children of Character in an Indulgent Age* (Hyperion, 2001); www.dankindlon.com.

Dr. Kindlon, a child psychiatrist, outlines the seven deadly syndromes of overindulgence, drawing both from his clinical experience as well as a study of hundreds of parents and children from middle- and upper-income families that he conducted in 2000. His simple, sound advice helps guide parents through the pitfalls of emotional overindulgence so they can teach the good character skills their children need to thrive in the world today.

Juliet Schor, *Born to Buy: The Commercialized Child and the New Consumer Culture* (Scribner, 2004).

Consumer expert Juliet Schor explains how society heavily markets to children, resulting in a generation of overly commercial pint-sized consumers. The media not only influences what these children purchase, she warns in this book, but also how they feel about themselves. Schor includes guidelines for teachers and parents trying to stem this dangerous rip tide.

Other Parenting Resources

Connect with Kids Network, Inc. (CWKN): a leading producer and syndicator of television, print, and Internet products that focus on the health, education, and well-being of children. Through CWKN's Web site, parents can order resource guides and video documentaries (for children in grades three through five, six through eight, and nine through twelve) giving information about and advice on dealing with key social and behavioral issues (such as divorce, drugs, driving skills, diversity, Internet use, and more). For more information, contact:

CWK Network, Inc.
6285 Barfield Road
2nd Floor
Atlanta, GA 30328
Phone: 888-891-6020
Web site: www.connectingwithkids.com

Teen Research Unlimited (TRU): This company was founded in 1982 as the first marketing-research firm to specialize exclusively in teenagers and remains the only full-service marketing-research firm dedicated to studying this group. TRU is also the only youth research firm to provide syndicated, qualitative, and quantitative research. The company's Web site tracks teen trends and also offers many of their findings and statistics. For more information, contact:

Teen Research Unlimited
707 Skokie Boulevard
7th Floor
Northbrook, IL 60062
Phone: 847-564-3440
Web site: www.teenresearch.com

Financial Literacy and Prosperity

Catherine Ponder, *The Dynamic Laws of Prosperity* (De Vorss & Company; revised edition, 1985).
    This great motivational book, originally written in 1962, is my all-time favorite book on creating a prosperity consciousness, and I turn to it again and again. Catherine Ponder explains how our attitudes and our thoughts about prosperity shape our lives, and she encourages us to seek a more satisfying life that includes health, wealth, and happiness. I also recommend Ponder's books *The Millionaires of Genesis: Their Prosperity Secrets for You!* (DeVorss, 1976) and *The Prosperity Secret of the Ages: How to Channel a Golden River of Riches into Your Life* (Prentice-Hall, 1964).

Napoleon Hill, *Think and Grow Rich* (Briggs Pub., revised edition, 2003); www.naphill.org.
    This classic book, written in 1937 right after the Great Depression, offers tried-and-true methods for applying the Law of Attraction, which states that we attract those things that match our vibration on all levels: emotional, mental, and spiritual. Hill explains how our thoughts manifest themselves into their physical equivalents. In other words, if we continually think thoughts of poverty and are motivated by fear, then poverty will be our experience. But if we have a burning desire to be successful and are willing to give something back to the world in order to accomplish it, then

the universe will take care of the details and supply the people, places, and means by which we can achieve our goals.

Hill's book is based on the experience of more than five hundred individuals (mostly men, including such notables as Henry Ford, Andrew Carnegie, and Thomas Edison) who began from scratch and achieved great wealth because of their ideas, thoughts, and organized plans. Though the writing is dated and sexist, the principles outlined contain so much value and wisdom that I simply took what was good and left the rest. I studied this book thoroughly, and followed the suggestions to the letter.

James Allen, *As a Man Thinketh* (DeVorss & Company, 1979).

This classic from James Allen is based on the Bible verse "As a man thinketh, so he is." Allen sees the mind as a garden, with what you reap being what you sow. In this book, he teaches how each of us has the power to create what happens in our lives based largely on what we think and the way we think it.

Suze Orman, *The Courage to Be Rich: Creating a Life of Material and Spiritual Abundance* (Riverhead Books, 1999); www.suzeorman.com.

We all tend to use money as an excuse for not living our lives fully in accordance with our inner wisdom. Suze Orman's work as a broker and financial expert has led her to the truth that money is not the key to happiness (or health), but it certainly can be a powerful ally along the path we take to get there. Our success, she teaches, depends on having the courage to break familial patterns of shame, to shed the poverty mentality behind which so many of us cloak our dissatisfaction, and to allow abundance on every level to flow freely into our lives. Her book gives your courage a healthy motivational nudge.

Suze Orman, *The Nine Steps to Financial Freedom: Practical and Spiritual Steps So You Can Stop Worrying* (Crown Publishers, 1997); www.suzeorman.com.

What I like most about Suze Orman's approach to money is that she acknowledges the connection between our past emotional experiences with money and our present financial situation. She lists three internal blocks to wealth: fear, anger, and shame—all emotions. Our emotions, Suze explains, are what determine how much we have and how much we get to keep. She has helped me release some old resentment that needed to leave my life. And she has also helped me see that, ultimately, it was clarity about money that helped launch me into a new life during menopause when, she quipped, "you also went through money-pause." I have found Suze's stories convincing and highly motivating; I hope you find Suze's financial wisdom as bracing as I have.

David Bach, *Smart Women Finish Rich: 7 Steps to Achieving Financial Security and Funding Your Dreams* (Broadway Books, 2002); www.finishrich.com.

This guide to money management for women is based on the author's belief that financial planning is as much an emotional issue as it is an intellectual one. David Bach's nine-step program teaches readers how to save for the future, spend wisely today, and align their money with their values at all times. This revised and updated edition also covers teaching your kids about money.

Robert Kiyosaki and Sharon Lechter, C.P.A., *Rich Dad, Poor Dad: What the Rich Teach Their Kids About Money That the Poor and Middle Class Do Not* (Doubleday, 1999); www.richdad.com.

You've all heard the phrase "The rich get richer while the poor stay that way or get poorer." Kiyosaki explains why in this book, teaching readers how to apply this principle in their own lives. He discusses the importance of seeing yourself as a "business" rather than just an "employee." He also explains the crucial difference between working for money (living from paycheck to paycheck) and learning how to create cash flow or passive income through investing in our own businesses or those of others. The same team also wrote *Rich Dad, Poor Dad for Teens: The Secrets About Money That You Don't Learn in School!* (Warner Books, 2004).

Kiyosaki also offers a board game, *Cash Flow 101*, which, though expensive, taught me more than I could have learned from reading a dozen books after playing the game just twice. The game has an eerie way of reflecting back to each player his or her beliefs and behaviors about money. The idea is to get out of the "rat race" (living from paycheck to paycheck) and into the fast track, which is reached when your monthly passive income exceeds your monthly expenses. I guarantee you that playing this game will change the way you look at every purchase you make. The game comes in board versions and CD-Rom versions. In addition to the basic *Cash Flow 101*, Kiyosaki also offers a version for kids (*Cash Flow for Kids*) as well as an advanced version teaching the skills of technical investing (*Cash Flow 202*).

Randy Gage, *Accept Your Abundance!: Why You Are Supposed to Be Wealthy* (Prime Concepts Group Inc, 2003) and *101 Keys to Your Prosperity: Insights on Health, Happiness and Abundance in Your Life* (Prime Concepts Group Inc, 2003); www.prosperityuniverse.com.

Prosperity guru and multimillionaire Randy Gage challenges people to change their limiting beliefs on all levels. Randy, once an alcoholic who washed dishes for a living, is quite a character and a very dynamic and funny speaker. One of my favorite phrases is "You can't out-give the universe." And Randy lives by this credo—his business spends more on charitable contributions than any other expense. For more information, contact:

Prime Concepts Group, Inc.
1807 S. Eisenhower St.
Wichita, KS 67209-2810
Phone: 800-432-GAGE (800-432-4243)
Web site: www.ProsperityUniverse.com

George S. Clason, *The Richest Man in Babylon* (Signet Book, reissue edition, 2004).

This inspirational money-management best-seller presents eleven ancient Babylonian tales that reveal the keys to financial success. The ancient wisdom it shares provides simple but powerful solutions for financial success that have stood the test of time.

Paul Zane Pilzer, *Unlimited Wealth: The Theory and Practice of Economic Alchemy* (Crown Publishers, 1990); www.paulzanepilzer.com.

Economist Paul Zane Pilzer, a professor of finance at New York University and former adviser to the Reagan and Bush administrations, explains why new and creative economic thinking is essential for success today. He teaches readers that the key to this is using their creativity to identify technological gaps and to design new goods and services to fill them.

Prosperity for You: This Web site (www.prosperityconcepts.com), maintained by prosperity coach Ken Partain, is dedicated to sharing ideas about prosperity and creating an e-community of like-minded people who want to learn and share their experiences. The site takes a holistic view, with tips relating not only to wealth but also to health and relationships.

Pro$perity Network: The mission of this upbeat Web site (www.prosperity network.com) is to "perpetuate the universal spiritual laws of prosperity, healing, and success to empower individuals to realize their divine birthrights of unlimited health, wealth, success, prosperity and abundance." You can sign up for a (free) monthly lesson on prosperity, as well as a monthly affirmation; the site also sells books and audiotapes on prosperity, as well as various additional prosperity products (including a wide variety of affirmation cards and even posters).

Resources for Role Models for Girls

The Role Model Project for Girls: This project, sponsored by Women's Work and designed for girls ages nine to sixteen, includes a page filled with professional careers open to women. Click on any category, and a girl can read information women have shared about how they got their careers and what they're like. The idea is to show the wide range of nontraditional careers open to women, and to offer advice to girls interested in considering those career paths. Eventually, the data will be made available on a CD. To visit the project, follow this link: www.womenswork.org/girls/about. html.

American Girls collection: This collection consists of eight different 18-inch dolls, their accessories, and several series of books telling stories from the lives of these fictional nine-year-old heroines (each living during a distinctive time in our country's history). The company describes its mission as "celebrating girls," and indeed, its products spark girls' imaginations and feed their intellectual curiosity. For more information, contact American Girl at 800-845-0005; www.americangirl.com.

Recommended Reading for Feeling Beautiful

Carole Jackson, *Color Me Beautiful: Discover Your Natural Beauty Through the Colors That Make You Look Great & Feel Fabulous!* (Acropolis Books, 1980); www.colormebeautiful.com.

The book that had everyone in the '80s asking, "What season are you?" Carole Jackson explains how to use your personal attributes (such as skin tone, hair color, and eye color) to determine what colors look best on you—both for makeup and clothing.

Hema Sundaram, M.D., *Face Value: The Truth About Beauty—And a Guilt-Free Guide to Finding It* (Rodale, 2003).

Dr. Sundaram gives women everywhere the permission we all need to feel beautiful, inside and out—along with practical and sage advice for making the right decisions about everything from face creams to face lifts.

Chapter 13: Eating for Life

Recommended Reading

Erika Schwartz, M.D., *The Teen Weight-Loss Solution: The Safe and Effective Path to Health and Self-Confidence* (William Morrow, 2004).

Dr. Schwartz, a specialist in women's health, explains the connection between hormones and weight gain and outlines a plan for using natural hormones and supplements to help balance raging teen hormones and improve mood and energy level, as well as optimize weight loss.

Walter C. Willett, M.D., with Patrick J. Skerrett, *Eat, Drink and Be Healthy: The Harvard Medical School Guide to Healthy Eating* (Simon & Schuster Source, 2001).

Based on research from Harvard Medical School and the Harvard School of Public Health, this revolutionary book turns the USDA food pyramid on its pointed head. Dr. Willett, one of the world's most distinguished nutrition researchers, explains that the old model is not only wrong but downright dangerous, and he offers a new model based on decades of research. The book also discusses supplements and offers recipes and menus.

Pamela Peeke, M.D., M.P.H., *Fight Fat After Forty: The Revolutionary Three-Pronged Approach That Will Break Your Stress-Fat Cycle and Make You Healthy, Fit, and Trim for Life* (Viking, 2000); www.drpeeke.com.

Dr. Peeke, a researcher with the National Institutes of Health, documents the connection between toxic stress and toxic weight gain—the kind of weight that accumulates in the abdomen and puts women at risk for heart disease and premature death. Toxic stress can come from any daily challenge, but a number of circumstances make it especially common in women over forty: the resurfacing of childhood trauma, perfectionism, relationship changes such as divorce and caregiving, job stress, acute or chronic illness, dieting, and the effects of menopause. This explanation certainly clicks with me. I invite you to read this book, then get out your calendar and do some detective work to see if you, too, have a stress pattern that could be leading to weight gain and uncover how you might reverse that.

Diana Schwarzbein, M.D., *The Schwarzbein Principle: The Truth About Losing Weight, Being Healthy, and Feeling Younger* (Health Communications, 1999); www.SchwarzbeinPrinciple.com

Dr. Schwarzbein pulls together the building blocks of the modern-day human's dietary puzzle, the result being a comprehensive guidebook to how food works at the cellular level to create or break our health. Prefaced by sections on aging, cholesterol and fat, heart disease, insulin resistance, and cancer, this book weighs in historical, vegetarian, and other lifestyle concerns and culminates in a four-week meal plan. Dr. Schwarzbein gives explanations for how to achieve an evolutionarily balanced diet, gain a handle on eating disorders, and construct a healing and maintenance program that fits modern-day needs, including a starting sampler of recipes. I also recommend Dr. Schwarzbein's *Schwarzbein Principle Cookbook* (Health Communications, 1999) and the *Schwarzbein Principle Vegetarian Cookbook* (Health Communications, 1999).

Kathleen DesMaisons, Ph.D., *Potatoes, Not Prozac: A Natural Seven-Step Dietary Plan to Control Your Cravings and Lose Weight, Recognize How Foods Affect the Way You Feel, and Stabilize the Level of Sugar in Your Blood* (Simon & Schuster, 1999).

I heartily recommend this book to anyone who has ever struggled with weight control. Dr. DesMaisons reveals the relationship between diet, beta-endorphins, and self-esteem, recognizing the crucial role that beta-endorphins play in regulating brain chemistry, mood, and appetite. Learn how brain chemistry is affected by what and when we eat. If you are one of an estimated 20 million people who are children or grandchildren of alcoholics or crave alcohol, then you can benefit from taking these simple actions: 1) eat breakfast, 2) have protein at each meal, 3) cut down on sugars, and 4) read this book.

Kathleen DesMaisons, Ph.D., *The Sugar Addict's Total Recovery Program* (Ballantine, 2000).

Dr. DesMaisons offers concrete information about specific foods and the biochemistry of sugar addiction in this book. Her research has uncovered three important factors that contribute to the start of sugar addiction and which, when balanced, are the keys to recovery from it: blood sugar, serotonin, and beta-endorphins. She has created an easy-to-follow, seven-step plan to break sugar addiction, which she outlines here in practical detail. Dr. DesMaisons's program acknowledges that recovery from sugar or any other addiction is a process, not an event. If you are a true sugar addict, every weight-loss diet you'll ever try is doomed to failure until you understand and apply the principles put forth so compellingly in this book.

H. Leighton Steward, Morrison Bethea, Sam Andrews, and Luis A. Balart, *The New Sugar Busters: Cut Sugar to Trim Fat* (Ballantine Books, 2003); www.sugarbusters.com.

The basic equation in this easy-to-understand book is simply put: Too Much Sugar = Too Much Insulin. Excess sugar consumption has been linked to myriad health problems, including depression, impaired immune function, and weight gain. If you suspect your diet may contain too much sugar or that you are sugar-sensitive, this book can help you evaluate your dietary needs more clearly. It contains meal plans and recipes that have helped many people lose or maintain their weight, as well as balance hormones, insulin, and eicosanoid levels.

Geneen Roth, *When Food Is Love: Exploring the Relationship Between Eating and Intimacy* (Dutton, 1991); www.geneenroth.com.

If you are facing the emotional dimensions of overeating, read this book. No one has ever written more eloquently or helpfully on the subject of eating and emotions. Whenever I read Geneen's work, I feel spiritually nourished and hopeful.

Geneen Roth, *Appetites: On the Search for True Nourishment* (Dutton, 1996); www.geneenroth.com.

What do women *really* want? Using eating as a metaphor for feminine desire in contemporary American culture, Geneen Roth examines the depths of our search for true nourishment, intimacy, friendship, health, and success.

Nutritional Plans and Information

Council for Responsible Nutrition (CRN): a Washington-based trade association representing ingredient suppliers and manufacturers in the dietary supplement industry. CRN's Web site contains detailed information on supplements, including basic information on and links to studies about a wide array of herbs and botanicals. One page (www.crnusa.org/about_label.html) gives clear and detailed information on how to read a supplement label. The council's downloadable publication, *The Benefits of Nutritional Supplements,* is a particularly enlightening document that shares much research that supports taking nutritional supplements at higher levels than the RDA to prevent chronic disease. For more information, contact:

Council for Responsible Nutrition (CRN)
1828 L Street, NW, Suite 900
Washington, DC 20036-5114
Phone: 202-776-7936
Web site: www.crnusa.org

Ray Strand, M.D., a family physician in South Dakota and the author of *Releasing Fat: Developing Healthy Lifestyles That Have a Side Effect of Permanent Fat Loss* (Health Concepts Publishing, 2003); www.bionutri tion.org.

Dr. Strand, a specialist in nutritional medicine, presents cutting-edge medical evidence explaining why so many diets don't work. He's been applying these truths in his private medical practice for over eight years. Not only are insulin-resistant patients improving their health and lifestyles, they are beginning to release fat for the first time in their lives.

Dr. Strand's Web site offers information about beating insulin resistance, including instructions on eating a healthy diet, following the right exercise program, and taking dietary supplements. The site includes detailed information about the glycemic index as well as recommended foods to help you prevent insulin resistance and maximize your health.

For information about the glycemic index, see Resources for Chapter 3.

Intuitive Resources

Mona Lisa Schulz, M.D., Ph.D., is a neuropsychiatrist and neuroscientist who is also a gifted medical intuitive. Dr. Schulz does several different types of intuitive readings, including a reading on a family to ascertain the emotional patterns present in the family dynamics that are affecting a child's health. (Note: Dr. Schulz does not make medical diagnoses during readings.) For more information or to make an appointment, call Dr. Schulz at 207-846-6497 or visit her Web site, www.drmonalisa.com.

Daily Vitamin and Mineral Supplements for Teens
(See also Resources for Chapter 3.)

USANA's Body Rox (based on USANA Essentials supplements for adults) is specifically formulated to meet the nutritional demands of teenagers and has been recently reformulated to add 50 percent more calcium and magnesium, as well as extra antioxidants. For more information, contact:

USANA
3838 West Parkway Boulevard
Salt Lake City, UT 84120
Phone: 888-950-9595
Web site: www.usana.com

Calcium Supplements for Teens

USANA's Body Rox Chewable Active Calcium: This chewable product (recommended for ages 12 through 18) contains a balanced formula of calcium, magnesium, silicon, and vitamin D, providing complete nutritional support for optimal bone development. For more information, contact:

> USANA
> 3838 West Parkway Boulevard
> Salt Lake City, UT 84120
> Phone: 888-872-6272
> Web site: www.usana.com

Nature's Way Calcium Complex: This supplement is formulated with a 2:1 calcium-to-magnesium ratio. Three tablets contain 500 mg calcium and 250 mg magnesium; additional ingredients include zinc, copper, manganese, boron, vitamin D_3, vitamin K, vitamin B_6, folic acid, and horsetail (silica). This product contains no yeast, milk, lactose, wheat, sugar, soy, or corn. For more information, contact:

> Emerson Ecologics, Inc.
> 7 Commerce Drive
> Bedford, NH 03110
> Phone: 800-654-4432
> Web site: www.emersonecologics.com

Sources for Omega-3 Supplements

(See Resources for Chapter 3.)

Information on Eating Disorders

The National Eating Disorders Association (NEDA) is the largest not-for-profit organization in the United States. NEDA works to prevent eating disorders and to provide treatment referrals to those suffering from anorexia, bulimia, and binge eating disorder and those concerned with body image and weight issues. NEDA's Web site offers tons of information on eating disorders, and includes an Eating Disorders Survival Guide, links to treatment providers in your area, and even a page called "Tips for Kids on Eating Well and Feeling Good About Yourself." For more information, contact:

> The National Eating Disorders Association (NEDA)
> 603 Stewart St., Suite 803
> Seattle, WA 98101
> Phone: 206-382-3587
> Web site: www.edap.org

Healthy Shakes and Bars for Quick, Nutritious Meals or Snacks

The following drink mixes and snack bars provide healthy alternatives to fast food when you don't have time to cook a meal. To make thick, rich shakes, add ice or fruit to the drink mixes (or even ingredients like vanilla extract, honey, or a bit of peanut butter) and whip them up in a blender. Keep some of the bars in your desk drawer or purse for those times when you get the munchies and peanut M&Ms are the healthiest thing in the snack machine.

Revival Soy meal replacement drink: Of the numerous soy products on the market, this is my favorite. Developed by doctors, Revival contains 160 mg of soy isoflavones per serving, the equivalent of six servings of soy per day. The higher the amount of isoflavones in a soy product, the greater the benefits. Revival comes in eight flavors (I especially like the chocolate) and three different sweetener options (fructose, Splenda, and unsweetened). For more information, contact:

> Revival Soy
> 1031 E. Mountain St.
> Building 302
> Kernersville, NC 27284
> Phone: 800-REVIVAL (800-738-4825)
> Web site: www.revivalsoy.com

Revival Cool Krispy Protein Bars: These crunchy, puffed soy crisps are blended with a variety of delicious flavors, including peanuts, chocolate chips, marshmallow, and apple. One serving of these bars equals six servings of regular soy foods. For more information, contact Revival.

Revival Low-Carb Bars: These very flavorful bars combine a high-protein content minimal carbs (from three to eight net impact carbs per bar). For more information, contact Revival.

USANA'S Nutrimeal drink mix: This meal replacement drink blends low-glycemic carbohydrates, high-quality soy protein (12 grams per serving), and healthy fat (3.5 grams) in the ideal ratio. It also contains six grams of dietary fiber. The drink mix comes in three flavors. For more information, contact:

> USANA
> 3838 West Parkway Boulevard
> Salt Lake City, UT 84120
> Phone: 888-950-9595
> Web site: www.usana.com

USANA Iced Lemon Fibergy Bar: These all-natural, low-glycemic, high-fiber bars are also high in omega-3 fatty acids (from flaxseed) and potassium. Each bar has only 1.5 grams of fat. For more information, contact USANA.

USANA Nutrition Bars: A delicious, healthy low-glycemic snack providing healthy carbohydrates, proteins, and fats that is one of my personal favorites. Nutrition Bars are available in two flavors—wild berry (with 8 grams of protein) and peanut crunch (with 12 grams of protein). For more information, contact USANA.

For information about Omega Smart Bars (an organic snack bar high in omega-3s and with a low glycemic index, available through Emerson Ecologics), see the Resources for Chapter 3.

For information about Nutiva's Hempseed Bars (an organic snack bar high in omega-3 and omega-6 fatty acids, protein, and vitamin E; available through Emerson Ecologics) see the Resources for Chapter 3.

KETO Shakes: These thick, filling shakes offer ideal high-protein, low-carb meal replacement, with 24 grams of protein and only 1 to 3 grams of fat per serving. KETO shakes come in more than 10 flavors with no added sugar, aspartame, or saccharin. I often use a half scoop of KETO mix to add protein and flavor to other blender drinks. KETO products are available nationwide, or visit www.keto.com.

Chapter 14: The School of Friendship

Recommended Reading

Rosalind Wiseman, *Queen Bees & Wannabes: Helping Your Daughter Survive Cliques, Gossip, Boyfriends, and Other Realities of Adolescence* (Crown Publishers, 2002); www.rosalindwiseman.com.

This groundbreaking book tells the candid truth about the power that cliques wield over adolescent girls today, revealing how shockingly mean girls can be toward one another. Rosalind Wiseman (who founded a nonprofit company dedicated to empowering teenage girls) talked to thousands of girls in researching this book. She also helps parents identify what specific role their daughters and their daughters' friends have taken on, as well as gives advice on how to empower girls so they can be who they truly are instead of who they think they are supposed to be. Wiseman also helps parents identify what their parenting styles are and understand how their own backgrounds and biases affect their relationships with their daughters. Wiseman's next book (*Surviving the Hive*) will center on parents and how they deal with each other in much the same way.

Rachel Simmons, *Odd Girl Out: The Hidden Culture of Aggression in Girls* (Harcourt, 2002).

A Vassar graduate, Rhodes scholar, and now an expert on female aggression, Rachel Simmons interviewed three hundred girls in thirty schools to write *Odd Girl Out*. She tells the down-and-dirty reality about how girls have created a culture where they not only bully each other, but where that bullying is sanctioned and encouraged by the tribe. She also shares some innovative ideas for how teachers, parents, and girls themselves can turn this painful trend around.

Lyn Mikel Brown, Ph.D., *Girlfighting: Betrayal and Rejection Among Girls* (New York University Press, 2003).

Psychologist and Colby College professor Lyn Mikel Brown details how the gossipy, competitive, cliquish nature of adolescent girls today is far from a harmless stage they will outgrow and is instead downright dangerous. She spoke with more than four hundred girls to research this book, which also offers good solutions for how we can change this damaging culture and teach our daughters to build more self-esteem and nurture their self-worth.

Vicki Crompton and Ellen Zelda Kessner, *Saving Beauty from the Beast: How to Protect Your Daughter from an Unhealthy Relationship* (Little, Brown, 2003).

One in three girls between the ages of ten and eighteen has been physically assaulted by a boyfriend, according to the Centers for Disease Control. Authors Vicki Crompton and Ellen Zelda Kessner know that statistic all too well. Crompton's daughter was murdered by her boyfriend when she was fifteen, while Kessner's adult daughter was also killed by violence. Hoping to prevent more stories like their own, these mothers wrote *Saving Beauty from the Beast* to warn parents of the danger signs that could indicate their daughters are in physically or mentally abusive relationships.

Jeanne Safer, Ph.D., *The Normal One: Life with a Difficult or Damaged Sibling* (Free Press, 2002); www.thenormalone.com.

This book by psychotherapist Jeanne Safer, who herself grew up with an emotionally ill brother, brings to light for the first time the specific challenges "normal" siblings face in families that include an emotionally or physically disadvantaged child. In her research, Dr. Safer interviewed sixty "normal" siblings about the ways they consciously and unconsciously compensated for their siblings' problems, including premature maturity, perfectionistic tendencies, and guilt about their own health. She also offers tools for helping such adult siblings heal the often-ignored and unacknowledged pain their family dynamics involved.

Shelley Taylor, Ph.D., *The Tending Instinct: How Nurturing Is Essential for Who We Are and How We Live* (Times Books, 2002).

Psychologist and stress research expert Dr. Shelley Taylor of UCLA explores her groundbreaking research showing that women respond to stress differently from men. Instead of being hardwired with the fight-or-flight response, women are biologically driven to respond with what Dr. Taylor dubs the "tend and befriend" response—they turn toward the open arms and willing ears of their friends, and soothe their jangled nerves through tending to and nurturing others. This altruistic, cooperative tendency, Dr. Taylor explains, provides an essential balance to the classic male fight-or-flight response—a balance she says is crucial for the survival of the species.

Alice Domar, Ph.D., *Self-Nurture: Learning to Care for Yourself as Effectively as You Care for Everyone Else* (Viking, 2000).

Harvard psychologist and stress management expert Dr. Alice Domar explains that women's self-sacrificing tendencies to take care of everyone else before themselves can lead to physical, emotional, and spiritual exhaustion. Just as the flight attendants instruct us to put on our own oxygen masks before helping any children seated next to us, Dr. Domar, the director of the Mind/Body Center for Women's Health at Harvard Medical School, shows us why and how putting ourselves first is a win-win situation for everyone. Using stories, meditations, and various other exercises, Dr. Domar outlines a comprehensive, year-long program designed to teach women how to nurture themselves. As Dr. Domar says, we don't have to give up our lives to enrich them.

Louise Hay, *You Can Heal Your Life* (Hay House, 1987) and *Heal Your Body A–Z: The Mental Causes for Physical Illness and How to Overcome Them* (Hay House, 1998); www.hayhouse.com.

I've been a big fan of Louise Hay's and her healing affirmations for years. Her approach works miracles! Louise teaches that the changes in our lives (and our bodies) that are loved into existence are permanent, while the changes that happen through self-abuse and denial will always be transient. Louise also writes a helpful, empowering newsletter that you can subscribe to through Hay House's Web site.

Resources for Helping Girls Bond Instead of Bicker

The Ophelia Project: an organization that promotes healthy character development and mentoring relationships through awareness, education, and advocacy. Dedicated to creating a culture that is emotionally, physically, and socially safe, the Ophelia Project offers expertise in covert peer aggression and other issues unique to girls. The organization targets relational aggression (such as gossip, spreading rumors, and exclusion) and teaches adolescents to treat their peers with respect. The project offers tools for parents and schools, advocacy programs for communities, and workshops and seminars. For more information, contact:

The Ophelia Project
P.O. Box 8736
Erie, PA 16505-0736
Web page: www.opheliaproject.org

Stop Bullying Now!: The Web site (www.stopbullyingnow.hrsa.gov) of this anti-bullying campaign, created as a joint effort of the U.S. Department of Health and Human Services, the Health Resources and Services Administration, and the Maternal and Child Health Bureau, includes games and "webisodes" for girls ages nine through thirteen. The site also offers an on-line resource kit for adults (including teachers and school administrators, mental health professionals, and youth leaders, among others).

Operation Respect: a nonprofit organization sharing educational resources with schools, camps, and other organizations focused on children and youth that help encourage more compassionate, safe, and respectful environments for our children. Founded by Peter Yarrow of the famous 1960s folk group Peter, Paul & Mary, the organization has developed a series of three *Don't Laugh at Me* (DLAM) programs, aimed at different grade levels. These programs use catchy music and videos along with other curriculum elements developed by the Resolving Conflict Creatively Program (RCCP) of Educators for Social Responsibility (ESR). The organization also offers an online bulletin board for kids to share their stories, ask questions, and offer some of their own solutions to other kids' queries. For more information, contact:

Operation Respect
2 Penn Plaza, 5th Floor
New York, NY 10121
Phone: 212-904-5243
Web site: www.dontlaugh.org

Dialectic Behavioral Therapy (DBT)

(See Resources for Room One)

Chapter 15: Puberty

Recommended Reading

Mary Pipher, Ph.D., *Reviving Ophelia: Saving the Selves of Adolescent Girls* (Putnam, 1994).

Clinical psychologist Mary Pipher writes about how young girls today lose their sense of self when they hit adolescence, often developing depression, eating disorders, and even suicidal thoughts at an alarming rate— thanks to the model-thin and skin-deep standards of beauty our culture espouses. Dr. Pipher also offers strategies to fight this alarming trend.

Cheryl Dellasega, Ph.D., *Surviving Ophelia: Mothers Share Their Wisdom in Navigating the Tumultuous Teenage Years* (Perseus, 2001).

In response to Mary Pipher's *Reviving Ophelia,* Dr. Dellasega, a clinician at Penn State's College of Medicine, shares her own heart-wrenching experience with her teenage daughter in this compilation of stories and poems from mothers of other "Ophelias" across the U.S. An appendix lists resources for mothers and daughters who need help navigating the teen years.

Sara Shandler, *Ophelia Speaks: Adolescent Girls Write About Their Search for Self* (HarperPerennial, 1999).

Amherst, MA, native Sara Shandler read *Reviving Ophelia* when she was sixteen and was so affected by it that she created a forum for teen girls to speak out on similar issues. This book, written when Sara was an undergraduate at Wesleyan University, is a collection of those voices, written by girls from age twelve to eighteen, from all religions and socioeconomic classes nationwide.

Anne Cameron, *Daughters of Copper Woman* (Harbour Publishing Co., 2002).

Anne Cameron's underground classic has been revised to include material cut from the original (published in 1981) as well as new material. In this book, she retells myths from northwest-coast Native American tribes that celebrate the awesome spiritual power and beauty of being a woman.

Celebrating a Girl's First Menstrual Period

Mary Dillon and Shinan Barclay, *Flowering Woman: Moontime for Kory: A Story of a Girl's Rites of Passage into Womanhood* (Sunlight Productions, 1988).

This beautifully illustrated book tells the fictional story of an indigenous girl named Kory and how the grandmothers of her tribe help usher her into womanhood, showing her how sacred being a woman really is. The book gently touches on the issues of sex, pregnancy, and passion, in addition to menstruation.

Barbara Biziou, *The Joy of Ritual: Spiritual Recipes to Celebrate Milestones, Ease Transitions, and Make Every Day Sacred* (Golden Books, 1999); www.joyofritual.com.

Biziou, a teacher of what she terms "practical spirituality," describes simple but meaningful ceremonies for everyday routines as well as rites of passage that you can design to fit your own circumstances and beliefs, with an emphasis on celebration and healing—even for sad events such as miscarriage. Biziou has also written *The Joy of Family Rituals: Recipes for Everyday Living* (Golden Books, 2000).

Joan Morais, *A Time to Celebrate: A Celebration of a Girl's First Menstrual Period* (Lua Publishing, 2003); joanmorais.com.

This splendid and empowering book for young girls and their families portrays the menstrual period as the gift it really is. Joan Morais gives practical, uplifting, and straightforward advice for recognizing and celebrating this event, just like any other special occasion. She also includes charts for girls to use to keep track of their periods and feelings, and a journal for writing thoughts and creative expressions.

Janet Lucy and Terri Allison, *Moon Mother, Moon Daughter: Myths and Rituals That Celebrate a Girl's Coming-of-Age* (Fair Winds Press, 2002).

Authors Janet Lucy (a teacher and therapist) and Terri Allison (a child development educator) have four daughters between them, ranging from ages ten to sixteen. This joyous book explores different coming-of-age traditions and offers activities for mothers and daughters to do together to help them bond during this often tumultuous time.

Kristi Meisenbach Boyland, *The Seven Sacred Rites of Menarche: The Spiritual Journey of the Adolescent Girl* (Santa Monica Press, 2001).

This book provides a remarkable blueprint for honoring and nurturing a girl's spirit. Kristi Meisenbach Boyland's book describes seven stepping stones all girls face on their spiritual journey from maidenhood to womanhood. She also shares her ideas for creating rites-of-passage ceremonies, including poignant ceremonies for mothers and daughters to share.

The First Moon: Passage to Womanhood: This special ceremonial kit helps mothers and daughters celebrate a girl's first period. Created by Helynna Brooke and her mother, Ann Short, after Helynna decided to design such a ceremony for her own daughter, and later, for other young women in her family. The company's Web site includes an extensive resources page with dozens of books, tapes, and other resources. For more information, contact:

> The Brooke Company
> 1342 38th Avenue
> San Francisco, CA 94122
> Phone: 888-965-4812
> Web site: www.celebrategirls.com

Celebrating Menstruation (and Being a Woman in General)

The Red Spot (www.onewoman.com/redspot): This hip Web site done with a sense of humor is a wonderful resource for young girls. It includes detailed biological information about the reproductive system, menstruation, and the hormone cycle (you'll love the dancing uterus); coming-of-age lore from different cultures around the globe; and a great section of straight talk about what it's like to get your period, written in a positive and encouraging style girls will appreciate. There's even a forum where girls share their stories, thoughts, and feelings about their periods.

Kami McBride, *105 Ways to Celebrate Menstruation* (Living Awareness Institute, 2003); www.livingawareness.com.

I just adored this light, fun, and empowering book, and I think every woman and girl should read it. Kami McBride explains how we can use menstruation as a tool for personal growth and even self-healing. A gifted herbalist specializing in women's health, she includes recipes for herbal formulas.

Lara Owen, *Honoring Menstruation: A Time of Self-Renewal* (Crossing Press, 1998); www.laraowen.com.

This graceful and empowering book on menstruation is filled with insights about the power and value of a woman's menstrual cycle, going way beyond the function of reproduction. Lara Owen draws on various cultural traditions as well as personal experience (and the experiences of other women) to show how your period represents a time for physical and spiritual renewal that allows you to tap more deeply in to your inner wisdom. This revised and expanded version (originally entitled *Her Blood Is Gold*) includes a section on natural healing methods for menstrual symptoms.

The Red Web Foundation: A foundation dedicated to creating a positive view of the menstrual cycle (in its entirety from menarche through menopause) for girls and women through education and community. The group is also committed to women rediscovering meaning in their cycles because, as their Web site states, "When we learn how to live wisely with lifecycles, we learn to ground our self-esteem in profound internal wisdom. Body image and menstrual cycles are interlinking facets of women's total health and well-being." For more information, contact:

> The Red Web Foundation
> 93 Rocca Drive
> Fairfax, CA 94930
> Phone: 888-965-4812
> Web site: www.theredweb.org

The Museum of Menstruation and Women's Health: Once displayed (from 1994 through 1998) in the Washington, D.C., area home of Harry Finley, the museum is now a virtual museum available via cybertour. The topics covered include everything from menstrual huts used in other cultures to menstrual art (not for the squeamish), all chosen for their ability to illustrate the history of woman's health and the culture of menstruation. For more information, contact:

MUM
P.O. Box 2398
Landover Hills Branch
Hyattsville, MD 20784-2398
Phone: 301-459-4450
Web site: www.mum.org/armensza.htm

My Monthly Cycles (www.mymonthlycycles.com) is a free site that allows you to keep track of your cycle, calculate your ovulation, and even arrange to send yourself e-mail reminders about things like monthly breast exams.

ROOM THREE: FOURTEEN TO TWENTY-ONE YEARS

Chapter 16: Aphrodite Rising

Recommended Reading

Linda E. Savage, Ph.D., *Reclaiming Goddess Sexuality: The Power of the Feminine Way* (Hay House, 1999); www.goddesstherapy.com.

Dr. Savage, a licensed psychologist, marriage and family therapist, and sex therapist, blends what the Western world knows about women's sexuality with wisdom from the ancient Goddess cultures. Sexuality is sacred, she teaches, while sharing step-by-step advice for using this concept to make your intimate relationships deeper, more balanced, and more fulfilling.

Marija Gimbutas, Ph.D., *The Civilization of the Goddess: The Old World of Europe* (HarperSanFrancisco, 1991).

The late Dr. Gimbutas, once a research fellow at Harvard and later a professor at UCLA, uses archaeological evidence to paint a picture of the Neolithic European world as a peaceful, goddess-worshipping, female-governed civilization that valued men and women equally—promoting the theory that our culture is indeed based on a rich matriarchal heritage.

Riane Eisler, Ph.D., *The Chalice and the Blade: Our History, Our Future* (Harper & Row, 1987).

Dr. Eisler, a cultural historian and evolutionary theorist who is president of the nonprofit Center for Partnership Studies, documents the shift from egalitarian goddess-worshipping cultures that were present on the earth in prehistoric days to the authoritarian, patriarchal, and often violent society that dictated that men should control and dominate women. A futurist, Dr. Eisler envisions a cooperative society with more humane values for everyone on the horizon.

Morton Kelsey and Barbara Kelsey, *The Sacrament of Sexuality: The Spirituality and Psychology of Sex* (Vega Books, 2002).

This book, written by an Episcopal priest and his wife, explains how parents' attitudes about sex and even the physical affection they show for one another and family members shape their children's ideas about sexuality. The Kelseys, who rely heavily on Jungian concepts, discuss many varieties of sexual expression (including homosexuality) as well as why and how our sexuality relates to our spirituality.

Helen Fisher, Ph.D., *Anatomy of Love: The Natural History of Monogamy, Adultery, and Divorce* (Norton, 1992); www.helenfisher.com.

Dr. Fisher, an anthropologist at Rutgers University and formerly with the American Museum of Natural History, has conducted extensive research on the evolution and future of human sex, love, and marriage as well as gender differences in the brain and behavior. In this book, she offers biologically driven, neurochemical explanations for why and how people in different cultures around the world flirt, fall in love, marry, and either stay together or part. She is also the author of *Why We Love: The Nature and Chemistry of Romantic Love* (Henry Holt, 2004); *The First Sex: The Natural Talents of Women and How They Are Changing the World* (Random House, 1999); and *The Sex Contract: The Evolution of Human Behavior* (William Morrow, 1992).

Dorothy Tennov, *Love and Limerence: The Experience of Being in Love* (Scarborough House, 1999).

Originally published twenty years ago, this classic delves into the psychology of emotion, describing an involuntary and temporary state the author coined as "limerence," which is roughly equivalent to falling in love. This emotionally dependent state includes longing for the other person to reciprocate, as well as obsessively thinking about the person and even being irrational about his or her positive attributes.

Naomi Wolf, *Promiscuities: The Secret Struggle for Womanhood* (Random House, 1997).

An expert on the effects of popular culture on women's self-image, Naomi Wolf writes about her own coming of age in San Francisco's hippie-charged Haight-Ashbury during the late '60s and '70s in describing what she sees as women's struggle to express their sexuality while simultaneously satisfing society's standards of behavior. The Madonna-whore attitude prevalent in our culture, she says, leaves few healthy outlets for girls' normal sexual desires. The book also goes into such topics as abortion, the sex industry, and even sexual violence and the effects such things have on girls' ideas about themselves and their sexuality.

Jalaja Bonheim, Ph.D., *Aphrodite's Daughters: Women's Sexual Stories and The Journey of the Soul* (Simon & Schuster, 1997); www.jalajabonheim.com.

Therapist Jalaja Bonheim shares the stories of dozens of women from a wide variety of spiritual traditions and backgrounds about how their sexual experiences have ultimately been entwined with their spiritual growth. Bonheim's interest in the subject began on a trip to India, when she met an older woman who had been a sexual priestess in the Tantric tradition.

Kami McBride, *105 Ways to Celebrate Menstruation*. (See Resources for Room Two, page 703.)

Sources for Information on Teen Sexuality and Preventing Pregnancy

The National Campaign to Prevent Teen Pregnancy: a nonprofit, nonpartisan organization begun in 1996 with the goal to reduce the rate of teen pregnancy by one-third before the year 2005. The section on the campaign's Web site that is specifically for teens has lots of useful information and straight talk, including direct quotes from other teens about sex, pregnancy, contraception, parents, the media, and even religion. Teens who take the quiz about teen sex and pregnancy will discover the results from a recent poll showing that about 35 percent of girls in the U.S. will get pregnant before they turn twenty, and that 63 percent of all teens (and 70 percent of teen girls) who have already had sex wished that they had waited. For more information, contact:

> The National Campaign to Prevent Teen Pregnancy
> 1776 Massachusetts Ave., NW, Suite 200
> Washington, DC 20036
> Phone: 202-478-8500
> Web site: www.teenpregnancy.org

Planned Parenthood Federation of America (PPFA): the world's largest voluntary reproductive health care organization. Founded in 1916 as America's first birth control clinic, Planned Parenthood espouses that women should be in charge of their own destinies. The organization's main Web site contains a huge amount of information about sexuality, pregnancy, and birth control, including an extremely helpful and detailed guide for parents (including a page on what children need to know and at what ages they need to know it).

Teenwire is PPFA's separate Web site just for teens, which includes extensive information on sexuality and relationships. "True Tales of a Teen Mom" and "How to Put On a Condom" (with a video using a plastic model) are just two examples of what you'll find here. For more information, contact:

> Planned Parenthood Federation of America
> 434 West 33rd Street
> New York, NY 10001
> Phone: 212-541-7800
> Web site: www.plannedparenthood.org and www.teenwire.com

Chapter 17: Addictions

Recommended Reading

Andrew Weil, M.D., and Winifred Rosen, *From Chocolate to Morphine: Everything You Need to Know About Mind-Altering Drugs* (Houghton Mifflin, 2004); www.drweil.com.

This recently revised book aimed at parents and their children gives an unbiased description of the ways a wide variety of drugs affect the mind and body and discusses the difference between drug use and drug abuse. The information includes side effects, precautions, and alternatives for both legal drugs like caffeine and antihistamines as well as the illegal variety.

Cynthia Kuhn, Scott Swartzwelder, and Wilkie Wilson, *Just Say Know: Talking with Kids About Drugs and Alcohol* (W.W. Norton & Co., 2002).

Written by professors in pharmacology and psychology at Duke University Medical Center, this book provides parents with tools for talking with their children about the health risks and legal dangers of alcohol and other drugs. Written in a straightforward and easily understood style, this book covers just about every form of drug being used and abused today, including steroids. The authors also wrote *Buzzed: The Straight Facts About the Most Used and Abused Drugs from Alcohol to Ecstasy* (W.W. Norton & Co., revised in 2003) and *Pumped: Straight Facts for Athletes About Drugs, Supplements and Training* (W.W. Norton & Co., 2000).

Nancy Goodman, *It Was Food vs. Me . . . and I Won* (Viking Press, 2004).

A former binge eater shares the story of how she overcame a lifelong obsession with food. This candid book gives advice on separating food from emotion, taking the fear out of food by learning to safely feed your cravings, and how to redirect your energy from what you eat and how much you weigh to who you really are—and how to learn to love that person.

Natural Remedies for Depression

Because certain prescription antidepressant drugs (SSRIs) have been recently shown to increase risk of suicide and suicidal feelings in young people, parents may want to consider other options for their children. In addition to cognitive-behavioral and interpersonal therapy (not to mention support groups), many alternative therapies used in various combinations can help lessen the need for drugs. They include massage; music, art, and play therapy; biofeedback; meditation or prayer; physical exercise; and nutritional supplements and herbs. Several studies have shown that the herb St. John's wort, for example, helps mild to moderate cases of depression. (The herb's active ingredient, hypericin, increases the levels of the neurotransmitters that maintain normal mood and emotional stability.) I recommend:

Vitanica's St. John's Wort: Each capsule of this product contains 300 mg of *Hypericum perforatum* (St. John's wort extract), standardized to 0.3 percent hypericin along with 100 mg of St. John's wort dried and powdered buds. For more information, contact:

Emerson Ecologics, Inc.
7 Commerce Drive
Bedford, NH 03110
Phone: 800-654-4432
Web site: www.emersonecologics.com

Resources for Helping Teens to Quit Smoking

Gotta Quit: a Web site (www.gottaquit.com) from the Monroe County, NY, Department of Health. The site offers lots of information about how to quit smoking and offers powerful tools such as goal-setting opportunities that make use of e-mailed reminders containing information you provide and quit coaches trained by the University of Rochester Medical Center who are available for live chat.

Crazyworld: an eerily entertaining and very informative Web site (www.thetruth.com) designed as an Internet amusement park filled with dire facts about smoking and the dangers of tobacco. The site manages to educate (and horrify) without sounding preachy (and includes a subtle but constantly updated notice showing how many people have died tobacco-related deaths since the viewer has entered the site). Crazyworld is part of The Truth, an anti-tobacco media campaign sponsored by the American Legacy Foundation (created by the $206 settlement reached by 46 state attorneys general and the tobacco industry).

Resources for Fighting Drug and Alcohol Addiction and Abuse

Parents. The anti-drug: This site (www.theantidrug.com) contains a wealth of information about drug abuse and the drugs teens are most likely to abuse, including marijuana, ecstasy, cocaine, club drugs, and methamphetamine (or meth) in addition to drugs like Ritalin and steroids. This site also includes advice on how to talk to your children about alcohol and drugs and how to look for signs that your child may be in trouble. One section includes sharing from teens themselves about experimenting with drugs, peer pressure, talking to parents, and more.

The National Youth Violence Prevention Resource Center: an organization sponsored by several federal agencies (most notably, the Centers for Disease Control and Prevention) dedicated to reducing violence of all types in children's lives. The group's Web site includes a variety of warning signs for a number of problems, including teen depression and suicide, substance abuse, dating violence, and more.

The section for teens helps answer such questions as how to help a friend who is depressed, what to do if someone you know is planning to commit a violent act, and what to do if you or a friend is the victim of teasing. For more information, contact:

National Youth Violence Prevention Resource Center
P.O. Box 10809
Rockville, MD 20849-0809
Phone: 866-SAFE-YOUTH (866-723-3968)
Web site: www.safeyouth.org/scripts/index.asp

Check Yourself: This site (www.checkyourself.com), supported by the Partnership for a Drug-Free America, invites teens to consider if their substance use is at risk for becoming substance abuse. Drug quizzes, decision games, short films, and real teen stories can help teens figure out where they are now and where they're headed with drugs and alcohol. Resources for getting help if needed are also included.

Free Vibe: This Web site (www.freevibe.com), maintained by the National Youth Anti-Drug Media Campaign, gives kids straight facts on drug and alcohol abuse. The site gives drug facts, tells what to do if a friend needs help, gives kids a forum to share their own stories, and encourages getting involved with other activities ("anti-drugs") instead. There's even a page on what to do if your parents do drugs or drink too much.

Mothers Against Drunk Driving (MADD): Founded in 1980 by Candy Lightner and a small band of other mothers, this grassroots activist organization fighting drinking and driving has grown to one of the largest crime victims organizations in the world. For more information, contact:

MADD National Office
511 E. John Carpenter Freeway, suite 700
Irving, TX 75062
Phone: 800-GET-MADD (800-438-6233)
Web site: www.madd.org

Students Against Destructive Decisions (SADD): Although the original mission of SADD was convincing kids not to drink and drive, its mission today is much broader. SADD is now a peer leadership organization dedicated to preventing destructive decisions of many types, particularly underage drinking, drug use, impaired driving, teen violence, and teen depression and suicide. For more information, contact:

SADD National Office
P.O. Box 800
Marlborough, MA 01752
Phone: 877-SADD-INC (877-723-3462)
Web site: www.sadd.org

Monitoring the Future (MTF): an ongoing study that gathers data on trends in smoking and drug use in U.S. secondary school students, college students, and young adults. The study is conducted by the Institute for Social Research at the University of Michigan. For more information, contact:

> Survey Research Center
> 1355 ISR Building
> P.O. Box 1248
> Ann Arbor, MI 48106
> Phone: 734-764-8365
> Web site: www.monitoringthefuture.org

Alcoholics Anonymous: the group that's been helping alcoholics stop drinking, one day at a time, ever since the 1930s. One page on A.A.'s Web site specifically addressed to teens gives a quiz designed to help them decide if drinking has become a problem for them. The site also gives contact information on local chapters across the country and has a link to the text of "The Big Book," what A.A. members call the text *Alcoholics Anonymous* (Alcoholics Anonymous World Services, revised edition, 2000). For more information, contact:

> Alcoholics Anonymous General Service Office
> P.O. Box 459, Grand Central Station
> New York, NY 10163
> Phone: 212-870-3400
> Web site: www.aa.org

Support for Compulsive Overeating

Overeaters Anonymous (OA): This worldwide, twelve-step fellowship and recovery program from compulsive overeating is modeled after Alcoholics Anonymous. OA addresses more than just weight loss and also promotes physical, emotional, and spiritual well-being. OA doesn't promote any particular eating plan or diet, but members (not all of whom are obese) are encouraged to develop their own food plan with a health care professional and a sponsor. For more information, contact:

> Overeaters Anonymous
> World Service Office
> P.O. Box 44020
> Rio Rancho, NM 87174-4020
> Phone: 505-891-2664
> Web site: www.overeatersanonymous.org

Information on Eating Disorders

(See Resources for Room Two, page 697.)

Chapter 18: Self-Care Basics

Recommended Reading

Margaret Bullitt-Jonas, *Holy Hunger: A Woman's Journey from Food Addiction to Spiritual Fulfillment* (Vintage, 2000); www.holyhunger.com.

Episcopal minister Bullitt-Jonas's incredibly touching memoir shares the story of how her economically privileged childhood with an alcoholic father and an emotionally reclusive mother spawned a food addiction, and how she eventually recovered—through her faith in a higher power and help from the twelve-step program Overeaters Anonymous.

Herbert Benson, M.D., with Miriam Z. Klipper, *The Relaxation Response* (updated and expanded edition, Quill, 2001); www.herbertbenson.com.

First published in 1975, this groundbreaking book demystified meditation and brought it from the realm of the gurus to within reach of the general public. The authors cite studies showing that the Relaxation Response not only reduces stress but also lowers blood pressure and helps reduce risk for heart disease. The technique Benson, a Harvard researcher, teaches is simple and requires just ten to twenty minutes a day. Although a plethora of good books about meditation exist today, this classic is still excellent for a basic understanding of the techniques and instructions for how to get started.

Dennis Lewis, *Free Your Breath, Free Your Life: How Conscious Breathing Can Relieve Stress, Increase Vitality, and Help You Live More Fully* (Shambhala, 2004); www.breath.org/dennislewis.html.

The most compelling and complete book on breathing I've ever read, this is "must" reading for everyone who is interested in optimum health. Dennis Lewis's illustrated guidebook and its simple exercises teach how being conscious of your breath can significantly improve your physical and emotional health.

Vitamin and Mineral Supplements

(See Resources for Chapter 3.)

Sources for Omega-3 and DHA

(See Resources for Chapter 3.)

Recommended Reading on Fitness

(See Resources for Room Two, page 687.)

Resources for Helping Your Children Stay Healthy

KidsHealth: an award-winning Web site (www.kidshealth.org) created by the Center for Children's Health Media at the Nemours Foundation. The site offers accurate and updated health information on a wide variety of subjects in separate areas for kids, teens, and parents—each with its own design, age-appropriate content, and tone. The kids' section (which includes animated cartoons and games) covers nutrition, keeping fit, avoiding smoking and alcohol, caffeine, sleep, and even things like bad breath. The teen section deals with sexuality, drugs and alcohol, eating problems, and a host of other teen-oriented health issues.

Resources for Overcoming Fatigue

Jacob Teitelbaum, M.D., *From Fatigued to Fantastic!* (Avery Pub. Group, 2001); www.endfatigue.com.

Dr. Teitelbaum is not only a leading researcher in the fields of chronic fatigue and fibromyalgia, he's suffered from both conditions himself. In this updated and revised edition of his book, he discusses the newest findings about these conditions and his treatment advice, which combines over-the-counter drugs, diet modification, vitamin and mineral supplements, acupuncture, massage, chiropractic medicine, herbal supplements, and psychotherapy.

Skin Care Resources

Sensé Skincare Products: Made by USANA, Sensé's formulas are self-preserving and contain a blend of pure botanicals, antioxidants, and active ingredients that can help renew your skin's surface, prevent the appearance of fine lines, and even help reverse sun damage when used on a regular basis. These pharmaceutical-grade complexes are tested by dermatologists, allergists, and ophthalmologists for quality and safety, and then tested again for effectiveness by an independent, third-party laboratory. For more information, contact:

> USANA
> 3838 West Parkway Boulevard
> Salt Lake City, UT 84120
> Phone: 888-950-9595
> Web site: www.usana.com

Trienelle Skin Care Products: These excellent physician-formulated products (manufactured by Aspen Benefits Group) contain tocotrienols, a recently discovered high-potency form of vitamin E that is far more effective at quelling free-radical damage and therefore maintaining healthy-looking skin than regular vitamin E (D-alpha tocopherol). Trienelle also contains a wide variety of other skin-specific antioxidants, such as coenzyme Q-10, alpha hydroxy acids, proanthocyanidins, and a clinically proven, collagen-supporting ingredient known as microcollagen pentapeptides. For more information, contact:

Aspen Benefits Group
7950 Meadowlark, Suite B
Coeur d'Alene, ID 83815
Phone: 800-539-5195
Web site: www.trienelle.com

Resources for Cosmetic Laser Treatments and Other Dermatologic Procedures

Laser News, Inc.: an Internet site (www.lasernews.com) offering current information about lasers and laser surgery. It's maintained by Stanford professor Randal Pham, M.D., an aesthetic and refractive laser surgeon whose specialty is research on laser technology used on the face. The site offers information on recently approved procedures as well as on potential laser technologies that may soon be available.

American Academy of Dermatology: a section of the AAD's main Web site offers lots of information on a wide variety of cosmetic procedures and advice for how to choose a dermatologist. See this link: www.skincarephysi cians.com/agingskinnet. The site also has links to a resource for finding physicians who are AAD members in your area. For more information, contact:

American Academy of Dermatology
930 E. Woodfield Road
Schaumburg, IL 60173
Phone: 847-330-0230
Web site: www.aad.org

Sources for Relieving Menstrual Cramps

Menastil: a homeopathic, topically applied product (distributed by Synaptic Systems) made of pure essential oils. Menastil's active ingredient is calendula oil, recognized by the FDA and the homeopathic Pharmacopoeia U.S. for its use in temporary relief of menstrual pain. For more information, contact:

Synaptic Systems, LLC
1117 Perimeter Center West, Suite W-211
Atlanta, GA 30338-5444
Phone: 770-350-8050
Web site: www.menastil.com

Soothing Flow, or Xiao Yao Wan Plus: the supplemental form of bupleurum (Xiao Yao Wan, sometimes spelled Hsiao Yao Wan) that I recommend for PMS, menstrual cramps, and perimenopausal symptoms. This supplement contains paeonia, a well-known female tonic. For more information, contact:

Quality Life Herbs
P.O. Box 565
Yarmouth, ME 04096
Phone: 207-842-4929
Web site: www.qualitylifeherbs.com

Traditional Chinese medicine (acupuncture) (See Resources for Room One, page 681.)

Guided Imagery and Visualization Tapes

Cognitive behavioral therapy is, at its core, a way to retrain your habitual thoughts and emotions so that your biochemistry and bodily responses change over time. This takes time and effort, but it works. Though working directly with a therapist is ideal, you can do a lot on your own using guided Imagery or visualization tapes. I recommend:

Louise Hay's *Overcoming Fears* audio program: This popular visualization program (available on audiocassette and CD) from metaphysical teacher Louise Hay will help you transform your deeply held beliefs that the world is an inescapably stressful place. This audio program directs you in changing your perception and biochemistry over time so that you begin to attract experiences of safety, security, and peace. As you feel safer and more peaceful more often, your stress hormone levels will level off, and so will your tendency to store fat as "protection." You will experience noticeable results in how you feel and think about yourself and your life after just one month of listening to this program consistently each day. Louise Hay is also the author of twenty-seven books, including *You Can Heal Your Life* (Hay House, 1987) and *Empowering Women* (Hay House, 1997). For more information, contact:

Hay House, Inc.
P.O. Box 5100
Carlsbad, CA 92018-5100
Phone: 800-654-5126
Web site: www.Hayhouse.com

Belleruth Naparstek's *Weight Loss* audio program: If you're faced with the emotional dimensions of overeating, this guided imagery weight loss audio program (available on cassette and CD) will help you transform your body and your biochemistry by showing you how to send healthy fat-burning messages to your body. I am uplifted and inspired every time I listen to it. If you listen consistently at least once per day, in one month you will experience noticeable results in how you feel and think about yourself and your life. This product doubled weight loss in a placebo-controlled pilot study at Canyon Ranch. For more information, contact:

Health Journeys
891 Moe Dr., Suite C
Akron, OH 44310
Phone: 800-800-8661
Web site: www.healthjourneys.com

For Help with Caffeine Detox

Elson M. Haas, M.D.'s Caffeine Support and Detox Nutrient Program: Dr. Haas, founder and director of the Preventive Medical Center of Marin in San Rafael, CA., specializes in family and nutritional medicine and detoxification. He is the author of several books, including *Staying Healthy with the Seasons* (Celestial Arts, originally published in 1981 but fully revised in 2003) and *The New Detox Diet* (Celestial Arts, 2004), among others.

His caffeine detox program is completely outlined both in his book *Staying Healthy with Nutrition* (Celestial Arts, 1992) and on the Internet at the following Web page:

www.healthy.net/library/books/haas/detox/caffeine.htm

Both print and Internet versions include a detailed explanation of what caffeine is and how it affects the body; charts of how much caffeine is contained in various foods, beverages, and over-the-counter drugs and products we commonly consume; the symptoms of caffeine abuse and caffeine withdrawal; herbal caffeine substitutes; and his nutrition- and supplement-based program for successfully detoxing from caffeine.

Chapter 19: The Read World

Recommended Reading

Walter Starcke, *The Third Appearance* (Guadalupe Press, 2004); www.walterstarcke.com.

This is the latest metaphysical book from spiritual teacher Walter Starcke (a pupil of Joel Goldsmith's for almost two decades), who challenges our understanding of God and of life in leading us toward a personal experience of our Divine Humanity.

Barbara Ehrenrich, Ph.D., *Nickel and Dimed: On (Not) Getting By in America* (Metropolitan Books, 2001).

For three months, Barbara Ehrenrich moved around the country, living in the cheapest housing she could find and accepting minimal-paying jobs (such as a waitress, a hotel maid, a house cleaner, a nursing home aide, and a sales clerk at Wal-Mart, all positions that paid between $6 and $7 per hour), to see firsthand how the working poor in the U.S. live. What she experienced and shares in this book is sometimes touching, sometimes horrifying, but definitely eye-opening.

Ronald D. Siegel, Psy.D., Michael H. Urdang, and Douglas R. Johnson, M.D., *Back Sense: A Revolutionary Approach to Halting the Cycle of Chronic Back Pain* (Broadway Books, 2001); www.backsense.org.

I highly recommend this wonderful book, written by three men who are themselves former chronic back pain sufferers, to everyone with chronic back problems. The first of my patients who read this book got out of bed and off narcotics for the first time in months. The authors assert that truly bad backs are rare, and that many back problems may well begin with an injury, but they become chronic conditions because of stress (which causes painfully tight muscles) and inactivity (which makes you lose conditioning, leaving you more vulnerable to additional injury).

William B. Salt II, M.D., and Neil F. Neimark, M.D., *Irritable Bowel Syndrome and the MindBodySpirit Connection: 7 Steps for Living a Healthy Life with a Functional Bowel Disorder, Crohn's Disease or Colitis* (revised edition, Parkview Pub., 2002).

This fully revised edition of Dr. Salt's excellent resource is essential reading for everyone who encounters this common condition. Dr. Salt, a clinical associate professor in medicine at Ohio State University, and Dr. Neimark, a family practitioner and professor of medicine at the University of California, Irvine, outline a treatment plan that taps in to the strongest medicine that exists—the body's ability to heal itself.

Jacob Teitelbaum, M.D., *From Fatigued to Fantastic!* (See *Resources* for Chapter 18.)

The Effects of Competition

Self-Determination Theory (SDT)—an approach to human motivation and personality: this Web site (www.psych.rochester.edu/SDT) offers an overview of SDT, which involves how we make decisions to do the things that we do (our autonomy). The site explains SDT and offers a publications page with links to a large number of studies about the theory.

The Holmes-Rahe Social Readjustment Rating Scale

The most recent research shows that the specific experiences we have in life don't affect our health nearly as much as how we view those experiences and how we respond to them. Even so, the Holmes-Rahe Social Readjustment Rating Scale is still useful in seeing the relative impact various potentially stressful situations might have on our lives. To see a list of the items for adults and youths (and have your score automatically tallied), visit the following Web page: www.markhenri.com/health/stress.html.

Chapter 20: The Legacy Continues

Recommended Reading

Jerry Hicks and Esther Hicks, *Ask and It Is Given: Learning to Manifest Your Desires* (Hay House, 2004); www.askanditisgiven.com.

Jerry and Esther Hicks channel a nonphysical entity identified as Abraham, whose teachings fill this book and explain how our relationships, health, finances, careers, and indeed every aspect of our lives are influenced by certain universal laws. By understanding these laws and allowing ourselves to follow the positive flow of the universe, Abraham teaches, we can manifest our innermost desires.

Melvin Morse, M.D., with Paul Perry, *Transformed by the Light: The Powerful Effect of Near-Death Experiences on People's Lives* (Villard Books, 1992); www.melvinmorse.com.

This book, based on the results of the largest study on near-death experiences (NDEs) ever done, details the extraordinary physical, emotional, and spiritual changes for the better that people experience after NDEs. In some, the experiences seemed to alter their bodies' electromagnetic forces (making watches and computers go crazy). Others found they suddenly had the ability to heal, while some found they had greater intellectual abilities. All report less fear of death and a higher zest for life. The authors have also written *Closer to the Light: Learning from Children's Near-Death Experiences* (G.K. Hall, 1991).

Catherine Ponder, *The Dynamic Laws of Healing* (Parker Publishing Co., 1966).

Unity minister Catherine Ponder, the author of more than a dozen books, begins this one with this powerful statement: "The shocking truth about healing is that you have healing power within you." She then outlines how to tap in to that healing ability by using the power of the mind and by following the series of spiritual "laws" through which healing works.

Sinclair Browning, *Feathers Brush My Heart: True Stories of Mothers Touching Their Daughters' Lives After Death* (Warner Books, 2002).

Mystery writer Sinclair Browning tells her own story as well as those of more than seventy other women who have received comforting signs or even life-saving warnings from their deceased mothers. Browning's sign, for example, is finding white feathers in places that would normally defy explanation.

Hope Edelman, *Motherless Daughters: The Legacy of Loss* (Addison-Wesley Publishing, 1994); www.hopeedelman.com.

In this touching book, freelance writer Hope Edelman shares her story of losing her mother to breast cancer when Edelman was seventeen, as well as the stories of other women of all ages across the country who lost their mothers through death as well as through abandonment and other forms of separation. Edelman details the stages of grief women go through when they lose their mothers and discusses the many ways such a loss can affect daughters at various stages in their lives (from young girls taking on the role of their mothers at home with their fathers and younger siblings to adult women experiencing fear of abandonment in romantic relationships).

Edelman also compiled *Letters from Motherless Daughters: Words of Courage, Grief, and Healing* (Addison-Wesley Publishing, 1995), a companion volume drawing from the letters she received after her first book was published. She's grouped the letters according to the number of years since the mother's death so each chapter can clearly address the issues appropriate to that stage. Edelman also includes information on starting or joining a mother-loss support group. She is currently writing a book called *Motherless Mothers* about the issues motherless women face when they become parents themselves.

Resources for Forgiveness

Fred Luskin, Ph.D., *Forgive for Good: A Proven Prescription for Health and Happiness* (HarperSanFrancisco, 2002); www.learningtoforgive.com.

Dr. Luskin, formerly director of the Stanford Forgiveness Project and now at the Stanford Center on Conflict and Negotiation, offers scientific evidence that forgiveness reduces anger, depression, hopelessness, and stress and leads to feelings of optimism, hope, compassion, and self-confidence.

Dr. Luskin's audio program (available on cassette or CD), *The Nine Steps of Forgiveness*, includes on one side a forty-five-minute presentation of his nine steps for learning to forgive, and on the other side two guided forgiveness visualizations. One of the visualizations deals with self-forgiveness. For more information, visit his Web site at the following link: www.learningtoforgive.com.

The International Forgiveness Institute (IFI): This nonprofit organization was founded in 1994 to promote the findings of fourteen years of research done on interpersonal forgiveness at the University of Wisconsin–Madison. Currently, IFI has set its sights on international goals, piloting a program in Northern Ireland at eleven schools in Belfast. The aim of the project is to expose an entire generation of children from first grade through the end of high school to forgiveness training in the hopes that as this generation grows into adults, they may be better able to handle the conflicts that have

torn their country apart and get closer to bringing about peace in their life-
times. For more information, contact:

International Forgiveness Institute
1127 University Ave. #201
Madison, WI 53715
Phone: 608-251-6484
Web site: www.forgiveness-institute.org

Index

Page numbers of illustrations appear in italics.

About the Author

CHRISTIANE NORTHRUP, M.D., is the author of the *New York Times* bestselling books *Women's Bodies, Women's Wisdom* and *The Wisdom of Menopause* and host of five public television specials, including *Mother-Daughter Wisdom*. A board-certified obstetrician-gynecologist, she trained at Dartmouth Medical School and Tufts New England Medical Center. Throughout her more than twenty-five years of clinical experience, she has pioneered the partnership between conventional and complementary medicine. Her work has been featured on *The Oprah Winfrey Show*, the *Today* show, and *Good Morning America*, among many other TV programs. She lives in Maine and is the mother of two adult daughters.

Visit Dr. Northrup's Web site at www.drnorthrup.com.